Sports Illustrated KIDS

YEAR IN SPORTS 2008

from the Editors of SPORTS ILLUSTRATED KIDS

SCHOLASTIC REFERENCE

AN IMPRINT OF

SCHOLASTIC

COVER PHOTOGRAPHY CREDITS
Peyton Manning: John Iacono
David Wright: Erick W. Rasco
Clint Dempsey: Simon Bruty
Carmelo Anthony: John W. McDonough
Annika Sorenstam: Darren Carroll
Shaun White: Al Tielemans
Danica Patrick: Brian Spurlock/US Presswire

BACK-COVER PHOTOGRAPHY CREDITS
John David Booty: Peter Read Miller
Cheryl Ford: Allen Einstein/NBAE/Getty Images
Sidney Crosby: Lou Capozzola

SPORTS ILLUSTRATED KIDS Year in Sports 2008 was prepared by Touchpoint Sports of White Plains, N.Y.

Editorial Director: Morin Bishop	Art Director: Barbara Chilenskas
Managing Editor: Reed Richardson	Photo Editor: John Blackmar
Associate Editors: Chris Freeburn, Max Berry	Editorial Intern: Monica Perschetz

SPORTS ILLUSTRATED KIDS Year in Sports 2008 is a production of SPORTS ILLUSTRATED KIDS and SPORTS ILLUSTRATED KIDS Books: Bob Der, Managing Editor; Michael Northrop, Project Editor; Edward Duarte, Designer; Gina Houseman, Photo Researcher; André Carter, Gary Gramling, Ted Keith, Sachin Shenolikar, and Justin Tejada, Contributors

Scholastic Reference staff: Brenda Murray, Assistant Editor; Karyn Browne, Managing Editor; Susan Casel, Production Editor; Becky Terhune, Art Director; Jess White, Manufacturing Coordinator

ISBN 13: 978-0-439-91659-2
ISBN 10: 0-439-91659-3

10 9 8 7 6 5 4 3   08 09 10

Printed in the U.S.A. 23
First printing, December 2007

CONTENTS

Indianapolis quarterback Peyton Manning finally won "the big one," leading the Colts to victory in Super Bowl XLI in Miami, Florida.

The Colts defense, which struggled during the regular season, carried the load in gritty playoff wins over the Chiefs and Ravens. But when Indy fell behind the Patriots in the first half of the AFC title game, 21–3, Peyton and the offense took center stage. The Colts scored 32 second-half points to win, 38–34.

Playing in his first Super Bowl, Manning led the Colts to a 29–17 victory over the Bears. It was the first Super Bowl ever played in the rain, and Manning's efficient play earned him MVP honors. The Colts defense did its part too, forcing five turnovers.

Chargers running back LaDainian Tomlinson dominated the regular season, breaking the single-season touchdown record with 31. Despite his play, his team couldn't avoid another disappointing postseason, losing to the Patriots in the AFC Divisional playoffs.

The Bears took the NFC crown despite the inconsistent play of their quarterback, Rex Grossman, while Saints signal caller Drew Brees nearly carried New Orleans to the Super Bowl. Brees, a former Charger, led the NFL in passing yards (4,418), and the Saints went from a 3–13 laughingstock to the NFC title game. Their run finally came to an end in snowy Chicago.

The Jets (4–12 in 2005) and Ravens (6–10) enjoyed turnaround seasons as well. Both teams reached the playoffs.

The Eagles seemed doomed when star QB Donovan McNabb suffered a season-ending knee injury, but backup Jeff Garcia led Philly to the NFC East title.

The defending champion Steelers fell to 8–8. Quarterback Ben Roethlisberger was hurt in a motorcycle accident during the preseason, and then threw a league-high 23 interceptions when the games counted. Head coach Bill Cowher announced he would retire after 15 seasons leading the Steelers. Another legendary coach, the Cowboys' Bill Parcells, called it quits after just his fourth year in Big D.

All-Pro running back Tiki Barber of the Giants shocked the NFL by also announcing he was retiring, but several new superstars seemed ready to take Tiki's place. Tennessee's rookie quarterback Vince Young showed a knack for the big play. After going 4–12 in 2005, and starting 0–3 in 2006, the Titans went 8–5 after Young took over as the starter. Chicago Bears defensive back/kick returner Devin Hester set a single-season NFL record with six return TDs during the regular season. Then he became the first player to run back the Super Bowl's opening kickoff for a score. And for the champs, Colts running back Joseph Addai led all rookies in total yards from scrimmage.

AFC TEAMS
Baltimore Ravens
Buffalo Bills
Cincinnati Bengals
Cleveland Browns
Denver Broncos
Houston Texans
Indianapolis Colts
Jacksonville Jaguars
Kansas City Chiefs
Miami Dolphins
New England Patriots
New York Jets
Oakland Raiders
Pittsburgh Steelers
San Diego Chargers
Tennessee Titans

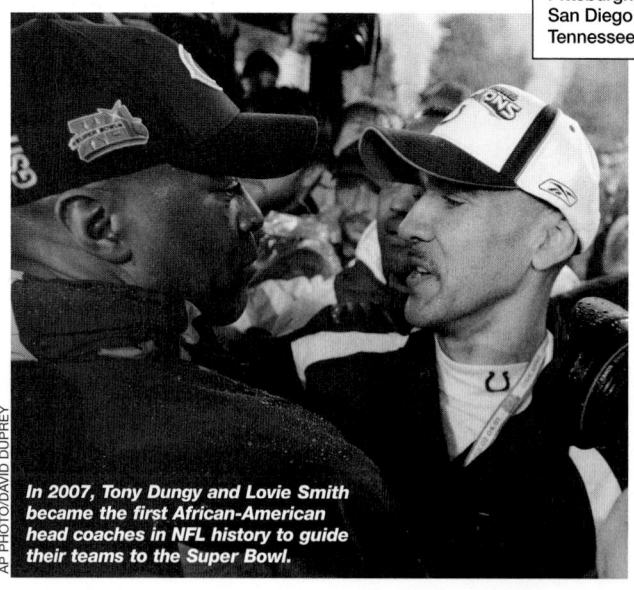

In 2007, Tony Dungy and Lovie Smith became the first African-American head coaches in NFL history to guide their teams to the Super Bowl.

AP PHOTO/DAVID DUPREY

Colts quarterback Peyton Manning was named the MVP of Super Bowl XLI.

AL TELEMANS

JOHN W. MCDONOUGH

Running back LaDainian Tomlinson of the San Diego Chargers scored an NFL record 31 touchdowns in 2006.

NFC TEAMS

Arizona Cardinals
Atlanta Falcons
Carolina Panthers
Chicago Bears
Dallas Cowboys
Detroit Lions
Green Bay Packers
Minnesota Vikings
New Orleans Saints
New York Giants
Philadelphia Eagles
San Francisco 49ers
Seattle Seahawks
St. Louis Rams
Tampa Bay Buccaneers
Washington Redskins

2006 NFL FINAL STANDINGS

AFC EAST						
TEAM	W	L	T	PCT	PF	PA
y-Patriots	12	4	0	.750	385	237
x-Jets	10	6	0	.625	316	295
Bills	7	9	0	.438	300	311
Dolphins	6	10	0	.375	260	283

AFC NORTH						
TEAM	W	L	T	PCT	PF	PA
yz-Ravens	13	3	0	.812	353	201
Bengals	8	8	0	.500	373	331
x-Steelers	8	8	0	.500	353	315
Browns	4	12	0	.250	238	356

AFC SOUTH						
TEAM	W	L	T	PCT	PF	PA
y-Colts	12	4	0	.750	427	360
Titans	8	8	0	.500	324	400
Jaguars	8	8	0	.500	371	274
Texans	6	10	0	.375	267	366

AFC WEST						
TEAM	W	L	T	PCT	PF	PA
*yz-Chargers	14	2	0	.875	492	303
x-Chiefs	9	7	0	.562	331	315
Broncos	9	7	0	.562	319	305
Raiders	2	14	0	.125	168	332

NFC EAST						
TEAM	W	L	T	PCT	PF	PA
y-Eagles	10	6	0	.625	398	328
x-Cowboys	9	7	0	.562	425	350
x-Giants	8	8	0	.500	355	362
Redskins	5	11	0	.312	307	376

NFC NORTH						
TEAM	W	L	T	PCT	PF	PA
*yz-Bears	13	3	0	.812	427	255
Packers	8	8	0	.500	301	366
Vikings	6	10	0	.375	282	327
Lions	3	13	0	.188	305	398

NFC SOUTH						
TEAM	W	L	T	PCT	PF	PA
yz-Saints	10	6	0	.625	413	322
Panthers	8	8	0	.500	270	305
Falcons	7	9	0	.438	292	328
Buccaneers	4	12	0	.250	211	353

NFC WEST						
TEAM	W	L	T	PCT	PF	PA
y-Seahawks	9	7	0	.562	335	341
Rams	8	8	0	.500	367	381
49ers	7	9	0	.438	298	412
Cardinals	5	11	0	.312	314	389

* clinched home-field advantage throughout the playoffs, x-clinched playoff berth, y-clinched division title, z-clinched first-round bye

KEY W=win; L=loss; T=tie; PCT=winning percentage; PF=points for; PA=points against

2006 NFL PLAYOFFS

AFC — Indianapolis Colts 23 / Kansas City Chiefs 8 · Indianapolis Colts 15 / Baltimore Ravens 6 · Indianapolis Colts 38 · San Diego Chargers 21 / New England Patriots 34 · New England Patriots 37 / New York Jets 16 · New England Patriots 24

INDIANAPOLIS COLTS 29 — Chicago Bears 17

NFC — Seattle Seahawks 21 / Dallas Cowboys 20 · Seattle Seahawks 24 · Chicago Bears 39 / Chicago Bears 27 · New Orleans Saints 27 · New Orleans Saints 14 · Philadelphia Eagles 24 / Philadelphia Eagles 23 · New York Giants 20

WILD CARD · DIV. PLAYOFF · CONF. CHAMPIONSHIP · CONF. CHAMPIONSHIP · DIV. PLAYOFF · WILD CARD

AFC WILD-CARD GAMES

INDIANAPOLIS COLTS 23
KANSAS CITY CHIEFS 8

	1Q	2Q	3Q	4Q	T
COLTS	6	3	7	7	23
CHIEFS	0	0	8	0	8

1ST QUARTER
FG Ind: Adam Vinatieri, 48 yd, 8:41. Drive: 10 plays, 39 yards in 4:51.
FG Ind: Adam Vinatieri, 19 yd, 2:09. Drive: 10 plays, 68 yards in 4:57.
2ND QUARTER
FG Ind: Adam Vinatieri, 50 yd, 0:00. Drive: 6 plays, 33 yards in 0:50.
3RD QUARTER
TD Ind: Joseph Addai, 6 yd run (Adam Vinatieri kick), 4:14. Drive: 12 plays, 89 yards in 6:56.
TD Kan: Tony Gonzalez, 6 yd pass from Trent Green (Trent Green pass to Kris Wilson for 2-pt. conversion), 0:08. Drive: 8 plays, 60 yards in 4:06.
4TH QUARTER
TD Ind: Reggie Wayne, 5 yd pass from Peyton Manning (Adam Vinatieri kick), 10:16. Drive: 9 plays, 71 yards in 4:52.

NEW ENGLAND PATRIOTS 37
NY JETS 16

	1Q	2Q	3Q	4Q	T
PATRIOTS	7	10	6	14	37
JETS	3	7	3	3	16

1ST QUARTER
TD NE: Corey Dillion, 11 yd run (Stephen Gostkowski kick), 11:53. Drive: 10 plays, 65 yards in 3:07.
FG NYJ: Mike Nugent, 28 yd, 2:36. drive: 4 plays, 5 yards in 1:30.
2ND QUARTER
TD NYJ: Jerricho Cotchery, 77 yd pass from Chad Pennington (Mike Nugent kick), 14:45. Drive: 3 plays, 80 yards in 0:17.
FG NE: Stephen Gostkowski, 20 yd, 10:57. Drive: 10 plays, 56 yards in 3:48.
TD NE: Daniel Graham, 1 yd pass from Tom Brady (Stephen Gostkowski kick), 0:11. Drive: 15 plays, 80 yards in 6:54.
3RD QUARTER
FG NYJ: Mike Nugent, 21 yd, 8:19. Drive: 13 plays, 73 yards in 6:41.
FG NE: Stephen Gostkowski, 40 yd, 4:22. Drive: 8 plays, 52 yards in 3:57.
FG NE: Stephen Gostkowski, 28 yd, 0:04. Drive: 4 plays, 5 yards in 1:39.
4TH QUARTER
FG NYJ: Mike Nugent, 37 yd, 11:39. Drive: 8 plays, 61 yards in 3:25.
TD NE: Kevin Faulk, 7 yd pass from Tom Brady (Stephen Gostkowski kick), 5:16. Drive: 13 plays, 63 yards in 6:23.
TD NE: Asante Samuel, 36 yd interception return (Stephen Gostkowski kick), 4:54.

TRIVIA CHALLENGE

With the Colts' victory in Super Bowl XLI, Tony Dungy became just the third person in NFL history to have won Super Bowls as both a head coach and a player. Name the other two.

Mike Ditka (coach–Chicago Bears, player–Dallas Cowboys); Tom Flores (coach–Oakland Raiders, player–Kansas City Chiefs).

NFC WILD-CARD GAMES

SEATTLE SEAHAWKS 21
DALLAS COWBOYS 20

	1Q	2Q	3Q	4Q	T
SEAHAWKS	3	3	7	8	21
COWBOYS	3	7	7	3	20

1ST QUARTER
FG Sea: Josh Brown, 23 yd, 11:13. Drive: 9 plays, 55 yards in 3:47.
FG Dal: Martin Gramatica, 50 yd, 4:50. Drive: 5 plays, 11 yards in 2:21.
2ND QUARTER
FG Sea: Josh Brown, 30 yd, 8:23. Drive: 13 plays, 54 yards in 5:14.
TD Dal: Patrick Crayton, 13 yd pass from Tony Romo (Martin Gramatica kick), 0:11. Drive: 10 plays, 76 yards in 5:03.
3RD QUARTER
TD Sea: Jerramy Stevens, 15 yd pass from Matt Hasselbeck (Josh Brown kick), 6:08. Drive: 12 plays, 62 yards in 6:45.
TD Dal: Miles Austin, 93 yd kick return (Martin Gramatica kick), 5:57.
4TH QUARTER
FG Dal: Martin Gramatica, 29 yd, 10:15. Drive: 8 plays, 46 yards in 4:26.
SAFETY Sea: 6:32
TD Sea: Jerramy Stevens, 37 yd pass from Matt Hasselbeck (Matt Hasselbeck 2-pt. conversion pass to Deion Branch failed), 4:24. Drive: 4 plays, 50 yards in 2:08.

PHILADELPHIA EAGLES 23
NEW YORK GIANTS 20

	1Q	2Q	3Q	4Q	T
EAGLES	0	17	3	3	23
GIANTS	7	3	0	10	20

1ST QUARTER
TD NYG: Plaxico Burress, 17 yd pass from Eli Manning (Jay Feely kick), 11:44. Drive: 7 plays, 67 yards in 3:16.
2ND QUARTER
TD Phi: Brian Westbrook, 49 yd run (David Akers kick), 14:11. Drive: 7 plays, 84 yards in 2:47.
FG Phi: David Akers, 19 yd, 9:34. Drive: 7 plays, 36 yards in 2:59.
FG NYG: Jay Feely, 20 yd, 4:45. Drive: 11 plays, 78 yards in 4:49.
TD Phi: Donte Stallworth, 28 yd pass from Jeff Garcia (David Akers kick), 1:01. Drive: 10 plays, 80 yards in 3:44.
3RD QUARTER
FG Phil: David Akers, 48 yd, 2:37. Drive: 10 plays, 45 yards in 4:35.
4TH QUARTER
FG NYG: Jay Feely, 24 yd, 14:50. Drive: 7 plays, 65 yards in 2:47.
TD NYG: Plaxico Burress, 11 yd pass from Eli Manning (Jay Feely kick), 5:04. Drive: 13 plays, 80 yards in 7:09.
FG Phi: David Akers, 38 yd, 0:00. Drive: 10 plays, 46 yards in 5:04.

AFC DIVISIONAL GAMES

INDIANAPOLIS COLTS 15
BALTIMORE RAVENS 6

	1Q	2Q	3Q	4Q	T
COLTS	6	3	3	3	15
RAVENS	0	3	0	3	6

1ST QUARTER
FG Ind: Adam Vinatieri, 23 yd, 8:04. Drive: 11 plays, 49 yards in 4:43.
FG Ind: Adam Vinatieri, 42 yd, 5:36. Drive: 4 plays, 8 yards in 1:38.
2ND QUARTER
FG Bal: Matt Stover, 40 yd, 14:56. Drive: 5 plays, 19 yards in 2:15.
FG Ind: Adam Vinatieri, 51 yd, 3:15. Drive: 13 plays, 65 yards in 6:00.
3RD QUARTER
FG Ind: Adam Vinatieri, 48 yd, 10:57. Drive: 9 plays, 54 yards in 4:03.
4TH QUARTER
FG Bal: Matt Stover, 51 yd, 13:03. Drive: 11 plays, 62 yards in 7:40.
FG Ind: Adam Vinatieri, 35 yd, 0:23. Drive: 13 plays, 47 yards in 7:16.

NEW ENGLAND PATRIOTS 24
SAN DIEGO CHARGERS 21

	1Q	2Q	3Q	4Q	T
PATRIOTS	3	7	3	11	24
CHARGERS	0	14	0	7	21

1ST QUARTER
FG NE: Stephen Gostkowski, 50 yd, 0:40. Drive: 9 plays, 33 yards in 4:35.
2ND QUARTER
TD SD: LaDainian Tomlinson, 2 yd run (Nate Kaeding kick), 7:19. Drive: 9 plays, 48 yards in 4:31.
TD SD: Michael Turner, 6 yd run (Nate Kaeding kick), 2:04. Drive: 4 plays, 77 yards in 2:23.
TD NE: Jabar Gaffney, 6 yd pass from Tom Brady (Stephen Gostkowski kick), 0:08. Drive: 11 plays, 72 yards in 1:56.
3RD QUARTER
FG NE: Stephen Gostkowski, 34 yd, 2:11. Drive: 7 plays, 15 yards in 3:09.
4TH QUARTER
TD SD: LaDainian Tomlinson, 3 yd run (Nate Kaeding kick), 8:35. Drive: 9 plays, 83 yards in 4:44.
TD NE: Reche Caldwell, 4 yd pass from Tom Brady (Kevin Faulk run for 2-pt. conversion), 4:36. Drive: 5 plays, 32 yards in 1:40.
FG NE: Stephen Gostkowski, 31 yd, 1:10. Drive: 8 plays, 72 yards in 2:20.

FAST FACT

The Indianapolis Colts and the New England Patriots have played each other in the AFC playoffs three out of the last four years.

NFC DIVISIONAL GAMES

NEW ORLEANS SAINTS 27
PHILADELPHIA EAGLES 24

	1Q	2Q	3Q	4Q	T
SAINTS	3	10	14	0	27
EAGLES	0	14	7	3	24

1ST QUARTER
FG NO: John Carney, 33 yd, 9:24. Drive: 5 plays, 35 yards in 2:05.
2ND QUARTER
FG NO: John Carney, 23 yd, 14:46. Drive: 6 plays, 59 yards in 1:33.
TD Phi: Donte Stallworth, 75 yd pass from Jeff Garcia (David Akers kick), 13:38. Drive: 3 plays, 76 yards in 1:08.
TD NO: Reggie Bush, 4 yd run (John Carney kick), 5:19. Drive: 14 plays, 78 yards in 8:19.
TD Phi: Brian Westbrook, 1 yd run (David Akers kick), 0:50. Drive: 11 plays, 80 yards in 4:29.
3RD QUARTER
TD Phi: Brian Westbrook, 62 yd run (David Akers kick), 13:25. Drive: 3 plays, 80 yards in 1:35.
TD NO: Deuce McAllister, 5 yd run (John Carney kick), 9:36. Drive: 7 plays, 63 yards in 3:49.
TD NO: Deuce McAllister, 11 yd pass from Drew Brees (John Carney kick), 1:05. Drive: 9 plays, 84 yards in 6:21.
4TH QUARTER
FG Phi: David Akers, 24 yd, 11:08. Drive: 9 plays, 64 yards in 4:57.

CHICAGO BEARS 27
SEATTLE SEAHAWKS 24

	1Q	2Q	3Q	4Q	OT	T
BEARS	7	14	0	3	3	27
SEAHAWKS	0	14	10	0	0	24

1ST QUARTER
TD Chi: Thomas Jones, 9 yd run (Robbie Gould kick), 8:35. Drive: 12 plays, 80 yards in 6:25.
2ND QUARTER
TD Sea: Nate Burleson, 16 yd pass from Matt Hasselbeck (Josh Brown kick), 14:54. Drive: 9 plays, 71 yards in 3:54.
TD Chi: Bernard Berrian, 68 yd pass from Rex Grossman (Robbie Gould kick), 14:36. Drive: 1 play, 68 yards in 0:18.
TD Sea: Shaun Alexander, 4 yd run (Josh Brown kick), 2:29. Drive: 5 plays, 26 yards in 1:50.
TD Chi: Thomas Jones, 7 yd run (Robbie Gould kick), 0:48. Drive: 7 plays, 57 yards in 1:41.
3RD QUARTER
FG Sea: Josh Brown, 40 yd, 9:56. Drive: 9 plays, 49 yards in 5:04.
TD Sea: Shaun Alexander, 13 yd run (Josh Brown kick), 4:57. Drive: 7 plays, 51 yards in 2:25.
4TH QUARTER
FG Chi: Robbie Gould, 41 yd, 4:24. Drive: 12 plays, 48 yards in 5:51.
OT
FG Chi: Robbie Gould, 49 yd, 10:02. Drive: 7 plays, 34 yards in 2:49.

AFC CONFERENCE CHAMPIONSHIP

INDIANAPOLIS COLTS 38
NEW ENGLAND PATRIOTS 34

	1Q	2Q	3Q	4Q	T
COLTS	3	3	15	17	38
PATRIOTS	7	14	7	6	34

1ST QUARTER
TD NE: Logan Mankins, 0 yd fumble return (Stephen Gostkowski kick), 7:24.
FG Ind: Adam Vinatieri, 42 yd, 0:48. Drive: 14 plays, 56 yards in 6:36.
2ND QUARTER
TD NE: Corey Dillon, 7 yd run (Stephen Gostkowski kick), 10:18. Drive: 11 plays, 72 yards in 5:30.
TD NE: Asante Samuel, 39 yd interception return (Stephen Gostkowski kick), 9:25.
FG Ind: Adam Vinatieri, 26 yd, 0:07. Drive: 15 plays, 80 yards in 2:59.
3RD QUARTER
TD Ind: Peyton Manning, 1 yd run (Adam Vinatieri kick), 8:13. Drive: 14 plays, 76 yards in 6:47.
TD Ind: Dan Klecko, 1 yd pass from Peyton Manning (Peyton Manning pass to Marvin Harrison for 2 pt. conversion), 4:00. Drive: 6 plays, 76 yards in 2:50.
TD Jabar Gaffney, 6 yd pass from Tom Brady (Stephen Gostkowski kick), 1:25. Drive: 5 plays, 21 yards in 2:35.
4TH QUARTER
TD Ind: Jeff Saturday, 0 yd fumble return (Adam Vinatieri kick), 13:24.
FG NE: Stephen Gostkowski, 28 yd, 7:42. Drive: 6 plays, 33 yards in 2:44.
FG Ind: Adam Vinatieri, 36 yd, 5:31. Drive: 5 plays, 59 yards in 2:11.
FG NE: Stephen Gostkowski, 43 yd, 3:49. Drive: 5 plays, 29 yards in 1:42.
TG Ind: Joseph Addai, 3 yd run (Adam Vinatieri kick), 1:00. Drive: 7 plays, 80 yards in 1:17.

NFC CONFERENCE CHAMPIONSHIP

CHICAGO BEARS 39
NEW ORLEANS SAINTS 14

	1Q	2Q	3Q	4Q	T
BEARS	3	13	2	21	39
SAINTS	0	7	7	0	14

1ST QUARTER
FG Chi: Robbie Gould, 19 yd, 0:41. Drive: 11 plays, 35 yards in 4:44.
2ND QUARTER
FG Chi: Robbie Gould, 43 yd, 13:40. Drive: 4 plays, 5 yards in 1:53.
FG Chi: Robbie Gould, 24 yd, 8:52. Drive: 8 plays, 43 yards in 3:25.
TD Chi: Thomas Jones, 2 yd run (Robbie Gould kick), 1:56. Drive: 8 plays, 69 yards in 3:55.
TD NO: Marques Colston, 13 yd pass from Drew Brees (John Carney kick), 0:46. Drive: 8 plays, 73 yards in 1:10.
3RD QUARTER
TD NO: Reggie Bush, 88 yd pass from Drew Brees (John Carney kick), 12:20. Drive: 2 plays, 93 yards in 0:53.
SAFETY Chi: Intentional grounding penalty on Drew Brees enforced in end zone, 5:27.
4TH QUARTER
TD Chi: Bernard Berrian, 33 yd pass from Rex Grossman (Robbie Gould kick), 14:23. Drive: 5 plays, 85 yards in 2:24.
TD Chi: Cedric Benson, 12 yd run (Robbie Gould kick), 11:37. Drive: 4 plays, 26 yards in 2:04.
TD Chi: Thomas Jones, 15 yd run (Robbie Gould kick), 4:19. Drive: 5 plays, 30 yards in 3:02.

SUPER BOWL XLI

INDIANAPOLIS COLTS 29
CHICAGO BEARS 17

FEBRUARY 4, 2007
DOLPHIN STADIUM, MIAMI, FLORIDA

	1Q	2Q	3Q	4Q	T
COLTS	6	10	6	7	29
BEARS	14	0	3	0	17

1ST QUARTER
TD Chi: Devin Hester, 92 yd kick return (Robbie Gould kick), 14:46.
TD Ind: Reggie Wayne, 53 yd pass from Peyton Manning, 6:50. Drive: 9 plays, 80 yards in 4:30.
TD Chi: Muhsin Muhammad, 4 yd pass from Rex Grossman (Robbie Gould kick), 4:34. Drive: 4 plays, 57 yards in 2:00.

2ND QUARTER
FG Ind: Adam Vinatieri, 29 yd, 11:17. Drive: 8 plays, 47 yards in 3:52.
TD Ind: Dominic Rhodes, 1 yd run (Adam Vinatieri kick), 6:09. Drive: 7 plays, 58 yards in 3:08.
3RD QUARTER
FG Ind: Adam Vinatieri, 24 yd, 7:26. Drive: 13 plays, 56 yards in 7:34.
FG Ind: Adam Vinatieri, 20 yd, 3:16. Drive: 6 plays, 62 yards in 2:07.
FG Chi: Robbie Gould, 44 yd, 1:14. Drive: 6 plays, 14 yards in 2:02.
4TH QUARTER
TD Ind: Kelvin Hayden, 56 yd interception return (Adam Vinatieri kick), 11:44.

LEGENDS

Earl Campbell led the NFL in rushing in 1978, 1979, and 1980.

■ **Earl Campbell, running back,** b. March 29, 1955, Tyler, Texas. With a compact, solid frame atop thick, muscular legs, Earl Campbell was famous for running over tacklers rather than around them. After winning the 1977 Heisman Trophy while playing at Texas, he became the number one overall pick in the 1978 draft. In his first NFL season, Campbell earned NFL Rookie of the Year honors, rumbling for 1,450 yards and leading the Houston Oilers to the AFC Championship game. In 1979, he again led the NFL in rushing yards and was named NFL MVP. In 1980, he not only led the league with 1,934 rushing yards, but he also set a new NFL single-season record with 373 carries. His role as an offensive workhorse took its toll on his body, however. After being traded to the New Orleans Saints in 1984, Campbell totalled only 833 yards over the final 24 games of his career, which ended after the 1985 season. During his eight-year career, Campbell gained 9,407 yards, scored 74 touchdowns, and was named to the All-Pro team five times. He was inducted into the Pro Football Hall of Fame in 1991, and in 1999, *The Sporting News* ranked him 33rd on their list of the 100 Greatest Football Players.

■ **Nick Buoniconti, linebacker,** b. December 15, 1940, Springfield, Massachusetts. At 5' 11", 220 pounds, Buoniconti was considered too small to play linebacker by many pro football scouts. He proved them wrong, though, and was named to the AFL All-Star team five out of his first seven seasons with the Boston Patriots. After being traded to Miami in 1969, Buoniconti became the core of the famed "No Name" defense that helped the Dolphins win two straight Super Bowls in 1973 and 1974. He was inducted into the Pro Football Hall of Fame in 2001.

■ **Marv Levy, coach,** b. August 3, 1925, Chicago, Illinois. Although Levy coached the Kansas City Chiefs from 1978 to 1982, he is best known for his 12 seasons as head coach of the Buffalo Bills from 1986 to 1997. As the Bills' head coach, Levy instituted a fast-paced, "no huddle" offense that powered Buffalo to four straight Super Bowl appearances from 1991 to 1994 (the Bills lost all four games). Over his 17 seasons coaching in the NFL, Levy's record was 143–112 during the regular season and 11–8 in the playoffs. He was inducted into the Pro Football Hall of Fame in 2001.

SUPER BOWL XLI (cont.)

TEAM STATS

	COLTS	BEARS
First Downs	24	11
Rushing	12	3
Passing	11	8
Penalty	1	0
3rd-Down Conversions	8–18	3–10
4th-Down Conversions	0–1	0–1
Total Net Yards	430	265
Total Plays	81	48
Average Gain	5.3	5.5
Net Yards Rushing	191	111
Rushes	42	19
Avg. Per Rush	4.5	5.8

	COLTS	BEARS
Net Yards Passing	239	154
Comp.-Att.	25–38	20–28
Yards Per Pass	6.3	5.5
Sacked-Yards Lost	1–8	1–11
Had Intercepted	1	2
Punts-Average	4–40.5	5–45.2
Return Yards	225	147
Punts-Returns	3–42	1–3
Kickoffs-Returns	4–89	6–138
Int.-Returns	2–94	1–6
Penalties-Yards	6–40	4–35
Fumbles-Lost	2–2	4–3
Time of Pos.	38:04	21:56

PLAYER STATISTICS: COLTS

OFFENSE

PASSING	COMP-ATT	YDS	TD	INT
Peyton Manning	25-38	247	1	1

RUSHING	ATT	YDS	TD	LG
Dominic Rhodes	21	113	1	36
Joseph Addai	19	77	0	14
Dallas Clark	1	1	0	1
Peyton Manning	1	0	0	0

RECEIVING	REC	YDS	TD	LG
Joseph Addai	10	66	0	12
Reggie Wayne	2	61	1	53
Marvin Harrison	5	59	0	22
Dallas Clark	4	36	0	17
Bryan Fletcher	2	9	0	6
Dominic Rhodes	1	8	0	8
Ben Utecht	1	8	0	8

DEFENSE	T-A	SCK	INT	FF
Gary Brackett	6-2	0.0	0	0
Cato June	5-2	0.0	0	0
Antoine Bethea	4-0	0.0	0	0
Kelvin Hayden	4-1	0.0	1	0
Rob Morris	4-0	0.0	0	0
Nicholas Harper	3-0	0.0	0	0
Jason David	2-0	0.0	0	0
Marlin Jackson	2-0	0.0	0	0
Anthony McFarland	2-0	0.1	0	0
Rocky Boiman	1-0	0.0	0	0
Ryan Diem	1-0	0.0	0	0
Bryan Fletcher	1-0	0.0	0	0
Freddy Keiaho	1-0	0.0	0	0
Robert Mathis	1-1	0.0	0	0
Aaron Moorehead	1-0	0.0	0	0
Dexter Reid	1-0	0.0	0	0
Bob Sanders	1-1	0.0	1	1
Raheem Brock	0-1	0.0	0	0

PLAYER STATISTICS: BEARS

OFFENSE

PASSING	COMP–ATT	YDS	TD	INT
Rex Grossman	20–28	165	1	2

RUSHING	ATT	YDS	TD	LG
Thomas Jones	15	112	0	52
Rex Grossman	2	0	0	0
Cedric Benson	2	-1	0	4

RECEIVING	REC	YDS	TD	LG
Desmond Clark	6	64	0	18
Bernard Berrian	4	38	0	14
Muhsin Muhammad	3	35	1	22
Thomas Jones	4	18	0	14
Jason McKie	2	8	0	4
Rashied Davis	1	2	0	2

DEFENSE	T–A	SCK	INT	FF
Lance Briggs	11–2	0.0	0	0
Danieal Manning	7–1	0.0	0	0
Brian Urlacher	7–3	0.0	0	0
Charles Tillman	6–4	0.0	0	1
Tank Johnson	4–1	0.5	0	0
Ian Scott	4–0	0.0	0	0
Nathan Vasher	4–2	0.0	0	0
Chris Harris	3–1	0.0	1	0
Alex Brown	2–0	0.0	0	0
Ricky Manning	2–0	0.0	0	0
Adewale Ogunleye	2–0	0.0	0	0
Mark Anderson	1–1	0.5	0	0
Brendon Ayanbadejo	1–0	0.0	0	0
Alfonso Boone	1–0	0.0	0	0
Roberto Garza	1–0	0.0	0	0
Rex Grossman	1–0	0.0	0	0
Hunter Hillenmeyer	1–5	0.0	0	0
Todd Johnson	1–1	0.0	0	0
Thomas Jones	1–0	0.0	0	0
Adrian Peterson	1–0	0.0	0	0
Patrick Mannelly	0–1	0.0	0	0

KEY COMP-ATT=completions-attempts; YDS=yards; TD=touchdowns; INT=interceptions;
ATT=attempts; LG=long; REC=receptions; T-A=tackles-assists; SCK=sacks; FF=forced fumbles

THE ASSOCIATED PRESS 2006 ALL-PRO TEAM

OFFENSE

QUARTERBACK Drew Brees, New Orleans Saints

RUNNING BACKS LaDainian Tomlinson, San Diego Chargers; Larry Johnson, Kansas City Chiefs

FULLBACK Lorenzo Neal, San Diego Chargers

TIGHT END Antonio Gates, San Diego Chargers

WIDE RECEIVERS Marvin Harrison, Indianapolis Colts; Chad Johnson, Cincinnati Bengals

TACKLES Jamaal Brown, New Orleans Saints; Willie Anderson, Cincinnati Bengals

GUARDS Shawn Andrews, Philadelphia Eagles; Alan Faneca, Pittsburgh Steelers

CENTER Olin Kreutz, Chicago Bears

KICKER Robbie Gould, Chicago Bears

KICK RETURNER Devin Hester, Chicago Bears

Jason Taylor,
Miami Dolphins

DEFENSE

ENDS Jason Taylor, Miami Dolphins; Julius Peppers, Carolina Panthers

TACKLES Jamal Williams, San Diego Chargers; Kevin Williams, Minnesota Vikings

OUTSIDE LINEBACKERS Shawne Merriman, San Diego Chargers; Adalius Thomas, Baltimore Ravens

INSIDE LINEBACKERS Brian Urlacher, Chicago Bears; Zach Thomas, Miami Dolphins

CORNERBACKS Rashean Mathis, Jacksonville Jaguars; Champ Bailey, Denver Broncos

SAFETIES Brian Dawkins, Philadelphia Eagles; Ed Reed, Baltimore Ravens

PUNTER Brian Moorman, Buffalo Bills

2006 REGULAR-SEASON RESULTS — AFC

BALTIMORE RAVENS

WEEK	OPPONENT	SCORE	W/L/T
1	at Buccaneers	27–0	W
2	RAIDERS	28–6	W
3	at Browns	15–14	W
4	CHARGERS	16–13	W
5	at Broncos	3–13	L
6	PANTHERS	21–23	L
7	BYE WEEK	—	—
8	at Saints	35–22	W
9	BENGALS	26–20	W
10	at Titans	27–26	W
11	FALCONS	24–10	W
12	STEELERS	27–0	W
13	at Bengals	7–13	L
14	at Chiefs	20–10	W
15	BROWNS	27–17	W
16	at Steelers	31–7	W
17	BILLS	19–7	W

BUFFALO BILLS

WEEK	OPPONENT	SCORE	W/L/T
1	at Patriots	17–19	L
2	at Dolphins	16–6	W
3	JETS	20–28	L
4	VIKINGS	17–12	W
5	at Bears	7–40	L
6	at Lions	17–20	L
7	PATRIOTS	6–28	L
8	BYE WEEK	—	—
9	PACKERS	24–10	W
10	at Colts	16–17	L
11	at Texans	24–21	W
12	JAGUARS	27–24	W
13	CHARGERS	21–24	L
14	at Jets	31–13	W
15	DOLPHINS	21–0	W
16	TITANS	29–30	L
17	at Ravens	7–19	L

CINCINNATI BENGALS

WEEK	OPPONENT	SCORE	W/L/T
1	at Chiefs	23–10	W
2	BROWNS	34–17	W
3	at Steelers	28–20	W
4	PATRIOTS	13–38	L
5	BYE WEEK	—	—
6	at Buccaneers	13–14	L
7	PANTHERS	17–14	W
8	FALCONS	27–29	L
9	at Ravens	20–26	L
10	CHARGERS	41–49	L
11	at Saints	31–16	W
12	at Browns	30–0	W
13	RAVENS	13–7	W
14	RAIDERS	27–10	W
15	at Colts	16–34	L
16	at Broncos	23–24	L
17	STEELERS	17–23	L

CLEVELAND BROWNS

WEEK	OPPONENT	SCORE	W/L/T
1	SAINTS	14–19	L
2	at Bengals	17–34	L
3	RAVENS	14–15	L
4	at Raiders	24–21	W
5	at Panthers	12–20	L
6	BYE WEEK	—	—
7	BRONCOS	7–17	L
8	JETS	20–13	W
9	at Chargers	25–32	L
10	at Falcons	17–13	W
11	STEELERS	20–24	L
12	BENGALS	0–30	L
13	CHIEFS	31–28	W
14	at Steelers	7–27	L
15	at Ravens	17–27	L
16	BUCCANEERS	7–22	L
17	at Texans	6–14	L

Note: Home games are capitalized.

2006 REGULAR-SEASON RESULTS — AFC (cont.)

DENVER BRONCOS

WEEK	OPPONENT	SCORE	W/L/T
1	at Rams	10–18	L
2	CHIEFS	9–6	W
3	at Patriots	17–7	W
4	BYE WEEK	—	—
5	RAVENS	13–3	W
6	RAIDERS	13–3	W
7	at Browns	17–7	W
8	COLTS	31–34	L
9	at Steelers	31–20	W
10	at Raiders	17–13	W
11	CHARGERS	27–35	L
12	at Chiefs	10–19	L
13	SEAHAWKS	20–23	L
14	at Chargers	20–48	L
15	at Cardinals	37–20	W
16	BENGALS	24–23	W
17	49ers	23–26	L

HOUSTON TEXANS

WEEK	OPPONENT	SCORE	W/L/T
1	EAGLES	10–24	L
2	at Colts	24–43	L
3	REDSKINS	15–31	L
4	DOLPHINS	17–15	W
5	BYE WEEK	—	—
6	at Cowboys	6–34	L
7	JAGUARS	27–7	W
8	at Titans	22–28	L
9	at Giants	10–14	L
10	at Jaguars	13–10	W
11	BILLS	21–24	L
12	at Jets	11–26	L
13	at Raiders	23–14	W
14	TITANS	20–26	L
15	at Patriots	7–40	L
16	COLTS	27–24	W
17	BROWNS	14–6	W

INDIANAPOLIS COLTS

WEEK	OPPONENT	SCORE	W/L/T
1	at Giants	26–21	W
2	TEXANS	43–24	W
3	JAGUARS	21–14	W
4	at Jets	31–28	W
5	TITANS	14–13	W
6	BYE WEEK	—	—
7	REDSKINS	36–22	W
8	at Broncos	34–31	W
9	at Patriots	27–20	W
10	BILLS	17–16	W
11	at Cowboys	14–21	L
12	EAGLES	45–21	W
13	at Titans	17–20	L
14	at Jaguars	17–44	L
15	BENGALS	34–16	W
16	at Texans	24–27	L
17	DOLPHINS	27–22	W

JACKSONVILLE JAGUARS

WEEK	OPPONENT	SCORE	W/L/T
1	COWBOYS	24–17	W
2	STEELERS	9–0	W
3	at Colts	14–21	L
4	at Redskins	30–36	L
5	JETS	41–0	W
6	BYE WEEK	—	—
7	at Texans	7–27	L
8	at Eagles	13–6	W
9	TITANS	37–7	W
10	TEXANS	10–13	L
11	GIANTS	26–10	W
12	at Bills	24–27	L
13	at Dolphins	24–10	W
14	COLTS	44–17	W
15	at Titans	17–24	L
16	PATRIOTS	21–24	L
17	at Chiefs	30–35	L

KANSAS CITY CHIEFS

WEEK	OPPONENT	SCORE	W/L/T
1	BENGALS	10–23	L
2	at Broncos	6–9	L
3	BYE WEEK	—	—
4	49ers	41–0	W
5	at Cardinals	23–20	W
6	at Steelers	7–45	L
7	CHARGERS	30–27	W
8	SEAHAWKS	35–28	W
9	at Rams	31–17	W
10	at Dolphins	10–13	L
11	RAIDERS	17–13	W
12	BRONCOS	19–10	W
13	at Browns	28–31	L
14	RAVENS	10–20	L
15	at Chargers	9–20	L
16	at Raiders	20–9	W
17	JAGUARS	35–30	W

MIAMI DOLPHINS

WEEK	OPPONENT	SCORE	W/L/T
1	at Steelers	17–28	L
2	BILLS	6–16	L
3	TITANS	13–10	W
4	at Texans	15–17	L
5	at Patriots	10–20	L
6	at Jets	17–20	L
7	PACKERS	24–34	L
8	BYE WEEK	—	—
9	at Bears	31–13	W
10	CHIEFS	13–10	W
11	VIKINGS	24–20	W
12	at Lions	27–10	W
13	JAGUARS	10–24	L
14	PATRIOTS	21–0	W
15	at Bills	0–21	L
16	JETS	10–13	L
17	at Colts	22–27	L

2006 REGULAR-SEASON RESULTS — AFC (cont.)

NEW ENGLAND PATRIOTS

WEEK	OPPONENT	SCORE	W/L/T
1	BILLS	19–17	W
2	at Jets	24–17	W
3	BRONCOS	7–17	L
4	at Bengals	38–13	W
5	DOLPHINS	20–10	W
6	BYE WEEK	–	–
7	at Bills	28–6	W
8	at Vikings	31–7	W
9	COLTS	20–27	L
10	JETS	14–17	L
11	at Packers	35–0	W
12	BEARS	17–13	W
13	LIONS	28–21	W
14	at Dolphins	0–21	L
15	TEXANS	40–7	W
16	at Jaguars	24–21	W
17	at Titans	40–23	W

NEW YORK JETS

WEEK	OPPONENT	SCORE	W/L/T
1	at Titans	23–16	W
2	PATRIOTS	17–24	L
3	at Bills	28–20	W
4	COLTS	28–31	L
5	at Jaguars	0–41	L
6	DOLPHINS	20–17	W
7	LIONS	31–24	W
8	at Browns	13–20	L
9	BYE WEEK	–	–
10	at Patriots	17–14	W
11	BEARS	0–10	L
12	TEXANS	26–11	W
13	at Packers	38–10	W
14	BILLS	13–31	L
15	at Vikings	26–13	W
16	at Dolphins	13–10	W
17	RAIDERS	23–3	W

OAKLAND RAIDERS

WEEK	OPPONENT	SCORE	W/L/T
1	CHARGERS	0–27	L
2	at Ravens	6–28	L
3	BYE WEEK	–	–
4	BROWNS	21–24	L
5	at 49ers	20–34	L
6	at Broncos	3–13	L
7	CARDINALS	22–9	W
8	STEELERS	20–13	W
9	at Seahawks	0–16	L
10	BRONCOS	13–17	L
11	at Chiefs	13–17	L
12	at Chargers	14–21	L
13	TEXANS	14–23	L
14	at Bengals	10–27	L
15	RAMS	0–20	L
16	CHIEFS	9–20	L
17	at Jets	3–23	L

PITTSBURGH STEELERS

WEEK	OPPONENT	SCORE	W/L/T
1	DOLPHINS	28–17	W
2	at Jaguars	0–9	L
3	BENGALS	20–28	L
4	BYE WEEK	–	–
5	at Chargers	13–23	L
6	CHIEFS	45–7	W
7	at Falcons	38–41	L
8	at Raiders	13–20	L
9	BRONCOS	20–31	L
10	SAINTS	38–31	W
11	at Browns	24–20	W
12	at Ravens	0–27	L
13	BUCCANEERS	20–3	W
14	BROWNS	27–7	W
15	at Panthers	37–3	W
16	RAVENS	7–31	L
17	at Bengals	23–17	W

SAN DIEGO CHARGERS

WEEK	OPPONENT	SCORE	W/L/T
1	at Raiders	27–0	W
2	TITANS	40–7	W
3	BYE WEEK	–	–
4	at Ravens	13–16	L
5	STEELERS	23–13	W
6	at 49ers	48–19	W
7	at Chiefs	27–30	L
8	RAMS	38–24	W
9	BROWNS	32–25	W
10	at Bengals	49–41	W
11	at Broncos	35–27	W
12	RAIDERS	21–14	W
13	at Bills	24–21	W
14	BRONCOS	48–20	W
15	CHIEFS	20–9	W
16	at Seahawks	20–17	W
17	CARDINALS	27–20	W

TENNESSEE TITANS

WEEK	OPPONENT	SCORE	W/L/T
1	JETS	16–23	L
2	at Chargers	7–40	L
3	at Dolphins	10–13	L
4	COWBOYS	14–45	L
5	at Colts	13–14	L
6	at Redskins	25–22	W
7	BYE WEEK	–	–
8	TEXANS	28–22	W
9	at Jaguars	7–37	L
10	RAVENS	26–27	L
11	at Eagles	31–13	W
12	GIANTS	24–21	W
13	COLTS	20–17	W
14	at Texans	26–20	W
15	JAGUARS	24–17	W
16	at Bills	30–29	W
17	PATRIOTS	23–40	L

2006 REGULAR-SEASON RESULTS – NFC

ARIZONA CARDINALS

WEEK	OPPONENT	SCORE	W/L/T
1	49ERS	34–27	W
2	at Seahawks	10–21	L
3	RAMS	14–16	L
4	at Falcons	10–32	L
5	CHIEFS	20–23	L
6	BEARS	23–24	L
7	at Raiders	9–22	L
8	at Packers	14–31	L
9	BYE WEEK	–	–
10	COWBOYS	10–27	L
11	LIONS	17–10	W
12	at Vikings	26–31	L
13	at Rams	34–20	W
14	SEAHAWKS	27–21	W
15	BRONCOS	20–37	L
16	at 49ers	26–20	W
17	at Chargers	20–27	L

DID YOU KNOW?

AFC teams have won eight out of the last 10 Super Bowls, but from 1985 through 1997, teams from the NFC won 13 Super Bowls in a row.

FAST FACT

Members of the Indianapolis Colts received $73,000 each for winning Super Bowl XLI. The Chicago Bears share was $38,000 per player.

TODAY'S STARS

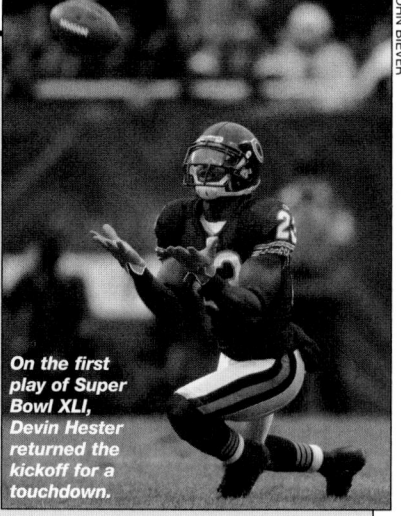

JOHN BIEVER

■ **Devin Hester, kick returner,** b. November 4, 1982, Riviera Beach, Florida. After an All-America collegiate career as a punt and kickoff returner at the University of Miami (Fla.), Hester made an immediate impact during his rookie NFL season in 2006. He scored an NFL single-season record six return touchdowns in his first 13 weeks with the Chicago Bears, including a 108-yard return of a missed field goal that tied for the longest play in NFL history. Hester continued his impressive play in the postseason by becoming the first player in Super Bowl history to return the game's opening kickoff for a touchdown. He was named to the 2007 Pro Bowl team.

On the first play of Super Bowl XLI, Devin Hester returned the kickoff for a touchdown.

■ **Drew Brees, quarterback,** b. January 15, 1979, Austin, Texas. After leading Purdue to the Rose Bowl and winning Academic All-America Player of the Year honors in 2000, Brees was drafted by San Diego in 2001. While with the Chargers, he was voted to the Pro Bowl after the 2004 and 2005 seasons. He signed with New Orleans as a free agent in 2006 and, thanks to his league-leading 4,418 passing yards, Brees led the Saints to their first NFC Championship game.

■ **Steven Jackson, running back,** b. July 22, 1983, Las Vegas, Nevada. Drafted out of Oregon State by St. Louis in 2004, Jackson split time with Marshall Faulk during his first two seasons. But in 2006, Jackson had a breakout year, leading the NFL with 2,334 total yards from scrimmage (1,528 rushing yards and 806 receiving yards) as well as scoring 16 touchdowns. For his performance, he was named to the 2007 Pro Bowl team.

ATLANTA FALCONS

WEEK	OPPONENT	SCORE	W/L/T
1	at Panthers	20–6	W
2	BUCCANEERS	14–3	W
3	at Saints	3–23	L
4	CARDINALS	32–10	W
5	BYE WEEK	—	—
6	GIANTS	14–27	L
7	STEELERS	41–38	W
8	at Bengals	29–27	W
9	at Lions	14–30	L
10	BROWNS	13–17	L
11	at Ravens	10–24	L
12	SAINTS	13–31	L
13	at Redskins	24–14	W
14	at Buccaneers	17–6	W
15	COWBOYS	28–38	L
16	PANTHERS	3–10	L
17	at Eagles	17–24	L

CAROLINA PANTHERS

WEEK	OPPONENT	SCORE	W/L/T
1	FALCONS	6–20	L
2	at Vikings	13–16	L
3	at Buccaneers	26–24	W
4	SAINTS	21–18	W
5	BROWNS	20–12	W
6	at Ravens	23–21	W
7	at Bengals	14–17	L
8	COWBOYS	14–35	L
9	BYE WEEK	—	—
10	BUCCANEERS	24–10	W
11	RAMS	15–0	W
12	at Redskins	13–17	L
13	at Eagles	24–27	L
14	GIANTS	13–27	L
15	STEELERS	3–37	L
16	at Falcons	10–3	W
17	at Saints	31–21	W

CHICAGO BEARS

WEEK	OPPONENT	SCORE	W/L/T
1	at Packers	26–0	W
2	LIONS	34–7	W
3	at Vikings	19–16	W
4	SEAHAWKS	37–6	W
5	BILLS	40–7	W
6	at Cardinals	24–23	W
7	BYE WEEK	—	—
8	49ERS	41–10	W
9	DOLPHINS	13–31	L
10	at Giants	38–20	W
11	at Jets	10–0	W
12	at Patriots	13–17	L
13	VIKINGS	23–13	W
14	at Rams	42–27	W
15	BUCCANEERS	34–31	W
16	at Lions	26–21	W
17	PACKERS	7–26	L

DALLAS COWBOYS

WEEK	OPPONENT	SCORE	W/L/T
1	at Jaguars	17–24	L
2	REDSKINS	27–10	W
3	BYE WEEK	—	—
4	at Titans	45–14	W
5	at Eagles	24–38	L
6	TEXANS	34–6	W
7	GIANTS	22–36	L
8	at Panthers	35–14	W
9	at Redskins	19–22	L
10	at Cardinals	27–10	W
11	COLTS	21–14	W
12	BUCCANEERS	38–10	W
13	at Giants	23–20	W
14	SAINTS	17–42	L
15	at Falcons	38–28	W
16	EAGLES	7–23	L
17	LIONS	31–39	L

DETROIT LIONS

WEEK	OPPONENT	SCORE	W/L/T
1	SEAHAWKS	6–9	L
2	at Bears	7–34	L
3	PACKERS	24–31	L
4	at Rams	34–41	L
5	at Vikings	17–26	L
6	BILLS	20–17	W
7	at Jets	24–31	L
8	BYE WEEK	—	—
9	FALCONS	30–14	W
10	49ERS	13–19	L
11	at Cardinals	10–17	L
12	DOLPHINS	10–27	L
13	at Patriots	21–28	L
14	VIKINGS	20–30	L
15	at Packers	9–17	L
16	BEARS	21–26	L
17	at Cowboys	39–31	W

GREEN BAY PACKERS

WEEK	OPPONENT	SCORE	W/L/T
1	BEARS	0–26	L
2	SAINTS	27–34	L
3	at Lions	31–24	W
4	at Eagles	9–31	L
5	RAMS	20–23	L
6	BYE WEEK	—	—
7	at Dolphins	34–24	W
8	CARDINALS	31–14	W
9	at Bills	10–24	L
10	at Vikings	23–17	W
11	PATRIOTS	0–35	L
12	at Seahawks	24–34	L
13	JETS	10–38	L
14	at 49ers	30–19	W
15	LIONS	17–9	W
16	VIKINGS	9–7	W
17	at Bears	26–7	W

Note: Home games are capitalized.

2006 REGULAR-SEASON RESULTS — NFC (cont.)

MINNESOTA VIKINGS

WEEK	OPPONENT	SCORE	W/L/T
1	at Redskins	19–16	W
2	PANTHERS	16–13	W
3	BEARS	16–19	L
4	at Bills	12–17	L
5	LIONS	26–17	W
6	BYE WEEK	—	—
7	at Seahawks	31–13	W
8	PATRIOTS	7–31	L
9	at 49ers	3–9	L
10	PACKERS	17–23	L
11	at Dolphins	20–24	L
12	CARDINALS	31–26	W
13	at Bears	13–23	L
14	at Lions	30–20	W
15	JETS	13–26	L
16	at Packers	7–9	L
17	RAMS	21–41	L

NEW ORLEANS SAINTS

WEEK	OPPONENT	SCORE	W/L/T
1	at Browns	19–14	W
2	at Packers	34–27	W
3	FALCONS	23–3	W
4	at Panthers	18–21	L
5	BUCCANEERS	24–21	W
6	EAGLES	27–24	W
7	BYE WEEK	—	—
8	RAVENS	22–35	L
9	at Buccaneers	31–14	W
10	at Steelers	31–38	L
11	BENGALS	16–31	L
12	at Falcons	31–13	W
13	49ERS	34–10	W
14	at Cowboys	42–17	W
15	REDSKINS	10–16	L
16	at Giants	30–7	W
17	PANTHERS	21–31	L

NEW YORK GIANTS

WEEK	OPPONENT	SCORE	W/L/T
1	COLTS	21–26	L
2	at Eagles	30–24	W
3	at Seahawks	30–42	L
4	BYE WEEK	—	—
5	REDSKINS	19–3	W
6	at Falcons	27–14	W
7	at Cowboys	36–22	W
8	BUCCANEERS	17–3	W
9	TEXANS	14–10	W
10	BEARS	20–38	L
11	at Jaguars	10–26	L
12	at Titans	21–24	L
13	COWBOYS	20–23	L
14	at Panthers	27–13	W
15	EAGLES	22–36	L
16	SAINTS	7–30	L
17	at Redskins	34–28	W

PHILADELPHIA EAGLES

WEEK	OPPONENT	SCORE	W/L/T
1	at Texans	24–10	W
2	GIANTS	24–30	L
3	at 49ers	38–24	W
4	PACKERS	31–9	W
5	COWBOYS	38–24	W
6	at Saints	24–27	L
7	at Buccaneers	21–23	L
8	JAGUARS	6–13	L
9	BYE WEEK	—	—
10	REDSKINS	27–3	W
11	TITANS	13–31	L
12	at Colts	21–45	L
13	PANTHERS	27–24	W
14	at Redskins	21–19	W
15	at Giants	36–22	W
16	at Cowboys	23–7	W
17	FALCONS	24–17	W

SAN FRANCISCO 49ERS

WEEK	OPPONENT	SCORE	W/L/T
1	at Cardinals	27–34	L
2	RAMS	20–13	W
3	EAGLES	24–38	L
4	at Chiefs	0–41	L
5	RAIDERS	34–20	W
6	CHARGERS	19–48	L
7	BYE WEEK	—	—
8	at Bears	10–41	L
9	VIKINGS	9–3	W
10	at Lions	19–13	W
11	SEAHAWKS	20–14	W
12	at Rams	17–20	L
13	at Saints	10–34	L
14	PACKERS	19–30	L
15	at Seahawks	24–14	W
16	CARDINALS	20–26	L
17	at Broncos	26–23	W

SEATTLE SEAHAWKS

WEEK	OPPONENT	SCORE	W/L/T
1	at Lions	9–6	W
2	CARDINALS	21–10	W
3	GIANTS	42–30	W
4	at Bears	6–37	L
5	BYE WEEK	—	—
6	at Rams	30–28	W
7	VIKINGS	13–31	L
8	at Chiefs	28–35	L
9	RAIDERS	16–0	W
10	RAMS	24–22	W
11	at 49ers	14–20	L
12	PACKERS	34–24	W
13	at Broncos	23–20	W
14	at Cardinals	21–27	L
15	49ERS	14–24	L
16	CHARGERS	17–20	L
17	at Buccaneers	23–7	W

2006 REGULAR-SEASON RESULTS — NFC (cont.)

ST. LOUIS RAMS

WEEK	OPPONENT	SCORE	W/L/T
1	BRONCOS	18–10	W
2	at 49ers	13–20	L
3	at Cardinals	16–14	W
4	LIONS	41–34	W
5	at Packers	23–20	W
6	SEAHAWKS	28–30	L
7	BYE WEEK	—	—
8	at Chargers	24–38	L
9	CHIEFS	17–31	L
10	at Seahawks	22–24	L
11	at Panthers	0–15	L
12	49ERS	20–17	W
13	CARDINALS	20–34	L
14	BEARS	27–42	L
15	at Raiders	20–0	W
16	REDSKINS	37–31	W
17	at Vikings	41–21	W

TAMPA BAY BUCCANEERS

WEEK	OPPONENT	SCORE	W/L/T
1	RAVENS	0–27	L
2	at Falcons	3–14	L
3	PANTHERS	24–26	L
4	BYE WEEK	—	—
5	at Saints	21–24	L
6	BENGALS	14–13	W
7	EAGLES	23–21	W
8	at Giants	3–17	L
9	SAINTS	14–31	L
10	at Panthers	10–24	L
11	REDSKINS	20–17	W
12	at Cowboys	10–38	L
13	at Steelers	3–20	L
14	FALCONS	6–17	L
15	at Bears	31–34	L
16	at Browns	22–7	W
17	SEAHAWKS	7–23	L

WASHINGTON REDSKINS

WEEK	OPPONENT	SCORE	W/L/T
1	VIKINGS	16–19	L
2	at Cowboys	10–27	L
3	at Texans	31–15	W
4	JAGUARS	36–30	W
5	at Giants	3–19	L
6	TITANS	22–25	L
7	at Colts	22–36	L
8	BYE WEEK	—	—
9	COWBOYS	22–19	W
10	at Eagles	3–27	L
11	at Buccaneers	17–20	L
12	PANTHERS	17–13	W
13	FALCONS	14–24	L
14	EAGLES	19–21	L
15	at Saints	16–10	W
16	at Rams	31–37	L
17	GIANTS	28–34	L

DID YOU KNOW?

In 2006, LaDainian Tomlinson set new NFL single-season records for rushing touchdowns (28), total touchdowns (31), and total points scored (186).

2006 INDIVIDUAL LEADERS — AFC

TOUCHDOWNS	TEAM	TD	RSH	REC	RET	PTS
LaDainian Tomlinson	SD	31	28	3	0	186
Larry Johnson	KC	19	17	2	0	114
Maurice Jones-Drew	JAC	16	13	2	1	96
Willie Parker	PIT	16	13	3	0	96
Corey Dillon	NE	13	13	0	0	78
Marvin Harrison	IND	12	0	12	0	72
Rudi Johnson	CIN	12	12	0	0	72
Reggie Wayne	IND	9	0	9	0	54
Jamal Lewis	BAL	9	9	0	0	54
Chris Henry	CIN	9	0	9	0	54
T.J. Houshmandzadeh	CIN	9	0	9	0	54
Javon Walker	DEN	9	1	8	0	54
Antonio Gates	SD	9	0	9	0	54

KEY TD=touchdowns; RSH=rushing touchdowns;
REC=receiving touchdowns; RET=returns; PTS=points

2006 INDIVIDUAL LEADERS — AFC (cont.)

KICKING	TEAM	FGM	FGA	LONG	XPM	XPA	PTS
Matt Stover	BAL	28	30	52	37	37	121
Jason Elam	DEN	27	29	51	34	34	115
Olindo Mare	MIA	26	36	52	22	22	100
Josh Scobee	JAC	26	32	48	41	41	119
Nate Kaeding	SD	26	29	54	58	58	136
Adam Vinatieri	IND	25	28	48	38	38	113
Shayne Graham	CIN	25	30	51	42	40	115
Mike Nugent	NYJ	24	27	54	35	34	106
Lawerence Tynes	KC	24	31	53	36	35	107
Rian Lindell	BUF	23	25	53	33	33	102

PASSER RATING	TEAM	YDS	ATT	COMP	TD	INT	LONG	RATING
Peyton Manning	IND	4,397	557	362	31	9	68	101.0
Damon Huard	KC	1,878	244	148	11	1	78	98.0
Carson Palmer	CIN	4,035	520	324	28	13	74	93.9
Philip Rivers	SD	3,388	460	284	22	9	57	92.0
Tom Brady	NE	3,529	516	319	24	12	62	87.9
J.P. Losman	BUF	3,051	429	268	19	14	83	84.9
Chad Pennington	NYJ	3,352	485	313	17	16	71	82.6
Steve McNair	BAL	3,050	468	295	16	12	87	82.5
David Carr	HOU	2,767	442	302	11	12	53	82.1
David Garrard	JAC	1,735	241	145	10	9	49	80.5

RECEPTIONS	TEAM	REC	YDS	AVG	TD	LONG
Andre Johnson	HOU	103	1,147	11.1	5	53
Marvin Harrison	IND	95	1,366	14.4	12	68
Laveranues Coles	NYJ	91	1,098	12.1	6	58
T.J. Houshmandzadeh	CIN	90	1,081	12.0	9	40
Kellen Winslow	CLE	89	875	9.8	3	40
Chad Johnson	CIN	87	1,369	15.7	7	74
Reggie Wayne	IND	86	1,310	15.2	9	51
Lee Evans	BUF	82	1,292	15.8	8	83
Jerricho Cotchery	NYJ	82	961	11.7	6	71
Hines Ward	PIT	74	975	13.2	6	70

WESLEY HITT / WIREIMAGE.COM

**Andre Johnson,
Houston Texans**

RUSHING	TEAM	YDS	ATT	AVG	TD	LONG
LaDainian Tomlinson	SD	1,815	348	5.2	28	85
Larry Johnson	KC	1,789	416	4.3	17	47
Willie Parker	PIT	1,494	337	4.4	13	76
Rudi Johnson	CIN	1,309	341	3.8	12	22
Travis Henry	TEN	1,211	270	4.5	7	70
Fred Taylor	JAC	1,146	231	5.0	5	76
Jamal Lewis	BAL	1,132	314	3.6	9	52
Joseph Addai	IND	1,081	226	4.8	7	41
Tatum Bell	DEN	1,025	233	4.4	2	51
Ronnie Brown	MIA	1,008	241	4.2	5	47
Willis McGahee	BUF	990	259	3.8	6	57

KEY FGM=field goals made; FGA=field goals attempted; XPM=extra points made; XPA=extra points attempted; PTS=points; YDS=yards; ATT=attempts; COMP=completions; TD=touchdowns; INT=interceptions; REC=receptions; AVG=average

2006 INDIVIDUAL LEADERS — AFC (cont.)

RECEIVING YARDS	TEAM	REC	YDS	AVG	TD	LONG
Chad Johnson	CIN	87	1,369	15.7	7	74
Marvin Harrison	IND	95	1,366	14.4	12	68
Reggie Wayne	IND	86	1,310	15.2	9	51
Lee Evans	BUF	82	1,292	15.8	8	83
Andre Johnson	HOU	103	1,147	11.1	5	53
Laveranues Coles	NYJ	91	1,098	12.1	6	58
Javon Walker	DEN	69	1,084	15.7	8	83
T.J. Houshmandzadeh	CIN	90	1,081	12.0	9	40
Hines Ward	PIT	74	975	13.2	6	70
Jerricho Cotchery	NYJ	82	961	11.7	6	71

**Shawne Merriman,
San Diego Chargers**

ROBERT BECK

INTERCEPTIONS	TEAM	INT	YDS	TD	LONG
Asante Samuel	NE	10	120	0	33
Champ Bailey	DEN	10	162	1	70
Rashean Mathis	JAC	8	146	0	55
Nnamdi Asomugha	OAK	8	59	1	24
Chris McAlister	BAL	6	121	2	60
Kevin Kaesviharn	CIN	6	24	0	22
Dawan Landry	BAL	5	101	1	37
Ed Reed	BAL	5	70	1	37
Daven Holly	CLE	5	127	1	57
Sean Jones	CLE	5	46	0	19
Chris Hope	TEN	5	105	1	61

SACKS	TEAM	SACKS	TACKLES*
Shawne Merriman	SD	17	62
Aaron Schobel	BUF	14	53
Jason Taylor	MIA	13.5	60
Trevor Pryce	BAL	13	47
Shaun Phillips	SD	11.5	65
Adalius Thomas	BAL	11	83
Kamerion Wimbley	CLE	11	62
Derrick Burgess	OAK	11	50
Robert Geathers	CIN	10.5	42
Bobby McCray	JAC	10	35

PUNTING	TEAM	NO.	YDS	AVG	NAVG	LG	TB	BLK	IN 20	RET	RET AVG	RET TD
Shane Lechler	OAK	77	3,660	47.5	36.4	67	19	0	19	34	12.9	0
Kyle Larson	CIN	77	3,428	44.5	38.6	67	11	0	26	42	5.6	0
Hunter Smith	IND	47	2,085	44.4	34.5	61	5	0	14	25	13.1	1
Dustin Colquitt	KC	71	3,145	44.3	39.3	72	5	0	23	32	7.9	0
Ben Graham	NYJ	72	3,182	44.2	37.8	69	11	0	26	28	7.3	0
Dave Zastudil	CLE	81	3,563	44.0	38.4	61	7	0	28	43	7.3	0
Brian Moorman	BUF	92	4,012	43.6	39.2	66	7	0	33	36	7.4	0
Josh Miller	NE	43	1,848	43.0	35.8	62	7	0	12	18	9.4	1

2006 INDIVIDUAL LEADERS — NFC

TOUCHDOWNS	TEAM	TD	RSH	REC	RET	PTS
Marion Barber	DAL	16	14	2	0	96
Steven Jackson	STL	16	13	3	0	96
Terrell Owens	DAL	13	0	13	0	78
Brian Westbrook	PHI	11	7	4	0	66
Deuce McAllister	NO	11	10	0	0	66
Darrell Jackson	SEA	10	0	10	0	60
Plaxico Burress	NYG	10	0	10	0	60
Torry Holt	STL	10	0	10	0	60
Brandon Jacobs	NYG	9	9	0	0	54
Reggie Brown	PHI	9	1	8	0	54

KEY NO.=number; NAVG=net average; LG=long; TB=touchback; BLK=blocked; IN 20=inside 20-yard line; RET=returned; RET AVG=return average; RET TD=returned for a touchdown

*Unassisted tackles

2006 INDIVIDUAL LEADERS — NFC (cont.)

KICKING	TEAM	FGM	FGA	LONG	XPM	XPA	PTS
Robbie Gould	CHI	32	36	49	47	47	143
Jeff Wilkins	STL	32	37	53	35	35	131
Jason Hanson	DET	29	33	53	30	30	117
Joe Nedney	SF	26	35	51	29	29	116
Neil Rackers	ARI	28	37	50	32	32	116
Dave Rayner	GB	26	35	54	32	31	109
Josh Brown	SEA	25	31	54	36	36	111
John Kasay	CAR	24	27	54	28	28	100
Jay Feely	NYG	23	27	47	38	38	107
John Carney	NO	23	25	51	47	46	115

PASSER RATING	TEAM	YDS	ATT	COMP	TD	INT	LONG	RATING
Drew Brees	NO	4,418	554	356	26	11	86	96.2
Donovan McNabb	PHI	2,647	316	180	18	6	87	95.5
Tony Romo	DAL	2,903	337	220	19	13	56	95.1
Marc Bulger	STL	4,301	588	370	24	8	67	92.9
Mark Brunell	WAS	1,789	260	162	8	4	74	86.5
Jake Delhomme	CAR	2,805	431	263	17	11	72	82.6
Jon Kitna	DET	4,208	596	372	21	22	60	79.9
Eli Manning	NYG	3,244	522	301	24	18	55	77.0
Matt Hasselbeck	SEA	2,442	371	210	18	15	72	76.0
Michael Vick	ATL	2,474	388	204	20	13	55	75.7
Alex Smith	SF	2,890	442	257	16	16	75	74.8

RECEPTIONS	TEAM	REC	YDS	AVG	TD	LONG
Mike Furrey	DET	98	1,086	11.1	6	31
Torry Holt	STL	93	1,188	12.8	10	67
Donald Driver	GB	92	1,295	14.1	8	82
Steven Jackson	STL	90	806	9.0	3	64
Reggie Bush	NO	88	742	8.4	2	74
Terrell Owens	DAL	85	1,180	13.9	13	56
Anquan Boldin	ARI	83	1,203	14.5	4	64
Steve Smith	CAR	83	1,166	14.0	8	72
Roy Williams	DET	82	1,310	16.0	7	60
Brian Westbrook	PHI	77	699	9.1	4	52

RECEIVING YARDS	TEAM	REC	YDS	AVG	TD	LONG
Roy Williams	DET	82	1,310	16.0	7	60
Donald Driver	GB	92	1,295	14.1	8	82
Anquan Boldin	ARI	83	1,203	14.5	4	64
Torry Holt	STL	93	1,188	12.8	10	67
Terrell Owens	DAL	85	1,180	13.9	13	56
Steve Smith	CAR	83	1,166	14.0	8	72
Issac Bruce	STL	74	1,098	14.8	3	45
Mike Furrey	DET	98	1,086	11.1	6	31
Joey Galloway	TB	62	1,057	17.0	7	64
Terry Glenn	DAL	70	1,047	15.0	6	54

Donald Driver,
Green Bay Packers

DAMIAN STROHMEYER

2006 INDIVIDUAL LEADERS — NFC (cont.)

RUSHING	TEAM	YDS	ATT	AVG	TD	LONG
Frank Gore	SF	1,695	312	5.4	8	72
Tiki Barber	NYG	1,662	327	5.1	5	55
Steven Jackson	STL	1,528	346	4.4	13	59
Brian Westbrook	PHI	1,217	240	5.1	7	71
Chester Taylor	MIN	1,216	303	4.0	6	95
Thomas Jones	CHI	1,210	296	4.1	6	30
Edgerrin James	ARI	1,159	337	3.4	6	18
Ladell Batts	WAS	1,154	245	4.7	4	26
Warrick Dunn	ATL	1,140	286	4.0	4	90
Julius Jones	DAL	1,084	267	4.1	4	77

PETER READ MILLER

**Frank Gore,
San Francisco 49ers**

INTERCEPTIONS	TEAM	INT	YDS	TD	LONG
Charles Woodson	GB	8	61	1	23
Walt Harris	SF	8	84	1	42
Lito Sheppard	PHI	6	157	1	102
Roy Williams	DAL	5	33	0	27
Ricky Manning	CHI	5	113	1	54
Charles Tillman	CHI	5	32	0	13
Brian Dawkins	PHI	4	38	0	38
Adrian Wilson	ARI	4	146	1	99
Darren Sharper	MIN	4	10	0	10

SACKS	TEAM	SACKS	TACKLES*
Aaron Kampman	GB	15.5	89
Julius Peppers	CAR	13	57
Leonard Little	STL	13	58
Mark Anderson	CHI	12	28
DeMarcus Ware	DAL	11.5	71
Will Smith	NO	10.5	49
Julian Peterson	SEA	10	89
Chike Okeafor	ARI	8.5	52
Trent Cole	PHI	8	62
Karlos Dansby	ARI	8	80
Cory Redding	DET	8	47

TRIVIA CHALLENGE

Who is the only head coach in NFL history to have appeared in six Super Bowls?

Don Shula (Baltimore-III; Miami-VI–VIII, XVII, XIX)

PUNTING	TEAM	NO.	YDS	AVG	NAVG	LG	TB	BLK	IN 20	RET	RET AVG	RET TD
Mat McBriar	DAL	56	2,697	48.2	38.6	75	10	0	22	31	10.8	0
Jason Baker	CAR	98	4,483	45.7	39.0	70	12	0	31	60	6.4	1
Ryan Plackemeier	SEA	84	3,778	45.0	37.3	72	15	0	25	38	9.0	0
Nick Harris	DET	66	2,967	45.0	38.2	67	9	0	18	38	7.0	1
Scott Player	ARI	66	2,965	44.9	34.5	58	3	0	18	44	12.8	1
Andy Lee	SF	81	3,625	44.8	36.8	66	9	0	22	35	13.2	1
Jon Ryan	GB	84	3,739	44.5	35.7	66	12	0	17	55	9.1	1
Brad Maynard	CHI	77	3,404	44.2	37.6	65	7	0	24	38	9.7	0
Steven Weatherford	NO	77	3,369	43.8	37.5	59	10	0	19	40	7.0	0
Josh Bidwell	TB	93	4,045	43.5	36.8	59	7	0	20	50	9.7	1

*Unassisted tackles

TEAM-BY-TEAM STATS — AFC

BALTIMORE RAVENS

PASSING

PLAYER	ATT	COMP	YDS	PCT COMP	YDS/ATT	TD	INT	RATING
Steve McNair	468	295	3,050	63.0	6.5	16	12	82.5

RUSHING

PLAYER	NO.	YDS	AVG	LG	TD
Jamal Lewis	314	1,132	3.6	52	9
Mike Anderson	39	183	4.7	34	1
Musa Smith	36	153	4.3	30	0
Steve McNair	45	119	2.6	19	1
Ovie Mughelli	12	50	4.2	12	0
Kyle Boller	22	34	1.5	10	0

RECEIVING

PLAYER	NO.	YDS	AVG	LG	TD
Mark Clayton	67	939	14.0	87	5
Todd Heap	73	765	10.5	30	6
Derrick Mason	68	750	11.0	38	2
Demetrius Williams	22	396	18.0	77	2
Ovie Mughelli	21	182	8.7	30	2
Daniel Wilcox	20	166	8.3	35	3

KICKING

PLAYER	FGM	FGA	PCT	XPM	XPA
Matt Stover	28	30	93.3	37	37

PUNTING

PLAYER	NO.	AVG	NET AVG	TB	IN 20	LG	BLK
Sam Koch	86	43.0	37.6	3	30	61	0

INTERCEPTIONS Chris McAlister, 6   **SACKS** Trevor Pryce, 13

BUFFALO BILLS

PASSING

PLAYER	ATT	COMP	YDS	PCT COMP	YDS/ATT	TD	INT	RATING
J.P. Losman	429	268	3,051	62.5	7.1	19	14	84.9

RUSHING

PLAYER	NO.	YDS	AVG	LG	TD
Willis McGahee	259	990	3.8	57	6
Anthony Thomas	107	378	3.5	19	2
J.P. Losman	38	140	3.7	15	1
Roscoe Parrish	2	18	9.0	11	0
Peerless Price	5	18	3.6	9	0

RECEIVING

PLAYER	NO.	YDS	AVG	LG	TD
Lee Evans	82	1,292	15.8	83	8
Josh Reed	34	410	12.1	52	2
Peerless Price	49	402	8.2	25	3
Roscoe Parrish	23	320	13.9	51	2
Robert Royal	23	233	10.1	33	0
Willis McGhee	18	156	8.7	56	0
Anthony Thomas	22	139	6.3	18	0

KICKING

PLAYER	FGM	FGA	PCT	XPM	XPA
Rian Lindell	23	25	92.0	33	33

PUNTING

PLAYER	NO.	AVG	NET AVG	TB	IN 20	LG	BLK
Brian Moorman	92	43.6	39.2	9	33	66	0

INTERCEPTIONS London Fletcher-Baker, 4   **SACKS** Aaron Schobel, 14

KEY	ATT=attempts; COMP=completions; YDS=yards; PCT COMP=completion percentage; YDS/ATT=yards per attempt; TD=touchdowns; INT=interceptions; NO.=number; AVG=average; LG=long; FGM=field goals made; FGA=field goals attempted; PCT=percentage; XPM=extra points made; XPA=extra points attempted; NET AVG=net average; TB=touchbacks; IN 20=inside 20-yard line; BLK=blocked

CINCINNATI BENGALS

PASSING

PLAYER	ATT	COMP	YDS	PCT COMP	YDS/ATT	TD	INT	RATING
Carson Palmer	520	324	4,035	62.3	7.8	28	13	93.9
Anthony Wright	3	3	31	100.0	10.3	0	0	109.7

RUSHING

PLAYER	NO.	YDS	AVG	LG	TD
Rudi Johnson	341	1,309	3.8	22	12
Kenny Watson	25	138	5.5	18	1
Chris Perry	10	57	5.7	18	0
Jeremi Johnson	15	56	3.7	15	1
Carson Palmer	26	37	1.4	11	0
Chad Johnson	6	24	4.0	8	0

RECEIVING

PLAYER	NO.	YDS	AVG	LG	TD
Chad Johnson	87	1,369	15.7	74	7
T.J. Houshmandzadeh	90	1,081	12.0	40	9
Chris Henry	36	605	16.8	71	9
Reggie Kelly	21	254	12.1	32	1
Kenny Watson	23	213	9.3	46	0
Rudi Johnson	23	124	5.4	18	0
Tony Stewart	14	120	8.6	26	1

KICKING

PLAYER	FGM	FGA	PCT	XPM	XPA
Shayne Graham	25	30	83.3	40	42

PUNTING

PLAYER	NO.	AVG	NET AVG	TB	IN 20	LG	BLK
Kyle Larson	77	44.5	38.6	11	26	67	0

INTERCEPTIONS Kevin Kaesviharn, 6   SACKS Robert Geathers, 10.5

CLEVELAND BROWNS

PASSING

PLAYER	ATT	COMP	YDS	PCT COMP	YDS/ATT	TD	INT	RATING
Charlie Frye	392	252	2,454	64.3	6.3	10	17	72.2
Derek Anderson	117	66	793	56.4	6.8	5	8	63.1

RUSHING

PLAYER	NO.	YDS	AVG	LG	TD
Reuben Droughns	220	758	3.4	22	4
Charlie Frye	47	215	4.6	17	3
Jason Wright	62	189	3.0	18	0
Jerome Harrison	20	60	3.0	15	0
Derek Anderson	4	47	11.8	33	0
Dennis Northcutt	3	32	10.7	16	0

RECEIVING

PLAYER	NO.	YDS	AVG	LG	TD
Braylon Edwards	61	884	14.5	75	6
Kellen Winslow	89	875	9.8	40	3
Joe Jurevicius	40	495	12.4	52	3
Steve Heiden	36	249	6.9	13	2
Dennis Northcutt	22	228	10.4	43	0
Reuben Droughns	27	169	6.3	24	0
Josh Cribbs	10	91	9.1	14	0
Jason Wright	6	82	13.7	54	0

KICKING

PLAYER	FGM	FGA	PCT	XPM	XPA
Phil Dawson	21	29	72.4	25	25

PUNTING

PLAYER	NO.	AVG	NET AVG	TB	IN 20	LG	BLK
Dave Zastudil	81	44.0	38.4	7	28	61	0

INTERCEPTIONS Sean Jones, Daven Holly, 5   SACKS Kamerion Wimbley, 11

DENVER BRONCOS

PASSING

PLAYER	ATT	COMP	YDS	PCT COMP	YDS/ATT	TD	INT	RATING
Jake Plummer	317	175	1,994	55.2	6.3	11	13	68.8

RUSHING

PLAYER	NO.	YDS	AVG	LG	TD
Tatum Bell	233	1,025	4.4	51	2
Mike Bell	157	677	4.3	48	8
Javon Walker	9	123	13.7	72	1
Jake Plummer	36	112	3.1	19	1
Cecil Sapp	10	80	8.0	28	0

RECEIVING

PLAYER	NO.	YDS	AVG	LG	TD
Javon Walker	69	1,084	15.7	83	8
Rod Smith	52	512	9.8	20	3
Brandon Marshall	20	309	15.5	71	2
Tony Scheffler	18	286	15.9	29	4
David Kircus	9	187	20.8	45	0
Stephen Alexander	18	160	8.9	24	2
Mike Bell	20	158	7.9	24	0
Tatum Bell	24	115	4.8	16	0

KICKING

PLAYER	FGM	FGA	PCT	XPM	XPA
Jason Elam	27	29	93.1	34	34

PUNTING

PLAYER	NO.	AVG	NET AVG	TB	IN 20	LG	BLK
Paul Ernster	80	41.7	36.6	7	23	61	0

INTERCEPTIONS Champ Bailey, 10   **SACKS** Elvis Dumervil, 8.5

HOUSTON TEXANS

PASSING

PLAYER	ATT	COMP	YDS	PCT COMP	YDS/ATT	TD	INT	RATING
David Carr	442	302	2,767	68.3	6.3	11	12	82.1

RUSHING

PLAYER	NO.	YDS	AVG	LG	TD
Ron Dayne	151	612	4.1	19	5
Wali Lundy	124	476	3.8	35	4
Samkon Gado	54	217	4.0	34	1
David Carr	53	195	3.7	16	2
Chris Taylor	28	123	4.4	17	1

RECEIVING

PLAYER	NO.	YDS	AVG	LG	TD
Andre Johnson	103	1,147	11.1	53	5
Eric Moulds	57	557	9.8	29	1
Owen Daniels	34	352	10.4	33	5
Wali Lundy	33	204	6.2	15	0
Kevin Walter	17	160	9.4	15	0
Jeb Putzier	13	125	9.6	26	0
Jameel Cook	18	107	5.9	15	0

KICKING

PLAYER	FGM	FGA	PCT	XPM	XPA
Kris Brown	19	25	76.0	26	27

PUNTING

PLAYER	NO.	AVG	NET AVG	TB	IN 20	LG	BLK
Chad Stanley	76	41.6	36.7	5	15	62	0

INTERCEPTIONS Demarcus Faggins, Dunta Robinson, 2   **SACKS** Jason Babin, 5

INDIANAPOLIS COLTS

PASSING

PLAYER	ATT	COMP	YDS	PCT COMP	YDS/ATT	TD	INT	RATING
Peyton Manning	557	362	4,397	65.0	7.9	31	9	101.0

RUSHING

PLAYER	NO.	YDS	AVG	LG	TD
Joseph Addai	226	1,081	4.8	41	7
Dominic Rhodes	187	641	3.4	17	5
Peyton Manning	23	36	1.6	12	4

RECEIVING

PLAYER	NO.	YDS	AVG	LG	TD
Marvin Harrison	95	1,366	14.4	68	12
Reggie Wayne	86	1,310	15.2	51	9
Ben Utecht	37	377	10.2	26	0
Dallas Clark	30	367	12.2	40	4
Joseph Addai	40	325	8.1	21	1
Dominic Rhodes	36	251	7.0	27	0
Bryan Fletcher	18	202	11.2	26	2

KICKING

PLAYER	FGM	FGA	PCT	XPM	XPA
Adam Vinatieri	25	28	89.3	38	38

PUNTING

PLAYER	NO.	AVG	NET AVG	TB	IN 20	LG	BLK
Hunter Smith	47	44.4	34.5	5	14	61	0

INTERCEPTIONS Nick Harper, Cato June, 3   SACKS Robert Mathis, 9.5

JACKSONVILLE JAGUARS

PASSING

PLAYER	ATT	COMP	YDS	PCT COMP	YDS/ATT	TD	INT	RATING
David Garrard	241	145	1,735	60.2	7.2	10	9	80.5
Byron Leftwich	183	108	1,159	59.0	6.3	7	5	79.0

RUSHING

PLAYER	NO.	YDS	AVG	LG	TD
Fred Taylor	231	1,146	5.0	76	5
Maurice Jones-Drew	166	941	5.7	74	
David Garrard	47	250	5.3	20	0
Alvin Pearman	19	89	4.7	12	1
Byron Leftwich	25	41	1.6	7	2
Reggie Williams	7	33	4.7	10	0

RECEIVING

PLAYER	NO.	YDS	AVG	LG	TD
Matt Jones	41	643	15.7	49	4
Reggie Williams	52	616	11.8	48	4
Ernest Wilford	36	524	14.6	41	2
Maurice Jones-Drew	46	436	9.5	51	2
George Wrighster	39	353	9.1	23	3
Fred Taylor	23	242	10.5	36	1
Marcedes Lewis	13	126	9.7	31	1
Cortez Hankton	5	48	9.6	15	0
Kyle Brady	5	37	7.4	13	0

KICKING

PLAYER	FGM	FGA	PCT	XPM	XPA
Josh Scobee	26	32	81.2	41	41

PUNTING

PLAYER	NO.	AVG	NET AVG	TB	IN 20	LG	BLK
Chris Hanson	72	40.6	33.4	7	20	58	0

INTERCEPTIONS Rashean Mathis, 8   SACKS Bobby McCray, 10

KANSAS CITY CHIEFS

PASSING

PLAYER	ATT	COMP	YDS	PCT COMP	YDS/ATT	TD	INT	RATING
Damon Huard	244	148	1,878	60.7	7.7	11	1	98.0

RUSHING

PLAYER	NO.	YDS	AVG	LG	TD
Larry Johnson	416	1,789	4.3	47	17
Michael Bennett	36	200	5.6	41	0
Trent Green	19	59	3.1	10	0
Dee Brown	10	24	2.4	7	0
Ronnie Cruz	5	19	3.8	7	0
Eddie Kennison	4	16	4.0	9	0

RECEIVING

PLAYER	NO.	YDS	AVG	LG	TD
Tony Gonzalez	73	900	12.3	57	5
Eddie Kennison	53	860	16.2	51	5
Samie Parker	41	561	13.7	43	1
Larry Johnson	41	410	10.0	78	2
Dante Hall	26	204	7.8	19	2
Kris Wilson	15	132	8.8	19	3
Michael Bennett	9	77	8.6	14	0
Jason Dunn	4	40	10.0	15	0

KICKING

PLAYER	FGM	FGA	PCT	XPM	XPA
Lawrence Tynes	24	31	77.4	35	36

PUNTING

PLAYER	NO.	AVG	NET AVG	TB	IN 20	LG	BLK
Dustin Colquitt	71	44.3	39.3	5	23	72	0

INTERCEPTIONS Ty Law, 4   SACKS Tamba Hali, 8

MIAMI DOLPHINS

PASSING

PLAYER	ATT	COMP	YDS	PCT COMP	YDS/ATT	TD	INT	RATING
Joey Harrington	388	223	2,236	57.5	5.8	12	15	68.2
Daunte Culpepper	134	81	929	60.4	6.9	2	3	77.0

RUSHING

PLAYER	NO.	YDS	AVG	LG	TD
Ronnie Brown	241	1,008	4.2	47	5
Sammy Morris	92	400	4.3	55	1
Chris Chambers	8	95	11.9	39	0
Travis Minor	19	74	3.9	9	0

RECEIVING

PLAYER	NO.	YDS	AVG	LG	TD
Marty Booker	55	747	13.6	52	6
Wes Welker	67	687	10.3	38	1
Chris Chambers	59	677	11.5	46	4
Randy McMichael	62	640	10.3	24	3
Ronnie Brown	33	276	8.4	24	0
Derek Hagan	21	221	10.5	24	1
Sammy Morris	21	162	7.7	44	0

KICKING

PLAYER	FGM	FGA	PCT	XPM	XPA
Olindo Mare	26	36	72.2	22	22

PUNTING

PLAYER	NO.	AVG	NET AVG	TB	IN 20	LG	BLK
Donnie Jones	85	42.8	35.7	10	28	64	0

INTERCEPTIONS Jason Taylor, Renaldo Hill, 2   SACKS Jason Taylor, 13.5

NEW ENGLAND PATRIOTS

PASSING

PLAYER	ATT	COMP	YDS	PCT COMP	YDS/ATT	TD	INT	RATING
Tom Brady	516	319	3,529	61.8	6.8	24	12	87.9

RUSHING

PLAYER	NO.	YDS	AVG	LG	TD
Corey Dillon	199	812	4.1	50	13
Laurence Maroney	175	745	4.3	41	6
Kevin Faulk	25	123	4.9	11	1
Heath Evans	27	117	4.3	35	0
Tom Brady	49	102	2.1	22	1
Chad Jackson	4	22	5.5	14	0

RECEIVING

PLAYER	NO.	YDS	AVG	LG	TD
Reche Caldwell	61	760	12.5	62	4
Benjamin Watson	49	643	13.1	40	3
Troy Brown	43	384	8.9	23	4
Kevin Faulk	43	356	8.3	43	2
Doug Gabriel	25	344	13.8	45	3
Daniel Graham	21	235	11.2	29	2
Laurence Maroney	22	194	8.8	31	1
David Thomas	11	159	14.5	36	1
Chad Jackson	13	152	11.7	35	3
Corey Dillon	15	147	9.8	52	0

KICKING

PLAYER	FGM	FGA	PCT	XPM	XPA
Stephen Gostkowski	20	26	76.9	43	44

PUNTING

PLAYER	NO.	AVG	NET AVG	TB	IN 20	LG	BLK
Josh Miller	43	43.0	35.8	7	12	62	0

INTERCEPTIONS Asante Samuel, 10   SACKS Rosevelt Colvin, 8.5

NEW YORK JETS

PASSING

PLAYER	ATT	COMP	YDS	PCT COMP	YDS/ATT	TD	INT	RATING
Chad Pennington	485	313	3,352	64.5	6.9	17	16	82.6

RUSHING

PLAYER	NO.	YDS	AVG	LG	TD
Leon Washington	151	650	4.3	23	4
Cedric Houston	113	374	3.3	31	5
Kevin Barlow	131	370	2.8	12	6
Chad Pennington	35	109	3.1	15	0

RECEIVING

PLAYER	NO.	YDS	AVG	LG	TD
Laveranues Coles	91	1,098	12.1	58	6
Jerricho Cotchery	82	961	11.7	71	6
Justin McCareins	23	347	15.1	50	1
Chris Baker	31	300	9.7	28	4
Leon Washington	25	270	10.8	64	0
Tim Dwight	16	112	7.0	15	0

KICKING

PLAYER	FGM	FGA	PCT	XPM	XPA
Mike Nugent	24	27	88.9	34	35

PUNTING

PLAYER	NO.	AVG	NET AVG	TB	IN 20	LG	BLK
Ben Graham	72	44.2	37.8	11	26	69	0

INTERCEPTIONS Andre Dyson, Kerry Rhodes, 4   SACKS Bryan Thomas, 8.5

OAKLAND RAIDERS

PASSING

PLAYER	ATT	COMP	YDS	PCT COMP	YDS/ATT	TD	INT	RATING
Andrew Walter	276	147	1,677	53.3	6.1	3	13	55.8
Aaron Brooks	192	110	1,105	57.3	5.8	3	8	61.7

RUSHING

PLAYER	NO.	YDS	AVG	LG	TD
Justin Fargas	178	659	3.7	48	1
LaMont Jordan	114	434	3.8	59	2
Zack Crockett	39	163	4.2	17	0
Aaron Brooks	22	124	5.6	23	0

RECEIVING

PLAYER	NO.	YDS	AVG	LG	TD
Ronald Curry	62	727	11.7	39	1
Randy Moss	42	553	13.2	51	3
Alvis Whitted	27	299	11.1	33	0
Randal Williams	28	293	10.5	28	0
Courtney Anderson	25	285	11.4	35	2
John Madsen	11	146	13.3	57	1
ReShard Lee	20	138	6.9	15	0
Justin Fargas	13	91	7.0	21	0
Doug Gabriel	5	84	16.8	28	0

KICKING

PLAYER	FGM	FGA	PCT	XPM	XPA
Sebastian Janikowski	18	25	72.0	16	16

PUNTING

PLAYER	NO.	AVG	NET AVG	TB	IN 20	LG	BLK
Shane Lechler	77	47.5	36.4	19	19	67	0

INTERCEPTIONS Nnamdi Asomugha, 8   **SACKS** Derrick Burgess, 11

PITTSBURGH STEELERS

PASSING

PLAYER	ATT	COMP	YDS	PCT COMP	YDS/ATT	TD	INT	RATING
Ben Roethlisberger	469	280	3,513	59.7	7.5	18	23	75.4
Charlie Batch	53	31	492	58.5	9.3	5	0	121.0

RUSHING

PLAYER	NO.	YDS	AVG	LG	TD
Willie Parker	337	1,494	4.4	76	13
Najeh Davenport	60	221	3.7	48	1
Ben Roethlisberger	32	98	3.1	20	2
Verron Haynes	15	78	5.2	13	0
Hines Ward	2	30	15.0	21	0
John Kuhn	2	18	9.0	16	0
Charlie Batch	13	15	1.2	12	0

RECEIVING

PLAYER	NO.	YDS	AVG	LG	TD
Hines Ward	74	975	13.2	70	6
Santonio Holmes	49	824	16.8	67	2
Nate Washington	35	624	17.8	49	4
Cedrick Wilson	37	504	13.6	38	1
Heath Miller	34	393	11.6	87	5
Willie Parker	31	222	7.2	25	3
Najeh Davenport	15	193	12.9	32	1
Verron Haynes	18	95	5.3	16	0

KICKING

PLAYER	FGM	FGA	PCT	XPM	XPA
Jeff Reed	20	27	74.1	41	41

PUNTING

PLAYER	NO.	AVG	NET AVG	TB	IN 20	LG	BLK
Chris Gardocki	65	41.3	36.7	4	11	56	0

INTERCEPTIONS Troy Polamalu, Bryant McFadden, 3   **SACKS** Joey Porter, 7

SAN DIEGO CHARGERS

PASSING

PLAYER	ATT	COMP	YDS	PCT COMP	YDS/ATT	TD	INT	RATING
Philip Rivers	460	284	3,388	61.7	7.4	22	9	92.0
LaDainian Tomlinson	3	2	20	66.7	6.7	2	0	125.0

RUSHING

PLAYER	NO.	YDS	AVG	LG	TD
LaDainian Tomlinson	348	1,815	5.2	85	28
Michael Turner	80	502	6.3	73	2
Lorenzo Neal	29	140	4.8	43	1
Philip Rivers	48	49	1.0	15	0
Andrew Pinnock	4	25	6.3	15	0

RECEIVING

PLAYER	NO.	YDS	AVG	LG	TD
Antonio Gates	71	924	13.0	57	9
Eric Parker	48	659	13.7	38	0
LaDainian Tomlinson	56	508	9.1	51	3
Vincent Jackson	27	453	16.8	55	6
Keenan McCardell	36	437	12.1	28	0
Malcom Floyd	15	210	14.0	46	3
Brandon Manumaleuna	14	91	6.5	19	3
Lorenzo Neal	17	83	4.9	21	0

KICKING

PLAYER	FGM	FGA	PCT	XPM	XPA
Nate Kaeding	26	29	89.7	58	58

PUNTING

PLAYER	NO.	AVG	NET AVG	TB	IN 20	LG	BLK
Mike Scifres	69	41.9	38.2	2	35	71	0

INTERCEPTIONS Quentin Jammer, 4   SACKS Shawne Merriman, 17

TENNESSEE TITANS

PASSING

PLAYER	ATT	COMP	YDS	PCT COMP	YDS/ATT	TD	INT	RATING
Vince Young	357	184	2,199	51.5	6.2	12	13	66.7
Kerry Collins	90	42	549	46.7	6.1	1	6	42.3

RUSHING

PLAYER	NO.	YDS	AVG	LG	TD
Travis Henry	270	1,211	4.5	70	7
Vince Young	83	552	6.7	39	7
LenDale White	61	244	4.0	26	0
Chris Brown	41	156	3.8	21	0
Ahmard Hall	7	21	3.0	11	0

RECEIVING

PLAYER	NO.	YDS	AVG	LG	TD
Drew Bennett	46	737	16.0	39	3
Bobby Wade	33	461	14.0	25	2
Brandon Jones	27	384	14.2	53	4
Bo Scaife	29	370	12.8	34	2
Ben Troupe	13	150	11.5	32	2
Ahmard Hall	15	138	9.2	28	0
Roydell Williams	8	121	15.1	20	0
David Givens	8	104	13.0	27	0

KICKING

PLAYER	FGM	FGA	PCT	XPM	XPA
Rob Bironas	22	28	78.6	32	32

PUNTING

PLAYER	NO.	AVG	NET AVG	TB	IN 20	LG	BLK
Craig Hentrich	88	42.7	37.3	10	32	73	0

INTERCEPTIONS Chris Hope, 5   SACKS Kyle Vanden Bosch, 6.5

TEAM-BY-TEAM STATS — NFC

ARIZONA CARDINALS

PASSING

PLAYER	ATT	COMP	YDS	PCT COMP	YDS/ATT	TD	INT	RATING
Matt Leinart	377	214	2,547	56.8	6.8	11	12	74.0
Kurt Warner	168	108	1,377	64.3	8.0	6	5	89.3

RUSHING

PLAYER	NO.	YDS	AVG	LG	TD
Edgerrin James	337	1,159	3.4	18	6
Matt Leinart	22	49	2.2	14	2
Marcel Shipp	17	41	2.4	9	4
Obafemi Ayanbadejo	9	37	4.1	11	0
Anquan Boldin	5	28	5.6	18	0

RECEIVING

PLAYER	NO.	YDS	AVG	LG	TD
Anquan Boldin	83	1,203	14.5	64	4
Larry Fitzgerald	69	946	13.7	57	6
Bryant Johnson	40	740	18.5	58	4
Edgerrin James	38	217	5.7	14	0
Troy Walters	23	209	9.1	26	2
Leonard Pope	16	161	10.0	33	0
Obafemi Ayanbadejo	17	139	8.2	27	0
Adam Bergen	15	111	7.4	17	1

KICKING

PLAYER	FGM	FGA	PCT	XPM	XPA
Neil Rackers	28	37	75.7	32	32

PUNTING

PLAYER	NO.	AVG	NET AVG	TB	IN 20	LG	BLK
Scott Player	66	44.9	34.5	3	18	58	0

INTERCEPTIONS Adrian Wilson, 4   **SACKS** Chike Okeafor, 8.5

ATLANTA FALCONS

PASSING

PLAYER	ATT	COMP	YDS	PCT COMP	YDS/ATT	TD	INT	RATING
Michael Vick	388	204	2,474	52.6	6.4	20	13	75.7
Matt Schaub	27	18	208	66.7	7.7	1	2	71.2

RUSHING

PLAYER	NO.	YDS	AVG	LG	TD
Warrick Dunn	286	1,140	4.0	90	4
Michael Vick	123	1,039	8.4	51	2
Jerious Norwood	99	633	6.4	78	2

RECEIVING

PLAYER	NO.	YDS	AVG	LG	TD
Alge Crumpler	56	780	13.9	46	8
Roddy White	30	506	16.9	55	0
Michael Jenkins	39	436	11.2	34	7
Ashley Lelie	28	430	15.4	51	1
Warrick Dunn	22	170	7.7	18	1
Justin Griffith	23	168	7.3	16	3
Jerious Norwood	12	102	8.5	32	0

KICKING

PLAYER	FGM	FGA	PCT	XPM	XPA
Morten Andersen	20	23	87.0	27	27

PUNTING

PLAYER	NO.	AVG	NET AVG	TB	IN 20	LG	BLK
Michael Koenen	76	42.1	35.9	6	25	65	0

INTERCEPTIONS DeAngelo Hall, 4   **SACKS** Rod Coleman, 6

KEY ATT=attempts; COMP=completions; YDS=yards; PCT COMP=completion percentage; YDS/ATT=yards per attempt; TD=touchdowns; INT=interceptions; NO.=number; AVG=average; LG=long; FGM=field goals made; FGA=field goals attempted; PCT=percentage; XPM=extra points made; XPA=extra points attempted; NET AVG=net average; TB=touchbacks; IN 20=inside 20-yard line; BLK=blocked

CAROLINA PANTHERS

PASSING

PLAYER	ATT	COMP	YDS	PCT COMP	YDS/ATT	TD	INT	RATING
Jake Delhomme	431	263	2,805	61.0	6.5	17	11	82.6

RUSHING

PLAYER	NO.	YDS	AVG	LG	TD
DeShaun Foster	227	897	4.0	43	3
DeAngelo Williams	121	501	4.1	31	1
Brad Hoover	22	73	3.3	17	1
Steve Smith	8	61	7.6	24	1
Nick Goings	11	52	4.7	28	0

RECEIVING

PLAYER	NO.	YDS	AVG	LG	TD
Steve Smith	83	1,166	14.0	72	8
Keyshawn Johnson	70	815	11.6	40	4
Drew Carter	28	357	12.8	42	3
DeAngelo Williams	33	313	9.5	41	1
Kris Mangum	21	170	8.1	19	1
DeShaun Foster	32	159	5.0	14	0
Michael Gaines	15	146	9.7	19	0

KICKING

PLAYER	FGM	FGA	PCT	XPM	XPA
John Kasay	24	27	88.9	28	28

PUNTING

PLAYER	NO.	AVG	NET AVG	TB	IN 20	LG	BLK
Jason Baker	98	45.7	39.0	12	31	70	0

INTERCEPTIONS Richard Marshall, Ken Lucas, Chris Gamble, 3   **SACKS** Julius Peppers, 13

CHICAGO BEARS

PASSING

PLAYER	ATT	COMP	YDS	PCT COMP	YDS/ATT	TD	INT	RATING
Rex Grossman	480	262	3,193	54.6	6.7	23	20	73.9
Brian Griese	32	18	220	56.3	6.9	1	2	62.0

RUSHING

PLAYER	NO.	YDS	AVG	LG	TD
Thomas Jones	296	1,210	4.1	30	6
Cedric Benson	157	647	4.1	30	6
Adrian Peterson	10	41	4.1	11	2
Jason McKie	8	18	2.3	7	0
Bernard Berrian	2	5	2.5	5	0

RECEIVING

PLAYER	NO.	YDS	AVG	LG	TD
Muhsin Muhammad	60	863	14.4	40	5
Bernard Berrian	51	775	15.2	62	6
Desmond Clark	45	626	13.9	33	6
Rashied Davis	22	303	13.8	31	2
Mark Bradley	14	282	20.1	75	3

KICKING

PLAYER	FGM	FGA	PCT	XPM	XPA
Robbie Gould	32	36	88.9	47	47

PUNTING

PLAYER	NO.	AVG	NET AVG	TB	IN 20	LG	BLK
Brad Maynard	77	44.2	37.6	7	24	65	0

INTERCEPTIONS Ricky Manning, Charles Tillman, 5   **SACKS** Mark Anderson, 12

DALLAS COWBOYS

PASSING

PLAYER	ATT	COMP	YDS	PCT COMP	YDS/ATT	TD	INT	RATING
Tony Romo	337	220	2,903	65.3	8.6	19	13	95.1
Drew Bledsoe	169	90	1,164	53.3	6.9	7	8	69.2

RUSHING

PLAYER	NO.	YDS	AVG	LG	TD
Julius Jones	267	1,084	4.1	77	4
Marion Barber	135	654	4.8	25	14
Tony Romo	34	102	3.0	16	0
Tyson Thompson	13	30	2.3	7	1
Drew Bledsoe	8	28	3.5	11	2

RECEIVING

PLAYER	NO.	YDS	AVG	LG	TD
Terrell Owens	85	1,180	13.9	56	13
Terry Glenn	70	1,047	15.0	54	6
Jason Whitten	64	754	11.8	42	1
Patrick Crayton	36	516	14.3	53	4
Marion Barber	23	196	8.5	26	2
Julius Jones	9	142	15.8	39	0
Anthony Fasano	14	126	9.0	22	0

KICKING

PLAYER	FGM	FGA	PCT	XPM	XPA
Mike Vanderjagt	13	18	72.2	33	33

PUNTING

PLAYER	NO.	AVG	NET AVG	TB	IN 20	LG	BLK
Mat McBriar	56	48.2	38.6	10	22	75	0

INTERCEPTIONS Roy Williams, 5   SACKS DeMarcus Ware, 11.5

DETROIT LIONS

PASSING

PLAYER	ATT	COMP	YDS	PCT COMP	YDS/ATT	TD	INT	RATING
Jon Kitna	596	372	4,208	62.4	7.1	21	22	79.9

RUSHING

PLAYER	NO.	YDS	AVG	LG	TD
Kevin Jones	181	689	3.8	52	6
Arlen Harris	49	158	3.2	20	1
Jon Kitna	34	156	4.6	18	2
Aveion Cason	24	94	3.9	16	0

RECEIVING

PLAYER	NO.	YDS	AVG	LG	TD
Roy Williams	82	1,310	16.0	60	7
Mike Furrey	98	1,086	11.1	31	6
Kevin Jones	61	520	8.5	26	2
Dan Campbell	21	308	14.7	30	4
Corey Bradford	14	164	11.7	23	0
Az-Zahir Hakim	17	147	8.6	23	0
Arlen Harris	18	132	7.3	20	0
Marcus Pollard	12	100	8.3	22	0
Mike Williams	8	99	12.4	21	1

KICKING

PLAYER	FGM	FGA	PCT	XPM	XPA
Jason Hanson	29	33	87.9	30	30

PUNTING

PLAYER	NO.	AVG	NET AVG	TB	IN 20	LG	BLK
Nick Harris	66	42.0	38.2	9	18	67	0

INTERCEPTIONS Terrence Holt, Jamar Fletcher, Dré Bly, 3   SACKS Corey Redding, 8

GREEN BAY PACKERS

PASSING

PLAYER	ATT	COMP	YDS	PCT COMP	YDS/ATT	TD	INT	RATING
Brett Favre	613	343	3,885	56.0	6.3	18	18	72.7
Aaron Rodgers	15	6	46	40.0	3.1	0	0	48.2

RUSHING

PLAYER	NO.	YDS	AVG	LG	TD
Ahman Green	266	1,059	4.0	70	5
Vernand Morency	91	421	4.6	39	2
Noah Herron	37	150	4.1	19	1

RECEIVING

PLAYER	NO.	YDS	AVG	LG	TD
Donald Driver	92	1,295	14.1	82	8
Greg Jennings	45	632	14.0	75	3
Ahman Green	46	373	8.1	20	1
Ruvell Martin	21	358	17.0	36	1
Bubba Franks	25	232	9.3	19	0
Noah Herron	29	211	7.3	16	2
David Martin	21	198	9.4	23	2

KICKING

PLAYER	FGM	FGA	PCT	XPM	XPA
Dave Rayner	26	35	74.3	31	32

PUNTING

PLAYER	NO.	AVG	NET AVG	TB	IN 20	LG	BLK
Jon Ryan	84	44.5	35.7	12	17	66	0

INTERCEPTIONS Charles Woodson, 8   SACKS Aaron Kampman, 15.5

MINNESOTA VIKINGS

PASSING

PLAYER	ATT	COMP	YDS	PCT COMP	YDS/ATT	TD	INT	RATING
Brad Johnson	439	270	2,750	61.5	6.3	9	15	72.0
Tarvaris Jackson	81	47	475	58.0	5.9	2	4	62.5

RUSHING

PLAYER	NO.	YDS	AVG	LG	TD
Chester Taylor	303	1,216	4.0	95	6
Artose Pinner	43	190	4.4	21	3
Mewelde Moore	24	131	5.5	15	0
Ciatrick Fason	18	99	5.5	15	1
Brad Johnson	29	82	2.8	10	1

RECEIVING

PLAYER	NO.	YDS	AVG	LG	TD
Travis Taylor	57	651	11.4	36	3
Mewelde Moore	46	468	10.2	50	1
Troy Williamson	37	455	12.3	46	0
Jermaine Wiggins	46	386	8.4	24	1
Marcus Robinson	29	381	13.1	40	4
Billy McMullen	23	307	13.3	40	2
Chester Taylor	42	288	6.9	24	2

KICKING

PLAYER	FGM	FGA	PCT	XPM	XPA
Ryan Longwell	21	25	84.0	27	28

PUNTING

PLAYER	NO.	AVG	NET AVG	TB	IN 20	LG	BLK
Chris Kluwe	93	42.3	35.6	7	28	68	0

INTERCEPTIONS Antoine Winfield, Dwight Smith, Darren Sharper, 4   SACKS Darrion Scott, 5.5

FOOTBALL PRO

NEW ORLEANS SAINTS

PASSING

PLAYER	ATT	COMP	YDS	PCT COMP	YDS/ATT	TD	INT	RATING
Drew Brees	554	356	4,418	64.3	8.0	26	11	96.2

RUSHING

PLAYER	NO.	YDS	AVG	LG	TD
Deuce McAllister	244	1,057	4.3	57	10
Reggie Bush	155	565	3.6	18	6
Mike Karney	11	33	3.0	8	1

RECEIVING

PLAYER	NO.	YDS	AVG	LG	TD
Marques Colston	70	1,038	14.8	86	8
Devery Henderson	32	745	23.3	76	5
Reggie Bush	88	742	8.4	74	2
Joe Horn	37	679	18.4	72	4
Terrance Copper	23	385	16.7	48	3
Deuce McAllister	30	198	6.6	24	0
Aaron Stecker	19	190	10.0	48	0
Mark Campbell	18	164	9.1	33	0

KICKING

PLAYER	FGM	FGA	PCT	XPM	XPA
John Carney	23	25	92.0	46	47

PUNTING

PLAYER	NO.	AVG	NET AVG	TB	IN 20	LG	BLK
Steven Weatherford	77	43.8	37.5	10	19	59	0

INTERCEPTIONS Four tied with 2   SACKS Will Smith, 10.5

NEW YORK GIANTS

PASSING

PLAYER	ATT	COMP	YDS	PCT COMP	YDS/ATT	TD	INT	RATING
Eli Manning	522	301	3,244	57.7	6.2	24	18	77.0

RUSHING

PLAYER	NO.	YDS	AVG	LG	TD
Tiki Barber	327	1,662	5.1	55	5
Brandon Jacobs	96	423	4.4	16	9
Chad Morton	1	22	22.0	22	0

RECEIVING

PLAYER	NO.	YDS	AVG	LG	TD
Plaxico Burress	63	988	15.7	55	10
Jeremy Shockey	66	623	9.4	25	7
Tiki Barber	58	465	8.0	28	0
Amani Toomer	32	360	11.3	44	3
Tim Carter	22	253	11.5	27	2
David Tyree	19	197	10.4	33	2
Brandon Jacobs	11	149	13.5	43	0

KICKING

PLAYER	FGM	FGA	PCT	XPM	XPA
Jay Feely	23	27	85.2	38	38

PUNTING

PLAYER	NO.	AVG	NET AVG	TB	IN 20	LG	BLK
Jeff Feagles	77	40.2	37.0	3	27	54	0

INTERCEPTIONS Seven tied with 2   SACKS Osi Umenyiora, 6

PHILADELPHIA EAGLES

PASSING

PLAYER	ATT	COMP	YDS	PCT COMP	YDS/ATT	TD	INT	RATING
Donovan McNabb	316	180	2,647	57.0	8.4	18	6	95.5
Jeff Garcia	188	116	1,309	61.7	7.0	10	2	95.8

RUSHING

PLAYER	NO.	YDS	AVG	LG	TD
Brian Westbrook	240	1,217	5.1	71	7
Correll Buckhalter	83	345	4.2	20	2
Donovan McNabb	32	212	6.6	37	3
Jeff Garcia	25	87	3.5	12	0
Ryan Moats	22	69	3.1	13	0

RECEIVING

PLAYER	NO.	YDS	AVG	LG	TD
Reggie Brown	46	816	17.7	60	8
Donte Stallworth	38	725	19.1	84	5
Brian Westbrook	77	699	9.1	52	4
L.J. Smith	50	611	12.2	65	5
Hank Baskett	22	464	21.1	89	2
Greg Lewis	24	348	14.5	45	2
Correll Buckhalter	24	256	10.7	55	1
Matt Schobel	14	214	15.3	60	2

KICKING

PLAYER	FGM	FGA	PCT	XPM	XPA
David Akers	18	23	78.3	48	48

PUNTING

PLAYER	NO.	AVG	NET AVG	TB	IN 20	LG	BLK
Dirk Johnson	78	42.6	34.9	11	21	60	0

INTERCEPTIONS Lito Sheppard, 6   SACKS Trent Cole, 8

SAN FRANCISCO 49ERS

PASSING

PLAYER	ATT	COMP	YDS	PCT COMP	YDS/ATT	TD	INT	RATING
Alex Smith	442	257	2,890	58.1	6.5	16	16	74.8

RUSHING

PLAYER	NO.	YDS	AVG	LG	TD
Frank Gore	312	1,695	5.4	72	8
Alex Smith	44	147	3.3	22	2
Michael Robinson	38	116	3.1	33	2
Bryan Gilmore	7	94	13.4	22	0

RECEIVING

PLAYER	NO.	YDS	AVG	LG	TD
Antonio Bryant	40	733	18.3	72	3
Arnaz Battle	59	686	11.6	56	3
Frank Gore	61	485	8.0	39	1
Eric Johnson	34	292	8.6	26	2
Vernon Davis	20	265	13.3	52	3
Bryan Gilmore	8	150	18.8	75	1
Maurice Hicks	13	137	10.5	33	1
Michael Robinson	9	47	5.2	12	0

KICKING

PLAYER	FGM	FGA	PCT	XPM	XPA
Joe Nedney	29	35	82.9	29	29

PUNTING

PLAYER	NO.	AVG	NET AVG	TB	IN 20	LG	BLK
Andy Lee	81	44.8	36.8	9	22	66	0

INTERCEPTIONS Walt Harris, 8   SACKS Brandon Moore, 6.5

SEATTLE SEAHAWKS

PASSING

PLAYER	ATT	COMP	YDS	PCT COMP	YDS/ATT	TD	INT	RATING
Matt Hasselbeck	371	210	2,442	56.6	6.6	18	15	76.0
Seneca Wallace	141	82	927	58.2	6.6	8	7	76.2

RUSHING

PLAYER	NO.	YDS	AVG	LG	TD
Shaun Alexander	252	896	3.6	33	7
Maurice Morris	161	604	3.8	29	0
Mack Strong	33	149	4.5	17	1
Seneca Wallace	12	122	10.2	37	0

RECEIVING

PLAYER	NO.	YDS	AVG	LG	TD
Darrell Jackson	63	956	15.2	72	10
Deion Branch	53	725	13.7	38	4
D.J. Hackett	45	610	13.6	47	4
Bobby Engram	24	290	12.1	25	1
Jerramy Stevens	22	231	10.5	26	4
Nate Burleson	18	192	10.7	36	2
Mack Strong	29	159	5.5	13	0
Itula Mili	10	69	6.9	15	0

KICKING

PLAYER	FGM	FGA	PCT	XPM	XPA
Josh Brown	25	31	80.6	36	36

PUNTING

PLAYER	NO.	AVG	NET AVG	TB	IN 20	LG	BLK
Ryan Plackemeier	84	45.0	37.3	15	25	72	0
Josh Brown	2	24.5	24.5	0	1	28	0

INTERCEPTIONS Ken Hamlin, 3   **SACKS** Julian Peterson, 10

ST. LOUIS RAMS

PASSING

PLAYER	ATT	COMP	YDS	PCT COMP	YDS/ATT	TD	INT	RATING
Marc Bulger	588	370	4,301	62.9	7.3	24	8	92.9

RUSHING

PLAYER	NO.	YDS	AVG	LG	TD
Steven Jackson	346	1,528	4.4	59	13
Stephen Davis	40	177	4.4	16	0
Marc Bulger	18	44	2.4	29	0
Matt Turk	2	19	9.5	16	0

RECEIVING

PLAYER	NO.	YDS	AVG	LG	TD
Torry Holt	93	1,188	12.8	67	10
Issac Bruce	74	1,098	14.8	45	3
Steven Jackson	90	806	9.0	64	3
Kevin Curtis	40	479	12.0	42	4

KICKING

PLAYER	FGM	FGA	PCT	XPM	XPA
Jeff Wilkins	32	37	86.5	35	35

PUNTING

PLAYER	NO.	AVG	NET AVG	TB	IN 20	LG	BLK
Matt Turk	72	43.5	38.3	5	26	74	0
Jeff Wilkins	3	30.3	27.7	0	3	33	0

INTERCEPTIONS Four tied with 3   **SACKS** Leonard Little, 13

TAMPA BAY BUCCANEERS

PASSING

PLAYER	ATT	COMP	YDS	PCT COMP	YDS/ATT	TD	INT	RATING
Bruce Gradkowski	328	177	1,661	54.0	5.1	9	9	65.9
Tim Rattay	101	61	748	60.4	7.4	4	2	88.2
Chris Simms	106	58	585	54.7	5.5	1	7	46.3

RUSHING

PLAYER	NO.	YDS	AVG	LG	TD
Cadillac Williams	225	798	3.5	38	1
Michael Pittman	50	245	4.9	32	1
Mike Alstott	60	171	2.9	17	3
Bruce Gradkowski	41	161	3.9	14	0
Earnest Graham	11	59	5.4	17	0

RECEIVING

PLAYER	NO.	YDS	AVG	LG	TD
Joey Galloway	62	1,057	17.0	64	7
Michael Pittman	47	405	8.6	25	0
Michael Clayton	33	356	10.8	27	1
Ike Hilliard	34	339	10.0	44	2
Alex Smith	35	250	7.1	27	3
Mike Alstott	25	222	8.9	24	1
Cadillac Williams	30	196	6.5	21	0
Anthony Becht	18	115	6.4	13	1
Maurice Stovall	7	102	14.6	27	0
Mike Alstott	21	85	4.0	18	0

KICKING

PLAYER	FGM	FGA	PCT	XPM	XPA
Matt Bryant	17	22	77.3	22	23

PUNTING

PLAYER	NO.	AVG	NET AVG	TB	IN 20	LG	BLK
Josh Bidwell	93	43.5	36.8	7	20	59	0

INTERCEPTIONS Derrick Brooks, Ronde Barber, 3 SACKS Greg Spires, Dewayne White, Ellis Wyms, 5

WASHINGTON REDSKINS

PASSING

PLAYER	ATT	COMP	YDS	PCT COMP	YDS/ATT	TD	INT	RATING
Mark Brunell	260	162	1,789	62.3	6.9	8	4	86.5
Jason Campbell	207	110	1,297	53.1	6.3	10	6	76.5

RUSHING

PLAYER	NO.	YDS	AVG	LG	TD
Ladell Betts	245	1,154	4.7	26	4
Clinton Portis	127	523	4.1	38	7
T.J. Duckett	38	132	3.5	19	2
Antwaan Randle El	19	118	6.2	20	0
Jason Campbell	24	107	4.5	15	0

RECEIVING

PLAYER	NO.	YDS	AVG	LG	TD
Santana Moss	55	790	14.4	68	6
Chris Cooley	57	734	12.9	66	6
Ladell Betts	53	445	8.4	34	1
Brandon Lloyd	23	365	15.9	52	0
Antwaan Randle El	32	351	11.0	34	3
Clinton Portis	17	170	10.0	74	0
James Thrash	12	151	12.6	27	1

KICKING

PLAYER	FGM	FGA	PCT	XPM	XPA
John Hall	9	11	81.8	9	9
Shaun Suisham	8	9	81.8	12	12

PUNTING

PLAYER	NO.	AVG	NET AVG	TB	IN 20	LG	BLK
Derrick Frost	81	42.9	36.7	7	27	60	0

INTERCEPTIONS Six tied with 1   SACKS Andre Carter, 6

SUPER BOWL RESULTS

SUPER BOWL	DATE	WINNER	LOSER	SCORE	SITE	ATTENDANCE
XLI	2-4-07	Colts	Bears	29–17	Miami, FL	74,512
XL	2-5-06	Steelers	Seahawks	21–10	Detroit, MI	68,206
XXXIX	2-6-05	Patriots	Eagles	24–21	Jacksonville, FL	78,125
XXXVIII	2-1-04	Patriots	Panthers	32–29	Houston, TX	71,525
XXXVII	1-26-03	Buccaneers	Raiders	48–21	San Diego, CA	67,603
XXXVI	2-3-02	Patriots	Rams	20–17	New Orleans, LA	72,922
XXXV	1-28-01	Ravens	Giants	34–7	Tampa, FL	71,921
XXXIV	1-30-00	Rams	Titans	23–16	Atlanta, GA	72,625
XXXIII	1-31-99	Broncos	Falcons	34–19	Miami, FL	74,803
XXXII	1-25-98	Broncos	Packers	31–24	San Diego, CA	68,912
XXXI	1-26-97	Packers	Patriots	35–21	New Orleans, LA	72,301
XXX	1-28-96	Cowboys	Steelers	27–17	Tempe, AZ	76,347
XXIX	1-29-95	49ers	Chargers	49–26	Miami, FL	74,107
XXVIII	1-30-94	Cowboys	Bills	30–13	Atlanta, GA	72,817
XXVII	1-31-93	Cowboys	Bills	52–17	Pasadena, CA	98,374
XXVI	1-26-92	Redskins	Bills	37–24	Minneapolis, MN	63,130
XXV	1-27-91	Giants	Bills	20–19	Tampa, FL	73,813
XXIV	1-28-90	49ers	Broncos	55–10	New Orleans, LA	72,919
XXIII	1-22-89	49ers	Bengals	20–16	Miami, FL	75,129
XXII	1-31-88	Redskins	Broncos	42–10	San Diego, CA	73,302
XXI	1-25-87	Giants	Broncos	39–20	Pasadena, CA	101,063
XX	1-26-86	Bears	Patriots	46–10	New Orleans, LA	73,818
XIX	1-20-85	49ers	Dolphins	38–16	Stanford, CA	84,059
XVIII	1-22-84	Raiders	Redskins	38–9	Tampa, FL	72,920
XVII	1-30-83	Redskins	Dolphins	27–17	Pasadena, CA	103,667
XVI	1-24-82	49ers	Bengals	26–21	Pontiac, MI	81,270
XV	1-25-81	Raiders	Eagles	27–10	New Orleans, LA	76,135
XIV	1-20-80	Steelers	Rams	31–19	Pasadena, CA	103,985
XIII	1-21-79	Steelers	Cowboys	35–31	Miami, FL	79,484
XII	1-15-78	Cowboys	Broncos	27–10	New Orleans, LA	76,400
XI	1-9-77	Raiders	Vikings	32–14	Pasadena, CA	103,438
X	1-18-76	Steelers	Cowboys	21–17	Miami, FL	80,187
IX	1-12-75	Steelers	Vikings	16–6	New Orleans, LA	80,997
VIII	1-13-74	Dolphins	Vikings	24–7	Houston, TX	71,882
VII	1-14-73	Dolphins	Redskins	14–7	Los Angeles, CA	90,182
VI	1-16-72	Cowboys	Dolphins	24–3	New Orleans, LA	81,023
V	1-17-71	Colts	Cowboys	16–13	Miami, FL	79,204
IV	1-11-70	Chiefs	Vikings	23–7	New Orleans, LA	80,562
III	1-12-69	Jets	Colts	16–7	Miami, FL	75,389
II	1-14-68	Packers	Raiders	33–14	Miami, FL	75,546
I	1-15-67	Packers	Chiefs	35–10	Los Angeles, CA	61,946

SUPER BOWL MVPS

SUPER BOWL	PLAYER/TEAM	POSITION	SUPER BOWL	PLAYER/TEAM	POSITION
XLI	Peyton Manning, Colts	QB	XX	Richard Dent, Bears	DE
XL	Hines Ward, Steelers	WR	XIX	Joe Montana, 49ers	QB
XXXIX	Deion Branch, Patriots	WR	XVIII	Marcus Allen, Raiders	RB
XXXVIII	Tom Brady, Patriots	QB	XVII	John Riggins, Redskins	RB
XXXVII	Dexter Jackson, Buccaneers	S	XVI	Joe Montana, 49ers	QB
XXXVI	Tom Brady, Patriots	QB	XV	Jim Plunkett, Raiders	QB
XXXV	Ray Lewis, Ravens	LB	XIV	Terry Bradshaw, Steelers	QB
XXXIV	Kurt Warner, Rams	QB	XIII	Terry Bradshaw, Steelers	QB
XXXIII	John Elway, Broncos	QB	XII (tie)	Randy White, Cowboys	DT
XXXII	Terrell Davis, Broncos	RB		Harvey Martin, Cowboys	DE
XXXI	Desmond Howard, Packers	KR	XI	Fred Biletnikoff, Raiders	WR
XXX	Larry Brown, Cowboys	DB	X	Lynn Swann, Steelers	WR
XXIX	Steve Young, 49ers	QB	IX	Franco Harris, Steelers	RB
XXVIII	Emmitt Smith, Cowboys	RB	VIII	Larry Csonka, Dolphins	RB
XXVII	Troy Aikman, Cowboys	QB	VII	Jake Scott, Dolphins	S
XXVI	Mark Rypien, Redskins	QB	VI	Roger Staubach, Cowboys	QB
XXV	Ottis Anderson, Giants	RB	V	Chuck Howley, Cowboys	LB
XXIV	Joe Montana, 49ers	QB	IV	Len Dawson, Chiefs	QB
XXIII	Jerry Rice, 49ers	WR	III	Joe Namath, Jets	QB
XXII	Doug Williams, Redskins	QB	II	Bart Starr, Packers	QB
XXI	Phil Simms, Giants	QB	I	Bart Starr, Packers	QB

KEY QB=quarterback; S=safety; LB=linebacker; RB=running back; KR=kick returner; DB=defensive back; WR=wide receiver; DE=defensive end; DT=defensive tackle

TRIVIA CHALLENGE

1 In 2006, New Orleans Saints RB Reggie Bush set a new NFL rookie record in which offensive category?
a. **Most passing yards**
b. **Most rushing yards**
c. **Most receptions**

Reggie Bush

2 Through 2006, which NFL team had gone the longest—8 seasons—without making an appearance in the playoffs?
a. **Arizona Cardinals**
b. **Buffalo Bills**
c. **Detroit Lions**

3 In 2006, for the first time in NFL history, two brothers starting at QB played against each other. Name their two teams.
a. **Eagles and Buccaneers**
b. **Giants and Colts**
c. **Seahawks and Giants**

4 2006 NFL Rookie of the Year Vince Young set a new single-season rushing record for rookie QBs. How many yards did he gain?
a. **166**
b. **302**
c. **552**

Vince Young

5 In what year did the Colts franchise move from Baltimore to Indianapolis in the middle of the night?
a. **1974**
b. **1984**
c. **1994**

Thurman Thomas was inducted into the Pro Football Hall of Fame in 2007.

6 What penalty is given to a team whose QB throws a forward pass from beyond the line of scrimmage?
a. **None**
b. **15 yards**
c. **5 yards and loss of down**

7 The NFL's oldest stadium was built in 1924. What is its name?
a. **Soldier Field**
b. **Fenway Park**
c. **Texas Stadium**

8 In the NFL, the player with the ball must physically touch the ground in the end zone to score a touchdown.
a. **True**
b. **False**

9 New Orleans head coach Sean Payton won NFL Coach of the Year honors in 2006, leading the Saints to a 10–6 regular season record and their first appearance in the NFC Championship game. What was the Saints' record in 2005?
a. **7–9**
b. **5–11**
c. **3–13**

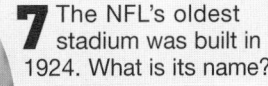

Sean Payton

10 Which jersey number was shared by QBs Joe Montana, Vinny Testaverde, and Jake Plummer?
a. **7**
b. **16**
c. **19**

11 During his career, Bills RB Thurman Thomas rushed for more than 1,000 yards in eight straight years. How many other players have done this?
a. **Zero**
b. **Three**
c. **Ten**

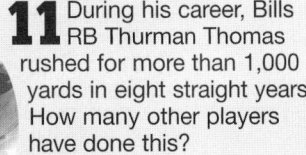

Trivia Challenge: 1. c; 2. a; 3. b; 4. c; 5. b; 6. c; 7. a; 8. b; 9. c; 10. b; 11. b

**Emmitt Smith,
Dallas Cowboys**

BILL FRAKES

ALL-TIME NFL INDIVIDUAL
STATISTICAL LEADERS — CAREER LEADERS

SCORING

PLAYER	YRS	TD	FG	PAT	PTS
†Morten Andersen	24	0	540	825	2,437
Gary Anderson	23	0	538	820	2,434
George Blanda	26	9	335	942	2,002
†John Carney	17	0	413	510	1,749
Norm Johnson	18	0	366	638	1,736
†Matt Stover	17	0	408	491	1,715
Nick Lowery	18	0	383	562	1,711
Jan Stenerud	19	0	373	580	1,699
†Jason Elam	14	0	368	568	1,672
Eddie Murray	19	0	352	538	1,594
Al Del Greco	17	0	347	543	1,584
†Jason Hanson	15	0	356	469	1,537
Steve Christie	15	6	336	468	1,476
Pat Leahy	18	0	304	558	1,470
Jim Turner	16	1	304	521	1,439
Matt Bahr	17	0	300	522	1,422
Mark Moseley	16	0	300	482	1,382
Jim Bakken	17	0	282	534	1,380
Fred Cox	15	0	282	519	1,365
Lou Groza	17	1	234	641	1,349

RUSHING

PLAYER	YRS	ATT	YDS	AVG	LG	TD
Emmitt Smith	15	4,409	18,355	4.2	75	164
Walter Payton	13	3,838	16,726	4.4	76	110
Barry Sanders	10	3,062	15,269	5.0	85	99
Curtis Martin	11	3,518	14,101	4.0	70	90
Jerome Bettis	13	3,479	13,662	3.9	71	91
Eric Dickerson	11	2,996	13,259	4.4	85	90
Tony Dorsett	12	2,936	12,739	4.3	99	77
Jim Brown	9	2,359	12,312	5.2	80	106
Marshall Faulk	12	2,836	12,279	4.3	71	100
Marcus Allen	16	3,022	12,243	4.1	61	123
Franco Harris	13	2,949	12,120	4.1	75	91
Thurman Thomas	13	2,877	12,074	4.2	80	65
John Riggins	14	2,916	11,352	3.9	66	104
†Corey Dillon	10	2,618	11,241	4.3	96	82
O.J. Simpson	11	2,404	11,236	4.7	94	61
Ricky Watters	10	2,622	10,643	4.1	57	78
†Tiki Barber	10	2,216	10,448	4.7	95	55
Eddie George	9	2,865	10,441	3.6	76	68
†Edgerrin James	8	2,525	10,385	4.1	72	70
Ottis Anderson	14	2,562	10,273	4.0	76	81
Earl Campbell	8	2,187	9,407	4.3	81	74

TOUCHDOWNS

PLAYER	YRS	RUSH	REC	RET	TD
Jerry Rice	20	10	197	0	208
Emmitt Smith	15	164	11	0	175
Marcus Allen	16	123	21	1	145
†Marshall Faulk	13	100	36	0	136
Cris Carter	16	0	130	1	131
Jim Brown	9	106	20	0	126
Walter Payton	13	110	15	0	125
†Marvin Harrison	11	0	122	0	122
†Terrell Owens	11	2	114	0	116
John Riggins	14	104	12	0	116

PLAYER	YRS	RUSH	REC	RET	TD
Lenny Moore	12	63	48	2	113
†LaDainian Tomlinson	6	100	11	0	111
Barry Sanders	10	99	10	0	109
†Shaun Alexander	7	96	11	0	107
Tim Brown	17	1	100	4	105
Don Hutson	11	3	99	3	105
Steve Largent	14	1	100	0	101
†Randy Moss	9	0	101	0	101
Franco Harris	13	91	9	0	100
†Curtis Martin	11	90	10	0	100

PASSING — EFFICIENCY*

PLAYER	YRS	ATT	COMP	PCT COMP	YDS	YDS/ATT	TD	INT	RATING
Steve Young	15	4,149	2,667	64.3	33,124	7.98	232	107	96.8
†Peyton Manning	9	4,890	3,131	64.0	37,586	7.69	275	139	94.4
†Kurt Warner	9	2,508	1,645	65.6	20,591	8.21	125	83	93.8
Joe Montana	15	5,391	3,409	63.2	40,551	7.52	273	139	92.3
†Daunte Culpepper	8	2,741	1,759	64.2	21,091	7.69	137	86	90.8
†Marc Bulger	6	2,106	1,357	64.4	16,233	7.71	95	59	91.3
†Tom Brady	7	3,064	1,896	61.9	21,564	7.04	147	78	88.4
†Trent Green	13	3,527	2,143	60.8	26,963	7.64	157	92	87.5
†Matt Hasselbeck	8	2,576	1,552	60.2	18,367	7.13	114	72	86.6
Dan Marino	17	8,358	4,967	59.4	61,361	7.34	420	252	85.1

PASSING — YARDS

PLAYER	YRS	ATT	COMP	PCT COMP	YDS
Dan Marino	17	8,358	4,967	59.4	61,361
†Brett Favre	16	8,224	5,021	61.1	57,500
John Elway	16	7,250	4,123	56.9	51,475
Warren Moon	17	6,823	3,988	58.4	49,325
Fran Tarkenton	18	6,467	3,686	57.0	47,003
†Vinny Testaverde	20	6,529	3,693	56.6	45,281

PLAYER	YRS	ATT	COMP	PCT COMP	YDS
†Drew Bledsoe	14	6,717	3,839	57.2	44,611
Dan Fouts	15	5,604	3,297	58.8	43,040
Joe Montana	15	5,391	3,409	63.2	40,551
Johnny Unitas	18	5,186	2,830	54.6	40,239
Dave Krieg	19	5,311	3,105	58.5	38,147
Boomer Esiason	14	5,205	2,969	57.0	37,920

*1,500 or more attempts. The passer ratings are based on performance standards established for completion percentage, interception percentage, touchdown percentage, and average gain. Passers are allocated points according to how their marks compare with those standards.
†Active in 2006

KEY YRS=years; TD=touchdowns; FG=field goals; PAT=extra points; PTS=points; ATT=attempts; AVG=average; LG=long; RUSH=rushing; REC=receiving; RET=returns; COMP=completions; PCT COMP=completion percentage; YDS/ATT=yards per attempt; INT=interceptions; COMP YDS=completion yards

ALL-TIME NFL INDIVIDUAL STATISTICAL LEADERS (cont.)

PASSING — TOUCHDOWNS

PLAYER	TD
Dan Marino	420
†Brett Favre	414
Fran Tarkenton	342
John Elway	300
Warren Moon	291
Johnny Unitas	290
†Peyton Manning	275
Joe Montana	273
†Vinny Testaverde	270
Dave Krieg	261
Sonny Jurgensen	255
Dan Fouts	254
†Drew Bledsoe	251
Boomer Esiason	247
John Hadl	244
Len Dawson	239
Jim Kelly	237

SACKS

PLAYER	SACKS
Bruce Smith	200.0
Reggie White	198.0
Kevin Greene	160.0
Chris Doleman	150.5
Richard Dent	137.5

Note: Officially compiled since 1982

Eric Dickerson,
Los Angeles Rams

INTERCEPTIONS

PLAYER	YRS	NO.	YDS	AVG	LG	TD
Paul Krause	16	81	1,185	14.6	81	3
Emlen Tunnell	14	79	1,282	16.2	55	4
Rod Woodson	17	71	1,483	20.9	98	12
Dick "Night Train" Lane	14	68	1,207	17.8	80	5
Ken Riley	15	65	596	9.2	66	5

RECEIVING — RECEPTIONS

PLAYER	YRS	NO.	YDS	AVG	LG	TD
Jerry Rice	20	1,549	22,895	14.8	96	197
Cris Carter	16	1,101	13,899	12.6	80	130
Tim Brown	17	1,094	14,934	13.7	80	100
†Marvin Harrison	11	1,022	13,697	13.4	80	122
Andre Reed	16	951	13,198	13.9	83	87
Art Monk	16	940	12,721	13.5	79	68
†Isaac Bruce	13	887	13,376	15.1	80	80
Jimmy Smith	12	862	12,287	14.3	75	67
†Keenan McCardell	15	861	11,117	12.9	76	62
Irving Fryar	17	851	12,785	15.0	80	84
†Rod Smith	12	849	11,389	13.4	85	68
Larry Centers	14	827	6,797	8.2	54	28
Steve Largent	14	819	13,089	16.0	74	100

RECEIVING — YARDS

PLAYER	YDS
Jerry Rice	22,895
Tim Brown	14,934
James Lofton	14,004
Cris Carter	13,899
Henry Ellard	13,777
†Marvin Harrison	13,697
†Issac Bruce	13,376
Andre Reed	13,198
Steve Largent	13,089
Irving Fryar	12,785
Art Monk	12,721

† Active in 2006

SINGLE-SEASON LEADERS

SCORING — POINTS

PLAYER	YEAR	TD	PAT	FG	PTS
LaDainian Tomlinson, Chargers	2006	31	0	0	186
Paul Hornung, Packers	1960	15	41	15	176
Shaun Alexander, Seahawks	2005	28	0	0	168
Gary Anderson, Vikings	1998	0	59	35	164
Jeff Wilkins, Rams	2003	0	46	39	163
Priest Holmes, Chiefs	2003	27	0	0	162
Mark Moseley, Redskins	1983	0	62	33	161
Marshall Faulk, Rams	2000	26	0	0	160
Gino Cappelletti, Patriots	1964	7	36	25	155
Emmitt Smith, Cowboys	1995	25	0	0	150
Chip Lohmiller, Redskins	1991	0	56	31	149

Note: Cappelletti's 1964 total includes a 2-point conversion.

TOUCHDOWNS

PLAYER	YEAR	RUSH	REC	RET	TOTAL
LaDainian Tomlinson, Chargers	2006	28	3	0	31
Shaun Alexander, Seahawks	2005	27	1	0	28
Priest Holmes, Chiefs	2003	27	0	0	27
Marshall Faulk, Rams	2000	18	8	0	26
Emmitt Smith, Cowboys	1995	25	0	0	25
John Riggins, Redskins	1983	24	0	0	24
Priest Holmes, Chiefs	2002	21	3	0	24
O.J. Simpson, Bills	1975	16	7	0	23
Jerry Rice, 49ers	1987	1	22	0	23

FIELD GOALS

PLAYER	YEAR	ATT	NO.
Neil Rackers, Cardinals	2005	42	40
Jeff Wilkins, Rams	2003	42	39
Olindo Mare, Dolphins	1999	46	39
John Kasay, Panthers	1996	45	37
Mike Vanderjagt, Colts	2003	37	37
Cary Blanchard, Colts	1996	40	36

Five tied with 35 (Jay Feely, 2005).

RUSHING — YARDS GAINED

PLAYER	YEAR	ATT	YDS	AVG
Eric Dickerson, Rams	1984	379	2,105	5.6
Jamal Lewis, Ravens	2003	387	2,066	5.3
Barry Sanders, Lions	1997	335	2,053	6.1
Terrell Davis, Broncos	1998	392	2,008	5.1
O.J. Simpson, Bills	1973	332	2,003	6.0
Earl Campbell, Oilers	1980	373	1,934	5.2
Barry Sanders, Lions	1994	331	1,883	5.7
Ahman Green, Packers	2003	355	1,883	5.3
Shaun Alexander, Seahawks	2005	370	1,880	5.1
Jim Brown, Browns	1963	291	1,863	6.4
Tiki Barber, Giants	2005	357	1,860	5.1

SINGLE-SEASON LEADERS (cont.)

RUSHING — AVERAGE GAIN

PLAYER	YEAR	AVG
Beattie Feathers, Bears	1934	8.44
Randall Cunningham, Eagles	1990	7.98
Michael Vick, Falcons	2004	7.50
Michael Vick, Falcons	2002	6.88
Bobby Douglass, Bears	1972	6.87

Minimum 100 attempts.

RUSHING — TOUCHDOWNS

PLAYER	YEAR	NO.
LaDainian Tomlinson, Chargers	2006	28
Shaun Alexander, Seahawks	2005	27
Priest Holmes, Chiefs	2003	27
Emmitt Smith, Cowboys	1995	25
John Riggins, Redskins	1983	24

PASSING — YARDS GAINED

PLAYER	YEAR	ATT	COMP	PCT	YDS
Dan Marino, Dolphins	1984	564	362	64.2	5,084
Kurt Warner, Rams	2001	546	375	68.7	4,830
Dan Fouts, Chargers	1981	609	360	59.1	4,802
Dan Marino, Dolphins	1986	623	378	60.7	4,746
Daunte Culpepper, Vikings	2004	548	379	69.2	4,717
Dan Fouts, Chargers	1980	589	348	59.1	4,715
Warren Moon, Oilers	1991	655	404	61.7	4,690
Warren Moon, Oilers	1990	584	362	62.0	4,689
Rich Gannon, Raiders	2002	618	418	67.6	4,689
Neil Lomax, Cardinals	1984	560	345	61.6	4,614
Peyton Manning, Colts	2004	497	336	67.6	4,557

PASSER RATING

PLAYER	YEAR	RATING
Peyton Manning, Colts	2004	121.1
Steve Young, 49ers	1994	112.8
Joe Montana, 49ers	1989	112.4
Daunte Culpepper, Vikings	2004	110.9
Milt Plum, Browns	1960	110.4
Sammy Baugh, Redskins	1945	109.9
Kurt Warner, Rams	1999	109.2

PASSING — TOUCHDOWNS

PLAYER	YEAR	NO.
Peyton Manning, Colts	2004	49
Dan Marino, Dolphins	1984	48
Dan Marino, Dolphins	1986	44
Kurt Warner, Rams	1999	41
Brett Favre, Packers	1996	39
Daunte Culpepper, Vikings	2004	39

Four tied with 36.

RECEIVING — RECEPTIONS

PLAYER	YEAR	NO.	YDS
Marvin Harrison, Colts	2002	143	1,722
Herman Moore, Lions	1995	123	1,686
Cris Carter, Vikings	1994	122	1,256
Jerry Rice, 49ers	1995	122	1,848
Cris Carter, Vikings	1995	122	1,371
Isaac Bruce, Rams	1995	119	1,781
Torry Holt, Rams	2003	117	1,696
Jimmy Smith, Jaguars	1999	116	1,636
Marvin Harrison, Colts	1999	115	1,663
Rod Smith, Broncos	2001	113	1,343

Four tied with 112.

RECEIVING — YARDS GAINED

PLAYER	YEAR	YDS
Jerry Rice, 49ers	1995	1,848
Isaac Bruce, Rams	1995	1,781
Charley Hennigan, Oilers	1961	1,746
Marvin Harrison, Colts	2002	1,722
Torry Holt, Lions	2003	1,696
Herman Moore, Lions	1995	1,686

RECEIVING — TOUCHDOWNS

PLAYER	YEAR	NO.
Jerry Rice, 49ers	1987	22
Mark Clayton, Dolphins	1984	18
Sterling Sharpe, Packers	1994	18

Eight tied with 17.

INTERCEPTIONS

PLAYER	YEAR	NO.
Dick "Night Train" Lane, Rams	1952	14
Dan Sandifer, Redskins	1948	13
Spec Sanders, N.Y. Yankees	1950	13
Lester Hayes, Raiders	1980	13

Nine tied with 12.

SACKS

PLAYER	YEAR	NO.
Michael Strahan, N.Y. Giants	2001	22.5
Mark Gastineau, Jets	1984	22.0
Reggie White, Eagles	1987	21.0
Chris Doleman, Vikings	1989	21.0
Lawrence Taylor, N.Y. Giants	1986	20.5

PRO BOWL RESULTS

DATE	RESULT	DATE	RESULT	DATE	RESULT
2-10-07	AFC 31, NFC 28	2-7-99	AFC 23, NFC 10	2-3-91	AFC 23, NFC 21
2-12-06	NFC 23, AFC 17	2-1-98	AFC 29, NFC 24	2-4-90	NFC 27, AFC 21
2-13-05	AFC 38, NFC 27	2-2-97	AFC 26, NFC 23	1-29-89	NFC 34, AFC 3
2-8-04	NFC 55, AFC 52	2-4-96	NFC 20, AFC 13	2-7-88	AFC 15, NFC 6
2-2-03	AFC 45, NFC 20	2-5-95	AFC 41, NFC 13	2-1-87	AFC 10, NFC 6
2-9-02	AFC 38, NFC 30	2-6-94	NFC 17, AFC 3	2-2-86	NFC 28, AFC 24
2-4-01	AFC 38, NFC 17	2-7-93	AFC 23, NFC 20	1-27-85	AFC 22, NFC 14
2-6-00	NFC 51, AFC 31	2-2-92	NFC 21, AFC 15	1-29-84	NFC 45, AFC 3

PRO BOWL RESULTS (cont.)

DATE	RESULT	DATE	RESULT	DATE	RESULT
2-6-83	NFC 20, AFC 19	1-21-68	AFL East 25, West 24	1-15-56	East 31, West 30
1-31-82	AFC 16, NFC 13	1-22-67	NFL East 20, West 10	1-16-55	West 26, East 19
2-1-81	NFC 21, AFC 7	1-21-67	AFL East 30, West 23	1-17-54	East 20, West 9
1-27-80	NFC 37, AFC 27	1-15-66	NFL East 36, West 7	1-10-53	N. Conf. 27, A. Conf. 7
1-29-79	NFC 13, AFC 7	1-15-66	AFL All-Stars 30, Buffalo 19	1-12-52	N. Conf. 30, A. Conf. 13
1-23-78	NFC 14, AFC 13	1-16-65	AFL West 38, East 14	1-14-51	A. Conf. 28, N. Conf. 27
1-17-77	AFC 24, NFC 14	1-10-65	NFL West 34, East 14	12-27-42	NFL All-Stars 17, Washington 14
1-26-76	NFC 23, AFC 20	1-19-64	AFL West 27, East 24		
1-20-75	NFC 17, AFC 10	1-12-64	NFL West 31, East 17	1-4-42	Chi. Bears 35, NFL All-Stars 24
1-20-74	AFC 15, NFC 13	1-13-63	NFL East 30, West 20		
1-21-73	AFC 33, NFC 28	1-13-63	AFL West 21, East 14	12-29-40	Chi. Bears 28, NFL All-Stars 14
1-23-72	AFC 26, NFC 13	1-14-62	NFL West 31, East 30		
1-24-71	NFC 27, AFC 6	1-7-62	AFL West 47, East 27	1-14-40	Green Bay 16, NFL All-Stars 7
1-18-70	NFL West 16, East 13	1-15-61	West 35, East 31		
1-17-70	AFL West 26, East 3	1-17-60	West 38, East 21	1-15-39	N.Y. Giants 13, Pro All-Stars 10
1-19-69	NFL West 10, East 7	1-11-59	East 28, West 21		
1-19-69	AFL West 38, East 25	1-12-58	West 26, East 7		
1-21-68	NFL West 38, East 20	1-13-57	West 19, East 10		

2007 NFL DRAFT — FIRST ROUND

April 28–29, 2007, New York, NY

PICK	TEAM	PLAYER	POS.	HT.	WT.	SCHOOL
1	Oakland	JaMarcus Russell	QB	6-6	263	Louisiana State
2	Detroit	Calvin Johnson	WR	6-4	237	Georgia Tech
3	Cleveland	Joe Thomas	OT	6-6	313	Wisconsin
4	Tampa Bay	Gaines Adams	DE	6-5	260	Clemson
5	Arizona	Levi Brown	OT	6-4	328	Penn State
6	Washington	LaRon Landry	FS	6-2	205	Louisiana State
7	Minnesota	Adrian Peterson	RB	6-2	218	Oklahoma
8	Atlanta	Jamaal Anderson	DE	6-6	279	Arkansas
9	Miami	Ted Ginn Jr.	WR	6-0	180	Ohio State
10	Houston	Amobi Okoye	DT	6-2	287	Louisville
11	San Francisco	Patrick Wills	ILB	6-1	240	Mississippi
12	Buffalo	Marshawn Lynch	RB	5-11	217	California
13	St. Louis	Adam Carriker	DE	6-6	292	Nebraska
14	N.Y. Jets	Darrelle Revis	CB	6-0	197	Pittsburgh
15	Pittsburgh	Lawrence Timmons	OLB	6-3	232	Florida State
16	Green Bay	Justin Harrell	DT	6-4	305	Tennessee
17	Denver	Jarvis Moss	DE	6-6	251	Florida
18	Cincinnati	Leon Hall	CB	5-11	193	Michigan
19	Tennessee	Michael Griffin	FS	6-0	195	Texas
20	N.Y. Giants	Aaron Ross	CB	6-1	192	Texas
21	Jacksonville	Reggie Nelson	FS	6-0	193	Florida
22	Cleveland	Brady Quinn	QB	6-3	226	Notre Dame
23	Kansas City	Dwayne Bowe	WR	6-2	217	Louisiana State
24	New England	Brandon Meriweather	FS	5-11	192	Miami (Florida)
25	Carolina	Jon Beason	OLB	6-0	236	Miami (Forida)
26	Dallas	Anthony Spencer	DE	6-3	266	Purdue
27	New Orleans	Robert Meachem	WR	6-3	211	Tennessee
28	San Francisco	Joe Staley	OT	6-5	302	Central Michigan
29	Baltimore	Ben Grubbs	G	6-3	314	Auburn
30	San Diego	Craig Davis	WR	6-1	207	Louisiana State
31	Chicago	Greg Olsen	TE	6-4	252	Miami (Florida)
32	Indianapolis	Anthony Gonzalez	WR	6-0	195	Ohio State

KEY QB=quarterback; RB=running back; WR=wide receiver; CB=cornerback; DE=defensive end; OLB=outside linebacker; OT=offensive tackle; FS=free safety; DT=defensive tackle; C=center; TE=tight end; G=guard

Once again, chaos and controversy ruled college football in 2006. For the fifth time in the nine-year history of the Bowl Championship Series (BCS), multiple teams staked a claim to be in the national title game.

The only team that was a sure bet to play in the big game was top-ranked Ohio State. Led by Heisman Trophy-winning QB Troy Smith, the Buckeyes rolled into the title tilt undefeated and outscoring their opponents by 25.9 points per game.

In early December, three teams were fighting for the second spot in the BCS national championship game. Heading into the final Saturday of the regular season, USC (10–1), Michigan (11–1), and Florida (11–1) were ranked second, third, and fourth, respectively. All USC had to do to hold off the other two teams was beat crosstown rival UCLA. But the Bruins beat the Trojans for the first time since 1998.

Later that night, the Gators beat Arkansas in the SEC Championship Game. A debate began about which one-loss team — Florida or Michigan — deserved to play Ohio State. Michigan argued that its only blemish came in a three-point loss on the road against the top-ranked Buckeyes. Florida claimed that the tough SEC schedule it had to play was more impressive. The voters sided with the Gators. Florida jumped Michigan in the BCS rankings and moved into second place.

Still, with what seemed like a compromise candidate at number two, the Buckeyes looked ready to be crowned national champions. But a funny thing happened once the ball was kicked off. Led by senior quarterback Chris Leak and an ultra-fast defense, the Gators devoured the Buckeyes, 41–7.

It was the school's second football national championship, and it made Florida the first school to hold the football and men's basketball titles at the same time.

Meanwhile, the drama that took place in the Fiesta Bowl on New Year's night made the annual BCS controversy seem like a tea party. Underdog Boise State went playground and beat powerhouse Oklahoma, 43–42, in what will surely go down as one of the greatest college football games ever.

Trailing 35–28 in the fourth quarter, the Broncos scored a touchdown on a "hook-and-ladder" play with seven seconds left to force overtime. On that play, Drisan James caught a pass at OU's 35-yard line and then flipped the ball to fellow receiver Jerard Rabb. Rabb then raced down the sideline for the score. In overtime, Boise State receiver Vinny Perretta threw a five-yard TD pass to make the score 42–41. Then, instead of playing to tie the game, the Broncos went for two and won the game on a modified "Statue of Liberty" play.

Senior quarterback Chris Leak completed 25 of 36 passes for 213 yards and threw for one touchdown in Florida's 41–14 victory over Ohio State in the BCS championship game.

ROBERT BECK

FINAL 2006 COLLEGE FOOTBALL POLLS

THE ASSOCIATED PRESS

TEAM	RECORD	POINTS
1. Florida	13–1	1,624
2. Ohio State	12–1	1,492
3. LSU	11–2	1,452
4. USC	11–2	1,389
5. Boise State	13–0	1,383
6. Louisville	12–1	1,338
7. Wisconsin	12–1	1,288
8. Michigan	11–2	1,145
9. Auburn	11–2	1,112
10. West Virginia	11–2	1,035
11. Oklahoma	11–3	933
12. Rutgers	11–2	884
13. Texas	10–3	772
14. California	10–3	697
15. Arkansas	10–4	677
16. BYU	11–2	673
17. Notre Dame	10–3	553
18. Wake Forest	11–3	551
19. Virginia Tech	10–3	407
20. Boston College	10–3	353
21. Oregon State	10–4	291
22. TCU	11–2	279
23. Georgia	9–4	204
24. Penn State	9–4	183
25. Tennessee	9–4	181

USA TODAY COACHES

TEAM	RECORD	POINTS
1. Florida	13–1	1,575
2. Ohio State	12–1	1,435
3. LSU	11–2	1,418
4. USC	11–2	1,345
5. Wisconsin	12–1	1,328
6. Boise State	13–0	1,275
7. Louisville	12–1	1,270
8. Auburn	11–2	1,119
9. Michigan	11–2	1,092
10. West Virginia	11–2	1,012
11. Oklahoma	11–3	849
12. Rutgers	11–2	841
13. Texas	10–3	791
14. California	10–3	716
15. BYU	11–2	615
16. Arkansas	10–4	592
17. Wake Forest	11–3	535
18. Virginia Tech	10–3	494
19. Notre Dame	10–3	485
20. Boston College	10–3	388
21. TCU	11–2	339
22. Oregon State	10–4	206
23. Tennessee	9–4	202
24. Hawaii	11–3	152
25. Penn State	9–4	142

2006–07 COLLEGE BOWL AND PLAYOFF RESULTS

BOWL GAME	DATE	SITE	RESULT
BCS CHAMPIONSHIP	Jan. 8	Glendale, Arizona	Florida 41, Ohio State 14
GMAC	Jan. 7	Mobile, Alabama	Southern Miss 28, Ohio 7
INTERNATIONAL	Jan. 6	Toronto, Canada	Cincinnati 27, Western Michigan 24
SUGAR	Jan. 3	New Orleans, Louisiana	Louisiana State 41, Notre Dame 14
ORANGE	Jan. 2	Miami, Florida	Louisville 24, Wake Forest 13
FIESTA	Jan. 1	Glendale, Arizona	Boise State 43, Oklahoma 42 (OT)
ROSE	Jan. 1	Pasadena, California	USC 32, Michigan 18
COTTON	Jan. 1	Dallas, Texas	Auburn 17, Nebraska 14
GATOR	Jan. 1	Jacksonville, Florida	West Virginia 38, Georgia Tech 35
CAPITAL ONE	Jan. 1	Orlando, Florida	Wisconsin 17, Arkansas 14
OUTBACK	Jan. 1	Tampa, Florida	Penn State 20, Tennessee 10
MPC COMPUTERS	Dec. 31	Boise, Idaho	Miami (Florida) 21, Nevada 20
CHICK-FIL-A	Dec. 30	Atlanta, Georgia	Georgia 31, Virginia Tech 24
ALAMO	Dec. 30	San Antonio, Texas	Texas 26, Iowa 24
MEINEKE CAR CARE	Dec. 30	Charlotte, North Carolina	Boston College 25, Navy 24
CHAMPS SPORTS	Dec. 29	Orlando, Florida	Maryland 24, Purdue 7
INSIGHT	Dec. 29	Tempe, Arizona	Texas Tech 44, Minnesota 41 (OT)
LIBERTY	Dec. 29	Memphis, Tennessee	South Carolina 44, Houston 36
SUN	Dec. 29	El Paso, Texas	Oregon State 39, Missouri 38
MUSIC CITY	Dec. 29	Nashville, Tennessee	Kentucky 28, Clemson 20
HOLIDAY	Dec. 28	San Diego, California	California 45, Texas A&M 10
TEXAS	Dec. 28	Houston, Texas	Rutgers 37, Kansas State 10
INDEPENDENCE	Dec. 28	Shreveport, Louisiana	Oklahoma State 34, Alabama 31
EMERALD	Dec. 27	San Francisco, California	Florida State 44, UCLA 27
MOTOR CITY	Dec. 26	Detroit, Michigan	Cent. Michigan 31, Middle Tenn. St. 14
HAWAII	Dec. 24	Honolulu, Hawaii	Hawaii 41, Arizona State 24
ARMED FORCES	Dec. 23	Fort Worth, Texas	Utah 25, Tulsa 13
NEW MEXICO	Dec. 23	Albuquerque, New Mexico	San Jose State 20, New Mexico 12
PAPAJOHNS.COM	Dec. 23	Birmingham, Alabama	South Florida 24, East Carolina 7
NEW ORLEANS	Dec. 22	Lafayette, Louisiana	Troy 41, Rice 17
LAS VEGAS	Dec. 21	Las Vegas, Nevada	BYU 38, Oregon 8
POINSETTIA	Dec. 19	San Diego, California	TCU 37, Northern Illinois 7

Troy Smith threw 30 TD passes in 2006.

JOHN BIEVER

2006 HEISMAN VOTING

PLAYER, SCHOOL	POSITION	1ST	2ND	3RD	TOTAL
Troy Smith, Ohio State	QB	801	62	13	2,540
Darren McFadden, Arkansas	RB	45	298	147	878
Brady Quinn, Notre Dame	QB	13	276	191	782
Steve Slaton, West Virginia	RB	6	51	94	214
Mike Hart, Michigan	RB	5	58	79	210
Colt Brennan, Hawaii	QB	6	44	96	202
Ray Rice, Rutgers	RB	1	16	44	79
Ian Johnson, Boise State	RB	1	13	44	73
Dwayne Jarrett, USC	WR	1	11	22	47
Calvin Johnson, Georgia Tech	WR	1	8	24	43

2006 AP ALL-AMERICA TEAM

OFFENSE

QB Troy Smith, Ohio State, senior
RB Darren McFadden, Arkansas, sophomore
Steve Slaton, West Virginia, sophomore
WR Dwayne Jarrett, USC, junior
Calvin Johnson, Georgia Tech, junior
TE Matt Spaeth, Minnesota, senior
C Dan Mozes, West Virginia, senior
OL Josh Beekman, Boston College, senior
Justin Blalock, Texas, senior
Jake Long, Michigan, senior
Joe Thomas, Wisconsin, senior
K Justin Medlock, UCLA, sophomore
AP DeSean Jackson, California, sophomore

DEFENSE

DL Glenn Dorsey, LSU, junior
Quinn Pitcock, Ohio State, senior
LaMarr Woodley, Michigan, senior
Gaines Adams, Clemson, senior
LB James Laurinaitis, Ohio State, sophomore
Paul Posluszny, Penn State, senior
Patrick Willis, Mississippi, senior
DB Leon Hall, Michigan, senior
Daymeion Hughes, California, senior
LaRon Landry, LSU, senior
Reggie Nelson, Florida, junior
P Daniel Sepulveda, Baylor, senior

KEY
QB=quarterback;
RB=running back;
WR=wide receiver;
TE=tight end; C=center;
OL=offensive lineman;
K=kicker; DL=defensive
lineman; LB=linebacker;
DB=defensive back;
P=punter; AP=all purpose

2006 NCAA DIVISION I-A CONFERENCE STANDINGS

Atlantic Coast Conference

TEAM	CONFERENCE				OVERALL			
	W	L	PF	PA	W	L	PF	PA
Atlantic Division								
Wake Forest	6	2	175	145	11	3	302	215
Boston College	5	3	189	133	10	3	338	204
Maryland	5	3	171	198	9	4	284	284
Clemson	5	3	209	136	8	5	425	210
Florida State	3	5	180	166	7	6	345	258
North Carolina State	2	6	137	174	3	9	210	262
Coastal Division								
Georgia Tech	7	1	213	155	9	5	349	257
Virginia Tech	6	2	186	93	10	3	336	143
Virginia	4	4	124	116	5	7	181	214
Miami (Florida)	3	5	127	127	7	6	255	201
North Carolina	2	6	109	221	3	9	216	366
Duke	0	8	124	280	0	12	179	406

Big East Conference

TEAM	CONFERENCE				OVERALL			
	W	L	PF	PA	W	L	PF	PA
Louisville	6	1	247	141	12	1	491	212
Rutgers	5	2	182	146	11	2	387	186
West Virginia	5	2	259	186	11	2	505	282
South Florida	4	3	145	133	9	4	299	220
Cincinatti	4	3	152	141	8	5	274	255
Pittsburgh	2	5	172	207	6	6	381	274
Connecticut	1	6	140	238	4	8	257	324
Syracuse	1	6	81	186	4	8	209	295

KEY W=win; L=loss; PF=points for; PA=points against

2006 NCAA DIVISION I-A CONFERENCE STANDINGS (cont.)

Big Ten Conference

TEAM	CONFERENCE				OVERALL			
	W	L	PF	PA	W	L	PF	PA
Ohio State	8	0	305	92	12	1	450	166
Wisconsin	7	1	245	116	12	1	380	157
Michigan	7	1	213	104	11	2	380	207
Penn State	5	3	135	117	9	4	290	187
Purdue	5	3	165	179	8	6	364	374
Minnesota	3	5	202	243	6	7	376	338
Indiana	3	5	179	302	5	7	277	394
Iowa	2	6	174	192	6	7	310	269
Northwestern	2	6	125	240	4	8	198	314
Michigan State	1	7	148	241	4	8	302	341
Illinois	1	7	155	220	2	10	235	321

Big 12 Conference (North)

TEAM	CONFERENCE				OVERALL			
	W	L	PF	PA	W	L	PF	PA
Nebraska	6	2	236	173	9	5	428	256
Missouri	4	4	214	178	8	5	391	254
Kansas State	4	4	188	218	7	6	296	309
Kansas	3	5	234	225	6	6	348	306
Colorado	2	6	160	199	2	10	196	267
Iowa State	1	7	120	262	4	8	226	369

Big 12 Conference (South)

TEAM	CONFERENCE				OVERALL			
	W	L	PF	PA	W	L	PF	PA
Oklahoma	7	1	208	121	11	3	424	242
Texas	6	2	270	173	10	3	467	238
Texas A&M	5	3	193	174	9	4	362	267
Texas Tech	4	4	240	235	8	5	422	326
Oklahoma State	3	5	264	243	7	6	458	333
Baylor	3	5	194	320	4	8	283	391

Conference USA (East)

TEAM	CONFERENCE				OVERALL			
	W	L	PF	PA	W	L	PF	PA
Southern Mississippi	6	2	213	132	9	5	356	260
East Carolina	5	3	188	154	7	6	280	270
Marshall	4	4	233	222	5	7	311	351
Univierity of Central Florida (UCF)	3	5	173	211	4	8	232	345
Alabama-Birmingham	2	6	177	220	3	9	225	297
Memphis	1	7	193	256	2	10	281	365

Conference USA (West)

TEAM	CONFERENCE				OVERALL			
	W	L	PF	PA	W	L	PF	PA
Houston	7	1	275	173	10	4	462	329
Rice	6	2	255	244	7	6	350	432
Tulsa	5	3	226	155	8	5	360	262
Southern Methodist (SMU)	4	4	216	212	6	6	325	294
Texas-El Paso	3	5	202	246	5	7	328	375
Tulane	2	6	130	256	4	8	224	400

Mid-American Conference (East)

TEAM	CONFERENCE				OVERALL			
	W	L	PF	PA	W	L	PF	PA
Ohio	7	1	197	119	9	5	276	253
Kent State	5	3	172	140	6	6	214	241
Akron	3	5	153	187	5	7	236	271
Bowling Green	3	5	166	214	4	8	234	340
Miami (Ohio)	2	6	164	187	2	10	222	304
Buffalo	1	7	201	314	2	10	220	431

FAST FACT

In the past 50 years, only two schools have won at least a share of the Division I-A college football title in back-to-back seasons more than once: Alabama (1964–65 and 1978–79) and Nebraska (1970–71 and 1994–95).

2006 NCAA DIVISION I-A CONFERENCE STANDINGS (cont.)

Mid-American Conference (West)

TEAM	CONFERENCE				OVERALL			
	W	L	PF	PA	W	L	PF	PA
Central Michigan	7	1	235	145	10	4	416	312
Western Michigan	6	2	177	148	8	5	299	259
Northern Illinois	5	3	207	144	7	6	331	275
Ball State	5	3	225	184	5	7	326	309
Toledo	3	5	157	204	5	7	281	332
Eastern Michigan	1	7	106	174	1	11	167	322

Mountain West Conference

TEAM	CONFERENCE				OVERALL			
	W	L	PF	PA	W	L	PF	PA
Brigham Young	8	0	317	113	11	2	478	191
Texas Christian (TCU)	6	2	237	113	11	2	380	160
Utah	5	3	232	171	8	5	363	258
Wyoming	5	3	164	187	6	6	258	264
New Mexico	4	4	189	207	6	7	284	312
Air Force	3	5	172	201	4	8	279	302
San Diego State	3	5	119	230	3	9	170	325
Colorado State	1	7	113	196	4	8	202	263
University of Nevada-Las Vegas (UNLV)	1	7	158	283	2	10	238	382

Pacific-Ten Conference

TEAM	CONFERENCE				OVERALL			
	W	L	PF	PA	W	L	PF	PA
Southern California (USC)	7	2	242	131	11	2	396	197
California	7	2	280	173	10	3	427	251
Oregon State	6	3	207	182	10	4	389	311
California-Los Angeles (UCLA)	5	4	198	169	7	6	299	259
Oregon	4	5	255	238	7	6	383	345
Arizona State	4	5	216	247	7	6	348	326
Arizona	4	5	152	167	6	6	199	235
Washington State	4	5	208	212	6	6	295	277
Washington	3	6	186	225	5	7	262	311
Stanford	1	8	74	274	1	11	127	377

Southeastern Conference (East)

TEAM	CONFERENCE				OVERALL			
	W	L	PF	PA	W	L	PF	PA
Florida	7	1	178	126	13	1	416	189
Tennessee	5	3	212	172	9	4	362	254
Georgia	4	4	185	168	9	4	327	229
Kentucky	4	4	163	207	8	5	347	369
South Carolina	3	5	147	146	8	5	346	243
Vanderbilt	1	7	131	206	4	8	264	284

Southeastern Conference (West)

TEAM	CONFERENCE				OVERALL			
	W	L	PF	PA	W	L	PF	PA
Arkansas	7	1	221	134	10	4	404	256
Auburn	6	2	162	133	11	2	322	181
Louisiana State University (LSU)	6	2	220	131	11	2	438	164
Alabama	2	6	133	175	6	7	298	250
Mississippi (Ole Miss)	2	6	123	182	4	8	188	275
Mississippi State	1	7	127	222	3	9	221	309

Sun Belt Conference

TEAM	CONFERENCE				OVERALL			
	W	L	PF	PA	W	L	PF	PA
Troy	6	1	177	136	8	5	296	289
Middle Tennessee State	6	1	204	92	7	6	296	302
Arkansas State	4	3	126	143	6	6	182	289
Florida Atlantic	4	3	129	100	5	7	181	299
Louisiana-Lafayette	3	4	126	151	6	6	248	296
Louisiana-Monroe	3	4	162	113	4	8	262	267
North Texas	2	5	76	147	3	9	154	304
Florida International	0	7	54	172	0	12	115	313

Western Athletic Conference

TEAM	CONFERENCE				OVERALL			
	W	L	PF	PA	W	L	PF	PA
Boise State	8	0	333	160	13	0	516	229
Hawaii	7	1	438	196	11	3	656	337
San Jose State	5	3	192	172	9	4	324	270
Nevada	5	3	260	142	8	5	391	249
Fresno State	4	4	203	214	4	8	276	339
Idaho	3	5	149	272	4	8	203	417
New Mexico State	2	6	230	262	4	8	374	369
Louisiana Tech	1	7	153	345	3	10	242	542
Utah State	1	7	123	318	1	11	130	462

Independents

TEAM	OVERALL			
	W	L	PF	PA
Notre Dame	10	3	403	310
Navy	9	4	367	261
Army	3	9	232	335
Temple	1	11	131	496

2006 NCAA DIVISION I-AA CONFERENCE STANDINGS

Atlantic 10 Conference (North)

TEAM	CONFERENCE				OVERALL			
	W	L	PF	PA	W	L	PF	PA
Massachusetts	8	0	222	89	13	2	413	200
New Hampshire	5	3	249	212	9	4	459	312
Maine	5	3	141	76	6	5	217	144
Northeastern	4	4	166	215	5	6	200	290
Rhode Island	2	6	137	252	5	6	200	290
Hofstra	1	7	131	174	2	9	185	246

Atlantic 10 Conference (South)

TEAM	CONFERENCE				OVERALL			
	W	L	PF	PA	W	L	PF	PA
James Madison	7	1	289	135	9	3	389	201
Villanova	5	3	176	187	6	5	247	273
Towson	4	4	172	215	7	4	236	237
Richmond	3	5	153	171	6	5	272	199
Delaware	3	5	239	255	5	6	289	285
William & Mary	1	7	143	237	3	8	209	283

Big Sky Conference

TEAM	CONFERENCE				OVERALL			
	W	L	PF	PA	W	L	PF	PA
Montana	8	0	264	140	12	2	385	225
Portland State	6	2	200	99	7	4	245	202
Montana State	6	2	170	145	8	5	261	286
Northern Arizona	5	3	291	202	6	5	378	296
Sacramento State	4	4	142	196	4	7	168	288
Weber State	3	5	171	205	4	7	201	265
Eastern Washington	3	5	180	167	3	8	214	296
Idaho State	1	7	173	237	2	9	255	330

Big South Conference

TEAM	CONFERENCE				OVERALL			
	W	L	PF	PA	W	L	PF	PA
Coastal Carolina	4	0	142	94	9	3	411	297
Charleston Southern	2	2	92	101	9	2	300	199
Gardner-Webb	2	2	100	135	6	5	270	329
Liberty	2	2	122	107	6	5	259	172
Virginia Military Institute	0	4	112	131	1	10	199	433

SIKIDS.com

Visit our website for the latest stats and sports info.

2006 NCAA DIVISION I-AA CONFERENCE STANDINGS (cont.)

Gateway Conference

TEAM	CONFERENCE				OVERALL			
	W	L	PF	PA	W	L	PF	PA
Youngstown State	6	1	227	126	11	3	440	323
Illinois State	5	2	212	150	9	4	377	262
Northern Iowa	5	2	208	162	7	4	341	249
Southern Illinois	4	3	218	162	9	4	448	256
Western Kentucky	4	3	173	154	6	5	258	263
Western Illinois	2	5	192	209	5	6	333	277
Missouri State	1	6	108	206	2	9	194	308
Indiana State	1	6	126	295	1	10	236	493

Great West Conference

TEAM	CONFERENCE				OVERALL			
	W	L	PF	PA	W	L	PF	PA
North Dakota State	4	0	151	73	10	1	374	147
South Dakota State	3	1	110	111	7	4	235	235
California Polytechnic	2	2	83	111	7	4	248	162
University of California-Davis	1	3	89	80	6	5	309	227
Southern Utah	0	4	49	107	3	8	215	276

Ivy League

TEAM	CONFERENCE				OVERALL			
	W	L	PF	PA	W	L	PF	PA
Princeton	6	1	166	129	9	1	233	179
Yale	6	1	177	111	8	2	257	208
Harvard	4	3	177	138	7	3	267	192
Cornell	3	4	123	162	5	5	189	217
Pennsylvania	3	4	153	129	5	5	228	191
Columbia	2	5	66	135	5	5	150	163
Brown	2	5	140	157	3	7	225	241
Dartmouth	2	5	105	146	2	8	147	254

Metro Atlantic Athletic Conference

TEAM	CONFERENCE				OVERALL			
	W	L	PF	PA	W	L	PF	PA
Duquesne	3	1	126	48	7	3	285	155
Marist	3	1	110	88	4	7	200	291
Iona	2	2	77	67	3	7	147	174
La Salle	1	3	50	135	3	7	146	255
St Peter's	1	3	97	122	2	8	154	347

Mid-Eastern Athletic Conference

TEAM	CONFERENCE				OVERALL			
	W	L	PF	PA	W	L	PF	PA
Hampton	7	1	290	92	10	2	410	174
Delaware State	6	2	207	141	8	3	335	192
South Carolina State	6	2	228	137	7	4	298	204
Florida A&M	5	3	213	233	7	4	273	327
Morgan State	4	4	160	166	5	6	199	242
Howard	4	4	139	150	5	6	180	237
Bethune-Cookman	3	5	220	207	4	7	310	253
Norfolk State	1	7	159	242	4	7	251	289
North Carolina A&T	0	8	93	341	0	11	114	475

Northeast Conference

TEAM	CONFERENCE				OVERALL			
	W	L	PF	PA	W	L	PF	PA
Monmouth (New Jersey)	6	1	177	83	10	2	286	152
Albany	5	2	162	85	7	4	224	143
Robert Morris	5	2	157	99	7	4	234	161
Stony Brook	5	2	220	144	5	6	242	278
Central Connecticut State	4	3	210	134	8	3	363	192
St. Francis (Pennsylvania)	2	5	130	267	3	8	227	398
Sacred Heart	1	6	108	207	2	9	189	300
Wagner	0	7	63	208	4	7	180	233

Ohio Valley Conference

TEAM	CONFERENCE				OVERALL			
	W	L	PF	PA	W	L	PF	PA
Eastern Illinois	7	1	197	100	8	5	297	275
Tennessee-Martin	6	1	182	104	9	3	298	188
Tennessee State	5	2	159	122	6	5	241	242
Eastern Kentucky	5	3	195	168	6	5	238	240
Jacksonville State	5	3	256	131	6	5	285	193
Tennessee Tech	4	4	159	191	4	7	192	296
Southeast Missouri State	2	6	114	208	4	7	203	307
Stamford	1	7	106	195	3	8	166	250
Murray State	0	8	115	264	1	10	195	386

Patriot League

TEAM	CONFERENCE				OVERALL			
	W	L	PF	PA	W	L	PF	PA
Lehigh	5	1	189	102	6	5	299	222
Lafayette	5	1	211	113	6	6	316	270
Holy Cross	4	2	161	129	7	4	275	235
Bucknell	3	3	78	134	6	5	222	268
Colgate	3	3	159	126	4	7	246	243
Fordham	1	5	103	193	3	8	158	289
Georgetown	0	6	81	185	2	9	164	287

Pioneer Football League (North)

TEAM	CONFERENCE				OVERALL			
	W	L	PF	PA	W	L	PF	PA
San Diego	7	0	349	87	11	1	514	155
Drake	6	1	186	103	9	2	303	168
Butler	2	5	82	210	3	8	156	331
Dayton	1	6	166	194	4	6	250	259
Valparaiso	1	6	104	289	3	8	212	378

Pioneer Football League (South)

TEAM	CONFERENCE				OVERALL			
	W	L	PF	PA	W	L	PF	PA
Davidson	5	2	236	172	6	4	295	228
Jacksonville (Florida)	4	3	173	192	4	6	206	323
Morehead State	2	5	147	196	2	9	218	322

Southern Conference

TEAM	CONFERENCE				OVERALL			
	W	L	PF	PA	W	L	PF	PA
Appalachian State	7	0	255	98	14	1	528	223
Furman	6	1	172	130	8	4	295	255
Wofford	5	2	209	107	7	4	329	213
Citadel	4	3	172	169	5	6	264	314
Elon	2	5	140	212	5	6	253	256
Chattanooga-Tennessee	2	5	125	223	3	8	201	304
Georgia Southern	2	5	139	154	3	8	235	260
Western Carolina	0	7	97	216	2	9	159	316

Southland Conference

TEAM	CONFERENCE				OVERALL			
	W	L	PF	PA	W	L	PF	PA
McNeese State	5	1	157	111	7	5	303	271
Sam Houston State	4	2	155	126	6	5	263	285
Stephen F. Austin	4	2	129	88	4	7	204	232
Texas State	3	3	135	119	5	6	244	248
Nicholls State	2	4	65	117	4	7	189	228
Northwestern State	2	4	109	120	4	7	187	249
Southeastern Louisiana	1	5	104	173	2	9	181	351

DID YOU KNOW?

In 2006, Michigan averaged 110,026 fans per home football game, beating Penn State's home attendance average of 107,567. That mark gave the Wolverines their ninth straight attendance title. Two other schools also topped the 100,000 mark in 2006: Tennessee at 105,789 and Ohio State at 105,096. The all-time single-season home attendance average record is 111,175, set by Michigan in 1999.

2006 NCAA DIVISION I-AA CONFERENCE STANDINGS (cont.)

Southwestern Athletic Conference (East)

TEAM	CONFERENCE				OVERALL			
	W	L	PF	PA	W	L	PF	PA
Alabama A&M	6	3	215	181	9	3	285	228
Alcorn State	5	4	234	230	6	5	263	260
Jackson State	5	4	238	222	6	5	311	273
Mississippi Valley State (MVSU)	5	4	178	186	6	5	199	245
Alabama State	5	4	189	172	5	6	199	227

Southwestern Athletic Conference (West)

TEAM	CONFERENCE				OVERALL			
	W	L	PF	PA	W	L	PF	PA
Arkansas-Pine Bluff	7	2	269	216	8	4	333	305
Southern University	4	5	226	224	5	6	276	280
Texas Southern	3	6	168	240	3	8	203	329
Grambling State	3	6	247	212	3	8	295	281
Prairie View A&M	2	7	119	200	3	7	156	200

Independents

TEAM	OVERALL			
	W	L	PF	PA
Central Arkansas	8	3	303	221
Winston-Salem	5	6	190	188
Austin Peay	3	8	245	271
Savannah State	2	9	108	379

2006 NCAA INDIVIDUAL LEADERS: DIVISION I-A

SCORING

	TD	PTS
Ian Johnson, Boise State	25	152
Ahmad Bradshaw, Marshall	21	126
Jarett Dillard, Rice	21	126
Arthur Carmody, Louisville	0	123
Ray Rice, Rutgers	20	120
Garrett Wolfe, Northern Illinois	19	116
Jorvorskie Lane, Texas A&M	19	114
Pat McAfee, West Virginia	0	113
Justin Medlock, UCLA	0	113
Alexis Serna, Oregon State	0	111

FIELD GOALS

	FGM	FGA	PCT
Justin Medlock, UCLA	28	32	87.5
Sam Swank, Wake Forest	23	31	74.2
Jeremy Ito, Rutgers	22	29	75.9
Alexis Serna, Oregon State	22	29	75.9
Kevin Kelly, Penn State	22	34	64.7
Arthur Carmody, Louisville	21	25	84.0

RUSHING

	G	CARRIES	YDS	AVG	TD
Garrett Wolfe, Northern Illinois	13	309	1,928	6.2	18
Ray Rice, Rutgers	13	335	1,794	5.4	20
Steve Slaton, West Virginia	13	248	1,744	7.0	16
Ian Johnson, Boise State	12	276	1,714	6.2	25
Darren McFadden, Arkansas	14	284	1,647	5.8	14
P. J. Hill, Wisconsin	13	311	1,569	5.1	15
Mike Hart, Michigan	13	318	1,562	4.9	14
Ahmad Bradshaw, Marshall	12	249	1,523	6.1	19
Tashard Choice, Georgia Tech	14	297	1,473	5.0	12
Dwayne Wright, Fresno State	12	261	1,462	5.6	11
Jon Cornish, Kansas	12	250	1,457	5.8	8

Ian Johnson, Boise State

AP PHOTO/MATT YORK

KEY TD=touchdowns; PTS=points; FGM=field goals made; FGA=field goals attempted; PCT=percentage; G=games; YDS=yards; AVG=average; TD=touchdowns

TODAY'S STARS

■ **John David Booty, quarterback,**
b. January 3, 1985, Shreveport, Louisiana.
After two years as backup to Heisman Trophy, winner Matt Leinart, Booty became the Trojans starter in 2006 as a junior. On the way to leading USC to a 10–2 regular season record, he passed for nearly 3,000 yards and 29 touchdowns, while throwing only nine interceptions. Then, in USC's 32–18 victory over Michigan in the Rose Bowl, he blistered the Wolverines with 391 passing yards and four touchdowns, setting high expecations for his senior season.

■ **Mike Hart, running back,** b. April 9, 1986, Syracuse, New York. In 2004, Hart scored nine touchdowns and set a Michigan freshman record by rushing for 1,455 yards. After a hamstring injury cut short his playing time during his sophomore season, he returned in 2006 to rush for 14 touchdowns and 1,562 yards, the fifth-highest single-season rushing yard total in Michigan history. For his junior-year performance, Hart came in fifth in the Heisman Trophy balloting. He looks to be among the strong favorites to win the award in 2007.

■ **DeSean Jackson, wide receiver,** b. December 1, 1986, Long Beach, California. As a freshman in 2005, Jackson quickly proved he could be a dynamic scoring threat for the Cal Bears, scoring touchdowns on his first career pass reception and first career punt return. As a sophomore, Jackson continued to improve, racking up nearly 1,000 receiving yards and nine touchdown catches, the most in the Pac-10. In addition, he scored four punt return touchdowns in 2006 and has now scored on five out of 26 career punt returns. His explosive performance as a punt returner in 2006 earned him first-team All-America honors.

John David Booty will be a leading Heisman Trophy candidate in 2007.

ROBERT BECK

2006 NCAA INDIVIDUAL LEADERS: DIVISION I-A (cont.)

PASSING EFFICIENCY	ATTS	COMP PCT	YDS	INT	TD	RATING
Colt Brennan, Hawaii	559	72.6	5,549	12	58	186.0
John Beck, BYU	417	69.3	3,885	8	32	169.1
JaMarcus Russell, LSU	342	67.8	3,129	8	28	167.0
Tyler Palko, Pittsburgh	322	68.3	2,871	9	25	163.2
Kevin Kolb, Houston	432	67.6	3,809	4	30	162.7
Jared Zabransky, Boise State	288	66.3	2,587	8	23	162.6
Troy Smith, Ohio State	311	65.3	2,542	6	30	161.9
Colt McCoy, Texas	318	68.2	2,570	7	29	161.8
Brian Brohm, Louisville	313	63.6	3,049	5	16	159.1
Justin Willis, SMU	270	67.4	2,047	6	26	158.4

KEY ATTS=attempts; COMP PCT=completion percentage; YDS=yards; INT=interceptions; TD=touchdowns

FAST FACT

Boston College has the longest current streak of bowl game wins in the nation, having won a bowl trophy in seven straight seasons. The Eagles' last loss in post-season play was to Colorado in the 1999 Insight Bowl.

2006 NCAA INDIVIDUAL LEADERS: DIVISION I-A (cont.)

RECEIVING	G	REC	YDS	YDS/G	TD
Chris Williams, New Mexico State	12	92	1,425	118.8	12
Johnnie Lee Higgins, UTEP	12	82	1,319	109.9	13
Joel Filani, Texas Tech	13	91	1,300	100.0	13
Robert Meachem, Tennessee	13	71	1,298	99.8	11
Sammy Stroughter, Oregon State	14	74	1,293	92.4	5
Harry Douglas, Louisville	13	70	1,265	97.3	6
Jarett Dillard, Rice	13	91	1,247	95.9	21
Davone Bess, Hawaii	14	96	1,220	87.1	15
Calvin Johnson, Georgia Tech	14	76	1,202	85.9	15
Adarius Bowman, Oklahoma State	13	60	1,181	90.9	12

INTERCEPTIONS	INT	YDS	TD
Stanley Franks, Idaho	9	220	1
Dwight Lowery, San Jose State	9	111	0
Daymeion Hughes, California	8	113	2
Ryan Smith, Florida	8	44	0
Quintin Demps, UTEP	7	61	0
John Talley, Duke	7	150	1
Tony Taylor, Geoia	7	97	1
DeJuan Tribble, Boston College	7	108	3
Eric Weddle, Utah	7	80	2
Trae Williams, South Florida	7	8	0

**Calvin Johnson,
Georgia Tech**

BOB ROSATO

2006 NCAA INDIVIDUAL LEADERS: DIVISION I-AA

SCORING	TD	PTS
Kevin Richardson, Appalachian State	31	186
Arkee Whitlock, Southern Illinois	25	150
Jerome Felton, Furman	23	140
Marcus Mason, Youngstown State	23	138
Clifton Dawson, Harvard	22	132
Justise Hairston, Central Connecticut State	20	120
Mike McLeod, Yale	20	120
Dan Carpenter, Montana	0	113
Steve Baylark, Massachusetts	18	108
Willie Cashmore, Drake	18	108
Chris Fletcher, Austin Peay	18	108
Herb Donaldson, Western Illinois	18	108

FIELD GOALS	FGM	FGA	PCT
Dan Carpenter, Montana	24	30	80.0
Blake Bercegeay, McNeese State	18	20	90.0
Rob Zarilli, Hofstra	18	21	85.7
Robert Weeks, Northwestern State	18	24	75.0
Brian Wingert, Northern Iowa	17	23	73.9
Andrew Paterini, Hampton	16	21	76.2
Chris Koepplin, Massachusetts	16	23	69.6
Craig Coffin, Southern Illinois	15	16	93.8
Brett Bergstrom, Eastern Washington	15	18	83.3

RUSHING	G	CARRIES	YDS	AVG	TD
Steve Baylark, Massachusetts	14	338	1,960	5.8	15
Justise Hairston, Central Connecticut State	11	277	1,847	6.7	20
Marcus Mason, Youngstown State	12	302	1,847	6.1	23
Arkee Whitlock, Southern Illinois	13	317	1,828	5.8	25
Pierre Rembert, Illinois State	13	355	1,743	4.9	16
Kevin Richardson, Appalachian State	15	302	1,676	5.6	30
Scott Phaydavong, Drake	11	277	1,613	5.8	10
Herb Donaldson, Western Illinois	11	233	1,417	6.1	18
Donald Chapman, Tennessee-Martin	11	269	1,412	6.1	18
Chris Fletcher, Austin Peay	11	255	1,401	5.5	16

TRIVIA CHALLENGE

Which school has had five players finish as runner-up for the Heisman Trophy, the most of any college?

Oklahoma (Kurt Burris, 1954; Greg Pruitt, 1972; Billy Sims, 1979; Josh Heupel, 2000; Adrian Peterson, 2004).

KEY   G=games; REC=receptions; YDS=yards; YDS/G=yards per game; TD=touchdowns; INT=interceptions;
PTS=points; FGM=field goals made; FGA=field goals attempted; PCT=percentage; AVG=average

PASSING EFFICIENCY

	ATTS	COMP PCT	YDS	INT	TD	RATING
Joshua Johnson, San Diego	371	66.3	3,320	5	34	169.0
Jason Murrietta, Northern Arizona	329	65.0	2,827	5	34	168.3
Tyler Thigpen, Coastal Carolina	339	64.0	3,296	11	29	167.4
Chris Wallace, Arkansas-Pine Bluff	211	61.1	2,023	9	20	164.4
Justin Rascati, James Madison	231	66.2	2,045	6	20	164.0
Liam Coen, Massachusetts	334	65.0	3,016	10	26	160.5
Nick Hill, Southern Illinois	196	61.7	1,721	4	15	156.7
Princeton Shepherd, Hampton	222	67.6	1,750	4	17	155.5
Collin Drafts, Charleston Southern	319	69.9	2,665	14	21	153.0
Ricky Santos, New Hampshire	432	67.8	3,125	7	29	147.5

RECEIVING

	G	REC	YDS	YDS/G	TD
William Mayfield, Appalachian State	15	64	1,129	75.3	5
David Ball, New Hampshire	12	93	1,114	92.8	13
Lanis Frederick, Austin Peay	11	77	1,101	100.1	7
Jerome Simpson, Coastal Carolina	12	61	1,077	89.8	16
Bruce Hocker, Duquesne	10	61	1,070	107.0	16
Steve Ogden, Valparaiso	11	55	1,048	95.3	8
Terrell Hudgins, Elon	9	69	1,027	114.1	8
Micheal Jefferson, Montana State	13	66	1,023	78.7	9
Alex Watson, Northern Arizona	11	82	1,017	92.5	15
Maurice Price, Charleston Southern	11	103	985	89.5	10
Nick Ruhe, Dayton	10	49	977	97.7	3

INTERCEPTIONS

	INT	YDS	TD
Dre Dokes, Northern Iowa	7	116	1
Jonathan Barsi, California-Davis	6	102	1
Steward Franks, Arkansas-Pine Bluff	6	96	0
Tristan Jackson, Central Arkansas	6	81	1
Frank Moore, Alabama A&M	6	50	0
Chris Parsons, Northern Iowa	6	34	0
Bobbie Williams, Bethune-Cookman	6	25	0
Brent Webber, Sacramento State	6	23	0
Jean-Pierre Marshall, Mississippi Valley	6	2	0

**Joshua Johnson,
San Diego**

DID YOU KNOW?

Since 1985, Georgia Southern has played in eight Division I-AA championship games and won three pairs of back-to-back titles (1985–86, '89–90, and 1999–2000).

AP PHOTO/MIA MALAFRONTE

KEY ATTS=attempts; COMP PCT=completion percentage; YDS=yards; INT=interceptions; TD=touchdowns; G=games; REC=receptions; YDS/G=yards per game

NATIONAL CHAMPIONSHIPS

YEAR	CHAMPION	RECORD	HEAD COACH
2006	Florida	13–1	Urban Meyer
2005	Texas	13–0	Mack Brown
2004	USC	13–0	Pete Carroll
2003	USC	12–1	Pete Carroll
(split)	LSU	13–1	Nick Saban
2002	Ohio State	14–0	Jim Tressel
2001	Miami (Florida)	12–0	Larry Coker
2000	Oklahoma	13–0	Bob Stoops
1999	Florida State	12–0	Bobby Bowden
1998	Tennessee	13–0	Phillip Fulmer
1997	Michigan	12–0	Lloyd Carr
(split)	Nebraska (ESPN)	13–0	Tom Osborne
1996	Florida	12–1	Steve Spurrier
1995	Nebraska	12–0–0	Tom Osborne
1994	Nebraska	13–0–0	Tom Osborne
1993	Florida State	12–1–0	Bobby Bowden
1992	Alabama	13–0–0	Gene Stallings
1991	Miami (Florida)	12–0–0	Dennis Erickson
(split)	Washington (CNN)	12–0–0	Don James
1990	Colorado	11–1–1	Bill McCartney
(split)	Georgia Tech (UPI)	11–0–1	Bobby Ross
1989	Miami (Florida)	11–1–0	Dennis Erickson
1988	Notre Dame	12–0–0	Lou Holtz
1987	Miami (Florida)	12–0–0	Jimmy Johnson
1986	Penn State	12–0–0	Joe Paterno
1985	Oklahoma	11–1–0	Barry Switzer
1984	Brigham Young	13–0–0	LaVell Edwards
1983	Miami (Florida)	11–1–0	Howard Schnellenberger
1982	Penn State	11–1–0	Joe Paterno
1981	Clemson	12–0–0	Danny Ford
1980	Georgia	12–0–0	Vince Dooley
1979	Alabama	12–0–0	Bear Bryant
1978	Alabama	11–1–0	Bear Bryant
(split)	USC (UPI)	12–1–0	John Robinson
1977	Notre Dame	11–1–0	Dan Devine
1976	Pittsburgh	12–0–0	Johnny Majors
1975	Oklahoma	11–1–0	Barry Switzer
1974	Oklahoma (AP)	11–0–0	Barry Switzer
(split)	USC (UPI)	10–1–1	John McKay
1973	Notre Dame	11–0–0	Ara Parseghian
(split)	Alabama (UPI)	11–1–0	Bear Bryant
1972	USC	12–0–0	John McKay
1971	Nebraska	13–0–0	Bob Devaney
1970	Nebraska	11–0–1	Bob Devaney
(split)	Texas (UPI)	10–1–0	Darrell Royal
1969	Texas	11–0–0	Darrell Royal
1968	Ohio State	10–0–0	Woody Hayes
1967	USC	10–1–0	John McKay
1966	Notre Dame	9–0–1	Ara Parseghian
1965	Alabama	9–1–1	Bear Bryant
(split)	Michigan State (UPI)	10–1–0	Duffy Daugherty
1964	Alabama	10–1–0	Bear Bryant

Note: National Champion selectors: Helms Athletic Foundation (H), 1883–1935; The Dickinson System (D), 1924–40; The Associated Press (AP), 1936–present; United Press International (UPI), 1958–90; *USA Today*/CNN (CNN), 1991–96; *USA Today*/ESPN (ESPN), 1997–present. In 1996, the NCAA introduced overtime to break ties.

NATIONAL CHAMPIONSHIPS (cont.)

YEAR	CHAMPION	RECORD	HEAD COACH	YEAR	CHAMPION	RECORD	HEAD COACH
1963	Texas	11–0–0	Darrell Royal	1926	Alabama (H)	9–0–1	Wallace Wade
1962	USC	11–0–0	John McKay	(split)	Stanford (D)(H)	10–0–1	Pop Warner
1961	Alabama	11–0–0	Bear Bryant	1925	Alabama (H)	10–0–0	Wallace Wade
1960	Minnesota	8–2–0	Murray Warmath	(split)	Dartmouth (D)	8–0–0	Jesse Hawley
1959	Syracuse	11–0–0	Ben Schwartzwalder	1924	Notre Dame	10–0–0	Knute Rockne
1958	Louisiana State	11–0–0	Paul Dietzel	1923	Illinois	8–0–0	Bob Zuppke
1957	Auburn	10–0–0	Shug Jordan	1922	Cornell	8–0–0	Gil Dobie
(split)	Ohio State (UPI)	9–1–0	Woody Hayes	1921	Cornell	8–0–0	Gil Dobie
1956	Oklahoma	10–0–0	Bud Wilkinson	1920	California	9–0–0	Andy Smith
1955	Oklahoma	11–0–0	Bud Wilkinson	1919	Harvard	9–0–1	Bob Fisher
1954	Ohio State	10–0–0	Woody Hayes	1918	Pittsburgh	4–1–0	Pop Warner
(split)	UCLA (UPI)	9–0–0	Red Sanders	1917	Georgia Tech	9–0–0	John Heisman
1953	Maryland	10–1–0	Jim Tatum	1916	Pittsburgh	8–0–0	Pop Warner
1952	Michigan State	9–0–0	Biggie Munn	1915	Cornell	9–0–0	Al Sharpe
1951	Tennessee	10–1–0	Robert Neyland	1914	Army	9–0–0	Charley Daly
1950	Oklahoma	10–1–0	Bud Wilkinson	1913	Harvard	9–0–0	Percy Haughton
1949	Notre Dame	10–0–0	Frank Leahy	1912	Harvard	9–0–0	Percy Haughton
1948	Michigan	9–0–0	Bennie Oosterbaan	1911	Princeton	8–0–2	Bill Roper
1947	Notre Dame	9–0–0	Frank Leahy	1910	Harvard	8–0–1	Percy Haughton
(split)	Michigan	10–0–0	Fritz Crisler	1909	Yale	10–0–0	Howard Jones
1946	Notre Dame	8–0–1	Frank Leahy	1908	Pennsylvania	11–0–1	Sol Metzger
1945	Army	9–0–0	Red Blaik	1907	Yale	9–0–1	Bill Knox
1944	Army	9–0–0	Red Blaik	1906	Princeton	9–0–1	Bill Roper
1943	Notre Dame	9–1–0	Frank Leahy	1905	Chicago	10–0–0	Amos Alonzo Stagg
1942	Ohio State	9–1–0	Paul Brown	1904	Pennsylvania	12–0–0	Carl Williams
1941	Minnesota	8–0–0	Bernie Bierman	1903	Princeton	11–0–0	Art Hillebrand
1940	Minnesota	8–0–0	Bernie Bierman	1902	Michigan	11–0–0	Fielding Yost
1939	Texas A&M (AP)	11–0–0	Homer Norton	1901	Michigan	11–0–0	Fielding Yost
(split)	USC (D)	8–0–2	Howard Jones	1900	Yale	12–0–0	Malcolm McBride
1938	TCU (AP)	11–0–0	Dutch Meyer	1899	Harvard	10–0–1	Benjamin H. Dibblee
(split)	Notre Dame (D)	8–1–0	Elmer Layden	1898	Harvard	11–0–0	W. Cameron Forbes
1937	Pittsburgh	9–0–1	Jock Sutherland	1897	Pennsylvania	15–0–0	George W. Woodruff
1936	Minnesota	7–1–0	Bernie Bierman	1896	Princeton	10–0–1	Garrett Cochran
1935	Minnesota (H)	8–0–0	Bernie Bierman	1895	Pennsylvania	14–0–0	George W. Woodruff
(split)	SMU (D)	12–1–0	Matty Bell	1894	Yale	16–0–0	William C. Rhodes
1934	Minnesota	8–0–0	Bernie Bierman	1893	Princeton	11–0–0	Tom Trenchard
1933	Michigan	8–0–0	Harry Kipke	1892	Yale	13–0–0	Walter Camp
1932	USC (H)	10–0–0	Howard Jones	1891	Yale	13–0–0	Walter Camp
(split)	Michigan (D)	8–0–0	Harry Kipke	1890	Harvard	11–0–0	G. Stewart/G.Adams
1931	USC	10–1–0	Howard Jones	1889	Princeton	10–0–0	Edgar Poe
1930	Notre Dame	10–0–0	Knute Rockne	1888	Yale	13–0–0	Walter Camp
1929	Notre Dame	9–0–0	Knute Rockne	1887	Yale	9–0–0	Harry W. Beecher
1928	Georgia Tech (H)	10–0–0	Bill Alexander	1886	Yale	9–0–1	Robert N. Corwin
(split)	USC (D)	9–0–1	Howard Jones	1885	Princeton	9–0–0	Charles DeCamp
1927	Illinois	7–0–1	Bob Zuppke	1884	Yale	8–0–1	Eugene L. Richards
				1883	Yale	8–0–0	Ray Tompkins

MAJOR BOWL GAME RESULTS

ROSE BOWL

DATE	RESULT	DATE	RESULT
2007	USC 32, Michigan 18	1989	Michigan 22, USC 14
2006	Texas 41, USC 38	1988	Michigan State 20, USC 17
2005	Texas 38, Michigan 37	1987	Arizona State 22, Michigan 15
2004	USC 28, Michigan 14	1986	UCLA 45, Iowa 28
2003	Oklahoma 34, Washington State 14	1985	USC 20, Ohio State 17
2002	Miami 37, Nebraska 14	1984	UCLA 45, Illinois 9
2001	Washington 34, Purdue 24	1983	UCLA 24, Michigan 14
2000	Wisconsin 17, Stanford 9	1982	Washington 28, Iowa 0
1999	Wisconsin 38, UCLA 31	1981	Michigan 23, Washington 6
1998	Michigan 21, Washington State 16	1980	USC 17, Ohio State 16
1997	Ohio State 20, Arizona State 17	1979	USC 17, Michigan 10
1996	USC 41, Northwestern 32	1978	Washington 27, Michigan 20
1995	Penn State 38, Oregon 20	1977	USC 14, Michigan 6
1994	Wisconsin 21, UCLA 16	1976	UCLA 23, Ohio State 10
1993	Michigan 38, Washington 31	1975	USC 18, Ohio State 17
1992	Washington 34, Michigan 14	1974	Ohio State 42, USC 21
1991	Washington 46, Iowa 34	1973	USC 42, Ohio State 17
1990	USC 17, Michigan 10	1972	Stanford 13, Michigan 12

ROSE BOWL (cont.)

DATE	RESULT	DATE	RESULT
1971	Stanford 27, Ohio State 17	1942	Oregon State 20, Duke 16
1970	USC 10, Michigan 3	1941	Stanford 21, Nebraska 13
1969	Ohio State 27, USC 16	1940	USC 14, Tennessee 0
1968	USC 14, Indiana 3	1939	USC 7, Duke 3
1967	Purdue 14, USC 13	1938	California 13, Alabama 0
1966	UCLA 14, Michigan State 12	1937	Pittsburgh 21, Washington 0
1965	Michigan 34, Oregon State 7	1936	Stanford 7, SMU 0
1964	Illinois 17, Washington 7	1935	Alabama 29, Stanford 13
1963	USC 42, Wisconsin 37	1934	Columbia 7, Stanford 0
1962	Minnesota 21, UCLA 3	1933	USC 35, Pittsburgh 0
1961	Washington 17, Minnesota 7	1932	USC 21, Tulane 12
1960	Washington 44, Wisconsin 8	1931	Alabama 24, Washington State 0
1959	Iowa 38, California 12	1930	USC 47, Pittsburgh 14
1958	Ohio State 10, Oregon 7	1929	Georgia Tech 8, California 7
1957	Iowa 35, Oregon State 19	1928	Stanford 7, Pittsburgh 6
1956	Michigan State 17, UCLA 14	1927	Stanford 7, Alabama 7
1955	Ohio State 20, USC 7	1926	Alabama 20, Washington 19
1954	Michigan State 28, UCLA 20	1925	Notre Dame 27, Stanford 10
1953	USC 7, Wisconsin 0	1924	Washington 14, Navy 14
1952	Illinois 40, Stanford 7	1923	USC 14, Penn State 3
1951	Michigan 14, California 6	1922	California 0, Washington & Jefferson 0
1950	Ohio State 17, California 14	1921	California 28, Ohio State 0
1949	Northwestern 20, California 14	1920	Harvard 7, Oregon 6
1948	Michigan 49, USC 0	1919	Great Lakes 17, Mare Island 0
1947	Illinois 45, UCLA 14	1918	Mare Island 19, Camp Lewis 7
1946	Alabama 34, USC 14	1917	Oregon 14, Pennsylvania 0
1945	USC 25, Tennessee 0	1916	Washington State 14, Brown 0
1944	USC 29, Washington 0	1902	Michigan 49, Stanford 0
1943	Georgia 9, UCLA 0		

Note: From 1903–15, no Rose Bowl football game was held. In 1903, polo replaced football. From 1904–1915, chariot races were held. Football returned in 1916.

ORANGE BOWL

DATE	RESULT	DATE	RESULT
January 2, 2007	Louisville 24, Wake Forest 13	January 1, 1977	Ohio State 27, Colorado 10
January 3, 2006	Penn State 26, Florida State 23	January 1, 1976	Oklahoma 14, Michigan 6
January 4, 2005	USC 55, Oklahoma 19	January 1, 1975	Notre Dame 13, Alabama 11
January 1, 2004	Miami (Florida) 16, Florida State 14	January 1, 1974	Penn State 16, LSU 9
January 2, 2003	USC 38, Iowa 17	January 1, 1973	Nebraska 40, Notre Dame 6
January 2, 2002	Florida 56, Maryland 23	January 1, 1972	Nebraska 38, Alabama 6
January 3, 2001	Oklahoma 13, Florida State 2	January 1, 1971	Nebraska 17, LSU 12
January 1, 2000	Michigan 35, Alabama 34 (OT)	January 1, 1970	Penn State 10, Missouri 3
January 2, 1999	Florida 31, Syracuse 10	January 1, 1969	Penn State 15, Kansas 14
January 2, 1998	Nebraska 42, Tennessee 17	January 1, 1968	Oklahoma 26, Tennessee 24
December 31, 1996	Nebraska 41, Virginia Tech 21	January 2, 1967	Florida 27, Georgia Tech 12
January 1, 1996	Florida State 31, Notre Dame 26	January 1, 1966	Alabama 39, Nebraska 28
January 1, 1995	Nebraska 24, Miami (Florida) 17	January 1, 1965	Texas 21, Alabama 17
January 1, 1994	Florida State 18, Nebraska 16	January 1, 1964	Nebraska 13, Auburn 7
January 1, 1993	Florida State 27, Nebraska 14	January 1, 1963	Alabama 17, Oklahoma 0
January 1, 1992	Miami (Florida) 22, Nebraska 0	January 1, 1962	LSU 25, Colorado 7
January 1, 1991	Colorado 10, Notre Dame 9	January 2, 1961	Missouri 21, Navy 14
January 1, 1990	Notre Dame 21, Colorado 6	January 1, 1960	Georgia 14, Missouri 0
January 2, 1989	Miami (Florida) 23, Nebraska 3	January 1, 1959	Oklahoma 21, Syracuse 6
January 1, 1988	Miami (Florida) 20, Oklahoma 14	January 1, 1958	Oklahoma 48, Duke 21
January 1, 1987	Oklahoma 42, Arkansas 8	January 1, 1957	Colorado 27, Clemson 21
January 1, 1986	Oklahoma 25, Penn State 10	January 2, 1956	Oklahoma 20, Maryland 6
January 1, 1985	Washington 28, Oklahoma 17	January 1, 1955	Duke 34, Nebraska 7
January 2, 1984	Miami (Florida) 31, Nebraska 30	January 1, 1954	Oklahoma 7, Maryland 0
January 1, 1983	Nebraska 21, LSU 20	January 1, 1953	Alabama 61, Syracuse 6
January 1, 1982	Clemson 22, Nebraska 15	January 1, 1952	Georgia Tech 17, Baylor 14
January 1, 1981	Oklahoma 18, Florida State 17	January 1, 1951	Clemson 15, Miami (Florida) 14
January 1, 1980	Oklahoma 24, Florida State 7	January 2, 1950	Santa Clara 21, Kentucky 13
January 1, 1979	Oklahoma 31, Nebraska 24	January 1, 1949	Texas 41, Georgia 28
January 2, 1978	Arkansas 31, Oklahoma 6	January 1, 1948	Georgia Tech 20, Kansas 14

MAJOR BOWL GAME RESULTS (cont.)

ORANGE BOWL (cont.)

DATE	RESULT	DATE	RESULT
January 1, 1947	Rice 8, Tennessee 0	January 1, 1940	Georgia Tech 21, Missouri 7
January 1, 1946	Miami (Florida) 13, Holy Cross 6	January 2, 1939	Tennessee 17, Oklahoma 0
January 1, 1945	Tulsa 26, Georgia Tech 12	January 1, 1938	Auburn 6, Michigan State 0
January 1, 1944	LSU 19, Texas A&M 14	January 1, 1937	Duquesne 13, Mississippi State 12
January 1, 1943	Alabama 37, Boston College 21	January 1, 1936	Catholic 20, Mississippi 19
January 1, 1942	Georgia 40, TCU 26	January 1, 1935	Bucknell 26, Miami (Florida) 0
January 1, 1941	Mississippi State 14, Georgetown 7		

SUGAR BOWL

DATE	RESULT	DATE	RESULT
January 3, 2007	LSU 41, Notre Dame 14	January 1, 1970	Mississippi 27, Arkansas 22
January 2, 2006	West Virginia 38, Georgia 35	January 1, 1969	Arkansas 16, Georgia 2
January 3, 2005	Auburn 16, Virginia Tech 13	January 1, 1968	LSU 20, Wyoming 13
January 4, 2004	LSU 21, Oklahoma 14	January 2, 1967	Alabama 34, Nebraska 7
January 1, 2003	Georgia 26, Florida State 13	January 1, 1966	Missouri 20, Florida 18
January 1, 2002	LSU 47, Illinois 34	January 1, 1965	LSU 13, Syracuse 10
January 2, 2001	Miami (Florida) 37, Florida 20	January 1, 1964	Alabama 12, Mississippi 7
January 4, 2000	Florida State 46, Virginia Tech 29	January 1, 1963	Mississippi 17, Arkansas 13
January 1, 1999	Ohio State 24, Texas A&M 14	January 1, 1962	Alabama 10, Arkansas 3
January 1, 1998	Florida State 31, Ohio State 14	January 2, 1961	Mississippi 14, Rice 6
January 2, 1997	Florida 52, Florida State 20	January 1, 1960	Mississippi 21, LSU 0
December 31, 1995	Virginia Tech 28, Texas 10	January 1, 1959	LSU 7, Clemson 0
January 2, 1995	Florida State 23, Florida 17	January 1, 1958	Mississippi 39, Texas 7
January 1, 1994	Florida 41, West Virginia 7	January 1, 1957	Baylor 13, Tennessee 7
January 1, 1993	Alabama 34, Miami (Florida) 13	January 2, 1956	Georgia Tech 7, Pittsburgh 0
January 1, 1992	Notre Dame 39, Florida 28	January 1, 1955	Navy 21, Mississippi 0
January 1, 1991	Tennessee 23, Virginia 22	January 1, 1954	Georgia Tech 42, West Virginia 19
January 1, 1990	Miami (Florida) 33, Alabama 25	January 1, 1953	Georgia Tech 24, Mississippi 7
January 2, 1989	Florida State 13, Auburn 7	January 1, 1952	Maryland 28, Tennessee 13
January 1, 1988	Auburn 16, Syracuse 16	January 1, 1951	Kentucky 13, Oklahoma 7
January 1, 1987	Nebraska 30, LSU 15	January 2, 1950	Oklahoma 35, LSU 0
January 1, 1986	Tennessee 35, Miami (Florida) 7	January 1, 1949	Oklahoma 14, North Carolina 6
January 1, 1985	Nebraska 28, LSU 10	January 1, 1948	Texas 27, Alabama 7
January 2, 1984	Auburn 9, Michigan 7	January 1, 1947	Georgia 20, North Carolina 10
January 1, 1983	Penn State 27, Georgia 23	January 1, 1946	Oklahoma State 33, Saint Mary's 13
January 1, 1982	Pittsburgh 24, Georgia 20	January 1, 1945	Duke 29, Alabama 26
January 1, 1981	Georgia 17, Notre Dame 10	January 1, 1944	Georgia Tech 20, Tulsa 18
January 1, 1980	Alabama 24, Arkansas 9	January 1, 1943	Tennessee 14, Tulsa 7
January 1, 1979	Alabama 14, Penn State 7	January 1, 1942	Fordham 2, Missouri 0
January 2, 1978	Alabama 35, Ohio State 6	January 1, 1941	Boston College 19, Tennessee 13
January 1, 1977	Pittsburgh 27, Georgia 3	January 1, 1940	Texas A&M 14, Tulane 13
December 31, 1975	Alabama 13, Penn State 6	January 2, 1939	TCU 15, Carnegie Mellon 7
December 31, 1974	Nebraska 13, Florida 10	January 1, 1938	Santa Clara 6, LSU 0
December 31, 1973	Notre Dame 24, Alabama 23	January 1, 1937	Santa Clara 21, LSU 14
December 31, 1972	Oklahoma 14, Penn State 0	January 1, 1936	TCU 3, LSU 2
January 1, 1972	Oklahoma 40, Auburn 22	January 1, 1935	Tulane 20, Temple 14
January 1, 1971	Tennessee 34, Air Force 13		

COTTON BOWL

DATE	RESULT	DATE	RESULT
January 1, 2007	Auburn 17, Nebraska 14	January 1, 1991	Miami (Florida) 46, Texas 3
January 2, 2006	Alabama 13, Texas Tech 10	January 1, 1990	Tennessee 31, Arkansas 27
January 1, 2005	Tennessee 38, Texas A&M 7	January 2, 1989	UCLA 17, Arkansas 3
January 2, 2004	Mississippi 31, Oklahoma State 28	January 1, 1988	Texas A&M 35, Notre Dame 10
January 1, 2003	Texas 35, LSU 20	January 1, 1987	Ohio State 28, Texas A&M 12
January 1, 2002	Oklahoma 10, Arkansas 3	January 1, 1986	Texas A&M 36, Auburn 16
January 1, 2001	Kansas State 35, Tennessee 21	January 1, 1985	Boston College 45, Houston 28
January 1, 2000	Arkansas 27, Texas 6	January 2, 1984	Georgia 10, Texas 9
January 1, 1999	Texas 38, Mississippi State 11	January 1, 1983	SMU 7, Pittsburgh 3
January 1, 1998	UCLA 29, Texas A&M 23	January 1, 1982	Texas 14, Alabama 12
January 1, 1997	BYU 19, Kansas State 15	January 1, 1981	Alabama 30, Baylor 2
January 1, 1996	Colorado 38, Oregon 6	January 1, 1980	Houston 17, Nebraska 14
January 2, 1995	USC 55, Texas Tech 14	January 1, 1979	Notre Dame 35, Houston 34
January 1, 1994	Notre Dame 24, Texas A&M 21	January 2, 1978	Notre Dame 38, Texas 10
January 1, 1993	Notre Dame 28, Texas A&M 3	January 1, 1977	Houston 30, Maryland 21
January 1, 1992	Florida State 10, Texas A&M 2	January 1, 1976	Arkansas 31, Georgia 10

LEGENDS

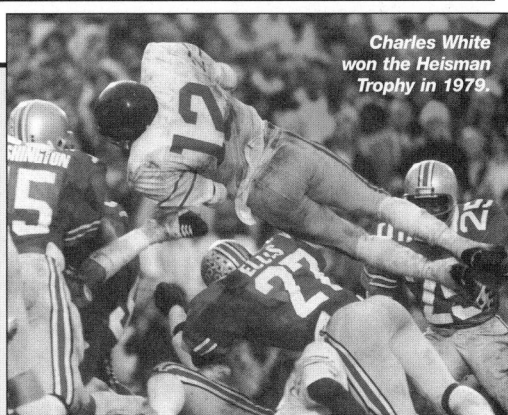

Charles White won the Heisman Trophy in 1979.

RICHARD MACKSON

■ **Charles White, running back,** b. January 22, 1958, Los Angeles, California. As one of the talented running backs that earned USC the nickname of "Tailback U," White led the Trojans in rushing for three straight years from 1977 to 1979. In 1978, as a junior, White helped the Trojans to a share of the 1978 national championship and was named co-MVP of the Rose Bowl. During his senior year, White gained 1,804 rushing yards during the regular season and was again named MVP of the Rose Bowl after steamrolling over Ohio State for 247 yards in USC's 17–16 victory. By the time White was awarded the Heisman Trophy at the end of the 1979 season, he had rushed for 5,598 yards during his regular season college career—the second-highest total in NCAA history —and had either set or matched 21 other NCAA, Pac-10, USC, or Rose Bowl records.

■ **Tim Rattay, quarterback,** b. March 15, 1977, Elyria, Ohio. In only three years at Louisiana Tech, Rattay proved to be one of the most productive passers in college football history. From 1997 through 1999, he passed for 12,746 yards and set all-time NCAA records for most completions per game (30.8), most pass attempts per game (47.0), and most passing yards per game (386.2).

■ **Dave Rimington, center,** b. May 22, 1960, Omaha, Nebraska. From 1979 to 1982, Rimington anchored a legendarily powerful Nebraska offensive line. In 1981 and 1982, he became the first (and only) player to win back-to-back Outland Trophys, the award given to the best lineman in America. In addition, Rimington was also named to both All-America and Academic All-America teams during his career. His play defined the position so well that since 2000, the award for best center in college football has been named after him. Rimington was inducted into the College Football Hall of Fame in 1997.

MAJOR BOWL GAME RESULTS (cont.)

COTTON BOWL (cont.)

DATE	RESULT	DATE	RESULT
January 1, 1975	Penn State 41, Baylor 20	January 1, 1960	Syracuse 23, Texas 14
January 1, 1974	Nebraska 19, Texas 3	January 1, 1959	TCU 0, Air Force 0
January 1, 1973	Texas 17, Alabama 13	January 1, 1958	Navy 20, Rice 7
January 1, 1972	Penn State 30, Texas 6	January 1, 1957	TCU 28, Syracuse 27
January 1, 1971	Notre Dame 24, Texas 11	January 2, 1956	Mississippi 14, TCU 13
January 1, 1970	Texas 21, Notre Dame 17	January 1, 1955	Georgia Tech 14, Arkansas 6
January 1, 1969	Texas 36, Tennessee 13	January 1, 1954	Rice 28, Alabama 6
January 1, 1968	Texas A&M 20, Alabama 16	January 1, 1953	Texas 16, Tennessee 0
December 31, 1966	Georgia 24, SMU 9	January 1, 1952	Kentucky 20, TCU 7
January 1, 1966	LSU 14, Arkansas 7	January 1, 1951	Tennessee 20, Texas 14
January 1, 1965	Arkansas 10, Nebraska 7	January 2, 1950	Rice 27, North Carolina 13
January 1, 1964	Texas 28, Navy 6	January 1, 1949	SMU 21, Oregon 13
January 1, 1963	LSU 13, Texas 0	January 1, 1948	SMU 13, Penn State 13
January 1, 1962	Texas 12, Mississippi 7	January 1, 1947	Arkansas 0, LSU 0
January 2, 1961	Duke 7, Arkansas 6		

MAJOR BOWL GAME RESULTS (cont.)

COTTON BOWL (cont.)

DATE	RESULT
January 1, 1946	Texas 40, Missouri 27
January 1, 1945	Oklahoma State 34, TCU 0
January 1, 1944	Texas 7, Randolph Field 7
January 1, 1943	Texas 14, Georgia Tech 7

DATE	RESULT
January 1, 1942	Alabama 29, Texas A&M 21
January 1, 1941	Texas A&M 13, Fordham 12
January 1, 1940	Clemson 6, Boston College 3
January 2, 1939	St. Mary's (CA) 20, Texas Tech 13
January 1, 1938	Rice 28, Colorado 14
January 1, 1937	TCU 16, Marquette 6

FIESTA BOWL

DATE	RESULT
January 2, 2007	Boise State 43, Oklahoma 42 (OT)
January 2, 2006	Ohio State 34, Notre Dame 20
January 1, 2005	Utah 35, Pittsburgh 7
January 2, 2004	Ohio State 35, Kansas St. 28
January 3, 2003	Ohio State 31, Miami (Florida) 24
January 1, 2002	Oregon 38, Colorado 16
January 1, 2001	Oregon State 41, Notre Dame 9
January 2, 2000	Nebraska 31, Tennessee 21
January 4, 1999	Tennessee 23, Florida State 16
December 31, 1997	Kansas State 35, Syracuse 18
January 1, 1997	Penn State 38, Texas 15
January 2, 1996	Nebraska 62, Florida 24
January 2, 1995	Colorado 41, Notre Dame 24
January 1, 1994	Arizona 29, Miami (Florida) 0
January 1, 1993	Syracuse 26, Colorado 22
January 1, 1992	Penn State 42, Tennessee 17
January 1, 1991	Louisville 34, Alabama 7
January 1, 1990	Florida State 41, Nebraska 17

DATE	RESULT
January 2, 1989	Notre Dame 34, West Virginia 21
January 1, 1988	Florida State 31, Nebraska 28
January 2, 1987	Penn State 14, Miami (Florida) 10
January 1, 1986	Michigan 27, Nebraska 23
January 1, 1985	UCLA 39, Miami (Florida) 37
January 2, 1984	Ohio State 28, Pittsburgh 23
January 1, 1983	Arizona State 32, Oklahoma 21
January 1, 1982	Penn State 26, USC 10
December 26, 1980	Penn State 31, Ohio State 19
December 25, 1979	Pittsburgh 16, Arizona 10
December 25, 1978	Arkansas 10, UCLA 10
December 25, 1977	Penn State 42, Arizona State 30
December 25, 1976	Oklahoma 41, Wyoming 7
December 26, 1975	Arizona State 17, Nebraska 14
December 28, 1974	Oklahoma State 16, BYU 6
December 21, 1973	Arizona State 28, Pittsburgh 7
December 23, 1972	Arizona State 49, Missouri 35
December 27, 1971	Arizona State 45, Florida State 38

BCS NATIONAL CHAMPIONSHIP GAME

DATE	RESULT
January 8, 2007	Florida 41, Ohio State 14

NCAA DIVISION I-AA CHAMPIONSHIPS

YEAR	WINNER	RUNNER-UP	SCORE	YEAR	WINNER	RUNNER-UP	SCORE
2006	Appalachian State	Massachusetss	28–17	1991	Youngstown State	Marshall	25–17
2005	Appalachian State	Northern Iowa	21–16	1990	Georgia Southern	Nevada-Reno	36–13
2004	James Madison	Montana	31–21	1989	Georgia Southern	Stephen F. Austin	37–34
2003	Delaware	Colgate	40–0	1988	Furman	Georgia Southern	17–12
2002	Western Kentucky	McNeese State	34–14	1987	Louisiana Monroe	Marshall	43–42
2001	Montana	Furman	13–6	1986	Georgia Southern	Arkansas State	48–21
2000	Georgia Southern	Montana	27–25	1985	Georgia Southern	Furman	44–42
1999	Georgia Southern	Youngstown State	59–24	1984	Montana State	Louisiana Tech	19–6
1998	Massachusetts	Georgia Southern	55–43	1983	Southern Illinois	Western Carolina	43–7
1997	Youngstown State	McNeese State	10–9	1982	Eastern Kentucky	Delaware	17–14
1996	Marshall	Montana	49–29	1981	Idaho State	Eastern Kentucky	34–23
1995	Montana	Marshall	22–20	1980	Boise State	Eastern Kentucky	31–29
1994	Youngstown State	Boise State	28–14	1979	Eastern Kentucky	Lehigh	30–7
1993	Youngstown State	Marshall	17–5	1978	Florida A&M	Massachusetts	35–28
1992	Marshall	Youngstown State	31–28				

HEISMAN MEMORIAL TROPHY

Awarded to the nation's best college player by the Downtown Athletic Club (DAC) of New York City. The trophy is named after John W. Heisman, who coached Georgia Tech to the national championship in 1917 and later served as DAC athletic director.

YEAR	WINNER, COLLEGE	RUNNER-UP, COLLEGE
2006	Troy Smith, Ohio State	Darren McFadden, Arkansas
2005	Reggie Bush, USC	Vince Young, Texas
2004	*† Matt Leinart, USC	Adrian Peterson, Oklahoma
2003	* Jason White, Oklahoma	Larry Fitzgerald, Pittsburgh
2002	Carson Palmer, USC	Brad Banks, Iowa
2001	Eric Crouch, Nebraska	Rex Grossman, Florida

*Juniors (all others were seniors)
†Winners who played for national championship teams the same year

HEISMAN MEMORIAL TROPHY (cont.)

YEAR	WINNER, COLLEGE	RUNNER-UP, COLLEGE
2000	Chris Weinke, Florida State	Josh Heupel, Oklahoma
1999	Ron Dayne, Wisconsin	Joe Hamilton, Georgia Tech
1998	Ricky Williams, Texas	Michael Bishop, Kansas State
1997	†Charles Woodson, Michigan	Peyton Manning, Tennessee
1996	†Danny Wuerffel, Florida	Troy Davis, Iowa State
1995	Eddie George, Ohio State	Tommie Frazier, Nebraska
1994	Rashaan Salaam, Colorado	Ki-Jana Carter, Penn State
1993	†Charlie Ward, Florida State	Heath Shuler, Tennessee
1992	Gino Torretta, Miami (Florida)	Marshall Faulk, San Diego State
1991	* Desmond Howard, Michigan	Casey Weldon, Florida State
1990	* Ty Detmer, BYU	Raghib Ismail, Notre Dame
1989	* Andre Ware, Houston	Anthony Thompson, Indiana
1988	* Barry Sanders, Oklahoma State	Rodney Peete, USC
1987	Tim Brown, Notre Dame	Don McPherson, Syracuse
1986	Vinny Testaverde, Miami (Florida)	Paul Palmer, Temple
1985	Bo Jackson, Auburn	Chuck Long, Iowa
1984	Doug Flutie, Boston College	Keith Byars, Ohio State
1983	Mike Rozier, Nebraska	Steve Young, BYU
1982	* Herschel Walker, Georgia	John Elway, Stanford
1981	Marcus Allen, USC	Herschel Walker, Georgia
1980	George Rogers, South Carolina	Hugh Green, Pittsburgh
1979	Charles White, USC	Billy Sims, Oklahoma
1978	* Billy Sims, Oklahoma	Chuck Fusina, Penn State
1977	Earl Campbell, Texas	Terry Miller, Oklahoma State
1976	†Tony Dorsett, Pittsburgh	Ricky Bell, USC
1975	Archie Griffin, Ohio State	Chuck Muncie, California
1974	* Archie Griffin, Ohio State	Anthony Davis, USC
1973	John Cappelletti, Penn State	John Hicks, Ohio State
1972	Johnny Rodgers, Nebraska	Greg Pruitt, Oklahoma
1971	Pat Sullivan, Auburn	Ed Marinaro, Cornell
1970	Jim Plunkett, Stanford	Joe Theismann, Notre Dame
1969	Steve Owens, Oklahoma	Mike Phipps, Purdue
1968	O.J. Simpson, USC	Leroy Keyes, Purdue
1967	Gary Beban, UCLA	O.J. Simpson, USC
1966	Steve Spurrier, Florida	Bob Griese, Purdue
1965	Mike Garrett, USC	Howard Twilley, Tulsa
1964	John Huarte, Notre Dame	Jerry Rhome, Tulsa
1963	* Roger Staubach, Navy	Billy Lothridge, Georgia Tech
1962	Terry Baker, Oregon State	Jerry Stovall, LSU
1961	Ernie Davis, Syracuse	Bob Ferguson, Ohio State
1960	Joe Bellino, Navy	Tom Brown, Minnesota
1959	Billy Cannon, LSU	Rich Lucas, Penn State
1958	Pete Dawkins, Army	Randy Duncan, Iowa
1957	John David Crow, Texas A&M	Alex Karras, Iowa
1956	Paul Hornung, Notre Dame	Johnny Majors, Tennessee
1955	Howard Cassady, Ohio State	Jim Swink, TCU
1954	Alan Ameche, Wisconsin	Kurt Burris, Oklahoma
1953	John Lattner, Notre Dame	Paul Giel, Minnesota
1952	Billy Vessels, Oklahoma	Jack Scarbath, Maryland
1951	Dick Kazmaier, Princeton	Hank Lauricella, Tennessee
1950	* Vic Janowicz, Ohio State	Kyle Rote, SMU
1949	†Leon Hart, Notre Dame	Charlie Justice, North Carolina
1948	* Doak Walker, SMU	Charlie Justice, North Carolina
1947	†John Lujack, Notre Dame	Bob Chappius, Michigan
1946	Glenn Davis, Army	Charley Trippi, Georgia
1945	*†Doc Blanchard, Army	Glenn Davis, Army
1944	Les Horvath, Ohio State	Glenn Davis, Army
1943	Angelo Bertelli, Notre Dame	Bob Odell, Pennsylvania
1942	Frank Sinkwich, Georgia	Paul Governali, Columbia
1941	†Bruce Smith, Minnesota	Angelo Bertelli, Notre Dame
1940	Tom Harmon, Michigan	John Kimbrough, Texas A&M
1939	Nile Kinnick, Iowa	Tom Harmon, Michigan
1938	†Davey O'Brien, TCU	Marshall Goldberg, Pittsburgh
1937	Clint Frank, Yale	Byron White, Colorado
1936	Larry Kelley, Yale	Sam Francis, Nebraska
1935	Jay Berwanger, Chicago	Monk Meyer, Army

*Juniors (all others were seniors)
†Winners who played for national championship teams the same year
 Note: Former Heisman winners and members of the national media cast votes with ballots allowing for three names (3 points for first, 2 points for second, and 1 point for third).

MAXWELL AWARD

Given to the nation's most outstanding college football player by the Maxwell Football Club of Philadelphia.

YEAR	PLAYER, COLLEGE	YEAR	PLAYER, COLLEGE
2006	Brady Quinn, Notre Dame	1970	Jim Plunkett, Stanford
2005	Vince Young, Texas	1969	Mike Reid, Penn State
2004	Jason White, Oklahoma	1968	O.J. Simpson, USC
2003	Eli Manning, Mississippi	1967	Gary Beban, UCLA
2002	Larry Johnson, Penn State	1966	Jim Lynch, Notre Dame
2001	Ken Dorsey, Miami (Florida)	1965	Tommy Nobis, Texas
2000	Drew Brees, Purdue	1964	Glenn Ressler, Penn State
1999	Ron Dayne, Wisconsin	1963	Roger Staubach, Navy
1998	Ricky Williams, Texas	1962	Terry Baker, Oregon State
1997	Peyton Manning, Tennessee	1961	Bob Ferguson, Ohio State
1996	Danny Wuerffel, Florida	1960	Joe Bellino, Navy
1995	Eddie George, Ohio State	1959	Rich Lucas, Penn State
1994	Kerry Collins, Penn State	1958	Pete Dawkins, Army
1993	Charlie Ward, Florida State	1957	Bob Reifsnyder, Navy
1992	Gino Torretta, Miami (Florida)	1956	Tommy McDonald, Oklahoma
1991	Desmond Howard, Michigan	1955	Howard Cassidy, Ohio State
1990	Ty Detmer, BYU	1954	Ron Beagle, Navy
1989	Anthony Thompson, Indiana	1953	John Lattner, Notre Dame
1988	Barry Sanders, Oklahoma State	1952	John Lattner, Notre Dame
1987	Don McPherson, Syracuse	1951	Dick Kazmaier, Princeton
1986	Vinny Testaverde, Miami (Florida)	1950	Reds Bagnell, Pennsylvania
1985	Chuck Long, Iowa	1949	Leon Hart, Notre Dame
1984	Doug Flutie, Boston College	1948	Chuck Bednarik, Pennsylvania
1983	Mike Rozier, Nebraska	1947	Doak Walker, SMU
1982	Herschel Walker, Georgia	1946	Charley Trippi, Georgia
1981	Marcus Allen, USC	1945	Doc Blanchard, Army
1980	Hugh Green, Pittsburgh	1944	Glenn Davis, Army
1979	Charles White, USC	1943	Bob Odell, Pennsylvania
1978	Chuck Fusina, Penn State	1942	Paul Governali, Columbia
1977	Ross Browner, Notre Dame	1941	Bill Dudley, Virginia
1976	Tony Dorsett, Pittsburgh	1940	Tom Harmon, Michigan
1975	Archie Griffin, Ohio State	1939	Nile Kinnick, Iowa
1974	Steve Joachim, Temple	1938	Davey O'Brien, TCU
1973	John Cappelletti, Penn State	1937	Clint Frank, Yale
1972	Brad Van Pelt, Michigan State		
1971	Ed Marinaro, Cornell		

VINCE LOMBARDI/ROTARY AWARD

Given to the most outstanding college lineman of the year. The award is sponsored by the Rotary Club of Houston, Texas.

YEAR	PLAYER, COLLEGE	YEAR	PLAYER, COLLEGE
2006	LaMarr Woodley, Michigan	1984	Tony Degrate, Texas
2005	A.J. Hawk, Ohio State	1983	Dean Steinkuhler, Nebraska
2004	David Pollack, Georgia	1982	Dave Rimington, Nebraska
2003	Tommie Harris, Oklahoma	1981	Kenneth Sims, Texas
2002	Terrell Suggs, Arizona State	1980	Hugh Green, Pittsburgh
2001	Julius Peppers, North Carolina	1979	Brad Budde, USC
		1978	Bruce Clark, Penn State
2000	Jamal Reynolds, Florida State	1977	Ross Browner, Notre Dame
1999	Corey Moore, Virginia Tech	1976	Wilson Whitley, Houston
1998	Dat Nguyen, Texas A&M	1975	Lee Roy Selmon, Oklahoma
1997	Grant Wistrom, Nebraska	1974	Randy White, Maryland
1996	Orlando Pace, Ohio State	1973	John Hicks, Ohio State
1995	Orlando Pace, Ohio State	1972	Rich Glover, Nebraska
1994	Warren Sapp, Miami (Florida)	1971	Walt Patulski, Notre Dame
1993	Aaron Taylor, Notre Dame	1970	Jim Stillwagon, Ohio State
1992	Marvin Jones, Florida State		
1991	Steve Emtman, Washington		
1990	Chris Zorich, Notre Dame		
1989	Percy Snow, Michigan State		
1988	Tracy Rocker, Auburn		
1987	Chris Spielman, Ohio State		
1986	Cornelius Bennett, Alabama		
1985	Tony Casillas, Oklahoma		

Lamarr Woodley, Michigan

DAMIAN STROHMEYER

DID YOU KNOW?

A record six college quarterbacks were picked in the first round of the 1983 NFL Draft. Four of these six ended up playing in a Super Bowl and three of these QBs were eventually inducted into the Pro Football Hall of Fame.

DAVEY O'BRIEN NATIONAL QUARTERBACK AWARD

Given to the nation's top quarterback by the Davey O'Brien Educational and Charitable Trust of Fort Worth. Named for TCU Hall of Fame quarterback Davey O'Brien.

YEAR	PLAYER, COLLEGE	YEAR	PLAYER, COLLEGE
2006	Troy Smith, Ohio State	1993	Charlie Ward, Florida State
2005	Vince Young, Texas	1992	Gino Torretta, Miami (Florida)
2004	Jason White, Oklahoma	1991	Ty Detmer, BYU
2003	Jason White, Oklahoma	1990	Ty Detmer, BYU
2002	Brad Banks, Iowa	1989	Andre Ware, Houston
2001	Eric Crouch, Nebraska	1988	Troy Aikman, UCLA
2000	Chris Weinke, Florida State	1987	Don McPherson, Syracuse
1999	Joe Hamilton, Georgia Tech	1986	Vinny Testaverde, Miami (Florida)
1998	Michael Bishop, Kansas State	1985	Chuck Long, Iowa
1997	Peyton Manning, Tennessee	1984	Doug Flutie, Boston College
1996	Danny Wuerffel, Florida	1983	Steve Young, BYU
1995	Danny Wuerffel, Florida	1982	Todd Blackledge, Penn State
1994	Kerry Collins, Penn State	1981	Jim McMahon, BYU

TRIVIA CHALLENGE

1 This school won the 2006 NCAA Division I-A championships in both football and men's basketball, a first in the history of collegiate sports.
a. Florida State
b. Florida
c. North Carolina

2 In 1993, Florida State's Charlie Ward became the second African-American QB to win the Heisman Trophy. Who was the first?
a. Andre Ware
b. Doug Williams
c. Warren Moon

Charlie Ward, Florida State

3 Which school holds the all-time record for most college football victories?
a. Notre Dame
b. Nebraska
c. Michigan

4 At the 2006 Fiesta Bowl, which team used trick plays to both tie the score with 0:07 left in regulation and then win the game in overtime on a two-point conversion?
a. LSU
b. USC
c. Boise State

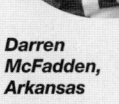

Darren McFadden, Arkansas

5 Which former Ohio State running back is the only player to have won the Heisman Trophy twice?
a. Archie Griffin
b. Eddie George
c. Antonio Pittman

6 In college football, if a player lands on his stomach while catching a pass at the one-yard line, and then rolls into the end zone untouched, what is the ruling?
a. Touchdown!
b. Complete pass, down at the one.

7 Which state played host to five bowl games in 2006, including the Alamo, Cotton, and Armed Forces Bowls?
a. Florida
b. Arizona
c. Texas

8 In 2006, Arkansas RB Darren McFadden came in second in the Heisman Trophy voting behind Ohio State QB Troy Smith. Which player came in third in the voting?
a. Dwayne Jarrett, WR, USC
b. Brady Quinn, QB, Notre Dame
c. Mike Hart, RB, Michigan

Trivia Challenge: 1. b; 2. a; 3. c; 4. c; 5. a; 6. b; 7. c; 8. b.

BASEBALL

Second-year phenom Ryan Howard of the Philadelphia Phillies hit 58 home runs and drove in 149 runs in 2006.

CHUCK SOLOMON

A new crop of young baseball stars took center stage in 2006. Big league games featured more new stars than at any time since the early 1990s, when players like Ken Griffey Jr., Frank Thomas, Mike Piazza, and Randy Johnson were making names for themselves.

The American League Central champion Minnesota Twins provided the best example of the major league youth movement. The Twins' lineup got a boost from 23-year-old AL batting champion Joe Mauer and 25-year-old AL MVP Justin Morneau. The Twins' rotation was strengthened by 22-year-old Francisco Liriano.

The New York Mets cruised to the best record in the National League, thanks largely to two young All-Stars: shortstop Jose Reyes and third baseman David Wright. The NL MVP award went to Ryan Howard of the Philadelphia Phillies, who blasted 58 homers in his second big league season.

Fresh talent also helped some teams exceed expectations. Flamethrowing AL Rookie of the Year Justin Verlander was one of several young hurlers who powered the Detroit Tigers to their first winning season since 1993. Detroit finished with 95 wins and captured the AL wild card. In the NL, the Florida Marlins, whose roster included a whopping 22 rookies, hung in the NL wild-card race until the season's final week. Marlins shortstop Hanley Ramirez ended up winning NL Rookie of the Year honors, and his 22-year-old teammate, Anibal Sanchez, threw the first no-hitter in the major leagues in more than two years.

Of course, the game's established stars weren't going to let the newcomers make all the headlines. The biggest milestone of the season was pulled off by one of the game's oldest players, San Francisco Giants slugger Barry Bonds. Bonds battled injuries and controversy, but he still managed to slug his 715th home run in May. That blast moved him past Babe Ruth and into second place on the all-time list. He finished the season with 734 homers, just 21 shy of Hank Aaron's all-time record.

Power hitting enjoyed a surge all over the majors in 2006. In addition to Howard's 58 home runs, 10 other players hit at least 40 homers. Among them was Alfonso Soriano, who had 46 home runs and 41 stolen bases for the Washington Nationals. Soriano, who went on to sign with the Cubs after the season ended, was just the fourth "40-40" player in baseball history.

Though the Mets and Yankees both finished with 97 wins—the best records in their respective leagues—neither New York team made it to their stop in a "Subway Series." The Yankees were devoured by the Tigers in four games in an AL Division Series. The Mets were weakened by injuries to their starting pitching and lost to the Cardinals in an exciting, seven-game NL Championship Series.

St. Louis entered the postseason in a slump, but the Redbirds righted themselves just in time. They bounced the San Diego Padres in four games before upending the heavily-favored Mets. In the World Series, St. Louis took advantage of some embarrassing Detroit fielding (eight errors in five games) and got clutch hitting from Series MVP David Eckstein. For the Cardinals, it was their tenth World Series title, and their first since 1982. And who secured the final out in this season of new stars? It was Adam Wainwright, the Cardinals' 25-year-old rookie closer.

2006 MAJOR LEAGUE BASEBALL FINAL STANDINGS

NATIONAL LEAGUE

EASTERN DIVISION

TEAM	W	L	PCT	GB	HOME	AWAY
NY Mets	97	65	.599	-	50-31	47-34
Philadelphia	85	77	.525	12	41-40	44-37
Atlanta	79	83	.488	18	40-41	39-42
Florida	78	84	.481	19	42-39	36-45
Washington	71	91	.438	26	41-40	30-51

CENTRAL DIVISION

TEAM	W	L	PCT	GB	HOME	AWAY
St. Louis	83	78	.516	-	49-31	34-47
Houston	82	80	.506	1.5	44-37	38-43
Milwaukee	80	82	.494	3.5	42-39	38-43
Pittsburgh	75	87	.463	8.5	48-33	27-54
Cincinnati	67	95	.414	16.5	43-38	24-57
Chicago Cubs	66	96	.407	17.5	36-45	30-51

WESTERN DIVISION

TEAM	W	L	PCT	GB	HOME	AWAY
San Diego	88	74	.543	-	43-38	45-36
†LA Dodgers	88	74	.543	-	49-32	39-42
San Francisco	76	85	.472	11.5	33-47	43-38
Arizona	76	86	.469	12	39-42	37-44
Colorado	76	86	.469	12	44-37	32-49

†Wild-card team

AMERICAN LEAGUE

EASTERN DIVISION

TEAM	W	L	PCT	GB	HOME	AWAY
NY Yankees	97	65	.599	-	50-31	47-34
Toronto	87	75	.537	10	50-31	37-44
Boston	86	76	.531	11	48-33	38-43
Baltimore	70	92	.432	27	40-41	30-51
Tampa Bay	61	101	.377	36	41-40	20-61

CENTRAL DIVISION

TEAM	W	L	PCT	GB	HOME	AWAY
Minnesota	96	66	.593	-	54-27	42-39
†Detroit	95	67	.586	1	46-35	49-32
Chicago Sox	90	72	.556	6	49-32	41-40
Cleveland	78	84	.481	18	44-37	34-47
Kansas City	62	100	.383	34	34-47	28-53

WESTERN DIVISION

TEAM	W	L	PCT	GB	HOME	AWAY
Oakland	93	69	.574	-	49-32	44-37
LA Angels	89	73	.549	4	45-36	44-37
Texas	80	82	.494	13	39-42	41-40
Seattle	78	84	.481	15	44-37	34-47

†Wild-card team

The only Tigers pitcher to have success in the World Series was Kenny Rogers, who won Game 2 for Detroit.

Cardinals shortstop David Eckstein batted .364 in the Fall Classic, earning World Series MVP honors.

MAJOR LEAGUE TEAMS

NATIONAL LEAGUE
Arizona Diamondbacks
Atlanta Braves
Chicago Cubs
Cincinnati Reds
Colorado Rockies
Florida Marlins
Houston Astros
Los Angeles Dodgers
Milwaukee Brewers
New York Mets
Philadelphia Phillies
Pittsburgh Pirates
San Diego Padres
San Francisco Giants
St. Louis Cardinals
Washington Nationals

AMERICAN LEAGUE
Baltimore Orioles
Boston Red Sox
Chicago White Sox
Cleveland Indians
Detroit Tigers
Kansas City Royals
Los Angeles Angels
Minnesota Twins
New York Yankees
Oakland Athletics
Seattle Mariners
Tampa Bay Devil Rays
Texas Rangers
Toronto Blue Jays

BASEBALL

MLB 2006 PLAYOFFS – NATIONAL LEAGUE

NATIONAL LEAGUE DIVISION SERIES

October 3	Cardinals 5, Padres 1	October 7	Padres 3, Cardinals 1
October 5	Cardinals 2, Padres 0	October 8	Padres 2, Cardinals 6

(CARDINALS WON SERIES, 3–1)

October 4	Dodgers 5, Mets 6	October 7	Mets 9, Dodgers 5
October 5	Dodgers 1, Mets 4		

(METS WON SERIES, 3–0)

NATIONAL LEAGUE CHAMPIONSHIP SERIES

October 12	Cardinals 0, Mets 2	October 17	Mets 2, Cardinals 4
October 13	Cardinals 9, Mets 6	October 18	Cardinals 2, Mets 4
October 14	Mets 0, Cardinals 5	October 19	Cardinals 3, Mets 1
October 15	Mets 12, Cardinals 5		

(CARDINALS WON SERIES, 4–3)

GAME 1

											R	H	E
Cardinals	0	0	0	0	0	0	0	0	0		0	4	0
Mets	0	0	0	0	0	2	0	0	x		2	6	0

W—NYM: Glavine. **L**—StL: Weaver. **SV**—Wagner.
LOB—NYM: 7; StL: 6. **2B**—NYM: Delgado 2. **HR**—NYM:
Beltran. **SB**—NYM: Green. **IBB**—NYM: Wright. **T**—2:52. **A**—
56,311.

Recap: After Mets starter Tom Glavine danced around several
Cardinals' threats early in the game, Carlos Beltran took
advantage of the only mistake that Jeff Weaver made all
night. Beltran hit a home run in the sixth inning that was the
difference in a 2-0 win. Glavine was helped by excellent
defense from Endy Chavez, David Wright, and Beltran, who
became the first Mets outfielder with a home run and an
assist in the same postseason game. The Mets' bullpen took
care of the last two innings and Albert Pujols, at least for one
day, turned out to be a non-factor.

GAME 2

											R	H	E
Cardinals	0	2	2	0	0	0	2	0	3		9	10	1
Mets	3	1	0	0	1	1	0	0	0		6	9	2

W—StL: Kinney. **L**—NYM: Wagner. **LOB**—StL: 8; NYM: 9.
2B—StL: Molina, Pujols, Spiezio; NYM: Reyes, Chavez, Lo
Duca. **3B**—StL: Spiezio. **HR**—StL: Edmonds, Taguchi; NYM:
Delgado 2. **SB**—StL: Eckstein. **GIDP**—NYM: Valentin,
Beltran. **HBP**—NYM: Tucker. **E**—StL: Belliard; NYM:
Delgado. **T**—3:58. **A**—56,349.

Recap: Scott Spiezio started in place of injured Scott Rolen
and ended up as the Cardinals' hitting standout. Spiezio
drove in three runs with a two-run triple in the seventh and an
RBI double in the ninth. Mets closer Billy Wagner entered the
game in the top of the ninth, trying to preserve a 6–6 tie.
Instead, Taguchi hit a tiebreaking homer and the Cardinals
added two more runs on a pair of doubles and a single, making
the score 9–6 by the time Wagner was removed from the
game.

GAME 3

											R	H	E
Mets	0	0	0	0	0	0	0	0	0		0	3	0
Cardinals	2	3	0	0	0	0	0	0	X		5	8	0

W—StL: Suppan. **L**—NYM: Trachsel. **LOB**—NYM 3; StL: 8.
3B—NYM: Reyes; StL: Spiezio **HR**—StL: Suppan. **SB**—
NYM: Beltran. **T**—2:53. **A**—47,053.

Recap: Cards starter Jeff Suppan pitched brilliantly, allowing
New York just three harmless hits over eight innings of work.
The two runs produced by Scott Spiezio's two-out triple in the
first inning proved to be all the offense the Cards would

need. Mets starter Steve Trachsel, on the other hand, had a
miserable night, walking five and allowing five earned runs
in less than two innings. The Mets bullpen shut down the
St. Louis offense the rest of the way, but Suppan never let
the Mets back in the game. He even helped his own cause
with a solo home run in the second inning to extend the
Cardinal lead.

GAME 4

											R	H	E
Mets	0	0	2	0	3	6	1	0	0		12	14	1
Cardinals	0	1	1	0	1	0	2	0	0		5	11	1

W—NYM: Perez. **L**—StL: Thompson. **LOB**—NYM: 8; StL: 5.
2B— NYM: Delgado, Valentin. **3B**—StL: Encarnacion.
HR—NYM: Beltran 2, Wright, Delgado; StL: Eckstein,
Edmonds, Molina. **SB**—StL: Belliard. **GIDP**—StL:
Encarnacion, Spiezio, Rodriguez. **HBP**—StL: Eckstein.
E—StL: Belliard; NYM: Delgado. **T**—3:31. **A**—46,600.

Recap: The Mets offense finally made an appearance as
New York bashed four home runs, including a pair from
Carlos Beltran, to even the series and ensure a Game 6 in
Shea Stadium. Oliver Perez pitched just well enough to
keep the Mets in it until the offense exploded in the fifth and
sixth innings to put the game out of reach. Cardinals
righthander Brad Thompson relieved Anthony Reyes to start
the fifth inning, but offered no relief at all. He lasted just one-
third of an inning and allowed three runs (two earned) on a
Carlos Delgado home run that put the Mets in front 5–2.
New York never looked back after that.

GAME 5

											R	H	E
Mets	0	0	0	2	0	0	0	0	0		2	8	0
Cardinals	0	0	0	2	1	1	0	0	X		4	10	0

W—StL: Weaver. **L**—NYM: Glavine. **SV**—Wainwright.
LOB—StL: 10; NYM: 8. **2B**—StL: Wilson; NYM: Chavez,
Green, Valentin, Wright. **3B**—StL: Miles. **HR**—StL: Pujols,
Duncan. **SB**—StL: Eckstein. **IBB**—StL: Pujols, Edmonds.
T—3:26. **A**—46,496.

Recap: With the score tied 2–2, St. Louis shortstop David
Eckstein led off the fifth inning with a single, then scored the
go-ahead run on a double by Preston Wilson. Mets starter
Tom Glavine, who had been brilliant in his previous two
playoff starts, was outpitched by the Cards' Jeff Weaver.
Weaver combined with the St. Louis bullpen to limit the
Mets offense to just two runs. Albert Pujols, held in check
for most of the series, hit a solo home run to get the
Cardinals offense started in the fourth inning.

NATIONAL LEAGUE CHAMPIONSHIP SERIES (cont.)

GAME 6											
Cardinals	0	0	0	0	0	0	0	2	2	**7**	**1**
Mets	1	0	0	1	0	0	2	0	x	**4**	**10**	**0**

W—NYM: Maine. **L**—StL: Carpenter. **LOB**—StL: 8; NYM: 7. **2B**—StL: Rolen, Taguchi. **HR**—NYM: Reyes. **GIDP**—StL: Rolen, Duncan; NYM: Valentin. **SB**—StL: Eckstein; NYM: Reyes 2, Tucker. **HBP**—StL: Encarnacion; NYM: Green. **IBB**—StL: Pujols. **E**—StL: Rolen. **T**—2:56. **A**—56,334.

Recap: Right-hander John Maine tossed 5⅓ shutout innings for the Mets. He allowed just two hits, both of them in the first inning, when he escaped a bases-loaded jam without allowing a run. Jose Reyes then led off the bottom of the inning with a solo homer off St. Louis ace Chris Carpenter to get the Mets offense on track. Shawn Green singled in a run in the fourth inning, and Paul Lo Duca put the game out of reach by driving in two with a single in the seventh.

GAME 7											
Cardinals	0	1	0	0	0	0	0	2	**3**	**6**	**1**
Mets	1	0	0	0	0	0	0	0	**1**	**4**	**1**

W—StL: Flores **L**—NYM: Heilman. **SV**—Wainwright. **LOB**—NYM: 11; StL: 6. **2B**—StL: Eckstein; NYM: Beltran. **HR**—StL: Molina. **GIDP**—StL: Encarnacion. **HBP**—NYM: Valentin; StL: Eckstein. **IBB**—StL: Pujols 2; NYM: Green. **E**—StL: Rolen; NYM: Delgado. **T**—3:23. **A**—56,357.

Recap: Cardinals righthander Jeff Suppan turned in another brilliant performance. He allowed one run on a David Wright single in the first inning before settling down and holding the Mets hitless until he was removed after walking the leadoff hitter in the eighth inning. Closer Adam Wainwright entered the game in the ninth and allowed a pair of hits and a walk to load the bases but struck out Carlos Beltran looking to end the game and the Series. The Mets' Oliver Perez pitched well, allowing the Cardinals just a single run in six innings of work, but Aaron Heilman allowed a two-run homer by St. Louis catcher Yadier Molina in the top of the ninth, giving St. Louis the margin of victory.

MLB 2006 PLAYOFFS – AMERICAN LEAGUE

AMERICAN LEAGUE DIVISION SERIES

October 3	Tigers 4, Yankees 8	October 6	Yankees 0, Tigers 6
October 5	Tigers 4, Yankees 3	October 7	Yankees 3, Tigers 8

(TIGERS WON SERIES, 3–1)

October 3	Athletics 3, Twins 2	October 6	Twins 3, Athletics 8
October 4	Athletics 5, Twins 2		

(ATHLETICS WON SERIES, 3–0)

AMERICAN LEAGUE CHAMPIONSHIP SERIES

October 10	Tigers 5, Athletics 1	October 13	Athletics 0, Tigers 3
October 11	Tigers 8, Athletics 5	October 14	Athletics 3, Tigers 6

(TIGERS WON SERIES, 4–0)

GAME 1											
Tigers	0	0	2	3	0	0	0	0	0	**5**	**11**	**1**
Athletics	0	0	0	0	0	0	0	1	0	**1**	**8**	**1**

W—Det: Robertson. **L**—Oak: Zito. **LOB**—Det: 11; Oak: 9. **2B**—Oak: Payton 2, Bradley; Det: Granderson, Inge. **HR**—Det: Inge, Rodriguez. **GIDP**—Oak: Scutaro, Bradley, Kotsay 2. **E**—StL: Jimenez; Det: Guillen. **T**—3:20. **A**—35,655.

Recap: The Detroit Tigers overwhelmed the Oakland A's 5–1 in the opening game of the ALCS. Detroit third baseman Brandon Inge went three-for-three, driving in two runs on a solo home run in the third inning and a double in the fourth. Catcher Ivan Rodriguez also homered for the Tigers. Starter Nate Robertson and the Detroit bullpen combined to hold the A's to a single run on an eighth-inning double by Oakland leftfielder Jay Payton. A's ace Barry Zito wasn't sharp, allowing five runs on seven hits in just 3⅔ innings.

GAME 2											
Tigers	0	1	0	4	0	2	0	0	1	**8**	**11**	**0**
Athletics	1	0	2	0	0	1	1	0	0	**5**	**11**	**0**

W—Det: Verlander. **L**—Oak: Loaiza. **SV**—Jones. **LOB**—Det: 5; Oak: 8. **2B**—Det: Guillen, Monroe; Oak: Kotsay 2. **HR**—Det: Gomez, Granderson. Oak: Bradley 2, Chavez. **GIDP**—Det: Ordonez. **SAC**—Det: Monroe, Inge. **IBB**—Det: Polanco. **E**—Oak: Jimenez. **T**—3:06. **A**—36,168.

Recap: Tigers second baseman Placido Polanco ignited the Detroit offense. He went three-for-four, reached base four times and raised his batting average to .440 (11 for 25) in the postseason. Estaban Loaiza, the A's starter, was unable to tame the Tigers. Despite being staked to leads in the first and third innings, Loaiza gave back all of the runs (and then some) in the second and fourth frames to put the A's in the hole. He allowed seven runs on nine hits over six innings. In the top of the fourth, after falling behind 3-1, the Tigers roared back and scored four runs on four hits, one walk and a sacrifice fly. They never trailed again.

KEY — W=winning pitcher; L=losing pitcher; SV=save; E=errors; LOB=left on base; S=sacrifice; SF=sacrifice fly; 2B=double; 3B=triple; HR=home run; SB=stolen bases; CS=caught stealing; HBP=hit by pitch; GIDP=grounded into double plays; IBB=intentional walk; PB=passed ball; T=time; A=attendance

AMERICAN LEAGUE CHAMPIONSHIP SERIES (cont.)

GAME 3

Athletics	0	0	0	0	0	0	0	0	0	0	**0**	**2**	**0**
Tigers	2	0	0	0	1	0	0	0	X		**3**	**6**	**0**

W—Det: Rogers. **L**—Oak: Harden. **SV**—Jones. **LOB**—Oak: 3; Det: 9. **2B**—Det: Polanco. **HR**—Det: Monroe. **GIDP**—Oak: Jimenez, Kielty; Det: Guillen. **HBP**—Oak: Thomas. **SB**—Det: Granderson, Infante. **T**—2:57. **A**—41,669.

Recap: Detroit leadoff hitter Curtis Granderson walked three times, including in the first inning, when he came around to score the first run of the game. The middle of the A's batting order—Milton Bradley, Frank Thomas, Jay Payton and Eric Chavez—went a combined 0-for-12 in the game. A's starter Rich Harden struggled with his control in the first, walking Granderson on four pitches. Harden then proceeded to allow back-to-back singles to Craig Monroe and Placido Polanco, who knocked in Granderson. Monroe scored the second run of the game on a fielder's choice grounder by Magglio Ordonez. The A's never seriously threatened the Tigers' lead.

GAME 4

Athletics	2	0	0	1	0	0	0	0	0		**3**	**8**	**1**
Tigers	0	0	0	0	2	1	0	0	3		**6**	**11**	**0**

W—Det: Ledezma. **L**—Oak: Street. **LOB**—Oak: 9; Det: 8. **2B**—Oak: Bradley, Chavez; Det: Granderson, Monroe. **HR**—Oak: Payton; Det: Ordonez. **GIDP**—Oak: Thomas; Det: Guillen. **IBB**—Det: Inge. **E**—Oak: Chavez. **T**—3.23. **A**—42,967.

Recap: Magglio Ordonez sealed this one with a game-winning three-run homer in the bottom of the ninth. Placido Polanco had three hits, including a single in the ninth inning that preceded Ordonez's blast. Polanco batted .529 in the Tigers' four-game ALCS sweep, and was named MVP of the series. Frank Thomas went 0-for-3 in this game, stranding three baserunners in the process, and finished 0-for-13 in the series. At the bottom of the fifth, with the A's holding a 3-0 lead, the Tigers suddenly got back into the game, thanks to back-to-back RBI doubles by Curtis Granderson and Craig Moore. The Tigers advanced to the World Series for the first time since 1984.

2006 WORLD SERIES

October 21	Cardinals 7, Tigers 2	October 26	Tigers 4, Cardinals 5
October 22	Cardinals 1, Tigers 6	October 27	Tigers 2, Cardinals 4
October 24	Tigers 0, Cardinals 5		

(ST. LOUIS CARDINALS WON SERIES, 4–1)

GAME 1

Cardinals	0	1	3	0	0	3	0	0	0		**7**	**8**	**2**
Tigers	1	0	0	0	0	0	0	0	1		**2**	**4**	**3**

W—StL: A. Reyes. **L**—Det: Verlander. **LOB**—StL: 4, Det: 4. **2B**—StL: Duncan, Rolen; Det: Monroe. **HR**—StL: Pujols, Rolen; Det: Monroe. **E**—StL: Encarnacion, Rolen; Det: Inge 2, Verlander. **T**—2:54. **A**—42,479.

Recap: Rest can be overrated. The St. Louis Cardinals managed just fine in Game 1 of the World Series after their seven-game slugfest with the Mets. Rookie Anthony Reyes easily outpitched Detroit rookie Justin Verlander, lasting into the ninth inning. Albert Pujols made Detroit pay for pitching to him, and Scott Rolen also homered to help St. Louis cruise past the Tigers 7–2. First base was open and Chris Duncan was on second when Pujols stepped to the plate with two outs in the third inning and St. Louis ahead 2–1. Verlander challenged him right away with a 93 mph fastball that the slugger drove over the right-field fence for a 4–1 lead. The three-run cushion was more than enough for Reyes, who retired 17 consecutive batters before Carlos Guillen's seventh-inning single. The right-hander was finally lifted after Craig Monroe's homer on the first pitch of the ninth, and Braden Looper was brought in to finish the game.

GAME 2

Cardinals	0	0	0	0	0	0	0	0	1		**1**	**4**	**1**
Tigers	2	0	0	0	1	0	0	0	X		**3**	**10**	**1**

W—Det: Rogers. **L**—StL: Weaver. **SV**—Jones. **LOB**—StL: 7; Det: 10. **2B**—StL: Edmonds; Det: Guillen. **3B**—Det: Guillen. **HR**—Det: Monroe. **SAC**—Det: Santiago. **GIDP**—StL: Eckstein; Det: Granderson, Rodriguez. **HBP**—StL: Wilson; Det: Casey, Polanco. **E**—StL: Pujols; Det: Jones. **T**—2:55. **A**—42,533.

Recap: An embarrassing error by Detroit closer Todd Jones helped St. Louis get within two runs in Game 2 and the Cardinals loaded the bases with two outs in the ninth inning for Yadier Molina. But Jones got Molina to hit an easy grounder to shortstop, preserving a 3-1 victory that tied the World Series at a game apiece. Craig Monroe hit a solo shot in the first and Carlos Guillen, who went three-for-three with a walk in the game, doubled in what ended up being the winning run in the same inning. But it was Kenny Rogers' smudged throwing hand that drew all the attention. After Cardinals' manager LaRussa mentioned it to the home plate umpire during the first inning, Rogers was warned to clean off whatever it was, and his hand looked noticeably cleaner for the rest of the game. Still, his breaking balls befuddled the big bats in the Cardinals' lineup all night, and he gave up only three hits over eight-plus innings to earn the victory.

GAME 3

Tigers	0	0	0	0	0	0	0	0	0		**0**	**3**	**1**
Cardinals	0	0	0	2	0	0	2	1	X		**5**	**7**	**0**

W—StL: Carpenter. **L**—Det: Robertson. **LOB**—StL: 11; Det: 2. **2B**—StL: Pujols, Edmonds, Molina. **GIDP**—StL: Rolen; Det: Inge. **IBB**—StL: Molina, Edmonds. **HBP**—StL: Pujols. **E**—Det: Zumaya. **T**—3:03. **A**—46,513.

Recap: Chris Carpenter was every bit the ace the St. Louis Cardinals expected. Only Brandon Inge made it as far as third base for Detroit, hitting a single and then advancing on a sacrifice and a wild pitch in the third inning. Edmonds started the Cardinals scoring in the fourth, rifling a double down the right-field line with the bases loaded. St Louis then put the game away for good in the seventh, scoring two more runs on a throwing error from Detroit reliever Joel Zumaya.

GAME 4

Team	1	2	3	4	5	6	7	8	9	R	H	E
Tigers	0	1	2	0	0	0	0	1	0	4	10	1
Cardinals	0	0	1	1	0	0	2	1	X	5	9	0

W—StL: Wainwright. **L**—Det: Zumaya. **LOB**—StL: 9; Det: 9.
2B—StL: Eckstein, Molina, Rolen 2; Det: Granderson, Rodriguez, Inge. **HR**—Det: Casey. **GIDP**—StL: Duncan. **SB**—StL: Miles; Det: Guillen. **IBB**—StL: Miles, Pujols; Det: Inge. **E**—Det: Rodney. **T**—3:35. **A**—46,470.

Recap: Fernando Rodney's error in the pivotal seventh inning was the fourth by a Detroit pitcher in the World Series—breaking a record—and the Cardinals went on to win 5–4 and take a 3–1 series lead. Rodney fielded a sacrifice bunt cleanly in front of the mound, turned and threw to first base, but the toss went far over 5'10" Placido Polanco's head. David Eckstein scored on the error to tie it at 3–3. Eckstein went 4-for-5 with two RBIs, including the game-winner, a two-out double in the eighth inning. Detroit's bats reawakened in Game 4 and they tied the game at four apiece in the top of the eighth. The RBI double by Inge was one of four extra-base hits by the Tigers on the night. However, Detroit's stumbling defense cost them once again. Two miscues in the Busch Stadium outfield, one by Monroe, one by Granderson, fueled a seventh-inning Cardinals rally that gave St. Louis its first lead of the night.

GAME 5

Team	1	2	3	4	5	6	7	8	9	R	H	E
Tigers	0	0	2	0	0	0	0	1	0	2	5	2
Cardinals	0	0	1	0	2	0	0	1	X	4	8	1

W—StL: Weaver. **L**—Det: Verlander. **SV**—StL: Wainwright. **LOB**—StL: 8; Det: 6. **HR**—Det: Casey. **2B**—Det: Casey 2, Inge. **E**—StL: Duncan; Det: Inge, Verlander. **T**—2:56. **A**—46,638.

Recap: "I think we shocked the world," Cardinals center-fielder Jim Edmonds said. Moments earlier, Wainwright had struck out Brandon Inge for the final out, sealing the Cardinals' Game 5 victory and the franchise's tenth World Series title. "No one believed in us, but we believed in ourselves," added David Eckstein, the 5'7" shortstop who was selected as Series MVP after batting .364. St. Louis had gone ahead on Eckstein's infield single in the second when Inge threw the ball low and wide to first. Tigers starter Verlander also continued the Tigers' fielding woes. He threw away a routine force out at third during the bottom of the fourth that eventually led to a 3–2 lead for St. Louis. That error raised the Tigers' World Series total to eight, and their eight unearned runs in the Series were the most allowed by a team in forty years. Rolen added a big run with a two-out RBI single in the seventh, extending his postseason hitting streak to 10 games.

TODAY'S STARS

New York Mets shortstop Jose Reyes led the major leagues in steals and triples in 2006.

■ **Jose Reyes, shortstop,** b. June 11, 1983, Villa Gonzalez, Dominican Republic. Just 23 years old, Reyes had a breakout season in 2006. He was named to his first All-Star team and won the Silver Slugger award. Reyes also became the first major leaguer to bat .300, steal more than 50 bases, and hit at least 15 triples, 20 doubles, and 10 home runs in a single season since Honus Wagner did it in 1908.

■ **Alfonso Soriano, outfielder,** b. January 7, 1976, San Pedro de Macoris, Dominican Republic. After an off-season trade from the Texas Rangers to the Washington Nationals forced him to move to left field, Soriano responded by leading the National League with 22 outfield assists in 2006. The five-time All-Star also hit 46 homers and swiped 41 bases, becoming only the fourth player in major league history to join the "40-40" club. After debuting with the New York Yankees in 1999, Soriano played in the Bronx for five seasons, winning World Series rings in 1999 and 2000. Prior to the start of the 2004 season, Soriano was traded to Texas as part of the blockbuster deal that brought Alex Rodriguez to New York. He was on the move again after 2006, signing an eight-year deal with the Cubs.

■ **Johan Santana, pitcher,** b. March 13, 1979, Tovar, Venezuela. Santana has become the most dominant pitcher in the major leagues over the past few years, going 67-22 since 2003 and winning AL Cy Young awards in 2004 and 2006. And in 2006, Santana played a pivotal role in the Twins' amazing late-season surge, as Minnesota came back from an 11½-game deficit in early June to win the AL Central on the last day of the season.

MLB 2006 PLAYOFFS COMPOSITE BOX SCORES

NATIONAL LEAGUE CHAMPIONSHIP SERIES

ST. LOUIS CARDINALS

BATTING	AB	R	H	HR	RBI	BA
Eckstein	26	3	6	1	1	.231
Belliard	25	0	6	0	2	.240
Molina	23	2	7	2	6	.348
Edmonds	22	5	5	2	4	.227
Encarnacion	22	1	4	0	2	.182
Pujols	22	5	7	1	1	.318
Rolen	21	4	5	0	0	.238
Spiezio	17	3	4	0	5	.235
Wilson	17	2	3	0	1	.176
Duncan	8	1	1	1	1	.125
Carpenter	4	0	1	0	0	000
Rodriguez	4	0	0	0	0	.000
Weaver	4	0	1	0	0	.250
Miles	3	0	2	0	0	.667
Suppan	3	1	1	1	1	.333
Taguchi	3	1	3	1	3	1.00

PITCHING	G	IP	H	BB	SO	ERA
Suppan	2	15.0	5	6	6	0.60
Weaver	2	11.2	10	4	2	3.09
Carpenter	2	11.0	13	4	5	5.73
Looper	3	4.2	7	0	1	5.79
Reyes	1	4.0	3	4	4	4.50
Flores	4	3.2	2	0	3	0.00
Johnson	4	3.2	2	1	5	2.45
Kinney	3	3.1	3	1	4	0.00
Wainwright	3	3.0	2	1	4	0.00
Thompson	2	0.2	3	0	1	27.0

NEW YORK METS

BATTING	AB	R	H	HR	RBI	BA
Reyes	32	5	9	1	2	.281
Lo Duca	29	3	6	0	3	.207
Beltran	27	8	8	3	4	.296
Chavez	27	1	5	0	0	.185
Wright	25	2	4	1	2	.160
Valentin	24	0	6	0	5	.250
Delgado	23	5	7	3	9	.304
Green	23	2	7	0	2	.304
Perez	5	0	0	0	0	.000
Tucker	5	1	2	0	0	.400
Glavine	4	0	0	0	0	.000
Floyd	3	0	0	0	0	.000
Franco	2	0	0	0	0	.000
Maine	2	0	0	0	0	.000
Oliver	2	0	0	0	0	.000
Hernandez	1	0	0	0	0	.000

PITCHING	G	IP	H	BB	SO	ERA
Perez	2	11.2	13	3	7	4.63
Glavine	2	11.0	11	5	4	2.45
Maine	2	9.1	4	9	8	2.89
Oliver	1	6.0	3	1	3	0.00
Bradford	5	5.1	3	0	2	0.00
Heilman	3	4.1	4	1	5	4.15
Mota	5	4.1	4	2	2	4.15
Feliciano	3	3.2	2	0	1	3.00
Wagner	3	2.2	7	1	0	16.87

AMERICAN LEAGUE CHAMPIONSHIP SERIES

DETROIT TIGERS

BATTING	AB	R	H	HR	RBI	BA
Ordonez	17	3	4	2	6	.235
Polanco	17	2	9	0	2	.529
Guillen	16	1	3	0	0	.188
Rodriguez	16	2	2	1	1	.125
Granderson	15	4	5	1	2	.333
Monroe	14	5	6	1	4	.429
Inge	12	3	4	1	3	.333
Gomez	9	1	4	1	4	.444
Santiago	7	0	0	0	0	.000
Thames	5	1	0	0	0	.000
Perez	4	0	0	0	0	.000
Casey	3	0	1	0	0	.333
Infante	2	0	1	0	0	.500

PITCHING	G	IP	H	BB	SO	ERA
Rogers	1	7.1	2	2	6	0.00
Bonderman	1	6.2	6	2	3	4.05
Verlander	1	5.1	7	1	6	6.75
Robertson	1	5.0	6	3	4	0.00
Rodney	3	3.2	1	1	4	0.00
Jones	3	3.0	3	1	2	0.00
Ledezma	2	2.2	2	1	1	3.38
Grilli	2	1.0	1	3	1	0.00
Zumaya	1	1.0	1	0	0	9.00
Walker	1	0.1	0	0	1	0.00

OAKLAND ATHLETICS

BATTING	AB	R	H	HR	RBI	BA
Bradley	18	4	9	2	5	.500
Kendall	17	0	5	0	0	.294
Kotsay	16	3	4	0	0	.250
Scutaro	15	0	1	0	0	.067
Payton	14	1	4	1	2	.286
Chavez	13	1	3	1	2	.231
Thomas	13	0	0	0	0	.000
Jimenez	12	0	2	0	0	.167
Swisher	10	0	1	0	0	.100
Kielty	2	0	0	0	0	.000
Melhouse	1	0	0	0	0	.000
Kiger	0	0	0	0	0	.000

PITCHING	G	IP	H	BB	SO	ERA
Loaiza	1	6.0	9	1	5	10.50
Harden	1	5.2	5	5	4	4.76
Haren	1	5.0	7	2	7	5.40
Kennedy	4	3.2	2	2	2	0.00
Zito	1	3.2	7	3	0	12.27
Gaudin	3	3.1	2	3	1	0.00
Street	2	3.1	4	0	3	10.80
Blanton	1	2.0	0	2	2	0.00
Calero	3	2.0	3	1	1	0.00

KEY AB=at-bats; R=runs; H=hits; HR=home runs; RBI=runs batted in; BA=batting average; G=games; IP=innings pitched; BB=bases on balls; SO=strikeouts; ERA=earned run average

2006 WORLD SERIES COMPOSITE BOX SCORES

DETROIT TIGERS

BATTING	AB	R	H	HR	RBI	BA
Granderson	21	1	2	0	0	.095
Monroe	20	3	3	2	2	.150
Ordonez	19	2	2	0	0	.105
Rodriguez	19	1	3	0	1	.158
Casey	17	2	9	2	5	.529
Guillen	17	2	6	0	2	.353
Inge	17	0	6	0	1	.353
Polanco	17	0	0	0	0	.000
Santiago	5	0	1	0	0	.200
Gomez	3	0	0	0	0	.000
Infante	1	0	0	0	0	.000
Thames	1	0	0	0	0	.000
Pitchers	4	0	0	0	0	.000

PITCHING	G	IP	H	BB	SO	ERA
Verlander	2	11.0	12	5	12	5.73
Rogers	1	8.0	2	3	5	0.00
Bonderman	1	5.1	6	4	4	3.38
Robertson	1	5.0	5	3	3	3.60
Rodney	4	4.0	5	4	5	4.50
Zumaya	3	3.0	1	3	3	3.00
Grilli	2	1.2	0	1	0	0.00
Jones	2	1.2	3	0	0	0.00
Ledezma	2	1.1	2	0	1	0.00
Miner	1	0.2	0	0	0	0.00
Walker	1	0.1	0	0	1	0.00

ST. LOUIS CARDINALS

BATTING	AB	R	H	HR	RBI	BA
Eckstein	22	3	8	0	4	.364
Rolen	19	5	8	1	2	.421
Edmonds	17	1	4	0	4	.235
Molina	17	3	7	0	1	.412
Pujols	15	3	3	1	2	.200
Belliard	12	0	0	0	0	.000
Taguchi	11	3	2	0	0	.182
Wilson	10	1	2	0	1	.200
Duncan	8	1	1	0	1	.125
Encarnacion	8	0	0	0	1	.000
Miles	6	2	1	0	0	.167
Spiezio	4	0	0	0	0	.000
Pitchers	9	0	0	0	0	.000

PITCHING	G	IP	H	BB	SO	ERA
Weaver	2	13.0	13	2	14	2.77
Carpenter	1	8.0	3	0	6	0.00
Reyes	1	8.0	4	1	4	2.25
Suppan	1	6.0	8	2	4	4.50
Wainwright	3	3.0	2	1	5	0.00
Looper	3	2.1	1	0	1	3.86
Flores	1	1.0	1	0	0	0.00
Johnson	2	1.0	0	0	1	0.00
Kinney	2	1.0	0	2	1	0.00
Thompson	1	0.2	0	0	1	0.00

DID YOU KNOW?

In July of 2006, Alex Rodriguez hit his 450th home run, making him the youngest player (at age 30 years 359 days old) in major league history to reach that milestone. A-Rod is one of only eight players in major league history to reach 2,000 hits before they turned 31 years old.

2006 MLB INDIVIDUAL LEADERS

NATIONAL LEAGUE BATTING

BATTING AVERAGE	
Freddy Sanchez, Pit	.344
Miguel Cabrera, Fla	.339
Albert Pujols, StL	.331
Garrett Atkins, Col	.329
Matt Holliday, Col	.326
Paul Lo Duca, NYM	.318
Lance Berkman, Hou	.315
Ryan Howard, Phil	.313
David Wright, NYM	.311
Chase Utley, Phi	.309

HITS	
Juan Pierre, Chi	.204
Chase Utley, Phil	.203
Freddy Sanchez, Pit	.200
Garrett Atkins, Col	.198
Rafael Furcal, LAD	.196
Matt Holliday, Col	.196
Miguel Cabrera, Fla	.195
Jose Reyes, NYM	.194
Jimmy Rollins, Phi	.191
Hanley Ramirez, Fla	.185

DOUBLES	
Freddy Sanchez, Pit	53
Luis Gonzalez, Ari	52
Miguel Cabrera, Fla	50
Garrett Atkins, Col	48
Scott Rolen, StL	48
Ryan Zimmerman	47

TRIPLES	
Jose Reyes, NYM	17
Juan Pierre, Chi	13
Dave Roberts, SD	13
Steve Finley, SF	12
Kenny Lofton, LAD	12
Hanley Ramirez, Fla	11

HOME RUNS	
Ryan Howard, Phil	58
Albert Pujols, StL	49
Alfonso Soriano, Was	46
Lance Berkman, Hou	45
Carlos Beltran, NYM	41
Andruw Jones, Atl	41
Adam Dunn, Cin	40
Carlos Delgado, NYM	38
Aramis Ramirez, Chi	38
Jason Bay, Pit	35

RUNS SCORED	
Chase Utley, Phi	131
Carlos Beltran, NYM	127
Jimmy Rollins, Phi	127
Jose Reyes, NYM	122
Matt Holliday, Col	119
Albert Pujols, StL	119
Hanley Ramirez, Fla	119
Alfonso Soriano, Was	119
Garrett Atkins, Col	117
Rafael Furcal, LAD	113
Miguel Cabrera, Fla	112

TOTAL BASES	
Ryan Howard, Phi	383
Alfonso Soriano, Was	362
Albert Pujols, StL	359
Matt Holliday, Col	353
Chase Utley, Phi	347

STOLEN BASES	
Jose Reyes, NYM	64
Juan Pierre, Chi	58
Hanley Ramirez, Fla	51
Dave Roberts, SD	49
Felipe Lopez, Was	44

RUNS BATTED IN	
Ryan Howard, Phil	149
Albert Pujols, StL	137
Lance Berkman, Hou	136
Andruw Jones, Atl	129
Garrett Atkins, Col	120
Aramis Ramirez, Chi	119
Carlos Beltran, NYM	116
David Wright, NYM	116
Miguel Cabrera, Fla	114
Carlos Delgado, NYM	114

SLUGGING PERCENTAGE	
Albert Pujols, StL	.671
Ryan Howard, Phi	.659
Lance Berkman, Hou	.621
Carlos Beltran, NYM	.594
Matt Holliday, Col	.586

ON-BASE PERCENTAGE	
Albert Pujols, StL	.431
Miguel Cabrera, Fla	.430
Nick Johnson, Was	.428
Ryan Howard, Phi	.425
Lance Berkman, Hou	.420

BASES ON BALLS	
Barry Bonds, SF	115
Adam Dunn, Cin	112
Nick Johnson, Was	110
Ryan Howard, Phi	108
Brian Giles, SD	104

Trevor Hoffman, Padres

NATIONAL LEAGUE PITCHING

EARNED RUN AVERAGE	
Roy Oswalt, Hou	2.98
Chris Carpenter, StL	3.09
Brandon Webb, Ari	3.10
Bronson Arroyo, Cin	3.29
Carlos Zambrano, Chi	3.41
Chris Young, SD	3.46
John Smoltz, Atl	3.49
Jason Schmidt, SF	3.59
Derek Lowe, LAD	3.63
Clay Hensley, SD	3.71

SAVES	
Trevor Hoffman, SD	46
Billy Wagner, NYM	40
Joe Borowski, FLA	36
Tom Gordon, Phi	34
Jason Isringhausen, StL	33
Brad Lidge, Hou	32
Brian Fuentes, Col	31
Chad Cordero, Was	29
Ryan Dempster, Chil	24

Note: Players listed under batting average must have had at least 3.1 plate appearances per game.

WINS	
Aaron Harang, Cin	16
Derek Lowe, LAD	16
Brad Penny, LAD	16
John Smoltz, Atl	16
Brandon Webb, Ari	16
Carlos Zambrano, Chi	16

Five tied with 15.

GAMES PITCHED	
Salomón Torres, Pit	94
Matt Capps, Pit	85
Jon Rauch, Was	85
Bob Howry, Chi	84
Mike Stanton, SF	82

INNINGS PITCHED	
Bronson Arroyo, Cin	240.2
Brandon Webb, Ari	235.0
Aaron Harang, Cin	234.1
John Smoltz, Atl	232.0
Dontrelle Willis, Fla	223.1

SHUTOUTS	
Chris Carpenter. StL	3
Brandon Webb, Ari	3

STRIKEOUTS	
Aaron Harang, Cin	216
Jake Peavy, SD	215
John Smoltz, Atl	211
Carlos Zambrano, Chi	210
Brett Myers, Phi	189
Bronson Arroyo, Cin	184
Chris Carpenter, StL	184
Jason Schmidt, SF	180
Matt Cain, SF	179

COMPLETE GAMES	
Aaron Harang, Cin	6
Chris Carpenter, StL	5
Brandon Webb, Ari	5
Dontrelle Willis, Fla	4
Bronson Arroyo, Cin	3

AMERICAN LEAGUE BATTING

BATTING AVERAGE

Joe Mauer, Min	.347
Derek Jeter, NYY	.343
Robinson Cano, NYY	.342
Miguel Tejada, Bal	.330
Vladimir Guerrero, LAA	.329
Ichiro Suzuki, Sea	.322
Justin Morneau, Min	.321
Manny Ramírez, Bos	.321
Carlos Guillen, Det	.320

HITS

Ichiro Suzuki, Sea	224
Michael Young, Tex	217
Derek Jeter, NYY	214
Miguel Tejada, Bal	214
Vladimir Guerrero, LAA	200
Gary Matthews, Tex	194
Justin Morneau, Min	190
Grady Sizemore, Cle	190
Vernon Wells, Tor	185

DOUBLES

Grady Sizemore, Cle	53
Michael Young, Tex	52
Mike Lowell, Bos	47
Lyle Overbay, Tor	46
Orlando Cabrera, LAA	45
Mark Teixeira, Tex	45

TRIPLES

Carl Crawford, TB	16
Grady Sizemore, Cle	11
Curtis Granderson, Det	9
Ichiro Suzuki, Sea	9
Chone Figgins, LAA	8

HOME RUNS

David Ortiz, Bos	54
Jermaine Dye, Chi	44
Travis Hafner, Cle	42
Jim Thome, Chi	42
Frank Thomas, Oak	42
Troy Glaus, Tor	39
Jason Giambi, NYY	37
Paul Konerko, Chi	35
Manny Ramírez, Bos	35
Alex Rodriguez, NYY	35

RUNS SCORED

Grady Sizemore, Cle	134
Derek Jeter, NYY	118
Johnny Damon, Bos	115
David Ortiz, Bos	115
Alex Rodríguez, NYY	113
Ichiro Suzuki, Sea	110
Jim Thome, Chi	108
Nick Swisher, Oak	106
Troy Glaus, Tor	105
Jermaine Dye, Chi	103

TOTAL BASES

David Ortiz, Bos	355
Grady Sizemore, Cle	349
Jermaine Dye, Chi	335
Vladimir Guerrero, LAA	335
Justin Morneau, Min	331

STOLEN BASES

Carl Crawford, TB	58
Chone Figgins, LAA	52
Corey Patterson	45
Ichiro Suzuki, Sea	45
Scott Podsednik	33

RUNS BATTED IN

David Ortiz, Bos	137
Justin Morneau, Min	130
Raul Ibanez, Sea	123
Alex Rodríguez, NYY	121
Jermaine Dye, Chi	120
Travis Hafner, Cle	117
Vladimir Guerrero, LAA	116
Frank Thomas, Oak	114
Jason Giambi, NYY	113
Paul Konerko, Chi	113

SLUGGING PERCENTAGE

Travis Hafner, Cle	.659
David Ortiz, Bos	.636
Jermaine Dye, Chi	.622
Manny Ramírez, Bos	.619
Jim Thome, Chi	.598

ON-BASE PERCENTAGE

Travis Hafner, Cle	.439
Manny Ramírez, Bos.	.439
Joe Mauer, Min	.429
Derek Jeter, NYY	.417
Jim Thome, Chi	.416

BASES ON BALLS

David Ortiz, Bos	119
Jason Giambi, NYY	110
Jim Thome, Chi	107
Travis Hafner, Cle	100
Manny Ramírez, Bos	100

David Ortiz, Red Sox

AMERICAN LEAGUE PITCHING

WINSLOW TOWNSON

EARNED RUN AVERAGE

Johan Santana, Min	2.77
Roy Halladay, Tor	3.19
C.C. Sabathia, Cle	3.22
Mike Mussina, NYY	3.51
John Lackey, LAA	3.56
Kelvim Escobar, LAA	3.61
Justin Verlander, Det	3.63
Chien-Ming Wang, NYY	3.63
Erik Bedard, Bal	3.76
Barry Zito, Oak	3.83

SAVES

Francisco Rodríguez, LAA	47
Bobby Jenks, Chi	41
B.J. Ryan, Tor	38
Todd Jones, Det	37
Huston Street, Oak	37
Joe Nathan, Min	36
J.J. Putz, Sea	36
Jonathan Papelbon, Bos	35
Mariano Rivera, NYY	34
Chris Ray, Bal	33

WINS

Johan Santana, Min	19
Chien-Ming Wang, NYY	19
Jon Garland, Chi	18
Freddy Garcia, Chi	17
Randy Johnson, NYY	17
Kenny Rogers, Det	17
Justin Verlander, Det	17

Six tied with 16.

GAMES PITCHED

Scott Proctor, NYY	83
Shawn Camp, TB	75
Juan Rincon, Minn	75
Scot Shields, LAA	74
Kyle Farnsworth, NYY	72
J.J. Putz, Sea	72

INNINGS PITCHED

Johan Santana, Min	233.2
Danny Haren, Oak	223.2
Barry Zito, Oak	221.0
Roy Halladay, Tor	220.0

STRIKEOUTS

Johan Santana, Min	245
Jeremy Bonderman	202
John Lackey, LAA	190
Javier Vazquez, Chi	184
Curt Schilling, Bos	183
Danny Haren, Oak	176
Felix Hernandez, Sea	176
Randy Johnson, NYY	172
Mike Mussina, NYY	172
C.C. Sabathia, Cle	172

COMPLETE GAMES

C.C. Sabathia, Cle	6
Roy Halladay, Tor	4
Kris Benson, Bal	3

Three tied with 3.

SHUTOUTS

John Lackey, LAA	2
C.C. Sabathia, Cle	2
Jeremy Sowers, Cle	2
Jake Westbrook, Cle	2

2005 REGULAR SEASON TEAM STATS

NATIONAL LEAGUE

TEAM BATTING

TEAM BATTING	G	AB	R	H	2B	3B	HR	RBI	TB	BB	SO	SB	OBP	SLG	BA
Los Angeles	162	5,628	820	1,552	307	58	153	787	2,434	601	959	128	.348	.432	.276
Colorado	162	5,562	813	1,504	325	54	157	761	2,408	561	1,108	85	.341	.433	.270
Atlanta	162	5,583	849	1,510	312	26	222	818	2,540	526	1,169	52	.337	.455	.270
St. Louis	161	5,522	781	1,484	292	27	184	745	2,382	531	922	59	.337	.431	.269
Chicago	162	5,587	716	1,496	271	46	166	677	2,357	395	928	121	.319	.422	.268
Arizona	162	5,645	773	1,506	331	38	160	743	2,393	504	965	76	.331	.424	.267
Philadelphia	162	5,687	865	1,518	294	41	216	823	2,542	626	1,203	92	.347	.447	.267
New York	162	5,558	834	1,469	323	41	200	800	2,474	547	1,071	146	.334	.445	.264
Florida	162	5,502	758	1,454	309	42	182	713	2,393	497	1,249	110	.331	.435	.264
Pittsburgh	162	5,558	691	1,462	286	17	141	656	2,205	459	1,200	68	.327	.397	.263
San Diego	162	5,576	731	1,465	298	38	161	698	2,322	564	1,104	123	.332	.416	.263
Washington	162	5,495	746	1,437	322	22	164	695	2,295	594	1,156	123	.338	.418	.262
San Francisco	161	5,472	746	1,418	297	52	163	711	2,308	494	891	58	.324	.422	.259
Milwaukee	162	5,433	730	1,400	301	20	180	695	2,281	502	1,233	71	.327	.420	.258
Cincinnati	162	5,515	749	1,419	291	12	217	718	2,385	614	1,192	124	.336	.432	.257
Houston	162	5,521	735	1,407	275	27	174	708	2,258	585	1,076	79	.332	.409	.255

TEAM PITCHING

TEAM PITCHING	W	L	ERA	CG	SHO	SV	INN	H	R	ER	BB	SO
San Diego	88	74	3.87	4	11	50	1,463.2	1,385	679	629	468	1,097
Houston	82	80	4.08	5	12	42	1,468.2	1,425	719	666	480	1,160
New York	97	65	4.14	5	12	43	1,461.1	1,402	731	673	527	1,161
Los Angeles	88	74	4.23	1	10	40	1,460.1	1,524	751	686	492	1,068
Florida	78	84	4.37	6	6	41	1,433.1	1,465	772	696	622	1,088
Arizona	76	86	4.48	8	9	34	1,459.2	1,503	788	727	536	1,115
Cincinnati	80	82	4.51	9	10	36	1,445.2	1,576	801	725	464	1,053
Pittsburgh	67	95	4.52	2	10	39	1,435.0	1,545	797	720	620	1,060
St. Louis	83	78	4.54	6	9	38	1,429.2	1,475	762	721	504	970
Philadelphia	85	77	4.60	4	6	42	1,460.1	1,561	812	747	512	1,138
Atlanta	79	83	4.60	6	6	38	1,441.1	1,529	805	736	572	1,049
San Francisco	76	85	4.63	7	9	37	1,429.2	1,422	790	735	584	992
Colorado	76	86	4.66	5	8	34	1,447.1	1,549	812	749	553	952
Chicago	66	96	4.74	2	7	29	1,439.0	1,396	834	758	687	1,250
Milwaukee	75	87	4.82	7	8	43	1,425.2	1,454	833	763	514	1,145
Washington	71	91	5.03	1	3	32	1,436.1	1,535	872	803	584	960

AMERICAN LEAGUE

TEAM BATTING

TEAM BATTING	G	AB	R	H	2B	3B	HR	RBI	TB	BB	SO	SB	OBP	SLG	BA
Minnesota	162	5,602	810	1,608	275	34	143	754	2,380	490	872	101	.347	.425	.287
New York	162	5,651	930	1,608	326	21	210	902	2,607	646	1,053	139	.363	.461	.285
Toronto	162	5,596	809	1,591	348	27	199	778	2,590	514	906	65	.348	.463	.284
Cleveland	162	5,619	870	1,576	351	27	196	839	2,569	556	1,204	55	.349	.457	.280
Chicago	162	5,657	868	1,586	291	20	236	839	2,625	502	1,056	93	.342	.464	.280
Texas	162	5,659	835	1,571	357	23	183	799	2,523	505	1,061	53	.338	.446	.278
Baltimore	162	5,610	768	1,556	288	20	164	727	2,376	474	878	121	.339	.424	.277
Los Angeles	162	5,609	766	1,539	309	29	159	737	2,383	486	914	148	.334	.425	.274
Detroit	162	5,642	822	1,548	294	40	203	785	2,531	430	1,133	60	.329	.449	.274
Seattle	162	5,670	756	1,540	266	42	172	703	2,406	404	974	106	.325	.424	.272
Kansas City	162	5,589	757	1,515	335	37	124	718	2,296	474	1,040	65	.332	.411	.271
Boston	162	5,619	820	1,510	327	16	192	777	2,445	672	1,056	51	.351	.435	.269
Oakland	162	5,500	771	1,429	266	22	175	735	2,264	650	976	61	.340	.412	.260
Tampa Bay	162	5,474	689	1,395	267	33	190	650	2,298	441	1,106	134	.314	.420	.255

TEAM PITCHING

TEAM PITCHING	W	L	ERA	CG	SHO	SV	INN	H	R	ER	BB	SO
Detroit	95	67	3.84	3	16	46	1,448.0	1,420	675	618	489	1,003
Minnesota	96	66	3.95	1	6	40	1,439.1	1,490	683	632	356	1,164
Los Angeles	89	73	4.04	5	12	50	1,452.2	1,410	732	652	471	1,164
Oakland	93	69	4.21	5	11	54	1,451.2	1,525	727	679	529	1,003
Toronto	87	75	4.37	6	6	42	1,428.1	1,447	754	694	504	1,076
Cleveland	78	84	4.41	13	13	24	1,423.1	1,583	782	698	429	948
New York	97	65	4.41	5	8	43	1,443.2	1,463	767	708	496	1,019
Seattle	78	84	4.60	6	6	47	1,446.2	1,500	792	739	560	1,067
Texas	80	82	4.60	3	8	42	1,431.1	1,558	784	731	496	972
Chicago	90	72	4.61	5	11	46	1,449.0	1,534	794	743	433	1,012
Boston	86	76	4.83	3	6	46	1,441.1	1,570	825	773	509	1,070
Tampa Bay	61	101	4.96	3	7	33	1,420.1	1,600	856	782	606	979
Baltimore	70	92	5.35	5	9	35	1,419.0	1,579	899	843	613	1,016
Kansas City	62	100	5.65	3	5	35	1,426.1	1,648	971	896	637	904

KEY G=games; GS=games started; AB=at bat; R=run; H=hit; 2B=double; 3B=triple; HR=home run; RBI=run batted in; TB=total bases; BB=walk; SO=strikeout; SB=stolen base; OBP=on-base percentage; SLG=slugging percentage; BA=batting average; W=win; L=loss; ERA=earned run average; CG=complete games; SHO=shutouts; SV=saves; INN=innings; ER=earned runs

NATIONAL LEAGUE TEAM-BY-TEAM STATS

ARIZONA DIAMONDBACKS

BATTING	G	AB	R	H	2B	3B	HR	RBI	TB	BB	SO	SB	OBP	SLG	BA
Chad Tracy	154	597	91	168	41	0	20	80	269	54	129	5	.343	.451	.281
Luis Gonzalez	153	586	93	159	52	2	15	73	260	69	58	0	.352	.444	.271
Orlando Hudson	157	579	87	166	34	9	15	67	263	61	78	9	.354	.454	.287
Eric Byrnes	143	562	82	150	37	3	26	79	271	34	88	25	.313	.482	.267
Conor Jackson	140	485	75	141	26	1	15	79	214	54	73	1	.368	.441	.291
Johnny Estrada	115	414	43	125	26	0	11	71	184	13	40	0	.328	.444	.302
Craig Counsell	105	372	56	95	14	4	4	30	129	31	47	15	.327	.347	.255
Jeff DaVanon	87	221	38	64	12	4	5	35	99	31	42	10	.371	.448	.290
Stephen Drew	59	209	27	66	13	7	5	23	108	14	50	2	.357	.517	.316
Damion Easley	90	189	24	44	6	1	9	28	79	21	30	1	.323	.418	.233
Chris Snyder	61	184	19	51	9	0	6	32	78	22	39	0	.349	.424	.277
Carlos Quentin	57	166	23	42	13	3	9	32	88	15	34	1	.342	.530	.253
Tony Clark	79	132	13	26	4	0	6	16	48	13	40	0	.279	.364	.197
Andy Green	73	86	15	16	4	0	1	6	23	13	20	1	.293	.267	.186

PITCHING	W–L	ERA	G	GS	CG	SV	INN	H	R	ER	BB	SO
Brandon Webb	16-8	3.10	33	33	5	0	235.0	216	91	81	50	178
Livan Hernandez	13-13	4.83	34	34	0	0	235.0	246	125	116	78	128
Miguel Baptista	11-8	4.58	34	33	3	0	206.1	231	116	105	84	110
Claudio Vargas	12-10	4.83	31	30	0	0	167.2	185	101	90	52	123
Enrique Gonzalez	3-7	5.67	22	18	3	0	106.1	114	71	67	34	66
Juan Cruz	5-6	4.18	31	15	0	0	94.2	80	45	44	47	88
Brandon Medders	5-3	3.64	60	0	0	0	71.2	76	37	29	28	47
Brandon Lyon	2-4	3.89	68	0	0	0	69.1	68	32	30	22	46
Jorge Julio	2-4	4.23	62	0	0	16	66.0	52	35	31	35	88
Luis Vizcaino	4-6	3.58	70	0	0	0	65.1	51	26	26	29	72
Jose Valverde	2-3	5.84	44	0	0	18	49.1	50	32	32	22	69
Greg Aquino	2-0	4.47	42	0	0	0	48.1	54	27	24	24	51
Edgar Gonzalez	3-4	4.22	11	5	0	0	42.2	45	20	20	9	28
Tony Pena	3-4	5.58	25	0	0	1	30.2	36	21	19	8	21
Jason Grimsley	1-2	4.88	19	0	0	0	27.2	30	15	15	8	10

ATLANTA BRAVES

BATTING	G	AB	R	H	2B	3B	HR	RBI	TB	BB	SO	SB	OBP	SLG	BA
Jeff Francoeur	162	651	83	169	24	6	29	103	292	23	132	1	.293	.449	.260
Egar Renteria	149	598	100	175	40	2	14	70	261	62	89	17	.361	.436	.293
Andruw Jones	156	565	107	148	29	0	41	129	300	82	127	4	.363	.531	.262
Marcus Giles	156	565	107	148	29	0	41	129	300	82	127	4	.363	.531	.262
Adam LaRoche	149	492	89	140	38	1	32	90	276	55	128	0	.354	.561	.285
Brian McCann	130	442	61	147	34	0	24	93	253	41	54	2	.388	.572	.333
Chipper Jones	110	411	87	133	28	3	26	86	245	61	73	6	.409	.596	.324
Ryan Langerhans	131	315	46	76	16	3	7	28	119	50	91	1	.350	.378	.241
Matt Diaz	124	297	37	97	15	4	7	32	141	11	49	5	.364	.475	.327
Willy Aybar	79	243	32	68	18	0	4	30	98	28	36	1	.364	.403	.280
Pete Orr	102	154	22	39	3	4	1	8	53	5	30	2	.277	.344	.253
Todd Pratt	62	135	14	28	6	0	4	19	46	12	43	1	.272	.341	.207
Daryle Ward	98	130	17	40	10	0	7	26	71	15	27	0	.380	.546	.308
Scott Thorman	55	128	13	30	11	0	5	14	56	5	21	1	.263	.438	.234
Brian Jordan	48	91	11	21	2	0	3	10	32	7	23	0	.287	.352	.231
John Smoltz	33	64	5	8	3	0	0	4	11	4	27	0	.176	.172	.125

PITCHING	W–L	ERA	G	GS	CG	SV	INN	H	R	ER	BB	SO
John Smoltz	16-9	3.49	35	35	3	0	232.0	221	93	90	55	211
Tim Hudson	13-12	4.86	35	35	2	0	218.1	235	129	118	79	141
Chuck James	11-4	3.78	25	18	0	0	119.0	101	54	50	47	91
Oscar Villarreal	9-1	3.61	58	4	0	0	92.1	93	41	37	27	55
John Thomson	2-7	4.82	18	15	0	0	80.1	93	55	43	32	46
Horacio Ramirez	5-5	4.48	14	14	0	0	76.1	85	42	38	31	37
Lance Cormier	4-5	4.89	29	0	0	0	73.2	90	44	40	39	43
Ken Ray	1-1	4.52	69	0	0	5	67.2	66	36	34	38	50
Kyle Davies	3-7	8.38	14	0	1	0	63.1	90	60	59	33	51
Danys Baez	5-6	4.53	57	0	0	9	59.2	60	35	30	17	39
Macay McBride	4-1	3.65	71	0	0	1	56.2	53	28	23	32	46
Chad Paronto	2-3	3.18	65	0	0	0	56.2	53	23	20	19	41
Tyler Yates	2-5	3.96	56	0	0	1	28.0	42	23	22	31	46
Chris Reitsma	1-2	8.68	27	0	0	18	26.0	46	27	27	8	13

CHICAGO CUBS

BATTING	G	AB	R	H	2B	3B	HR	RBI	TB	BB	SO	SB	OBP	SLG	BA
Juan Pierre	162	699	87	204	32	13	3	40	271	32	38	58	.330	.338	.292
Aramis Ramirez	157	594	93	173	38	4	38	119	333	50	63	2	.352	.561	.291
Ronny Cedeno	151	534	51	131	18	7	6	41	181	17	109	8	.271	.339	.245
Jacque Jones	149	533	73	152	31	1	27	81	266	35	116	9	.334	.499	.285
Matt Murton	144	455	70	135	22	3	13	62	202	45	62	5	.365	.444	.297
Michael Barrett	107	375	54	115	25	3	16	53	194	33	41	0	.368	.517	.307
Henry Blanco	74	241	23	64	15	2	6	37	101	14	38	0	.304	.419	.266
Neifi Perez	87	236	27	60	13	1	2	24	81	5	21	0	.266	.343	.254
John Mabry	107	210	16	43	8	1	5	25	68	23	57	0	.283	.324	.205
Ceaser Izturis	54	192	14	47	9	1	1	18	61	12	14	1	.295	.318	.245
Phil Nevin	67	179	26	49	4	0	12	33	89	17	52	0	.335	.497	.274

PITCHING	W–L	ERA	G	GS	CG	SV	INN	H	R	ER	BB	SO
Carlos Zambrano	16-7	3.41	33	33	0	0	214.0	162	91	81	115	210
Sean Marshall	6-9	5.59	24	24	0	0	125.2	132	85	78	59	77
Rich Hill	6-7	4.17	17	16	2	0	99.1	83	51	46	39	90
Carlos Marmol	5-7	6.08	19	13	0	0	77.0	71	54	52	59	59
Bob Howry	4-5	3.17	84	0	0	5	76.2	70	28	27	17	71
Roberto Novoa	2-1	4.26	66	0	0	0	76.0	77	47	36	32	53
Ryan Dempster	1-9	4.80	74	0	0	24	75.0	77	47	40	36	67
Glendon Rusch	3-8	7.46	25	9	0	0	66.1	86	57	55	33	59
Will Ohman	1-1	4.13	78	0	0	0	65.1	51	30	30	34	74
Scott Eyre	1-3	3.38	74	0	0	0	61.1	61	25	23	30	73
Angel Guzman	0-6	7.39	15	10	0	0	56.0	68	48	46	37	60

CINCINNATI REDS

BATTING	G	AB	R	H	2B	3B	HR	RBI	TB	BB	SO	SB	OBP	SLG	BA
Adam Dunn	160	561	99	131	24	0	40	92	275	112	194	7	.365	.490	.234
Brandon Phillips	149	536	65	148	28	1	17	75	229	35	88	25	.324	.427	.276
Scott Hatteberg	141	456	62	132	28	0	13	51	199	74	41	2	.389	.436	.289
Royce Clayton	137	454	49	117	30	1	2	40	155	30	85	14	.307	.341	.258
Ryan Freel	132	454	67	123	30	2	8	27	181	57	98	37	.363	.399	.271
Rich Aurilia	122	440	61	132	25	1	23	70	228	34	51	3	.349	.518	.300
Ken Griffey, Jr.	109	428	62	108	19	0	27	72	208	39	78	0	.316	.486	.252
Edwin Encarnacion	117	406	60	112	33	1	15	72	192	41	78	6	.359	.473	.276
David Ross	90	247	37	63	15	1	21	52	143	37	75	0	.353	.579	.255
Jason LaRue	72	191	22	37	5	0	8	21	66	27	51	1	.317	.346	.194
Javier Valentin	92	186	24	50	6	1	8	27	82	13	29	0	.313	.441	.269
Chris Denorfia	49	106	14	30	6	0	1	7	39	11	21	1	.356	.368	.283
Juan Castro	54	95	8	27	5	1	2	14	40	5	13	0	.320	.421	.284

PITCHING	W–L	ERA	G	GS	CG	SV	INN	H	R	ER	BB	SO
Bronson Arroyo	14-11	3.29	35	35	3	0	240.2	222	98	88	64	184
Aaron Harang	16-11	3.76	36	35	6	0	234.1	242	109	98	56	216
Eric Milton	8-8	5.19	26	26	0	0	152.2	163	94	88	42	90
Elizardo Ramirez	4-9	5.37	21	19	0	0	104.0	123	70	62	29	69
Todd Coffey	6-7	3.58	81	0	0	8	78.0	85	34	31	27	60
Ryan Franklin	6-7	4.54	66	0	0	0	77.1	86	42	39	33	43
Brandon Claussen	3-8	6.19	14	5	0	0	77.0	93	56	53	28	57
David Weathers	4-4	3.54	67	0	0	12	73.2	61	31	29	34	50
Gary Majewski	4-4	4.61	65	14	0	0	70.1	79	38	36	29	43
Kyle Lohse	3-5	4.57	12	0	0	0	63.0	70	33	32	19	51
Bill Bray	3-2	4.09	48	0	0	2	50.2	57	27	23	18	39

COLORADO ROCKIES

BATTING	G	AB	R	H	2B	3B	HR	RBI	TB	BB	SO	SB	OBP	SLG	BA
Garrett Atkins	157	602	117	198	48	1	29	120	335	79	76	4	.409	.556	.329
Matt Holliday	155	602	119	196	45	5	34	114	353	47	110	10	.387	.584	.326
Todd Helton	145	546	94	165	40	5	15	81	260	91	64	3	.404	.476	.302
Brad Hawpe	150	499	67	146	33	6	22	84	257	74	123	5	.383	.515	.293
Clint Barmes	131	478	57	105	26	4	7	56	160	22	72	5	.264	.335	.220
Jamey Carroll	136	463	84	139	23	5	5	36	187	56	66	10	.377	.404	.300
Cory Sullivan	126	386	47	103	26	10	2	30	155	32	100	10	.321	.402	.267
Vinny Castilla	87	275	26	63	10	0	5	27	88	9	49	0	.258	.320	.229
Kazuo Matsui	70	243	32	65	12	3	3	26	92	16	46	10	.310	.379	.267
Yorvit Torrealba	65	223	23	55	16	3	7	43	98	11	49	4	.293	.439	.247
Choo Freeman	88	173	24	41	6	3	2	18	59	14	42	5	.298	.341	.237
Ryan Spilborghs	67	167	26	48	6	3	4	21	72	14	30	5	.337	.431	.287
Luis Gonzalez	61	149	7	36	9	1	2	14	53	4	27	1	.269	.356	.242
Danny Ardoin	35	109	12	21	5	1	0	2	28	8	27	0	.261	.257	.193
Jason Smith	49	99	9	26	1	0	5	13	42	7	29	3	.324	.424	.263

PITCHING	W–L	ERA	G	GS	CG	SV	INN	H	R	ER	BB	SO
Aaron Cook	9-15	4.23	32	32	0	0	212.2	242	107	100	55	92
Jason Jennings	9-13	3.78	32	32	3	0	212.0	206	94	89	85	142
Jeff Francis	13-11	4.16	32	32	1	0	199.0	187	101	92	69	117
Josh Fogg	11-9	5.49	31	31	1	0	172.0	206	115	105	60	93
Byung-Hyun Kim	8-12	5.57	27	27	0	0	155.0	179	103	96	61	129
Jose Mesa	1-5	3.86	79	0	0	1	72.1	73	32	31	36	39
Ramon Ramirez	4-3	3.46	61	0	0	0	67.2	58	28	26	27	61
Brian Fuentes	3-4	3.44	66	0	0	30	65.1	50	25	25	26	73
Tom Martin	2-0	5.07	68	0	0	0	60.1	62	37	34	25	46
Ray King	1-4	4.43	67	5	0	1	44.2	56	26	22	20	23
Manny Corpas	1-2	3.62	35	0	0	0	32.1	36	13	13	8	27
David Cortes	3-1	4.30	30	0	0	0	29.1	35	14	14	6	14
Jeremy Affeldt	4-2	6.91	27	0	0	1	27.1	31	23	21	13	20

FLORIDA MARLINS

BATTING	G	AB	R	H	2B	3B	HR	RBI	TB	BB	SO	SB	OBP	SLG	BA
Hanley Ramirez	158	633	119	185	46	11	17	59	304	56	128	51	.353	.480	.292
Dan Uggla	154	611	105	172	26	7	27	90	293	48	123	6	.339	.480	.282
Miguel Cabrera	158	576	112	195	50	2	26	114	327	86	108	9	.430	.568	.339
Josh Willingham	142	502	62	139	28	2	26	74	249	54	109	2	.356	.496	.227
Mike Jacobs	136	469	54	123	37	1	20	77	222	45	105	3	.325	.473	.262
Miguel Olivo	127	430	52	113	22	3	16	58	189	9	103	2	.287	.440	.263
Alfredo Amezaga	132	334	42	87	9	3	3	19	111	33	46	20	.332	.332	.260
Jeremy Hermida	99	307	37	77	19	1	5	28	113	33	70	4	.332	.368	.251
Cody Ross	101	269	34	61	12	2	13	46	116	22	65	1	.293	.431	.227
Reggie Abercrombie	111	255	39	54	12	2	5	24	85	18	78	6	.271	.333	.212
Wes Helms	140	240	30	79	19	5	10	47	138	21	55	0	.390	.575	.329
Joe Borchard	108	230	30	53	7	1	10	28	92	28	66	0	.322	.400	.230
Matt Treanor	67	157	12	36	6	1	2	14	50	19	34	0	.328	.318	.229
Chris Aguila	47	95	5	22	8	1	0	7	32	9	26	2	.298	.337	.232

PITCHING	W–L	ERA	G	GS	CG	SV	INN	H	R	ER	BB	SO
Dontrelle Willis	12-12	3.87	34	34	4	0	223.1	234	106	96	83	160
Scott Olsen	12-10	4.04	31	31	0	0	180.2	160	94	81	75	166
Josh Johnson	12-7	3.10	31	24	0	0	157.0	136	63	54	68	133
Ricky Nolasco	11-11	4.82	35	22	0	0	140.0	157	86	75	41	99
Brian Moehler	7-11	6.57	29	21	0	0	122.0	164	95	89	38	58
Anibal Sanchez	10-3	2.83	18	17	2	0	114.1	90	39	36	46	72
Matt Herges	2-3	4.31	66	0	0	0	71.0	94	42	34	28	36
Joe Borowski	3-3	3.75	72	0	0	36	69.2	63	31	29	33	64
Randy Messenger	2-7	5.67	59	0	0	0	60.1	72	42	38	24	45
Jason Vargas	1-2	7.33	12	5	0	0	43.1	50	39	35	30	25

BASEBALL

HOUSTON ASTROS

BATTING	G	AB	R	H	2B	3B	HR	RBI	TB	BB	SO	SB	OBP	SLG	BA
Craig Biggio	145	548	79	172	33	0	21	62	231	40	84	3	.306	.422	.246
Lance Berkman	152	536	95	156	29	0	45	136	333	98	106	3	.420	.621	.315
Willy Taveras	149	529	83	136	19	5	1	30	179	34	88	33	.333	.338	.278
Adam Everett	150	514	52	149	28	6	6	59	181	34	71	9	.290	.352	.239
Brad Ausmus	139	439	37	138	16	1	2	39	125	45	71	3	.308	.285	.230
Morgan Ensberg	127	387	67	137	17	1	23	58	179	101	96	1	.396	.463	.235
Mike Lamb	126	381	70	100	22	3	12	45	181	35	55	2	.361	.475	.307
Chris Burke	123	366	58	76	23	1	9	40	153	27	77	11	.347	.418	.276
Jason Lane	112	288	44	79	10	0	15	45	113	49	75	1	.318	.392	.201
Aubrey Huff	68	224	31	58	10	1	13	38	107	26	39	0	.341	.478	.250
Luke Scott	65	214	31	46	19	6	10	37	133	30	43	2	.426	.621	.336
Eric Munson	53	141	10	24	6	0	5	19	49	11	32	0	.269	.348	.199
Eric Bruntlett	73	119	11	25	8	0	0	10	41	13	21	3	.351	.345	.277
Orlando Palmeiro	103	119	2	17	6	1	0	17	38	6	17	1	.294	.319	.252

PITCHING	W–L	ERA	G	GS	CG	SV	INN	H	R	ER	BB	SO
Roy Oswalt	15-8	2.98	33	32	2	0	220.2	220	76	73	38	166
Andy Pettitte	14-13	4.20	36	35	2	0	214.1	238	114	100	70	178
Wandy Rodriguez	9-10	5.64	30	24	0	0	135.2	154	96	85	63	98
Roger Clemens	7-6	2.30	19	19	0	0	113.1	89	34	29	29	102
Taylor Buchholz	6-10	5.89	22	19	1	0	113.0	107	80	74	34	77
Fernando Nieve	3-3	4.20	40	11	0	0	96.1	87	46	45	41	70
Chad Qualls	7-3	3.76	81	0	0	0	88.2	76	38	37	28	56
Brad Lidge	1-5	5.28	78	0	0	32	75.0	69	47	44	36	104
Dan Wheeler	3-5	2.52	75	0	0	9	71.1	58	22	20	24	68
Dave Borkowski	3-2	4.69	40	0	0	0	71.0	70	38	37	23	52

LOS ANGELES DODGERS

BATTING	G	AB	R	H	2B	3B	HR	RBI	TB	BB	SO	SB	OBP	SLG	BA
Rafael Furcal	159	654	113	196	32	9	15	63	291	73	98	37	.369	.445	.300
J.D. Drew	146	494	84	140	34	6	20	100	246	89	106	2	.393	.498	.283
Nomar Garciaparra	122	469	82	142	31	2	20	93	237	42	30	3	.367	.505	.303
Kenny Lofton	129	469	79	141	15	12	3	41	189	45	42	32	.360	.403	.301
Russell Martin	121	415	65	117	26	4	10	65	181	45	57	10	.355	.436	.282
Jeff Kent	115	407	61	119	27	3	14	68	194	55	69	1	.385	.477	.292
Andre Either	126	396	50	122	20	7	11	55	189	34	77	5	.365	.477	.308
Wilson Betemit	143	373	49	98	23	0	18	53	175	36	102	3	.326	.469	.263
Marlon Anderson	134	279	43	83	16	4	12	38	143	25	49	4	.354	.513	.297
Jose Cruz	86	223	34	52	16	1	5	17	85	43	54	5	.353	.381	.233
Olmedo Saenz	103	179	30	53	15	0	11	48	101	14	47	0	.363	.564	.296
Ramon Martinez	82	176	20	49	7	1	2	24	64	15	20	0	.339	.364	.278
Matt Kemp	52	154	30	39	7	1	7	23	69	9	53	6	.289	.448	.253
Julio Lugo	49	146	16	32	5	1	0	10	39	12	29	6	.278	.267	.219
Jason Repko	69	130	21	33	5	1	3	16	49	15	24	10	.345	.377	.254
Bill Mueller	32	107	12	27	7	1	0	15	43	17	9	1	.357	.402	.252

PITCHING	W–L	ERA	G	GS	CG	SV	INN	H	R	ER	BB	SO
Derek Lowe	16-8	3.63	35	34	1	0	218.0	221	97	88	55	123
Greg Maddux	15-14	4.20	34	34	0	0	210.0	219	109	98	37	117
Brad Penny	16-9	4.33	34	33	0	0	189.0	206	94	91	54	148
Brett Tomko	8-7	4.73	44	15	0	0	112.1	123	67	59	29	76
Aaron Sele	8-6	4.53	28	15	0	0	103.1	120	57	52	30	57
Chad Billingsley	7-4	3.80	18	16	0	0	90.0	92	43	38	58	59
Takashi Saito	6-2	2.07	72	0	0	24	78.1	48	19	18	23	107
Jonathan Broxton	4-1	2.59	68	0	0	3	76.1	61	25	22	33	97
Mark Hendrickson	2-7	4.68	18	12	0	0	75.0	92	45	39	28	48
Joe Beimel	2-1	2.96	62	0	0	2	70.0	70	26	23	21	30
Jae Seo	2-4	5.78	19	10	0	0	67.0	75	45	43	25	49

MILWAUKEE BREWERS

BATTING	G	AB	R	H	2B	3B	HR	RBI	TB	BB	SO	SB	OBP	SLG	BA
Prince Fielder	157	569	82	154	35	1	28	81	275	59	125	7	.347	.483	.271
Bill Hall	148	537	101	145	39	4	35	85	297	63	162	8	.345	.553	.270
David Bell	145	504	60	136	27	4	10	63	201	50	68	3	.337	.399	.270
Geoff Jenkis	147	484	62	131	26	1	17	70	210	56	129	4	.357	.434	.271
Brady Clark	138	415	51	109	14	2	4	29	139	43	60	3	.348	.335	.263
Carlos Lee	102	388	60	111	18	0	28	81	213	38	39	12	.347	.549	.286
Rickie Weeks	95	359	73	100	15	3	8	34	145	30	92	19	.363	.404	.279
Damian Miller	101	331	34	83	28	0	6	38	129	33	86	0	.322	.390	.251
Jeff Cirillo	112	263	33	84	16	0	3	23	109	21	33	1	.369	.414	.319
Corey Koskie	76	257	29	67	23	0	12	33	126	29	58	1	.343	.490	.261
Corey Hart	87	237	32	67	13	2	9	33	111	17	58	5	.328	.468	.283
Tony Graffanino	60	236	34	66	17	3	2	27	95	20	37	2	.345	.403	.280
Gabe Gross	117	208	42	57	15	0	9	38	99	36	60	1	.382	.476	.274

PITCHING	W–L	ERA	G	GS	CG	SV	INN	H	R	ER	BB	SO
Chris Capuano	11-12	4.03	34	34	3	0	221.1	229	108	99	47	174
Dave Bush	12-11	4.41	34	32	3	0	210.0	201	111	103	38	166
Doug Davis	11-11	4.91	34	34	1	0	203.1	206	118	111	102	159
Ben Sheets	6-7	3.82	17	17	0	0	106.0	105	47	45	11	116
Tomo Ohka	4-5	4.82	18	18	0	0	97.0	98	58	52	35	50
Jose Capellan	4-2	4.40	61	0	0	0	71.2	65	37	35	31	58
Derrick Turnbow	4-9	6.87	64	0	0	24	56.1	56	51	43	39	69
Geremi Gonzalez	4-2	5.79	24	4	0	0	56.0	71	43	36	23	44
Carlos Villanueva	2-2	3.69	10	6	0	0	53.2	43	22	22	11	39
Dan Kolb	2-2	4.84	53	0	0	1	48.1	53	28	26	20	26
Matt Wise	5-6	3.86	40	0	0	2	44.1	45	24	19	14	27
Zach Jackson	2-2	5.40	8	7	0	0	38.1	48	26	23	14	22
Ricky Helling	0-2	4.11	20	2	0	0	35.0	25	17	16	15	32

NEW YORK METS

BATTING	G	AB	R	H	2B	3B	HR	RBI	TB	BB	SO	SB	OBP	SLG	BA
Jose Reyes	153	647	122	194	30	17	19	81	315	53	81	64	.354	.487	.300
David Wright	154	582	96	181	40	5	26	116	309	66	113	20	.381	.531	.311
Shawn Green	149	530	73	147	31	3	15	66	229	45	82	4	.344	.432	.277
Carlos Delgado	144	524	89	139	30	2	38	114	287	74	120	0	.361	.548	.265
Paul Lo Duca	124	512	80	163	39	1	5	49	219	24	38	3	.355	.428	.318
Carlos Beltran	140	510	127	140	38	1	41	116	303	95	99	18	.388	.594	.275
Jose Valentin	137	384	56	104	24	3	18	62	188	37	71	6	.330	.490	.271
Endy Chavez	133	353	48	108	22	5	4	42	152	24	44	12	.348	.431	.306
Cliff Floyd	97	332	45	81	19	1	11	44	135	29	58	6	.324	.407	.244
Chris Woodward	83	222	25	48	10	1	3	25	69	23	55	1	.289	.311	.216
Lastings Milledge	56	166	14	40	7	2	4	22	63	12	39	1	.310	.380	.241
Julio Franco	95	165	14	45	10	0	2	26	61	13	49	6	.330	.370	.273
Ramon Castro	40	126	13	30	7	0	4	12	49	15	40	0	.322	.389	.238
Eli Marrero	55	93	11	19	4	0	6	15	41	15	31	5	.324	.441	.204
Ricky Ledee	70	85	8	16	6	0	2	9	28	6	16	1	.242	.329	.188

PITCHING	W–L	ERA	G	GS	CG	SV	INN	H	R	ER	BB	SO
Tom Glavine	15-7	3.82	32	32	0	0	198.0	202	94	84	62	131
Steve Trachsel	15-8	4.97	30	30	1	0	164.2	185	94	91	78	79
Orlando Hernandez	11-11	4.66	29	29	1	0	162.1	155	90	84	61	164
Pedro Martinez	9-8	4.48	23	23	0	0	132.2	108	72	66	39	137
Oliver Perez	3-13	6.55	22	22	1	0	112.2	129	90	82	68	102
John Maine	6-5	3.62	16	16	1	0	90.0	69	40	36	33	71
Aaron Heilman	4-5	3.60	74	74	0	0	87.0	73	37	35	28	73
Darren Oliver	4-1	3.62	45	45	0	0	81.0	70	33	31	21	60
Billy Wagner	3-2	3.44	70	0	0	40	72.1	59	22	18	21	94
Dave Williams	5-4	6.52	14	13	0	0	69.0	93	52	50	20	32
Roberto Hernandez	0-3	3.11	68	0	0	2	63.2	61	32	22	32	48
Chad Bradford	4-2	2.90	70	6	0	2	62.0	59	22	20	13	45
Pedro Feliciano	7-2	2.09	64	0	0	0	60.1	56	15	14	20	54
Duaner Sanchez	5-1	2.60	49	0	0	0	55.1	43	19	16	24	44
Alay Soler	2-3	6.00	8	8	1	0	45.0	50	33	30	21	23
Brian Bannister	2-1	4.26	8	6	0	0	38.0	34	18	18	22	19

PHILADELPHIA PHILLIES

BATTING	G	AB	R	H	2B	3B	HR	RBI	TB	BB	SO	SB	OBP	SLG	BA
Jimmy Rollins	158	689	127	191	45	9	25	83	329	57	80	36	.334	.478	.277
Chase Utley	160	658	131	203	40	4	32	102	347	63	132	15	.379	.527	.309
Ryan Howard	159	581	104	182	25	1	58	149	383	108	181	0	.425	.659	.313
Pat Burrell	144	462	80	119	24	1	29	95	232	98	131	0	.388	.502	.258
Shane Victorino	153	415	70	119	19	8	6	46	172	24	54	4	.346	.414	.287
Aaron Rowand	109	405	59	106	24	3	12	47	172	18	76	10	.321	.425	.262
Bobby Abreu	98	339	61	94	25	2	8	65	147	91	86	20	.427	.434	.277
Abraham Nunez	123	322	42	68	10	2	2	32	88	41	58	1	.303	.273	.211
David Dellucci	132	264	41	77	14	5	13	39	140	28	62	1	.369	.530	.292
Mike Lieberthal	67	209	22	57	14	0	9	36	98	8	19	0	.316	.469	.273
Chris Coste	65	198	25	65	14	0	7	32	100	10	31	0	.376	.505	.328
Jose Hernandez	85	152	12	40	4	1	3	19	55	12	40	0	.317	.362	.263
Sal Fasano	50	140	9	34	8	0	4	10	54	5	47	0	.284	.386	.243
Jeff Conine	28	100	11	28	6	1	1	17	39	5	12	0	.327	.390	.280
Carlos Ruiz	27	69	5	18	1	1	3	10	30	5	8	0	.316	.435	.261

PITCHING	W–L	ERA	G	GS	CG	SV	INN	H	R	ER	BB	SO
Brett Myers	12-7	3.91	31	31	1	0	198.0	194	93	86	63	189
Jon Lieber	9-11	4.93	27	27	2	0	168.0	196	100	92	24	100
Ryan Madson	11-9	5.69	50	17	0	2	134.1	176	92	85	50	99
Cole Hamels	9-8	4.08	23	23	0	0	132.1	117	66	60	48	145
Cory Lidle	8-7	4.74	21	21	0	0	125.1	132	74	66	39	98
Geoff Geary	7-1	2.96	81	0	0	1	91.1	103	34	30	20	60
Aaron Fultz	3-1	4.54	66	1	0	0	71.1	80	39	36	28	62
Rick White	4-1	5.15	64	0	0	1	64.2	72	44	37	22	40
Tom Gordon	3-4	3.34	59	0	0	34	59.1	53	23	22	22	68
Randy Wolf	4-0	5.56	12	12	0	0	56.2	63	37	35	33	44
Gavin Floyd	4-3	7.29	11	11	1	0	54.1	70	48	44	32	34
Jamie Moyer	5-2	4.03	8	8	0	0	51.1	49	25	23	7	26

PITTSBURGH PIRATES

BATTING	G	AB	R	H	2B	3B	HR	RBI	TB	BB	SO	SB	OBP	SLG	BA
Freddy Sanchez	157	582	85	200	53	6	6	85	275	31	52	3	.378	.473	.344
Jason Bay	159	570	101	163	29	3	35	109	303	102	156	11	.396	.532	.286
Jack Wilson	142	543	70	148	27	1	8	35	201	33	65	4	.316	.370	.273
Jose Castillo	148	518	54	131	25	0	14	65	198	32	98	6	.299	.382	.253
Xavier Nady	130	468	57	131	28	1	17	63	212	30	85	3	.337	.453	.280
Ronny Paulino	129	442	37	137	19	0	6	55	174	34	79	0	.360	.394	.310
Jose Bautista	117	400	58	94	20	3	16	51	168	46	110	2	.335	.420	.235
Chris Duffy	84	314	46	80	14	3	2	18	106	19	71	26	.317	.338	.255
Jeromy Burnitz	111	313	35	72	12	0	16	49	132	22	74	1	.289	.422	.230
Nate McLouth	106	270	50	63	16	2	7	16	104	18	59	10	.320	.385	.233
Craig Wilson	85	255	38	68	11	2	13	41	122	24	88	1	.339	.478	.267
Sean Casey	59	213	30	63	15	0	3	29	87	23	22	0	.377	.408	.296
Joe Randa	89	206	23	55	13	0	4	28	80	16	26	0	.316	.388	.267
Ryan Doumit	61	149	15	31	9	0	6	17	58	15	42	0	.322	.389	.208

PITCHING	W–L	ERA	G	GS	CG	SV	INN	H	R	ER	BB	SO
Zach Duke	10-15	4.47	34	34	2	0	215.1	255	116	107	68	117
Ian Snell	14-11	4.74	32	32	0	0	186.0	198	104	98	74	169
Paul Maholm	8-10	4.76	30	30	0	0	176.0	202	98	93	81	117
Victor Santos	5-9	5.70	25	19	0	0	115.1	150	80	73	42	81
Salomon Torres	3-6	3.28	94	0	0	12	93.1	98	42	34	38	72
Matt Capps	9-1	3.79	85	0	0	1	80.2	81	37	34	12	56
John Grabow	4-2	4.13	72	0	0	0	69.2	68	34	32	30	66
Tom Gorzelanny	2-5	3.79	11	11	0	0	61.2	50	29	26	31	40
Damaso Marte	1-7	3.70	75	0	0	0	58.1	51	30	24	31	63
Mike Gonzalez	3-4	2.17	54	0	0	24	54.0	42	13	13	31	64
Shawn Chacon	2-3	5.48	9	9	0	0	46.0	47	32	28	27	27

ST. LOUIS CARDINALS

BATTING	G	AB	R	H	2B	3B	HR	RBI	TB	BB	SO	SB	OBP	SLG	BA
Juan Encarnacion	153	557	74	155	25	5	19	79	247	30	86	6	.317	.443	.278
Albert Pujols	143	535	119	177	33	1	49	137	359	92	50	7	.431	.671	.331
Scott Rolen	142	521	94	154	48	1	22	95	270	56	69	7	.369	.518	.296
Preston Wilson	135	501	58	132	25	2	17	72	212	29	121	12	.307	.423	.263
David Eckstein	123	500	68	146	18	1	2	23	172	31	41	7	.350	.344	.292
Aaron Miles	135	426	48	112	20	5	2	30	148	38	42	2	.324	.347	.263
Yadier Molina	129	417	29	90	26	0	6	49	134	26	41	1	.274	.321	.216
Jim Edmonds	110	350	52	90	18	0	19	70	165	53	101	4	.350	.471	.257
So Taguchi	134	316	46	84	19	1	2	31	111	32	48	11	.335	.351	.266
Chris Duncan	90	280	60	82	11	3	22	43	165	30	69	0	.363	.589	.293
Scott Spiezio	119	276	44	75	15	4	13	52	137	37	66	1	.366	.496	.272
Hector Luna	76	223	27	65	14	1	4	21	93	21	34	5	.355	.417	.291
Ronnie Belliard	54	194	20	46	9	1	5	23	72	15	36	0	.295	.371	.237
John Rodriguez	102	183	31	55	12	3	2	19	79	21	45	0	.374	.432	.301
Gary Bennett	60	157	13	35	5	0	4	22	52	11	30	0	.274	.331	.223

PITCHING	W–L	ERA	G	GS	CG	SV	INN	H	R	ER	BB	SO
Chris Carpenter	15-8	3.09	32	32	5	0	221.2	194	81	76	43	184
Jason Marquis	14-16	6.02	33	33	0	0	194.1	221	136	130	75	96
Jeff Suppan	12-7	4.12	32	32	0	0	190.0	207	100	87	69	104
Jorge Sosa	3-11	5.42	45	13	0	4	118.0	138	79	71	40	75
Mark Mulder	6-7	7.14	17	17	0	0	93.1	124	77	74	35	50
Anthony Reyes	5-8	5.06	17	17	1	0	85.1	84	48	48	34	72
Jeff Weaver	5-4	5.18	15	15	0	0	83.1	99	49	48	26	45
Josh Hancock	3-3	4.09	62	0	0	1	77.0	70	37	35	23	50
Adam Wainwright	2-1	3.12	61	0	0	3	75.0	64	26	26	22	72
Braden Looper	9-3	3.56	69	0	0	0	73.1	76	30	29	20	41
Sidney Ponson	4-4	5.24	14	13	0	0	68.2	82	42	40	29	33
Jason Isringhausen	4-8	3.55	59	0	0	33	58.1	47	25	23	38	52

SAN DIEGO PADRES

BATTING	G	AB	R	H	2B	3B	HR	RBI	TB	BB	SO	SB	OBP	SLG	BA
Brian Giles	158	604	87	159	37	1	14	83	240	104	60	9	.374	.397	.263
Adrian Gonzalez	156	570	83	173	38	1	24	82	285	52	113	0	.362	.500	.304
Mike Cameron	141	552	88	148	34	9	22	83	266	71	142	25	.355	.482	.268
Josh Barfield	150	539	72	151	32	3	13	58	228	30	81	21	.318	.423	.280
Dave Roberts	129	499	80	146	18	13	2	44	196	51	61	49	.360	.393	.293
Todd Walker	138	442	56	123	22	2	9	53	176	55	38	2	.356	.398	.278
Khalil Greene	121	412	56	101	26	2	15	55	176	39	87	5	.320	.427	.245
Mike Piazza	126	339	39	113	19	1	22	68	200	34	66	0	.342	.501	.283
Geoff Blum	109	276	27	70	17	1	4	34	101	17	51	0	.293	.336	.254
Mark Bellhorn	115	253	26	48	11	2	8	27	87	32	90	0	.285	.344	.190
Josh Bard	93	231	28	78	19	0	9	40	124	27	39	1	.406	.537	.338
Eric Young	56	128	19	26	5	0	3	13	40	13	16	8	.281	.313	.203
Ben Johnson	58	120	19	30	5	2	4	12	51	14	36	3	.333	.425	.250
Rob Bowen	94	94	22	23	5	0	3	13	37	13	26	0	.339	.394	.245

PITCHING	W–L	ERA	G	GS	CG	SV	INN	H	R	ER	BB	SO
Jake Peavy	11-14	4.09	32	32	2	0	202.1	187	93	92	62	215
Clay Hensley	11-12	3.71	37	29	1	0	187.0	174	82	77	76	122
Chris Young	11-5	3.46	31	31	0	0	179.1	134	72	69	69	164
Woody Williams	12-5	3.65	25	24	0	0	145.1	152	68	59	35	72
Chan Ho Park	7-7	4.81	24	21	1	0	136.2	146	81	73	44	96
Mike Thompson	4-5	4.99	19	16	0	0	92.0	103	56	51	30	35
Scott Linebrink	7-4	3.57	73	0	0	2	75.2	70	31	30	22	68
Trevor Hoffman	0-2	2.14	65	0	0	46	63.0	48	16	15	13	50
Brian Sweeney	2-0	3.20	37	0	0	2	56.1	53	22	20	16	23
Jon Adkins	2-1	3.98	55	0	0	0	52.1	55	26	24	20	30
Alan Embree	4-3	3.27	73	0	0	0	52.1	50	21	19	15	53
Cla Meredith	5-1	1.07	45	0	0	0	50.2	30	6	6	6	37

SAN FRANCISCO GIANTS

BATTING	G	AB	R	H	2B	3B	HR	RBI	TB	BB	SO	SB	OBP	SLG	BA
Pedro Feliz	160	603	75	147	30	5	22	98	258	33	112	1	.281	.428	.244
Omar Vizquel	153	579	88	171	28	10	4	58	225	56	51	24	.361	.389	.295
Randy Winn	149	573	82	150	33	5	11	56	227	48	63	10	.324	.396	.262
Ray Durham	137	498	79	146	34	7	26	93	268	51	61	7	.360	.538	.293
Steve Finley	139	426	66	105	21	12	6	40	168	46	55	7	.320	.394	.246
Barry Bonds	130	367	74	99	17	0	26	77	200	115	51	3	.454	.545	.270
Moises Alou	98	345	52	104	17	1	22	74	197	28	31	2	.352	.571	.301
Eliezer Alfonzo	87	286	27	76	18	2	12	39	133	9	74	1	.302	.465	.266
Mark Sweeney	114	259	32	65	16	2	5	37	99	28	50	0	.330	.382	.251
Shea Hillenbrand	60	234	33	58	22	0	9	29	97	7	40	0	.275	.415	.248
Lance Niekro	66	199	27	49	8	2	5	31	77	11	32	0	.286	.387	.246
Mike Matheny	47	160	10	37	4	0	3	18	54	9	30	0	.276	.338	.231

PITCHING	W–L	ERA	G	GS	CG	SV	INN	H	R	ER	BB	SO
Jason Schmidt	11-9	3.59	32	32	3	0	213.1	189	94	85	80	180
Matt Morris	10-15	4.98	33	33	2	0	207.2	218	123	115	63	117
Matt Cain	13-12	4.15	32	31	1	0	190.2	157	93	88	87	179
Noah Lowry	7-10	4.74	27	27	1	0	159.1	166	89	84	56	84
Jamey Wright	6-10	5.19	34	21	0	0	156.0	167	95	90	64	79
Brad Hennessey	5-6	4.26	34	12	0	1	99.1	92	53	47	42	42
Kevin Correia	2-0	3.49	48	0	0	0	69.2	64	27	27	22	57
Mike Stanton	7-7	3.99	82	0	0	8	67.2	70	30	30	27	48
Steve Kline	4-3	3.66	72	0	0	1	51.2	53	24	21	26	33
Jeremy Accardo	1-3	4.91	38	0	0	3	40.1	38	23	22	11	40
Jonathan Sanchez	3-1	4.95	27	4	0	0	40.0	38	26	22	23	33
Armando Benitez	4-2	3.52	41	0	0	17	38.1	39	15	15	21	31

WASHINGTON NATIONALS

BATTING	G	AB	R	H	2B	3B	HR	RBI	TB	BB	SO	SB	OBP	SLG	BA
Alfonso Soriano	159	647	119	179	41	2	46	95	362	67	147	41	.351	.560	.277
Felipe Lopez	156	617	98	169	27	3	11	52	235	81	102	44	.358	.381	.274
Ryan Zimmerman	157	614	84	176	47	3	20	110	289	61	148	11	.351	.471	.287
Austin Kearns	150	537	86	142	33	2	24	86	251	76	82	9	.363	.467	.264
Nick Johnson	147	500	100	145	46	0	23	77	260	110	76	10	.428	.520	.290
Jose Vidro	126	463	52	134	26	1	7	47	183	41	87	1	.348	.395	.289
Brian Schneider	124	410	30	105	18	0	4	55	135	38	48	2	.320	.329	.256
Jose Guillen	69	241	28	52	15	1	9	40	96	15	30	1	.276	.398	.216
Marlon Byrd	78	197	28	44	8	1	5	18	69	22	55	3	.317	.350	.223
Ryan Church	71	196	22	54	17	1	10	35	103	26	70	6	.366	.526	.276
Robert Fick	60	128	14	34	4	0	2	9	44	10	34	1	.324	.344	.266
Damian Jackson	67	116	16	23	6	1	4	10	43	12	83	1	.295	.371	.198
Bernie Castro	42	110	18	25	1	3	0	10	32	9	50	7	.286	.291	.227
Nook Logan	27	90	13	27	3	1	1	8	35	6	37	2	.337	.389	.300
Alex Escobar	33	87	14	31	3	2	4	18	50	8	17	2	.394	.575	.356

PITCHING	W–L	ERA	G	GS	CG	SV	INN	H	R	ER	BB	SO
Ramon Ortiz	11-16	5.57	33	33	0	0	190.2	230	127	118	64	104
Tony Armas	9-12	5.03	30	30	0	0	154.0	167	96	86	64	97
Michael O'Connor	3-8	4.80	21	20	0	0	105.0	96	61	56	45	59
Jon Rauch	4-5	3.35	85	0	0	2	91.1	78	37	34	36	86
Pedro Astacio	5-5	5.98	17	17	1	0	90.1	109	64	60	31	42
Chad Cordero	7-4	3.19	68	0	0	29	73.1	59	27	26	22	69
Jason Bergmann	0-2	6.68	29	6	0	0	64.2	81	49	48	27	54
Saul Rivera	3-0	3.43	54	0	0	1	60.1	59	28	23	32	41
Billy Traber	4-5	6.44	54	8	0	0	43.1	53	33	31	14	25
John Patterson	1-2	4.43	8	8	0	0	40.2	36	21	20	9	42
Zach Day	2-5	6.75	8	8	0	0	40.0	51	32	30	21	19
Shaw Hill	1-3	4.66	6	6	0	0	36.2	43	20	19	12	16

AMERICAN LEAGUE TEAM-BY-TEAM STATS

BALTIMORE ORIOLES

BATTING	G	AB	R	H	2B	3B	HR	RBI	TB	BB	SO	SB	OBP	SLG	BA
Miguel Tejada	162	648	99	214	37	0	24	100	323	46	83	6	.379	.498	.330
Melvin Mora	155	624	96	171	25	0	16	83	244	54	112	11	.342	.391	.274
Brian Roberts	138	563	85	161	34	3	10	55	231	55	83	36	.347	.410	.286
Ramon Hernandez	144	501	66	138	29	2	23	91	240	43	56	1	.343	.479	.275
Nick Markakis	147	491	72	143	25	2	16	62	220	43	68	2	.351	.448	.291
Corey Patterson	135	463	75	128	19	5	16	53	205	21	58	45	.314	.443	.276
Kevin Millar	132	430	64	117	26	0	15	64	188	59	84	1	.374	.437	.272
Jeff Connie	114	389	43	103	20	3	9	49	156	35	43	3	.325	.401	.265
Jay Gibbons	90	343	34	95	23	0	13	46	157	32	60	0	.341	.458	.277
Brandon Fahey	91	251	36	59	8	2	2	23	77	23	32	3	.307	.307	.235
Chris Gomez	55	132	14	45	7	0	2	17	58	7	17	1	.387	.439	.341
David Newhan	39	131	14	33	4	0	4	18	49	7	45	4	.294	.374	.252
Luis Matos	55	121	14	25	7	1	2	5	40	10	49	7	.278	.331	.207
Chris Widger	36	93	6	16	3	0	1	9	22	11	41	0	.255	.237	.172
Fernando Tatis	28	56	7	14	6	1	2	8	28	6	38	0	.313	.500	.250
Luis Terrerol	27	40	4	8	1	0	1	6	12	1	23	0	.238	.300	.200

PITCHING	W–L	ERA	G	GS	CG	SV	INN	H	R	ER	BB	SO
Erik Bedard	15-11	3.76	33	33	0	0	196.1	196	92	82	69	171
Rodrigo Lopez	9-18	5.90	36	29	0	0	189.0	234	129	124	59	136
Kris Benson	11-12	4.82	30	30	3	0	183.0	199	105	98	58	88
Daniel Cabrera	9-10	4.74	26	26	2	0	148.0	130	82	78	104	157
Adam Loewen	6-6	5.37	22	19	0	0	112.1	111	72	67	62	98
Bruce Chen	0-7	6.93	40	12	0	0	98.2	137	81	76	35	70
Chris Ray	4-4	2.73	61	0	0	33	66.0	45	22	20	27	51
La Troy Hawkins	3-2	4.48	60	0	0	0	60.1	73	30	30	15	27
Todd Williams	2-4	4.74	62	0	0	1	57.0	76	36	36	19	24
Chris Britton	0-2	3.35	52	0	0	1	53.2	46	22	22	17	41
Sendy Rleal	1-1	4.44	42	0	0	0	46.2	48	25	25	23	19
Russ Ortiz	0-3	8.48	20	5	0	0	40.1	59	39	39	18	23
Kurt Birkins	5-2	4.94	35	0	0	0	31.0	25	19	19	16	27
John Halama	3-1	6.14	17	1	0	0	29.1	38	20	20	13	12
Julio Manon	0-1	5.40	22	0	0	0	20.0	23	13	13	16	22

BOSTON RED SOX

BATTING	G	AB	R	H	2B	3B	HR	RBI	TB	BB	SO	SB	OBP	SLG	BA
Mark Loretta	155	635	75	181	33	0	5	59	229	49	63	4	.345	.361	.285
Mike Lowell	153	573	79	163	47	1	20	80	272	47	61	2	.339	.475	.284
Kevin Youkilis	147	569	100	159	42	2	13	72	244	91	120	5	.381	.429	.279
David Ortiz	151	558	115	160	29	2	54	137	355	119	117	1	.413	.636	.287
Manny Ramirez	130	449	79	144	27	1	35	102	278	100	102	0	.439	.619	.321
Coco Crisp	105	413	58	109	22	2	8	36	159	31	67	22	.317	.385	.264
Alex Gonzalez	111	388	48	99	24	2	9	50	154	22	67	1	.299	.397	.255
Trot Nixon	114	381	59	102	24	0	8	52	150	60	56	0	.373	.394	.268
Jason Varitek	103	365	46	87	19	2	12	55	146	46	87	1	.325	.400	.238
Javier Lopez	94	342	36	86	20	1	8	35	132	20	76	0	.297	.386	.251
Eric Hinske	109	277	43	75	17	2	13	34	135	35	79	2	.353	.487	.271
Wily Mo Pena	84	276	36	83	15	2	11	42	135	20	90	0	.349	.489	.301
Alex Cora	96	235	31	56	7	2	1	18	70	19	29	6	.312	.298	.238
Doug Mirabelli	59	161	12	31	6	0	6	25	55	11	54	0	.261	.342	.193
Gabe Kapler	72	130	21	33	7	0	2	12	46	14	15	1	.340	.354	.254
Dustin Pedroia	31	89	5	17	4	0	2	7	27	7	7	0	.258	.303	.191

PITCHING	W–L	ERA	G	GS	CG	SV	INN	H	R	ER	BB	SO
Josh Beckett	16-11	5.01	33	33	0	0	204.2	191	120	114	74	158
Curt Schilling	15-7	3.97	31	31	0	0	204.0	220	90	90	28	183
Tim Wakefield	7-11	4.63	23	23	1	0	140.0	135	80	72	51	90
Jason Johnson	3-12	6.35	20	20	0	0	106.1	149	81	75	35	50
Julian Tavarez	5-4	4.47	58	6	1	1	98.2	110	54	49	44	56
Jon Lester	7-2	4.76	15	15	0	0	81.1	91	43	43	43	60
Jonathan Papelbon	4-2	0.92	59	0	0	35	68.1	40	8	7	13	75
Matt Clement	5-5	6.61	12	12	0	0	65.1	77	50	48	38	43
Mike Timlin	6-6	4.36	68	0	0	9	64.0	78	33	31	16	30
Kyle Snyder	4-5	6.56	17	11	0	0	60.1	87	51	44	20	57
Manny Delcarmen	2-0	5.06	50	0	0	0	53.1	68	32	30	17	45
Keith Foulke	3-1	4.35	44	0	0	0	49.2	52	24	24	7	36
David Wells	2-3	4.98	8	8	0	0	47.0	64	30	26	8	24
Rudy Seanez	2-1	4.82	41	0	0	0	46.2	51	28	25	26	48

CHICAGO WHITE SOX

BATTING	G	AB	R	H	2B	3B	HR	RBI	TB	BB	SO	SB	OBP	SLG	BA
Paul Konerko	152	566	97	177	30	0	35	113	312	60	104	1	.381	.551	.313
Tadahito Iguchi	138	555	97	156	24	0	18	67	234	59	110	11	.352	.422	.281
Joe Crede	150	544	76	154	31	0	30	94	275	28	58	0	.323	.506	.283
Jermain Dye	146	539	103	170	27	3	44	120	335	59	118	7	.385	.622	.315
Scot Podesdnik	139	524	86	137	27	6	3	45	185	54	96	40	.330	.353	.261
A.J. Pierzynski	140	509	65	150	24	0	16	64	222	22	72	1	.333	.436	.295
Jim Thome	143	490	108	141	26	0	42	109	293	107	147	0	.416	.598	.288
Juan Uribe	132	463	53	109	28	2	21	71	204	13	82	1	.257	.441	.235
Brian N. Anderson	134	365	46	82	23	1	8	33	131	30	90	4	.290	.359	.225
Alex Clinton	91	288	35	82	10	3	5	41	113	10	35	10	.310	.392	.285
Rob Mackowiak	112	255	31	74	12	1	5	23	103	28	59	5	.365	.404	.290
Pablo Ozuna	79	189	25	62	12	2	2	17	84	7	16	6	.365	.444	.328
Ross Gload	77	156	22	51	8	2	3	18	72	6	15	6	.354	.462	.327
Sandy Alomar	19	46	5	10	3	0	1	8	16	3	7	0	.255	.348	.217
Ryan Sweeney	18	35	1	8	0	0	0	5	8	0	7	0	.229	.229	.229

PITCHING	W–L	ERA	G	GS	CG	SV	INN	H	R	ER	BB	SO
Freddy Garcia	17-9	4.53	33	33	1	0	216.1	228	116	109	48	135
Jon Garland	18-7	4.51	33	32	1	0	211.1	247	112	106	41	112
Mark Buehrle	12-13	4.99	32	32	1	0	204.0	247	124	113	48	98
Javier Vazquez	11-12	4.84	33	32	1	0	202.2	206	116	109	56	184
Jose Contreras	13-9	4.27	30	30	1	0	196.0	194	101	93	55	134
Brandon McCarthy	4-7	4.68	53	2	0	0	84.2	77	44	44	33	69
Bobby Jenks	3-4	4.00	67	0	0	41	69.2	66	32	31	31	80
Neal Cotts	5-3	5.17	70	0	0	1	54.0	64	33	31	24	43
Matt Thornton	1-2	3.33	63	0	0	2	54.0	46	20	20	21	49
David Riske	1-2	3.89	41	0	0	0	44.0	40	20	19	17	28
Cliff Politte	2-2	8.70	30	0	0	0	30.0	47	30	29	15	15
Mike MacDougal	1-1	1.55	29	0	0	1	29.0	21	5	5	6	21
Charlie Haeger	1-1	3.44	7	1	0	1	18.1	12	10	7	13	19

CLEVELAND INDIANS

BATTING	G	AB	R	H	2B	3B	HR	RBI	TB	BB	SO	SB	OBP	SLG	BA
Grady Sizemore	162	655	134	190	53	11	28	76	349	78	153	22	.375	.533	.290
Victor Martinez	153	572	82	181	37	0	16	93	266	71	78	0	.391	.465	.316
Jhonny Peralta	149	569	84	146	28	3	13	68	219	56	152	0	.323	.385	.257
Jason Michaels	123	494	77	132	32	1	9	55	193	43	101	9	.326	.391	.267
Travis Hafner	129	454	100	140	31	1	42	117	299	100	111	0	.439	.659	.308
Casey Blake	109	401	63	113	20	1	19	68	192	45	93	6	.356	.479	.282
Aaron Boone	104	354	50	89	19	1	7	46	131	27	62	5	.314	.370	.251
Ronnie Belliard	93	350	43	102	21	0	8	44	147	21	45	2	.337	.420	.291
Joe Inglett	64	201	26	57	8	3	2	21	77	14	39	5	.332	.383	.284
Ryan Garko	50	185	28	54	12	0	7	45	87	14	37	0	.359	.470	.292
Andy Marte	50	164	20	37	15	1	5	23	69	13	38	0	.287	.421	.226
Shin-shie Choo	49	157	23	44	12	3	3	22	71	18	50	5	.360	.452	.280
Todd Hollandsworth	56	156	21	37	12	1	6	27	69	4	33	0	.253	.454	.237

PITCHING	W–L	ERA	G	GS	CG	SV	INN	H	R	ER	BB	SO
Jake Westbrook	15-10	4.17	32	32	3	0	211.1	247	106	98	55	109
Cliff Lee	14-11	4.40	33	33	1	0	200.2	224	114	98	58	129
C.C. Sabathia	12-11	3.22	28	28	6	0	192.2	182	83	69	44	172
Paul Byrd	10-9	4.88	31	31	1	0	179.0	232	120	97	38	88
Jeremy Sowers	7-4	3.57	14	14	2	0	88.1	85	36	35	20	35
Fausto Carmona	1-10	5.42	38	7	0	0	74.2	88	46	45	31	58
Fernando Cabrera	3-3	5.19	51	0	0	0	60.2	53	36	35	32	71
Rafael Betancourt	3-4	3.81	50	0	0	3	56.2	52	25	24	11	48
Jason Davis	3-2	3.74	39	0	0	1	55.1	67	28	23	14	37
Guillermo Mota	1-3	6.21	34	0	0	0	37.2	45	27	26	19	27
Bob Wickman	1-4	4.18	29	0	0	15	28.0	29	15	13	11	17
Brian Sikorski	2-1	4.58	17	0	0	0	19.2	20	10	10	4	24
Jeremy Guthrie	0-0	6.98	9	1	0	0	19.1	24	15	15	15	14
Edward Mujica	0-1	2.95	10	0	0	0	18.1	25	6	6	0	12

DETROIT TIGERS

BATTING	G	AB	R	H	2B	3B	HR	RBI	TB	BB	SO	SB	OBP	SLG	BA
Curtis Granderson	159	596	90	155	31	9	19	68	261	66	174	8	.335	.438	.260
Magglio Ordonez	155	593	82	177	32	1	24	104	283	45	87	1	.350	.477	.298
Ivan Rodriguez	136	547	74	164	28	4	13	69	239	26	86	8	.332	.437	.300
Carlos Guillen	153	543	100	174	41	5	19	85	282	71	87	20	.400	.519	.320
Brandon Inge	159	542	83	137	29	2	27	83	251	43	128	7	.313	.463	.253
Craig Monroe	147	541	89	138	35	2	28	92	261	37	126	2	.301	.482	.255
Placido Polanco	110	461	58	136	18	1	4	52	168	17	27	1	.329	.364	.295
Chris Shelton	115	373	50	102	16	4	16	47	174	34	107	1	.340	.466	.273
Matt Staires	117	348	42	86	21	0	13	51	146	40	86	0	.328	.420	.247
Marcus Thames	110	348	61	89	20	2	26	60	191	37	92	1	.333	.549	.256
Omar Infante	78	224	35	62	11	4	4	25	93	14	45	3	.325	.415	.277
Sean Casey	53	184	17	45	7	0	5	30	67	10	21	0	.286	.364	.245
Dmitri Young	48	172	19	43	4	1	7	23	70	11	39	1	.293	.407	.250
Vance Wilson	56	152	18	43	9	0	5	18	67	2	33	0	.304	.441	.283
Alexis Gomez	62	103	17	28	5	2	1	6	40	6	21	4	.318	.388	.272
Ramon Santiago	43	80	9	18	1	1	0	3	21	1	14	2	.244	.263	.225

PITCHING	W–L	ERA	G	GS	CG	SV	INN	H	R	ER	BB	SO
Jeremy Bonderman	14-8	4.08	34	34	0	0	214.0	214	104	97	64	202
Nate Robertson	13-13	3.84	32	32	1	0	208.2	206	98	89	67	137
Kenny Rogers	17-8	3.84	34	33	0	0	204.0	195	97	87	62	99
Justin Verlander	17-9	3.63	30	30	1	0	186.0	187	78	75	60	124
Zach Miner	7-6	4.84	27	16	1	0	93.0	100	53	50	32	59
Joel Zumaya	6-3	1.94	62	0	0	1	83.1	56	20	18	42	97
Fernando Rodney	7-4	3.52	63	0	0	7	71.2	51	36	28	34	65
Todd Jones	2-6	3.94	62	0	0	37	64.0	70	31	28	11	28
Jason Grilli	2-3	4.21	51	0	0	0	62.0	61	31	29	25	31
Wilfredo Ledezma	3-3	3.58	24	7	0	0	60.1	60	28	24	23	39
Mike Maroth	5-2	4.19	13	9	0	0	53.2	64	26	25	16	24
Jamie Walker	0-1	2.81	56	0	0	0	48.0	47	15	15	8	37
Roman Colon	2-0	4.89	20	1	0	1	38.2	46	21	21	14	25
Bobby Seay	0-0	6.46	14	0	0	0	15.1	14	11	11	9	12
Jordan Tata	0-0	6.14	8	0	0	0	14.2	14	11	10	7	6

KANSAS CITY ROYALS

BATTING	G	AB	R	H	2B	3B	HR	RBI	TB	BB	SO	SB	OBP	SLG	BA
Mark Grudzielanek	134	548	85	163	32	4	7	52	224	28	69	7	.331	.409	.297
Emil Brown	147	527	77	151	41	2	15	81	241	59	95	10	.358	.457	.287
David DeJesus	119	491	83	145	36	7	8	56	219	43	70	3	.364	.446	.295
Angel Berroa	132	474	45	111	18	1	9	54	158	14	88	5	.259	.333	.234
Mark Teahen	109	393	70	114	21	7	18	69	203	40	85	3	.357	.517	.290
Joey Gathright	134	383	59	91	12	3	1	41	112	42	75	7	.321	.292	.238
John Buck	114	371	37	91	21	1	11	50	147	26	84	2	.306	.396	.245
Reggie Sanders	88	325	45	80	23	1	11	49	138	28	86	1	.304	.425	.246
Doug Mientkiewicz	91	314	37	89	24	2	4	43	129	35	50	2	.359	.411	.283
Esteban German	106	279	44	91	18	5	3	34	128	40	49	4	.422	.459	.326
Shane Costa	72	237	23	65	20	1	3	23	96	6	29	3	.304	.405	.274
Tony Graffanino	69	220	34	59	16	0	5	32	90	25	31	1	.346	.409	.268
Mike Sweeney	60	217	23	56	15	0	8	33	95	28	48	0	.349	.438	.258
Ryan Shealy	51	193	29	54	10	1	7	36	87	15	50	0	.338	.451	.280

PITCHING	W–L	ERA	G	GS	CG	SV	INN	H	R	ER	BB	SO
Mark Redman	11-10	5.71	29	29	2	0	167.0	202	110	106	63	76
Scott Elarton	4-9	5.34	20	20	0	0	114.2	117	73	68	52	49
Runelvys Hernandez	6-10	6.48	21	21	1	0	109.2	145	87	79	48	50
Luke Hudson	7-6	5.12	26	15	0	0	102.0	109	62	58	38	64
Jimmy Gobble	4-6	5.14	60	6	0	2	84.0	95	51	48	29	80
Joel Peralta	1-3	4.40	64	0	0	1	73.2	74	37	36	17	57
Ambiorix Burgos	4-5	5.52	68	1	0	18	73.1	83	49	45	37	72
Jeremy Affeldt	4-6	5.91	27	9	0	0	70.0	71	51	46	42	28
Odalis Perez	2-4	5.64	12	12	0	0	67.0	80	44	42	18	48
Andrew Sisco	1-3	7.10	65	0	0	1	58.1	66	47	46	40	52
Todd Wellemeyer	1-2	3.63	28	0	0	1	57.0	48	25	23	37	37
Elmer Dessens	5-7	4.50	43	0	0	2	54.0	63	31	27	36	36

BASEBALL

LOS ANGELES ANGELS

BATTING	G	AB	R	H	2B	3B	HR	RBI	TB	BB	SO	SB	OBP	SLG	BA
Orlando Cabrera	153	607	95	171	45	1	9	72	245	55	101	27	.335	.404	.282
Vladimir Guerrero	156	607	92	200	34	1	33	116	335	50	108	15	.382	.552	.329
Chone Figgins	155	604	93	161	23	8	9	62	227	65	84	52	.336	.376	.267
Garrett Anderson	141	543	63	152	28	2	17	85	235	38	50	1	.323	.433	.280
Adam Kennedy	139	451	50	123	26	6	4	55	173	39	48	16	.334	.384	.273
Juan Rivera	124	448	65	139	27	0	23	85	235	33	64	0	.362	.525	.310
Maicer Izturis	104	352	64	103	21	3	5	44	145	38	41	14	.365	.412	.293
Mike Napoli	99	268	47	61	13	0	16	42	122	51	71	2	.360	.455	.228
Howie Kendrick	72	267	25	76	21	1	4	30	111	9	44	6	.314	.416	.285
Robb Quinlan	86	234	28	75	11	1	9	32	115	7	44	2	.344	.491	.321
Jose Molina	78	225	18	54	17	0	4	22	83	9	64	1	.273	.369	.240
Tim Salmon	76	211	30	56	8	2	9	27	95	29	21	0	.361	.450	.265
Kendry Morales	57	197	21	46	10	1	5	22	73	17	41	1	.293	.371	.285
Dallas McPherson	40	115	16	30	4	0	7	13	54	6	26	1	.298	.478	.321
Darin Erstad	40	95	8	21	8	1	0	5	31	6	18	1	.279	.326	.221

PITCHING	W–L	ERA	G	GS	CG	SV	INN	H	R	ER	BB	SO
John Lackey	13-11	3.56	33	33	3	0	217.2	203	98	86	72	190
Ervin Santana	16-8	4.28	33	33	0	0	204.0	181	106	97	70	141
Kelvim Escobar	11-14	3.61	30	30	1	0	189.1	192	93	76	50	147
Jered Weaver	11-2	2.56	19	19	0	0	123.0	94	36	35	33	105
Hector Carrasco	7-3	3.41	56	3	0	1	100.1	93	42	38	27	72
Jeff Weaver	3-10	6.29	16	16	0	0	88.2	114	68	62	21	62
Scot Shields	7-7	2.87	74	0	0	2	87.2	70	30	28	24	84
Kevin Gregg	3-4	4.14	32	3	0	0	78.1	88	41	36	21	71
Francisco Rodriguez	2-3	1.73	69	0	0	47	73.0	52	16	14	28	98
Joe Saunders	7-3	4.71	13	13	0	0	70.2	71	42	37	29	51
Brendan Donnelly	6-0	3.94	62	0	0	0	64.0	58	32	28	28	53
Bartolo Colon	1-5	5.11	10	10	1	0	56.1	71	39	32	11	31

MINNESOTA TWINS

BATTING	G	AB	R	H	2B	3B	HR	RBI	TB	BB	SO	SB	OBP	SLG	BA
Justin Morneau	157	592	97	190	37	1	34	130	331	53	93	3	.375	.559	.321
Luis Castillo	142	584	84	173	22	6	3	49	216	56	53	25	.358	.370	.296
Michael Cuddyer	150	557	102	158	41	5	24	109	281	62	130	6	.362	.504	.284
Torii Hunter	147	557	86	155	21	2	31	98	273	45	108	12	.336	.490	.278
Joe Mauer	140	521	86	181	36	4	13	84	264	79	54	8	.429	.507	.347
Nick Punto	135	459	73	133	21	7	1	45	171	47	68	17	.352	.373	.290
Rondell White	99	337	32	83	17	1	7	38	123	11	54	1	.276	.365	.246
Jason Bartlett	99	333	44	103	18	2	2	32	131	22	46	10	.367	.393	.309
Lew Ford	104	234	40	53	6	1	4	18	73	16	43	9	.287	.312	.226
Jason Kubel	73	220	23	53	8	0	8	26	85	12	45	2	.279	.386	.241
Phil Nevin	62	218	28	46	9	0	10	35	85	31	54	0	.313	.390	.211
Jason Tyner	62	218	29	68	5	2	0	18	77	11	18	4	.345	.353	.312
Mike Redmond	47	179	20	61	13	0	0	23	74	4	18	0	.365	.413	.341
Tony Batista	50	178	24	42	12	0	5	21	69	15	27	0	.303	.388	.236
Shannon Stewart	44	174	21	51	5	1	2	21	64	14	19	3	.347	.368	.293
Juan Castro	50	156	10	36	5	2	1	14	48	6	23	1	.258	.308	.231
Luis Rodriguez	59	115	11	27	4	0	2	6	37	14	16	0	.315	.322	.235

PITCHING	W–L	ERA	G	GS	CG	SV	INN	H	R	ER	BB	SO
Johan Santana	19-6	2.77	34	34	1	0	233.2	186	79	72	47	245
Carlos Silva	11-15	5.94	36	31	0	0	180.1	246	130	119	32	70
Brad Radke	12-9	4.32	28	28	0	0	162.1	197	87	78	32	83
Francisco Liriano	12-3	2.16	28	16	0	1	121.0	89	31	29	24	144
Boof Bosner	7-6	4.22	18	18	0	0	100.1	104	50	47	14	84
Scott Baker	5-8	6.37	16	16	0	0	83.1	114	63	59	16	62
J.D. Crain	4-5	3.52	68	0	0	1	76.2	79	31	30	18	60
Juan Rincon	3-1	2.91	75	0	0	1	74.1	76	30	24	24	65
Matt Guerrier	1-0	3.36	39	1	0	1	69.2	78	29	26	21	37
Joe Nathan	7-0	1.58	64	0	0	36	68.1	38	12	12	16	86
Kyle Lohse	2-5	7.07	22	8	0	0	63.2	80	50	50	25	18
Wille Eyre	1-0	5.31	42	0	0	0	59.1	75	36	35	22	59

NEW YORK YANKEES

BATTING

BATTING	G	AB	R	H	2B	3B	HR	RBI	TB	BB	SO	SB	OBP	SLG	BA
Derek Jeter	154	623	118	214	39	3	14	97	301	69	102	34	.417	.483	.343
Johnny Damon	149	593	115	169	35	5	24	80	286	67	85	25	.359	.482	.285
Alex Rodriguez	154	572	113	166	26	1	35	121	299	90	139	15	.392	.523	.290
Robinson Cano	122	482	62	165	41	1	15	78	253	18	54	5	.365	.525	.342
Jorge Posada	143	465	65	129	27	2	23	93	229	64	97	3	.374	.492	.277
Melky Cabrera	130	460	75	129	26	2	7	50	180	56	59	12	.360	.391	.280
Jason Giambi	139	446	92	113	25	0	37	113	249	110	106	2	.413	.558	.253
Bernie Williams	131	420	65	118	29	0	12	61	183	33	53	2	.332	.436	.281
Andy Phillips	110	246	30	59	11	3	7	29	97	15	56	3	.281	.394	.240
Miguel Cairo	81	222	28	53	12	3	0	30	71	13	31	13	.280	.320	.239
Bobby Abreu	58	309	37	69	16	0	7	42	106	33	52	10	.419	.507	.330
Hideki Matsui	51	172	32	52	9	0	8	29	85	27	23	1	.393	.494	.302
Gary Sheffield	39	151	22	45	5	0	6	25	68	13	16	5	.355	.450	.298
Aaron Guiel	63	132	25	32	6	0	7	18	59	14	31	2	.338	.447	.242

PITCHING

PITCHING	W–L	ERA	G	GS	CG	SV	INN	H	R	ER	BB	SO
Chien-Ming Wang	19-6	3.63	34	33	2	1	218.0	233	92	88	52	76
Randy Johnson	17-11	5.00	33	33	2	0	205.0	194	125	114	60	172
Mike Mussina	15-7	3.51	32	32	1	0	197.1	184	88	77	35	172
Jaret Wright	11-7	4.49	30	27	0	0	140.1	157	76	70	57	84
Scott Proctor	6-4	3.52	83	0	0	1	102.1	89	41	40	33	89
Ron Villone	3-3	5.04	70	0	0	0	80.1	75	48	45	51	72
Mariano Rivera	5-5	1.80	63	0	0	34	75.0	61	16	15	11	55
Kyle Farnsworth	3-6	4.36	72	0	0	6	66.0	62	34	32	28	75
Shawn Chacon	5-3	7.00	17	11	0	0	63.0	77	55	49	36	35
Cory Lidle	4-3	5.16	10	9	0	0	45.1	49	26	26	19	32
Jeff Karstens	2-1	3.80	8	6	0	0	42.2	40	20	18	11	16
Mike Myers	1-2	3.23	62	0	0	0	30.2	29	14	11	10	22
Aaron Small	0-3	8.46	11	3	0	0	27.2	42	29	26	12	12
Brian Bruney	1-1	0.87	19	0	0	0	20.2	14	2	2	15	25
Darrell Rasner	3-1	4.43	6	3	0	0	20.1	18	10	10	5	11

OAKLAND ATHLETICS

BATTING

BATTING	G	AB	R	H	2B	3B	HR	RBI	TB	BB	SO	SB	OBP	SLG	BA
Jay Payton	142	557	78	168	32	3	10	59	233	22	52	8	.325	.418	.296
Nick Swisher	157	556	106	141	24	2	35	95	274	97	152	1	.372	.493	.254
Jason Kendall	143	552	76	163	23	0	1	50	189	53	54	11	.367	.342	.295
Mark Kotsay	129	502	57	138	29	3	7	59	194	44	55	6	.332	.386	.275
Eric Chavez	137	485	74	117	24	2	22	72	211	84	100	3	.351	.435	.241
Frank Thomas	137	466	77	126	11	0	39	114	254	81	81	0	.381	.545	.270
Mark Ellis	124	441	64	110	25	1	11	52	170	40	76	4	.319	.385	.249
Marco Scutaro	117	365	52	97	21	6	5	41	145	50	66	5	.350	.397	.266
Bobby Crosby	96	358	42	82	12	0	9	40	121	36	76	8	.298	.338	.229
Milton Bradley	96	351	53	97	14	2	14	52	157	51	65	10	.370	.447	.276
Dan Johnson	91	286	30	67	13	1	9	37	109	40	45	0	.323	.381	.234
Bobby Kielty	81	270	35	73	20	1	8	36	119	22	49	2	.329	.441	.270
Adam Melhuse	49	128	10	28	8	0	4	18	48	9	34	0	.278	.375	.219
Antonio Perez	57	98	10	10	5	1	1	8	20	10	44	0	.185	.204	.102
D'Angelo Jimenez	28	71	8	13	3	0	1	8	19	16	13	0	.333	.268	.183

PITCHING

PITCHING	W–L	ERA	G	GS	CG	SV	INN	H	R	ER	BB	SO
Dan Haren	14-13	4.12	34	34	2	0	223.0	224	109	102	45	176
Barry Zito	16-10	3.83	34	34	0	0	221.0	211	99	94	99	151
Joe Blanton	16-12	4.82	32	31	1	0	194.1	241	111	104	58	107
Estaban Loaiza	11-9	4.89	26	26	2	0	154.2	179	92	84	40	97
Kirk Saarloos	7-7	4.75	35	16	0	2	121.1	149	70	64	53	52
Brad Halsey	5-4	4.67	52	7	0	0	94.1	108	53	49	46	67
Chad Gaudin	4-2	3.09	55	0	0	2	64.0	51	24	22	42	36
Kiko Calero	3-2	3.41	70	0	0	2	58.0	50	22	22	24	67
Justin Duchscherer	2-1	2.91	53	0	0	9	55.2	52	18	18	9	51
Rich Harden	4-0	4.24	9	9	0	0	46.2	31	22	22	26	49
Joe Kennedy	4-1	2.31	39	0	0	1	35.0	34	10	9	13	29

BASEBALL

SEATTLE MARINERS

BATTING	G	AB	R	H	2B	3B	HR	RBI	TB	BB	SO	SB	OBP	SLG	BA
Ichiro Suzuki	161	695	110	224	20	9	9	49	289	49	71	45	.370	.416	.322
Raul Ibanez	159	626	103	181	33	5	33	123	323	65	115	2	.353	.516	.289
Adrian Beltre	156	620	88	166	39	4	25	89	288	47	118	11	.328	.465	.268
Jose Lopez	151	603	78	170	28	8	10	79	244	26	80	5	.319	.405	.282
Richie Sexson	158	591	75	156	40	0	34	107	298	64	154	1	.338	.504	.264
Yuniesky Betancourt	157	558	68	161	28	6	8	47	225	17	54	11	.310	.403	.289
Kenji Johjima	144	506	61	147	25	1	18	76	228	20	46	3	.332	.451	.291
Ben Broussard	144	432	61	125	21	0	21	63	209	26	103	2	.331	.484	.289
Carl Everett	92	308	37	70	8	0	11	33	111	29	57	1	.297	.360	.227
William Bloomquist	102	251	36	62	6	2	1	15	75	24	40	16	.320	.299	.247
Jeremy Reed	67	212	27	46	6	5	6	17	80	11	31	2	.260	.377	.217
Eduardo Perez	80	186	22	47	10	0	9	33	84	18	33	0	.324	.452	.253
Rene Rivera	35	99	8	15	4	0	2	4	25	3	29	1	.184	.253	.152
Chris Snelling	36	96	14	24	6	1	3	8	41	13	38	2	.360	.457	.250
Adam Jones	32	74	6	16	4	0	1	8	23	2	22	3	.237	.311	.216

PITCHING	W–L	ERA	G	GS	CG	SV	INN	H	R	ER	BB	SO
Felix Hernandez	12-14	4.52	31	31	2	0	191.1	195	105	96	60	176
Jarrod Washburn	8-14	4.67	31	31	0	0	187.0	198	103	97	55	103
Gil Meche	11-8	4.48	32	32	1	0	186.2	183	106	93	84	156
Joel Pineiro	8-13	6.36	40	25	1	1	165.2	209	123	117	64	87
Jamie Moyer	6-12	4.39	25	25	2	0	160.0	179	85	78	44	82
Jack Woods	7-4	4.20	37	8	0	1	105.0	115	51	49	53	66
J.J. Putz	4-1	2.30	72	0	0	36	78.1	59	20	20	13	104
Rafael Soriano	1-2	2.25	53	0	0	2	60.0	44	15	15	21	65
Julio Mateo	9-4	4.19	48	0	0	0	53.2	62	27	25	22	31
George Sherrill	2-4	4.28	72	0	0	1	40.0	30	19	19	27	42
Emiliano Fruto	2-2	5.50	23	0	0	1	36.0	34	24	22	24	34
Cha Seung Baek	4-1	3.67	6	6	0	0	34.1	26	15	14	13	23
Sean Green	0-0	4.50	24	0	0	0	32.0	34	16	16	13	15
Eddie Guardado	1-3	5.48	28	0	0	5	23.0	29	14	14	11	22

TAMPA BAY DEVIL RAYS

BATTING	G	AB	R	H	2B	3B	HR	RBI	TB	BB	SO	SB	OBP	SLG	BA
Carl Crawford	151	600	89	183	20	16	18	77	302	27	84	46	.331	.469	.301
Ty Wigginton	122	444	55	122	25	1	24	79	221	32	97	4	.330	.498	.275
Jorge Cantu	107	413	40	103	18	2	14	62	167	26	91	1	.295	.404	.249
Jonny Gomes	117	385	53	83	21	1	20	59	166	61	116	1	.325	.431	.216
Rocco Baldelli	92	364	59	110	24	6	16	57	194	14	70	1	.339	.533	.302
Travis Lee	114	343	35	77	11	2	11	31	125	42	73	5	.312	.364	.224
Damon Hollins	121	333	37	76	20	0	15	33	141	19	64	3	.269	.423	.228
Greg Norton	98	294	47	87	15	0	17	45	153	35	69	1	.374	.520	.296
Julio Lugo	73	289	53	89	17	1	12	27	144	27	47	18	.373	.498	.308
Tomas Perez	99	241	31	51	12	0	2	16	69	5	44	1	.224	.286	.212
Aubrey Huff	63	230	26	65	15	1	8	28	106	24	25	0	.348	.461	.283
Toby Hall	64	221	15	51	13	0	8	23	88	8	17	0	.261	.398	.231
Dioner Navarro	56	193	23	47	7	0	4	20	66	20	33	1	.316	.342	.244
Ben Zobrist	52	183	10	41	6	2	2	18	57	10	26	2	.260	.311	.224

PITCHING	W–L	ERA	G	GS	CG	SV	INN	H	R	ER	BB	SO
Scott Kazmir	10-8	3.24	24	24	1	0	144.2	132	59	52	52	163
Casey Fossum	6-6	5.33	25	25	0	0	130.0	136	89	77	63	88
James Shields	6-8	4.84	21	21	1	0	124.2	141	69	67	38	104
Seth McClung	6-12	6.29	39	15	0	6	103.0	120	77	72	68	59
Tim Corcoran	5-9	4.38	21	16	0	0	90.1	92	48	44	48	59
Jae Seo	1-8	5.00	17	16	0	0	90.0	122	56	50	31	39
Mark Hendrickson	4-8	3.81	13	13	1	0	89.2	81	42	38	34	51
Ruddy Lugo	2-4	3.81	64	0	0	0	85.0	75	39	36	37	48
Shamp Camp	7-4	4.68	75	0	0	4	75.0	93	43	39	19	53
Brian Meadows	3-6	5.17	53	0	0	8	69.2	90	43	40	15	35
Doug Waechter	1-4	6.62	11	10	0	0	53.0	67	40	39	19	25
Jason Hammel	0-6	7.77	9	9	0	0	44.0	61	38	38	19	25
J.P. Howell	1-3	5.10	8	8	0	0	42.1	52	25	24	14	33

TEXAS RANGERS

BATTING	G	AB	R	H	2B	3B	HR	RBI	TB	BB	SO	SB	OBP	SLG	BA
Michael Young	162	691	93	217	52	3	14	103	317	48	96	7	.356	.459	.314
Mark Teixeira	162	628	99	177	45	1	33	110	323	89	128	2	.371	.514	.282
Gary Matthews	147	620	102	194	44	6	19	79	307	58	99	10	.371	.495	.313
Hank Blalock	152	591	76	157	26	3	16	89	237	51	98	1	.325	.401	.266
Mark DeRosa	136	520	78	154	40	2	13	74	237	44	102	4	.357	.456	.296
Ian Kinsler	120	423	65	121	27	1	14	55	192	40	64	11	.347	.454	.286
Rod Baraias	97	344	49	88	20	0	11	41	141	17	51	0	.298	.410	.256
Kevin Mench	87	320	36	91	18	1	12	50	147	23	42	1	.338	.459	.284
Brad Wilkerson	95	320	56	71	15	2	15	44	135	37	116	3	.306	.422	.222
Gerald Laird	78	243	46	72	20	1	7	22	115	12	54	3	.332	.473	.296
Carlos Lee	59	236	42	76	19	1	9	35	124	20	26	7	.369	.525	.322
Nelson Cruz	41	140	15	29	3	0	6	22	50	7	32	1	.261	.385	.223
Jerry Hairston	63	88	17	18	3	1	0	6	23	9	20	2	.286	.261	.205
Jason Botts	20	50	8	11	4	0	1	6	18	9	18	0	.317	.360	.220

PITCHING	W–L	ERA	G	GS	CG	SV	INN	H	R	ER	BB	SO
Kevin Millwood	16-12	4.52	34	34	2	0	215.0	228	114	108	53	157
Vincente Padilla	15-10	4.50	33	33	0	0	200.0	206	108	100	70	156
John Koronka	7-7	5.69	23	23	0	0	125.0	145	80	79	47	61
Joaquin Benoit	1-1	4.86	56	0	0	2	79.2	68	49	43	38	85
Kameron Loe	3-6	5.86	15	15	1	0	78.1	105	54	51	22	34
Robinson Tejeda	5-5	4.28	14	14	0	0	73.2	83	40	35	32	40
Rick Bauer	3-1	3.55	58	1	0	2	71.0	73	31	28	25	35
John Rheinecker	4-6	5.86	21	13	0	0	70.2	104	46	46	19	28
Adam Eaton	7-4	5.12	13	13	0	0	65.0	78	38	37	24	43
Mike Wood	3-3	5.71	23	7	0	0	64.2	86	51	41	23	29
Akinori Otsuka	2-4	2.11	63	0	0	32	59.2	53	17	14	11	47
Ron Mahay	1-3	3.95	62	0	0	0	57.0	54	30	25	28	56
Francisco Cordero	7-4	4.81	49	0	0	6	48.2	49	27	26	16	54
C.J. Wilson	2-4	4.06	44	0	0	1	44.1	39	23	20	18	43
Scott Feldman	0-2	3.92	36	0	0	0	41.1	42	19	18	10	30
Wes Littleton	2-1	1.73	33	0	0	1	36.1	23	7	7	13	17

TORONTO BLUE JAYS

BATTING	G	AB	R	H	2B	3B	HR	RBI	TB	BB	SO	SB	OBP	SLG	BA
Vernon Wells	154	611	91	185	40	5	32	106	331	54	90	17	.357	.542	.303
Lyle Overbay	157	581	82	181	46	1	22	92	295	55	96	5	.372	.508	.312
Aaron Hill	155	546	70	159	28	3	6	50	211	42	66	5	.349	.386	.291
Troy Glaus	153	540	105	136	27	0	38	104	277	86	134	3	.355	.513	.252
Reed Johnson	134	461	86	147	34	2	12	49	221	33	81	8	.390	.479	.319
Alex Rios	128	450	68	136	33	6	17	82	232	35	89	15	.349	.516	.302
Frank Catalanotto	128	437	56	131	36	2	7	56	192	52	37	1	.376	.439	.300
Bengie Molina	117	433	44	123	20	1	19	57	202	19	47	1	.319	.467	.284
Shea Hillenbrand	81	296	40	89	15	1	12	39	142	14	40	1	.342	.480	.301
Gregg Zaun	99	290	39	79	19	0	12	40	134	41	42	0	.363	.462	.272
John McDonald	104	260	35	58	7	3	3	23	80	16	41	7	.271	.308	.223
Russ Adams	90	251	31	55	14	1	3	28	80	22	41	1	.282	.319	.219
Edgardo Alfonzo	30	87	5	11	2	0	0	5	13	7	4	0	.200	.149	.126
Adam Lind	18	60	8	22	8	0	2	8	36	5	12	0	.415	.600	.367

PITCHING	W–L	ERA	G	GS	CG	SV	INN	H	R	ER	BB	SO
Roy Halladay	16-5	3.19	32	32	4	0	220.0	208	82	78	34	132
Ted Lilly	15-13	4.31	32	32	0	0	181.2	179	98	87	81	160
A.J. Burnett	10-8	3.98	21	21	2	1	135.2	138	67	60	39	118
Casey Janssen	6-10	5.07	19	17	0	0	94.0	103	58	53	21	44
Gustavo Chacin	9-4	5.05	17	17	0	0	87.1	90	49	49	38	47
Shaun Marcum	3-4	5.06	21	14	0	0	78.1	87	44	44	38	65
Scott Downs	6-2	4.09	59	5	0	1	77.0	73	38	35	30	61
B.J. Ryan	2-2	1.37	65	0	0	38	72.1	42	12	11	20	86
Josh Towers	2-10	8.42	15	12	0	0	62.0	93	62	58	17	35
Brian Tallet	3-0	3.81	44	1	0	0	54.1	45	24	23	31	37
Justin Speier	2-0	2.98	58	0	0	0	51.1	47	18	17	21	55
Jason Frasor	3-2	4.32	51	0	0	0	50.0	47	24	24	17	51
Brandon League	1-2	2.53	33	0	0	1	42.2	34	17	12	9	29

WORLD SERIES ALL-TIME RESULTS

Year	Result	Year	Result
2006	St. Louis (N) 4, Detroit (A) 1	1953	New York (A) 4, Brooklyn (N) 2
2005	Chicago (A) 4, Houston (N) 0	1952	New York (A) 4, Brooklyn (N) 3
2004	Boston (A) 4, St. Louis (N) 0	1951	New York (A) 4, New York (N) 2
2003	Florida (N) 4, New York (A) 2	1950	New York (A) 4, Philadelphia (N) 0
2002	Anaheim (A) 4, San Francisco (N) 3	1949	New York (A) 4, Brooklyn (N) 1
2001	Arizona (N) 4, New York (A) 3	1948	Cleveland (A) 4, Boston (N) 2
2000	New York (A) 4, New York (N) 1	1947	New York (A) 4, Brooklyn (N) 3
1999	New York (A) 4, Atlanta (N) 0	1946	St. Louis (N) 4, Boston (A) 3
1998	New York (A) 4, San Diego (N) 0	1945	Detroit (A) 4, Chicago (N) 3
1997	Florida (N) 4, Cleveland (A) 3	1944	St. Louis (N) 4, St. Louis (A) 2
1996	New York (A) 4, Atlanta (N) 2	1943	New York (A) 4, St. Louis (N) 1
1995	Atlanta (N) 4, Cleveland (A) 2	1942	St. Louis (N) 4, New York (A) 1
1994	Series canceled due to labor dispute.	1941	New York (A) 4, Brooklyn (N) 1
1993	Toronto (A) 4, Philadelphia (N) 2	1940	Cincinnati (N) 4, Detroit (A) 3
1992	Toronto (A) 4, Atlanta (N) 2	1939	New York (A) 4, Cincinnati (N) 0
1991	Minnesota (A) 4, Atlanta (N) 3	1938	New York (A) 4, Chicago (N) 0
1990	Cincinnati (N) 4, Oakland (A) 0	1937	New York (A) 4, New York (N) 1
1989	Oakland (A) 4, San Francisco (N) 0	1936	New York (A) 4, New York (N) 2
1988	Los Angeles (N) 4, Oakland (A) 1	1935	Detroit (A) 4, Chicago (N) 2
1987	Minnesota (A) 4, St. Louis (N) 3	1934	St. Louis (N) 4, Detroit (A) 3
1986	New York (N) 4, Boston (A) 3	1933	New York (N) 4, Washington (A) 1
1985	Kansas City (A) 4, St. Louis (N) 3	1932	New York (A) 4, Chicago (N) 0
1984	Detroit (A) 4, San Diego (N) 1	1931	St. Louis (N) 4, Philadelphia (A) 3
1983	Baltimore (A) 4, Philadelphia (N) 1	1930	Philadelphia (A) 4, St. Louis (N) 2
1982	St. Louis (N) 4, Milwaukee (A) 3	1929	Philadelphia (A) 4, Chicago (N) 1
1981	Los Angeles (N) 4, New York (A) 2	1928	New York (A) 4, St. Louis (N) 0
1980	Philadelphia (N) 4, Kansas City (A) 2	1927	New York (A) 4, Pittsburgh (N) 0
1979	Pittsburgh (N) 4, Baltimore (A) 3	1926	St. Louis (N) 4, New York (A) 3
1978	New York (A) 4, Los Angeles (N) 2	1925	Pittsburgh (N) 4, Washington (A) 3
1977	New York (A) 4, Los Angeles (N) 2	1924	Washington (A) 4, New York (N) 3
1976	Cincinnati (N) 4, New York (A) 0	1923	New York (A) 4, New York (N) 2
1975	Cincinnati (N) 4, Boston (A) 3	1922	New York (N) 4, New York (A) 0; 1 tie
1974	Oakland (A) 4, Los Angeles (N) 1	1921	New York (N) 5, New York (A) 3
1973	Oakland (A) 4, New York (N) 3	1920	Cleveland (A) 5, Brooklyn (N) 2
1972	Oakland (A) 4, Cincinnati (N) 3	1919	Cincinnati (N) 5, Chicago (A) 3
1971	Pittsburgh (N) 4, Baltimore (A) 3	1918	Boston (A) 4, Chicago (N) 2
1970	Baltimore (A) 4, Cincinnati (N) 1	1917	Chicago (A) 4, New York (N) 2
1969	New York (N) 4, Baltimore (A) 1	1916	Boston (A) 4, Brooklyn (N) 1
1968	Detroit (A) 4, St. Louis (N) 3	1915	Boston (A) 4, Philadelphia (N) 1
1967	St. Louis (N) 4, Boston (A) 3	1914	Boston (N) 4, Philadelphia (A) 0
1966	Baltimore (A) 4, Los Angeles (N) 0	1913	Philadelphia (A) 4, New York (N) 1
1965	Los Angeles (N) 4, Minnesota (A) 3	1912	Boston (A) 4, New York (N) 3; 1 tie
1964	St. Louis (N) 4, New York (A) 3	1911	Philadelphia (A) 4, New York (N) 2
1963	Los Angeles (N) 4, New York (A) 0	1910	Philadelphia (A) 4, Chicago (N) 1
1962	New York (A) 4, San Francisco (N) 3	1909	Pittsburgh (N) 4, Detroit (A) 3
1961	New York (A) 4, Cincinnati (N) 1	1908	Chicago (N) 4, Detroit (A) 1
1960	Pittsburgh (N) 4, New York (A) 3	1907	Chicago (N) 4, Detroit (A) 0; 1 tie
1959	Los Angeles (N) 4, Chicago (A) 2	1906	Chicago (A) 4, Chicago (N) 2
1958	New York (A) 4, Milwaukee (N) 3	1905	New York (N) 4, Philadelphia (A) 1
1957	Milwaukee (N) 4, New York (A) 3	1904	No series
1956	New York (A) 4, Brooklyn (N) 3	1903	Boston (A) 5, Pittsburgh (N) 3
1955	Brooklyn (N) 4, New York (A) 3		
1954	New York (N) 4, Cleveland (A) 0	Note: A=American League; N=National League	

WORLD SERIES – MOST VALUABLE PLAYERS

2006	David Eckstein, StL	1980	Mike Schmidt, Phil
2005	Jermaine Dye, Chi (A)	1979	Willie Stargell, Pitt
2004	Manny Ramirez, Bos	1978	Bucky Dent, NY (A)
2003	Josh Beckett, Fla	1977	Reggie Jackson, NY (A)
2002	Troy Glaus, Ana	1976	Johnny Bench, Cin
2001	Randy Johnson, Ari; Curt Schilling, Ari	1975	Pete Rose, Cin
2000	Derek Jeter, NY (A)	1974	Rollie Fingers, Oak
1999	Mariano Rivera, NY (A)	1973	Reggie Jackson, Oak
1998	Scott Brosius, NY (A)	1972	Gene Tenace, Oak
1997	Livan Hernandez, Fla	1971	Roberto Clemente, Pitt
1996	John Wetteland, NY (A)	1970	Brooks Robinson, Bal
1995	Tom Glavine, Atl	1969	Donn Clendenon, NY (N)
1994	Series canceled due to labor dispute.	1968	Mickey Lolich, Det
1993	Paul Molitor, Tor	1967	Bob Gibson, StL
1992	Pat Borders, Tor	1966	Frank Robinson, Bal
1991	Jack Morris, Min	1965	Sandy Koufax, LA
1990	Jose Rijo, Cin	1964	Bob Gibson, StL
1989	Dave Stewart, Oak	1963	Sandy Koufax, LA
1988	Orel Hershiser, LA	1962	Ralph Terry, NY (A)
1987	Frank Viola, Min	1961	Whitey Ford, NY (A)
1986	Ray Knight, NY (N)	1960	Bobby Richardson, NY (A)
1985	Bret Saberhagen, KC	1959	Larry Sherry, LA
1984	Alan Trammell, Det	1958	Bob Turley, NY (A)
1983	Rick Dempsey, Bal	1957	Lew Burdette, Mil
1982	Darrell Porter, StL	1956	Don Larsen, NY (A)
1981	Ron Cey, LA; Steve Yeager, LA; Pedro Guerrero, LA	1955	Johnny Podres, Bklyn

LEAGUE CHAMPIONSHIP SERIES

	NATIONAL LEAGUE		AMERICAN LEAGUE
2006	St. Louis (C) 4, New York (E) 3	2006	Detroit (WC) 4, Oakland (W) 0
2005	Houston (WC) 4, St. Louis (C) 2	2005	Chicago (C) 4, Los Angeles (W) 1
2004	St. Louis (C) 4, Houston (WC) 3	2004	Boston (WC) 4, New York (E) 3
2003	Florida (WC) 4, Chicago (C) 3	2003	New York (E) 4, Boston (WC) 3
2002	San Francisco (WC) 4, St. Louis (C) 1	2002	Anaheim (WC) 4, Minnesota (C) 1
2001	Arizona (W) 4, Atlanta (E) 1	2001	New York (E) 4, Seattle (W) 1
2000	New York (WC) 4, St. Louis (C) 1	2000	New York (E) 4, Seattle (WC) 2
1999	Atlanta (E) 4, New York (WC) 2	1999	New York (E) 4, Boston (WC) 1
1998	San Diego (W) 4, Atlanta (E) 2	1998	New York (E) 4, Cleveland (C) 2
1997	Florida (WC) 4, Atlanta (E) 2	1997	Cleveland (C) 4, Baltimore (E) 2
1996	Atlanta (E) 4, St. Louis (C) 3	1996	New York (E) 4, Baltimore (WC) 1
1995	Atlanta (E) 4, Cincinnati (C) 0	1995	Cleveland (C) 4, Seattle (W) 2
1994	Playoffs canceled due to labor dispute.	1994	Playoffs canceled due to labor dispute.
1993	Philadelphia (E) 4, Atlanta (W) 2	1993	Toronto (E) 4, Chicago (W) 2
1992	Atlanta (W) 4, Pittsburgh (E) 3	1992	Toronto (E) 4, Oakland (W) 2
1991	Atlanta (W) 4, Pittsburgh (E) 3	1991	Minnesota (W) 4, Toronto (E) 1
1990	Cincinnati (W) 4, Pittsburgh (E) 2	1990	Oakland (W) 4, Boston (E) 0
1989	San Francisco (W) 4, Chicago (E) 1	1989	Oakland (W) 4, Toronto (E) 1
1988	Los Angeles (W) 4, New York (E) 3	1988	Oakland (W) 4, Boston (E) 0
1987	St. Louis (E) 4, San Francisco (W) 3	1987	Minnesota (W) 4, Detroit (E) 1
1986	New York (E) 4, Houston (W) 2	1986	Boston (E) 4, California (W) 3
1985	St. Louis (E) 4, Los Angeles (W) 2	1985	Kansas City (W) 4, Toronto (E) 3
1984	San Diego (W) 3, Chicago (E) 2	1984	Detroit (E) 3, Kansas City (W) 0
1983	Philadelphia (E) 3, Los Angeles (W) 1	1983	Baltimore (E) 3, Chicago (W) 1
1982	St. Louis (E) 3, Atlanta (W) 0	1982	Milwaukee (E) 3, California (W) 2
1981	Los Angeles (W) 3, Montreal (E) 2	1981	New York (E) 3, Oakland (W) 0
1980	Philadelphia (E) 3, Houston (W) 2	1980	Kansas City (W) 3, New York (E) 0
1979	Pittsburgh (E) 3, Cincinnati (W) 0	1979	Baltimore (E) 3, California (W) 1
1978	Los Angeles (W) 3, Philadelphia (E) 1	1978	New York (E) 3, Kansas City (W) 1
1977	Los Angeles (W) 3, Philadelphia (E) 1	1977	New York (E) 3, Kansas City (W) 2
1976	Cincinnati (W) 3, Philadelphia (E) 0	1976	New York (E) 3, Kansas City (W) 2
1975	Cincinnati (W) 3, Pittsburgh (E) 0	1975	Boston (E) 3, Oakland (W) 0
1974	Los Angeles (W) 3, Pittsburgh (E) 1	1974	Oakland (W) 3, Baltimore (E) 1
1973	New York (E) 3, Cincinnati (W) 2	1973	Oakland (W) 3, Baltimore (E) 2
1972	Cincinnati (W) 3, Pittsburgh (E) 2	1972	Oakland (W) 3, Detroit (E) 2
1971	Pittsburgh (E) 3, San Francisco (W) 1	1971	Baltimore (E) 3, Oakland (W) 0
1970	Cincinnati (W) 3, Pittsburgh (E) 0	1970	Baltimore (E) 3, Minnesota (W) 0
1969	New York (E) 3, Atlanta (W) 0	1969	Baltimore (E) 3, Minnesota (W) 0

Note: WC=wild-card team; W=Western Division; E=Eastern Division; C=Central Division

NLCS MOST VALUABLE PLAYER

2006	Jeff Suppan, StL	1996	Javier Lopez, Atl	1986	Mike Scott, Hou
2005	Roy Oswalt, Hou	1995	Mike Devereaux, Atl	1985	Ozzie Smith, StL
2004	Albert Pujols, StL	1994	Playoffs canceled	1984	Steve Garvey, SD
2003	Ivan Rodriguez, Fla	1993	Curt Schilling, Phil	1983	Gary Matthews, Phil
2002	Benito Santiago, SF	1992	John Smoltz, Atl	1982	Darrell Porter, StL
2001	Craig Counsell, Ari	1991	Steve Avery, Atl	1981	Burt Hooton, LA
2000	Mike Hampton, NY	1990	R. Myers/R. Dibble, Cin	1980	Manny Trillo, Phil
1999	Eddie Perez, Atl	1989	Will Clark, SF	1979	Willie Stargell, Pitt
1998	Sterling Hitchcock, SD	1988	Orel Hershiser, LA	1978	Steve Garvey, LA
1997	Livan Hernandez, Fla	1987	Jeffrey Leonard, SF	1977	Dusty Baker, LA

ALCS MOST VALUABLE PLAYER

2006	Placido Polanco, Det	1997	Marquis Grissom, Cle	1988	Dennis Eckersley, Oak
2005	Paul Konerko, Chi	1996	Bernie Williams, NY	1987	Gary Gaetti, Min
2004	David Ortiz, Bos	1995	Orel Hershiser, Cle	1986	Marty Barrett, Bos
2003	Mariano Rivera, NY	1994	Playoffs canceled	1985	George Brett, KC
2002	Adam Kennedy, Ana	1993	Dave Stewart, Tor	1984	Kirk Gibson, Det
2001	Andy Pettitte, NY	1992	Roberto Alomar, Tor	1983	Mike Boddicker, Bal
2000	David Justice, NY	1991	Kirby Puckett, Min	1982	Fred Lynn, Cal
1999	Orlando Hernandez, NY	1990	Dave Stewart, Oak	1981	Graig Nettles, NY
1998	David Wells, NY	1989	Rickey Henderson, Oak	1980	Frank White, KC

ALL-STAR GAME

DATE	WINNER	SCORE	SITE	DATE	WINNER	SCORE	SITE
7-11-06	American	3–2	PNC Park, Pitt	7-11-67	National	2–1	Anaheim Stadium, Cal
7-12-05	American	7–5	Comerica Park, Det	7-12-66	National	2–1	Busch Stadium, StL
7-13-04	American	9–4	Minute Maid Park, Hou	7-13-65	National	6–5	Metropolitan Stadium, Min
7-15-03	American	7–6	U.S. Cellular Field, Chi				
7-9-02	Tie (11 inn)	7–7	Miller Park, Mil	7-7-64	National	7–4	Shea Stadium, NY
7-10-01	American	4–1	Safeco Field, Sea	7-9-63	National	5–3	Municipal Stadium, Cle
7-11-00	American	6–3	Turner Field, Atl	7-30-62	American	9–4	Wrigley Field, Chi
7-13-99	American	4–1	Fenway Park, Bos	7-10-62	National	3–1	D.C. Stadium, Wash
7-7-98	American	13–8	Coors Field, Col	7-31-61	Tie*	1–1	Fenway Park, Bos
7-8-97	American	3–1	Jacobs Field, Cle	7-11-61	National	5–4	Candlestick Park, SF
7-9-96	National	6–0	Veterans Stadium, Phil	7-13-60	National	6–0	Yankee Stadium, NY
7-11-95	National	3–2	The Ballpark in Arlington, Tex	7-11-60	National	5–3	Municipal Stadium, KC
				8-3-59	American	5–3	Memorial Coliseum, LA
7-12-94	National	8–7	Three Rivers Stadium, Pitt	7-7-59	National	5–4	Forbes Field, Pitt
7-13-93	American	9–3	Camden Yards, Bal	7-8-58	American	4–3	Memorial Stadium, Bal
7-14-92	American	13–6	Jack Murphy Stadium, SD	7-9-57	American	6–5	Sportsman's Park, StL
7-9-91	American	4–2	SkyDome, Tor	7-10-56	National	7–3	Griffith Stadium, Wash
7-10-90	American	2–0	Wrigley Field, Chi	7-12-55	National	6–5	County Stadium, Mil
7-11-89	American	5–3	Anaheim Stadium, Cal	7-13-54	American	11–9	Municipal Stadium, Cle
7-12-88	American	2–1	Riverfront Stadium, Cin	7-14-53	National	5–1	Crosley Field, Cin
7-14-87	National	2–0	Oakland Coliseum, Oak	7-8-52	National	3–2	Shibe Park, Phil
7-15-86	American	3–2	Astrodome, Hou	7-10-51	National	8–3	Briggs Stadium, Det
7-16-85	National	6–1	Metrodome, Min	7-11-50	National	4–3	Comiskey Park, Chi
7-10-84	National	3–1	Candlestick Park, SF	7-12-49	American	11–7	Ebbets Field, Bklyn
7-6-83	American	13–3	Comiskey Park, Chi	7-13-48	American	5–2	Sportsman's Park, StL
7-13-82	National	4–1	Olympic Stadium, Mon	7-8-47	American	2–1	Wrigley Field, Chi
8-9-81	National	5–4	Municipal Stadium, Cle	7-9-46	American	12–0	Fenway Park, Bos
7-8-80	National	4–2	Dodger Stadium, LA	1945	No game due to wartime travel restrictions.		
7-17-79	National	7–6	Kingdome, Sea	7-11-44	National	7–1	Forbes Field, Pitt
7-11-78	National	7–3	Jack Murphy Stadium, SD	7-13-43	American	5–3	Shibe Park, Phil
7-19-77	National	7–5	Yankee Stadium, NY	7-6-42	American	3–1	Polo Grounds, NY
7-13-76	National	7–1	Veterans Stadium, Phil	7-8-41	American	7–5	Briggs Stadium, Det
7-15-75	National	6–3	County Stadium, Mil	7-10-40	National	4–0	Sportsman's Park, StL
7-23-74	National	7–2	Three Rivers Stadium, Pitt	7-11-39	American	3–1	Yankee Stadium, NY
7-24-73	National	7–1	Royals Stadium, KC	7-6-38	National	4–1	Crosley Field, Cin
7-25-72	National	4–3	Atlanta Stadium, Atl	7-7-37	American	8–3	Griffith Stadium, Wash
7-13-71	American	6–4	Tiger Stadium, Det	7-7-36	National	4–3	Braves Field, Bos
7-14-70	National	5–4	Riverfront Stadium, Cin	7-8-35	American	4–1	Municipal Stadium, Cle
7-23-69	National	9–3	R.F.K. Memorial Stadium, Wash	7-10-34	American	9–7	Polo Grounds, NY
				7-6-33	American	4–2	Comiskey Park, Chi
7-9-68	National	1–0	Astrodome, Hou				

*Game called because of rain after nine innings.

ALL-STAR GAME – MOST VALUABLE PLAYERS

Year	Name, Team	Lg	Year	Name, Team	Lg	Year	Name, Team	Lg
2006	Michael Young, Tex	AL	1988	Terry Steinbach, Oak	AL	1971	Frank Robinson, Bal	AL
2005	Miguel Tejada, Bal	AL	1987	Tim Raines, Mon	NL	1970	Carl Yastrzemski, Bos	AL
2004	Alfonso Soriano, Tex	AL	1986	Roger Clemens, Bos	AL	1969	Willie McCovey, SF	NL
2003	Garret Anderson, Ana	AL	1985	LaMarr Hoyt, SD	NL	1968	Willie Mays, SF	NL
2002	None selected		1984	Gary Carter, Mon	NL	1967	Tony Perez, Cin	NL
2001	Cal Ripken, Jr., Bal	AL	1983	Fred Lynn, Cal	AL	1966	Brooks Robinson, Bal	AL
2000	Derek Jeter, NY	AL	1982	Dave Concepcion, Cin	NL	1965	Juan Marichal, SF	NL
1999	Pedro Martinez, Bos	AL	1981	Gary Carter, Mon	NL	1964	Johnny Callison, Phil	NL
1998	Roberto Alomar, Bal	AL	1980	Ken Griffey, Cin	NL	1963	Willie Mays, SF	NL
1997	Sandy Alomar, Cle	AL	1979	Dave Parker, Pitt	NL	1962	Maury Wills, LA	NL
1996	Mike Piazza, LA	NL	1978	Steve Garvey, LA	NL		Leon Wagner, LA	AL
1995	Jeff Conine, Fla	NL	1977	Don Sutton, LA	NL			
1994	Fred McGriff, Atl	NL	1976	George Foster, Cin	NL			
1993	Kirby Puckett, Min	AL	1975	Bill Madlock, Chi	NL			
1992	Ken Griffey, Jr., Sea	AL		Jon Matlack, NY	NL			
1991	Cal Ripken, Jr., Bal	AL	1974	Steve Garvey, LA	NL			
1990	Julio Franco, Tex	AL	1973	Bobby Bonds, SF	NL			
1989	Bo Jackson, KC	AL	1972	Joe Morgan, Cin	NL			

Michael Young, Rangers

DARREN CARROLL

REGULAR SEASON – MOST VALUABLE PLAYERS

NATIONAL LEAGUE

Ryan Howard won the 2006 NL MVP award.

CHUCK SOLOMON

YEAR	NAME AND TEAM	POSITION
2006	Ryan Howard, Phil	First Base
2005	Albert Pujols, StL	First Base
2004	Barry Bonds, SF	Outfield
2003	Barry Bonds, SF	Outfield
2002	Barry Bonds, SF	Outfield
2001	Barry Bonds, SF	Outfield
2000	Jeff Kent, SF	Second Base
1999	Chipper Jones, Atl	Third Base
1998	Sammy Sosa, Chi	Outfield
1997	Larry Walker, Col	Outfield
1996	Ken Caminiti, SD	Third Base
1995	Barry Larkin, Cin	Shortstop
1994	Jeff Bagwell, Hou	First Base
1993	Barry Bonds, SF	Outfield
1992	Barry Bonds, Pitt	Outfield
1991	Terry Pendleton, Atl	Third Base
1990	Barry Bonds, Pitt	Outfield
1989	Kevin Mitchell, SF	Outfield
1988	Kirk Gibson, LA	Outfield
1987	Andre Dawson, Chi	Outfield
1986	Mike Schmidt, Phil	Third Base
1985	Willie McGee, StL	Outfield
1984	Ryne Sandberg, Chi	Second Base
1983	Dale Murphy, Atl	Outfield
1982	Dale Murphy, Atl	Outfield
1981	Mike Schmidt, Phil	Third Base
1980	Mike Schmidt, Phil	Third Base
1979	Keith Hernandez, StL	First Base
	Willie Stargell, Pitt	First Base
1978	Dave Parker, Pitt	Outfield
1977	George Foster, Cin	Outfield
1976	Joe Morgan, Cin	Second Base
1975	Joe Morgan, Cin	Second Base
1974	Steve Garvey, LA	First Base
1973	Pete Rose, Cin	Outfield
1972	Johnny Bench, Cin	Catcher
1971	Joe Torre, StL	Third Base
1970	Johnny Bench, Cin	Catcher
1969	Willie McCovey, SF	First Base
1968	Bob Gibson, StL	Pitcher
1967	Orlando Cepeda, StL	First Base
1966	Roberto Clemente, Pitt	Outfield
1965	Willie Mays, SF	Outfield
1964	Ken Boyer, StL	Third Base
1963	Sandy Koufax, LA	Pitcher

YEAR	NAME AND TEAM	POSITION
1962	Maury Wills, LA	Shortstop
1961	Frank Robinson, Cin	Outfield
1960	Dick Groat, Pitt	Shortstop
1959	Ernie Banks, Chi	Shortstop
1958	Ernie Banks, Chi	Shortstop
1957	Hank Aaron, Mil	Outfield
1956	Don Newcombe, Bklyn	Pitcher
1955	Roy Campanella, Bklyn	Catcher
1954	Willie Mays, NY	Outfield
1953	Roy Campanella, Bklyn	Catcher
1952	Hank Sauer, Chi	Outfield
1951	Roy Campanella, Bklyn	Catcher
1950	Jim Konstanty, Phil	Pitcher
1949	Jackie Robinson, Bklyn	Second Base
1948	Stan Musial, StL	Outfield
1947	Bob Elliott, Bos	Third Base
1946	Stan Musial, StL	First Base, Outfield
1945	Phil Cavarretta, Chi	First Base
1944	Marty Marion, StL	Shortstop

BASEBALL

REGULAR SEASON – MOST VALUABLE PLAYERS (cont.)

NATIONAL LEAGUE

YEAR	NAME AND TEAM	POSITION
1943	Stan Musial, StL	Outfield
1942	Mort Cooper, StL	Pitcher
1941	Dolph Camilli, Bklyn	First Base
1940	Frank McCormick, Cin	First Base
1939	Bucky Walters, Cin	Pitcher
1938	Ernie Lombardi, Cin	Catcher
1937	Joe Medwick, StL	Outfield
1936	Carl Hubbell, NY	Pitcher
1935	Gabby Hartnett, Chi	Catcher
1934	Dizzy Dean, StL	Pitcher
1933	Carl Hubbell, NY	Pitcher
1932	Chuck Klein, Phil	Outfield
1931	Frankie Frisch, StL	Second Base
1930	No selection	
1929	Rogers Hornsby, Chi	Second Base
1928	Jim Bottomley, StL	First Base
1927	Paul Waner, Pitt	Outfield
1926	Bob O'Farrell, StL	Catcher
1925	Rogers Hornsby, StL	Second Base, Manager
1924	Dazzy Vance, Bklyn	Pitcher
1915-23	No selections	
1914	Johnny Evers, Bos	Second Base
1913	Jake Daubert, Bklyn	First Base
1912	Larry Doyle, NY	Second Base
1911	Wildfire Schulte, Chi	Outfield

AMERICAN LEAGUE

YEAR	NAME AND TEAM	POSITION
2006	Justin Morneau, Min	First Base
2005	Alex Rodriguez, NY	Third Base
2004	Vladimir Guerrero, Ana	Outfield
2003	Alex Rodriguez, Tex	Shortstop
2002	Miguel Tejada, Oak	Shortstop
2001	Ichiro Suzuki, Sea	Outfield
2000	Jason Giambi, Oak	First Base
1999	Ivan Rodriguez, Tex	Catcher
1998	Juan Gonzalez, Tex	Outfield
1997	Ken Griffey, Jr., Sea	Outfield
1996	Juan Gonzalez, Tex	Outfield
1995	Mo Vaughn, Bos	First Base
1994	Frank Thomas, Chi	First Base
1993	Frank Thomas, Chi	First Base
1992	Dennis Eckersley, Oak	Pitcher
1991	Cal Ripken, Jr., Bal	Shortstop
1990	Rickey Henderson, Oak	Outfield
1989	Robin Yount, Mil	Outfield
1988	Jose Canseco, Oak	Outfield
1987	George Bell, Tor	Outfield
1986	Roger Clemens, Bos	Pitcher
1985	Don Mattingly, NY	First Base
1984	Willie Hernandez, Det	Pitcher
1983	Cal Ripken, Jr., Bal	Shortstop
1982	Robin Yount, Mil	Shortstop
1981	Rollie Fingers, Mil	Pitcher
1980	George Brett, KC	Third Base
1979	Don Baylor, Cal	Outfield, DH
1978	Jim Rice, Bos	Outfield, DH
1977	Rod Carew, Min	First Base
1976	Thurman Munson, NY	Catcher
1975	Fred Lynn, Bos	Outfield
1974	Jeff Burroughs, Tex	Outfield
1973	Reggie Jackson, Oak	Outfield
1972	Dick Allen, Chi	First Base
1971	Vida Blue, Oak	Pitcher
1970	Boog Powell, Bal	First Base
1969	Harmon Killebrew, Min	Third Base, First Base

AMERICAN LEAGUE

YEAR	NAME AND TEAM	POSITION
1968	Denny McLain, Det	Pitcher
1967	Carl Yastrzemski, Bos	Outfield
1966	Frank Robinson, Bal	Outfield
1965	Zoilo Versalles, Min	Shortstop
1964	Brooks Robinson, Bal	Third Base
1963	Elston Howard, NY	Catcher
1962	Mickey Mantle, NY	Outfield
1961	Roger Maris, NY	Outfield
1960	Roger Maris, NY	Outfield
1959	Nellie Fox, Chi	Second Base
1958	Jackie Jensen, Bos	Outfield
1957	Mickey Mantle, NY	Outfield
1956	Mickey Mantle, NY	Outfield
1955	Yogi Berra, NY	Catcher
1954	Yogi Berra, NY	Catcher
1953	Al Rosen, Cle	Third Base
1952	Bobby Shantz, Phil	Pitcher
1951	Yogi Berra, NY	Catcher
1950	Phil Rizzuto, NY	Shortstop
1949	Ted Williams, Bos	Outfield
1948	Lou Boudreau, Cle	Shortstop
1947	Joe DiMaggio, NY	Outfield
1946	Ted Williams, Bos	Outfield
1945	Hal Newhouser, Det	Pitcher
1944	Hal Newhouser, Det	Pitcher
1943	Spud Chandler, NY	Pitcher
1942	Joe Gordon, NY	Second Base
1941	Joe DiMaggio, NY	Outfield
1940	Hank Greenberg, Det	Outfield
1939	Joe DiMaggio, NY	Outfield
1938	Jimmie Foxx, Bos	First Base
1937	Charlie Gehringer, Det	Second Base
1936	Lou Gehrig, NY	First Base
1935	Hank Greenberg, Det	First Base
1934	Mickey Cochrane, Det	Catcher
1933	Jimmie Foxx, Phil	First Base
1932	Jimmie Foxx, Phil	First Base
1931	Lefty Grove, Phil	Pitcher
1930	No selection	
1929	No selection	
1928	Mickey Cochrane, Phil	Catcher
1927	Lou Gehrig, NY	First Base
1926	George Burns, Cle	First Base
1925	Roger Peckinpaugh, Wash	Shortstop
1924	Walter Johnson, Wash	Pitcher
1923	Babe Ruth, NY	Outfield
1922	George Sisler, StL	First Base
1915–21	No selections	
1914	Eddie Collins, Phil	Second Base
1913	Walter Johnson, Wash	Pitcher
1912	Tris Speaker, Bos	Outfield
1911	Ty Cobb, Det	Outfield

FAST FACT

In 2006, players from the Minnesota Twins won the AL batting title (Joe Mauer), the AL Cy Young award (Johan Santana), and the AL MVP award (Justin Morneau). The last team to achieve this was the 1962 Los Angeles Dodgers with NL batting champ Tommy Davis, NL Cy Young winner Don Drysdale, and NL MVP Maury Wills.

REGULAR SEASON – ROOKIES OF THE YEAR

NATIONAL LEAGUE		AMERICAN LEAGUE	
2006	Hanley Ramirez, Fla (SS)	2006	Justin Verlander, Det (P)
2005	Ryan Howard, Phi (1B)	2005	Huston Street, Oak (P)
2004	Jason Bay, Pitt (OF)	2004	Bobby Crosby, Oak (SS)
2003	Dontrelle Willis, Fla (P)	2003	Angel Berroa, KC (SS)
2002	Jason Jennings, Col (P)	2002	Eric Hinske, Tor (3B)
2001	Albert Pujols, StL (3B)	2001	Ichiro Suzuki, Sea (OF)
2000	Rafael Furcal, Atl (SS)	2000	Kazuhiro Sasaki, Sea (P)
1999	Scott Williamson, Cin (P)	1999	Carlos Beltran, KC (OF)
1998	Kerry Wood, Chi (P)	1998	Ben Grieve, Oak (OF)
1997	Scott Rolen, Phil (3B)	1997	Nomar Garciaparra, Bos (SS)
1996	Todd Hollandsworth, LA (OF)	1996	Derek Jeter, NY (SS)
1995	Hideo Nomo, LA (P)	1995	Marty Cordova, Min (OF)
1994	Raul Mondesi, LA (OF)	1994	Bob Hamelin, KC (DH)
1993	Mike Piazza, LA (C)	1993	Tim Salmon, Cal (OF)
1992	Eric Karros, LA (1B)	1992	Pat Listach, Mil (SS)
1991	Jeff Bagwell, Hou (3B)	1991	Chuck Knoblauch, Min (2B)
1990	David Justice, Atl (OF)	1990	Sandy Alomar, Jr., Cle (C)
1989	Jerome Walton, Chi (OF)	1989	Gregg Olson, Bal (P)
1988	Chris Sabo, Cin (3B)	1988	Walt Weiss, Oak (SS)
1987	Benito Santiago, SD (C)	1987	Mark McGwire, Oak (1B)
1986	Todd Worrell, StL (P)	1986	Jose Canseco, Oak (OF)
1985	Vince Coleman, StL (OF)	1985	Ozzie Guillen, Chi (SS)
1984	Dwight Gooden, NY (P)	1984	Alvin Davis, Sea (1B)
1983	Darryl Strawberry, NY (OF)	1983	Ron Kittle, Chi (OF)
1982	Steve Sax, LA (2B)	1982	Cal Ripken, Jr., Bal (SS)
1981	Fernando Valenzuela, LA (P)	1981	Dave Righetti, NY (P)
1980	Steve Howe, LA (P)	1980	Joe Charboneau, Cle (OF)
1979	Rick Sutcliffe, LA (P)	1979	Alfredo Griffin, Tor (SS)
1978	Bob Horner, Atl (3B)		John Castino, Min (3B)
1977	Andre Dawson, Mon (OF)	1978	Lou Whitaker, Det (2B)
1976	Pat Zachry, Cin (P)	1977	Eddie Murray, Bal (DH)
	Butch Metzger, SD (P)	1976	Mark Fidrych, Det (P)
1975	John Montefusco, SF (P)	1975	Fred Lynn, Bos (OF)
1974	Bake McBride, StL (OF)	1974	Mike Hargrove, Tex (1B)
1973	Gary Matthews, SF (OF)	1973	Al Bumbry, Bal (OF)
1972	Jon Matlack, NY (P)	1972	Carlton Fisk, Bos (C)
1971	Earl Williams, Atl (C)	1971	Chris Chambliss, Cle (1B)
1970	Carl Morton, Mon (P)	1970	Thurman Munson, NY (C)
1969	Ted Sizemore, LA (2B)	1969	Lou Piniella, KC (OF)
1968	Johnny Bench, Cin (C)	1968	Stan Bahnsen, NY (P)
1967	Tom Seaver, NY (P)	1967	Rod Carew, Min (2B)
1966	Tommy Helms, Cin (2B)	1966	Tommie Agee, Chi (OF)
1965	Jim Lefebvre, LA (2B)	1965	Curt Blefary, Bal (OF)
1964	Dick Allen, Phil (3B)	1964	Tony Oliva, Min (OF)
1963	Pete Rose, Cin (2B)	1963	Gary Peters, Chi (P)
1962	Ken Hubbs, Chi (2B)	1962	Tom Tresh, NY (SS)
1961	Billy Williams, Chi (OF)	1961	Don Schwall, Bos (P)
1960	Frank Howard, LA (OF)	1960	Ron Hansen, Bal (SS)
1959	Willie McCovey, SF (1B)	1959	Bob Allison, Wash (OF)
1958	Orlando Cepeda, SF (1B)	1958	Albie Pearson, Wash (OF)
1957	Jack Sanford, Phil (P)	1957	Tony Kubek, NY (OF, SS)
1956	Frank Robinson, Cin (OF)	1956	Luis Aparicio, Chi (SS)
1955	Bill Virdon, StL (OF)	1955	Herb Score, Cle (P)
1954	Wally Moon, StL (OF)	1954	Bob Grim, NY (P)
1953	Junior Gilliam, Bklyn (2B)	1953	Harvey Kuenn, Det (SS)
1952	Joe Black, Bklyn (P)	1952	Harry Byrd, Phil (P)
1951	Willie Mays, NY (OF)	1951	Gil McDougald, NY (3B)
1950	Sam Jethroe, Bos (OF)	1950	Walt Dropo, Bos (1B)
1949	Don Newcombe, Bklyn (P)	1949	Roy Sievers, StL (OF)
1948*	Alvin Dark, Bos (SS)		
1947*	Jackie Robinson, Bklyn (1B)		

*One selection for both leagues

**Brandon Webb,
Diamondbacks**

REGULAR SEASON –
CY YOUNG AWARD WINNERS

*Johan Santana
of the Twins
led the AL in
wins, ERA and
strikeouts.*

(LEFT) CHUCK SOLOMON; JOHN BIEVER (SANTANA)

NATIONAL LEAGUE

YEAR	PITCHER	W–L	SV	ERA
2006	Brandon Webb, Ari	16–8	0	3.10
2005	Chris Carpenter, StL	21–5	0	2.83
2004	Roger Clemens, Hou	18–4	0	2.98
2003	Eric Gagne, LA	2–3	55	1.20
2002	Randy Johnson, Ari	24–5	0	2.32
2001	Randy Johnson, Ari	21–6	0	2.49
2000	Randy Johnson, Ari	19–7	0	2.64
1999	Randy Johnson, Ari	17–9	0	2.48
1998	Tom Glavine, Atl	20–6	0	2.47
1997	Pedro Martinez, Mon	17–8	0	1.90
1996	John Smoltz, Atl	24–8	0	2.94
1995	Greg Maddux, Atl	19–2	0	1.63
1994	Greg Maddux, Atl	16–6	0	1.56
1993	Greg Maddux, Atl	20–10	0	2.36
1992	Greg Maddux, Chi	20–11	0	2.18
1991	Tom Glavine, Atl	20–11	0	2.55
1990	Doug Drabek, Pitt	22–6	0	2.76
1989	Mark Davis, SD	4–3	44	1.85
1988	Orel Hershiser, LA	23–8	1	2.26
1987	Steve Bedrosian, Phil	5–3	40	2.83
1986	Mike Scott, Hou	18–10	0	2.22
1985	Dwight Gooden, NY	24–4	0	1.53
1984†	Rick Sutcliffe, Chi	16–1	0	2.69
1983	John Denny, Phil	19–6	0	2.37
1982	Steve Carlton, Phil	23–11	0	3.10
1981	Fernando Valenzuela, LA	13–7	0	2.48
1980	Steve Carlton, Phil	24–9	0	2.34
1979	Bruce Sutter, Chi	6–6	37	2.23
1978	Gaylord Perry, SD	21–6	0	2.72
1977	Steve Carlton, Phil	23–10	0	2.64
1976	Randy Jones, SD	22–14	0	2.74
1975	Tom Seaver, NY	22–9	0	2.38
1974	Mike Marshall, LA	15–12	21	2.42
1973	Tom Seaver, NY	19–10	0	2.08
1972	Steve Carlton, Phil	27–10	0	1.97
1971	Ferguson Jenkins, Chi	24–13	0	2.77
1970	Bob Gibson, StL	23–7	0	3.12
1969	Tom Seaver, NY	25–7	0	2.21
1968*	Bob Gibson, StL	22–9	0	1.12
1967	Mike McCormick, SF	22–10	0	2.85
1966	Sandy Koufax, LA (NL)	27–9	0	1.73
1965	Sandy Koufax, LA (NL)	26–8	2	2.04
1964	Dean Chance, LA (AL)	20–9	4	1.65
1963*	Sandy Koufax, LA (NL)	25–5	0	1.88
1962	Don Drysdale, LA (NL)	25–9	1	2.83
1961	Whitey Ford, NY (AL)	25–4	0	3.21
1960	Vernon Law, Pitt (NL)	20–9	0	3.08
1959	Early Wynn, Chi (AL)	22–10	0	3.17
1958	Bob Turley, NY (AL)	21–7	1	2.97
1957	Warren Spahn, Mil (NL)	21–11	3	2.69
1956*	Don Newcombe, Bklyn (NL)	27–7	0	3.06

* Won the MVP and Cy Young awards in the same season.
†NL games only. Sutcliffe pitched 15 games with Cleveland before being traded to the Cubs.
Note: One award was presented for both leagues from 1956-1966.

AMERICAN LEAGUE

YEAR	PITCHER	W–L	SV	ERA
2006	Johan Santana, Min	19–6	0	2.77
2005	Bartolo Colon, LA	21–8	0	3.48
2004	Johan Santana, Min	20–6	0	2.61
2003	Roy Halladay, Tor	22–7	0	3.25
2002	Barry Zito, Oak	23–5	0	2.75
2001	Roger Clemens, NY	20–3	0	3.51
2000	Pedro Martinez, Bos	18–6	0	1.74
1999	Pedro Martinez, Bos	23–4	0	1.55
1998	Roger Clemens, Tor	20–6	0	2.65
1997	Roger Clemens, Tor	21–7	0	2.05
1996	Pat Hentgen, Tor	20–10	0	3.22
1995	Randy Johnson, Sea	18–2	0	2.48
1994	David Cone, KC	16–5	0	2.94
1993	Jack McDowell, Chi	22–10	0	3.37
1992*	Dennis Eckersley, Oak	7–1	51	1.91
1991	Roger Clemens, Bos	18–10	0	2.62
1990	Bob Welch, Oak	27–6	0	2.95
1989	Bret Saberhagen, KC	23–6	0	2.16
1988	Frank Viola, Min	24–7	0	2.64
1987	Roger Clemens, Bos	20–9	0	2.97
1986*	Roger Clemens, Bos	24–4	0	2.48
1985	Bret Saberhagen, KC	20–6	0	2.87
1984*	Willie Hernandez, Det	9–3	32	1.92
1983	LaMarr Hoyt, Chi	24–10	0	3.66
1982	Pete Vuckovich, Mil	18–6	0	3.34
1981*	Rollie Fingers, Mil	6–3	28	1.04
1980	Steve Stone, Bal	25–7	0	3.23
1979	Mike Flanagan, Bal	23–9	0	3.08
1978	Ron Guidry, NY	25–3	0	1.74
1977	Sparky Lyle, NY	13–5	26	2.17
1976	Jim Palmer, Bal	22–13	0	2.51
1975	Jim Palmer, Bal	23–11	1	2.09
1974	Catfish Hunter, Oak	25–12	0	2.49
1973	Jim Palmer, Bal	22–9	1	2.40
1972	Gaylord Perry, Cle	24–16	1	1.92
1971*	Vida Blue, Oak	24–8	0	1.82
1970	Jim Perry, Min	24–12	0	3.03
1969	Denny McLain, Det	24–9	0	2.80
	(tie) Mike Cuellar, Bal	23–11	0	2.38
1968*	Denny McLain, Det	31–6	0	1.96
1967	Jim Lonborg, Bos	22–9	0	3.16

REGULAR SEASON – CAREER INDIVIDUAL BATTING

GAMES

Pete Rose	3,562
Carl Yastrzemski	3,308
Hank Aaron	3,298
Rickey Henderson	3,081
Ty Cobb	3,035
Eddie Murray	3,026
Stan Musial	3,026
Cal Ripken, Jr.	3,001
Willie Mays	2,992
Dave Winfield	2,973
Rusty Staub	2,951
Brooks Robinson	2,896
*Barry Bonds	2,860
Robin Yount	2,856
Al Kaline	2,834
Rafael Palmeiro	2,831
Harold Baines	2,830
Eddie Collins	2,826
Reggie Jackson	2,820
Frank Robinson	2,808
Honus Wagner	2,792

AT-BATS

Pete Rose	14,053
Hank Aaron	12,364
Carl Yastrzemski	11,988
Cal Ripken, Jr.	11,551
Ty Cobb	11,429
Eddie Murray	11,336
Robin Yount	11,008
Dave Winfield	11,003
Stan Musial	10,972
Rickey Henderson	10,961
Willie Mays	10,881
Paul Molitor	10,835
Brooks Robinson	10,654
Rafael Palmeiro	10,472
Honus Wagner	10,430
*Craig Biggio	10,359
George Brett	10,349
Lou Brock	10,332
Cap Anson	10,278
Luis Aparicio	10,230
Tris Speaker	10,195

HOME RUNS

Hank Aaron	755
*Barry Bonds	734
Babe Ruth	714
Willie Mays	660
Sammy Sosa	588
Frank Robinson	586
Mark McGwire	583
Harmon Killebrew	573
Rafael Palmeiro	569
*Ken Griffey, Jr.	563
Reggie Jackson	563
Mike Schmidt	548
Mickey Mantle	536
Jimmie Foxx	534
Willie McCovey	521
Ted Williams	521
Eddie Mathews	512
Ernie Banks	512
Mel Ott	511
Eddie Murray	504

HITS

Pete Rose	4,256
Ty Cobb	4,191
Hank Aaron	3,771
Stan Musial	3,630
Tris Speaker	3,514
Carl Yastrzemski	3,419
Cap Anson	3,418
Honus Wagner	3,415
Paul Molitor	3,319
Eddie Collins	3,315
Willie Mays	3,283
Eddie Murray	3,255
Nap Lajoie	3,242
Cal Ripken, Jr.	3,184
George Brett	3,154
Paul Waner	3,152
Robin Yount	3,142
Tony Gwynn	3,141
Dave Winfield	3,110
Rickey Henderson	3,055

BATTING AVERAGE**

Ty Cobb	.367
Rogers Hornsby	.358
Ed Delahanty	.346
Tris Speaker	.345
Ted Williams	.344
Billy Hamilton	.344
Dan Brouthers	.342
Harry Heilmann	.342
Babe Ruth	.342
Willie Keeler	.341
Bill Terry	.341
Lou Gehrig	.340
George Sisler	.340
Jesse Burkett	.338
Tony Gwynn	.338
Nap Lajoie	.338
Al Simmons	.334
Cap Anson	.333
Eddie Collins	.333
Paul Waner	.333

RUNS

Rickey Henderson	2,295
Ty Cobb	2,245
Hank Aaron	2,174
Babe Ruth	2,174
Pete Rose	2,165
*Barry Bonds	2,152
Willie Mays	2,062
Cap Anson	1,996
Stan Musial	1,949
Lou Gehrig	1,888
Tris Speaker	1,882
Mel Ott	1,859
Frank Robinson	1,829
Eddie Collins	1,821
Carl Yastrzemski	1,816
Ted Williams	1,798
Paul Molitor	1,782
*Craig Biggio	1,776
Charlie Gehringer	1,774
Jimmie Foxx	1,751
Honus Wagner	1,736

DOUBLES

Tris Speaker	792
Pete Rose	746
Stan Musial	725
Ty Cobb	723
George Brett	665
Nap Lajoie	657
Carl Yastrzemski	646
Honus Wagner	640
*Craig Biggio	637
Hank Aaron	624
Paul Molitor	605
Paul Waner	605
Cal Ripken, Jr.	603
*Barry Bonds	587
Rafael Palmeiro	585
Robin Yount	583
Cap Anson	581
Wade Boggs	578
Charlie Gehringer	574
Eddie Murray	560

TRIPLES

Sam Crawford	309
Ty Cobb	297
Honus Wagner	252
Jake Beckley	243
Roger Connor	233
Tris Speaker	222
Fred Clarke	220
Dan Brouthers	205
Joe Kelley	194
Paul Waner	191
Bid McPhee	188
Eddie Collins	187
Ed Delahanty	185
Sam Rice	184
Jesse Burkett	182
Ed Konetchy	182
Edd Roush	182
Buck Ewing	178
Rabbit Maranville	177
Stan Musial	177

BASES ON BALLS

*Barry Bonds	2,426
Rickey Henderson	2,190
Babe Ruth	2,062
Ted Williams	2,019
Joe Morgan	1,865
Carl Yastrzemski	1,845
Mickey Mantle	1,733
Mel Ott	1,708
Eddie Yost	1,614
Darrell Evans	1,605
Stan Musial	1,599
Pete Rose	1,566
Harmon Killebrew	1,559
*Frank Thomas	1,547
Lou Gehrig	1,508
Mike Schmidt	1,507
Eddie Collins	1,499
Willie Mays	1,464
Jimmie Foxx	1,452
Eddie Mathews	1,444

* Active in 2006.
** Minimum 5,000 at bats.
Note: Stats were compiled after the 2006 season.

REGULAR SEASON – CAREER INDIVIDUAL BATTING (CONT.)

Ted Williams is the all-time leader in on-base percentage and is second all-time in slugging percentage.

NATIONAL BASEBALL HALL OF FAME

ON-BASE PERCENTAGE**

Ted Williams	.482
Babe Ruth	.469
*Barry Bonds	.443
Lou Gehrig	.442
*Todd Helton	.430
Jimmie Foxx	.425
Ty Cobb	.424
Rogers Hornsby	.424
*Frank Thomas	.424
Mickey Mantle	.422
Edgar Martinez	.418
Stan Musial	.417
Tris Speaker	.417
Wade Boggs	.415
*Jason Giambi	.413
*Bobby Abreu	.412
*Manny Ramirez	.411
Mel Ott	.410
Mickey Cochrane	.409
Hank Greenberg	.409

TOTAL BASES

Hank Aaron	6,856
Stan Musial	6,134
Willie Mays	6,066
Ty Cobb	5,859
Babe Ruth	5,793
*Barry Bonds	5,784
Pete Rose	5,752
Carl Yastrzemski	5,539
Eddie Murray	5,397
Rafael Palmeiro	5,388
Frank Robinson	5,373
Dave Winfield	5,221
Cal Ripken, Jr.	5,168
Tris Speaker	5,101
Lou Gehrig	5,060
George Brett	5,044
Mel Ott	5,041
Jimmie Foxx	4,956
Ted Williams	4,884
Honus Wagner	4,862

STRIKEOUTS

Reggie Jackson	2,597
Sammy Sosa	2,194
Andres Galarraga	2,003
Jose Canseco	1,942
Willie Stargell	1,936
*Jim Thome	1,909
Mike Schmidt	1,883
Fred McGriff	1,882
Tony Perez	1,867
Dave Kingman	1,816
Bobby Bonds	1,757
Dale Murphy	1,748
Lou Brock	1,730
Mickey Mantle	1,710
Harmon Killebrew	1,699
Chili Davis	1,698
Dwight Evans	1,697
Rickey Henderson	1,694
Dave Winfield	1,686
*Craig Biggio	1,641

RUNS BATTED IN

Hank Aaron	2,297
Babe Ruth	2,213
Cap Anson	2,076
Lou Gehrig	1,995
Stan Musial	1,951
Ty Cobb	1,938
*Barry Bonds	1,930
Jimmie Foxx	1,922
Eddie Murray	1,917
Willie Mays	1,903
Mel Ott	1,860
Carl Yastrzemski	1,844
Ted Williams	1,839
Rafael Palmeiro	1,835
Dave Winfield	1,833
Al Simmons	1,827
Frank Robinson	1,812
Honus Wagner	1,732
Reggie Jackson	1,702
Cal Ripken, Jr.	1,695

SLUGGING PERCENTAGE**

Babe Ruth	.690
Ted Williams	.634
Lou Gehrig	.632
Jimmie Foxx	.609
*Barry Bonds	.608
Hank Greenberg	.605
*Manny Ramirez	.600
Mark McGwire	.588
*Vladimir Guerrero	.583
Joe DiMaggio	.579
Rogers Hornsby	.577

*Alex Rodriguez	.573
*Frank Thomas	.566
*Jim Thome	.565
Larry Walker	.565
Albert Belle	.564
Johnny Mize	.562
*Juan Gonzalez	.561
*Carlos Delgado	.559
Stan Musial	.559
*Ken Griffey, Jr.	.557

STOLEN BASES

Rickey Henderson	1,406
Lou Brock	938
Billy Hamilton	912
Ty Cobb	892
Tim Raines	808
Vince Coleman	752
Eddie Collins	745
Max Carey	738
Honus Wagner	722
Joe Morgan	689
Willie Wilson	668
Bert Campaneris	649
Otis Nixon	620
George Davis	616
Tom Brown	615
*Kenny Lofton	599
Dummy Hoy	594
Maury Wills	586
George Van Haltren	583
Ozzie Smith	580
Hugh Duffy	574

* Active in 2006.
**Minimum 5,000 at bats.

REGULAR SEASON – CAREER INDIVIDUAL PITCHING

GAMES

Jesse Orosco	1,251
John Franco	1,119
*Mike Stanton	1,109
Dennis Eckersley	1,071
Hoyt Wilhelm	1,070
Dan Plesac	1,064
Kent Tekulve	1,050
Lee Smith	1,022
Mike Jackson	1,005
Goose Gossage	1,002
Lindy McDaniel	987
*Jose Mesa	966
*Mike Timlin	961
*Roberto Hernandez	960
Rollie Fingers	944
Gene Garber	931
Cy Young	906
Sparky Lyle	899
Jim Kaat	898
Paul Assenmacher	884

LOSSES

Cy Young	316
Jim Galvin	310
Nolan Ryan	292
Walter Johnson	279
Phil Niekro	274
Gaylord Perry	265
Don Sutton	256
Jack Powell	254
Eppa Rixey	251
Bert Blyleven	250
Bobby Mathews	248
Robin Roberts	245
Warren Spahn	245
Steve Carlton	244
Early Wynn	244
Jim Kaat	237
Frank Tanana	236
Gus Weyhing	232
Tommy John	231
Bob Friend	230

EARNED RUN AVERAGE

Ed Walsh	1.82
Addie Joss	1.89
Al Spalding	2.04
Mordecai Brown	2.06
John Ward	2.10
Christy Mathewson	2.13
Tommy Bond	2.14
Rube Waddell	2.16
Walter Johnson	2.17
Ed Reulbach	2.28
Will White	2.28
Eddie Plank	2.35
Larry Corcoran	2.36
Eddie Cicotte	2.38
Candy Cummings	2.39
Doc White	2.39
Nap Rucker	2.42
George Bradley	2.43
Jim McCormick	2.43
Chief Bender	2.46

INNINGS PITCHED

Cy Young	7,356.0
Jim Galvin	6,003.1
Walter Johnson	5,914.1
Phil Niekro	5,404.1
Nolan Ryan	5,386.0
Gaylord Perry	5,350.1
Don Sutton	5,282.1
Warren Spahn	5,243.2
Steve Carlton	5,217.1
Grover Alexander	5,190.0
Kid Nichols	5,056.1
Tim Keefe	5,049.2
Bert Blyleven	4,970.0
Bobby Mathews	4,956.0
*Roger Clemens	4,817.2
Mickey Welch	4,802.0
Tom Seaver	4,782.2
Christy Mathewson	4,780.2
Tommy John	4,710.1
Robin Roberts	4,688.2

WINNING PERCENTAGE**

Al Spalding	.795
Spud Chandler	.717
*Pedro Martinez	.691
Whitey Ford	.690
Dave Foutz	.690
Bob Caruthers	.688
Don Gullett	.686
Lefty Grove	.680
Joe Wood	.672
Vic Raschi	.667
Larry Corcoran	.665
*Tim Hudson	.665
Christy Mathewson	.665
*Roger Clemens	.662
Sam Leever	.660
Sal Maglie	.657
*Randy Johnson	.656
Dick McBride	.656
Sandy Koufax	.655
Johnny Allen	.654

SHUTOUTS

Walter Johnson	110
Grover Alexander	90
Christy Mathewson	79
Cy Young	76
Eddie Plank	69
Warren Spahn	63
Nolan Ryan	61
Tom Seaver	61
Bert Blyleven	60
Don Sutton	58
Pud Galvin	57
Ed Walsh	57
Bob Gibson	56
Three Finger Brown	55
Steve Carlton	55
Jim Palmer	53
Gaylord Perry	53
Juan Marichal	52
Rube Waddell	50
Vic Willis	50

WINS

Cy Young	511
Walter Johnson	417
Grover Alexander	373
Christy Mathewson	373
Jim Galvin	365
Warren Spahn	363
Kid Nichols	361
*Roger Clemens	348
Tim Keefe	342
*Greg Maddux	314
Steve Carlton	329
John Clarkson	328
Eddie Plank	326
Nolan Ryan	324
Don Sutton	324
Phil Niekro	318
Gaylord Perry	314
Tom Seaver	311
Charley Radbourn	309
Mickey Welch	307

SAVES

*Trevor Hoffman	482
Lee Smith	478
John Franco	424
*Mariano Rivera	413
Dennis Eckersley	379
Jeff Reardon	390
Randy Myers	347
Rollie Fingers	341
John Wetteland	330
*Roberto Hernandez	326
*Troy Percival	324
*Jose Mesa	320
Rick Aguilera	318
Robb Nen	314
Tom Henke	311
Goose Gossage	310
Jeff Montgomery	304
Doug Jones	303
Bruce Sutter	300
*Rod Beck	286

COMPLETE GAMES

Cy Young	749
Jim Galvin	646
Tim Keefe	554
Walter Johnson	531
Kid Nichols	531
Bobby Mathews	525
Mickey Welch	525
Charley Radbourn	489
John Clarkson	485
Tony Mullane	468
Jim McCormick	466
Gus Weyhing	448
Grover Alexander	437
Christy Mathewson	434
Jack Powell	422
Eddie Plank	410
Will White	394
Amos Rusie	393
Vic Willis	388
Tommy Bond	386

*Active in 2006. **Minimum 100 victories.

REGULAR SEASON – CAREER INDIVIDUAL PITCHING (CONT.)

STRIKEOUTS		BASES ON BALLS	
Nolan Ryan	5,714	Nolan Ryan	2,795
*Roger Clemens	4,604	Steve Carlton	1,833
*Randy Johnson	4,544	Phil Niekro	1,809
Steve Carlton	4,136	Early Wynn	1,775
Bert Blyleven	3,701	Bob Feller	1,764
Tom Seaver	3,640	Bobo Newsom	1,732
Don Sutton	3,574	Amos Rusie	1,707
Gaylord Perry	3,534	Charlie Hough	1,665
Walter Johnson	3,508	Gus Weyhing	1,566
Phil Niekro	3,342	*Roger Clemens	1,549
Ferguson Jenkins	3,192	Red Ruffing	1,541
*Greg Maddux	3,169	Bump Hadley	1,442
Bob Gibson	3,117	Warren Spahn	1,434
*Curt Schilling	3,015	Earl Whitehill	1,431
*Pedro Martinez	2,998	*Randy Johnson	1,409
Jim Bunning	2,855	Tony Mullane	1,408
Mickey Lolich	2,832	*Tom Glavine	1,399
Cy Young	2,803	Sad Sam Jones	1,396
*John Smoltz	2,778	Jack Morris	1,390
Frank Tanana	2,773	Tom Seaver	1,390

Adam Dunn, Reds

DAMIAN STROHMEYER

REGULAR SEASON – INDIVIDUAL BATTING, SINGLE SEASON

HITS		TRIPLES		RUNS BATTED IN	
Ichiro Suzuki, 2004	262	Chief Wilson, 1912	36	Hack Wilson, 1930	191
George Sisler, 1920	257	Dave Orr, 1886	31	Lou Gehrig, 1931	184
Lefty O'Doul, 1929	254	Heinie Reitz, 1894	31	Hank Greenberg, 1937	183
Bill Terry, 1930	254	Perry Werden, 1893	29	Lou Gehrig, 1927	175
Al Simmons, 1925	253	Harry Davis, 1897	28	Jimmie Foxx, 1938	175
Rogers Hornsby, 1922	250	Sam Thompson, 1894	28	Lou Gehrig, 1930	174
Chuck Klein, 1930	250	George Davis, 1893	27	Babe Ruth, 1921	171
Ty Cobb, 1911	248	Sam Thompson, 1894	27	Chuck Klein, 1930	170
George Sisler, 1922	246	Jimmy Williams, 1899	27	Hank Greenberg, 1935	170
Ichiro Suzuki, 2001	242	John Reilly, 1890	26	Jimmie Foxx, 1932	169
Heinie Manush, 1928	241	George Treadway, 1894	26		
Babe Herman, 1930	241	Joe Jackson, 1912	26	STRIKEOUTS	

BATTING AVERAGE					
		Sam Crawford, 1914	26	Adam Dunn, 2004	195
Hugh Duffy, 1894	.440	Kiki Cuyler, 1925	26	Bobby Bonds, 1970	189
Tip O'Neill, 1887	.435			Jose Hernandez, 2002	188
Ross Barnes, 1872	.432	HOME RUNS		Bobby Bonds, 1969	187
Cal McVey, 1871	.431			Preston Wilson, 2000	187
R Barnes, 1876	.429	Barry Bonds, 2001	73	Rob Deer, 1987	186
Nap Lajoie, 1901	.426	Mark McGwire, 1998	70	Jose Hernandez, 2001	185
R Barnes, 1873	.425	Sammy Sosa, 1998	66	Pete Incaviglia, 1986	185
Rogers Hornsby, 1924	.424	Mark McGwire, 1999	65	Cecil Fielder, 1990	182
Ty Cobb, 1911	.420	Sammy Sosa, 2001	64	*Jim Thome, 2003	182
George Sisler, 1922	.420	Sammy Sosa, 1999	63	Mo Vaughn, 2000	181
Ty Cobb, 1912	.410	Roger Maris, 1961	61		
Ed Delahanty, 1899	.410	Babe Ruth, 1927	60	RUNS	
		Babe Ruth, 1921	59	Billy Hamilton, 1894	198
DOUBLES		Jimmie Foxx, 1932	58	Tom Brown, 1891	177
		Hank Greenberg, 1938	58	Babe Ruth, 1921	177
Earl Webb, 1931	67	Mark McGwire, 1997	58	Tip O'Neill, 1887	167
George Burns, 1926	64	Ryan Howard, 2006	58	Lou Gehrig, 1936	167
Joe Medwick, 1936	64			Billy Hamilton, 1895	166
Hank Greenberg, 1934	63	TOTAL BASES		Willie Keeler, 1894	165
Paul Waner, 1932	62	Babe Ruth, 1921	457	Joe Kelley, 1894	165
Charlie Gehringer, 1936	60	Rogers Hornsby, 1922	450	Arlie Latham, 1887	163
Tris Speaker, 1923	59	Lou Gehrig, 1927	447	Babe Ruth, 1928	163
Chuck Klein, 1930	59	Chuck Klein, 1930	445	Lou Gehrig, 1931	163
Todd Helton, 2000	59	Jimmie Foxx, 1932	438		
Billy Herman, 1936	57	Stan Musial, 1948	429		
Billy Herman, 1935	57	Sammy Sosa, 2001	425		
Carlos Delgado, 2000	57	Hack Wilson, 1930	423		
		Chuck Klein, 1932	420		
		Luis Gonzalez, 2001	419		
		Lou Gehrig, 1930	419		

REGULAR SEASON – INDIVIDUAL BATTING, SINGLE SEASON (CONT.)

STOLEN BASES		BASES ON BALLS		SLUGGING PERCENTAGE	
Hugh Nicol, 1887	138	Barry Bonds, 2004	232	Barry Bonds, 2001	.863
Rickey Henderson, 1982	130	Barry Bonds, 2002	198	Babe Ruth, 1920	.847
Arlie Latham, 1887	129	Barry Bonds, 2001	177	Babe Ruth, 1921	.846
Lou Brock, 1974	118	Babe Ruth, 1923	170	Barry Bonds, 2004	.812
Charlie Comiskey, 1887	117	Ted Williams, 1947	162	Barry Bonds, 2002	.799
John Ward, 1887	111	Ted Williams, 1949	162	Babe Ruth, 1927	.772
Billy Hamilton, 1889	111	Mark McGwire, 1998	162	Lou Gehrig, 1927	.765
Billy Hamilton, 1891	111	Ted Williams, 1946	156	Babe Ruth, 1923	.764
Vince Coleman, 1985	110	Eddie Yost, 1956	151	Rogers Hornsby, 1925	.756
Arlie Latham, 1888	109	Barry Bonds, 1996	151	Mark McGwire, 1998	.752
Vince Coleman, 1987	109	Babe Ruth, 1920	150	Jeff Bagwell, 1994	.750

REGULAR SEASON – INDIVIDUAL PITCHING, SINGLE SEASON

GAMES		LOSSES		SHUTOUTS	
Mike Marshall, 1974	106	John Coleman, 1883	48	George Bradley, 1876	16
Kent Tekulve, 1979	94	Will White, 1880	42	Grover Alexander, 1916	16
Salomon Torres, 2006	94	Larry McKeon, 1884	41	Jack Coombs, 1910	13
Mike Marshall, 1973	92	George Bradley, 1879	40	Bob Gibson, 1968	13
Kent Tekulve, 1978	91	Jim McCormick, 1879	40	Jim Galvin, 1884	12
Wayne Granger, 1969	90	Henry Porter, 1888	37	Ed Morris, 1886	12
Mike Marshall, 1979	90	Kid Carsey, 1891	37	Grover Alexander, 1915	12
Kent Tekulve, 1987	90	George Cobb, 1892	37	Tommy Bond, 1879	11
*Jim Brower, 2004	89	Stump Weidman, 1886	36	Charley Radbourn, 1884	11
Mark Eichhorn, 1987	89	Bill Hutchison, 1892	36	Dave Foutz, 1886	11
Steve Kline, 2001	89			Christy Mathewson, 1908	11
Paul Quantrill, 2003	89	WINNING PERCENTAGE		Ed Walsh, 1908	11
Julian Tavarez, 1997	89	Roy Face, 1959	.947	Walter Johnson, 1913	11
		Johnny Allen, 1937	.938	Sandy Koufax, 1963	11
GAMES STARTED		Phil Regan, 1966	.933	Dean Chance, 1964	11
Will White, 1879	75	Perry Werden, 1884	.923		
Jim Galvin, 1883	75	Larry Twitchell, 1887	.917	COMPLETE GAMES	
Jim McCormick, 1880	74	Greg Maddux, 1995	.905	Will White, 1879	75
Charley Radbourn, 1884	73	Randy Johnson, 1995	.900	Charley Radbourn, 1884	73
Guy Hecker, 1884	73	Ron Guidry, 1978	.893	Jim McCormick, 1880	72
Jim Galvin, 1884	72	Freddie Fitzsimmons, 1940	.889	Jim Galvin, 1883	72
John Clarkson, 1889	72	Lefty Grove, 1931	.886	Guy Hecker, 1884	72
John Clarkson, 1885	70	Bob Stanley, 1978	.882	Jim Galvin, 1884	71
Bill Hutchison, 1892	70	Preacher Roe, 1951	.880	Tim Keefe, 1883	68
Matt Kilroy, 1887	69			John Clarkson, 1885	68
		SAVES		John Clarkson, 1889	68
INNINGS PITCHED		Bobby Thigpen, 1990	57	Bill Hutchison, 1892	67
Will White, 1878	680.0	Eric Gagne, 2003	55		
Charley Radbourn, 1884	678.2	John Smoltz, 2002	55	STRIKEOUTS	
Guy Hecker, 1884	670.2	Randy Myers, 1993	53	Matt Kilroy, 1886	513
Jim McCormick, 1880	657.2	Trevor Hoffman, 1998	53	Toad Ramsey, 1886	499
Jim Galvin, 1883	656.1	Mariano Rivera, 2004	53	Hugh Daily, 1884	483
Jim Galvin, 1884	636.1	Eric Gagne, 2002	52	Dupee Shaw, 1884	451
Charley Radbourn, 1883	632.1	Dennis Eckersley, 1992	51	Charley Radbourn, 1884	441
John Clarkson, 1885	623.0	Rod Beck, 1998	51	Charlie Buffinton, 1884	417
Jim Devlin, 1876	622.0	Mariano Rivera, 2001	50	Guy Hecker, 1884	385
Bill Hutchison, 1892	622.0	Francisco Cordero, 2004	49	Nolan Ryan, 1973	383
		Dennis Eckersley, 1990	48	Sandy Koufax, 1965	382
WINS		Rod Beck, 1993	48	Bill Sweeney, 1884	374
Charley Radbourn, 1884	59	Jeff Shaw, 1998	48		
John Clarkson, 1885	53			BASES ON BALLS	
Guy Hecker, 1884	52	EARNED RUN AVERAGE		Amos Rusie, 1890	289
John Clarkson, 1889	49	Tim Keefe, 1880	0.86	Mark Baldwin, 1889	274
Charley Radbourn, 1883	48	Dutch Leonard, 1914	0.96	Amos Rusie, 1892	270
Charlie Buffinton, 1884	48	Three Finger Brown, 1906	1.04	Amos Rusie, 1891	262
Al Spalding, 1876	47	Bob Gibson, 1968	1.12	Mark Baldwin, 1890	249
John Ward, 1879	47	Christy Mathewson, 1909	1.14	Jack Stivetts, 1891	232
Jim Galvin, 1883	46	Walter Johnson, 1913	1.14	Mark Baldwin, 1891	227
Jim Galvin, 1884	46	Jack Pfiester, 1907	1.15	Phil Knell, 1891	226
Matt Kilroy, 1887	46	Addie Joss, 1908	1.16	Bob Barr, 1890	219
		Carl Lundgren, 1907	1.17	Amos Rusie, 1893	218
		Denny Driscoll, 1882	1.21		

REGULAR SEASON – INDIVIDUAL BATTING, SINGLE GAME

MOST RUNS		
7	Guy Hecker, Lou	Aug. 15, 1886

MOST HITS		
7	Wilbert Robinson, Bal	June 10, 1892
	Rennie Stennett, Pitt	Sept. 16, 1975

MOST HOME RUNS		
4	Bobby Lowe, Bos (N)	May 30, 1894
	Ed Delahanty, Phil	July 13, 1896
	Lou Gehrig, NY (A)	June 3, 1932
	Gil Hodges, Bklyn	Aug. 31, 1950
	Joe Adcock, Mil (N)	July 31, 1954
	Rocky Colavito, Cle	June 10, 1959
	Willie Mays, SF	April 30, 1961
	Mike Schmidt, Phi	April 17, 1976
	Bob Horner, Atl	July 6, 1986
	Mark Whiten, StL	Sept. 7, 1993
	Mike Cameron, Sea	May 2, 2002
	Shawn Green, LA	May 23, 2002
	Carlos Delgado, Tor	Sept. 25, 2003

MOST GRAND SLAMS		
2	Tony Lazzeri, NY (A)	May 24, 1936
	Jim Tabor, Bos (A)	July 4, 1939
	Rudy York, Bos (A)	July 27, 1946
	Jim Gentile, Bal	May 9, 1961
	Tony Cloninger, Atl	July 3, 1966
	Jim Northrup, Det	June 24, 1968
	Frank Robinson, Bal	June 26, 1970
	Robin Ventura, Chi (A)	Sept. 4, 1995
	Chris Hoiles, Bal	Aug. 14, 1998
	Fernando Tatis, StL	April 23, 1999
	Nomar Garciaparra, Bos	May 10, 1999
	Bill Mueller, Bos	July 29, 2003

MOST RBIS		
12	Jim Bottomley, StL	Sept. 16, 1924
	Mark Whiten, StL	Sept. 7, 1993

REGULAR SEASON – INDIVIDUAL PITCHING, SINGLE GAME

MOST INNINGS PITCHED		
26	Leon Cadore, Bklyn	May 1, 1920, tie 1–1
	Joe Oeschger, Bos (N)	May 1, 1920, tie 1–1

MOST RUNS ALLOWED		
24	Al Travers, Det	May 18, 1912

MOST HITS ALLOWED		
36	Jack Wadsworth, Lou	Aug. 17, 1894

MOST STRIKEOUTS		
20	Roger Clemens, Bos	April 29, 1986
	Roger Clemens, Bos	Sept. 18, 1996
	Kerry Wood, Chi (N)	May 6, 1998
	Randy Johnson, Ari	May 8, 2001

MOST WALKS ALLOWED		
16	Bill George, NY (N)	May 30, 1887
	George Van Haltren, Chi (N)	June 27, 1887
	Henry Gruber, Cle	April 19, 1890
	Bruno Haas, Phil (A)	June 2, 1915

MOST WILD PITCHES		
6	J.R. Richard, Hou	April 10, 1979
	Phil Niekro, Atl	Aug. 14, 1979
	Bill Gullickson, Mon	April 10, 1982

NOTABLE ACHIEVEMENTS

NO-HIT GAMES, NINE INNINGS OR MORE

NATIONAL LEAGUE

DATE		PITCHER AND GAME	DATE		PITCHER AND GAME
1876	July 15	George Bradley, StL vs. Hart 2–0	1893	Aug. 16	Bill Hawke, Bal vs. Wash 5–0
1880	June 12	John Richmond, Wor vs. Cle 1–0	1897	Sept. 18	Cy Young, Cle vs. Cin 6–0
		(perfect game)	1898	April 22	Ted Breitenstein, Cin vs. Pitt 11–0
	June 17	Monte Ward, Prov vs. Buf 5–0		April 22	Jim Hughes, Bal vs. Bos 8–0
		(perfect game)		July 8	Frank Donahue, Phil vs. Bos 5–0
	Aug. 19	Larry Corcoran, Chi vs. Bos 6–0		Aug. 21	Walter Thornton, Chi vs. Bklyn 2–0
	Aug. 20	Pud Galvin, Buff vs. Wor 1–0	1899	May 25	Deacon Phillippe, Lou vs. NY 7–0
1882	Sept. 20	Larry Corcoran, Chi vs. Wor 5–0		Aug. 7	Vic Willis, Bos vs. Wash 7–1
	Sept. 22	Tim Lovett, Bklyn vs. NY 4–0	1900	July 12	Noodles Hahn, Cin vs. Phil 4–0
1883	July 25	Hoss Radbourn, Prov vs. Cle 8–0	1901	July 15	Christy Mathewson, Cin vs. StL 5–0
	Sept. 13	Hugh Daily, Cle vs. Phil 1–0	1903	Sept. 18	Chick Fraser, Phil vs. Chi 10–0
1884	June 27	Larry Corcoran, Chi vs. Prov 6–0	1904	June 11	Bob Wicker, Chi vs. NY 1–0
	Aug. 4	Pud Galvin, Buf vs. Det 18–0			(hit in 10th; won in 12th)
1885	July 27	John Clarkson, Chi vs. Prov 4–0	1905	June 13	Christy Mathewson, NY vs. Chi 1–0
	Aug. 29	Charles Ferguson, Phil vs. Prov 1–0	1906	May 1	John Lush, Phil vs. Bklyn 6–0
1891	June 22	Tom Lovett, Bklyn vs. NY 4–0		July 20	Mal Eason, Bklyn vs. StL 2–0
	July 31	Amos Rusie, NY vs. Bklyn 6–0		Aug. 1	Harry McIntire, Bklyn vs. Pitt 0–1
1892	Aug. 6	Jack Stivetts, Bos vs. Bklyn 11–0			(hit in 11th; lost in 13th)
	Aug. 22	Alex Sanders, Lou vs. Bal 6–2	1907	May 8	Frank Pfeffer, Bos vs. Cin 6–0
	Oct. 15	Bumpus Jones, Cin vs. Pitt 7–1		Sept. 20	Nick Maddox, Pitt vs. Bklyn 2–1
		(first major league game)			

NOTABLE ACHIEVEMENTS

NO-HIT GAMES, NINE INNINGS OR MORE (CONT.)

NATIONAL LEAGUE

DATE		PITCHER AND GAME	DATE		PITCHER AND GAME
1908	July 4	George Wiltse, NY vs. Phil 1–0		April 30	Jim Maloney, Cin vs. Hou 10–0
		(10 innings)		May 1	Don Wilson, Hou vs. Cin 4–0
	Sept. 5	Nap Rucker, Bklyn vs. Bos 6–0		Aug. 19	Ken Holtzman, Chi vs. Atl 3–0
1909	April 15	Leon Ames, NY vs. Bklyn 0–3		Sept. 20	Bob Moose, Pitt vs. NY 4–0
		(hit in 10th; lost in 13th)	1970	June 12	Dock Ellis, Pitt vs. SD 2–0
1912	Sept. 6	Jeff Tesreau, NY vs. Phil 3–0		July 20	Bill Singer, LA vs. Phil 5–0
1914	Sept. 9	George Davis, Bos vs. Phil 7–0	1971	June 3	Ken Holtzman, Chi vs. Cin 1–0
1915	April 15	Rube Marquard, NY vs. Bklyn 2–0		June 23	Rick Wise, Phil vs. Cin 4–0
	Aug. 31	Jimmy Lavender, Chi vs. NY 2–0		Aug. 14	Bob Gibson, StL vs. Pitt 11–0
1916	June 16	Tom Hughes, Bos vs. Pitt 2–0	1972	April 16	Burt Hooton, Chi vs. Phil 4–0
1917	May 2	Jim Vaughn, Chi vs. Cin 0–1		Sept. 2	Milt Pappas, Chi vs. SD 8–0
		(hit in 10th; lost in 10th)		Oct. 2	Bill Stoneman, Mon vs. NY 7–0
	May 2	Fred Toney, Cin vs. Chi 1–0	1973	Aug. 5	Phil Niekro, Atl vs. SD 9–0
		(10 innings)	1975	Aug. 24	Ed Halicki, SF vs. NY 6–0
1919	May 11	Hod Eller, Cin vs. StL 6–0	1976	July 9	Larry Dierker, Hou vs. Mon 6–0
1922	May 7	Jesse Barnes, NY vs. Phil 6–0		Aug. 9	John Candelaria, Pitt vs. LA 2–0
1924	July 17	Jesse Haines, StL vs. Bos 5–0		Sept. 29	John Montefusco, SF vs. Atl 9–0
1925	Sept. 13	Dazzy Vance, Bklyn vs. Phil 10–1	1978	April 16	Bob Forsch, StL vs. Phil 5–0
1929	May 8	Carl Hubbell, NY vs. Pitt 11–0		June 16	Tom Seaver, Cin vs. StL 4–0
1934	Sept. 21	Paul Dean, StL vs. Bklyn 3–0	1979	April 7	Ken Forsch, Hou vs. Atl 6–0
1938	June 11	Johnny Vander Meer, Cin vs. Bos 3–0	1980	June 27	Jerry Reuss, LA vs. SF 8–0
	June 15	Johnny Vander Meer, Cin vs. Bklyn 6–0	1981	May 10	Charlie Lea, Mon vs. SF 4–0
1940	April 30	Tex Carleton, Bklyn vs. Cin 3–0		Sept. 26	Nolan Ryan, Hou vs. LA 5–0
1941	Aug. 30	Lon Warneke, StL vs. Cin 2–0	1983	Sept. 26	Bob Forsch, StL vs. Mon 3–0
1944	April 27	Jim Tobin, Bos vs. Bklyn 2–0	1986	Sept. 25	Mike Scott, Hou vs. SF 2–0
	May 15	Clyde Shoun, Cin vs. Bos 1–0	1988	Sept. 16	Tom Browning, Cin vs. LA 1–0
1946	April 23	Ed Head, Bklyn vs. Bos 5–0			(perfect game)
1947	June 18	Ewell Blackwell, Cin vs. Bos 6–0	1990	June 29	Fernando Valenzuela, LA vs. StL 6–0
1948	Sept. 9	Rex Barney, Bklyn vs. NY 2–0		Aug. 15	Terry Mulholland, Phil vs. SF 6–0
1950	Aug. 11	Vern Bickford, Bos vs. Bklyn 7–0	1991	May 23	Tommy Greene, Phil vs. Mon 2–0
1951	May 6	Cliff Chambers, Pitt vs. Bos 3–0		July 26	Mark Gardner, Mon vs. LA 0–1
1952	June 19	Carl Erskine, Bklyn vs. Chi 5–0			(hit in 10th, lost in 10th)
1954	June 12	Jim Wilson, Mil vs. Phil 2–0		July 28	Dennis Martinez, Mon vs. LA 2–0
1955	May 12	Sam Jones, Chi vs. Pitt 4–0			(perfect game)
1956	May 12	Carl Erskine, Bklyn vs. NY 3–0		Sept. 11	Kent Mercker (6), Mark Wohlers (2),
	Sept. 25	Sal Maglie, Bklyn vs. Phil 5–0			and Alejandro Pena (1), Atl vs. SD 1–0
1959	May 26	Harvey Haddix, Pitt vs. Mil 0–1	1992	Aug. 17	Kevin Gross, LA vs. SF 2–0
		(hit in 13th; lost in 13th)	1993	Sept. 8	Darryl Kile, Hou vs. NY 7–1
1960	May 15	Don Cardwell, Chi vs. StL 4–0	1994	April 8	Kent Mercker, Atl vs. LA 6–0
	Aug. 18	Lew Burdette, Mil vs. Phil 1–0	1995	June 3	Pedro Martinez, Mon vs. SD 1–0
	Sept. 16	Warren Spahn, Mil vs. Phil 4–0			(perfect through nine, hit in 10th)
1961	April 28	Warren Spahn, Mil vs. SF 1–0		July 14	Ramon Martinez, LA vs. Fla 7–0
1962	June 30	Sandy Koufax, LA vs. NY 5–0	1996	May 11	Al Leiter, Fla vs. Col 11–0
1963	May 11	Sandy Koufax, LA vs. SF 8–0		Sept. 17	Hideo Nomo, LA vs. Col 9–0
	May 17	Don Nottebart, Hou vs. Phil 4–1	1997	June 10	Kevin Brown, Fla vs. SF 9–0
	June 15	Juan Marichal, SF vs. Hou 1–0		July 12	Francisco Cordova (9) and
1964	April 23	Ken Johnson, Hou vs. Cin 0–1			Ricardo Rincon (1), Pitt vs. Col 3–0
	June 4	Sandy Koufax, LA vs. Phil 3–0	1999	June 25	Jose Jimenez, StL vs. Ari 1–0
	June 21	Jim Bunning, Phil vs. NY 6–0	2001	May 12	A.J. Burnett, Fla vs. SD 3–0
		(perfect game)		Sept. 3	Bud Smith, StL vs. SD 4–0
1965	June 14	Jim Maloney, Cin vs. NY 0–1	2003	April 27	Kevin Millwood, Phil vs. SF 1–0
		(hit in 11th; lost in 11th)		June 11	Roy Oswalt (1), Pete Munro (2⅔),
	Aug. 19	Jim Maloney, Cin vs. Chi 1–0			Kirk Saarloos (1⅓), Brad Lidge (2),
		(10 innings)			Octavio Dotel (1), and Billy Wagner (1),
	Sept. 9	Sandy Koufax, LA vs. Chi 1–0			Hou vs. NY 8–0
		(perfect game)	2004	May 18	Randy Johnson, Ari vs. Atl 2–0
1967	June 18	Don Wilson, Hou vs. Atl 2–0			(perfect game)
1968	July 29	George Culver, Cin vs. Phil 6–1	2006	Sept. 6	Anibal Sanchez, Fla vs. Ari 2–0
	Sept. 17	Gaylord Perry, SF vs. StL 1–0			
	Sept. 18	Ray Washburn, StL vs. SF 2–0			
1969	April 17	Bill Stoneman, Mon vs. Phil 7–0			

FAST FACT

Rookie Anibal Sanchez's no-hitter was the fourth no-hitter in the Florida Marlins' 14-year franchise history. The New York Mets have never had a pitcher throw a no-hitter in their 45-year history.

BASEBALL

NOTABLE ACHIEVEMENTS
NO-HIT GAMES, NINE INNINGS OR MORE (CONT.)

DATE		PITCHER AND GAME	DATE		PITCHER AND GAME
1901	May 9	Earl Moore, Cle vs. Chi 2–4	1956	July 14	Mel Parnell, Bos vs. Chi 4–0
		(hit in 10th; lost in 10th)		Oct. 8	Don Larsen, NY (A) vs. Bklyn (N) 2–0
1902	Sept. 20	Jimmy Callahan, Chi vs. Det 3–0			(World Series, perfect game)
1904	May 5	Cy Young, Bos vs. Phil 3–0	1957	Aug. 20	Bob Keegan, Chi vs. Wash 6–0
		(perfect game)	1958	July 20	Jim Bunning, Det vs. Bos 3–0
	Aug. 17	Jesse Tannehill, Bos vs. Chi 6–0		Sept. 20	Hoyt Wilhelm, Bal vs. NY 1–0
1905	July 22	Weldon Henley, Phil vs. StL 6–0	1962	May 5	Bo Belinsky, LA vs. Bal 2–0
	Sept. 6	Frank Smith, Chi vs. Det 15–0		June 26	Earl Wilson, Bos vs. LA 2–0
	Sept. 27	Bill Dinneen, Bos vs. Chi 2–0		Aug. 1	Bill Monbouquette, Bos vs. Chi 1–0
1908	June 30	Cy Young, Bos vs. NY 8–0		Aug. 26	Jack Kralick, Min vs. KC 1–0
	Sept. 18	Bob Rhoades, Cle vs. Bos 2–1	1965	Sept. 16	Dave Morehead, Bos vs. Cle 2–0
	Sept. 20	Frank Smith, Chi vs. Phil 1–0	1966	June 10	Sonny Siebert, Cle vs. Wash 2–0
	Oct. 2	Addie Joss, Cle vs. Chi 1–0	1967	April 30	Steve Barber (8⅔) and Stu Miller (⅓),
		(perfect game)			Bal vs. Det 1–2
1910	April 20	Addie Joss, Cle vs. Chi 1–0		Aug. 25	Dean Chance, Min vs. Cle 2–1
	May 12	Chief Bender, Phil vs. Cle 4–0		Sept. 10	Joel Horlen, Chi vs. Det 6–0
	Aug. 30	Tom Hughes, NY vs. Cle 0–5	1968	April 27	Tom Phoebus, Bal vs. Bos 6–0
		(hit in 10th; lost in 11th)		May 8	Catfish Hunter, Oak vs. Min 4–0
1911	July 29	Joe Wood, Bos vs. StL 5–0			(perfect game)
	Aug. 27	Ed Walsh, Chi vs. Bos 5–0	1969	Aug. 13	Jim Palmer, Bal vs. Oak 8–0
1912	July 4	George Mullin, Det vs. StL 7–0	1970	July 3	Clyde Wright, Cal vs. Oak 4–0
	Aug. 30	Earl Hamilton, StL vs. Det 5–1		Sept. 21	Vida Blue, Oak vs. Min 6–0
1914	May 14	Jim Scott, Chi vs. Wash 0–1	1973	April 27	Steve Busby, KC vs. Det 3–0
		(hit in 10th; lost in 10th)		May 15	Nolan Ryan, Cal vs. KC 3–0
	May 31	Joe Benz, Chi vs. Cle 6–1		July 15	Nolan Ryan, Cal vs. Det 6–0
1916	June 21	George Foster, Bos vs. NY 2–0		July 30	Jim Bibby, Tex vs. Oak 6–0
	Aug. 26	Joe Bush, Phil vs. Cle 5–0	1974	June 19	Steve Busby, KC vs. Mil 2–0
	Aug. 30	Dutch Leonard, Bos vs. StL 4–0		July 19	Dick Bosman, Cle vs. Oak 4–0
1917	April 14	Ed Cicotte, Chi vs. StL 11–0		Sept. 28	Nolan Ryan, Cal vs. Min 4–0
	April 24	George Mogridge, NY vs. Bos 2–1	1975	June 1	Nolan Ryan, Cal vs. Bal 1–0
	May 5	Ernie Koob, StL vs. Chi 1–0		Sept. 28	Vida Blue (5), Glenn Abbott (1),
	May 6	Bob Groom, StL vs. Chi 3–0			Paul Lindblad (1), and Rollie Fingers (2),
	June 23	Ernie Shore, Bos vs. Wash 4–0			Oak vs. Cal 5–0
		(perfect game)	1976	July 28	John Odom (5) and Francisco
1918	June 3	Dutch Leonard, Bos vs. Det 5–0			Barrios (4), Chi vs. Oak 2–1
1919	Sept. 10	Ray Caldwell, Cle vs. NY 3–0	1977	May 14	Jim Colborn, KC vs. Tex 6–0
1920	July 1	Walter Johnson, Wash vs. Bos 1–0		May 30	Dennis Eckersley, Cle vs. Cal 1–0
1922	April 30	Charlie Robertson, Chi vs. Det 2–0		Sept. 22	Bert Blyleven, Tex vs. Cal 6–0
		(perfect game)	1981	May 15	Len Barker, Cle vs. Tor 3–0
1923	Sept. 4	Sam Jones, NY vs. Phil 2–0			(perfect game)
	Sept. 7	Howard Ehmke, Bos vs. Phil 4–0	1983	July 4	Dave Righetti, NY vs. Bos 4–0
1926	Aug. 21	Ted Lyons, Chi vs. Bos 6–0		Sept. 29	Mike Warren, Oak vs. Chi 3–0
1931	April 29	Wes Ferrell, Cle vs. StL 9–0	1984	April 7	Jack Morris, Det vs. Chi 4–0
	Aug. 8	Bob Burke, Wash vs. Bos 5–0		Sept. 30	Mike Witt, Cal vs. Tex 1–0
1934	Sept. 18	Bobo Newsom, StL vs. Bos 1–2			(perfect game)
		(hit in 10th; lost in 10th)	1986	Sept. 19	Joe Cowley, Chi vs. Cal 7–1
1935	Aug. 31	Vern Kennedy, Chi vs. Cle 5–0	1987	April 15	Juan Nieves, Mil vs. Bal 7–0
1937	June 1	Bill Dietrich, Chi vs. StL 8–0	1990	April 11	Mark Langston (7) and Mike Witt (2),
1938	Aug. 27	Monte Pearson, NY vs. Cle 13–0			Cal vs. Sea 1–0
1940	April 16	Bob Feller, Cle vs. Chi 1–0		June 2	Randy Johnson, Sea vs. Det 2–0
		(Opening Day)		June 11	Nolan Ryan, Tex vs. Oak 5–0
1945	Sept. 9	Dick Fowler, Phil vs. StL 1–0		June 29	Dave Stewart, Oak vs. Tor 5–0
1946	April 30	Bob Feller, Cle vs. NY 1–0		July 1	Andy Hawkins, NY vs. Chi 0–4 (pitched
1947	July 10	Don Black, Cle vs. Phil 3–0			eight innings of nine-inning game)
	Sept. 3	Bill McCahan, Phil vs. Wash 3–0		Sept. 2	Dave Stieb, Tor vs. Cle 3–0
1948	June 30	Bob Lemon, Cle vs. Det 2–0	1991	May 1	Nolan Ryan, Tex vs. Tor 3–0
1951	July 1	Bob Feller, Cle vs. Det 2–1		July 13	Bob Milacki (6), Mike Flanagan (1),
	July 12	Allie Reynolds, NY vs. Cle 1–0			Mark Williamson (1), and Gregg
	Sept. 28	Allie Reynolds, NY vs. Bos 8–0			Olson (1), Bal vs. Oak 2–0
1952	May 15	Virgil Trucks, Det vs. Wash 1–0		Aug. 11	Wilson Alvarez, Chi vs. Bal 7–0
	Aug. 25	Virgil Trucks, Det vs. NY 1–0		Aug. 26	Bret Saberhagen, KC vs. Chi 7–0
1953	May 6	Bobo Holloman, StL vs. Phil 6–0	1993	April 22	Chris Bosio, Sea vs. Bos 7–0
		(first major league start)		Sept. 4	Jim Abbott, NY vs. Cle 4–0

NOTABLE ACHIEVEMENTS
NO-HIT GAMES, NINE INNINGS OR MORE (cont.)

DATE		PITCHER AND GAME	DATE		PITCHER AND GAME
1994	April 27	Scott Erickson, Min vs. Mil 6–0	1999	July 18	David Cone, NY vs. Mon 6–0
	July 28	Kenny Rogers, Tex vs. Cal 4–0			(perfect game)
		(perfect game)		Sept. 11	Eric Milton, Min vs. Ana 7–0
1996	May 14	Dwight Gooden, NY vs. Sea 2–0	2001	April 4	Hideo Nomo, Bos vs. Bal 3–0
1998	May 17	David Wells, NY vs. Min 4–0	2002	April 27	Derek Lowe, Bos vs. TB 10–0
		(perfect game)			

LONGEST HITTING STREAKS

NATIONAL LEAGUE			AMERICAN LEAGUE		
PLAYER AND TEAM	YEAR	G	PLAYER AND TEAM	YEAR	G
Willie Keeler, Bal	1897	44	Joe DiMaggio, NY	1941	56
Pete Rose, Cin	1978	44	George Sisler, StL	1922	41
Bill Dahlen, Chi	1894	42	Ty Cobb, Det	1911	40
Tommy Holmes, Bos	1945	37	Paul Molitor, Mil	1987	39
Jimmy Rollins, Phil	2005-06	36	Ty Cobb, Det	1917	35
Billy Hamilton, Phil	1894	38	Ty Cobb, Det	1912	34
Luis Castillo, Fla	2002	35	George Sisler, StL	1925	34
Fred Clarke, Lou	1895	35	John Stone, Det	1930	34
Chase Utley, Phil	2006	35	George McQuinn, StL	1938	34
Benito Santiago, SD	1987	34	Dom DiMaggio, Bos	1949	34
George Davis, NY	1893	33	Hal Chase, NY	1907	33
Rogers Hornsby, StL	1922	33	Heinie Manush, Wash	1933	33

TRIPLE CROWN WINNERS*

NATIONAL LEAGUE					AMERICAN LEAGUE				
PLAYER AND TEAM	YEAR	HR	RBI	BA	PLAYER AND TEAM	YEAR	HR	RBI	BA
Paul Hines, Prov	1878	4	50	.358	Nap Lajoie, Phil	1901	14	125	.422
Hugh Duffy, Bos	1894	18	145	.438	Ty Cobb, Det	1909	9	115	.377
Heinie Zimmerman, Chi **	1912	14	103	.372	Jimmie Foxx, Phil	1933	48	163	.356
Rogers Hornsby, StL	1922	42	152	.401	Lou Gehrig, NY	1934	49	165	.363
Rogers Hornsby, StL	1925	39	143	.403	Ted Williams, Bos	1942	36	137	.356
Chuck Klein, Phil	1933	28	120	.368	Ted Williams, Bos	1947	32	114	.343
Joe Medwick, StL	1937	31	154	.374	Mickey Mantle, NY	1956	52	130	.353
					Frank Robinson, Bal	1966	49	122	.316
					Carl Yastrzemski, Bos	1967	44	121	.326

* Player who leads in three categories: home runs, RBIs, and batting average.
** Zimmerman ranked first in RBIs as calculated by Ernie Lanigan, but only third as calculated by Information Concepts Inc.

TRIPLE CROWN PITCHERS***

NATIONAL LEAGUE											
PLAYER AND TEAM	YEAR	W	L	SO	ERA	PLAYER AND TEAM	YEAR	W	L	SO	ERA
Tommy Bond, Bos	1877	40	17	170	2.11	Hippo Vaughn, Chi	1918	22	10	148	1.74
Hoss Radbourn, Prov	1884	60	12	441	1.38	Grover Alexander, Chi	1920	27	14	173	1.91
Tim Keefe, NY	1888	35	12	333	1.74	Dazzy Vance, Bklyn	1924	28	6	262	2.16
John Clarkson, Bos	1889	49	19	284	2.73	Bucky Walters, Cin	1939	27	11	137	2.29
Amos Rusie, NY	1894	36	13	195	2.78	Sandy Koufax, LA	1963	25	5	306	1.88
Christy Mathewson, NY	1905	31	8	206	1.27	Sandy Koufax, LA	1965	26	8	382	2.04
Christy Mathewson, NY	1908	37	11	259	1.43	Sandy Koufax, LA	1966	27	9	317	1.73
Grover Alexander, Phil	1915	31	10	241	1.22	Steve Carlton, Phil	1972	27	10	310	1.97
Grover Alexander, Phil	1916	33	12	167	1.55	Dwight Gooden, NY	1985	24	4	268	1.53
Grover Alexander, Phil	1917	30	13	201	1.86	Randy Johnson, Ari	2002	24	5	334	2.32

AMERICAN LEAGUE											
PLAYER AND TEAM	YEAR	W	L	SO	ERA	PLAYER AND TEAM	YEAR	W	L	SO	ERA
Cy Young, Bos	1901	33	10	158	1.62	Lefty Gomez, NY	1934	26	5	158	2.33
Rube Waddell, Phil	1905	26	11	287	1.48	Lefty Gomez, NY	1937	21	11	194	2.33
Walter Johnson, Wash	1913	36	7	303	1.09	Hal Newhouser, Det	1945	25	9	212	1.81
Walter Johnson, Wash	1918	23	13	162	1.27	Roger Clemens, Tor	1997	21	7	292	2.05
Walter Johnson, Wash	1924	23	7	158	2.72	Roger Clemens, Tor	1998	20	6	271	2.64
Lefty Grove, Phil	1930	28	5	209	2.54	Pedro Martinez, Bos	1999	23	4	313	2.07
Lefty Grove, Phil	1931	31	4	175	2.06	Johan Santana, Min	2006	19	6	245	2.77

***Pitcher who leads in three categories: wins, strikeouts, and ERA.

NOTABLE ACHIEVEMENTS

CONSECUTIVE GAMES PLAYED, 500 OR MORE GAMES

NATIONAL LEAGUE AND AMERICAN LEAGUE

Cal Ripken, Jr.	2,632	Frank McCormick	652
Lou Gehrig	2,130	Sandy Alomar, Sr.	648
Everett Scott	1,307	Eddie Brown	618
Steve Garvey	1,207	Roy McMillan	585
Billy Williams	1,117	George Pinckney	577
Joe Sewell	1,103	Steve Brodie	574
Miguel Tejada	1,069	Aaron Ward	565
Stan Musial	895	Alex Rodriguez	546
Eddie Yost	829	Candy LaChance	540
Gus Suhr	822	Buck Freeman	535
Nellie Fox	798	Fred Luderus	533
Pete Rose	745	Clyde Milan	511
Dale Murphy	740	Charlie Gehringer	511
Richie Ashburn	730	Vada Pinson	508
Ernie Banks	717	Tony Cuccinello	504
Pete Rose	678	Charlie Gehringer	504
Earl Averill	673	Omar Moreno	503

UNASSISTED TRIPLE PLAYS

PLAYER AND TEAM	DATE	POS	OPP	OPP BATTER
Neal Ball, Cle	7-19-09	SS	Bos	Amby McConnell
Bill Wambsganss, Cle	10-10-20	2B	Bklyn	Clarence Mitchell
George Burns, Bos	9-14-23	1B	Cle	Frank Brower
Ernie Padgett, Bos	10-6-23	SS	Phil	Walter Holke
Glenn Wright, Pitt	5-7-25	SS	StL	Jim Bottomley
Jimmy Cooney, Chi	5-30-27	SS	Pitt	Paul Waner
Johnny Neun, Det	5-31-27	1B	Cle	Homer Summa
Ron Hansen, Wash	7-30-68	SS	Cle	Joe Azcue
Mickey Morandini, Phil	9-20-92	2B	Pitt	Jeff King
John Valentin, Bos	7-15-94	SS	Min	Marc Newfield
Randy Velarde, Oak	5-29-00	2B	NYY	Shane Spencer
Rafael Furcal, Atl	5-10-03	SS	StL	Woody Williams

PENNANT WINNERS (PAST 50 YEARS)

NATIONAL LEAGUE

YEAR	TEAM	MANAGER	W	L	PCT	GA
2006	St. Louis Cardinals (C)	Tony La Russa	83	78	.516	1.5
2005	Houston Astros (WC)	Phil Garner	89	73	.549	-11
2004	St. Louis (C)	Tony La Russa	105	57	.648	13
2003	Florida (WC)	Jack McKeon	91	71	.562	-10
2002	San Francisco (WC)	Dusty Baker	95	66	.590	-2.5
2001	Arizona (W)	Bob Brenly	92	70	.568	2
2000	New York (WC)	Bobby Valentine	94	68	.580	-6.5
1999	Atlanta (E)	Bobby Cox	103	59	.636	6.5
1998	San Diego (W)	Bruce Bochy	98	64	.605	9.5
1997	Florida (WC)	Jim Leyland	92	70	.568	-9
1996	Atlanta (E)	Bobby Cox	96	66	.593	8
1995	Atlanta (E)	Bobby Cox	90	54	.625	21
1994	Season ended Aug. 11 due to labor dispute.					
1993	Philadelphia (E)	Jim Fregosi	97	65	.599	3
1992	Atlanta (W)	Bobby Cox	98	64	.605	8
1991	Atlanta (W)	Bobby Cox	94	68	.580	1
1990	Cincinnati (W)	Lou Piniella	91	71	.562	5
1989	San Francisco (W)	Roger Craig	92	70	.568	3
1988	Los Angeles (W)	Tommy Lasorda	94	67	.584	7
1987	St. Louis (E)	Whitey Herzog	95	67	.586	3
1986	New York (E)	Dave Johnson	108	54	.667	21.5
1985	St. Louis (E)	Whitey Herzog	101	61	.623	3
1984	San Diego (W)	Dick Williams	92	70	.568	12
1983	Philadelphia (E)	Pat Corrales/Paul Owens	90	72	.556	6
1982	St. Louis (E)	Whitey Herzog	92	70	.568	3
1981**	Los Angeles (W)	Tommy Lasorda	63	47	.573	**
1980	Philadelphia (E)	Dallas Green	91	71	.562	1
1979	Pittsburgh (E)	Chuck Tanner	98	64	.605	2
1978	Los Angeles (W)	Tommy Lasorda	95	67	.586	2.5
1977	Los Angeles (W)	Tommy Lasorda	98	64	.605	10

GA = Games Ahead. **First half 36–21; second half 27–26, in season split by strike; defeated Houston in playoff for Western Division title.

LEGENDS

Rollie Fingers, relief pitcher, b. August 25, 1946, Steubenville, Ohio. Fingers, whose real first name is Roland, began his career as a starting pitcher, but he became a great relief pitcher and helped change the way teams used their bullpens. Fingers dominated opposing hitters during the early 1970s. He won three World Series with the Oakland A's and was named the 1974 World Series MVP. After a stint with the Padres, Fingers rejuvenated his career in Milwaukee, going 6–3 with a 1.04 ERA and 28 saves for the Brewers in 1981. He won both the AL Cy Young award and league MVP honors that year. The seven-time All-Star finished his career with what was, at the time, a major league record 341 saves. He was inducted into the Baseball Hall of Fame in 1992.

Rollie Fingers won one game and saved two others for the Oakland A's in the 1974 World Series.

WALTER IOOSS, JR.

James "Cool Papa" Bell, outfielder, b. May 17, 1903, Starkville, Mississippi; d. March 7, 1991 St. Louis, Missouri. Perhaps the fastest baserunner of his era, Bell played centerfield for several Negro League teams from 1922 to 1950. During his career, he became well-known for stealing bases, turning sacrifice bunts into hits, and stretching singles into doubles and even triples. During the mid-1930s, Bell was on the roster of a legendary Pittsburgh Crawfords team that included Negro League stars Josh Gibson and Satchel Paige. In 1974, Bell was inducted into the Baseball Hall of Fame.

Yogi Berra, catcher, b. May 12, 1925, St. Louis, Missouri. Often thought of as the greatest catcher in the history of baseball, Berra symbolized the success of the Yankees of the late 1940s and 1950s. He won AL MVP awards in 1951, '54, and '55 and he helped the Yankees win ten World Series titles between 1947 and 1964. Berra, a 15-time All-Star, was inducted into the Baseball Hall of Fame in 1972.

PENNANT WINNERS (PAST 50 YEARS cont.)

NATIONAL LEAGUE

YEAR	TEAM	MANAGER	W	L	PCT	GA
1976	Cincinnati (W)	Sparky Anderson	102	60	.630	10
1975	Cincinnati (W)	Sparky Anderson	108	54	.667	20
1974	Los Angeles (W)	Walter Alston	102	60	.630	4
1973	New York (E)	Yogi Berra	82	79	.509	1.5
1972	Cincinnati (W)	Sparky Anderson	95	59	.617	10.5
1971	Pittsburgh (E)	Danny Murtaugh	97	65	.599	7
1970	Cincinnati (W)	Sparky Anderson	102	60	.630	14.5
1969	New York (E)	Gil Hodges	100	62	.617	8
1968	St. Louis	Red Schoendienst	97	65	.599	9
1967	St. Louis	Red Schoendienst	101	60	.627	10.5
1966	Los Angeles	Walter Alston	95	67	.586	1.5
1965	Los Angeles	Walter Alston	97	65	.599	2
1964	St. Louis	Johnny Keane	93	69	.574	1
1963	Los Angeles	Walter Alston	99	63	.611	6
1962#	San Francisco	Al Dark	103	62	.624	1
1961	Cincinnati	Fred Hutchinson	93	61	.604	4
1960	Pittsburgh	Danny Murtaugh	95	59	.617	7
1959‡	Los Angeles	Walter Alston	88	68	.564	2
1958	Milwaukee	Fred Haney	92	62	.597	8
1957	Milwaukee	Fred Haney	95	59	.617	8
1956	Brooklyn	Walter Alston	93	61	.604	1

Note: League Championship Series playoffs began in 1969. #Defeated Los Angeles, two games to one, in playoff for pennant. ‡Defeated Milwaukee, two games to none, in playoff for pennant. WC=Wild-card team, E=East division champion, W=West division champion.

PENNANT WINNERS (PAST 50 YEARS)

AMERICAN LEAGUE

YEAR	TEAM	MANAGER	W	L	PCT	GA
2006	Detroit Tigers (WC)	Jim Leyland	95	67	.586	-1
2005	Chicago White Sox (C)	Ozzie Guillen	99	63	.611	6
2004	Boston (WC)	Terry Francona	98	64	.605	-3
2003	New York (E)	Joe Torre	101	61	.623	6
2002	Anaheim (WC)	Mike Scioscia	99	63	.611	-4
2001	New York (E)	Joe Torre	95	65	.594	13.5
2000	New York (E)	Joe Torre	87	74	.540	2.5
1999	New York (E)	Joe Torre	98	64	.605	4
1998	New York (E)	Joe Torre	114	48	.704	22
1997	Cleveland (C)	Mike Hargrove	86	75	.534	6
1996	New York (E)	Joe Torre	92	70	.568	4
1995	Cleveland (C)	Mike Hargrove	100	44	.694	30
1994	Season ended Aug. 11 due to labor dispute.					
1993	Toronto (E)	Cito Gaston	95	67	.586	7
1992	Toronto (E)	Cito Gaston	96	66	.593	4
1991	Minnesota (W)	Tom Kelly	95	67	.586	8
1990	Oakland (W)	Tony La Russa	103	59	.636	9
1989	Oakland (W)	Tony La Russa	99	63	.611	7
1988	Oakland (W)	Tony La Russa	104	58	.642	13
1987	Minnesota (W)	Tom Kelly	85	77	.525	2
1986	Boston (E)	John McNamara	95	66	.590	5.5
1985	Kansas City (W)	Dick Howser	91	71	.562	1
1984	Detroit (E)	Sparky Anderson	104	58	.642	15
1983	Baltimore (E)	Joe Altobelli	98	64	.605	6
1982	Milwaukee (E)	Buck Rodgers, Harvey Kuenn	95	67	.586	1
1981	New York (E)	Gene Michael, Bob Lemon	59	48	.551	#
1980	Kansas City (W)	Jim Frey	97	65	.599	14
1979	Baltimore (E)	Earl Weaver	102	57	.642	8
1978†	New York (E)	Billy Martin, Bob Lemon	100	63	.613	1
1977	New York (E)	Billy Martin	100	62	.617	2.5
1976	New York (E)	Billy Martin	97	62	.610	10.5
1975	Boston (E)	Darrell Johnson	95	65	.594	4.5
1974	Oakland (W)	Al Dark	90	72	.556	5
1973	Oakland (W)	Dick Williams	94	68	.580	6
1972	Oakland (W)	Dick Williams	93	62	.600	5.5
1971	Baltimore (E)	Earl Weaver	101	57	.639	12
1970	Baltimore (E)	Earl Weaver	108	54	.667	15
1969	Baltimore (E)	Earl Weaver	109	53	.673	19
1968	Detroit	Mayo Smith	103	59	.636	12
1967	Boston	Dick Williams	92	70	.568	1
1966	Baltimore	Hank Bauer	97	63	.606	9
1965	Minnesota	Sam Mele	102	60	.630	7
1964	New York	Yogi Berra	99	63	.611	1
1963	New York	Ralph Houk	104	57	.646	10.5
1962	New York	Ralph Houk	96	66	.593	5
1961	New York	Ralph Houk	109	53	.673	8
1960	New York	Casey Stengel	97	57	.630	8
1959	Chicago	Al Lopez	94	60	.610	5
1958	New York	Casey Stengel	92	62	.597	10
1957	New York	Casey Stengel	98	56	.636	8
1956	New York	Casey Stengel	97	57	.630	9

Note: League Championship Series playoffs began in 1969.

†Defeated Boston in a one-game playoff.

#First half 34–22; second half 25–26, in season split by strike; defeated Milwaukee in playoff for Eastern Division title.

WC=Wild-card team, E=East division champ, W=West division champ.

The following is a list of big-time players who switched teams for the 2007 season.

Alfonso Soriano, leftfielder, Chicago Cubs One year after being traded from the Texas Rangers to the Washington Nationals, Soriano scored a big payday as a free agent in December 2006, signing an eight-year, $136-million contract with the Chicago Cubs. During the final five years of the contract, he will be paid $18 million a year, making him the fifth-highest player in the major leagues. Soriano's signing was only one of a number of aggressive off-season moves by the Cubs, who will be guided by new skipper Lou Piniella.

Andy Pettitte, pitcher, New York Yankees Seeking to recapture the magic that saw them win four World Series in five years from 1996 to 2000, the Yankees re-signed Andy Pettitte. The lefty, who makes his off-season home in Texas, had been pitching in Houston since 2004. He signed a one-year deal for $16 million, bringing his 18–6 career playoff record back to a Yankees team that hasn't made it past the ALCS since both he and Roger Clemens left after the 2003 season.

Daisuke Matsuzaka, pitcher, Boston Red Sox At 26 years old, Matsuzaka was already a proven starter with a 96-mph fastball and more than 100 career Japanese League wins. He was on the wish list of every GM in baseball this past winter. But it was the Red Sox who were willing to pay a whopping $51.1-million posting fee to his team, the Seibu Lions, just for the right to talk with him. After a dramatic, cross-country negotiating process, Boston finally signed "Dice-K" to a deal worth $52 million over the next six years.

Barry Zito, pitcher, San Francisco Giants Zito was considered one of the biggest free-agent prizes of the class of 2006 and the Giants landed him with a seven-year contract worth more than $120 million. A lefthander, Zito had compiled a 102-63 record in seven major league seasons with the Oakland A's. He won the AL Cy Young award in 2002. The Giants made their move after having lost their ace Jason Schmidt, who signed a three-year deal with the Dodgers.

JEFF ROBERSON

CHUCK SOLOMON

AP PHOTO/ASAHI BREWERIES, LTD./HO

AP PHOTO/JEFF CHIU

2007 YOUNG STARS TO WATCH

■ **Hanley Ramirez, shortstop, Florida Marlins** The 22-year-old Ramirez was named the 2006 NL Rookie of the Year after a stellar debut season. His 46 doubles were the most by a rookie since 2001, when Albert Pujols had 47 for the Cardinals, and his 51 steals were the most by a rookie since Ichiro Suzuki had 56 in 2001. Ramirez was the first NL rookie to ever have 110-plus runs and 50-plus stolen bases. He was only the fifth big-league player since 1900 to hit more than 45 doubles and steal more than 50 bases in a single season.

CHUCK SOLOMON

■ **Ryan Zimmerman, third baseman, Washington Nationals** Just 21 years old, Zimmerman had a banner year, batting .287, smacking 20 home runs, and driving in 110 RBIs in 2006, his first full season in the major leagues.

DAVID E. KLUTHO

■ **Jonathan Papelbon, pitcher, Boston Red Sox** Originally slated to be a starter in 2006, Papelbon took over the team's closer role in the second game of the season and converted his first 20 save opportunities. His 10 saves in the month of April set a major league rookie record. His season ended early due to a shoulder injury, but he still managed a 4-2 record with 35 saves and an ERA of 0.92. He was runner-up to pitching phenom Justin Verlander in AL Rookie of the Year voting.

JOHN IACONO

■ **Joe Mauer, catcher, Minnesota Twins** Mauer, a 23-year-old native Minnesotan, led the major leagues in 2006 with a red-hot .347 batting average. He also became the first catcher to lead the AL in batting. In May, Mauer also set a major league record when he reached base four or more times in five straight games.

JOHN BIEVER

DID YOU KNOW?

With their win in the 2006 World Series, the St. Louis Cardinals moved into sole possession of second place in total World Series titles with ten. The Philadelphia/Kansas City/Oakland A's are in third place with nine titles and the Brooklyn/Los Angeles Dodgers and Boston Red Sox are tied for fourth with six championships apiece.

TRIVIA CHALLENGE

1 Houston Astros second baseman Craig Biggio currently holds the all-time major league record in which unfortunate statistic?

a. **Most strikeouts**
b. **Most times hit-by-pitch**
c. **Most times caught stealing**

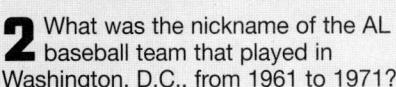

Craig Biggio

2 What was the nickname of the AL baseball team that played in Washington, D.C., from 1961 to 1971?

a. **Capitals**
b. **Senators**
c. **Generals**

3 What body of water lies just over the rightfield bleachers of AT&T Park, the homefield of the San Francisco Giants?

a. **Mays Bay**
b. **McCovey Cove**
c. **Bonds Pond**

4 If a pitcher throws a perfect game, exactly how many batters will he have faced when the game is over?

a. **27**
b. **33**
c. **21**

5 How many home runs did Albert Pujols hit in his first six major league seasons?

a. **188**
b. **225**
c. **250**

Albert Pujols

6 True or False: A manager can change his team's pitcher during the middle of an at-bat?

a. **True**
b. **False**

7 In which month is baseball's All-Star Game traditionally held?

a. **June**
b. **July**
c. **August**

8 If a batted baseball hits the foul pole while still in the air, what is the correct ruling?

a. **Fair: Ground-rule double!**
b. **Foul: Strike!**
c. **Fair: Home run!**

9 At the end of the 2006 season, Red Sox pitcher Curt Schilling had 3,015 career strikeouts. Which one of the following three active pitchers had more strikeouts than he did at that point?

a. **Greg Maddux**
b. **John Smoltz**
c. **Tom Glavine**

Curt Schilling

10 Which rookie pitcher got the start for the Detroit Tigers in Game 1 of the 2006 World Series?

a. **Justin Verlander**
b. **Jonathan Papelbon**
c. **Adam Wainwright**

11 In which year did the AL's designated hitter rule begin?

a. **1953**
b. **1973**
c. **1993**

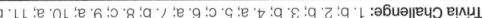

Ron Blomberg, the first DH in major league history

Trivia Challenge: 1. b; 2. b; 3. b; 4. a; 5. c; 6. a; 7. b; 8. c; 9. a; 10. a; 11. b

BASKETBALL MEN'S

The West was the best in 2006–07. The Dallas Mavericks and Phoenix Suns ruled the NBA regular season while the San Antonio Spurs were crowned kings of the league when they won the championship in June.

Dallas dominated regular season play with a 67–15 record. The Mavs became the first NBA team in history to have three win streaks of at least 12 games.

Forward Dirk Nowitzki won his first regular-season MVP award by averaging 24.6 points per game. Phoenix was on the Mavs' heels with a 61–21 record, including a 17-game win streak in December and January.

The Mavs and Suns provided plenty of highlights, but there was one black mark on the season: a brawl between the Denver Nuggets and New York Knicks on December 16. Six

players were suspended. Nuggets star Carmelo Anthony missed 15 games for punching Knicks guard Mardy Collins. Denver made news again on December 19, this time for picking up Allen Iverson in a trade with the Philadelphia 76ers.

The mood of the league turned festive during All-Star Weekend, which was held in Las Vegas, Nevada. The West beat the East, 153–132, thanks

Tony Parker (right) was named Finals MVP, marking the first time in four Spurs' titles that the trophy didn't go to Tim Duncan (left).

BOB ROSATO

NBA TEAMS

EASTERN CONFERENCE
Atlanta Hawks
Boston Celtics
Charlotte Bobcats
Chicago Bulls
Cleveland Cavaliers
Detroit Pistons
Indiana Pacers
Miami Heat
Milwaukee Bucks
New Jersey Nets
New York Knicks
Orlando Magic
Philadelphia 76ers
Toronto Raptors
Washington Wizards

WESTERN CONFERENCE
Dallas Mavericks
Denver Nuggets
Golden State Warriors
Houston Rockets
Los Angeles Clippers
Los Angeles Lakers
Memphis Grizzlies
Minnesota Timberwolves
New Orleans Hornets
Phoenix Suns
Portland Trail Blazers
Sacramento Kings
San Antonio Spurs
Seattle SuperSonics
Utah Jazz

to 31 points from MVP Kobe Bryant.

The opening round of the playoffs saw the greatest upset in tournament history when the eighth-seeded Golden State Warriors defeated Number 1 seed Dallas in six games. The Warriors had won nine of their last 10 games to sneak into the playoffs with a 42–40 record. They stayed hot and beat Dallas thanks to a swarming defense and impressive long-range shooting.

The Suns versus the Spurs was the heavyweight match-up of Round 2. The turning point of the series came in the final seconds of Game 4 when San Antonio's Robert Horry shoved Phoenix point guard Steve Nash, causing a scuffle. Suns forwards Amaré Stoudemire and Boris Diaw were suspended one game each for leaving the bench during the incident. San Antonio took the next two games and won the series, four games to two.

The most impressive individual performance of the playoffs came from the Cleveland Cavaliers superstar LeBron James, who scored 48 points in Game 5 of the Eastern Conference Finals against the Detroit Pistons. James scored Cleveland's final 25 points in the 109–107 double-overtime win. Cleveland went on to beat Detroit, four games to two.

Cleveland's first trip to the NBA Finals didn't last long. The experienced Spurs swept the series to win their fourth title in the last nine seasons. Spurs guard Tony Parker averaged 24.5 points per game and was named the Finals MVP.

LeBron James led the Cavs to their first-ever NBA Finals.

JOHN BIEVER

2006-07 NBA FINAL STANDINGS

Eastern Conference

ATLANTIC	W	L	PCT	GB
a-Toronto	47	35	.573	—
x-New Jersey	41	41	.500	6
Philadelphia	35	47	.427	12
New York	33	49	.402	14
Boston	24	58	.293	23

CENTRAL	W	L	PCT	GB
e-Detroit	53	29	.646	—
x-Cleveland	50	32	.610	3
x-Chicago	49	33	.598	4
Indiana	35	47	.427	18
Milwaukee	28	54	.341	25

SOUTHEAST	W	L	PCT	GB
se-Miami	44	38	.537	—
x-Washington	41	41	.500	3
x-Orlando	40	42	.488	4
Charlotte	33	49	.402	11
Atlanta	30	52	.366	14

Western Conference

NORTHWEST	W	L	PCT	GB
nw-Utah	51	31	.622	—
x-Denver	45	37	.549	6
Portland	32	50	.390	19
Minnesota	32	50	.390	19
Seattle	31	51	.378	20

PACIFIC	W	L	PCT	GB
p-Phoenix	61	21	.744	—
x-LA Lakers	42	40	.512	19
x-Golden State	42	40	.512	19
LA Clippers	40	42	.488	21
Sacramento	33	49	.402	28

SOUTHWEST	W	L	PCT	GB
w-Dallas	67	15	.817	—
x-San Antonio	58	24	.707	9
x-Houston	52	30	.634	15
New Orleans/Okla. City	39	43	.476	28
Memphis	22	60	.268	45

KEY x=clinched playoff berth; e=clinched Eastern Conference; a=clinched Atlantic Division; se=clinched Southeast Division; w=clinched Western Conference; nw=clinched Northwest Division; p=clinched Pacific Division; W=wins; L=losses; PCT=winning percentage; GB=games back

2007 NBA PLAYOFFS

EASTERN CONFERENCE					**WESTERN CONFERENCE**	

Detroit Pistons (4–0)
Detroit Pistons (4–2)
Orlando Magic
Detroit Pistons
Miami Heat
Chicago Bulls
Chicago Bulls (4–0)

Golden State Warriors
Dallas Mavericks
Golden State Warriors (4–2)
Utah Jazz
Utah Jazz (4–3)
Utah Jazz (4–1)
Houston Rockets

San Antonio Spurs
vs.
Cleveland Cavaliers
San Antonio Spurs won the series 4 games to 0

Toronto Raptors
New Jersey Nets
New Jersey Nets (4–2)
Cleveland Cavaliers (4–2)
Cleveland Cavaliers (4–0)
Cleveland Cavaliers (4–2)
Washington Wizards

San Antonio Spurs (4–2)
San Antonio Spurs (4–1)
San Antonio Spurs (4–1)
Denver Nuggets
Phoenix Suns (4–1)
Phoenix Suns
L.A. Lakers

FIRST ROUND · CONF. SEMIFINALS · CONF. FINALS · NBA FINALS · CONF. FINALS · CONF. SEMIFINALS · FIRST ROUND

NBA PLAYOFF RESULTS

FIRST ROUND
Eastern Conference
DETROIT PISTONS VS. ORLANDO MAGIC
GAME 1 April 21, 2007: Detroit 100, Orlando 92
GAME 2 April 23, 2007: Detroit 98, Orlando 90
GAME 3 April 26, 2007: Detroit 93, Orlando 77
GAME 4 April 28, 2007: Detroit 97, Orlando 93
DETROIT PISTONS WINS SERIES, 4–0

MIAMI HEAT VS. CHICAGO BULLS
GAME 1 April 21, 2007: Chicago 96, Miami 91
GAME 2 April 24, 2007: Chicago 107, Miami 89
GAME 3 April 27, 2007: Chicago 104, Miami 96
GAME 4 April 29, 2007: Chicago 92, Miami 79
CHICAGO BULLS WIN SERIES, 4–0

TORONTO RAPTORS VS. NEW JERSEY NETS
GAME 1 April 21, 2007: New Jersey 96, Toronto 91
GAME 2 April 24, 2007: Toronto 89, New Jersey 83
GAME 3 April 27, 2007: New Jersey 102, Toronto 89
GAME 4 April 29, 2007: New Jersey 102, Toronto 81
GAME 5 May 1, 2007: Toronto 99, New Jersey 96
GAME 6 May 4, 2007: New Jersey 98, Toronto 97
NEW JERSEY NETS WIN SERIES, 4–2

CLEVELAND CAVALIERS VS. WASHINGTON WIZARDS
GAME 1 April 22, 2007: Cleveland 97, Washington 82
GAME 2 April 25, 2007: Cleveland 109, Washington 102
GAME 3 April 28, 2007: Cleveland 98, Washington 92
GAME 4 April 30, 2007: Cleveland 97, Washington 90
CLEVELAND WIN SERIES, 4–0

Western Conference
DALLAS MAVERICKS VS. GOLDEN STATE WARRIORS
GAME 1 April 22, 2007: Golden State 97, Dallas 85
GAME 2 April 25, 2007: Dallas 112, Golden State 99
GAME 3 April 27, 2007: Golden State 109, Dallas 91
GAME 4 April 29, 2007: Golden State 103, Dallas 99
GAME 5 May 1, 2007: Dallas 118, Golden State 112
GAME 6 May 3, 2007: Golden State 111, Dallas 86
GOLDEN STATE WIN SERIES, 4–2

UTAH JAZZ VS. HOUSTON ROCKETS
GAME 1 April 21, 2007: Houston 84, Utah 75
GAME 2 April 23, 2007: Houston 98, Utah 90
GAME 3 April 26, 2007: Utah 81, Houston 67
GAME 4 April 28, 2007: Utah 98, Houston 85

GAME 5 April 30, 2007: Houston 96, Utah 92
GAME 6 May 3, 2007: Utah 94, Houston 82
GAME 7 May 5, 2007: Utah 103, Houston 99
UTAH JAZZ WIN SERIES, 4–3

SAN ANTONIO SPURS VS. DENVER NUGGETS
GAME 1 April 22, 2007: Denver 95, San Antonio 89
GAME 2 April 25, 2007: San Antonio 97, Denver 88
GAME 3 April 28, 2007: San Antonio 96, Denver 91
GAME 4 April 30, 2007: San Antonio 96, Denver 89
GAME 5 May 2, 2007: San Antonio 93, Denver 78
SAN ANTONIO SPURS WIN SERIES, 4-1

PHOENIX SUNS VS. LOS ANGELES LAKERS
GAME 1 April 22, 2007: Phoenix 95, Los Angeles 87
GAME 2 April 24, 2007: Phoenix 108, Los Angeles 98
GAME 3 April 26, 2007: Los Angeles 95, Phoenix 89
GAME 4 April 29, 2007: Phoenix 113, Los Angeles 100
GAME 5 May 2, 2007: Phoenix 119, Los Angeles 110
PHOENIX SUNS WIN SERIES, 4–1

CONFERENCE SEMIFINALS
Eastern Conference
DETROIT PISTONS VS. CHICAGO BULLS
GAME 1 May 5, 2007: Detroit 95, Chicago 69
GAME 2 May 7, 2007: Detroit 108, Chicago 871
GAME 3 May 10, 2007: Detroit 81, Chicago 74
GAME 4 May 13, 2007: Chicago 102, Detroit 87
GAME 5 May 15, 2007: Chicago 108, Detroit 92
GAME 6 May 17, 2007: Detroit 95, Chicago 85
DETROIT PISTONS WINS SERIES, 4–2

CLEVELAND CAVALIERS VS. NEW JERSEY NETS
GAME 1 May 6, 2007: Cleveland 81, New Jersey 77
GAME 2 May 8, 2007: Cleveland 102, New Jersey 92
GAME 3 May 12, 2007: New Jersey 96, Cleveland 85,
GAME 4 May 14, 2007: Cleveland 87, New Jersey 85
GAME 5 May 16, 2007: New Jersey 83, Cleveland 72
GAME 6 May 18, 2007: Cleveland 88, New Jersey 72
CLEVELAND CAVALIERS WIN SERIES, 4–2

Western Conference

SAN ANTONIO SPURS VS. PHOENIX SUNS
GAME 1 May 6, 2007: San Antonio 111, Phoenix 106
GAME 2 May 8, 2007: Phoenix 101, San Antonio 81
GAME 3 May 12, 2007: San Antonio 108, Phoenix 101
GAME 4 May 14, 2007: Phoenix 104, San Antonio 98
GAME 5 May 16, 2007: San Antonio 88, Phoenix 85
GAME 6 May 18, 2007: San Antonio 114, Phoenix 106
SAN ANTONIO SPURS WIN SERIES, 4–2

UTAH JAZZ VS. GOLDEN STATE WARRIORS
GAME 1 May 8, 2006: Utah 116, Golden State 112
GAME 2 May 10, 2006: Utah 127, Golden State 117 (OT)
GAME 3 May 12, 2006: Golden State 125, Utah 105
GAME 4 May 14, 2006: Utah 115, Golden State 101
GAME 5 May 16, 2006: Utah 100, Golden State 87
UTAH JAZZ WIN SERIES, 4–1

CONFERENCE FINALS

Western Conference

SAN ANTONIO SPURS VS. UTAH JAZZ
GAME 1 May 20, 2007: San Antonio 108, Utah 100
GAME 2 May 22, 2007: San Antonio 105, Utah 96
GAME 3 May 26, 2007: Utah 109, San Antonio 83
GAME 4 May 28, 2007: San Antonio 91, Utah 79
GAME 5 May 30, 2007: San Antonio 109, Utah 84
SAN ANTONIO SPURS WIN SERIES, 4–1

Eastern Conference

DETROIT PISTONS VS. CLEVELAND CAVALIERS
GAME 1 May 21, 2007: Detroit 79, Cleveland 76
GAME 2 May 24, 2007: Detroit 79, Cleveland 76
GAME 3 May 27, 2007: Cleveland 88, Detroit 82
GAME 4 May 29, 2007: Cleveland 91, Detroit 87
GAME 5 May 31, 2007: Cleveland 109, Detroit 107 (2OT)
GAME 6 June 2, 2007: Cleveland 98, Detroit 82
CLEVELAND CAVALIERS WIN SERIES, 4–2

NBA FINALS

SAN ANTONIO SPURS VS. CLEVELAND CAVALIERS
GAME 1 June 7, 2007: San Antonio 85, Cleveland 76
GAME 2 June 10, 2007: San Antonio 103, Cleveland 92
GAME 3 June 12, 2007: San Antonio 75, Cleveland 72
GAME 4 June 14, 2007: San Antonioi 83, Cleveland 82
SAN ANTONIO SPURS WIN SERIES, 4–0

NBA FINALS COMPOSITE BOX SCORE

SAN ANTONIO SPURS

PLAYER	GP	Field Goals		3-PT FG		Free Throws		Rebounds		A	STL	TO	BLK	AVG
		FGM	PCT	FGM	PCT	FTM	PCT	OFF	TOTAL					
Tony Parker	4	42	56.8	4	57.1	10	52.6	3	20	13	3	12	0	24.5
Tim Duncan	4	29	44.6	0	0.0	15	62.5	16	46	15	5	11	9	18.3
Manu Ginobili	4	18	36.7	10	43.5	25	83.3	1	23	10	5	9	0	17.8
Bruce Bowen	4	8	29.6	7	38.9	1	25.0	3	22	5	2	3	1	6.0
Fabricio Oberto	4	8	47.1	0	0.0	1	33.3	7	17	2	1	4	0	4.3
Francisco Elson	4	6	100.0	0	0.0	4	80.0	6	10	0	1	3	0	4.0
Michael Finley	4	6	26.1	1	8.3	2	66.7	1	8	3	5	2	0	3.8
Brent Barry	4	4	36.4	4	40.0	0	0.0	1	6	2	1	3	0	3.0
Robert Horry	4	3	33.3	3	37.5	3	75.0	4	18	13	1	5	5	3.0
Jacque Vaughn	4	4	57.1	0	0.0	0	0.0	1	5	4	0	0	0	2.0
Beno Udrih	2	0	0.0	0	0.0	0	0.0	0	0	0	0	0	0	0.0
TOTALS	**4**	**128**	**44.4**	**29**	**37.2**	**61**	**66.3**	**43**	**175**	**67**	**24**	**52**	**15**	**86.5**

CLEVELAND CAVALIERS

PLAYER	GP	Field Goals		3-PT FG		Free Throws		Rebounds		A	STL	TO	BLK	AVG
		FGM	PCT	FGM	PCT	FTM	PCT	OFF	TOTAL					
LeBron James	4	32	35.6	4	20.0	20	69.0	4	28	27	4	23	2	22.0
Drew Gooden	4	22	50.0	0	0.0	7	87.5	12	33	1	1	5	2	12.8
Daniel Gibson	4	18	43.9	6	31.6	1	100.0	1	7	10	6	0	0	10.8
Aleksandar Pavlovic	4	16	36.4	5	41.7	2	33.3	4	10	3	2	5	0	9.8
Zydrunas Ilgauskas	4	13	35.1	0	0.0	5	83.3	18	41	2	2	4	4	7.8
Anderson Varejao	4	10	66.7	0	0.0	10	62.5	6	21	3	5	2	2	7.5
Damon Jones	4	5	45.5	5	55.6	3	100.0	1	5	4	0	0	0	4.5
Donyell Marshall	4	5	31.3	2	18.2	3	75.0	2	9	5	3	2	0	3.8
Eric Snow	4	2	40.0	0	0.0	1	50.0	1	4	9	1	1	1	1.3
Larry Hughes	2	1	10.0	0	0.0	0	0.0	0	5	2	1	2	0	1.0
Ira Newble	1	0	0.0	0	0.0	0	0.0	0	1	0	0	0	0	0.0
Scot Pollard	1	0	0.0	0	0.0	0	0.0	0	0	0	0	0	0	0.0
Shannon Brown	1	0	0.0	0	0.0	0	0.0	0	0	0	0	0	0	0.0
TOTALS	**4**	**124**	**39.5**	**22**	**29.3**	**52**	**69.3**	**49**	**164**	**66**	**25**	**47**	**11**	**80.5**

KEY GP=games played; FGM=field goals made; PCT=percentage; FTM=free throws made; OFF=offensive; A=assists; STL=steals; TO=turnovers; BLK=blocks; AVG=average

NBA FINALS BOX SCORES

GAME 1

SAN ANTONIO SPURS 85

	MIN	FG M-A	FT M-A	REB O-T	A	PF	STL	TO	PTS
T. Parker	38	12-23	3-6	1-4	7	1	2	4	27
M. Finley	20	1-7	0-0	0-3	0	1	0	0	2
T. Duncan	39	10-17	4-5	5-13	1	2	2	2	24
B. Bowen	40	2-6	0-0	1-3	1	1	0	1	6
F. Oberto	17	0-2	0-0	2-4	2	3	0	1	0
M. Ginobili	28	5-12	3-4	0-8	0	3	1	2	16
R. Horry	23	1-3	0-0	0-1	6	2	1	3	3
F. Elson	16	2-2	1-1	3-6	0	1	0	0	5
J. Vaughn	10	1-3	0-0	1-1	1	0	0	0	2
B. Barry	8	0-0	0-0	0-0	0	1	0	1	0
B. Udrih	1	0-0	0-0	0-0	0	0	0	0	0
M. Bonner									DNP
TOTALS	240	34-75	11-16	13-43	18	15	6	14	85

Percentages: Field Goals—45.3%, 3-Point Field Goals: 6-16, 37.5%, (M. Finley 0-4, B. Bowen 2-4, M. Ginobili 3-5, R. Horry 1-3). Free-Throws: 68.8%. Team Rebounds: 8. Blocked Shots: 5 (T. Duncan 5)

CLEVELAND CAVALIERS 76

	MIN	FG M-A	FT M-A	REB O-T	A	PF	STL	TO	PTS
L. Hughes	23	1-5	0-0	0-3	0	2	0	0	2
A. Pavlovic	37	6-12	1-2	2-5	0	2	0	1	13
D. Gooden	26	6-9	2-2	1-4	0	4	1	2	14
L. James	44	4-16	4-4	1-7	4	1	1	6	14
Z. Ilgauskas	23	1-8	0-0	2-6	1	2	1	0	2
A. Varejao	31	3-6	4-7	3-4	0	3	0	1	10
D. Gibson	28	7-9	0-0	0-1	4	1	4	0	16
D. Marshall	16	2-5	0-0	0-2	0	1	1	1	5
D. Jones	12	0-0	0-0	0-0	0	0	0	0	0
E. Snow	1	0-0	0-0	0-0	0	0	0	0	0
S. Pollard									DNP
I. Newble									DNP
TOTALS	240	30-70	11-15	9-32	9	16	8	11	76

Percentages: Field Goals: 42.9%, 3-Point Field Goals: 5-15, 33.3%, (L. Hughes 0-1, A. Pavlovic 0-1, L. James 2-6, D. Gibson 2-3, D. Marshall 1-4). Free-Throws: 73.3%. Team Rebounds: 7. Blocked Shots: 2 (L. James 1, Z. Ilgauskas 1)

GAME 2

SAN ANTONIO SPURS 103

	MIN	FG M-A	FT M-A	REB O-T	A	PF	STL	TO	PTS
T. Parker	36	13-20	3-4	1-4	2	2	1	2	30
M. Finley	15	1-4	0-0	1-3	3	2	1	1	2
T. Duncan	36	9-16	5-7	4-9	8	4	0	1	23
B. Bowen	41	1-9	0-0	1-5	0	1	1	1	3
F. Oberto	20	2-3	0-2	1-4	0	3	0	1	4
M. Ginobili	28	5-11	11-11	0-6	2	5	3	3	25
R. Horry	26	1-3	2-2	2-9	4	3	0	0	5
F. Elson	13	3-3	0-0	2-3	0	3	0	1	6
J. Vaughn	12	1-2	0-0	0-3	2	0	0	0	2
B. Barry	12	1-6	0-0	0-2	1	0	0	0	3
B. Udrih	1	0-0	0-0	0-0	0	0	0	0	0
M. Bonner									DNP
TOTALS	240	37-77	21-26	12-46	21	23	6	10	103

Percentages: Field Goals: 48.1%, 3-Point Field Goals: 8-24, 33.3% (T. Parker 1-1, M. Finley 1-4, B. Bowen 1-6, M. Ginobili 4-6, R. Horry 1-2, B. Barry 1-6). Free-Throws: 80.8%. Team Rebounds: 3. Blocked Shots: 6 (R. Horry 5, B. Bowen 1)

CLEVELAND CAVALIERS 92

	MIN	FG M-A	FT M-A	REB O-T	A	PF	STL	TO	PTS
L. Hughes	20	0-5	0-0	0-2	2	1	1	2	0
A. Pavlovic	27	4-11	0-2	2-4	0	1	3	3	10
D. Gooden	24	6-12	1-1	3-6	0	2	0	0	13
L. James	38	9-21	7-11	3-7	6	3	1	6	25
Z. Ilgauskas	22	3-8	3-3	1-4	0	3	0	0	9
D. Gibson	32	6-12	1-1	0-1	0	3	1	0	15
A. Varejao	28	2-2	4-7	1-10	2	4	0	0	8
D. Marshall	21	1-4	2-2	1-2	3	2	1	0	5
D. Jones	15	2-4	0-0	1-3	0	0	0	0	6
E. Snow	11	0-1	1-2	1-2	2	0	0	0	1
S. Pollard	1	0-0	0-0	0-0	0	0	0	0	0
I. Newble	1	0-1	0-0	0-1	0	0	0	0	0
TOTALS	240	33-81	19-29	13-42	15	19	5	11	92

Percentages: Field Goals: 40.7%, 3-Point Field Goals: 7-19, 36.8% (L. Hughes 0-1, A. Pavlovic 2-5, D. Gooden 0-2, D. Gibson 2-5, D. Marshall 1-3, D. Jones 2-3, I. Newble 0-1). Free-Throws: 65.5%. Team Rebounds: 12. Blocked Shots: 2 (D. Gooden 1, Z. Ilgauskas 1)

GAME 3

SAN ANTONIO SPURS 75

	MIN	FG M-A	FT M-A	REB O-T	A	PF	STL	TO	PTS
T. Parker	39	7-17	2-4	1-5	3	0	0	3	17
M. Finley	24	3-7	0-0	0-2	1	1	4	1	7
T. Duncan	34	6-17	2-2	2-9	3	4	1	2	14
B. Bowen	44	4-6	1-4	0-9	1	1	1	1	13
F. Oberto	20	3-7	0-0	1-4	0	3	0	2	6
M. Ginobili	27	0-7	3-4	0-4	5	2	0	3	3
R. Horry	20	1-1	0-0	1-5	2	1	0	0	3
B. Barry	17	3-5	0-0	1-2	0	1	1	1	9
J. Vaughn	9	1-1	0-0	0-0	0	1	0	0	2
F. Elson	6	0-0	1-2	1-1	0	1	0	1	1
M. Bonner									DNP
B. Udrih									DNP
TOTALS	240	28-68	9-16	7-41	15	15	7	14	75

Percentages: Field Goals: 41.2%, 3-Point Field Goals: 10-19, 52.6% (T. Parker 1-3, M. Finley 1-3, B. Bowen 4-5, M. Ginobili 0-3, R. Horry 1-1, B. Barry 3-4). Free-Throws: 56.3%. Team Rebounds: 8. Blocked Shots: 2 (T. Duncan 2)

CLEVELAND CAVALIERS 72

	MIN	FG M-A	FT M-A	REB O-T	A	PF	STL	TO	PTS
D. Gibson	36	1-10	0-0	0-3	1	0	1	0	2
A. Pavlovic	42	5-15	1-2	0-0	3	3	0	1	13
D. Gooden	33	5-11	3-4	4-12	1	6	0	2	13
L. James	42	9-23	7-8	0-8	7	3	2	5	25
Z. Ilgauskas	32	6-13	0-1	10-18	0	2	1	3	12
D. Jones	18	1-2	0-0	0-1	2	1	0	0	3
E. Snow	17	0-0	0-0	0-1	5	0	1	0	0
A. Varejao	15	2-4	0-0	1-4	0	1	2	1	4
D. Marshall	6	0-1	0-0	0-1	0	1	0	0	0
D. Wesley									DNP
S. Pollard									DNP
S. Brown									DNP
TOTALS	240	29-79	11-15	15-48	19	17	7	12	72

Percentages: Field Goals: 36.7%, 3-Point Field Goals: 3-19, 15.8% (D. Gibson 0-5, A. Pavlovic 2-6, L. James 0-5, D. Jones 1-2, D. Marshall 0-1). Free-Throws: 73.3%. Team Rebounds: 4. Blocked Shots: 5 (D. Gooden 1, L. James 1, Z. Ilgauskas 1, A. Varejao 2)

KEY — MIN=minutes played; FG M-A=field goals made-attempted; FT M-A=free throws made-attempted; REB O-T=rebounds offensive-total; A=assists; PF=personal fouls; STL=steals; TO=turnovers; PTS=points; DNP=did not play

GAME 4

SAN ANTONIO 83

	MIN	FG M-A	FT M-A	REB O-T	A	PF	STL	TO	PTS
T. Parker	39	10-14	2-5	0-7	1	2	0	3	24
M. Finley	16	1-5	2-3	0-2	0	0	0	0	4
T. Duncan	40	4-15	4-10	5-15	3	3	2	6	12
B. Bowen	42	1-6	0-0	1-5	3	4	0	0	2
F. Oberto	25	3-5	1-1	3-5	0	2	1	0	7
M. Ginobili	33	8-19	8-10	1-5	3	5	1	1	27
R. Horry	19	0-2	1-2	1-3	1	1	0	2	1
F. Elson[11]	11	1-1	2-2	0-0	0	0	1	1	4
J. Vaughn	9	1-1	0-0	0-1	1	1	0	0	2
B. Barry	5	0-0	0-0	0-2	1	1	0	1	0
M. Bonner									DNP
B. Udrih									DNP
TOTALS	**240**	**29-68**	**20-34**	**11-45**	**13**	**19**	**5**	**14**	**83**

Percentages: Field Goals: 42.6%, 3-Point Field Goals: 5-19, 26.3% (T. Parker 2-3, M. Finley 0-2, B. Bowen 0-3, M. Ginobili 3-9, R. Horry 0-2). Free-Throws: 58.8%. Team Rebounds: 12. Blocked Shots: 2 (T. Duncan 2).

CLEVELAND 82

	MIN	FG M-A	FT M-A	REB O-T	A	PF	STL	TO	PTS
D. Gibson	44	4-13	0-0	1-2	5	4	0	0	10
A. Pavlovic	21	1-2	0-0	0-1	0	4	1	0	3
D. Gooden	27	5-9	1-1	4-11	0	2	0	1	11
L. James	46	10-30	2-6	0-6	10	1	0	6	24
Z. Ilgauskas	26	3-8	2-2	5-13	1	3	0	1	8
A. Varejao	24	3-6	2-2	1-3	1	4	3	0	8
D. Jones	20	2-4	3-3	0-1	2	1	0	0	9
D. Marshall	19	2-7	1-2	1-4	2	4	1	1	5
E. Snow	13	2-5	0-0	0-1	2	1	0	1	4
S. Brown	1	0-0	0-0	0-0	0	0	0	0	0
D. Wesley									DNP
S. Pollard									DNP
TOTALS	**240**	**32-84**	**11-16**	**12-42**	**23**	**24**	**5**	**10**	**82**

Percentages: Field Goals: 38.1%, 3-Point Field Goals: 7-22, 31.8% (D. Gibson 2-6, A. Pavlovic 1-2, L. James 2-7, D. Jones 2-4, D. Marshall 0-3). Free-Throws: 68.8%. Team Rebounds: 11. Blocked Shots 2 (Z. Ilgauskas 1, E. Snow 1).

In San Antonio's sweep of the Cleveland Cavaliers in the 2007 NBA Finals, Spurs forward Tim Duncan averaged 18.3 points, 11.5 rebounds, 3.8 assists, and 2.3 blocks per game.

LEGENDS

■ **Darryl Dawkins, center,** b. January 11, 1957, Orlando, Florida. One of the first players to come straight to the NBA from high school, Dawkins was known for his backboard-shattering dunks with the Philadelphia 76ers, which prompted the NBA to adopt a new, flexible-rim design. Dawkins went to the NBA finals with Sixers in 1977, 1980, and 1982. He also holds the NBA record for most personal fouls commited in one season (386, in 1984). After seven seasons with the Sixers, Dawkins was traded to the New Jersy Nets, where he spent five seasons. Dawkins then played briefly for Utah, Detroit, and Toronto before retiring from the NBA in 1989.

Dawkins shattered his first backboard in Kansas City in 1979.

PETER READ MILLER/SPORTS ILLUSTRATED

■ **Pete Maravich, guard,** b. June 22, 1947, Aliquippa, Pennsylvania; d. January 5, 1988, Pasadena, California. "Pistol" Pete Maravich was the first-round draft pick for the Atlanta Hawks in 1970 after setting 11 NCAA records during his three years with the LSU Tigers. Maravich also played for the New Orleans (and, later, Utah) Jazz and the Boston Celtics, where he briefly shared the court with Larry Bird. In his 10 years in the NBA, Maravich never won a championship. He is, however, 16th on the league's all-time scoring list, averaging 24.2 points over 658 games. He also led the league in scoring during the 1976-77 season, averaging 31.1 points per game, and was a five-time NBA All-Star. Eight years after his retirement from the NBA, Maravich died of a heart attack while playing a three-on-three pickup game in a California gym.

■ **Bob McAdoo, forward,** b. September 25, 1951, Greensboro, North Carolina. After being drafted by the expansion Buffalo Braves in 1972, McAdoo had an fantastic start to his NBA career. In his first four years in the league, he earned the NBA Rookie of the Year Award (1974), the league MVP Award (1975), and three straight scoring titles. During his early years in the league, McAdoo was traded several times before he finally found his spot with a championship team. In a surprising late-career resurgence in the early 1980's, McAdoo earned two championship rings in four finals appearances with the Los Angeles Lakers. A five-time NBA All-Star, McAdoo was elected to the Basketball Hall of Fame in 2000. He is currently an assistant coach for the Miami Heat.

2006–2007 NBA INDIVIDUAL LEADERS

JOHN W. MCDONOUGH

Kobe Bryant

SCORING

	GP	PTS	AVG
Kobe Bryant, Los Angeles Lakers	77	2,430	31.6
Carmelo Anthony, Denver Nuggets	65	1,181	28.9
Gilbert Arenas, Washington Wizards	74	2,105	28.4
LeBron James, Cleveland Cavaliers	78	2,132	27.3
Ray Allen, Seattle SuperSonics	55	1,454	26.4
Allen Iverson, Philadelphia/Denver	65	1,709	26.3

REBOUNDING

	GP	REB	AVG
Kevin Garnett, Minnesota Timberwolves	76	975	12.8
Tyson Chandler, NO/OKC Hornets	73	904	12.4
Dwight Howard, Orlando Magic	82	1,008	12.3
Carlos Boozer, Utah Jazz	74	867	11.7
Marcus Camby, Denver Nuggets	70	816	11.7
Ben Wallace, Chicago Bulls	77	821	10.7

ASSISTS

	GP	A	AVG
Steve Nash, Phoenix Suns	76	884	11.6
Deron Williams, Utah Jazz	80	745	9.3
Jason Kidd, New Jersey Nets	80	736	9.2
Chris Paul, NO/OKC Hornets	64	569	8.9
Baron Davis, Golden State Warriors	63	509	8.1

FIELD GOAL PERCENTAGE

	FGA	FGM	PCT
Mikki Moore, New Jersey Nets	506	308	.609
Dwight Howard, Orlando Magic	873	526	.603
Andris Biedrins, Golden State Warriors	581	348	.599
Eddy Curry, New York Knicks	1,016	585	.576
Amare Stoudemire, Phoenix Suns	1,055	607	.575

FREE THROW PERCENTAGE

	FTA	FTM	PCT
Kyle Korver, Philadelphia 76ers	209	191	.914
Matt Carroll, Charlotte Bobcats	208	188	.904
Dirk Nowitzki, Dallas Mavericks	551	498	.904
Ray Allen, Seattle SuperSonics	309	279	.903
Steve Nash, Phoenix Suns	247	222	.899
Earl Boykins, Denver/Milwaukee	245	220	.898

3-POINT FIELD GOAL PERCENTAGE

	FGA	FGM	PCT
Jason Kapono, Miami Heat	210	108	.514
Steve Nash, Phoenix Suns	343	156	.454
Brent Barry, San Antonio Spurs	287	128	.450
Luther Head, Houston Rockets	401	177	.441
Anthony Parker, Toronto Raptors	261	115	.441
Jason Terry, Dallas Mavericks	370	162	.440

STEALS

	GP	STL	AVG
Baron Davis, Golden State Warriors	63	135	2.1
Ron Artest, Sacramento Kings	70	149	2.1
Caron Butler, Washington Wizards	63	134	2.1
Andre Iguodala, Philadelphia 76ers	76	152	2.0
Gerald Wallace, Charlotte Bobcats	72	144	2.0

Marcus Camby

JOHN W. MCDONOUGH

BLOCKS

	GP	BLK	AVG
Marcus Camby, Denver Nuggets	70	231	3.3
Josh Smith, Atlanta Hawks	72	207	2.8
Jermaine O'Neal, Indiana Pacers	69	182	2.6
Emeka Okafor, Charlotte Bobcats	67	172	2.5
Tim Duncan, San Antonio Spurs	80	190	2.3

KEY GP=games played; PTS=points; AVG=average; REB=rebounds; A=assists; FGA=field goals attempted; FGM=field goals made; PCT=percentage; FTA=free throw attempts; FTM=free throws made; STL=steals; BLK=blocks

TEAM-BY-TEAM STATS

ATLANTA HAWKS

PLAYER	GP	MIN	Field Goals		3-PT FG	Free Throws		Rebounds		A	STL	TO	BLK	AVG
			FGM	PCT	FGA-FGM	FTM	PCT	OFF	TOTAL					
Joe Johnson	57	2,359	536	47.1	312-119	235	74.8	53	239	249	60	176	11	25.0
Josh Smith	72	2,647	436	43.9	152-38	268	69.3	165	621	236	101	227	207	16.4
Marvin Williams	64	2,179	306	43.3	45-11	216	81.5	84	337	121	52	127	30	13.1
Josh Childress	55	2,024	261	50.4	77-26	167	79.5	123	340	127	58	80	36	13.0
Zaza Pachulia	72	2,026	291	47.4	1-0	293	78.6	199	500	106	77	162	36	12.2
Tyronn Lue	56	1,488	218	41.6	161-56	144	88.3	19	104	201	24	85	0	11.4
Salim Stoudamire	61	1,034	177	41.6	155-56	61	89.7	6	74	61	21	55	2	7.7
Anthony Johnson	27	739	82	41.6	44-14	25	78.1	9	53	123	17	45	2	7.5
Shelden Williams	81	1,514	166	45.5	4-2	110	76.4	131	435	44	52	96	39	5.5
Speedy Claxton	42	1,054	91	32.7	28-6	33	55.0	12	81	185	72	75	4	5.3
Solomon Jones	58	666	65	50.8	1-0	59	78.7	49	136	11	11	25	42	3.3
Royal Ivey	53	539	64	44.8	16-5	24	68.6	15	51	45	24	31	4	3.0
Slava Medvedenko	14	81	12	41.4	2-1	17	85.0	4	14	2	0	5	2	3.0
Dijon Thompson	6	50	6	40.0	2-0	5	83.3	3	8	2	0	1	0	2.8
Lorenzen Wright	67	1,035	82	44.8	0-0	9	28.1	85	216	40	28	39	28	2.6
TEAM TOTALS	**82**	**19,880**	**2,831**	**44.4**	**1,038-341**	**1,677**	**76.1**	**976**	**3,288**	**1,573**	**609**	**1,306**	**446**	**93.7**
OPPONENTS	**82**		**2,953**	**46.6**	**1,236-465**	**1,699**	**73.4**	**948**	**3,318**	**1,732**	**597**	**1,247**	**421**	**98.4**

KEY GP=games played; MIN=minutes played; FGM=field goals made; PCT=percentage; FGA=field goals attempted; FTM=free throws made; OFF=offensive; A=assists; STL=steals; TO=turnovers; BLK=blocks; AVG=average

BOSTON CELTICS

PLAYER	GP	MIN	FGM	PCT	FGA-FGM	FTM	PCT	OFF	TOTAL	A	STL	TO	BLK	AVG
			Field Goals		3-PT FG	Free Throws		Rebounds						
Paul Pierce	47	1,740	373	43.9	275-107	320	79.6	39	277	194	48	152	13	25.0
Al Jefferson	69	2,319	453	51.4	1-0	201	68.1	237	756	88	48	136	106	16.0
Wally Szczerbiak	32	900	161	41.5	106-44	113	89.7	16	98	55	18	54	3	15.0
Delonte West	69	2,219	306	42.7	178-65	168	85.3	32	208	304	74	140	34	12.2
Ryan Gomes	73	2,275	338	46.7	42-16	189	81.1	125	407	119	48	105	13	12.1
Tony Allen	33	805	133	51.4	33-8	105	78.4	35	124	56	49	75	12	11.5
Gerald Green	81	1,780	310	41.9	258-95	128	80.5	68	208	83	41	120	24	10.4
Rajon Rondo	78	1,831	188	41.8	29-6	119	64.7	74	292	297	128	137	8	6.4
Allan Ray	47	710	100	38.6	116-48	42	76.4	18	69	43	20	42	3	6.2
Sebastian Telfair	78	1,578	176	37.1	128-37	90	81.8	17	108	218	43	98	11	6.1
Kevinn Pinkney	6	100	12	44.4	2-1	6	66.7	7	15	5	3	4	3	5.2
Kendrick Perkins	72	1,576	132	49.1	3-0	60	60.0	113	372	94	23	113	96	4.5
Leon Powe	63	720	79	44.6	2-0	106	73.6	97	215	10	14	47	22	4.2
Brian Scalabrine	54	1,027	77	40.3	110-44	18	78.3	24	105	59	23	44	18	4.0
Theo Ratliff	2	44	1	33.3	0-0	3	75.0	2	7	0	1	1	3	2.5
Michael Olowokandi	24	234	19	41.3	0-0	2	66.7	14	48	5	8	17	13	1.7
TEAM TOTALS	82	19,855	2,858	44.3	1,283-471	1,670	76.7	918	3,309	1,630	589	1,350	382	95.8
OPPONENTS	82		2,966	46.8	1,212-429	1,776	74.7	848	3,324	1,811	604	1,250	449	99.2

CHARLOTTE BOBCATS

PLAYER	GP	MIN	FGM	PCT	FGA-FGM	FTM	PCT	OFF	TOTAL	A	STL	TO	BLK	AVG
			Field Goals		3-PT FG	Free Throws		Rebounds						
Gerald Wallace	72	2,640	478	50.2	120-39	309	69.1	142	518	185	144	160	69	18.1
Emeka Okafor	67	2,329	394	53.2	0-0	175	59.3	258	757	80	57	111	172	14.4
Raymond Felton	78	2,832	393	38.4	312-103	204	79.7	51	267	545	118	230	10	14.0
Matt Carroll	72	1,878	285	43.3	267-111	188	90.4	35	207	91	53	73	9	12.1
Sean May	35	838	164	50.0	3-2	86	76.8	73	233	66	19	56	24	11.9
Adam Morrison	78	2,326	355	37.6	258-87	120	71.0	54	230	163	28	130	6	11.8
Walter Herrmann	48	936	174	52.7	115-53	41	77.4	28	139	26	17	32	7	9.2
Brevin Knight	45	1,273	152	41.9	18-1	103	80.5	14	115	296	67	95	3	9.1
Derek Anderson	50	1,190	126	42.9	152-54	93	87.7	29	113	133	52	56	7	8.0
Alan Anderson	17	256	37	45.7	20-5	19	82.6	11	32	21	7	22	0	5.8
Primoz Brezec	58	838	122	44.5	3-1	43	63.2	80	184	23	11	38	23	5.0
Jake Voskuhl	73	1,043	121	47.5	0-0	77	68.1	84	256	44	30	56	24	4.4
Jeff McInnis	38	702	71	39.2	8-1	22	68.8	14	62	124	14	42	0	4.3
Melvin Ely	24	245	23	38.3	0-0	24	68.6	12	39	14	2	23	6	2.9
Othella Harrington	26	220	25	44.6	0-0	17	77.3	13	38	6	1	15	1	2.6
Ryan Hollins	27	185	20	55.6	0-0	24	60.0	11	31	1	4	16	7	2.4
Eric Williams	5	33	4	30.8	2-0	4	57.1	2	3	1	1	2	0	2.4
Bernard Robinson	21	242	16	29.6	2-0	19	86.4	9	42	17	13	16	1	2.4
TEAM TOTALS	82	20,005	2,960	44.6	1,280-457	1,568	73.4	920	3,266	1,836	638	1,224	369	96.9
OPPONENTS	82		2,999	46.5	1,245-452	1,802	75.0	929	3,491	1,717	603	1,296	437	100.6

DID YOU KNOW?

Only Shaquille O'Neal, Michael Jordan, and Willis Reed have won the NBA MVP, All-Star Game MVP, and NBA Finals MVP awards in the same season.

CHICAGO BULLS

PLAYER	GP	MIN	Field Goals		3-PT FG	Free Throws		Rebounds						
			FGM	PCT	FGA-FGM	FTM	PCT	OFF	TOTAL	A	STL	TO	BLK	AVG
Ben Gordon	82	2,704	609	45.5	375-155	380	86.4	35	258	296	64	249	17	21.4
Luol Deng	82	3,071	630	51.7	7-1	279	77.7	148	579	204	97	153	48	18.8
Kirk Hinrich	80	2,839	475	44.8	337-140	237	83.5	32	274	500	100	191	23	16.6
Andres Nocioni	53	1,406	273	46.7	209-80	123	84.8	42	301	57	27	104	24	14.1
Chris Duhon	78	1,906	197	40.8	245-88	76	75.2	23	169	310	69	105	6	7.2
Ben Wallace	77	2,697	192	45.3	5-1	109	40.8	303	821	186	111	101	156	6.4
P.J. Brown	72	1,456	170	40.7	2-0	96	78.7	129	347	48	24	85	52	6.1
Tyrus Thomas	72	966	134	47.5	2-0	106	60.6	89	269	40	46	94	76	5.2
Malik Allen	60	638	107	41.5	1-0	28	82.4	42	119	16	17	21	16	4.0
Thabo Sefolosha	71	868	109	42.6	42-15	23	51.1	35	153	60	33	60	11	3.6
Michael Sweetney	48	385	58	43.3	0-0	37	56.1	45	120	28	9	42	11	3.2
Adrian Griffin	54	585	61	47.3	6-0	15	78.9	40	109	59	32	38	4	2.5
Viktor Khryapa	33	231	27	38.6	6-0	19	73.1	20	57	21	10	16	1	2.2
Andre Barrett	6	29	4	50.0	0-0	0	00.0	1	5	7	0	4	0	1.3
TEAM TOTALS	82	19,780	3,046	45.7	1,237-480	1,528	73.4	984	3,581	1,832	639	1,310	445	98.8
OPPONENTS	82		2,793	43.5	1,387-484	1,619	7.30	897	3,353	1,675	614	1,429	433	93.8

CLEVELAND CAVALIERS

PLAYER	GP	MIN	Field Goals		3-PT FG	Free Throws		Rebounds						
			FGM	PCT	FGA-FGM	FTM	PCT	OFF	TOTAL	A	STL	TO	BLK	AVG
LeBron James	78	3,190	772	47.6	310-99	489	69.8	83	526	470	125	250	55	27.3
Larry Hughes	70	2,596	381	40.0	222-74	209	67.6	41	267	256	89	154	26	14.9
Zydrunas Ilgauskas	78	2,130	385	48.5	1-0	155	80.7	242	599	123	48	141	98	11.9
Drew Gooden	80	2,238	371	47.3	6-1	142	71.4	263	681	88	70	115	28	11.1
Aleksandar Pavlovic	67	1,534	222	45.3	148-60	100	78.7	23	158	105	55	102	17	9.0
Donyell Marshall	81	1,360	209	42.4	271-95	53	66.3	86	323	46	39	67	43	7.0
Anderson Varejao	81	1,932	191	47.6	9-0	165	61.6	191	545	75	76	67	52	6.8
Damon Jones	60	1,173	137	38.6	231-89	30	68.2	9	66	94	16	36	2	6.6
Daniel Gibson	60	988	98	42.4	124-54	28	71.8	28	92	69	23	44	8	4.6
Eric Snow	82	1,929	135	41.7	4-0	72	63.7	35	188	330	55	111	16	4.2
Shannon Brown	23	202	28	37.8	25-7	10	71.4	6	21	10	7	14	3	3.2
Ira Newble	15	129	16	43.2	15-8	6	60.0	13	30	2	6	3	0	3.1
David Wesley	35	352	22	29.3	38-9	20	71.4	3	35	37	12	17	4	2.1
Scot Pollard	24	109	11	42.3	0-0	2	50.0	15	31	3	4	4	1	1.0
Dwayne Jones	4	18	0	00.0	0-0	3	50.0	1	6	0	0	2	0	0.8
TEAM TOTALS	82	19,880	2,978	44.7	1,404-494	1,484	69.5	1,039	3,568	1,708	625	1,177	353	96.8
OPPONENTS	82		2,838	44.8	1,231-405	1,539	73.4	807	3,268	1,649	540	1,254	349	92.9

DALLAS MAVERICKS

PLAYER	GP	MIN	Field Goals		3-PT FG	Free Throws		Rebounds		A	STL	TO	BLK	AVG
			FGM	PCT	FGA-FGM	FTM	PCT	OFF	TOTAL					
Dirk Nowitzki	78	2,820	673	50.2	173-72	498	90.4	122	693	263	52	167	62	24.6
Josh Howard	70	2,455	493	45.9	239-92	243	82.7	130	475	127	82	123	56	18.9
Jason Terry	81	2,846	514	48.4	370-162	160	80.4	41	231	422	81	152	17	16.7
Jerry Stackhouse	67	1,615	280	42.8	162-62	182	84.7	39	145	187	51	117	10	12.0
Devin Harris	80	2,081	292	49.2	50-14	215	82.4	45	196	296	96	146	21	10.2
Erick Dampier	76	1,915	209	62.6	0-0	119	62.3	217	566	44	24	107	82	7.1
Devean George	60	1,283	146	39.5	150-53	36	75.0	57	213	33	46	51	23	6.4
Greg Buckner	76	1,372	123	41.1	103-32	27	79.4	35	158	70	47	40	7	4.0
Anthony Johnson	40	561	60	41.1	29-11	21	72.4	13	48	78	16	31	1	3.8
Austin Croshere	61	727	78	35.1	91-26	45	86.5	33	186	44	14	33	6	3.7
Jose Barea	33	191	28	35.9	21-6	16	66.7	7	25	24	1	14	1	2.4
Kevin Willis	5	43	5	38.5	0-0	2	100.0	2	8	1	2	2	1	2.4
Pops Mensah-Bonsu	12	71	11	64.7	0-0	7	38.9	9	21	0	1	9	0	2.4
DeSagana Diop	81	1,480	71	47.0	1-0	48	55.8	166	438	30	40	63	113	2.3
Maurice Ager	32	214	22	31.4	15-5	20	60.6	1	21	7	4	15	3	2.2
Didier Ilunga-Mbenga	21	79	5	31.3	0-0	7	87.5	3	11	6	3	5	5	0.8
TEAM TOTALS	82	19,755	3,010	46.7	1,404-535	1,646	80.5	920	3,435	1,632	560	1,140	408	100.0
OPPONENTS	82		2,790	44.7	1,074-375	1,654	74.6	839	3,125	1,471	565	1,190	312	92.8

DENVER NUGGETS

PLAYER	GP	MIN	Field Goals		3-PT FG	Free Throws		Rebounds		A	STL	TO	BLK	AVG
			FGM	PCT	FGA-FGM	FTM	PCT	OFF	TOTAL					
Carmelo Anthony	65	2,486	691	47.6	149-40	459	80.8	143	391	249	77	234	23	28.9
Allen Iverson	50	2,121	430	45.4	144-50	331	75.9	16	152	359	90	202	12	24.8
Earl Boykins	31	877	156	41.3	110-41	119	90.8	23	63	132	25	52	2	15.2
J.R. Smith	63	1,471	284	44.1	382-149	102	81.0	30	143	91	49	85	9	13.0
Andre Miller	23	822	117	47.2	16-4	62	72.9	25	104	209	37	70	4	13.0
Nene	64	1,715	294	57.0	1-0	195	68.9	150	449	77	62	127	59	12.2
Marcus Camby	70	2,369	312	47.3	0-2	161	72.9	164	816	223	87	122	231	11.2
Kenyon Martin	2	63	8	50.0	1-0	3	25.0	6	20	1	0	5	0	9.5
Steve Blake	49	1,642	164	43.2	140-48	32	72.7	14	124	324	51	101	5	8.3
Linas Kleiza	79	1,488	200	42.2	221-83	115	85.2	77	266	45	28	79	14	7.6
Eduardo Najera	75	1,658	204	57.6	12-1	88	71.5	131	310	64	73	56	26	6.6
Joe Smith	11	148	23	47.9	1-0	10	83.3	13	40	3	6	13	7	5.1
Reggie Evans	66	1,127	117	54.4	0-0	91	49.7	156	460	45	42	95	16	4.9
Yakhouba Diawara	64	1,177	100	34.2	170-49	35	66.0	27	110	55	30	37	7	4.4
DerMarr Johnson	39	419	50	32.5	88-19	16	76.2	10	57	17	16	27	12	3.5
Anthony Carter	2	37	3	37.5	2-0	0	00.0	0	3	11	0	6	1	3.0
Julius Hodge	4	37	2	40.0	0-0	2	100.0	1	3	10	3	1	0	1.5
Jamal Sampson	22	125	9	64.3	1-0	6	42.9	15	48	5	2	10	7	1.1
TEAM TOTALS	82	19,780	3,164	46.5	1,440-484	1,827	74.6	1,001	3,559	1,920	678	1,352	435	105.4
OPPONENTS	82		3,257	46.0	1,569-554	1,438	73.9	1,006	3,467	2,010	680	1,343	424	103.7

DETROIT PISTONS

PLAYER	GP	MIN	Field Goals		3-PT FG	Free Throws		Rebounds							
			FGM	PCT	FGA-FGM	FTM	PCT	OFF	TOTAL	A	STL	TO	BLK	AVG
Richard Hamilton	75	2,763	547	46.8	129-44	347	86.1	75	282	285	59	159	15	19.8
Chauncey Billups	70	2,533	348	42.7	316-109	386	88.3	23	237	502	84	140	17	17.0
Tayshaun Prince	82	3,001	459	46.0	210-81	172	76.8	144	429	227	51	98	55	14.3
Rasheed Wallace	75	2,419	357	42.3	296-104	108	78.8	90	543	127	75	94	118	12.3
Chris Webber	43	1,277	200	48.9	6-2	84	63.6	87	288	127	42	74	26	11.3
Antonio McDyess	82	1,729	284	52.6	0-0	96	69.1	165	288	127	42	74	26	8.1
Ronald Murray	69	1,477	177	40.4	83-24	87	72.5	26	113	187	49	90	13	6.7
Amir Johnson	8	124	18	54.5	3-0	11	78.6	15	37	3	5	9	13	5.9
Nazr Mohammed	51	773	118	53.2	0-0	50	61.0	89	229	9	27	43	40	5.6
Carlos Delfino	82	1,372	156	41.5	138-46	70	78.7	67	266	88	46	61	8	5.2
Jason Maxiell	67	943	131	50.0	0-0	72	52.6	88	186	14	30	53	60	5.0
Lindsey Hunter	52	745	94	38.5	119-38	30	90.9	9	47	93	34	35	7	4.9
Dale Davis	46	464	33	44.6	0-0	17	65.4	59	137	12	10	15	34	1.8
Will Blalock	14	166	9	30.0	5-1	6	100.0	6	15	17	5	12	0	1.8
Ronald Dupree	19	94	11	35.5	0-0	3	33.3	5	17	5	5	3	1	1.3
TEAM TOTALS	82	19,880	2,942	45.4	1,305-449	1,539	77.4	948	3,322	1,768	583	1,001	472	96.0
OPPONENTS	82		2,819	44.5	1,205-409	1,484	74.0	973	3,376	1,647	521	1,205	290	91.8

GOLDEN STATE WARRIORS

PLAYER	GP	MIN	Field Goals		3-PT FG	Free Throws		Rebounds							
			FGM	PCT	FGA-FGM	FTM	PCT	OFF	TOTAL	A	STL	TO	BLK	AVG
Baron Davis	63	2,221	452	43.9	280-85	275	74.5	51	276	509	135	193	29	20.1
Al Harrington	42	1,355	272	45.6	175-73	96	68.1	80	270	98	40	78	14	17.0
Stephen Jackson	38	1,293	229	44.6	173-59	123	80.4	44	127	173	51	102	14	16.8
Monta Ellis	77	2,638	480	47.5	143-39	273	76.3	62	243	319	132	221	21	16.5
Mike Dunleavy	39	1,052	166	44.9	104-36	78	77.2	40	187	117	38	71	12	11.4
Jason Richardson	51	1,675	306	41.7	301-110	92	65.7	71	259	172	54	82	32	16.0
Mickael Pietrus	72	1,937	286	48.8	240-93	136	64.8	81	327	62	48	105	55	11.1
Matt Barnes	76	1,813	275	43.8	290-106	90	73.2	91	350	156	73	105	41	9.8
Andris Biedrins	82	2,382	348	59.9	0-0	87	52.1	251	762	88	67	119	136	9.5
Troy Murphy	26	667	81	45.0	59-22	47	71.2	37	157	60	21	29	17	8.9
Ike Diogu	17	222	44	53.0	0-0	35	79.5	21	63	5	3	18	11	7.2
Kelenna Azubuike	41	669	98	44.5	79-34	61	78.2	26	94	28	22	39	10	7.1
Anthony Roberson	20	227	44	42.3	55-21	2	66.7	2	21	10	12	13	0	5.6
Keith McLeod	26	379	41	39.0	23-9	47	88.7	3	21	45	17	23	3	5.3
Renaldo Major	1	27	2	20.0	0-0	1	50.0	0	2	0	2	1	0	5.0
Sarunas Jasikevicius	26	309	37	36.6	44-12	27	87.1	5	21	61	13	31	1	4.3
Dajuan Wagner	1	7	1	100.0	1-1	1	50.00	0	0	1	0	1	0	4.0
Josh Powell	30	289	41	52.6	0-0	22	73.3	17	69	18	5	24	12	3.5
Adonal Foyle	48	475	48	56.5	0-0	11	44.0	51	126	19	11	23	50	2.2
Patrick O'Bryant	16	119	10	31.3	0-0	11	64.7	7	21	9	6	8	8	1.9
TEAM TOTALS	82	19,755	3,261	46.3	1,967-700	1,515	71.7	940	3,396	1,950	750	1,309	466	106.5
OPPONENTS	82		3,171	46.2	1,664-609	1,814	75.0	1,074	3,807	2,023	680	1,525	399	106.9

HOUSTON ROCKETS

| PLAYER | GP | MIN | Field Goals | | 3-PT FG | Free Throws | | Rebounds | | | | | | |
			FGM	PCT	FGA-FGM	FTM	PCT	OFF	TOTAL	A	STL	TO	BLK	AVG
Yao Ming	48	1,624	423	51.6	2-0	356	86.2	101	452	94	17	167	94	25.0
Tracy McGrady	71	2,539	638	43.1	381-126	345	70.7	56	378	458	92	213	36	24.6
Rafer Alston	82	3,040	383	37.5	529-192	130	73.4	29	282	444	129	170	10	13.3
Luther Head	80	2,211	306	43.7	401-177	83	79.0	31	252	194	76	137	5	10.9
Shane Battier	82	2,988	292	44.6	373-157	88	77.9	67	338	175	79	72	60	10.1
Juwan Howard	80	2,123	309	46.5	0-0	155	82.4	138	470	131	29	112	8	9.7
Bonzi Wells	28	590	85	41.1	7-1	46	56.1	26	120	31	24	57	13	7.8
Chuck Hayes	78	1,714	192	57.3	0-0	55	61.8	204	521	47	70	64	18	5.6
Kirk Snyder	39	563	66	45.2	44-11	49	65.3	17	83	39	11	26	12	4.9
John Lucas III	47	383	62	39.7	59-15	15	78.9	9	36	33	17	15	0	3.3
Dikembe Mutombo	75	1,289	85	55.6	0-0	60	69.0	164	488	13	22	38	76	3.1
Vassilis Spanoulis	31	272	23	31.9	29-5	34	81.0	5	22	28	7	29	1	2.7
Jake Tsakalidis	13	132	9	40.9	0-0	12	80.0	18	40	3	1	3	1	2.3
Scott Padgett	24	198	15	30.6	29-8	6	54.5	11	45	8	4	8	3	1.8
Steve Novak	35	191	18	36.0	39-13	2	100.0	4	26	6	5	4	0	1.5
TEAM TOTALS	82	19,855	2,906	44.5	1,893-705	1,436	75.3	880	3,553	1,704	583	1,162	337	97.0
OPPONENTS	82		2,793	42.9	1,346-472	1,497	74.9	800	3,348	1,588	571	1,163	353	92.1

INDIANA PACERS

| PLAYER | GP | MIN | Field Goals | | 3-PT FG | Free Throws | | Rebounds | | | | | | |
			FGM	PCT	FGA-FGM	FTM	PCT	OFF	TOTAL	A	STL	TO	BLK	AVG
Jermaine O'Neal	69	2,459	498	43.6	7-0	343	76.7	153	661	167	50	203	182	19.4
Al Harrington	36	1,208	223	45.8	118-54	72	71.3	71	226	51	25	91	10	15.9
Stephen Jackson	37	1,186	180	41.9	138-41	120	82.2	17	95	114	33	81	20	14.1
Mike Dunleavy	43	1,529	218	45.4	120-34	133	79.2	44	244	111	46	78	10	14.0
Danny Granger	82	2,785	398	45.9	288-110	236	80.3	114	381	114	66	135	61	13.9
Jamaal Tinsley	72	2,243	346	38.9	193-61	172	72.0	60	240	494	117	200	25	12.8
Troy Murphy	42	1,185	185	46.0	88-36	61	77.2	63	257	66	25	49	25	11.1
Sarunas Jasikevicius	37	664	91	41.2	86-32	59	92.2	10	48	111	13	59	0	7.4
Marquis Daniels	45	800	129	45.9	26-6	56	70.0	26	82	57	27	55	7	5.1
Ike Diogu	42	538	83	45.4	0-0	77	80.2	54	140	20	5	49	15	5.8
Darrell Armstrong	81	1,275	156	41.4	214-72	73	78.5	34	135	191	70	76	6	5.6
Jeff Foster	75	1,740	122	47.1	1-0	78	63.9	252	608	57	62	70	37	4.3
Keith McLeod	22	339	32	38.6	22-7	22	88.0	1	22	45	7	23	2	4.2
Shawne Williams	46	556	75	46.9	52-19	11	55.0	33	83	22	6	24	8	3.9
David Harrison	24	190	30	51.7	0-0	11	50.0	9	42	6	5	26	12	3.0
Maceo Baston	47	405	49	64.5	7-3	37	78.7	21	74	16	12	32	18	2.9
Rawle Marshall	40	361	32	36.0	18-4	31	68.9	8	29	13	12	19	5	2.5
Josh Powell	7	64	2	13.3	0-0	8	66.7	7	19	3	0	5	0	1.7
Orien Greene	41	254	23	37.1	11-2	15	60.0	12	44	22	17	28	4	1.5
TEAM TOTALS	82	19,780	2,872	43.8	1,389-481	1,615	76.0	989	3,430	1,680	598	1,335	447	95.6
OPPONENTS	82		2,931	45.7	1,175-437	1,741	75.3	915	3,413	1,642	644	1,288	410	98.0

LOS ANGELES CLIPPERS

PLAYER	GP	MIN	Field Goals		3-PT FG	Free Throws		Rebounds		A	STL	TO	BLK	AVG
			FGM	PCT	FGA-FGM	FTM	PCT	OFF	TOTAL	A	STL	TO	BLK	AVG
Elton Brand	80	3,077	645	53.3	1-1	351	76.1	268	744	235	77	202	179	20.5
Corey Maggette	75	2,291	367	45.4	65-13	519	82.0	90	442	208	65	201	14	16.9
Cuttino Mobley	78	2,841	388	44.0	246-101	200	83.7	52	267	198	92	145	24	13.8
Sam Cassell	58	1,407	261	41.8	109-32	160	87.9	27	167	270	28	101	8	12.3
Tim Thomas	76	2,054	299	41.4	356-136	102	70.8	63	378	171	55	106	28	11.0
Chris Kaman	75	2,176	294	45.1	1-0	166	74.1	160	588	79	41	147	116	10.1
Shaun Livingston	54	1,611	208	46.3	16-5	82	70.7	56	184	274	59	108	29	9.3
Jason Hart	23	746	85	43.8	23-4	32	88.9	12	83	93	41	34	1	9.0
Quinton Ross	81	1,700	177	46.7	10-2	68	78.2	60	190	86	70	33	32	5.2
Daniel Ewing	61	712	65	40.4	44-14	35	77.8	9	73	90	32	50	4	2.9
Aaron Williams	38	374	29	54.7	1-0	18	81.8	27	85	7	7	18	14	2.0
Doug Christie	7	82	5	29.4	6-1	2	66.7	3	11	8	3	5	1	1.9
Paul Davis	31	180	22	42.3	0-0	7	70.0	21	44	7	6	8	5	1.6
James Singleton	53	376	30	36.6	14-3	22	75.9	36	106	17	15	17	17	1.6
Yaroslav Korolev	10	41	4	25.0	5-1	3	50.0	1	3	4	3	1	0	1.2
Luke Jackson	3	16	1	12.5	4-1	0	00.0	0	1	4	0	1	0	1.0
Alvin Williams	2	10	0	00.0	1-0	2	50.0	1	1	3	2	3	0	1.0
Will Conroy	4	35	0	00.0	0-0	0	00.0	2	5	8	0	2	0	0.0
TEAM TOTALS	82	19,730	2,880	45.6	903-314	1,769	78.8	888	3,372	1,762	596	1,239	472	95.6
OPPONENTS	82		2,912	45.2	1,341-455	1,602	74.8	843	3,220	1,722	582	1,132	321	96.1

LOS ANGELES LAKERS

PLAYER	GP	MIN	Field Goals		3-PT FG	Free Throws		Rebounds		A	STL	TO	BLK	AVG
			FGM	PCT	FGA-FGM	FTM	PCT	OFF	TOTAL	A	STL	TO	BLK	AVG
Kobe Bryant	77	3,140	813	46.3	398-137	667	86.8	75	439	413	111	255	36	31.6
Lamar Odom	56	2,202	319	46.8	182-54	198	70.0	102	547	270	53	163	32	15.9
Luke Walton	60	1,982	264	47.4	124-48	108	74.5	87	302	257	60	118	21	11.4
Smush Parker	82	2,457	342	43.6	301-110	113	64.6	45	206	228	119	153	10	11.1
Kwame Brown	41	1,132	143	59.1	1-0	59	44.0	81	244	75	39	76	49	8.4
Maurice Evans	76	1,732	234	43.2	133-48	122	78.7	93	221	74	38	57	14	8.4
Andrew Bynum	82	1,793	247	55.8	3-0	143	66.8	139	484	94	12	115	128	7.8
Brian Cook	65	1,018	185	45.3	115-46	34	72.3	61	215	65	25	51	27	6.9
Vladimir Radmanovic	55	986	134	42.4	118-40	53	72.6	53	180	66	25	69	18	6.6
Ronny Turiaf	72	1,087	147	54.9	1-0	89	66.4	88	259	63	17	52	78	5.3
Jordan Farmar	72	1,090	124	42.2	137-45	27	71.1	22	119	137	44	73	7	4.4
Sasha Vujacic	73	935	105	39.2	161-60	43	87.8	28	107	64	41	30	1	4.3
Shammond Williams	30	345	35	40.7	50-20	4	66.7	11	40	31	12	13	0	3.1
Aaron McKie	10	131	11	64.7	0-0	0	00.0	1	18	13	4	8	0	2.2
TEAM TOTALS	82	20,030	3,103	46.6	1,724-608	1,660	74.7	886	3,381	1,850	600	1,273	421	103.3
OPPONENTS	82		3,097	46.1	1,462-523	1,763	76.0	955	3,463	1,798	649	1,208	409	103.4

MEMPHIS GRIZZLIES

| PLAYER | GP | MIN | Field Goals | | 3-PT FG | Free Throws | | Rebounds | | | | | | |
			FGM	PCT	FGA-FGM	FTM	PCT	OFF	TOTAL	A	STL	TO	BLK	AVG
Pau Gasol	59	2,133	462	53.8	11-3	299	74.8	149	581	201	29	162	126	20.8
Mike Miller	70	2,740	465	46.0	498-202	161	79.3	52	378	298	54	179	18	18.5
Chucky Atkins	75	2,064	310	43.4	306-116	252	81.0	18	139	346	50	127	4	13.2
Hakim Warrick	82	2,152	373	52.4	8-0	299	77.1	130	420	75	43	161	30	12.7
Rudy Gay	78	2,103	321	42.2	143-52	152	72.7	93	348	100	71	140	74	10.8
Stromile Swift	54	1,029	161	46.5	5-0	97	72.4	85	250	17	30	69	62	7.8
Tarence Kinsey	48	967	139	45.7	46-13	78	79.6	29	97	41	53	46	1	7.7
Dahntay Jones	78	1,671	220	47.7	12-5	138	79.3	47	153	68	39	92	22	7.5
Damon Stoudamire	62	1,501	171	39.1	175-59	66	79.5	31	139	299	47	101	2	7.5
Kyle Lowry	10	175	14	36.8	8-3	25	89.3	12	31	32	14	12	1	5.6
Eddie Jones	29	561	57	37.7	74-22	25	73.5	14	61	33	22	23	2	5.6
Lawrence Roberts	54	969	94	45.2	2-0	95	72.5	101	261	30	36	36	13	5.2
Junior Harrington	29	543	57	41.6	26-7	31	67.4	12	68	89	21	52	5	5.2
Brian Cardinal	28	313	42	49.4	44-18	25	92.6	13	59	31	22	23	1	4.5
Alexander Johnson	59	753	91	53.8	0-0	78	66.1	50	181	17	25	47	35	4.4
Jake Tsakalidis	23	258	20	40.0	0-0	14	58.3	24	64	2	7	11	21	2.3
Scott Padgett	7	33	1	14.3	4-0	0	00.0	5	9	0	1	1	0	0.3
TEAM TOTALS	**82**	**19,980**	**2,998**	**46.5**	**1,362-500**	**1,835**	**76.1**	**866**	**3,241**	**1,680**	**564**	**1,343**	**407**	**101.6**
OPPONENTS	**82**		**3,287**	**48.6**	**1,480-576**	**1,603**	**75.9**	**965**	**3,448**	**2,062**	**681**	**1,253**	**450**	**106.7**

MIAMI HEAT

| PLAYER | GP | MIN | Field Goals | | 3-PT FG | Free Throws | | Rebounds | | | | | | |
			FGM	PCT	FGA-FGM	FTM	PCT	OFF	TOTAL	A	STL	TO	BLK	AVG
Dwyane Wade	51	1,931	472	49.1	79-21	432	80.7	51	239	384	107	216	62	27.4
Shaquille O'Neal	40	1,135	283	59.1	0-0	124	42.2	97	297	79	8	95	55	17.3
Jason Kapono	67	1,767	278	49.4	210-108	66	89.2	26	180	81	38	70	2	10.9
Jason Williams	61	1,865	235	41.3	295-100	94	91.3	18	141	322	58	100	1	10.9
Udonis Haslem	79	2,483	353	49.2	4-0	118	68.0	188	654	97	49	110	26	10.7
Eddie Jones	35	1,033	121	44.6	148-56	34	82.9	17	129	76	46	24	8	9.5
Alonzo Mourning	77	1,572	238	56.0	0-0	185	60.1	126	350	18	13	129	178	8.6
Antoine Walker	78	1,818	265	39.7	305-84	46	43.8	92	339	130	48	141	17	8.5
James Posey	71	1,919	186	43.1	259-97	81	82.7	66	357	94	71	55	23	7.7
Dorell Wright	66	1,292	162	44.5	34-5	64	74.4	40	272	95	41	65	46	6.0
Gary Payton	68	1,503	144	39.3	123-32	38	66.7	18	132	201	43	66	3	5.3
Robert Hite	12	136	19	31.7	23-5	8	66.7	4	16	8	3	6	2	4.3
Michael Doleac	56	698	82	46.9	1-0	36	87.8	44	155	22	18	30	15	3.6
Chris Quinn	42	408	48	36.6	57-20	25	67.6	6	30	65	15	21	0	3.4
Wayne Simien	8	93	9	39.1	0-0	5	71.4	5	11	4	2	3	0	2.9
Earl Barron	28	203	24	28.9	1-0	17	94.4	19	41	5	6	11	4	2.3
TEAM TOTALS	**82**	**19,855**	**2,919**	**46.4**	**1,539-528**	**1,393**	**69.0**	**817**	**3,343**	**1,681**	**566**	**1,201**	**442**	**94.6**
OPPONENTS	**82**		**2,895**	**44.4**	**1,495-531**	**1,513**	**74.2**	**921**	**3,388**	**1,656**	**562**	**1,185**	**314**	**95.5**

MILWAUKEE BUCKS

| PLAYER | GP | MIN | Field Goals | | 3-PT FG | Free Throws | | Rebounds | | | | | | |
			FGM	PCT	FGA-FGM	FTM	PCT	OFF	TOTAL	A	STL	TO	BLK	AVG
Michael Redd	53	2,036	477	46.5	306-117	345	82.9	42	196	124	63	122	9	26.7
Maurice Williams	68	2,472	468	44.6	228-79	159	85.5	54	329	416	85	202	6	17.3
Ruben Patterson	81	2,508	475	54.8	19-3	241	64.1	190	440	232	110	199	25	14.7
Earl Boykins	35	1,154	167	42.7	129-54	101	88.6	26	76	159	31	68	0	14.0
Charlie Bell	82	2,848	426	43.7	361-127	131	78.0	57	238	247	97	105	4	13.5
Andrew Bogut	66	2,258	348	55.3	5-1	112	57.7	168	584	198	49	150	35	12.3
Charlie Villanueva	39	984	180	47.0	86-29	73	82.0	62	228	36	24	54	12	11.8
Ersan Ilyasova	66	973	139	38.3	148-54	70	78.7	58	189	49	27	51	17	6.1
Dan Gadzuric	54	840	108	47.4	1-0	42	46.7	94	246	29	22	49	32	4.8
Brian Skinner	67	1,523	124	49.0	0-0	46	58.2	106	385	58	18	75	64	4.4
Lynn Greer	41	432	61	43.3	52-18	27	84.4	2	27	53	17	18	1	4.1
Steve Blake	33	583	45	34.9	68-19	11	55.0	7	45	84	10	28	3	3.6
David Noel	68	792	65	36.7	53-17	37	86.0	42	123	65	25	40	9	2.7
Julius Hodge	5	28	4	57.1	0-0	1	50.0	1	5	2	1	2	0	1.8
Damir Markota	30	170	19	36.5	16-6	7	63.6	11	31	6	3	15	1	1.7
Jared Reiner	27	244	15	34.9	0-0	3	30.0	21	71	13	5	14	6	1.2
Chris McCray	5	12	0	00.0	0-0	0	00.0	0	0	0	0	2	0	0.0
TEAM TOTALS	**82**	**19,855**	**3,121**	**46.5**	**1,472-524**	**1,406**	**73.3**	**941**	**3,213**	**1,771**	**587**	**1,240**	**224**	**99.7**
OPPONENTS	**82**		**3,201**	**48.0**	**1,537-565**	**1,564**	**74.2**	**1,062**	**3,530**	**2,077**	**615**	**1,284**	**433**	**104.0**

MINNESOTA TIMBERWOLVES

| PLAYER | GP | MIN | Field Goals | | 3-PT FG | Free Throws | | Rebounds | | | | | | |
			FGM	PCT	FGA-FGM	FTM	PCT	OFF	TOTAL	A	STL	TO	BLK	AVG
Kevin Garnett	76	2,995	638	47.6	56-12	416	83.5	183	975	313	89	205	126	22.4
Ricky Davis	81	3,021	506	46.5	310-123	239	83.9	54	315	385	80	210	23	17.0
Mark Blount	82	2,544	427	50.9	31-9	147	75.4	136	505	67	43	159	58	12.3
Randy Foye	82	1,879	300	43.4	185-68	164	85.4	49	218	232	53	152	21	10.1
Mike James	82	2,069	297	42.2	215-80	154	83.7	25	163	297	55	129	7	10.1
Craig Smith	82	1,537	246	53.1	6-0	116	62.4	149	416	49	51	74	18	7.4
Trenton Hassell	76	2,223	217	49.0	25-6	72	78.3	83	243	203	22	80	26	6.7
Troy Hudson	34	554	74	37.9	80-28	26	81.3	8	48	73	14	40	2	5.9
Marko Jaric	70	1,555	136	41.8	85-32	67	76.1	54	184	145	75	88	16	5.3
Rashad McCants	37	554	62	35.0	75-20	40	69.0	14	47	38	26	40	7	5.0
Bracey Wright	19	190	24	40.0	20-6	13	72.2	7	21	15	9	6	1	3.5
Justin Reed	41	318	40	37.4	0-0	26	86.7	15	46	17	5	22	3	2.6
Eddie Griffin	13	92	7	25.9	1-0	4	80.0	7	25	4	0	6	7	1.4
Mark Madsen	56	473	23	53.5	0-0	15	51.7	35	87	10	10	21	10	1.1
TEAM TOTALS	**82**	**20,005**	**2,997**	**46.1**	**1,089-384**	**1,499**	**79.2**	**819**	**3,293**	**1,848**	**532**	**1,278**	**325**	**96.1**
OPPONENTS	**82**		**3,075**	**46.0**	**1,488-518**	**1,510**	**76.0**	**958**	**3,395**	**1,782**	**583**	**1,163**	**360**	**99.7**

NEW JERSEY NETS

| PLAYER | GP | MIN | Field Goals | | 3-PT FG | Free Throws | | Rebounds | | A | STL | TO | BLK | AVG |
			FGM	PCT	FGA-FGM	FTM	PCT	OFF	TOTAL					
Vince Carter	82	3,126	726	45.4	437-156	462	80.2	114	492	393	82	217	30	25.2
Nenad Krstic	26	848	170	52.6	1-0	86	71.1	51	176	46	10	52	24	16.4
Richard Jefferson	55	1,956	303	45.6	145-52	239	73.3	48	240	148	34	120	8	16.3
Jason Kidd	80	2,933	369	40.6	361-124	179	77.8	135	655	736	127	213	23	13.0
Mikki Moore	79	2,082	308	60.9	1-0	160	68.1	145	403	74	46	113	60	9.8
Bostjan Nachbar	76	1,532	226	45.7	265-112	132	80.5	27	253	61	30	69	26	9.2
Eddie House	56	946	180	42.8	175-75	33	91.7	14	92	67	27	27	3	8.4
Marcus Williams	79	1,315	208	39.5	163-46	72	84.7	29	163	260	29	142	2	6.8
Antoine Wright	63	1,137	110	43.8	59-19	44	60.3	38	175	55	30	43	10	4.5
Josh Boone	61	669	99	57.9	0-0	56	54.4	64	176	10	11	33	21	4.2
Clifford Robinson	50	955	81	37.2	66-25	16	44.4	31	122	51	12	30	23	4.1
Hassan Adams	61	495	75	55.6	1-0	24	66.7	35	77	13	17	22	4	2.9
Jason Collins	80	1,844	55	36.4	2-0	59	46.5	90	316	46	40	73	38	2.1
Bernard Robinson	10	37	3	37.5	0-0	4	80.0	1	6	2	4	0	1	1.0
Mile Ilic	5	6	0	00.0	0-0	0	00.0	0	1	0	0	3	0	0.0
TEAM TOTALS	**82**	**19,880**	**2,913**	**45.7**	**1,676-609**	**1,566**	**72.7**	**822**	**3,347**	**1,962**	**499**	**1,212**	**273**	**97.6**
OPPONENTS	**82**		**2,911**	**45.0**	**1,455-519**	**1,723**	**76.2**	**867**	**3,393**	**1,805**	**584**	**1,188**	**369**	**98.3**

NEW ORLEANS/OKLAHOMA CITY HORNETS

| PLAYER | GP | MIN | Field Goals | | 3-PT FG | Free Throws | | Rebounds | | A | STL | TO | BLK | AVG |
			FGM	PCT	FGA-FGM	FTM	PCT	OFF	TOTAL					
David West	52	1,900	377	47.6	25-8	187	82.4	126	424	114	42	98	38	18.3
Peja Stojakovic	13	425	83	42.3	84-34	31	81.6	11	54	11	8	19	4	17.8
Chris Paul	64	2,353	381	43.7	143-50	292	81.8	54	280	569	118	161	3	17.3
Desmond Mason	75	2,575	407	45.2	0-0	214	66.3	124	345	115	52	192	22	13.7
Devin Brown	58	1,662	233	42.0	227-81	123	79.4	55	251	149	44	91	9	11.6
Bobby Jackson	56	1,330	204	39.4	165-54	130	77.4	42	178	141	50	78	6	10.6
Rasual Butler	81	2,223	314	39.8	363-134	56	64.4	42	256	63	40	67	54	10.1
Tyson Chandler	73	2,525	292	62.4	1-0	106	52.7	320	904	66	37	126	129	9.5
Jannero Pargo	82	1,710	283	40.9	209-81	104	85.2	20	180	203	53	122	4	9.2
Marc Jackson	56	1,025	159	41.0	1-0	90	87.4	62	192	58	21	65	7	7.3
Linton Johnson III	54	720	93	48.9	30-10	30	81.1	52	163	18	33	27	18	4.2
Hilton Armstrong	56	634	68	54.4	0-0	40	59.7	58	149	10	12	35	26	3.1
Cedric Simmons	43	534	55	41.7	0-0	16	48.5	44	107	12	8	22	23	2.9
Brandon Bass	21	162	15	34.1	1-0	12	75.0	13	43	3	2	10	3	2.0
Marcus Vinicius	13	103	7	46.7	7-3	5	71.4	2	11	5	2	6	1	1.7
TEAM TOTALS	**82**	**19,880**	**2,971**	**44.5**	**1,256-455**	**1,436**	**74.0**	**1,025**	**3,537**	**1,537**	**522**	**1,187**	**347**	**95.5**
OPPONENTS	**82**		**3,004**	**45.7**	**1,575-559**	**1,395**	**75.9**	**853**	**3,346**	**1,703**	**554**	**1,119**	**392**	**97.1**

NEW YORK KNICKS

PLAYER	GP	MIN	Field Goals FGM	PCT	3-PT FG FGA-FGM	Free Throws FTM	PCT	Rebounds OFF	TOTAL	A	STL	TO	BLK	AVG
Eddy Curry	81	2,849	585	57.6	1-1	405	61.5	195	571	68	34	295	40	19.5
Jamal Crawford	59	2,198	354	40.0	322-103	228	83.8	44	186	259	57	162	8	17.6
Stephon Marbury	74	2,748	395	41.5	345-123	297	76.9	36	213	403	71	179	10	16.4
Quentin Richardson	49	1,621	228	41.8	258-97	83	69.2	65	352	108	36	70	7	13.0
Steve Francis	44	1,237	140	40.8	111-42	175	82.9	33	157	170	41	100	12	11.3
David Lee	58	1,731	240	60.0	0-0	141	81.5	196	602	104	48	92	23	10.7
Nate Robinson	64	1,356	227	43.4	213-83	108	77.7	55	152	90	50	72	6	10.1
Channing Frye	72	1,896	298	43.3	18-3	85	78.7	91	395	67	36	100	42	9.5
Renaldo Balkman	68	1,064	139	50.5	27-5	51	56.7	97	294	44	57	49	44	4.9
Mardy Collins	52	777	87	38.2	47-13	48	58.5	28	104	83	32	57	3	4.5
Jared Jeffries	55	1,307	95	46.1	20-2	31	45.6	111	238	67	44	61	30	4.1
Malik Rose	65	810	74	39.8	8-2	42	80.8	47	175	65	26	65	9	3.0
Jerome James	41	273	33	41.8	0-0	10	55.6	21	66	3	6	23	15	1.9
Kelvin Cato	18	95	7	31.8	0-0	8	66.7	12	31	0	3	6	10	1.2
Randolph Morris	5	44	1	16.7	0-0	2	33.3	1	9	1	2	2	1	0.8
TEAM TOTALS	82	20,005	2,903	45.7	1,370-474	1,714	71.5	1,032	3,548	1,532	543	1,405	260	97.5
OPPONENTS	82		3,021	46.0	1,523-573	1,613	75.6	885	3,182	1,748	616	1,122	406	100.3

ORLANDO MAGIC

PLAYER	GP	MIN	Field Goals FGM	PCT	3-PT FG FGA-FGM	Free Throws FTM	PCT	Rebounds OFF	TOTAL	A	STL	TO	BLK	AVG
Dwight Howard	82	3,023	526	60.3	2-1	390	58.6	283	1,008	158	70	317	156	17.6
Grant Hill	65	2,009	342	51.8	12-2	248	76.5	53	237	138	61	144	25	14.4
Hedo Turkoglu	73	2,268	345	41.9	281-109	171	78.1	57	293	233	70	143	16	13.3
Jameer Nelson	77	2,331	376	43.0	194-65	183	82.8	50	236	330	73	184	5	13.0
Trevor Ariza	57	1,278	200	53.9	7-0	106	62.0	98	249	65	59	84	19	8.9
Darko Milicic	80	1,913	249	45.4	1-0	141	61.3	145	437	90	44	124	140	8.0
Keyon Dooling	66	1,435	188	41.0	96-31	114	80.9	22	86	112	52	72	15	7.9
Carlos Arroyo	72	1,304	203	42.5	51-14	132	79.5	31	134	202	39	90	2	7.7
Tony Battie	66	1,575	176	48.9	1-0	52	67.5	92	344	35	29	61	30	6.1
J.J. Redick	42	622	80	41.0	98-38	54	90.0	10	52	36	12	21	0	6.0
Keith Bogans	59	990	99	40.4	137-53	47	74.6	16	93	59	28	46	2	5.1
Travis Diener	26	288	34	42.5	50-18	12	80.0	3	18	35	4	13	0	3.8
Pat Garrity	33	277	22	31.4	32-11	16	88.9	12	42	14	7	14	0	2.2
Bo Outlaw	41	460	34	66.7	0-0	13	59.1	47	106	16	17	21	6	2.0
James Augustine	2	7	1	33.3	0-0	0	0.0	1	3	2	0	0	0	1.0
TEAM TOTALS	82	19,780	2,875	47.2	962-342	1,679	70.2	920	3,338	1,525	565	1,392	416	94.8
OPPONENTS	82		2,739	44.2	1,306-461	1,768	76.0	865	3,082	1,609	678	1,232	376	94.0

PHILADELPHIA 76ERS

PLAYER	GP	MIN	Field Goals FGM	PCT	3-PT FG FGA-FGM	Free Throws FTM	PCT	Rebounds OFF	TOTAL	A	STL	TO	BLK	AVG
Allen Iverson	15	640	151	41.3	53-12	154	88.5	7	41	109	33	66	1	31.2
Andre Iguodala	76	3,062	443	44.7	155-48	452	82.0	77	434	432	152	261	33	18.2
Kyle Korver	74	2,288	372	44.0	307-132	191	91.4	30	259	105	57	117	20	14.4
Andre Miller	57	2,144	307	46.4	19-1	160	80.8	72	248	416	73	152	6	13.6
Willie Green	74	1,842	357	41.1	157-51	74	69.6	42	159	112	56	106	4	11.3
Chris Webber	18	544	89	38.7	5-2	18	64.3	37	149	61	18	33	15	11.0
Samuel Dalembert	82	2,535	356	54.1	2-0	167	74.6	239	733	64	47	161	159	10.7
Joe Smith	54	1,355	191	44.5	4-0	115	84.6	107	360	46	31	63	20	9.2
Rodney Carney	67	1,169	182	46.4	72-25	53	60.9	39	128	26	38	43	23	6.6
Steven Hunter	70	1,605	188	57.7	0-0	74	49.0	114	335	26	13	65	76	6.4
Shavlik Randolph	13	179	23	47.9	0-0	12	54.5	19	54	4	7	9	10	4.5
Louis Williams	61	688	93	44.1	37-12	64	69.6	17	70	110	22	46	1	4.3
Kevin Ollie	53	919	81	43.3	2-0	37	82.2	8	74	130	21	47	1	3.8
Alan Henderson	38	418	43	64.2	0-0	33	70.2	48	107	10	9	12	12	3.1
Bobby Jones	44	336	43	46.2	9-1	23	56.1	22	57	16	11	18	1	2.5
Louis Amundson	10	87	6	40.0	0-0	4	40.0	13	28	1	1	5	8	1.6
Ivan McFarlin	11	41	5	38.5	1-0	5	71.4	7	11	1	0	1	0	1.4
Steven Smith	8	28	2	25.0	0-0	1	50.0	1	6	0	1	2	0	0.6
TEAM TOTALS	**82**	**19,880**	**2,932**	**45.8**	**823-284**	**1,637**	**76.7**	**899**	**3,252**	**1,669**	**590**	**1,258**	**390**	**94.9**
OPPONENTS	**82**		**3,039**	**46.3**	**1,424-503**	**1,452**	**75.4**	**969**	**3,373**	**1,825**	**606**	**1,280**	**320**	**98.0**

PHOENIX SUNS

PLAYER	GP	MIN	Field Goals FGM	PCT	3-PT FG FGA-FGM	Free Throws FTM	PCT	Rebounds OFF	TOTAL	A	STL	TO	BLK	AVG
Amare Stoudemire	82	3,689	607	57.5	3-0	457	78.1	222	786	84	78	232	110	20.4
Steve Nash	76	2,682	517	53.2	343-156	222	89.9	30	269	884	57	287	6	18.6
Leandro Barbosa	80	2,613	529	47.6	438-190	196	84.5	22	214	317	96	146	15	18.1
Shawn Marion	80	3,010	561	52.4	252-80	201	81.0	172	785	134	156	114	122	17.5
Raja Bell	78	2,917	410	43.2	496-205	118	77.6	48	251	196	50	83	22	14.7
Boris Diaw	73	2,268	306	53.8	45-15	82	68.3	91	317	352	28	154	38	9.7
James Jones	76	1,376	162	36.8	238-90	71	87.7	33	176	45	28	28	42	6.4
Marcus Banks	45	503	84	42.9	29-5	48	80.0	10	38	60	23	40	3	4.9
Kurt Thomas	67	1,208	126	48.6	1-0	56	78.9	86	379	24	24	35	29	4.6
Jalen Rose	29	246	38	44.2	47-21	11	91.7	3	23	16	5	9	2	3.7
Pat Burke	23	164	23	35.4	22-6	8	61.5	12	47	5	3	7	2	2.6
Eric Piatkowski	11	73	9	36.0	18-7	2	100.0	2	9	4	0	5	1	2.5
Jumaine Jones	18	138	14	27.5	32-10	2	100.0	6	23	1	5	7	1	2.2
Sean Marks	3	17	2	33.3	1-0	2	100.0	0	3	0	0	0	1	2.0
TEAM TOTALS	**82**	**19,905**	**3,388**	**49.4**	**1,965-785**	**1,476**	**80.8**	**737**	**3,320**	**2,122**	**553**	**1,189**	**394**	**110.2**
OPPONENTS	**82**		**3,238**	**45.7**	**1,387-504**	**1,458**	**76.7**	**1,008**	**3,512**	**1,548**	**566**	**1,242**	**304**	**102.9**

FAST FACT

With their win over the Dallas Mavericks, the Golden State Warriors became the first eighth-seeded team to defeat a top-seeded team in a best of seven NBA playoff series.

PORTLAND TRAIL BLAZERS

PLAYER	GP	MIN	Field Goals		3-PT FG	Free Throws		Rebounds		A	STL	TO	BLK	AVG
			FGM	PCT	FGA-FGM	FTM	PCT	OFF	TOTAL	A	STL	TO	BLK	AVG
Zach Randolph	68	2,425	600	46.7	48-14	394	81.9	199	688	147	53	215	15	23.6
Brandon Roy	57	2,015	349	45.6	146-55	202	83.8	58	250	230	67	116	10	16.8
Jarrett Jack	79	2,651	320	45.4	180-63	243	87.1	18	208	417	86	187	9	12.0
Travis Outlaw	67	1,532	246	43.4	37-10	143	79.0	65	217	52	61	66	74	9.6
LaMarcus Aldridge	63	1,392	241	50.3	2-0	83	72.2	144	312	24	22	43	73	9.0
Juan Dixon	55	1,243	189	42.6	143-52	60	83.3	16	85	82	49	77	7	8.9
Ime Udoka	75	2,144	237	46.1	219-89	66	74.2	95	279	112	71	73	17	8.4
Martell Webster	82	1,759	195	39.6	250-91	93	70.5	43	240	52	35	76	19	7.0
Jamaal Magloire	81	1,703	199	50.4	0-0	131	54.1	151	492	30	21	129	66	6.5
Fred Jones	24	449	43	38.4	27-7	22	84.6	7	33	53	18	17	4	4.8
Raef LaFrentz	27	352	39	38.2	23-2	20	76.9	25	70	8	7	13	11	3.7
Sergio Rodriguez	67	862	101	42.3	85-24	21	80.8	20	91	218	35	77	2	3.7
Dan Dickau	50	444	54	35.8	61-16	42	79.2	7	43	70	14	27	1	3.3
Stephen Graham	14	165	17	42.5	11-3	8	88.9	6	21	5	4	13	1	3.2
Joel Przybilla	43	701	37	47.4	0-0	10	37.0	59	168	12	10	40	67	2.0
Luke Schenscher	11	118	7	30.4	0-0	5	71.4	10	25	1	2	4	4	1.7
Jeremy Richardson	1	1	0	00.0	0-0	0	00.0	0	0	0	0	0	0	0.0
TEAM TOTALS	82	19,955	2,874	45.0	1,232-426	1,543	76.9	923	3,222	1,513	555	1,236	380	94.1
OPPONENTS	82		2,962	47.1	1,293-467	1,678	77.8	850	3,197	1,703	539	1,127	380	98.4

SACRAMENTO KINGS

PLAYER	GP	MIN	Field Goals		3-PT FG	Free Throws		Rebounds		A	STL	TO	BLK	AVG
			FGM	PCT	FGA-FGM	FTM	PCT	OFF	TOTAL	A	STL	TO	BLK	AVG
Kevin Martin	80	2,818	505	47.3	333-127	481	84.4	69	342	173	98	135	11	20.2
Ron Artest	70	2,641	458	44.0	260-93	307	74.0	102	454	235	149	146	43	18.8
Mike Bibby	82	2,784	471	40.4	481-173	288	83.0	39	263	388	88	197	6	17.1
Shareef Abdur-Rahim	80	2,015	310	47.4	20-3	170	72.6	122	398	109	53	116	40	9.9
Corliss Williamson	68	1,337	236	51.0	2-0	148	71.5	63	221	39	29	97	15	9.1
Brad Miller	63	1,783	224	45.3	33-5	115	77.2	79	401	224	38	108	39	9.0
John Salmons	79	2,135	236	45.6	112-40	159	77.9	47	264	254	73	119	27	8.5
Francisco Garcia	79	1,410	163	42.9	149-53	95	83.3	53	205	87	45	70	43	6.0
Kenny Thomas	62	1,412	146	48.2	1-0	39	51.3	134	377	76	43	90	16	5.3
Justin Williams	26	333	54	61.4	1-0	23	36.5	51	115	2	5	15	16	5.0
Ronnie Price	58	563	67	39.0	65-21	37	67.3	15	71	48	28	33	4	3.3
Jason Hart	13	100	15	50.0	6-3	10	90.9	2	15	10	3	4	0	3.3
Quincy Douby	42	359	48	38.1	50-12	11	73.3	11	37	15	15	15	4	2.8
Maurice Taylor	12	103	8	28.6	0-0	8	61.5	10	28	5	4	6	1	2.0
Vitaly Potapenko	3	13	0	00.0	0-0	0	00.0	0	2	0	0	2	0	0.0
TEAM TOTALS	82	19,805	2,941	45.0	1,513-530	1,891	76.5	797	3,193	1,665	671	1,194	265	101.3
OPPONENTS	82		3,147	47.2	1,524-557	1,600	75.7	907	3,555	1,840	572	1,335	405	103.1

SAN ANTONIO SPURS

PLAYER	GP	MIN	FGM	PCT	FGA-FGM	FTM	PCT	OFF	TOTAL	A	STL	TO	BLK	AVG
Tim Duncan	80	2,726	618	54.6	9-1	362	63.7	213	845	273	66	223	190	20.0
Tony Parker	77	2,499	570	52.0	38-15	274	78.3	34	250	420	82	191	6	18.6
Manu Ginobili	75	2,060	396	46.4	323-128	320	86.0	59	327	263	109	157	27	16.5
Michael Finley	82	1,823	273	41.2	286-104	90	91.8	34	223	108	32	46	16	9.0
Brent Barry	75	1,631	202	47.5	287-128	103	88.0	17	160	138	56	61	12	8.5
James White	6	137	18	43.9	7-2	12	80.0	3	20	5	3	5	1	8.3
Bruce Bowen	82	2,464	189	40.5	232-89	43	58.9	23	223	117	62	65	25	6.2
Francisco Elson	70	1,332	144	51.1	2-0	62	77.5	81	336	55	31	86	59	5.0
Matt Bonner	56	653	106	44.7	94-36	27	71.1	64	156	22	17	25	11	4.9
Beno Udrih	73	948	127	36.9	115-33	53	88.3	11	82	122	27	56	1	4.7
Fabricio Oberto	79	1,365	158	56.2	0-0	33	64.7	131	368	68	25	69	24	4.4
Robert Horry	68	1,124	90	35.9	149-50	38	59.4	73	229	77	45	44	41	3.9
Jackie Butler	11	103	16	45.7	0-0	9	90.0	6	22	5	2	10	0	3.7
Melvin Ely	6	65	6	30.0	0-0	7	58.3	3	14	4	4	5	2	3.2
Jacque Vaughn	64	760	71	42.5	2-1	49	75.4	8	68	131	24	40	2	3.0
Eric Williams	16	88	15	44.1	17-8	4	57.1	1	14	6	2	5	0	2.6
TEAM TOTALS	**82**	**19,780**	**2,999**	**47.4**	**1,561-595**	**1,486**	**75.1**	**761**	**3,337**	**1,814**	**587**	**1,136**	**417**	**98.5**
OPPONENTS	**82**		**2,860**	**44.3**	**1,101-368**	**1,300**	**74.0**	**828**	**3,207**	**1,416**	**579**	**1,176**	**337**	**90.1**

SEATTLE SUPERSONICS

PLAYER	GP	MIN	FGM	PCT	FGA-FGM	FTM	PCT	OFF	TOTAL	A	STL	TO	BLK	AVG
Ray Allen	55	2,219	505	43.8	443-165	279	90.3	57	247	228	82	154	11	26.4
Rashard Lewis	60	2,348	463	46.1	387-151	265	84.1	91	396	145	68	118	39	22.4
Chris Wilcox	82	2,586	433	52.9	6-0	240	68.4	178	629	82	70	127	38	13.5
Luke Ridnour	71	2,091	301	43.3	139-49	128	80.5	28	164	368	83	156	19	11.0
Nick Collison	82	2,378	318	50.0	2-0	154	77.4	229	666	82	48	123	66	9.6
Earl Watson	77	2,152	263	38.3	280-92	108	73.5	34	185	437	99	167	23	9.4
Damien Wilkins	82	2,037	262	43.5	122-50	150	88.2	87	229	156	92	116	16	8.8
Johan Petro	81	1,510	226	51.6	0-0	50	64.9	92	335	45	39	82	47	6.2
Mickael Gelabale	70	1,239	122	46.2	47-11	66	80.5	59	173	56	24	49	22	4.6
Mike Wilks	47	534	66	46.8	15-5	33	78.6	15	54	79	15	31	4	3.6
Danny Fortson	14	158	15	50.0	1-0	10	76.9	13	43	1	1	15	0	2.9
Andre Brown	38	271	42	56.8	1-0	9	60.0	26	74	2	6	29	4	2.4
Mouhamed Sene	28	169	18	36.7	0-0	17	58.6	16	45	0	3	11	12	1.9
Desmon Farmer	8	32	5	33.3	8-2	1	100.0	0	1	9	1	1	0	1.6
Andreas Glyniadakis	13	81	8	47.1	0-0	1	50.0	2	8	1	0	9	0	1.3
Randy Livingston	4	26	0	00.0	0-0	0	00.0	1	1	4	0	1	0	0.0
TEAM TOTALS	**82**	**19,830**	**3,047**	**46.0**	**1,451-525**	**1,511**	**79.1**	**928**	**3,250**	**1,695**	**631**	**1,268**	**301**	**99.1**
OPPONENTS	**82**		**3,126**	**47.6**	**1,437-519**	**1,596**	**75.1**	**954**	**3,362**	**1,870**	**590**	**1,233**	**341**	**102.0**

TORONTO RAPTORS

PLAYER	GP	MIN	Field Goals		3-PT FG	Free Throws		Rebounds		A	STL	TO	BLK	AVG
			FGM	PCT	FGA-FGM	FTM	PCT	OFF	TOTAL					
Chris Bosh	69	2,658	543	49.6	35-12	463	78.5	186	741	175	39	179	90	22.6
T.J. Ford	75	2,243	393	43.6	69-21	240	81.9	53	236	595	101	231	8	14.0
Anthony Parker	73	2,437	328	47.7	261-115	132	83.5	60	283	153	73	71	11	12.4
Andrea Bargnani	65	1,629	267	42.7	268-100	117	82.4	52	255	50	32	107	53	11.6
Juan Dixon	26	683	110	42.5	83-27	41	93.2	11	73	41	27	24	2	11.1
Morris Peterson	71	1,515	222	42.9	295-106	84	68.3	32	237	47	45	53	12	8.9
Jose Calderon	77	1,614	263	52.1	75-25	117	81.8	21	134	387	63	110	5	8.7
Jorge Garbajosa	67	1,909	222	42.0	193-66	57	73.1	48	330	125	78	64	15	8.5
Fred Jones	39	870	96	38.6	101-32	73	83.0	16	82	55	30	50	12	7.6
Joey Graham	79	1,319	192	49.5	31-9	110	84.0	55	248	44	30	49	4	6.4
Rasho Nesterovic	80	1,676	230	54.6	1-0	34	68.0	115	360	74	37	56	84	6.2
Luke Jackson	10	122	18	51.4	13-4	5	55.6	2	9	9	5	6	1	4.5
Kris Humphries	60	670	87	47.0	0-0	53	67.1	78	187	18	14	32	21	3.8
Darrick Martin	31	220	33	35.1	37-13	15	71.4	2	12	43	3	12	0	3.0
Uros Slokar	20	72	14	53.8	2-1	9	69.2	7	14	1	1	9	2	1.9
P.J. Tucker	17	83	11	50.0	0-0	8	57.1	11	23	3	2	6	0	1.8
Pape Sow	7	34	3	33.3	0-0	4	66.7	6	11	2	1	1	1	1.4
TEAM TOTALS	82	19,755	3,032	46.3	1,464-531	1,562	78.8	755	3,235	1,822	581	1,104	321	99.5
OPPONENTS	82		3,051	46.3	1,491-533	1,441	75.4	848	3,489	1,742	489	1,241	317	98.5

UTAH JAZZ

PLAYER	GP	MIN	FGM	PCT	FGA-FGM	FTM	PCT	OFF	TOTAL	A	STL	TO	BLK	AVG
Carlos Boozer	74	2,557	647	56.1	0-0	255	68.5	235	867	221	70	194	21	20.9
Mehmet Okur	80	2,664	490	46.2	336-129	296	76.5	160	579	156	36	125	38	17.6
Deron Williams	80	2,950	494	45.6	255-82	227	76.7	41	267	745	78	246	13	16.2
Matt Harpring	77	1,965	322	49.1	39-13	237	76.7	117	353	99	52	118	11	11.6
Derek Fisher	82	2,287	258	38.2	156-48	262	85.3	30	149	274	83	120	6	10.1
Andrei Kirilenko	70	2,049	197	47.1	75-16	174	72.8	88	329	202	74	135	144	8.3
Gordan Giricek	61	1,188	176	46.2	122-52	71	81.6	24	129	63	28	64	5	7.8
Paul Millsap	82	1,472	209	52.5	3-1	140	67.3	183	423	62	67	94	74	6.8
Ronnie Brewer	56	675	102	52.8	9-0	56	67.5	37	75	24	37	24	6	4.6
C.J. Miles	37	373	40	34.5	32-7	14	60.9	11	35	25	11	28	4	2.7
Rafael Araujo	28	248	27	41.5	0-0	18	62.1	22	66	10	6	17	2	2.6
Jarron Collins	82	913	75	44.1	0-0	54	65.1	71	171	60	13	37	8	2.5
Dee Brown	49	450	32	32.7	28-6	24	64.9	8	40	83	22	31	7	1.9
Roger Powell	3	13	0	00.0	1-0	2	100.0	3	3	0	0	3	0	0.7
TEAM TOTALS	82	19,805	3,069	47.4	1,056-354	1,830	74.3	1,030	3,486	2,024	577	1,277	339	101.5
OPPONENTS	82		2,819	45.5	1,424-506	1,943	76.7	813	3,036	1,552	623	1,230	438	98.6

TRIVIA CHALLENGE

What active basketball player has earned more All-NBA First Team mentions than any other, with nine?

A: Tim Duncan

WASHINGTON WIZARDS

| PLAYER | GP | MIN | Field Goals | | 3-PT FG | Free Throws | | Rebounds | | A | STL | TO | BLK | AVG |
			FGM	PCT	FGA-FGM	FTM	PCT	OFF	TOTAL					
Gilbert Arenas	74	2,942	647	41.8	584-205	606	84.4	61	338	443	139	236	13	28.4
Antawn Jamison	70	2,662	512	45.0	379-138	226	73.6	134	562	136	80	104	36	19.8
Caron Butler	63	2,474	451	46.3	72-18	283	86.3	147	467	233	134	181	17	19.1
DeShawn Stevenson	82	2,419	347	46.1	183-74	152	70.4	55	216	218	65	119	19	11.2
Darius Songaila	37	700	118	52.4	2-0	46	85.2	44	134	38	17	43	10	7.6
Jarvis Hayes	81	1,626	224	41.0	183-66	71	84.5	42	210	80	48	56	13	7.2
Antonio Daniels	80	1,761	172	44.2	63-19	208	83.2	18	151	290	39	69	9	7.1
Brendan Haywood	77	1,740	198	55.8	0-0	115	54.8	195	477	47	34	90	88	6.6
Etan Thomas	65	1,246	159	57.4	0-0	77	55.8	136	377	29	22	71	89	6.1
Andray Blatche	56	682	86	43.7	27-4	30	61.2	77	191	39	17	49	32	3.7
Roger Mason	62	492	59	33.0	102-33	14	87.5	7	45	35	13	19	6	2.7
Donell Taylor	47	369	56	40.0	17-3	11	52.4	14	53	45	17	25	3	2.7
Calvin Booth	44	380	31	47.0	2-1	6	60.0	27	81	18	4	9	29	1.6
Mike Hall	2	13	1	25.0	0-0	0	00.0	1	2	1	0	0	0	1.0
James Lang	11	55	4	44.4	0-0	3	60.0	5	11	2	0	2	3	1.0
Michael Ruffin	30	271	5	27.8	0-0	7	36.8	35	62	6	6	12	8	0.6
TEAM TOTALS	82	19,830	3,070	45.0	1,614-561	1,855	76.5	998	3,377	1,660	635	1,133	375	104.3
OPPONENTS	82		3,166	47.3	1,585-598	1,668	77.7	973	3,524	1,942	519	1,291	380	104.9

TODAY'S STARS

Amare Stoudemire entered the NBA after high school to earn money for his family.

BOB ROSATO

■ **Amaré Stoudemire, center,** b. November 16, 1982, Lake Wales, Florida. Stoudemire skipped college ans was the ninth overall pick in the 2002 NBA Draft. He had the most successful NBA season by any prep-to-pro rookie up to that point, winning the 2002–03 Rookie of the Year award. After missing most of the 2005–06 season due to knee problems, he was back to his old self in 2006–07, receiving his first All-NBA First Team mention along with Suns' teammate Steve Nash.

■ **Brandon Roy, guard,** b. July 23, 1984, Seattle, Washington. Roy played for the University of Washington for four years after removing his name from the 2002 NBA Draft to attend college. The Minnesota Timberwolves selected Roy as the sixth overall pick in the 2006 draft, but then traded his rights to the Portland Trail Blazers. In his first NBA season with the Blazers, Roy averaged 16.8 points and 4 assists per game and was chosen as the 2006-07 NBA Rookie of the Year, receiving 127 of 128 first place votes.

■ **Chris Bosh, forward,** b. March 24, 1984, Dallas, Texas. Selected fourth overall— after Lebron James, Carmelo Anthony, and Dwyane Wade—by the Toronto Raptors in the 2003 draft, Bosh led all rookies in rebounds and blocks and was selected to the All-Rookie NBA First Team for the 2003–04 season. After Vince Carter left the team in December 2004, Bosh became the new leader and face of the franchise, helping the team to its first-ever Atlantic division title in 2006–07.

NBA CHAMPIONS

SEASON	CHAMPION	SERIES	RUNNER-UP	WINNING COACH	FINALS MVP
2006–07	San Antonio	4-0	Cleveland	Gregg Popovich	Tony Parker, SA
2005–06	Miami	4-2	Dallas	Pat Riley	Dwyane Wade, Mia
2004–05	San Antonio	4-3	Detroit	Gregg Popovich	Tim Duncan, SA
2003–04	Detroit	4-1	L.A. Lakers	Larry Brown	Chauncey Billups, Det
2002–03	San Antonio	4-2	New Jersey	Gregg Popovich	Tim Duncan, SA
2001–02	L.A. Lakers	4-0	New Jersey	Phil Jackson	Shaquille O'Neal, L.A.
2000–01	L.A. Lakers	4-1	Philadelphia	Phil Jackson	Shaquille O'Neal, L.A.
1999–00	L.A. Lakers	4-2	Indiana	Phil Jackson	Shaquille O'Neal, L.A.
1998–99	San Antonio	4-1	New York	Gregg Popovich	Tim Duncan, SA
1997–98	Chicago	4-2	Utah	Phil Jackson	Michael Jordan, Chi
1996–97	Chicago	4-2	Utah	Phil Jackson	Michael Jordan, Chi
1995–96	Chicago	4-2	Seattle	Phil Jackson	Michael Jordan, Chi
1994–95	Houston	4-0	Orlando	Rudy Tomjanovich	Hakeem Olajuwon, Hou
1993–94	Houston	4-3	New York	Rudy Tomjanovich	Hakeem Olajuwon, Hou
1992–93	Chicago	4-2	Phoenix	Phil Jackson	Michael Jordan, Chi
1991–92	Chicago	4-2	Portland	Phil Jackson	Michael Jordan, Chi
1990–91	Chicago	4-1	L.A. Lakers	Phil Jackson	Michael Jordan, Chi
1989–90	Detroit	4-1	Portland	Chuck Daly	Isiah Thomas, Det
1988–89	Detroit	4-0	L.A. Lakers	Chuck Daly	Joe Dumars, Det
1987–88	L.A. Lakers	4-3	Detroit	Pat Riley	James Worthy, L.A.
1986–87	L.A. Lakers	4-2	Boston	Pat Riley	Magic Johnson, L.A.
1985–86	Boston	4-2	Houston	K.C. Jones	Larry Bird, Bos
1984–85	L.A. Lakers	4-2	Boston	Pat Riley	Kareem Abdul-Jabbar, L.A.
1983–84	Boston	4-3	L.A. Lakers	K.C. Jones	Larry Bird, Bos
1982–83	Philadelphia	4-0	L.A. Lakers	Billy Cunningham	Moses Malone, Phil
1981–82	L.A. Lakers	4-2	Philadelphia	Pat Riley	Magic Johnson, L.A.
1980–81	Boston	4-2	Houston	Bill Fitch	Cedric Maxwell, Bos
1979–80	L.A. Lakers	4-2	Philadelphia	Paul Westhead	Magic Johnson, L.A.
1978–79	Seattle	4-1	Washington	Lenny Wilkens	Dennis Johnson, Sea
1977–78	Washington	4-3	Seattle	Dick Motta	Wes Unseld, Wash
1976–77	Portland	4-2	Philadelphia	Jack Ramsay	Bill Walton, Port
1975–76	Boston	4-2	Phoenix	Tom Heinsohn	Jo Jo White, Bos
1974–75	Golden State	4-0	Washington	Al Attles	Rick Barry, GS
1973–74	Boston	4-3	Milwaukee	Tom Heinsohn	John Havlicek, Bos
1972–73	New York	4-1	L.A. Lakers	Red Holzman	Willis Reed, N.Y.
1971–72	L.A. Lakers	4-1	New York	Bill Sharman	Wilt Chamberlain, L.A.
1970–71	Milwaukee	4-0	Baltimore	Larry Costello	*Lew Alcindor, Mil
1969–70	New York	4-3	L.A. Lakers	Red Holzman	Willis Reed, N.Y.
1968–69	Boston	4-3	L.A. Lakers	Bill Russell	Jerry West, L.A.
1967–68	Boston	4-2	L.A. Lakers	Bill Russell	—
1966–67	Philadelphia	4-2	San Francisco	Alex Hannum	—
1965–66	Boston	4-3	L.A. Lakers	Red Auerbach	—
1964–65	Boston	4-1	L.A. Lakers	Red Auerbach	—
1963–64	Boston	4-1	San Francisco	Red Auerbach	—
1962–63	Boston	4-2	L.A. Lakers	Red Auerbach	—
1961–62	Boston	4-3	L.A. Lakers	Red Auerbach	—
1960–61	Boston	4-1	St. Louis	Red Auerbach	—
1959–60	Boston	4-3	St. Louis	Red Auerbach	—
1958–59	Boston	4-0	Minneapolis	Red Auerbach	—
1957–58	St. Louis	4-2	Boston	Alex Hannum	—
1956–57	Boston	4-3	St. Louis	Red Auerbach	—
1955–56	Philadelphia	4-1	Ft. Wayne	George Senesky	—
1954–55	Syracuse	4-3	Ft. Wayne	Al Cervi	—
1953–54	Minneapolis	4-3	Syracuse	John Kundla	—
1952–53	Minneapolis	4-1	New York	John Kundla	—
1951–52	Minneapolis	4-3	New York	John Kundla	—
1950–51	Rochester	4-3	New York	Les Harrison	—
1949–50	Minneapolis	4-2	Syracuse	John Kundla	—
1948–49	Minneapolis	4-2	Washington	John Kundla	—
1947–48	Baltimore	4-2	Philadelphia	Buddy Jeannette	—
1946–47	Philadelphia	4-1	Chicago	Ed Gottlieb	—

Note: The NBA did not name a Finals MVP from 1946–47 to 1967–68.
*Alcindor changed his name to Kareem Abdul-Jabbar after the 1970–71 season.

ALL-TIME INDIVIDUAL LEADERS

SCORING

MOST POINTS, CAREER	PTS	AVG
Kareem Abdul-Jabbar	38,387	24.6
Karl Malone	36,928	25.0
Michael Jordan	32,292	30.1
Wilt Chamberlain	31,419	30.1
Moses Malone	27,409	20.6
Elvin Hayes	27,313	21.0
Hakeem Olajuwon	26,946	21.8
Oscar Robertson	26,710	25.7
Dominique Wilkins	26,668	24.8
John Havlicek	26,395	20.8

HIGHEST SCORING AVERAGE, CAREER

Michael Jordan	30.1	1,072 games
Wilt Chamberlain	30.1	1,045 games
Allen Iverson	27.9	747 games
Elgin Baylor	27.4	846 games
Jerry West	27.0	932 games
Bob Pettit	26.4	792 games
George Gervin	26.2	791 games
Shaquille O'Neal	25.9	981 games
Oscar Robertson	25.7	1,040 games
Karl Malone	25.0	1,476 games

Note: Minimum 400 games or 10,000 points.

MOST POINTS, GAME		OPPONENT	DATE
100	Wilt Chamberlain, Phil	N.Y.	3/2/62
81	Kobe Bryant, LAL	Tor	1/22/06
73	Wilt Chamberlain, Phil	Chi	1/13/62
73	Wilt Chamberlain, SF	N.Y.	11/16/62
73	David Thompson, Den	Det	4/9/78
72	Wilt Chamberlain, SF	LAC	11/3/62
71	Elgin Baylor, LAL	N.Y.	11/15/60
71	David Robinson, SA	LAC	4/24/94
70	Wilt Chamberlain, SF	Syr	3/10/63
69	Michael Jordan, Chi	Clev	3/28/90

HIGHEST FIELD-GOAL PERCENTAGE, CAREER
.599 Artis Gilmore

Note: Minimum 2,000 field goals made.

HIGHEST FREE-THROW PERCENTAGE, CAREER
.904 Mark Price

Note: Minimum 1,200 free throws made.

3-POINT FIELD GOALS
Most 3-point Field Goals, Career:
  2,560 Reggie Miller, Indiana
Highest 3-point Field-Goal Percentage, Career:
  .454 Steve Kerr, San Antonio
Most 3-point Field Goals, Game:
  12 Kobe Bryant, L.A. Lakers vs. Seattle, 1/7/03
  12 Donyell Marshall, Toronto vs. Philadelphia,
  3/13/05

Note: First season of 3-point field goal: 1979–80.

*Steals have only been an official stat since the 1973–74 season.

Wilt Chamberlain (right) is the only NBA player to score 100 points in a game.

AP PHOTO

STEALS*

Most Steals, Career: 3,265 John Stockton, Utah
Most Steals, Game: 11 Kendall Gill, New Jersey vs.
  Miami, 4/3/99; Larry Kenon, San Antonio vs. Kansas
  City, 12/26/76

REBOUNDS

MOST REBOUNDS, CAREER

PLAYER	REBOUNDS	YRS	AVG
Wilt Chamberlain	23,924	14	22.9
Bill Russell	21,620	13	22.5
Kareem Abdul-Jabbar	17,440	20	11.2
Elvin Hayes	16,279	16	12.5
Moses Malone	16,212	19	12.2
Karl Malone	14,968	19	10.1
Robert Parish	14,715	21	9.1
Nate Thurmond	14,464	14	15.0
Walt Bellamy	14,241	14	13.7
Wes Unseld	13,769	13	14.0

MOST REBOUNDS, GAME

NO.	PLAYER, TEAM	OPPONENT	DATE
55	Wilt Chamberlain, Phil	Bos	11/24/60
51	Bill Russell, Bos	Syr	2/5/60
49	Bill Russell, Bos	Phil	11/16/57
49	Bill Russell, Bos	Det	3/11/65
45	Wilt Chamberlain, Phil	Syr	2/6/60
45	Wilt Chamberlain, Phil	L.A.	1/21/61

ASSISTS

MOST ASSISTS, CAREER

John Stockton	15,806
Mark Jackson	10,334
Magic Johnson	10,141
Oscar Robertson	9,887
Isiah Thomas	9,061

MOST ASSISTS, GAME

30 Scott Skiles, Orlando vs. Denver, 12/30/90

BLOCKS*

MOST BLOCKS, CAREER

Hakeem Olajuwon	3,830
Dikembe Mutombo	3,230
Kareem Abdul-Jabbar	3,189
Mark Eaton	3,064
David Robinson	2,954

MOST BLOCKS, GAME

17 Elmore Smith, L.A. Lakers vs. Portland, 10/28/73

*Blocks have only been an official stat since the 1973–74 season.

Oscar Robertson (right) was a 12-time NBA All-Star.

VERNON BIEVER/WIREIMAGE.COM

DID YOU KNOW?

Dirk Nowitzki is the first European-born player ever to recieve the NBA's Most Valuable Player award, and only the second German-born player to make it to the NBA Finals.

MOST VALUABLE PLAYER: MAURICE PODOLOFF TROPHY

JOHN BIEVER

SEASON	PLAYER, TEAM
2006–07	Dirk Nowitzki, Dallas
2005–06	Steve Nash, Phoenix
2004–05	Steve Nash, Phoenix
2003–04	Kevin Garnett, Minnesota
2002–03	Tim Duncan, San Antonio
2001–02	Tim Duncan, San Antonio
2000–01	Allen Iverson, Philadelphia
1999–00	Shaquille O'Neal, L.A. Lakers
1998–99	Karl Malone, Utah
1997–98	Michael Jordan, Chicago
1996–97	Karl Malone, Utah
1995–96	Michael Jordan, Chicago
1994–95	David Robinson, San Antonio
1993–94	Hakeem Olajuwon, Houston
1992–93	Charles Barkley, Phoenix
1991–92	Michael Jordan, Chicago
1990–91	Michael Jordan, Chicago
1989–90	Magic Johnson, L.A. Lakers
1988–89	Magic Johnson, L.A. Lakers
1987–88	Michael Jordan, Chicago
1986–87	Magic Johnson, L.A. Lakers
1985–86	Larry Bird, Boston
1984–85	Larry Bird, Boston
1983–84	Larry Bird, Boston
1982–83	Moses Malone, Philadelphia
1981–82	Moses Malone, Houston

Dirk Nowitzki, Dallas Mavericks

SEASON	PLAYER, TEAM
1980–81	Julius Erving, Philadelphia
1979–80	Kareem Abdul-Jabbar, L.A. Lakers
1978–79	Moses Malone, Houston
1977–78	Bill Walton, Portland
1976–77	Kareem Abdul-Jabbar, L.A. Lakers
1975–76	Kareem Abdul-Jabbar, L.A. Lakers
1974–75	Bob McAdoo, Buffalo
1973–74	Kareem Abdul-Jabbar, Milwaukee
1972–73	Dave Cowens, Boston
1971–72	Kareem Abdul-Jabbar, Milwaukee
1970–71	Lew Alcindor, Milwaukee*
1969–70	Willis Reed, New York
1968–69	Wes Unseld, Baltimore
1967–68	Wilt Chamberlain, Philadelphia
1966–67	Wilt Chamberlain, Philadelphia
1965–66	Wilt Chamberlain, Philadelphia
1964–65	Bill Russell, Boston
1963–64	Oscar Robertson, Cincinnati
1962–63	Bill Russell, Boston
1961–62	Bill Russell, Boston
1960–61	Bill Russell, Boston
1959–60	Wilt Chamberlain, Philadelphia
1958–59	Bob Pettit, St. Louis
1957–58	Bill Russell, Boston
1956–57	Bob Cousy, Boston
1955–56	Bob Pettit, St. Louis

*Alcindor changed his name to Kareem Abdul-Jabbar after the 1970–71 season.

ROOKIE OF THE YEAR: EDDIE GOTTLIEB TROPHY

SEASON	PLAYER, TEAM
2006–07	Brandon Roy, Portland
2005–06	Chris Paul, New Orleans
2004–05	Emeka Okafor, Charlotte
2003–04	LeBron James, Cleveland
2002–03	Amare Stoudemire, Phoenix
2001–02	Pau Gasol, Memphis
2000–01	Mike Miller, Orlando
1999–00	Steve Francis, Houston
	Elton Brand, Chicago
1998–99	Vince Carter, Toronto
1997–98	Tim Duncan, San Antonio
1996–97	Allen Iverson, Philadelphia
1995–96	Damon Stoudamire, Toronto
1994–95	Jason Kidd, Dallas
	Grant Hill, Detroit
1993–94	Chris Webber, Golden State
1992–93	Shaquille O'Neal, Orlando
1991–92	Larry Johnson, Charlotte
1990–91	Derrick Coleman, New Jersey
1989–90	David Robinson, San Antonio
1988–89	Mitch Richmond, Golden State
1987–88	Mark Jackson, New York
1986–87	Chuck Person, Indiana
1985–86	Patrick Ewing, New York
1984–85	Michael Jordan, Chicago
1983–84	Ralph Sampson, Houston
1982–83	Terry Cummings, San Diego
1981–82	Buck Williams, New Jersey
1980–81	Darrell Griffith, Utah
1979–80	Larry Bird, Boston
1978–79	Phil Ford, Kansas City
1977–78	Walter Davis, Phoenix
1976–77	Adrian Dantley, Buffalo
1975–76	Alvan Adams, Phoenix
1974–75	Keith Wilkes, Golden State
1973–74	Ernie DiGregorio, Buffalo
1972–73	Bob McAdoo, Buffalo
1971–72	Sidney Wicks, Portland
1970–71	Dave Cowens, Boston
	Geoff Petrie, Portland
1969–70	Lew Alcindor, Milwaukee*
1968–69	Wes Unseld, Baltimore
1967–68	Earl Monroe, Baltimore
1966–67	Dave Bing, Detroit

Brandon Roy averaged 16.8 points per game in 2006–07.

KEVIN REECE/ICON SMI

SEASON	PLAYER, TEAM
1965–66	Rick Barry, San Francisco
1964–65	Willis Reed, New York
1963–64	Jerry Lucas, Cincinnati
1962–63	Terry Dischinger, Chicago
1961–62	Walt Bellamy, Chicago
1960–61	Oscar Robertson, Cincinnati
1959–60	Wilt Chamberlain, Philadelphia
1958–59	Elgin Baylor, Minneapolis
1957–58	Woody Sauldsberry, Philadelphia
1956–57	Tom Heinsohn, Boston
1955–56	Maurice Stokes, Rochester
1954–55	Bob Pettit, Milwaukee
1953–54	Ray Felix, Baltimore
1952–53	Don Meineke, Ft. Wayne

*Alcindor changed his name to Kareem Abdul-Jabbar after the 1970–71 season.

Note: There were co-winners in 1999–00, 1994–95, and 1970–71.

DEFENSIVE PLAYER OF THE YEAR

SEASON	PLAYER, TEAM
2006–07	Marcus Camby, Denver
2005–06	Ben Wallace, Detroit
2004–05	Ben Wallace, Detroit
2003–04	Ron Artest, Indiana
2002–03	Ben Wallace, Detroit
2001–02	Ben Wallace, Detroit
2000–01	Dikembe Mutombo, Philadelphia/Atlanta
1999–00	Alonzo Mourning, Miami
1998–99	Alonzo Mourning, Miami
1997–98	Dikembe Mutombo, Atlanta
1996–97	Dikembe Mutombo, Atlanta
1995–96	Gary Payton, Seattle
1994–95	Dikembe Mutombo, Denver

SEASON	PLAYER, TEAM
1993–94	Hakeem Olajuwon, Houston
1992–93	Hakeem Olajuwon, Houston
1991–92	David Robinson, San Antonio
1990–91	Dennis Rodman, Detroit
1989–90	Dennis Rodman, Detroit
1988–89	Mark Eaton, Utah
1987–88	Michael Jordan, Chicago
1986–87	Michael Cooper, L.A. Lakers
1985–86	Alvin Robertson, San Antonio
1984–85	Mark Eaton, Utah
1983–84	Sidney Moncrief, Milwaukee
1982–83	Sidney Moncrief, Milwaukee

SIXTH MAN AWARD

SEASON	PLAYER, TEAM
2006–07	Leandro Barbosa, Phoenix
2005–06	Mike Miller, Memphis
2004–05	Ben Gordon, Chicago
2003–04	Antawn Jamison, Dallas
2002–03	Bobby Jackson, Sacramento
2001–02	Corliss Williamson, Detroit
2000–01	Aaron McKie, Philadelphia
1999–00	Rodney Rogers, Phoenix
1998–99	Darrell Armstrong, Orlando
1997–98	Danny Manning, Phoenix
1996–97	John Starks, New York
1995–96	Toni Kukoc, Chicago
1994–95	Anthony Mason, New York
1993–94	Dell Curry, Charlotte
1992–93	Clifford Robinson, Portland
1991–92	Detlef Schrempf, Indiana
1990–91	Detlef Schrempf, Indiana
1989–90	Ricky Pierce, Milwaukee
1988–89	Eddie Johnson, Phoenix
1987–88	Roy Tarpley, Dallas
1986–87	Ricky Pierce, Milwaukee
1985–86	Bill Walton, Boston
1984–85	Kevin McHale, Boston
1983–84	Kevin McHale, Boston
1982–83	Bobby Jones, Philadelphia

Leandro Barbosa holds the Suns' record for points scored by a rookie.

MOST IMPROVED PLAYER

SEASON	PLAYER, TEAM	SEASON	PLAYER, TEAM
2006–07	Monta Ellis, Golden State	1995–96	Gheorghe Muresan, Washington
2005–06	Boris Diaw, Phoenix Suns	1994–95	Dana Barros, Philadelphia
2004–05	Bobby Simmons, L.A. Clippers	1993–94	Don MacLean, Washington
2003–04	Zach Randolph, Portland	1992–93	Mahmoud Abdul-Rauf, Denver
2002–03	Gilbert Arenas, Golden State	1991–92	Pervis Ellison, Washington
2001–02	Jermaine O'Neal, Indiana	1990–91	Scott Skiles, Orlando
2000–01	Tracy McGrady, Orlando	1989–90	Rony Seikaly, Miami
1999–00	Jalen Rose, Indiana	1988–89	Kevin Johnson, Phoenix
1998–99	Darrell Armstrong, Orlando	1987–88	Kevin Duckworth, Portland
1997–98	Alan Henderson, Atlanta	1986–87	Dale Ellis, Seattle
1996–97	Isaac Austin, Miami	1985–86	Alvin Robertson, San Antonio

2007 NBA DRAFT – FIRST ROUND

June 28, 2007, New York, NY

1. Greg Oden, Portland
2. Kevin Durant, Seattle
3. Al Horford, Atlanta
4. Mike Conley Jr., Memphis
5. Jeff Green, Boston
6. Yi Jianlin, Milwaukee
7. Corey Brewer, Minnesota
8. Brandan Wright, Charlotte
9. Joakim Noah, Chicago
10. Spencer Hawes, Sacramento
11. Acie Law IV, Atlanta
12. Thaddeus Young, Philadelphia
13. Julian Wright, New Orleans
14. Al Thornton, LA Clippers
15. Rodney Stuckey, Detroit
16. Nick Young, Washington
17. Sean Williams, New Jersey
18. Marco Belinelli, Golden State
19. Javaris Crittenton, LA Lakers
20. Jason Smith, Miami
21. Daequan Cook, Philadelphia
22. Jared Dudley, Charlotte
23. Wilson Chandler, New York
24. Rudy Fernandez, Phoenix
25. Morris Almond, Utah
26. Aaron Brooks, Houston
27. Arron Afflalo, Detroit
28. Tiago Splitter, San Antonio
29. Alando Tucker, Phoenix
30. Petteri Koponen, Philadelphia

ALL-STAR GAME RESULTS

YEAR	RESULT	SITE	WINNING COACH	MOST VALUABLE PLAYER
2007	West 153, East 132	Las Vegas, NV	Mike D'Antoni	Kobe Bryant, L.A. Lakers
2006	East 122, West 120	Houston, TX	Flip Saunders	LeBron James, Cleveland
2005	East 125, West 115	Denver, CO	Stan Van Gundy	Allen Iverson, Philadelphia
2004	West 136, East 132	Los Angeles, CA	Flip Saunders	Shaquille O'Neal, L.A. Lakers
2003	West 155, East 145 (2 OT)	Atlanta, GA	Rick Adelman	Kevin Garnett, Minnesota
2002	West 135, East 120	Philadelphia, PA	Don Nelson	Kobe Bryant, L.A. Lakers
2001	East 111, West 110	Washington, DC	Larry Brown	Allen Iverson, Philadelphia
2000	West 137, East 126	Oakland, CA	Phil Jackson	Shaquille O'Neal, L.A. Lakers/ Tim Duncan, San Antonio
1999	Canceled due to lockout			
1998	East 135, West 114	New York, NY	Larry Bird	Michael Jordan, Chicago
1997	East 132, West 120	Cleveland, OH	Doug Collins	Glen Rice, Charlotte
1996	East 129, West 118	San Antonio, TX	Phil Jackson	Michael Jordan, Chicago
1995	West 139, East 112	Phoenix, AZ	Paul Westphal	Mitch Richmond, Sacramento
1994	East 127, West 118	Minneapolis, MN	Lenny Wilkens	Scottie Pippen, Chicago
1993	West 135, East 132	Salt Lake City, UT	Paul Westphal	Karl Malone/John Stockton, Utah
1992	West 153, East 113	Orlando, FL	Don Nelson	Magic Johnson, L.A. Lakers
1991	East 116, West 114	Charlotte, NC	Chris Ford	Charles Barkley, Philadelphia
1990	East 130, West 113	Miami, FL	Chuck Daly	Magic Johnson, L.A. Lakers
1989	West 143, East 134	Houston, TX	Pat Riley	Karl Malone, Utah
1988	East 138, West 133	Chicago, IL	Mike Fratello	Michael Jordan, Chicago
1987	West 154, East 149 (OT)	Seattle, WA	Pat Riley	Tom Chambers, Seattle
1986	East 139, West 132	Dallas, TX	K.C. Jones	Isiah Thomas, Detroit
1985	West 140, East 129	Indianapolis, IN	Pat Riley	Ralph Sampson, Houston
1984	East 154, West 145 (OT)	Denver, CO	K.C. Jones	Isiah Thomas, Detroit
1983	East 132, West 123	Los Angeles, CA	Billy Cunningham	Julius Erving, Philadelphia
1982	East 120, West 118	East Rutherford, NJ	Bill Fitch	Larry Bird, Boston
1981	East 123, West 120	Cleveland, OH	Billy Cunningham	Nate Archibald, Boston
1980	East 144, West 135 (OT)	Washington, DC	Billy Cunningham	George Gervin, San Antonio
1979	West 134, East 129	Detroit, MI	Lenny Wilkens	David Thompson, Denver
1978	East 133, West 125	Atlanta, GA	Billy Cunningham	Randy Smith, Buffalo
1977	West 125, East 124	Milwaukee, WI	Larry Brown	Julius Erving, Philadelphia
1976	East 123, West 109	Philadelphia, PA	Tom Heinsohn	Dave Bing, Washington
1975	East 108, West 102	Phoenix, AZ	K.C. Jones	Walt Frazier, New York
1974	West 134, East 123	Seattle, WA	Larry Costello	Bob Lanier, Detroit
1973	East 104, West 84	Chicago, IL	Tom Heinsohn	Dave Cowens, Boston
1972	West 112, East 110	Los Angeles, CA	Bill Sharman	Jerry West, L.A. Lakers
1971	West 108, East 107	San Diego, CA	Larry Costello	Lenny Wilkens, Seattle
1970	East 142, West 135	Philadelphia, PA	Red Holzman	Willis Reed, New York
1969	East 123, West 112	Baltimore, MD	Gene Shue	Oscar Robertson, Cincinnati
1968	East 144, West 124	New York, NY	Alex Hannum	Hal Greer, Philadelphia
1967	West 135, East 120	San Francisco, CA	Fred Schaus	Rick Barry, San Francisco
1966	East 137, West 94	Cincinnati, OH	Red Auerbach	Adrian Smith, Cincinnati
1965	East 124, West 123	St. Louis, MO	Red Auerbach	Jerry Lucas, Cincinnati
1964	East 111, West 107	Boston, MA	Red Auerbach	Oscar Robertson, Cincinnati
1963	East 115, West 108	Los Angeles, CA	Red Auerbach	Bill Russell, Boston
1962	West 150, East 130	St. Louis, MO	Fred Schaus	Bob Pettit, St. Louis
1961	West 153, East 131	Syracuse, NY	Paul Seymour	Oscar Robertson, Cincinnati
1960	East 125, West 115	Philadelphia, PA	Red Auerbach	Wilt Chamberlain, Philadelphia
1959	West 124, East 108	Detroit, MI	Ed Macauley	Bob Pettit, St. Louis/ Elgin Baylor, Minnesota
1958	East 130, West 118	St. Louis, MO	Red Auerbach	Bob Pettit, St. Louis
1957	East 109, West 97	Boston, MA	Red Auerbach	Bob Cousy, Boston
1956	West 108, East 94	Rochester, NY	Charley Eckman	Bob Pettit, St. Louis
1955	East 100, West 91	New York, NY	Al Cervi	Bill Sharman, Boston
1954	East 98, West 93 (OT)	New York, NY	Joe Lapchick	Bob Cousy, Boston
1953	West 79, East 75	Ft. Wayne, IN	John Kundla	George Mikan, Minnesota
1952	East 108, West 91	Boston, MA	Al Cervi	Paul Arizin, Philadelphia
1951	East 111, West 94	Boston, MA	Joe Lapchick	Ed Macauley, Boston

FAST FACT

The San Antonio Spurs' 2006–07 championship was the team's fourth title in nine years, making them the most successful pro sports franchise of the past decade.

TRIVIA CHALLENGE

Which player led the NBA in free-throw percentage during the 2006–07 season: Steve Nash, Richard Hamilton, or Kyle Korver?

A: Kyle Korver

TRIVIA CHALLENGE

1 Who is the only NBA player ever to average a triple double for an entire season?
a. Michael Jordan
b. Shaquille O'Neal
c. Oscar Robertson

2 What player holds the record for most assists in a single NBA game, with 30?
a. Scott Skiles
b. John Stockton
c. Steve Nash

3 Besides being former teammates with the Toronto Raptors, how else are Tracy McGrady and Vince Carter connected?
a. They are third cousins.
b. They are former classmates.
c. They own a restaurant together.

4 What player has led the league in technical fouls in each of the past three seasons?
a. Ron Artest
b. Rasheed Wallace
c. Allen Iverson

5 Julius "Dr. J" Erving was the first basketball player to achieve which off-court milestone?
a. He was pictured on a Wheaties box.
b. He marketed his own athletic shoes.
c. He established his own charity.

Julius Erving

6 Whose silhouette is the NBA logo based on?
a. Wilt Chabmerlain
b. Michael Jordan
c. Jerry West

7 Besides Wilt Chamberlain, who is the only player to win both the NBA's Rookie of the Year and MVP Awards during the same season?
a. Michael Jordan
b. Magic Johnson
c. Wes Unseld

8 Who was the youngest All-Star Game MVP in NBA history, receiving the honor at 21 years and 51 days old?
a. LeBron James
b. Isiah Thomas
c. Kobe Bryant

Trivia Challenge: 1. c; 2. a; 3. a; 4. b; 5. b; 6. c; 7. c; 8. a;

AP/WIREPHOTO

WORLD CHAMPIONSHIP OF BASKETBALL

YEAR	WINNER	RUNNER-UP	SCORE	SITE
2006	Spain	Greece	70–47	Saitama, Japan
2002	Yugoslavia	Argentina	84–77 (OT)	Indianapolis, Indiana
1998	Yugoslavia	Russia	64–62	Athens, Greece
1994*	United States	Russia	137–91	Toronto, Ontario, Canada
1990	Yugoslavia	Soviet Union	92–75	Buenos Aires, Argentina
1986	United States	Soviet Union	87–85	Madrid, Spain
1982	Soviet Union	United States	95–94	Cali, Colombia
1978	Yugoslavia	Soviet Union	82–81 (OT)	Manila, Philippines
1974	Soviet Union	Yugoslavia	†	San Juan, Puerto Rico
1970	Yugoslavia	Brazil	†	Ljubljana, Yugoslavia
1967	Soviet Union	Yugoslavia	†	Montevideo, Uruguay
1963	Brazil	Yugoslavia	†	Rio de Janeiro, Brazil
1959	Brazil	United States	†	Santiago, Chile
1954	United States	Brazil	†	Rio de Janeiro, Brazil
1950	Argentina	United States	†	Rio de Janeiro, Brazil

* U.S. professionals began competing in 1994. In 1998, an NBA labor dispute resulted in a boycott of the World Championship by NBA stars. Players from the Continental Basketball Association, European professional leagues, and U.S. colleges were used to fill the U.S. team's roster.
† Result determined by overall record in final round of competition.

BASKETBALL WOMEN'S

The WNBA sped things up in 2006, changing the shot clock from 30 seconds to 24. Diana Taurasi of the Phoenix Mercury thrived at the faster pace. The dynamic guard set a single-game record with 47 points. Lisa Leslie of the Los Angeles Sparks became the first WNBA player to reach 5,000 career points, finishing the season with 5,412.

Leslie also received her third league MVP award. The 6' 5" center finished in the top three in points and rebounds and had a league-best 17 double doubles. She helped power L.A. to the WNBA's best record (25-9). However, the Sparks sputtered out in the playoffs. They lost to the Sacramento Monarchs in the Western Conference Finals.

The Monarchs, led by All-Star Yolanda Griffith, were looking to repeat as champions. They surged to a 2–1 lead over the Detroit Shock in the best-of-five series and the title seemed to be in the bag, but Sacramento was grounded by the strong play of Finals MVP Deanna (Tweety) Nolan. Behind Nolan, the Shock came roaring back to win its second title in four years.

Every team in the league got to celebrate one thing this season: the 10th year of the WNBA. Media and fans named a WNBA All-Decade Team, and fans chose a Greatest Moment from the first 10 years: Teresa Weatherspoon's half-court buzzer-beater that won Game 2 of the 1999 WNBA Finals for the New York Liberty.

Deanna Nolan dominated opponents in the playoffs and was named MVP of the 2006 WNBA Finals. She led the Shock to its second WNBA championship in four years.

RON HOSKINS/NBAE/ GETTY IMAGES

FAST FACT

Lisa Leslie has played in the WNBA since the league began, in 1997.

2006 WNBA FINAL STANDINGS

EASTERN CONFERENCE

TEAM	W	L	PCT	GB
Connecticut	26	8	.765	—
Detroit	23	11	.676	3.0
Indiana	21	13	.618	8.0
Washington	18	16	.529	10.0
New York	11	23	.324	15.0
Charlotte	11	23	.324	15.0
Chicago	5	29	.147	21.0

WESTERN CONFERENCE

TEAM	W	L	PCT	GB
Los Angeles	25	9	.735	—
Sacramento	21	13	.618	4.0
Houston	18	16	.529	7.0
Seattle	18	16	.529	7.0
Phoenix	18	16	.529	7.0
San Antonio	13	21	.382	12.0
Minnesota	10	24	.294	15.0

Sparks center Lisa Leslie won her third WNBA MVP award in 2006.

2006 WNBA Playoffs

EASTERN CONFERENCE

Detroit Shock (2-0)
Indiana Fever
— Detroit Shock (2-1)

Connecticut Sun (2-0)
Washington Mystics
— Connecticut Sun

DETROIT SHOCK (3–2)

Sacramento Monarchs

WESTERN CONFERENCE

Sacramento Monarchs (2-0)
Los Angeles Sparks
— Sacramento Monarchs (2-0)
Houston Comets

Los Angeles Sparks (2-1)
Seattle Storm

2006 WNBA PLAYOFF RESULTS

EASTERN CONFERENCE SEMIFINALS

August 18: Sun 76, Mystics 61
August 20: Sun 58, Mystics 65
Connecticut Sun won series, 2–0

August 17: Shock 68, Fever 56
August 19: Shock 98, Fever 83
Detroit Shock won series, 2–0

WESTERN CONFERENCE SEMIFINALS

August 18: Storm 84, Sparks 72
August 20: Sparks 78, Storm 70
August 22: Sparks 68, Storm 63
Los Angeles Sparks won series, 2–1

August 17: Monarchs 93, Comets 78
August 19: Monarchs 92, Comets 64
Sacramento Monarchs won series, 2–0

EASTERN CONFERENCE FINALS

August 24: Shock 70, Sun 59
August 26: Sun 77, Shock 68
August 27: Shock 79, Sun 55
Detroit Shock won series, 2–1

WESTERN CONFERENCE FINALS

August 24: Monarchs 64, Sparks 61
Augsut 26: Monarchs 72, Sparks 58
Sacramento Monarchs won series, 2–0

WNBA FINALS

August 30: Monarchs 95, Shock 71
September 1: Shock 73, Monarchs 63
September 3: Monarchs 89, Shock 69
September 6: Shock 72, Monarchs 52
September 9: Shock 80, Monarchs 75
Detroit Shock won series, 3–2

WNBA FINALS COMPOSITE BOX SCORE

DETROIT SHOCK

PLAYER	GP	MPG	FG%	3P%	FT%	REBOUNDS/GAME OFF	DEF	TOTAL	APG	SPG	BPG	TO	PF	PPG
Deanna Nolan	5	33.8	.446	.400	.846	1.00	3.20	4.20	2.8	1.60	.40	3.40	2.00	17.8
Katie Smith	5	36.4	.470	.423	.706	0.40	1.40	1.80	3.4	.40	.00	3.00	2.80	17.0
Cheryl Ford	5	25.4	.583	.000	.786	2.20	6.40	8.80	1.2	1.40	.80	2.20	4.00	12.8
Plenette Pierson	5	19.2	.474	.000	.696	1.20	3.40	4.60	1.6	.60	1.40	1.40	3.00	6.8
Swin Cash	5	28.2	.344	.000	.818	2.20	3.60	5.80	3.6	.00	.20	3.00	1.80	6.2
Kara Braxton	5	16.2	.462	.000	.556	1.00	1.60	2.60	0.6	1.00	.40	1.60	3.00	5.8
Elaine Powell	5	14.4	.467	.000	.429	.60	1.20	1.80	1.6	1.00	.00	2.60	2.00	3.4
Ruth Riley	5	18.2	.250	.000	1.000	1.00	1.40	2.40	0.4	.40	1.80	1.60	3.00	2.0
Angelina Williams	4	3.8	.429	.000	.000	.50	0	.50	0	.25	.25	.50	.75	1.5
Kedra Holland-Corn	4	5.0	.000	.000	.000	.25	.25	.50	1.0	.25	.00	1.00	.50	0
Jacqueline Batteast	2	3.0	.000	.000	.000	0	0	0	0	0	0	0	.50	0
TEAM AVERAGES	5	200.0	.448	.366	.732	10.20	22.60	32.80	16.0	6.80	5.20	20.20	21.00	73.0

SACRAMENTO MONARCHS

PLAYER	GP	MPG	FG%	3P%	FT%	REBOUNDS/GAME OFF	DEF	TOTAL	APG	SPG	BPG	TO	PF	PPG
Yolanda Griffith	5	27.4	.420	.000	.781	2.80	4.60	7.40	1.8	1.20	1.00	1.40	2.80	13.4
Nicole Powell	5	28.2	.524	.529	.818	1.00	3.20	4.20	1.8	1.60	.20	1.40	2.80	12.4
Kara Lawson	5	32.0	.452	.480	.750	.60	1.00	1.60	0.8	1.00	.20	1.00	1.60	11.2
DeMya Walker	5	24.2	.426	.000	.857	2.20	1.20	3.40	2.2	.80	1.00	3.20	3.20	10.4
Kristin Haynie	5	17.2	.486	.357	1.000	.20	2.20	2.40	2.6	1.60	.00	.60	2.00	8.4
Hamchetou Maiga-Ba	5	13.6	.423	.000	1.000	1.00	.20	1.20	0.8	.60	.00	1.20	2.40	5.2
Ticha Penicheiro	5	20.0	.206	.000	.583	.00	1.60	1.60	2.8	1.20	.00	1.20	1.40	4.2
Rebekkah Brunson	5	17.2	.269	.000	.545	1.20	3.20	4.40	0.2	.20	.60	1.20	2.20	4.0
Erin Buescher	5	11.2	.385	1.000	.667	.80	.60	1.40	1.0	1.00	.20	.20	1.60	3.4
Scholanda Dorrell	5	8.2	.300	.500	1.000	.40	.40	.80	0.2	.40	.00	1.20	1.00	2.0
Kim Smith	3	1.3	.000	.000	.500	0	.33	.33	0	0	0	.67	0	0.3
TEAM AVERAGES	5	200.0	.407	.426	.743	10.20	18.40	28.60	14.2	9.60	3.20	14.40	21.00	74.8

WNBA FINALS GAME 1 MONARCHS 95, SHOCK 71 Time of Game: 2:06 Attendance: 11,268

8/30/2006 Palace of Auburn Hills, Detriot, Mich. Officials: June Courteau, Lamont Simpson, Michael Price

SACRAMENTO MONARCHS

PLAYER	POS	MIN	FGM-A	3GM-A	FTM-A	REBOUNDS OFF	DEF	TOT	A	STL	BLK	TO	PF	PTS
Kara Lawson	G	34	7-10	6-3	2-2	1	1	2	0	1	1	2	3	22
Ticha Penicheiro	G	21	1-3	0-2	1-2	0	3	3	6	2	0	3	1	3
Nicole Powell	F	27	8-12	4-7	1-1	1	2	3	4	3	0	1	4	21
DeMya Walker	F	18	7-12	0-0	3-3	3	1	4	2	0	0	2	4	17
Yolanda Griffith	C	26	7-11	0-0	3-4	2	3	5	3	1	2	3	3	17
Rebekkah Brunson		20	2-10	0-0	0-0	2	5	7	1	0	1	1	0	4
Kristin Haynie		16	1-3	0-2	2-2	1	3	4	2	5	0	1	0	4
Hamchetou Maiga-Ba	.	15	2-4	0-0	0-0	0	1	1	1	0	0	1	2	4
Erin Buescher		14	0-0	0-0	3-4	0	1	1	3	1	0	0	5	3
Sholanda Dorrell		5	0-1	0-0	0-0	1	0	1	0	0	0	1	1	0
Kim Smith		1	0-0	0-0	0-0	0	0	0	0	0	0	0	0	0
TOTA		200	35-66 (53.0%)	10-19 (52.6%)	15-18 (83.3%)	11	20	31	22	13	4	15	23	95

DETROIT SHOCK

PLAYER	POS	MIN	FGM-A	3GM-A	FTM-A	REBOUNDS OFF	DEF	TOT	A	STL	BLK	TO	PF	PTS
Katie Smith	G	37	7-15	4-6	3-4	1	1	2	2	2	0	4	1	21
Deanna Nolan	G	37	6-14	1-2	1-2	2	5	7	5	2	0	3	1	14
Cheryl Ford	F	29	9-13	0-0	7-11	3	5	8	1	2	3	1	3	25
Swin Cash	F	11	0-2	0-0	0-0	1	0	1	0	0	0	1	1	0
Ruth Riley	C	15	0-1	0-0	2-2	0	0	0	0	1	1	2	4	2
Plenette Pierson		23	1-3	0-0	1-2	3	2	5	4	0	0	3	3	3
Elaine Powell		22	0-3	0-0	2-2	0	2	2	2	2	0	2	1	2
Kara Braxton		14	2-4	0-0	0-0	1	3	4	3	1	0	5	4	4
Kedra Holland-Corn		7	0-1	0-1	0-0	0	0	0	1	0	0	2	0	0
Angelina Williams		3	0-0	0-0	0-0	0	0	0	0	0	0	1	1	0
TOTAL		200	25-56 (44.6%)	5-9 (55.6%)	16-23 (69.6%)	11	18	29	18	10	4	24	19	71

WNBA FINALS GAME 2 MONARCHS 63, SHOCK 73 Time of Game: 2:05 Attendance: 15,218

9/01/2006 Palace of Auburn Hills Detroit, Mich.   Officials: Lisa Mattingly, Sue Blauch, Kurt Walker

SACRAMENTO MONARCHS

PLAYER	POS	MIN	FGM-A	3GM-A	FTM-A	REBOUNDS OFF	DEF	TOT	A	STL	BLK	TO	PF	PTS
Kara Lawson	G	35	3-11	2-7	3-5	0	3	3	0	0	0	1	1	11
Ticha Penicheiro	G	23	0-8	0-3	0-0	0	0	0	2	3	0	0	2	0
Nicole Powell	F	30	2-6	0-1	1-1	0	5	5	0	0	1	1	3	5
DeMya Walker	F	24	4-9	0-0	2-2	2	0	2	2	1	1	5	5	10
Yolanda Griffith	C	29	4-9	0-0	6-8	3	5	8	2	2	1	2	1	14
Rebekkah Brunson		18	0-5	0-0	3-4	3	4	7	0	0	0	2	3	3
Kristin Haynie		16	5-9	1-3	0-0	0	2	2	3	1	0	2	2	11
Hamchetou Maiga-Ba		10	2-3	0-0	2-2	2	0	2	0	0	0	3	1	6
Erin Buescher		8	0-2	0-0	1-2	1	0	1	1	1	0	0	0	1
Scholanda Dorrell		4	1-2	0-1	0-0	0	0	0	0	0	0	0	1	2
TOTAL		200	24-64 (32.8%)	3-15 (20.0%)	18-24 (75.0%)	11	19	30	10	8	3	16	19	63

DETROIT SHOCK

PLAYER	POS	MIN	FGM-A	3GM-A	FTM-A	REBOUNDS OFF	DEF	TOT	A	STL	BLK	TO	PF	PTS
Deanna Nolan	G	40	8-20	1-3	4-4	2	1	3	4	1	0	4	1	21
Katie Smith	G	37	6-13	2-6	2-2	0	0	0	3	0	0	3	3	16
Swin Cash	F	33	5-9	0-0	1-1	3	5	8	5	0	0	2	1	11
Cheryl Ford	F	20	1-3	0-0	3-3	0	8	8	0	3	0	3	5	5
Ruth Riley	C	13	1-3	0-0	0-0	3	0	3	0	0	2	3	4	2
Kara Braxton		22	2-6	0-0	2-4	0	1	1	0	1	0	2	3	6
Plenette Pierson		21	3-3	0-0	0-1	1	3	4	2	2	3	1	3	6
Elaine Powell		11	3-5	0-0	0-1	0	1	1	1	1	0	3	3	6
TOTAL		200	29-62 (46.8%)	3-19 (33.3%)	12-16 (75.0%)	9	19	28	15	8	5	21	23	73

WNBA FINALS GAME 3 DETROIT 69, MONARCHS 89 Time of Game: 2:14 Attendance 14,253

9/03/2006 ARCO Arena, Sacramento, Calif.   Officials: Bob Trammell, Daryl Humphrey, Tina Napier

DETROIT SHOCK

PLAYER	POS	MIN	FGM-A	3GM-A	FTM-A	REBOUNDS OFF	DEF	TOT	A	STL	BLK	TO	PF	PTS
Deanna Nolen	G	36	9-17	0-1	4-5	0	5	5	0	1	0	6	2	22
Katie Smith	G	33	3-9	0-2	3-5	0	1	1	3	0	0	3	4	9
Swin Cash	F	30	2-5	0-0	4-4	0	5	5	3	0	0	3	2	8
Cheryl Ford	F	29	2-4	0-0	7-9	4	4	8	3	1	0	3	4	11
Ruth Riley	C	14	1-4	0-0	0-0	1	1	2	1	0	0	2	5	2
Kara Braxton		17	3-7	0-0	0-2	2	2	4	0	1	1	0	2	6
Plenetta Pierson		14	1-1	0-0	2-3	1	3	4	0	0	1	0	5	4
Elanie Powell		12	1-2	0-1	1-4	0	0	0	1	0	0	5	1	3
Kedra Holland-Corn		5	0-0	0-0	0-0	0	1	1	3	1	0	1	1	0
Angelina Williams		4	2-3	0-0	0-0	0	0	0	0	1	0	0	1	4
Jacqueline Batteast		3	0-1	0-1	0-0	0	0	0	0	0	0	0	1	0
TOTAL		200	24-53 (45.3%)	0-5 (.0%)	21-32 (65.6%)	8	22	30	14	5	2	23	28	69

SACRAMENTO MONARCHS

PLAYER	POS	MIN	FGM-A	3GM-A	FTM-A	REBOUNDS OFF	DEF	TOT	A	STL	BLK	TO	PF	PTS
Kara Lawson	G	26	0-5	0-2	0-0	0	0	0	2	3	0	0	2	0
Ticha Penicheiro	G	19	3-6	0-0	1-2	0	0	0	2	0	0	1	2	7
Nicole Powell	F	24	5-10	2-3	2-3	2	4	6	3	2	0	1	2	14
DeMya Walker	F	23	5-10	0-0	1-1	3	2	5	5	0	0	2	3	11
Yolanda Griffith	C	17	4-6	0-0	7-8	0	4	4	0	1	0	3	4	15
Rebekkah Brunson		19	3-4	0-0	3-7	1	1	2	0	1	0	1	1	9
Erin Buescher		19	4-7	1-1	2-3	3	2	5	0	2	0	1	3	11
Kristin Haynie		18	4-9	1-2	0-0	0	2	2	2	0	0	0	2	9
Sholanda Dorrell		16	2-2	2-2	2-2	0	1	1	0	0	0	0	2	8
Hamchetou Maiga-Ba		13	2-7	0-0	0-0	1	0	1	2	2	0	1	3	4
Kim Smith		2	0-0	0-0	1-2	0	1	1	0	0	0	1	0	1
TOTAL		200	32-66 (48.5%)	6-10 (60.0%)	19-28 (67.9%)	10	17	27	16	11	0	8	23	89

KEY POS=position; MIN=minutes; FGM-A=field goals made-attempts; 3GM-A=3-point field goals made-attempts; FTM-A=free throws made-attempts; TOT=total; A=assists; STL=steals; BLK=blocks; PTS=points

WNBA FINALS GAME 4 SHOCK 72, MONARCHS 52 Time of Game: 2:00 Attendance 14,213
9/06/2006 ARCO Arena, Sacramento, Calif.   Officials: June Courteau, Kurt Walker, Michael Price

DETROIT SHOCK

PLAYER	POS	MIN	FGM-A	3GM-A	FTM-A	OFF	DEF	TOT	A	STL	BLK	TO	PF	PTS
Katie Smith	G	39	8-17	3-8	3-4	1	3	4	3	0	0	2	3	22
Deanna Nolan	G	16	4-9	0-0	0-0	0	2	2	1	2	0	3	4	8
Swin Cash	F	30	4-12	0-0	0-0	5	1	6	5	0	1	3	3	8
Cheryl Ford	F	27	5-11	0-0	3-3	4	6	10	1	1	1	2	3	13
Ruth Riley	C	27	0-0	0-0	0-0	0	4	4	0	1	2	1	1	0
Elaine Powell		20	3-5	0-0	0-0	3	2	5	2	2	0	2	2	6
Kara Braxton		15	4-6	0-0	0-0	1	2	3	0	0	1	0	2	8
Plenette Pierson		13	1-5	0-0	0-0	0	4	4	1	0	2	0	1	5
Angelina Williams		5	1-3	0-2	3-4	1	0	1	0	0	1	1	1	2
Kedra Holland-Corn		4	0-1	0-0	0-0	1	0	1	0	0	0	1	1	0
Jaqueline Batteast		1	0-0	0-0	0-0	0	0	0	0	0	0	0	0	0
TOTAL		200	30-69 (43.5%)	3-10 (30.0%)	9-11 (81.8%)	16	24	40	13	6	8	15	21	72

SACRAMENTO MONARCHS

PLAYER	POS	MIN	FGM-A	3GM-A	FTM-A	OFF	DEF	TOT	A	STL	BLK	TO	PF	PTS
Kara Lawson	G	31	2-6	2-4	0-0	0	1	1	1	0	0	1	0	6
Ticha Penicheiro	G	17	2-9	0-1	2-2	0	3	3	2	1	0	1	2	6
Nicole Powell	F	32	5-7	2-3	1-2	1	0	1	1	2	0	3	1	13
DeMya Walker	F	24	3-9	0-0	0-1	1	2	3	1	0	3	4	0	6
Yolanda Griffith	C	30	3-13	0-0	4-6	5	6	11	2	0	1	2	4	10
Kristin Haynie		18	2-6	1-2	0-0	0	1	1	1	1	0	0	4	5
Rebekkah Brunson		14	0-3	0-0	0-0	0	4	4	0	0	1	1	3	0
Hamchetou Maiga-Ba		12	2-5	0-0	0-0	1	0	1	0	0	0	1	3	4
Erin Buescher		11	1-3	0-0	0-0	0	0	0	1	1	1	0	0	2
Sholanda Dorrell		6	0-2	0-0	0-0	1	0	1	0	0	0	1	1	0
Kim Smith		1	0-0	0-0	0-0	0	0	0	0	0	0	1	0	0
TOTAL		200	20-63 (31.7%)	5-10 (50.0%)	7-11 (73.7%)	9	26	26	9	5	6	15	18	52

WNBA FINALS GAME 5 MONARCHS 75, SHOCK 80 Time of Game: 2:12 Attendance 19,671
9/09/2006 Palace of Auburn Hills, Detriot, Mich. Officials: Bob Trammell, Lisa Mattingly, Tina Napier

SACRAMENTO MONARCHS

PLAYER	POS	MIN	FGM-A	3GM-A	FTM-A	OFF	DEF	TOT	A	STL	BLK	TO	PF	PTS
Kara Lawson	G	32	7-10	2-4	1-1	2	0	2	1	1	0	1	2	17
Ticha Penicheiro	G	18	1-8	0-1	3-6	0	2	2	2	0	0	1	0	5
DeMya Walker	F	31	4-14	0-0	0-0	2	1	3	1	3	1	3	4	8
Nicole Powell	F	25	2-7	1-3	4-4	1	5	6	1	1	0	1	4	9
Yolanda Griffith	C	33	3-11	0-0	5-6	4	5	9	2	2	1	0	3	11
Hamchetou Maiga-Ba		18	3-7	0-0	2-2	1	0	1	1	1	0	0	3	8
Kristin Haynie		17	5-8	2-5	1-1	0	3	3	5	1	0	0	2	13
Rebekkah Brunson		13	2-4	0-0	0-0	0	2	2	0	0	1	1	4	4
Sholanda Dorrell		7	0-3	0-1	0-0	0	1	1	1	2	0	3	0	0
Erin Buescher		2	0-1	0-0	0-0	0	0	0	0	0	0	0	0	0
TOTAL		200	27-73 (37.0%)	5-14 (35.7%)	16-20 (80.0%)	10	19	29	14	11	3	10	22	75

DETROIT SHOCK

PLAYER	POS	MIN	FGM-A	3GM-A	FTM-A	OFF	DEF	TOT	A	STL	BLK	TO	PF	PTS
Deanna Nolan	G	40	10-23	2-4	2-2	1	3	4	4	2	2	1	2	24
Katie Smith	G	36	7-12	2-4	1-2	0	2	2	6	0	0	3	3	17
Swin Cash	F	36	0-4	3-5	4-6	2	7	9	5	0	0	6	2	4
Cheryl Ford	F	21	4-5	0-0	2-2	0	10	10	1	0	0	2	5	10
Ruth Riley	C	23	1-4	0-0	2-2	1	2	3	1	0	4	0	1	4
Plenette Pierson		23	3-7	0-0	10-13	1	1	6	1	1	1	3	3	16
Kara Braxton		10	1-3	0-0	3-3	1	5	1	0	2	0	1	4	5
Elaine Powell		8	0-0	0-0	0-0	0	1	1	2	0	0	1	3	0
Kedra Holland-Corn		1	0-0	0-0	0-0	0	0	0	0	0	0	0	0	0
Angelina Williams		1	0-1	0-0	0-0	1	0	1	0	0	0	0	0	0
TOTAL		200	26-59 (44.1%)	4-8 (50.0%)	24-30 (80.0%)	7	30	37	20	5	7	17	23	80

WNBA CHAMPIONS

YEAR	CHAMPION	RUNNER-UP	FINALS MVP
2006	Detroit Shock	Sacramento Monarchs	Deanna Nolan
2005	Sacramento Monarchs	Connecticut Sun	Yolanda Griffith
2004	Seattle Storm	Connecticut Sun	Betty Lennox
2003	Detroit Shock	Los Angeles Sparks	Ruth Riley
2002	Los Angeles Sparks	New York Liberty	Lisa Leslie
2001	Los Angeles Sparks	Charlotte Sting	Lisa Leslie
2000	Houston Comets	New York Liberty	Cynthia Cooper
1999	Houston Comets	New York Liberty	Cynthia Cooper
1998	Houston Comets	Phoenix Mercury	Cynthia Cooper
1997	Houston Comets	New York Liberty	Cynthia Cooper

TEAM-BY-TEAM STATS

CHARLOTTE STING

PLAYER	GP	MIN	FIELD GOALS FGM	PCT	3-PT FG FGM	FGA	FREE THROWS FTM	PCT	REBOUNDS OFF	TOTAL	A	STL	TO	BLK	PPG
Tangela Smith	34	972	178	.421	31	85	58	.744	48	180	50	41	70	29	13.1
Tammy Sutton-Brown	30	800	118	.488	0	0	99	.639	70	176	20	26	71	55	11.2
Sheri Sam	34	990	137	.399	21	78	64	.627	53	172	90	55	73	3	10.6
Monique Currie	34	844	87	.332	16	55	149	.810	51	132	87	34	62	4	10.0
Kelly Mazzante	34	725	105	.379	64	167	28	.848	23	99	64	47	48	6	8.9
LaToya Bond	34	614	63	.399	10	46	57	.740	7	49	73	35	80	8	5.7
Helen Darling	29	607	51	.370	18	47	38	.691	13	59	82	35	73	3	5.4
Janel McCarville	30	421	54	.458	0	0	28	.636	40	105	25	17	28	20	4.5
Yelena Leuchanka	4	38	5	.500	0	0	2	.500	2	5	3	0	1	1	3.0
Tye'sha Fluker	31	324	30	.337	0	2	16	.727	26	66	9	2	21	14	2.5
Ayana Walker	25	181	17	.459	0	0	12	.571	11	31	3	10	4	10	1.8
Allison Feaster	32	309	19	.235	16	64	1	.500	3	20	21	13	14	2	1.7
STING	**34**	**6,825**	**864**	**.397**	**176**	**544**	**552**	**.710**	**347**	**1,094**	**527**	**315**	**574**	**155**	**72.2**
OPPONENTS	**34**	**–**	**911**	**.424**	**155**	**465**	**594**	**.751**	**370**	**1,240**	**522**	**286**	**619**	**125**	**75.6**

Note: The Charlotte Sting franchise was disbanded after the 2006 season.

CHICAGO SKY

PLAYER	GP	MIN	FIELD GOALS FGM	PCT	3-PT FG FGM	FGA	FREE THROWS FTM	PCT	REBOUNDS OFF	TOTAL	A	STL	TO	BLK	PPG
Candice Dupree	34	1,032	186	.457	0	5	95	.779	55	188	60	43	60	25	13.7
Bernadette Ngoyisa	30	627	122	.528	0	0	58	.592	65	170	28	14	60	7	10.1
Jia Perkins	30	841	105	.351	18	65	54	.806	33	107	97	43	56	13	9.4
Amanda Lassiter	32	778	93	.366	49	149	22	.710	25	88	65	42	57	17	8.0
Stacey Lovelace	34	623	95	.415	19	63	44	.786	48	136	22	19	53	20	7.4
Stacey Dales	34	454	52	.354	25	81	32	.696	6	27	40	9	32	1	7.0
Chelsea Newton	27	648	52	.335	13	49	59	.738	19	71	58	36	40	7	6.5
Deanna Jackson	22	328	49	.395	1	3	33	.647	32	66	13	9	22	3	6.0
Elaine Powell	14	251	26	.433	0	3	17	.708	7	25	37	13	26	3	4.9
Brooke Wyckoff	15	345	16	.242	10	43	8	.800	15	40	33	14	16	12	3.3
Coretta Brown	15	252	16	.271	12	44	4	.500	4	22	26	10	18	0	3.2
Katie Cronin	11	134	9	.300	4	13	2	.286	3	12	2	6	12	2	2.2
SKY	**34**	**6,800**	**858**	**.394**	**157**	**536**	**449**	**.698**	**357**	**1,037**	**509**	**277**	**527**	**125**	**68.3**
OPPONENTS	**34**	**–**	**971**	**.452**	**200**	**536**	**545**	**.740**	**379**	**1,239**	**623**	**262**	**535**	**120**	**79.0**

Note: Players with fewest minutes are not necessarily included in the boxscore. Team totals may not match the sum of listed players' totals.

KEY FGM=field goals made; PCT=percentage; FGA=field-goal attempts; FTM=free throws made; A=assists; STL=steals; BLK=blocks

CONNECTICUT SUN

| PLAYER | GP | MIN | FIELD GOALS | | 3-PT FG | | FREE THROWS | | REBOUNDS | | A | STL | TO | BLK | PPG |
			FGM	PCT	FGM	FGA	FTM	PCT	OFF	TOTAL					
Katie Douglas	32	1,002	179	.443	73	173	94	.839	38	121	79	62	73	4	16.4
Nykesha Sales	22	611	109	.429	32	80	36	.720	82	248	60	26	29	6	13.0
Taj McWilliams-Franklin	34	992	164	.498	1	8	81	.736	104	306	80	35	78	31	12.8
Asjha Jones	34	772	155	.463	5	19	62	.785	59	183	46	23	59	20	11.1
Margo Dydek	34	747	125	.494	1	4	69	.821	35	206	40	21	50	85	9.4
Lindsay Whalen	33	857	88	.389	8	62	112	.903	17	122	153	34	79	2	9.0
Erin Phillips	34	613	57	.393	24	70	44	.880	73	95	80	29	38	2	5.4
Jamie Carey	24	289	22	.379	14	40	5	1.000	16	17	32	7	14	0	2.6
Megan Mahoney	31	351	26	.306	7	29	17	.895	66	30	24	7	25	1	2.5
Laura Summerton	33	361	32	.432	3	5	16	.593	36	6	19	3	20	2	2.5
Lecoe Willingham	29	211	25	.472	6	10	7	.538	55	10	17	5	15	0	2.2
Brooke Queenan	4	10	0	.000	0	0	2	1.000	0	6	0	0	1	0	0.5
SUN	34	6,825	982	.443	174	510	545	.807	342	1,268	630	252	514	153	78.9
OPPONENTS	34	–	948	.402	163	508	358	.716	368	1,151	528	273	486	103	71.1

DETROIT SHOCK

| PLAYER | GP | MIN | FIELD GOALS | | 3-PT FG | | FREE THROWS | | REBOUNDS | | A | STL | TO | BLK | PPG |
			FGM	PCT	FGM	FGA	FTM	PCT	OFF	TOTAL					
Cheryl Ford	32	920	157	.498	0	0	129	.648	130	363	45	38	58	25	13.8
Deanna Nolan	34	1,088	172	.405	39	113	85	.850	32	153	124	47	86	11	13.8
Katie Smith	34	1,137	123	.407	59	161	93	.912	19	92	112	25	65	4	11.7
Swin Cash	34	990	124	.384	1	13	109	.762	63	168	106	20	88	11	10.5
Ruth Riley	34	875	115	.456	3	9	16	.889	36	165	52	18	54	49	7.3
Plenette Pierson	34	565	82	.456	0	3	56	.700	44	132	24	18	37	14	6.5
Kara Braxton	34	359	58	.406	0	2	30	.625	42	117	26	11	53	11	4.3
Kedra Holland-Corn	34	397	51	.359	28	84	10	.625	12	40	43	23	40	2	4.1
Angelina Williams	21	133	14	.326	2	8	11	.647	3	13	12	7	15	6	2.0
Jacqueline Batteast	26	178	15	.278	2	14	4	.571	13	25	7	2	4	3	1.4
Elaine Powell	11	120	3	.188	0	2	8	.571	7	13	15	3	9	0	1.3
SHOCK	34	6,825	919	.414	136	414	553	.741	408	1,288	572	213	537	137	74.3
OPPONENTS	34	–	784	.403	175	561	529	.754	324	1,084	474	275	507	108	70.1

HOUSTON COMETS

| PLAYER | GP | MIN | FIELD GOALS | | 3-PT FG | | FREE THROWS | | REBOUNDS | | A | STL | TO | BLK | PPG |
			FGM	PCT	FGM	FGA	FTM	PCT	OFF	TOTAL					
Tina Thompson	21	696	139	.457	40	96	74	.804	31	118	47	20	52	13	18.7
Sheryl Swoopes	31	1,111	180	.413	25	90	97	.764	34	183	115	64	74	9	15.5
Michelle Snow	34	995	178	.510	0	0	86	.667	78	269	47	33	88	38	13.0
Dominique Canty	15	431	54	.514	0	3	56	.727	12	52	44	17	35	0	10.9
Roneeka Hodges	33	698	87	.401	44	120	29	.744	11	65	32	16	36	4	7.5
Dawn Staley	34	1,018	84	.420	53	124	29	.806	25	75	133	35	76	5	7.4
Tamecka Dixon	23	591	69	.404	1	9	23	.821	19	60	54	13	58	2	7.0
Sancho Lyttle	29	380	40	.460	0	0	26	.619	40	114	8	25	18	4	3.7
Astou Ndiaye-Diatta	11	127	16	.457	0	0	3	.50	10	30	8	1	10	1	3.2
Kayte Christensen	6	88	8	.500	0	0	2	1.000	9	19	4	0	11	0	3.0
Mistie Williams	27	274	34	.531	0	0	11	.324	29	64	16	11	10	3	2.9
Tari Phillips	21	222	20	.665	0	0	19	.655	12	47	4	9	23	5	2.8
COMETS	**34**	**6,925**	**928**	**.442**	**169**	**472**	**482**	**.711**	**303**	**1,125**	**532**	**252**	**566**	**84**	**73.7**
OPPONENTS	**34**	**–**	**928**	**.416**	**148**	**496**	**445**	**.724**	**337**	**1,124**	**526**	**298**	**519**	**89**	**72.0**

INDIANA FEVER

| PLAYER | GP | MIN | FIELD GOALS | | 3-PT FG | | FREE THROWS | | REBOUNDS | | A | STL | TO | BLK | PPG |
			FGM	PCT	FGM	FGA	FTM	PCT	OFF	TOTAL					
Tamika Catchings	32	1,071	162	.407	32	107	165	.809	68	240	119	94	79	35	16.3
Tamika Whitmore	34	1,057	199	.457	15	38	115	.821	53	165	61	46	94	12	15.5
Anna DeForge	34	1,001	123	.393	48	127	54	.818	40	146	76	39	55	9	10.2
Tan White	34	745	113	.373	19	88	57	.750	32	82	52	27	51	9	8.9
Tully Bevilaqua	34	999	76	.411	76	185	38	.717	10	77	79	71	54	1	6.6
Ebony Hoffman	34	851	82	.394	0	8	54	.771	73	193	46	37	73	16	6.4
Linda Frohlich	20	169	26	.382	8	22	6	.750	14	35	9	5	13	0	3.3
La Tangela Atkinson	33	417	38	.437	5	17	18	.462	25	75	22	18	33	5	3.0
Olympia Scott	21	159	23	.434	0	1	4	.500	8	33	7	8	15	2	2.4
Kasha Terry	10	53	11	.579	0	0	1	.200	4	14	0	0	8	3	2.3
Charlotte Smith	18	173	12	.308	8	22	3	.750	9	24	7	3	13	1	1.9
Kristen Sharp	23	155	8	.229	3	15	3	1.000	3	9	23	7	8	0	1.0
FEVER	**34**	**6,850**	**873**	**.407**	**171**	**551**	**518**	**.766**	**339**	**1,094**	**501**	**354**	**528**	**93**	**71.6**
OPPONENTS	**34**	**–**	**883**	**.432**	**137**	**444**	**413**	**.739**	**288**	**1,061**	**507**	**259**	**617**	**105**	**68.1**

LOS ANGELES SPARKS

PLAYER	GP	MIN	FIELD GOALS		3-PT FG		FREE THROWS		REBOUNDS						
			FGM	PCT	FGM	FGA	FTM	PCT	OFF	TOTAL	A	STL	TO	BLK	PPG
Lisa Leslie	34	1,043	257	.511	8	20	158	.650	83	323	108	51	126	57	20.0
Chamique Holdsclaw	25	739	148	.470	3	15	76	.884	57	152	56	34	57	9	15.0
Mwadi Mabika	32	679	92	.377	32	96	56	.889	17	64	48	19	37	6	8.5
Temeka Johnson	32	808	102	.402	3	26	48	.800	15	97	161	47	70	1	8.0
Tamara Moore	34	634	68	.469	17	49	53	.803	16	71	65	33	38	8	6.1
Christie Thomas	27	539	65	.489	4	20	30	.638	43	143	26	20	42	14	6.1
Murriel Page	34	690	66	.471	0	3	35	.761	40	121	33	17	30	9	4.9
Lisa Willis	24	320	35	.385	19	52	22	.710	13	43	10	26	17	0	4.6
Jessica Moore	34	653	59	.434	0	2	29	.763	35	98	24	22	28	9	4.3
Doneeka Hodges	34	456	46	.319	18	61	21	.913	9	42	66	14	43	4	3.9
Brandi Davis	14	118	14	.264	7	33	6	.600	1	13	8	5	5	1	2.9
Tiffany Stansbury	4	23	3	.375	0	0	0	.000	6	7	2	1	2	0	1.5
Emmeline Ndongue	17	111	7	.259	0	0	6	.462	15	26	3	7	6	8	1.2
SPARKS	34	6,825	962	.438	111	377	540	.744	350	1,202	610	296	534	129	75.7
OPPONENTS	34	—	873	.400	196	570	534	.741	336	1,082	565	284	556	128	72.8

MINNESOTA LYNX

PLAYER	GP	MIN	FIELD GOALS		3-PT FG		FREE THROWS		REBOUNDS						
			FGM	PCT	FGM	FGA	FTM	PCT	OFF	TOTAL	A	STL	TO	BLK	PPG
Seimone Augustus	34	1,124	283	.456	30	85	148	.897	15	128	50	21	71	18	21.9
Nicole Ohlde	34	870	120	.453	0	1	87	.664	61	190	54	20	74	25	9.6
Amber Jacobs	34	861	96	.449	40	102	47	.825	17	90	115	26	90	2	8.2
Svetlana Abrosimova	34	724	99	.411	24	65	41	.661	44	106	54	34	61	1	7.7
Kristen Mann	33	894	92	.387	36	96	25	.735	23	113	94	19	50	7	7.4
Vanessa Hayden	33	424	68	.402	0	0	41	.621	41	115	19	6	44	44	5.4
Adrian Williams	32	488	60	.448	0	1	37	.536	40	149	8	25	19	8	4.9
Tamika Williams	31	672	65	.442	1	9	16	.444	73	174	21	16	37	1	4.7
Megan Duffy	31	387	33	.359	12	37	27	.692	10	29	36	9	24	0	3.4
Chandi Jones	6	38	5	.556	3	4	4	1.000	2	5	3	1	2	0	2.8
Tynesha Lewis	19	202	19	.345	1	11	7	.700	10	27	18	12	16	5	2.4
Shona Thorburn	22	141	5	.185	1	8	5	.625	4	18	19	4	14	2	.7
LYNX	34	6,825	945	.427	148	419	485	.712	340	1,144	491	193	530	113	74.2
OPPONENTS	34	—	1004	.434	179	542	548	.762	372	1,204	625	308	438	124	80.4

NEW YORK LIBERTY

PLAYER	GP	MIN	FIELD GOALS FGM	PCT	3-PT FG FGM	FGA	FREE THROWS FTM	PCT	REBOUNDS OFF	TOTAL	A	STL	TO	BLK	PPG
Becky Hammon	22	677	107	.425	37	108	72	.960	6	66	81	29	65	3	14.7
Shameka Christon	34	985	136	.391	52	156	99	.825	29	120	44	20	81	42	12.4
Cathrine Kraayeveld	34	901	106	.444	31	93	55	.764	46	158	32	16	62	15	8.8
Kelly Schmacher	21	536	58	.411	2	8	45	.714	38	116	23	3	35	25	7.8
Barbara Farris	34	943	95	.430	0	3	71	.724	56	178	51	21	65	5	7.7
Sherill Baker	34	614	97	.386	9	33	48	.857	23	56	35	46	50	2	7.4
Erin Thorn	27	379	55	.417	28	65	28	.903	9	38	33	6	21	1	6.1
Loree Moore	34	950	68	.338	35	96	37	.725	31	144	122	61	64	10	6.1
Asley Battle	33	459	54	.383	15	46	20	.800	13	62	29	31	39	3	4.3
Iciss Tillis	25	261	32	.360	6	29	16	.727	21	55	11	10	22	4	3.4
Christelle N'Garsanet	15	91	8	.276	0	2	11	.440	11	18	5	5	8	2	1.8
Emilie Gomis	2	14	0	.000	0	2	3	.750	0	0	0	1	1	0	1.5
LIBERTY	34	6,775	822	.397	216	645	512	.788	286	1,021	475	252	576	111	69.8
OPPONENTS	34	—	966	.449	171	461	553	.766	341	1,173	508	270	485	134	78.1

PHOENIX MERCURY

PLAYER	GP	MIN	FIELD GOALS FGM	PCT	3-PT FG FGM	FGA	FREE THROWS FTM	PCT	REBOUNDS OFF	TOTAL	A	STL	TO	BLK	PPG
Diana Taurasi	34	1,152	298	.452	121	305	143	.781	25	122	139	42	79	27	25.3
Cappie Pondexter	32	1,068	219	.442	47	126	139	.853	37	107	98	37	45	4	19.5
Penny Taylor	20	533	98	.445	24	65	57	.864	32	113	51	29	29	9	113.9
Kelly Miller	27	812	109	.421	30	79	48	.774	41	144	94	28	73	6	11.0
Kamila Vodichkova	28	737	111	.444	0	7	50	.769	46	187	41	28	53	19	9.7
Tamicha Jackson	3	54	10	.357	0	3	4	.667	1	4	7	6	4	1	8.0
Jennifer Lacy	33	506	61	.477	0	4	40	.690	42	102	14	12	45	12	4.9
Kristen Rasmussen	34	907	64	.512	6	14	12	.600	72	208	72	28	33	27	4.3
Belinda Snell	30	250	35	.389	20	63	10	1.00	11	39	19	15	17	3	3.3
Jennifer Derevjanik	31	460	38	.507	4	15	16	.615	11	57	68	23	25	7	3.1
Crystal Smith	23	209	21	.447	7	19	11	.917	4	22	22	17	18	0	2.6
Ann Strother	8	39	6	.429	4	10	0	.000	2	5	2	1	11	2	2.0
Mandisa Stevenson	2	18	1	.200	1	1	0	.000	1	2	0	1	2	1	1.5
MERCURY	34	6,900	1,079	.443	265	722	537	.785	334	1,145	640	275	517	127	87.1
OPPONENTS	34	—	1,023	.433	203	618	630	.739	408	1,283	578	231	483	126	84.7

SACRAMENTO MONARCHS

PLAYER	GP	MIN	FIELD GOALS		3-PT FG		FREE THROWS		REBOUNDS		A	STL	TO	BLK	PPG
			FGM	PCT	FGM	FGA	FTM	PCT	OFF	TOTAL					
Yolanda Griffith	34	854	134	.457	0	1	139	.751	87	219	56	44	66	16	12.0
Erin Buescher	34	663	117	.537	0	2	96	.750	78	134	35	33	55	14	9.7
Nicole Powell	34	886	116	.375	55	156	40	.816	25	124	61	42	47	15	9.6
DeMya Walker	23	438	79	.436	0	0	55	.655	55	37	32	15	36	7	9.3
Kara Lawson	34	749	96	.397	49	123	36	.923	11	65	56	20	43	4	8.1
Rebekkah Brunson	34	597	94	.461	0	0	44	.587	77	191	17	21	40	15	6.8
Ticha Penicheiro	34	846	58	.339	6	31	61	.792	8	97	149	48	67	6	5.4
Hamchetou Maiga-Ba	34	537	75	.475	0	1	27	.563	35	73	30	32	45	9	5.2
Scholanda Dorrell	33	502	64	.372	25	85	18	.818	9	36	17	29	39	4	5.2
Kristin Haynie	34	476	55	.364	9	30	21	.840	20	67	68	27	46	50	4.1
Kim Smith	31	313	28	.333	13	32	5	.556	11	39	20	9	22	0	2.4
Brittany Wilkins	4	14	3	.429	0	0	10	.000	0	0	1	0	2	0	1.5
MONARCHS	34	6,875	919	.420	157	461	542	.731	418	1,138	509	330	542	88	74.6
OPPONENTS	34	—	872	.431	156	507	504	.762	294	1,019	507	244	633	143	70.7

SAN ANTONIO SILVER STARS

PLAYER	GP	MIN	FIELD GOALS		3-PT FG		FREE THROWS		REBOUNDS		A	STL	TO	BLK	PPG
			FGM	PCT	FGM	FGA	FTM	PCT	OFF	TOTAL					
Sophia Young	34	1,055	154	.416	0	4	100	.730	85	257	50	57	45	13	12.0
Agnieszka Bibrzycka	32	752	130	.418	55	157	46	.868	10	66	48	26	47	12	11.3
Vickie Johnson	34	999	119	.375	23	69	76	.844	55	167	122	28	59	3	9.9
Shannon Johnson	32	875	104	.406	32	91	78	.804	31	95	117	60	75	5	9.9
LaToya Thomas	19	367	56	.452	0	0	45	.763	27	82	22	14	14	7	8.3
Katie Feenstra	34	636	100	.467	0	0	65	.619	74	209	14	12	69	26	7.8
Chantelle Anderson	23	414	59	.527	0	0	35	.778	28	85	15	7	29	10	6.7
Shanna Zolman	34	551	83	.379	48	127	12	.667	7	41	34	11	38	4	6.6
Kendra Wecker	34	572	75	.350	19	56	21	.778	22	84	47	11	32	3	5.6
Shyra Ely	12	136	12	.273	45	20	5	.577	5	31	10	2	13	0	3.4
Dalma Ivanyi	31	320	15	.268	2	9	15	.667	7	34	50	12	19	12	1.4
Jae Kingi-Cross	18	118	8	.444	2	6	7	.778	3	10	11	6	5	0	1.4
SILVER STARS	34	6,800	915	.406	189	556	504	.750	354	1,168	540	246	488	83	74.2
OPPONENTS	34	—	974	.431	165	459	490	.766	372	1,237	560	253	480	129	76.6

SEATTLE STORM

PLAYER	GP	MIN	FIELD GOALS FGM	PCT	3-PT FG FGM	FGA	FREE THROWS FTM	PCT	REBOUNDS OFF	TOTAL	A	STL	TO	BLK	PPG
Lauren Jackson	30	848	192	.535	29	77	170	.899	68	227	48	24	40	51	19.4
Betty Lennox	34	891	191	.452	29	90	54	.761	34	137	73	36	98	5	13.7
Sue Bird	34	1,065	137	.411	56	153	59	.868	24	102	162	61	88	5	11.4
Janell Burse	27	737	113	.511	1	1	73	.670	63	178	22	17	55	25	11.1
Wendy Palmer	5	120	16	.485	1	3	14	.737	13	38	3	5	10	3	9.4
Iziane Castro Marques	34	655	91	.469	25	65	39	.661	16	72	47	23	49	2	7.2
Barbara Turner	34	622	71	.447	10	40	64	.831	26	86	48	13	40	3	6.4
Tiffani Johnson	32	643	61	.415	0	0	28	.757	32	125	17	10	31	17	4.7
Tanisha Wright	33	508	42	.353	2	14	17	.844	19	60	41	11	53	2	3.8
Shaunzinski Gortman	20	265	20	.364	2	12	14	.778	9	48	17	11	25	2	2.8
Edwige Lawson	26	209	17	.378	5	19	4	.667	2	21	29	15	19	1	1.7
Ashley Robinson	17	197	9	.360	0	1	3	.300	18	45	7	6	12	8	1.2
STORM	**34**	**6,800**	**960**	**.452**	**160**	**475**	**544**	**.789**	**326**	**1,147**	**514**	**232**	**570**	**127**	**77.7**
OPPONENTS	**34**	**—**	**940**	**.424**	**164**	**484**	**490**	**.751**	**322**	**1,031**	**520**	**297**	**485**	**115**	**75.7**

WASHINGTON MYSTICS

PLAYER	GP	MIN	FIELD GOALS FGM	PCT	3-PT FG FGM	FGA	FREE THROWS FTM	PCT	REBOUNDS OFF	TOTAL	A	STL	TO	BLK	PPG
Alana Beard	32	994	232	.495	37	102	113	.758	23	149	98	59	90	25	19.2
DeLisha Milton-Jones	23	675	125	.472	34	79	51	.810	23	112	48	35	67	17	14.6
Chastity Melvin	34	999	153	.520	0	2	99	.656	82	199	25	31	61	14	11.9
Nikki Teasley	34	975	118	.371	52	151	76	.826	13	89	183	44	77	11	10.7
Nakia Sanford	34	885	112	.519	0	0	77	.616	69	134	36	28	72	21	8.9
Crystal Robinson	27	727	84	.402	26	92	25	.806	18	70	49	33	27	0	7.4
Coco Miller	34	658	84	.491	12	30	26	.897	36	91	59	34	49	4	6.1
Latasha Byears	26	330	48	.449	0	0	16	.800	37	87	10	12	35	2	4.3
Tamara James	21	160	19	.388	3	12	16	.889	9	16	3	4	10	2	2.7
Nikki Blue	24	181	14	.259	1	12	25	.806	7	20	36	18	18	0	2.3
Laurie Koehn	32	161	23	.500	22	42	3	.750	0	12	8	2	5	2	2.2
Zane Teilane	16	105	14	.538	0	0	1	.500	11	27	1	3	4	3	1.8
MYSTICS	**34**	**6,850**	**1016**	**.462**	**187**	**522**	**528**	**.738**	**330**	**1,100**	**576**	**306**	**541**	**113**	**80.8**
OPPONENTS	**34**	**—**	**909**	**.432**	**204**	**553**	**635**	**.746**	**321**	**1,041**	**583**	**252**	**573**	**89**	**78.1**

FAST FACT

Connecticut Sun center Margo Dydek has led the league in blocks for the past five years.

2006 WNBA INDIVIDUAL LEADERS

POINTS	GP	PTS	AVG
Diana Taurasi, Phoenix Mercury	34	860	25.3
Seimone Augustus, Minnesota Lynx	34	744	21.9
Lisa Leslie, Los Angeles Sparks	34	680	20.0
Lauren Jackson, Seattle Storm	30	583	19.5
Cappie Pondexter, Phoenix Mercury	32	624	19.5

REBOUNDS	GP	REB	AVG
Cheryl Ford, Detroit Shock	32	363	11.3
Taj McWilliams-Franklin, Conn. Sun	34	306	9.6
Lisa Leslie, Los Angeles Sparks	34	323	9.5
Michelle Snow, Houston Comets	34	269	7.9
Lauren Jackson, Seattle Storm	30	230	7.7

ASSISTS	GP	A	AVG
Nikki Teasley, Wash. Mystics	34	183	5.4
Temeka Johnson, L.A. Sparks	32	161	5.0
Sue Bird, Seattle Storm	34	162	4.8
Lindsay Whalen, Connecticut Sun	33	153	4.6
Diana Taurasi, Phoenix Mercury	34	139	4.0

FIELD-GOAL PERCENTAGE	FGM	FGA	PCT
Erin Buescher, Sac. Monarchs	117	218	.537
Lauren Jackson, Seattle Storm	193	361	.535
Bernadette Ngoyisa, Chicago Sky	122	231	.528
Chasity Melvin, Wash. Mystics	153	294	.520
Nakia Sanford, Wash. Mystics	112	216	.519

FREE-THROW PERCENTAGE	FTM	FTA	PCT
Becky Hammon, New York Liberty	72	75	.960
Katie Smith, Detroit Shock	93	102	.912
Lindsay Whalen, Connecticut Sun	112	124	.903
Lauren Jackson, Seattle Storm	170	189	.899
Seimone Augustus, Minnesota Lynx	148	165	.897

Indiana's Tamika Catchings (left) won the WNBA's Defensive Player of the Year award.

AP PHOTO/TOM STRICKLAND

3-POINT FIELD-GOAL PERCENTAGE	FGM	FGA	PCT
Erin Thorn, New York Liberty	28	65	.431
DeLisha Milton-Jones, Wash. Mystics	34	79	.430
Dawn Staley, Houston Comets	53	124	.427
Katie Douglas, Connecticut Sun	73	173	.422
Tina Thompson, Houston Comets	40	96	.417

STEALS	GP	STL	AVG
Tamika Catchings, Indiana Fever	32	94	2.94
Tully Bevilaqua, Indiana Fever	34	71	2.09
Sheryl Swoopes, Houston Comets	31	64	2.06
Katie Douglas, Connecticut Sun	32	62	1.94
Shannon Johnson, S.A. Silver Stars	32	60	1.88

BLOCKS	GP	BLK	AVG
Margo Dydek, Conn. Sun	34	85	2.50
Tammy Sutton-Brown, Chicago Sky	30	55	1.83
Lauren Jackson, Seattle Storm	30	51	1.70
Lisa Leslie, Los Angeles Sparks	34	57	1.68
Ruth Riley, Detroit Shock	34	49	1.44

TODAY'S STARS

Katie Douglas was named the MVP of the 2006 WNBA All-Star game.

REUTERS/RAY STUBBLEBINE (UNITED STATES)

■ **Katie Douglas, guard/forward,** b. May 7, 1979, Indianapolis, Indiana. Douglas, a six-year veteran, was named the MVP in her first career All-Star game in 2006. Through 2006, she had amassed 2,001 points, 675 rebounds, and 411 assists in her career. Douglas is a lanky 6'0" ball-handler who is also known for her tenacious defense. She helped power the Sun to back-to-back trips to the WNBA Finals in 2004 and 2005. In her collegiate career, Douglas led Purdue to the NCAA Women's Division I Championship in 1999 and was a two-time All-American in 2000 and 2001.

■ **Alana Beard, guard,** b. May 14, 1982, Shreveport, Louisiana. In only her third year in the league, Beard has established herself as one of the WNBA's best shooting guards. A two-time All-Star, Beard was the second overall pick in the 2005 WNBA draft. In college, Beard was a three-time All-American and helped Duke reach the NCAA Final Four in 2001 and 2003. She broke the Blue Devils' all-time scoring record, and her Duke jersey number (#20) has since been retired.

■ **Sue Bird, guard,** b. October 16, 1980, Syosset, New York. Although Bird has twice been named an All-Star (in 2005 and 2006), 2004 was the biggest year of her career. She helped lead the Seattle Storm to its first WNBA title. She also won a gold medal as the youngest member of the U.S. women's basketball team at the Summer Olympics in Athens, Greece. Bird played at the University of Connecticut during her college career and led the Huskies to the 2002 NCAA Division I title. She is among only six WNBA players to have won an NCAA championship, a WNBA championship, and an Olympic gold medal.

WNBA ALL-STAR GAME RESULTS

YEAR	RESULT	SITE	WINNING COACH	MVP
2006	East 98, West 82	New York, NY	Mike Thibault	Katie Douglas, Connecticut Sun
2005	West 122, East 99	Uncasville, CT	Anne Donovan	Sheryl Swoopes, Houston Comets
2004	U.S. National Team 74, WNBA All-Stars 58	New York, NY	Van Chancellor	Yolanda Griffith, Sacramento Monarchs
2003	West 84, East 75	New York, NY	Michael Cooper	Nikki Teasley, Los Angeles Sparks
2002	West 81, East 76	Washington, D.C.	Michael Cooper	Lisa Leslie, Los Angeles Sparks
2001	West 80, East 72	Orlando, FL	Van Chancellor	Lisa Leslie, Los Angeles Sparks
2000	West 73, East 61	Phoenix, AZ	Van Chancellor	Tina Thompson, Houston Comets
1999	West 79, East 61	New York, NY	Van Chancellor	Lisa Leslie, Los Angeles Sparks

2007 WNBA DRAFT

APRIL 4, 2007, CLEVELAND, OHIO

FIRST ROUND PICK TEAM	NAME/POSITION	SCHOOL	FIRST ROUND PICK TEAM	NAME/POSITION	SCHOOL
1. Phoenix	*Lindsey Harding, G	Duke	8. Houston	Ashley Shields, G	SW Tenn. St.
2. San Antonio	†Jessica Davenport, C	Ohio State	9. Indiana	Alison Bales, C	Duke
3. Chicago	Armintie Price, G	Mississippi	10. Chicago	Carla Thomas, F	Vanderbilt
4. Minnesota	Noelle Quinn, G	UCLA	11. Detroit	Ivory Latta, G	North Carolina
5. New York	Tiffany Jackson, F	Texas	12. Connecticut	Kamesha Hairston, F	Temple
6. Washington	Bernice Mosby, F	Baylor	13. Connecticut	Sandrine Gruda, C	France
7. Seattle	Katie Gearlds, G	Purdue			

* traded to Minnesota Lynx

† traded to New York Liberty

KEY G=guard; F=forward; C=center

LEGENDS

Sheryl Swoopes is second all-time in WNBA career points (4,376) and field goals made (1,643).

BARRY GOSSAGE/NBAE VIA GETTY IMAGES

■ **Sheryl Swoopes, forward,** b. March 25, 1971, Brownfield, Texas. Swoopes has been in the WNBA since its first season in 1997. During her nine-year career, she has been named league MVP three times. In addition to helping the Houston Comets win four WNBA titles, Swoopes has also won an NCAA Division I championship at Texas Tech and three Olympic gold medals as a member of the U.S. women's basketball teams in 1996, 2000 and 2004.

■ **Cheryl Miller, player/coach,** b. January 3, 1964, Riverside, California. Although Miller's basketball career ended before the WNBA began, she is considered one of the sport's legends. While playing her college ball at USC during the early 1980s, Miller was a four-time All-American and led the Trojans to two NCAA titles. Since retiring as a player, Miller has been a head coach at USC and for the Phoenix Mercury. Miller has been inducted into both the Basketball Hall of Fame and the Women's Basketball Hall of Fame.

■ **Cynthia Cooper, guard,** b. April 14, 1963, Chicago, Illinois. Cooper, along with Swoopes and Tina Thompson, comprised the powerful core of a Houston Comets dynasty that dominated the WNBA during the league's first four seasons. During her five-year WNBA career, which ended in 2003, Cooper became the first player in league history to reach the scoring milestones of 500, 1,000, 2,000, and 2,500 points. Currently, Cooper is head women's basketball coach at Prairie View A&M University.

DID YOU KNOW?

Phoenix Mercury head coach Paul Westhead led the Los Angeles Lakers to their seventh NBA championship in 1980.

WNBA TRIVIA

1 Which team has made it to the WNBA Finals in four different seasons only to fall short of winning the championship each time?
a. **New York Liberty**
b. **Los Angeles Sparks**
c. **Connecticut Sun**

2 Who is the all-time leading scorer in WNBA history?
a. **Chamique Holdsclaw**
b. **Tina Thompson**
c. **Lisa Leslie**

Seimone Augustus

3 Which of the following NBA rules is NOT the same in the WNBA?
a. **24-second shot clock**
b. **Game is divided into four quarters**
c. **Three-point line is 23 feet, 9 inches from the basket at the top of key**

4 How many teams played in the WNBA during the league's first season in 1997?
a. **8**
b. **10**
c. **14**

5 Where did Minnesota Lynx guard and 2006 WNBA Rookie of the Year Seimone Augustus go to college?
a. **Tennessee**
b. **LSU**
c. **Baylor**

6 Which WNBA franchise has won the most titles in league history, winning four straight between 1997 and 2000?
a. **New York Liberty**
b. **Houston Comets**
c. **Detroit Shock**

Trivia Challenge: 1. a; 2. c; 3. c; 4. a; 5. b; 6. b

AWARD WINNERS

YEAR	MVP	ROOKIE	DEFENSIVE	IMPROVED	SPORTSMANSHIP	COACH
2006	Lisa Leslie	Seimone Augustus	Tamika Catchings	Erin Buescher	Dawn Staley	Mike Thibault
2005	Sheryl Swoopes	Temeka Johnson	Tamika Catchings	Nicole Powell	Taj McWilliams-Franklin	John Whisenant
2004	Lisa Leslie	Diana Taurasi	Lisa Leslie	Kelly Miller/ Wendy Palmer	Teresa Edwards	Susie McConnell Serio
2003	Lauren Jackson	Cheryl Ford	Sheryl Swoopes	Michelle Snow	Edna Campbell	Bill Laimbeer
2002	Sheryl Swoopes	Tamika Catchings	Sheryl Swoopes	Coco Miller	Jennifer Gillom	Marianne Stanley
2001	Lisa Leslie	Jackie Stiles	Debbie Black	Janeth Arcain	Sue Wicks	Dan Hughes
2000	Sheryl Swoopes	Betty Lennox	Sheryl Swoopes	Tari Phillips	Susie McConnell Serio	Michael Cooper
1999	Yolanda Griffith	Chamique Holdsclaw	Yolanda Griffith	N/A	Dawn Staley	Van Chancellor
1998	Cynthia Cooper	Tracy Reid	Teresa Weatherspoon	N/A	Susie McConnell Serio	Van Chancellor
1997	Cynthia Cooper	N/A	Teresa Weatherspoon	N/A	Haixia Zheng	Van Chancellor

NEWCOMER*
1998 Susie McConnell Serio
1999 Yolanda Griffith

*No longer awarded

Sı KIDS.com
Visit our website for the latest stats and sports info.

The 2006–07 college basketball season began with one of the best freshmen classes in history stealing the spotlight. It ended with a team of veterans storming the record books, as the Florida Gators became the first repeat national champions in 15 years.

The new age minimum for NBA players went into effect for the 2006–07 season. That sent top hoops talent to college for at least one year, rather than straight to the pros after high school. Not surprisingly, freshmen had a huge impact. Arizona's Chase Budinger, Georgia Tech's Thaddeus Young, and North Carolina's trio of first-year starters (Ty Lawson, Wayne Ellington, and Brandan Wright) all made major contributions. But two freshmen towered above the rest: Ohio State's seven-foot center Greg Oden, and Texas' 6'9" small forward Kevin Durant.

Oden averaged 15.7 points, 9.6 rebounds, and 3.3 blocks per game and was named a first-team All-America player. He was joined by Durant, who was the only player in the nation to finish in the top five in both scoring (25.8) and rebounding (11.8). Durant went on to sweep the major national player of the year honors, making him the first freshman ever to do so.

The Longhorns hovered just outside the top title contenders. The Buckeyes joined a small group of schools (including Florida, Kansas, North Carolina, Wisconsin, Georgetown, and UCLA) that had a good shot at the national title. The Gators featured a star-studded starting lineup of Joakim Noah, Al

Florida's Corey Brewer was named the Most Outstanding Player of the Final Four.

AL TIELEMANS

Horford, Corey Brewer, Taurean Green, and Lee Humphrey. All five put the NBA on hold to defend their 2005–06 title, and the Gators entered the NCAA tournament as the top overall seed.

The 2006 Tournament was marked by the Cinderella run of 11th-seed George Mason to the Final Four, but there were no such surprises this year. By the Elite Eight, seven of the top eight seeds were still alive. The four teams who survived to reach the Final Four in Atlanta were all heavyweights: top seeds Florida and Ohio State and

number-two seeds UCLA and Georgetown.

The title game pitted the experienced Florida squad against Ohio State, home of the nation's best freshman class. Florida had beaten Ohio State by 26 points earlier in the season and, once again, the Gators proved their dominance. Florida rolled to an 84–75 victory and the school's second straight national title. Three months earlier, the Florida football team had routed Ohio State in the BCS national championship game. The Gators earned a new nickname: the School of Chomps.

NCAA MEN'S DIVISION I CHAMPIONSHIP BOX SCORE

FLORIDA GATORS: 84

PLAYER	POS	MIN	FG M-A	3-PT M-A	FT M-A	PF	PTS
Corey Brewer	F	36	4-12	3-8	2-2	2	13
Joakim Noah	F	21	1-3	0-0	6-6	4	8
Al Horford	C	34	6-15	0-0	6-8	3	18
Taurean Green	G	38	4-6	3-3	5-5	0	16
Lee Humphrey	G	34	5-8	4-7	0-0	1	14
M. Speights	F-C	6	1-2	0-0	0-0	3	2
Walter Hodge	G	11	2-2	0-0	1-1	1	5
Chris Richard	F-C	20	3-5	0-0	2-3	5	8
TOTALS			**26-53**	**10-18**	**22-25**	**19**	**84**
			(49.1%)	(55.6%)	(88.0%)		

OHIO STATE BUCKEYES: 75

PLAYER	POS	MIN	FG M-A	3-PT M-A	FT M-A	PF	PTS
G. Oden	C	38	10-15	0-0	5-8	4	25
J. Butler	G	36	1-7	1-6	0-0	3	3
M. Conley Jr.	G	34	7-13	1-3	5-6	3	20
R. Lewis	G	34	6-13	0-4	0-1	3	12
I. Harris	F	26	2-8	2-8	1-2	2	7
D. Lighty	G-F	13	2-3	0-1	0-0	1	4
D. Cook	G	9	1-2	0-1	0-0	1	2
M. Terwilliger	F-C	5	1-1	0-0	0-0	1	2
O. Hunter	F	5	0-2	0-0	0-0	2	0
TOTALS			**30-64**	**4-23**	**11-17**	**20**	**75**
			(46.9%)	(17.4%)	(64.7%)		

KEY POS=position; MIN=minutes played; FG M-A=field goals made-attempted; 3-PT M-A=3-point field goals made-attempted; FT M-A=free throws made-attempted; PF=personal fouls; PTS=points; F=forward; G=guard; C=center

TRIVIA CHALLENGE

In the 2007 semifinals, Florida defeated UCLA in a rematch of the 2006 championship game. When was the last time the defending national champion faced its title game opponent again in the following season's tournament?

1991 (Eventual champion Duke beat UNLV in the semifinals after losing to the Runnin' Rebels in the 1990 national title game.)

The national title game featured a battle between centers Al Horford (right) and Greg Oden.

REUTERS/HANS DERYK

USA TODAY/ESPN Coaches Top 25 Final Poll

RANK	SCHOOL	FINAL RECORD	POINTS
1	Florida	35-5	775
2	Ohio State	35-4	744
3	UCLA	30-6	699
4	Georgetown	30-7	694
5 (tie)	Kansas	33-5	627
(tie)	North Carolina	31-7	627
7	Memphis	33-4	594
8	Oregon	29-8	531
9	Texas A&M	27-7	521
10	Pittsburgh	29-8	459
11 (tie)	Southern Illinois	29-7	425
(tie)	Wisconsin	30-6	425
13	Butler	29-7	360
14	UNLV	30-7	309
15	USC	25-12	294
16	Texas	25-10	287
17	Washington State	26-8	280
18	Tennessee	24-11	238
19	Vanderbilt	22-12	234
20	Louisville	24-10	222
21	Nevada	29-5	217
22	Winthrop	29-5	108
23	Maryland	25-9	72
24	Virginia	21-11	56
25	Virginia Tech	22-12	54

NCAA MEN'S DIVISION I INDIVIDUAL LEADERS

SCORING

PLAYER	CLASS	GP	FG	3FG	FT	PTS	AVG
Reggie Williams, Virginia Military Institute	Jr.	33	338	76	176	928	28.1
Trey Johnson, Jackson State	Sr.	34	303	77	239	922	27.1
Morris Almond, Rice	Sr.	32	263	77	241	844	26.4
Kevin Durant, Texas	Fr.	33	289	80	188	846	25.6
Gary Neal, Towson	Sr.	32	267	93	183	810	25.3
Bo McCalebb, New Orleans	Jr.	31	287	26	176	776	25.0
Rodney Stuckey, Eastern Washington	So.	29	227	43	215	712	24.6
Gerald Brown, Loyola (Md.)	Jr.	29	205	58	175	643	22.2
Jaycee Carroll, Utah State	Jr.	34	247	80	150	724	21.3
Stephen Curry, Davidson	Fr.	33	233	117	117	700	21.2

KEY GP=games played; FG=field goals; 3FG=3-point field goals; FT=free throws; PTS=points; AVG=average; Fr.=freshman; So.=sophomore; Jr.=junior; Sr.=senior

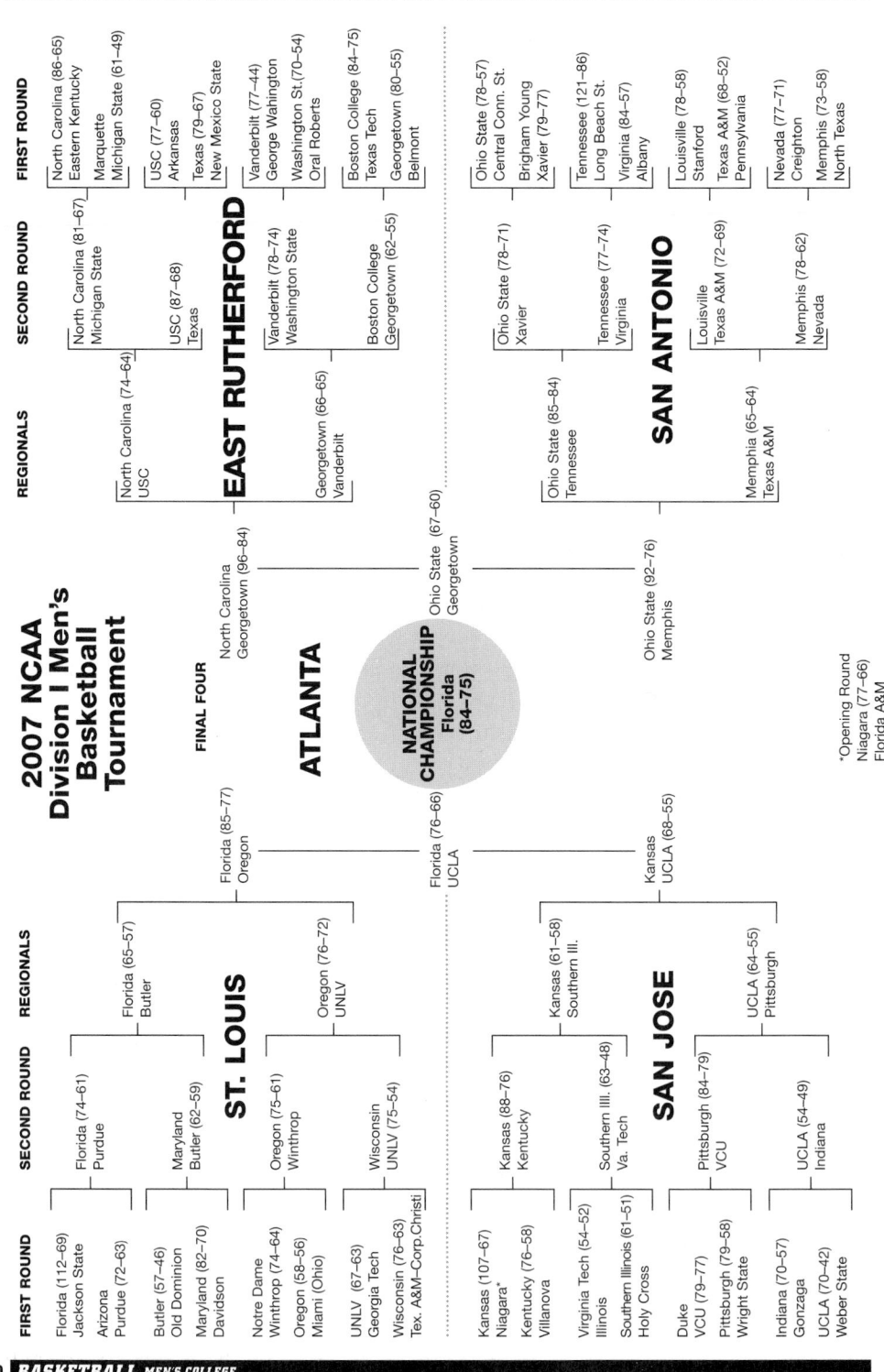

2007 NCAA Division I Men's Basketball Tournament

EAST RUTHERFORD

FIRST ROUND
- North Carolina (86–65)
- Eastern Kentucky
- Marquette
- Michigan State (61–49)
- USC (77–60)
- Arkansas
- Texas (79–67)
- New Mexico State
- Vanderbilt (77–44)
- George Wahington
- Washington St (70–54)
- Oral Roberts
- Boston College (84–75)
- Texas Tech
- Georgetown (80–55)
- Belmont

SECOND ROUND
- North Carolina (81–67)
- Michigan State
- USC (87–68)
- Texas
- Vanderbilt (78–74)
- Washington State
- Boston College
- Georgetown (62–55)

REGIONALS
- North Carolina (74–64)
- USC
- Georgetown (66–65)
- Vanderbilt

SAN ANTONIO

FIRST ROUND
- Ohio State (78–57)
- Central Conn. St.
- Brigham Young
- Xavier (79–77)
- Tennessee (121–86)
- Long Beach St.
- Virginia (84–57)
- Albany
- Louisville (78–58)
- Stanford
- Texas A&M (68–52)
- Pennsylvania
- Nevada (77–71)
- Creighton
- Memphis (73–58)
- North Texas

SECOND ROUND
- Ohio State (78–71)
- Xavier
- Tennessee (77–74)
- Virginia
- Louisville
- Texas A&M (72–69)
- Memphis (78–62)
- Nevada

REGIONALS
- Ohio State (85–84)
- Tennessee
- Memphis (65–64)
- Texas A&M

FINAL FOUR — ATLANTA

- North Carolina
- Georgetown (96–84)
- Ohio State (67–60)
- Georgetown
- Florida (85–77)
- Oregon
- Florida (76–66)
- UCLA
- Ohio State (92–76)
- Memphis
- Kansas
- UCLA (68–55)

NATIONAL CHAMPIONSHIP
Florida (84–75)

ST. LOUIS

REGIONALS
- Florida (65–57)
- Butler
- Oregon (76–72)
- UNLV

SECOND ROUND
- Florida (74–61)
- Purdue
- Maryland
- Butler (62–59)
- Oregon (75–61)
- Winthrop
- Wisconsin
- UNLV (75–54)

FIRST ROUND
- Florida (112–69)
- Jackson State
- Arizona
- Purdue (72–63)
- Butler (57–46)
- Old Dominion
- Maryland (82–70)
- Davidson
- Notre Dame
- Winthrop (74–64)
- Oregon (58–56)
- Miami (Ohio)
- UNLV (67–63)
- Georgia Tech
- Wisconsin (76–63)
- Tex. A&M-Corp.Christi

SAN JOSE

REGIONALS
- Kansas (61–58)
- Southern Ill.
- UCLA (64–55)
- Pittsburgh

SECOND ROUND
- Kansas (88–76)
- Kentucky
- Southern Ill. (63–48)
- Va. Tech
- Pittsburgh (84–79)
- VCU
- UCLA (54–49)
- Indiana

FIRST ROUND
- Kansas (107–67)
- Niagara*
- Kentucky (76–58)
- Villanova
- Virginia Tech (54–52)
- Illinois
- Southern Illinois (61–51)
- Holy Cross
- Duke
- VCU (79–77)
- Pittsburgh (79–58)
- Wright State
- Indiana (70–57)
- Gonzaga
- UCLA (70–42)
- Weber State

*Opening Round
Niagara (77–66)
Florida A&M

SOPHOMORE JUMP

Philadelphia Phillies first baseman Ryan Howard had a breakout year in 2006, his second season in the majors. The 26-year-old led the majors with 58 homers and 149 RBIs and was named the NL MVP.

OCHOA ON A ROLL

Despite not winning a major, 25-year-old Mexican phenom Lorena Ochoa proved she was among the best golfers in the world in 2006. Thanks to her six tournament wins and 20 top-10 finishes in 25 starts, she easily came in first on the LPGA Tour's money list. Ochoa was named the LPGA Rolex Player of the Year as well as the Associated Press Female Athlete of the Year.

D-TERMINED D-WADE

After only four years in the league, Heat guard Dwyane Wade has established himself as a true NBA superstar. In 2006, the 24-year-old Wade averaged more than 27 points per game and guided Miami to its first NBA title. Along the way, the three-time All-Star set an NBA record as the youngest player to reach 1,000 career points in the postseason.

ALEXANDER THE GREAT

In his first two seasons in the NHL, 22-year-old Washington Capitals left wing Alexander Ovechkin has been a scoring machine, consistently among the league leaders in both goals and points. In Ovechkin's rookie year, he scored 52 goals, making him one of only four players in NHL history to surpass 50 goals during their first season.

SASHA SKATES

Sasha Cohen, whose real first name is Alexandra, had a memorable year in 2006. The 22-year-old began by finishing first at the U.S. National Figure Skating Championships in January. Then she took the silver at the Winter Olympics one month later and won bronze at the World Championships in March.

AFP PHOTO/TIMOTHY A. CLARY

DYNAMO-MENTUM!

Dynamo forward Brian Ching drove home the winning goal in an overtime shootout to clinch Houston's victory in the 2006 MLS Cup. The Dynamo, who had moved from San Jose to Houston during the off-season, defeated the New England Revolution for the title. For New England, the loss marked their second straight MLS Cup defeat. In 2005, the Revolution lost to the Los Angeles Galaxy in the MLS Cup final.

ROARING BACK

The death of Tiger Woods' father, Earl, in early May of 2006 weighed heavily on Tiger. As a result, he played poorly at the U.S. Open in June and for the first time in his career he missed the cut at a major. But only five weeks later, Tiger began an amazing comeback by winning his 11th career major at the British Open. It was the first of six consecutive tournament victories. Included in this streak was Tiger's victory at the PGA Championship in August, a win that moved him into second place on the all-time major championship winners list. At the end of his roller-coaster year, Tiger was named the PGA Tour's Player of the Year for the eighth time.

TURN UP THE HEAT

Phoenix Mercury guard Diana Taurasi turned in one of the best offensive performances in WNBA history in 2006. Thriving under new Mercury head coach Paul Westhead's aggressive, up-tempo style, Taurasi led the WNBA in scoring. She set league records for most points scored in a single season (741) and in a single game (47).

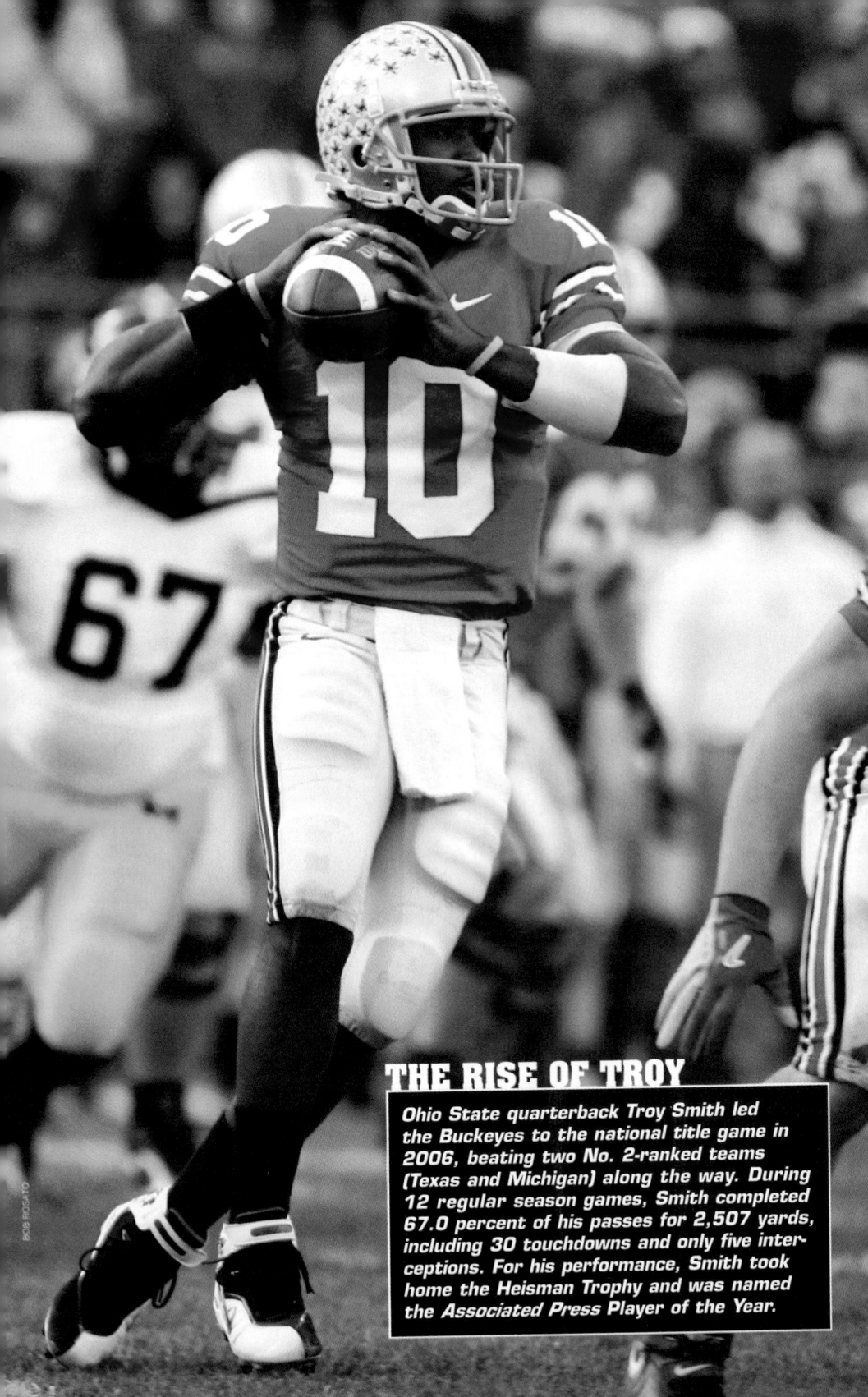

THE RISE OF TROY

Ohio State quarterback Troy Smith led the Buckeyes to the national title game in 2006, beating two No. 2-ranked teams (Texas and Michigan) along the way. During 12 regular season games, Smith completed 67.0 percent of his passes for 2,507 yards, including 30 touchdowns and only five interceptions. For his performance, Smith took home the Heisman Trophy and was named the *Associated Press* Player of the Year.

NOAH'S ARC

After leading the University of Florida to its first college basketball title in 2006, Gators forward Joakim Noah chose not to turn pro and instead returned for his junior year in 2007. Powered by Noah's strong inside game, Florida rose to the top of the polls and won its second straight national championship.

BILL FRAKES

RICCARDO S. SAVI/ WIREIMAGE.COM

SUPERPIPE SARAH

At the 2007 Winter X Games in Aspen, Colorado, 24-year-old Canadian skier Sarah Burke finally won a gold medal in the superpipe competition. Burke had competed in seven previous X Games without winning. But she wowed both the crowd and the judges on her first run by landing an amazing, 900-degree flip.

DAVID WALBERG

VICTORY LAP

After finishing second in the Nextel Cup standings in 2003 and 2004, Jimmie Johnson finally won the Cup in 2006. He was helped by an impressive five-win season, which included victories at the Daytona 500, as well as Talladega, Martinsville, and Indianapolis. His 2006 season money-winning total of $15,770,125 set a new NASCAR record.

ROCKIN' RODDICK

After a disappointing 2005 season that saw him lose in the first round at both Wimbledon and the U.S. Open, 23-year-old Andy Roddick regained his form in 2006. He made it to the final match of the U.S. Open in September, where he lost to Roger Federer in four sets, and he climbed from fourth to third on the year-end money list with $2,214,890 in winnings.

LOTTA IVORY

Senior guard Ivory Latta helped her University of North Carolina team reel off 24 straight wins to start the 2006–07 season. Latta, who stands only 5' 6", guided the Tar Heels to a Final Four appearance in 2006 (where her team lost to eventual champion Maryland). She was later named a consensus All-America as well as National Player of the Year by the U.S. Basketball Writers Association.

WITH OR WITHOUT WHEELS

Only five months after winning a gold medal in the snowboarding halfpipe event at the Winter Olympics in Turin, Italy, Shaun White took home the trophy for the skateboarding halfpipe event at the 2006 Dew Action Sports Tour stop in Denver, Colorado.

HOFF TO THE RACES

American swimmer Katie Hoff continued to impress in 2006. She won gold in the 200-meter freestyle and 400-meter individual medley events at the Pan Pacific Championships in August, only a few weeks after she set a new world record in the 200-meter individual medley at the U.S. National Championships. Having been the youngest member of the U.S. Olympic team as a 15-year-old in 2004, Hoff will be have plenty of experience under her cap by the time she competes in Beijing in 2008.

ROBERT BECK

CALL HIM MR. TOUCHDOWN

In 2006, San Diego Chargers running back LaDainian Tomlinson had a season for the ages. Tomlinson scored 31 touchdowns (28 of them rushing TDs) and 186 points, breaking previous NFL single-season records for touchdowns (28), rushing touchdowns (27), and points scored (176). For his incredible performance, "LT" was named to his fifth Pro Bowl and won the Associated Press's NFL MVP award.

NCAA MEN'S DIVISION I INDIVIDUAL LEADERS (cont.)

FIELD GOAL PERCENTAGE

PLAYER	CLASS	GP	FGM	FGA	PCT
Roy Hibbert, Georgetown	Jr.	32	156	225	69.3
Mike Freeman, Hampton	Fr.	30	162	239	67.8
Stuart Creason, Colorado State	Jr.	30	118	176	67.0
Florentino Valencia, Toledo	Sr.	31	159	239	66.5
Vladimir Kuljanin, UNC-Wilmington	Jr.	29	165	249	66.3
Brandan Wright, North Carolina	Fr.	33	208	314	66.2
Calvin Brown, Norfolk State	Sr.	30	152	233	65.2
Rome Sanders, Florida A&M	Sr.	34	168	259	64.9
Greg Dilligard, Illinois State	Sr.	31	128	198	64.6
Zach Andrews, Bradley	Sr.	33	147	228	64.5

Note: Minimum five field goals per game.

Roy Hibbert, Georgetown

FREE THROW PERCENTAGE

PLAYER	CLASS	GP	FTM	FTA	PCT
Ryan Toolson, Utah Valley State	So.	29	96	99	97.0
Derek Raivio, Gonzaga	Sr.	33	146	152	96.1
A.J. Graves, Butler	Jr.	32	137	143	95.8
Blake Ahearn, Missouri State	Sr.	32	109	117	93.2
Tristan Blackwood, Central Conn. State	Jr.	33	97	105	92.4
David Kool, Western Michigan	Fr.	29	99	108	91.7
Darren Cooper, Portland	Sr.	23	104	114	91.2
Mike Schachtner, Wis.-Green Bay	So.	33	104	114	91.2
Arvydas Eitutavicius, American Univ.	Sr.	30	95	105	90.5
Leemire Goldwire, UNC-Charlotte	Jr.	30	95	105	90.5

Note: Minimum 2.5 free throws made per game.

REBOUNDING

PLAYER	CLASS	GP	REB	AVG
Rashad Jones-Jennings, Ark.-Little Rock	Sr.	30	392	13.1
Chris Holm, Vermont	Sr.	32	287	12.1
Kentrell Gransberry, South Florida	Jr.	23	263	11.4
Kevin Durant, Texas	Fr.	33	373	11.3
Nick Fazekas, Nevada	Sr.	30	336	11.2
Obie Nwadike, Central Conn. St.	Sr.	30	326	10.9
Ryvon Covile, Detroit	Sr.	30	317	10.6
Glen Davis, LSU	Jr.	29	303	10.4
Jason Smith, Colorado State	Jr.	30	304	10.1
Jason Thompson, Rider	Jr.	31	312	10.1

ASSISTS

PLAYER	CLASS	GP	A	APG
Jared Jordan, Marist	Jr.	31	274	8.8
Jason Richards, Davidson	Jr.	33	242	7.3
Mustafa Shakur, Arizona	Sr.	30	207	6.9
D.J. Augustin, Texas	Fr.	33	221	6.7
Mike Conley Jr., Ohio State	Fr.	33	209	6.3
Eric Maynor, VCU	So.	33	208	6.3
Keenan Jones, Northwestern State	Sr.	32	200	6.3

3-POINT FIELD GOAL PERCENTAGE

PLAYER	CLASS	GP	3FGM	3FGA	PCT
Josh Carter, Texas A&M	So.	31	83	161	51.6
Jeremy Crouch, Bradley	Jr.	25	77	151	51.0
Stephen Sir, Northern Arizona	Sr.	30	124	253	49.0
Jimmy Baron, Rhode Island	So.	32	97	203	47.8
Josh Washington, Texas A&M-Corpus Christi	Sr.	31	89	187	47.6

Note: Minimum 2.5 three-point field goals made per game.

KEY GP=games played; FGM=field goals made; FGA=field goals attempted; PCT=percentage; FTM=free throws made; FTA=free throws attempted; REB=rebounds; AVG=average; A=assists; APG=assists per game; 3FGM=3-point field goals made; 3FGA=3-point field goals attempted

NCAA MEN'S DIVISION I INDIVIDUAL LEADERS (cont.)

STEALS

PLAYER	CLASS	GP	STL	SPG
Travis Holmes, Virginia Military Institute	So.	33	111	3.4
Paul Gause, Seton Hall	So.	29	90	3.1
Ledell Eackles, Campbell	Sr.	31	94	3.0
Ibrahim Jaaber, Pennsylvania	Sr.	30	90	3.0

Paul Gause, Seton Hall

BLOCKS

PLAYER	CLASS	GP	BLK	BPG
Mickell Gladness, Alabama A&M	Jr.	30	188	6.3
Stephane Lasme, Massachusetts	Sr.	31	156	5.0
Hasheem Thabeet, Connecticut	Fr.	31	119	3.8
McHugh Mattis, South Florida	Sr.	30	109	3.6

BOB ROSATO

KEY GP=games played; STL=steals; SPG=steals per game; BLK=blocks; BPG=blocks per game

DID YOU KNOW?

Florida became just the seventh school to win back-to-back NCAA Division I national championships in basketball. The other schools are Oklahoma A&M, Kentucky, San Francisco, Cincinnati, UCLA, and Duke.

TRIVIA CHALLENGE

1 What was unique about Florida's winning a second straight national championship in 2007?
a. First team to defeat Ohio State that year.
b. First team to win overtime title game.
c. First team to win back-to-back titles with the same starting five players.

2 In 2007, Kevin Durant became the second player in Texas history (and first freshman) to win the John Wooden Award, which is given annually to the best college basketball player in the nation. Name the first Longhorn player to win this award.
a. T.J. Ford
b. Chris Mihm
c. Royal Ivey

Kevin Durant

3 North Carolina holds the record for most trips to the Final Four. How many times have the Tar Heels made it to the semifinals?
a. 10
b. 16
c. 21

4 Unlike in the NBA, a college basketball player can no longer remain in the game once he commits his fifth foul.
a. True
b. False

5 In 2007, Bobby Knight won his 880th game, making him the winningest head coach in men's NCAA Division I history. Whose record did he break?
a. John Wooden
b. Mike Krzyzewski
c. Dean Smith

6 Name the last freshman to be named Most Outstanding Player of the NCAA tournament.
a. Pervis Ellison
b. Carmelo Anthony
c. Emeka Okafor

GREG NELSON

7 The NCAA's all-time leading scorer, Pete Maravich, was known by what nickname during his playing career?
a. "Pistol"
b. "The Shooter"
c. "Big Swish"

Trivia Challenge: 1. c; 2. a; 3. b; 4. a; 5. c; 6. b; 7. a.

NCAA MEN'S DIVISION I CHAMPIONSHIP RESULTS

YEAR	WINNER	SCORE	RUNNER-UP	THIRD PLACE	FOURTH PLACE	WINNING COACH
2007	Florida	84–75	Ohio State	UCLA*	Georgetown*	Billy Donovan
2006	Florida	73–57	UCLA	George Mason*	LSU*	Billy Donovan
2005	North Carolina	75–70	Illinois	Michigan State*	Louisville*	Roy Williams
2004	Connecticut	82-73	Georgia Tech	Duke*	Oklahoma State*	Jim Calhoun
2003	Syracuse	81-78	Kansas	Texas*	Marquette*	Jim Boeheim
2002	Maryland	64-52	Indiana	Kansas*	Oklahoma*	Gary Williams
2001	Duke	82-72	Arizona	Maryland*	Michigan State*	Mike Krzyzewski
2000	Michigan State	89-76	Florida	Wisconsin*	North Carolina*	Tom Izzo
1999	Connecticut	77-74	Duke	Michigan State*	Ohio State*	Jim Calhoun
1998	Kentucky	78-69	Utah	Stanford*	North Carolina*	Tubby Smith
1997	Arizona	84-79(OT)	Kentucky	Minnesota*	North Carolina*	Lute Olson
1996	Kentucky	76-67	Syracuse	Vacated‡	Mississippi State*	Rick Pitino
1995	UCLA	89-78	Arkansas	North Carolina*	Oklahoma State*	Jim Harrick
1994	Arkansas	76-72	Duke	Arizona*	Florida*	Nolan Richardson
1993	North Carolina	77-71	Vacated‡	Kansas*	Kentucky*	Dean Smith
1992	Duke	71-51	Vacated‡	Cincinnati*	Indiana*	Mike Krzyzewski
1991	Duke	72-65	Kansas	UNLV*	North Carolina*	Mike Krzyzewski
1990	UNLV	103-73	Duke	Arkansas*	Georgia Tech*	Jerry Tarkanian
1989	Michigan	80-79(OT)	Seton Hall	Duke*	Illinois*	Steve Fisher
1988	Kansas	83-79	Oklahoma	Arizona*	Duke*	Larry Brown
1987	Indiana	83-79	Syracuse	UNLV*	Providence*	Bobby Knight
1986	Louisville	74-73	Duke	Kansas*	LSU*	Denny Crum
1985	Villanova	72-69	Georgetown	St. John's (N.Y.)*	Vacated‡	Rollie Massimino
1984	Georgetown	66-64	Houston	Kentucky*	Virginia*	John Thompson
1983	North Carolina State	84-75	Houston	Georgia*	Louisville*	Jim Valvano
1982	North Carolina	54-52	Georgetown	Houston*	Louisville*	Dean Smith
1981	Indiana	63-62	North Carolina	Virginia	LSU	Bobby Knight
1980	Louisville	63-50	Vacated‡	Purdue	Iowa	Denny Crum
1979	Michigan State	59-54	Indiana State	DePaul	Penn	Jud Heathcote
1978	Kentucky	75-64	Duke	Arkansas	Notre Dame	Joe Hall
1977	Marquette	94-88	North Carolina	UNLV	UNC-Charlotte	Al McGuire
1976	Indiana	67-59	Michigan	UCLA	Rutgers	Bobby Knight
1975	UCLA	86-68	Kentucky	Louisville	Syracuse	John Wooden
1974	North Carolina State	92-85	Marquette	UCLA	Kansas	Norm Sloan
1973	UCLA	76-64	Memphis State	Indiana	Providence	John Wooden
1972	UCLA	87-66	Florida State	North Carolina	Louisville	John Wooden
1971	UCLA	81-76	Vacated‡	Vacated‡	Kansas	John Wooden
1970	UCLA	68-62	Jacksonville	New Mexico State	St. Bonaventure	John Wooden
1969	UCLA	80-69	Purdue	Drake	North Carolina	John Wooden
1968	UCLA	92-72	North Carolina	Ohio State	Houston	John Wooden
1967	UCLA	78-55	Dayton	Houston	North Carolina	John Wooden
1966	Texas Western	79-64	Kentucky	Duke	Utah	Don Haskins
1965	UCLA	72-65	Michigan	Princeton	Wichita State	John Wooden
1964	UCLA	91-80	Duke	Michigan	Kansas State	John Wooden
1963	Loyola (Ill.)	98-83	Cincinnati	Duke	Oregon State	George Ireland
1962	Cincinnati	60-58(OT)	Ohio State	Wake Forest	UCLA	Edwin Jucker
1961	Cincinnati	71-59	Ohio State	Vacated‡	Utah	Edwin Jucker
1960	Ohio State	70-65(OT)	California	Cincinnati	NYU	Fred Taylor
1959	California	75-55	West Virginia	Cincinnati	Louisville	Pete Newell
1958	Kentucky	71-70	Seattle	Temple	Kansas State	Adolph Rupp
1957	North Carolina	84-72	Kansas	San Francisco	Michigan State	Frank McGuire
1956	San Francisco	83–71	Iowa	Temple	SMU	Phil Woolpert
1955	San Francisco	77–63	La Salle	Colorado	Iowa	Phil Woolpert
1954	La Salle	92–76	Bradley	Penn State	USC	Kenneth Loeffler
1953	Indiana	69–68	Kansas	Washington	LSU	Branch McCracken
1952	Kansas	80–63	St. John's (N.Y.)	Illinois	Santa Clara	Forrest Allen
1951	Kentucky	68-58	Kansas State	Illinois	Oklahoma State	Adolph Rupp
1950	City College of N.Y.	71–68	Bradley	North Carolina State	Baylor	Nat Holman
1949	Kentucky	46–36	Oklahoma State	Illinois	Oregon State	Adolph Rupp
1948	Kentucky	58–42	Baylor	Holy Cross	Kansas State	Adolph Rupp
1947	Holy Cross	58–47	Oklahoma	Texas	City College of N.Y.	Alvin Julian
1946	Oklahoma A&M	43–40	North Carolina	Ohio St.	California	Hank Iba
1945	Oklahoma A&M	49–45	NYU	Arkansas*	Ohio State*	Hank Iba
1944	Utah	42–40 (OT)	Dartmouth	Iowa State*	Ohio State*	Vadal Peterson
1943	Wyoming	46–34	Georgetown	Texas*	DePaul*	Everett Shelton
1942	Stanford	53–38	Dartmouth	Colorado*	Kentucky*	Everett Dean
1941	Wisconsin	39–34	Washington State	Pittsburgh*	Arkansas*	Harold Foster
1940	Indiana	60–42	Kansas	Duquesne*	USC*	Branch McCracken
1939	Oregon	46–33	Ohio St.	Oklahoma*	Villanova*	Howard Hobson

* Tied for third place. ‡Student-athletes representing St. Joseph's (Pennsylvania) in 1961, Villanova in 1971, Western Kentucky in 1971, UCLA in 1980, Memphis State in 1985, Michigan in 1992 and 1993, and Massachusetts in 1996 were declared ineligible subsequent to the tournament. Under NCAA rules, the teams' and ineligible student-athletes' records were deleted, and the teams' places in the standings were vacated.

TODAY'S STARS

Ohio State teammates Mike Conley Jr. (right) and Greg Oden (left) won three state titles playing together in high school.

DAVID E. KLUTHO

■ **Mike Conley Jr., guard,** b. October 11, 1987, Fayetteville, Arkansas. Playing with his former high school teammate and fellow freshman Greg Oden, Conley helped the Buckeyes return to the NCAA title game for the first time in 45 years. Throughout the Buckeyes' tournament run, Conley ran Ohio State's offense like a veteran point guard, and averaged 16 points, 5 rebounds, and 5 assists per game. Although the Buckeyes couldn't overcome Florida's depth and experience in the national championship game, Conley was recognized for his outstanding play and was named to the 2007 freshman All-America team.

■ **Jeff Green, forward,** b. August 28, 1986, Hyattsville, Maryland. As a junior, Green proved to be a triple threat for Georgetown, leading the team in scoring (14.4 points per game) and ranking second in rebounds (6.2) and assists (3.2) per game. After helping the Hoyas win the 2007 Big East conference tournament, Green became a key part of Georgetown's Final Four run. For his play, Green was named a third-team All-America.

■ **Darren Collison, guard,** b. August 23, 1987, Rancho Cucamonga, California. After UCLA lost in the 2006 national title game during his freshman season, Collison made big improvements in every aspect of his game in 2007, more than doubling his scoring (12.2), assist (5.7), and steal (2.2) averages. Collison also helped the Bruins return to the Final Four thanks to one of the best three-point shooting averages in the country (44.7%) and his tenacious defense, which earned him National Defensive Player of the Year honors.

NCAA FINAL FOUR MOST OUTSTANDING PLAYERS

YEAR	WINNER, SCHOOL	YEAR	WINNER, SCHOOL	YEAR	WINNER, SCHOOL
2007	Corey Brewer, Florida	1983	Akeem Olajuwon, Houston*	1959	Jerry West, West Virginia*
2006	Joakim Noah, Florida	1982	James Worthy, North Carolina	1958	Elgin Baylor, Seattle*
2005	Sean May, North Carolina	1981	Isiah Thomas, Indiana	1957	Wilt Chamberlain, Kansas*
2004	Emeka Okafor, Connecticut	1980	Darrell Griffith, Louisville	1956	Hal Lear, Temple*
2003	Carmelo Anthony, Syracuse	1979	Earvin Johnson, Michigan State	1955	Bill Russell, San Francisco
2002	Juan Dixon, Maryland	1978	Jack Givens, Kentucky	1954	Tom Gola, La Salle
2001	Shane Battier, Duke	1977	Butch Lee, Marquette	1953	B.H. Born, Kansas*
2000	Mateen Cleaves, Michigan State	1976	Kent Benson, Indiana	1952	Clyde Lovellette, Kansas
1999	Richard Hamilton, Connecticut	1975	Richard Washington, UCLA	1951	Bill Spivey, Kentucky
1998	Jeff Sheppard, Kentucky	1974	David Thompson, N.C. State	1950	Irwin Dambrot, CCNY
1997	Miles Simon, Arizona	1973	Bill Walton, UCLA	1949	Alex Groza, Kentucky
1996	Tony Delk, Kentucky	1972	Bill Walton, UCLA	1948	Alex Groza, Kentucky
1995	Ed O'Bannon, UCLA	1971	Howard Porter, Villanova*†	1947	George Kaftan, Holy Cross
1994	Corliss Williamson, Arkansas	1970	Sidney Wicks, UCLA	1946	Bob Kurland, Oklahoma A&M
1993	Donald Williams, North Carolina	1969	Lew Alcindor, UCLA**	1945	Bob Kurland, Oklahoma A&M
1992	Bobby Hurley, Duke	1968	Lew Alcindor, UCLA**	1944	Arnie Ferrin, Utah
1991	Christian Laettner, Duke	1967	Lew Alcindor, UCLA**	1943	Ken Sailors, Wyoming
1990	Anderson Hunt, UNLV	1966	Jerry Chambers, Utah*	1942	Howard Dallmar, Stanford
1989	Glen Rice, Michigan	1965	Bill Bradley, Princeton*	1941	John Kotz, Wisconsin
1988	Danny Manning, Kansas	1964	Walt Hazzard, UCLA	1940	Marv Huffman, Indiana
1987	Keith Smart, Indiana	1963	Art Heyman, Duke	1939	Jimmy Hull, Ohio State*
1986	Pervis Ellison, Louisville	1962	Paul Hogue, Cincinnati		
1985	Ed Pinckney, Villanova	1961	Jerry Lucas, Ohio State*		
1984	Patrick Ewing, Georgetown	1960	Jerry Lucas, Ohio State		

* Not a member of the championship-winning team.
† Record later vacated.
** Now known as Kareem Abdul-Jabbar.

FAST FACT

The men's Division I NCAA basketball tournament expanded from 48 to 64 teams in 1985. The women's Division I tournament expanded to 64 teams in 1994.

NATIONAL INVITATION TOURNAMENT (NIT) CHAMPIONSHIP RESULTS

YEAR	WINNER	SCORE	RUNNER-UP	YEAR	WINNER	SCORE	RUNNER-UP
2007	West Virginia	78–73	Clemson	1972	Maryland	100–69	Niagara
2006	South Carolina	76–64	Michigan	1971	North Carolina	84–66	Georgia Tech
2005	South Carolina	60–57	St. Joseph's	1970	Marquette	65–53	St. John's (N.Y.)
2004	Michigan	62–55	Rutgers	1969	Temple	89–76	Boston College
2003	St. John's (N.Y.)	70–67	Georgetown	1968	Dayton	61–48	Kansas
2002	Memphis	72–62	South Carolina	1967	Southern Illinois	71–56	Marquette
2001	Tulsa	79–60	Alabama	1966	Brigham Young	97–84	NYU
2000	Wake Forest	71–61	Notre Dame	1965	St. John's (N.Y.)	55–51	Villanova
1999	California	61–60	Clemson	1964	Bradley	86–54	New Mexico
1998	Minnesota	79–72	Penn State	1963	Providence	81–66	Canisius
1997	Michigan	82–73	Florida State	1962	Dayton	73–67	St. John's (N.Y.)
1996	Nebraska	60–56	St. Joseph's	1961	Providence	62–59	St. Louis
1995	Virginia Tech	65–64 (OT)	Marquette	1960	Bradley	88–72	Providence
1994	Villanova	80–73	Vanderbilt	1959	St. John's (N.Y.)	76–71 (OT)	Bradley
1993	Minnesota	62–61	Georgetown	1958	Xavier	78–74 (OT)	Dayton
1992	Virginia	81–76	Notre Dame	1957	Bradley	84–83	Memphis State
1991	Stanford	78–72	Oklahoma	1956	Louisville	93–80	Dayton
1990	Vanderbilt	74–72	St. Louis	1955	Duquesne	70–58	Dayton
1989	St. John's (N.Y.)	73–65	St. Louis	1954	Holy Cross	71–62	Duquesne
1988	Connecticut	72–67	Ohio State	1953	Seton Hall	58–46	St. John's (N.Y.)
1987	Southern Miss.	84–80	La Salle	1952	La Salle	75–64	Dayton
1986	Ohio State	73–63	Wyoming	1951	BYU	62–43	Dayton
1985	UCLA	65–62	Indiana	1950	CCNY	69–61	Bradley
1984	Michigan	83–63	Notre Dame	1949	San Francisco	48–47	Loyola (Illinois)
1983	Fresno State	69–60	DePaul	1948	St. Louis	65–52	NYU
1982	Bradley	67–58	Purdue	1947	Utah	49–45	Kentucky
1981	Tulsa	86–84 (OT)	Syracuse	1946	Kentucky	46–45	Rhode Island
1980	Virginia	58–55	Minnesota	1945	DePaul	71–54	Bowling Green
1979	Indiana	53–52	Purdue	1944	St. John's (N.Y.)	47–39	DePaul
1978	Texas	101–93	North Carolina State	1943	St. John's (N.Y.)	48–27	Toledo
1977	St. Bonaventure	94–91	Houston	1942	West Virginia	47–45	Western Kentucky
1976	Kentucky	71–67	North Carolina-Charlotte	1941	Long Island Univ.	56–42	Ohio University
1975	Princeton	80–69	Providence	1940	Colorado	51–40	Duquesne
1974	Purdue	87–81	Utah	1939	Long Island Univ.	44–32	Loyola (Illinois)
1973	Virginia Tech	92–91 (OT)	Notre Dame	1938	Temple	60–36	Colorado

NCAA MEN'S DIVISION I ALL-TIME SINGLE-SEASON LEADERS

POINTS

PLAYER	YEAR	GP	FG	3FG	FT	PTS
Pete Maravich, LSU	1970	31	522	—	337	1,381
Elvin Hayes, Houston	1968	33	519	—	176	1,214
Frank Selvy, Furman	1954	29	427	—	355	1,209
Pete Maravich, LSU	1969	26	433	—	282	1,148
Pete Maravich, LSU	1968	26	432	—	274	1,138
Bo Kimble, Loyola Marymount	1990	32	404	92	231	1,131
Hersey Hawkins, Bradley	1988	31	377	87	284	1,125
Austin Carr, Notre Dame	1970	29	444	—	218	1,106
Austin Carr, Notre Dame	1971	29	430	—	241	1,101
Otis Birdsong, Houston	1977	36	452	—	186	1,090

Pete Maravich, LSU

SCORING AVERAGE

PLAYER	YEAR	GP	FG	FT	PTS	AVG
Pete Maravich, LSU	1970	31	522	337	1,381	44.5
Pete Maravich, LSU	1969	26	433	282	1,148	44.2
Pete Maravich, LSU	1968	26	432	274	1,138	43.8
Frank Selvy, Furman	1954	29	427	355	1,209	41.7
Johnny Neumann, Mississippi	1971	23	366	191	923	40.1

DID YOU KNOW?

KEY
GP=games played; FG=field goals; 3FG=3-point field goals; FT=free throws; PTS=points; AVG=average

In 1985, Georgetown reached the Final Four with John Thompson as its head coach and Patrick Ewing as its starting center. In 2007, their sons, John Thompson III and Patrick Ewing Jr., were the ones helping to lead the Hoyas back to the Final Four as head coach and player.

NCAA MEN'S DIVISION I SINGLE-SEASON LEADERS (cont.)

SCORING AVERAGE (CONT.)

PLAYER	YEAR	GP	FG	FT	PTS	AVG
Freeman Williams, Portland State	1977	26	417	176	1,010	38.8
Billy McGill, Utah	1962	26	394	221	1,009	38.8
Calvin Murphy, Niagara	1968	24	337	242	916	38.2
Austin Carr, Notre Dame	1970	29	444	218	1,106	38.1
Austin Carr, Notre Dame	1971	29	430	241	1,101	38.0

REBOUND AVERAGE (BEFORE 1973)

PLAYER	YEAR	GP	REB	AVG
Charlie Slack, Marshall	1955	21	538	25.6
Leroy Wright, Pacific	1959	26	652	25.1
Art Quimby, Connecticut	1955	25	611	24.4
Charlie Slack, Marshall	1956	22	520	23.6
Ed Conlin, Fordham	1953	26	612	23.5

REBOUND AVERAGE (SINCE 1973*)

PLAYER	YEAR	GP	REB	AVG
Kermit Washington, American Univ.	1973	25	511	20.4
Marvin Barnes, Providence	1973	30	571	19.0
Marvin Barnes, Providence	1974	32	597	18.7
Pete Padgett, Nevada	1973	26	462	17.8
Jim Bradley, Northern Illinois	1973	24	426	17.8

*Freshmen became eligible for varsity play before the 1972-73 season.

ASSISTS

PLAYER	YEAR	GP	A
Mark Wade, UNLV	1987	38	406
Avery Johnson, Southern Univ.	1988	30	399
Anthony Manuel, Bradley	1988	31	373
Avery Johnson, Southern Univ.	1987	31	333
Mark Jackson, St. John's (N.Y.)	1986	32	328

Mark Jackson, St. John's

FIELD GOAL PERCENTAGE

PLAYER	YEAR	FGM	FGA	PCT
Steve Johnson, Oregon State	1981	235	315	74.6
Dwayne Davis, Florida	1989	179	248	72.2
Keith Walker, Utica	1985	154	216	71.3
Steve Johnson, Oregon State	1980	211	297	71.0
Adam Mark, Belmont	2002	150	212	70.8

FREE THROW PERCENTAGE

PLAYER	YEAR	FTM	FTA	PCT
Blake Ahearn, Missouri State*	2004	117	120	97.5
Ryan Toolson, Utah Valley Sate	2006	96	99	97.0
Derek Raivio, Gonzaga	2006	146	152	96.1
Craig Collins, Penn State	1985	94	98	95.9
A.J. Graves, Butler	2006	137	143	95.8

3-POINT FIELD GOAL PERCENTAGE

PLAYER	YEAR	3FGM	3FGA	PCT
Glenn Tropf, Holy Cross	1988	52	82	63.4
Sean Wightman, Western Michigan	1992	48	76	63.2
Keith Jennings, East Tennessee State	1991	84	142	59.2
Dave Calloway, Monmouth	1989	48	82	58.5
Steve Kerr, Arizona	1988	114	199	57.3

* formerly Southwest Missouri State

FOCUS ON SPORT/GETTY IMAGES

KEY

GP=games played; FG=field goals; FT=free throws; PTS=points; AVG=average; REB=rebounds; A=assists; FGM=field goals made; FGA=field goals attempted; PCT=percentage; FTM=free throws made; FTA=free throws attempted; 3FGM=3-point field goals made; 3FGA=3-point field goals attempted

FAST FACT

For the 2006–07 season, Kevin Durant ranked fourth in the nation in both scoring average (25.6) and rebounds per game (11.3). The last player to be ranked in the top five in both categories in the same season was Adonal Foyle of Colgate, who did it in 1996–97.

STEALS

PLAYER	YEAR	GP	STL
Desmond Cambridge, Alabama A&M	2002	29	160
Mookie Blaylock, Oklahoma	1988	39	150
Aldwin Ware, Florida A&M	1988	29	142
Darron Brittman, Chicago State	1986	28	139
John Linehan, Providence	2002	31	139

David Robinson, Navy

BLOCKS

PLAYER	YEAR	GP	BLK
David Robinson, Navy	1986	35	207
Shawn James, Northeastern	2006	30	196
Mickell Gladness, Alabama A&M	2006	30	188
Adonal Foyle, Colgate	1997	28	180
Keith Closs, Central Connecticut State	1996	28	178

KEY GP=games played; STL=steals; BLK=blocks

JERRY WACHTER/SPORTS ILLUSTRATED

LEGENDS

Hakeem Olajuwon powered the University of Houston's famous "Phi Slamma Jamma" offense.

MANNY MILLAN/SPORTS ILLUSTRATED

■ **Christian Laettner, forward,** b. August 17, 1969, Angola, New York. As a key member of the powerful Duke teams of the early 1990s, Laettner is the only player in NCAA history to start in four consecutive Final Fours, and he still holds the all-time NCAA tournament records for most games played and points scored. During his first two trips to the Final Four in 1989 and '90, Laettner and the Blue Devils fell short. In his junior and senior seasons, though, he led Duke to back-to-back national titles. Perhaps the most memorable moment of his collegiate career came in the 1992 East regional final against Kentucky, when Laettner caught an 80-foot inbounds pass, turned, and drained a 17-foot jump shot at the buzzer to lift his team to a thrilling 104–103 overtime victory over the Wildcats.

■ **Hakeem Olajuwon, center,** b. January 21, 1963, Lagos, Nigeria. Although he didn't pick up a basketball until age 15, Olajuwon left his native Africa to play college basketball at the University of Houston in 1980. He quickly developed into one of the premier college centers in the country and helped the Cougars reach the Final Four three straight years. Although his teams never won a national title, Olajuwon was still named the NCAA tournament's Most Outstanding Player in 1983, marking the last time a player not on the championship team received the honor.

■ **Walt Hazzard, guard,** b. April 15, 1942, Wilmington, Delaware. Under the guidance of coach John Wooden, Hazzard and his backcourt partner Gail Goodrich began the UCLA dynasty when they led the team to an undefeated season and the school's first national title in 1964. The Bruins went on to win nine more over the next 11 seasons. Hazzard—who later changed his name to Mahdi Abdul-Rahman—was named first-team All-America in 1964 and Most Outstanding Player of the NCAA tournament.

The 2006–07 season cemented Candace Parker's status as one of the greatest players the women's game has ever seen. Tennessee's 6'4" forward averaged 19.6 points and 9.8 rebounds, dunked in a game four times, and was named the SEC Player of the Year. In April, the sophomore star led the Lady Vols (34–3) to their first national title in nine seasons.

At the start of the season, whether or not Maryland could repeat as national champions was the big question. The Terps had all five starters back from the year before, including second-team All-America forward Crystal Langhorne. Maryland had another strong season, but couldn't quite recapture the magic of its title run. The team went 28–6 and was upset in the second round of the NCAA Tournament by Mississippi.

It was Maryland's biggest rival that ruled the regular season. The Duke Blue Devils finished the regular season with a 29–0 record and were ranked number one in the polls. But things started heading south for Duke when they lost to North Carolina State in the ACC Tournament semifinals. Three weeks later, a second loss ended Duke's season. The top-seeded Blue Devils lost to fourth seed Rutgers, 53–52, in the NCAA tournament's Sweet Sixteen. Duke star guard Lindsey Harding missed two free throws with 0.1 seconds left in the second half that could have won or tied the game. On the bright side, Harding was later named the Naismith Player of the Year and was chosen number one overall in the 2007 WNBA Draft.

Rutgers' upset win over Duke gave the Scarlet Knights momentum that carried them to their first Final Four since 2000. The other Final Four teams were regulars. LSU made the Final Four for the fourth straight season. North Carolina made it for the second straight season. And, of course, there was Tennessee, which made its sixth Final Four in the past nine years.

Tennessee beat Rutgers, 59–46, in the national championship game. The Lady Vols dominated. They led by as many as 16 points in the second

Candace Parker was named Most Outstanding Player of the Final Four and led Tennessee to its seventh national title.

BILL FRAKES/SI

DID YOU KNOW?

Tennessee's Pat Summitt is the winningest head coach in NCAA Division I basketball history, with a career record of 947 wins and 180 losses. In February 2007, she became the first women's basketball coach featured on a box of Wheaties.

half and out-rebounded the Scarlet Knights, 40–30. The win gave Tennessee its seventh national title—the most in the history of women's college basketball. Hall of Fame coach Pat Summitt has been with the team for all seven titles. Parker had 17 points and 7 rebounds in the title game and was named the Most Outstanding Player of the Final Four. After the season, the 20-year-old became the youngest woman to win the John R. Wooden Player of the Year award.

Once known mainly for her dunking and raw talent, Parker has now established herself as a true winner. The icing on the cake for college hoops fans: She'll be back at Tennessee next season to try to bring *another* national championship to Knoxville.

After starting 2–4, Rutgers turned their season around, playing its way into the school's first national title game.

2007 NCAA WOMEN'S DIVISION I CHAMPIONSHIP BOX SCORE

TENNESSEE LADY VOLUNTEERS: 59

PLAYER	MIN	FG M-A	FT M-A	REB OFF	REB TOT	A	PF	PTS
Sidney Spencer	36	4–12	2–2	2	2	2	4	11
Candace Parker	39	5–15	7–10	2	7	3	3	17
Nicky Anosike	34	2–9	0–5	10	16	2	2	4
Shannon Bobbitt	32	4–9	1–2	2	3	0	1	13
Alexis Hornbuckle	37	2–8	0–0	3	7	1	2	4
Dominique Redding	11	0–0	0–0	0	0	0	0	0
Alberta Auguste	15	3–5	4–4	4	1	1	1	10
Alex Fuller	6	0–0	0–0	0	0	0	0	0
TOTALS		20–58 (34.5%)	14–23 (60.9%)	23	340	9	13	59

RUTGERS SCARLET KNIGHTS: 46

PLAYER	MIN	FG M-A	FT M-A	REB OFF	REB TOT	A	PF	PTS
Essence Carson	40	4–11	0–3	1	6	1	4	8
Heather Zurich	23	2–6	0–0	0	1	0	3	4
Kia Vaughn	34	9–15	2–3	7	10	2	4	20
Epiphanny Prince	26	0–0	2–4	1	3	2	4	2
Matee Ajavon	37	3–9	0–0	0	4	1	5	8
Dee Dee Jernigan	1	0–0	0–0	0	0	0	0	0
Kate Adams	1	0–0	0–0	0	0	0	0	0
Myia McCurdy	17	1–3	0–0	0	1	0	3	2
Judith Ray	15	0–3	0–0	1	2	0	0	0
Rashidat Junaid	6	1–2	0–0	1	3	0	1	2
TOTALS		20–49 (40.8%)	4–10 (40.0%)	11	30	6	22	46

KEY MIN=minutes played; FG M-A=field goals made-attempted; FT M-A=free throws made-attempted; REB=rebounds; OFF=offensive; TOT=total; A=assists; PF=personal fouls; PTS=points

USA TODAY/ESPN TOP 25 FINAL POLL

RANK	TEAM	RECORD	POINTS
1.	Tennessee	34–3	775
2.	Rutgers	27–9	727
3.	North Carolina	34–4	724
4.	LSU	30–8	678
5.	Connecticut	32–4	630
6.	Duke	32–2	597
7.	Purdue	31–6	569
8.	Arizona State	31–5	549
9.	Oklahoma	28–4	474
10.	Mississippi	24–11	434
11.	George Washington	28–4	408
12.	North Carolina State	25–10	404
13.	Georgia	27–7	387
14.	Maryland	28–6	368
15.	Bowling Green	31–4	306
16.	Stanford	29–5	298
17.	Vanderbilt	28–6	271
18.	Ohio State	28–4	201
19.	Florida State	24–10	198
20.	Baylor	26–8	189
21.	Texas A&M	25–7	181
22.	Marist	29–6	137
23.	Middle Tennessee St.	30–4	104
24.	Louisville	27–8	92
25.	Michigan State	24–9	79

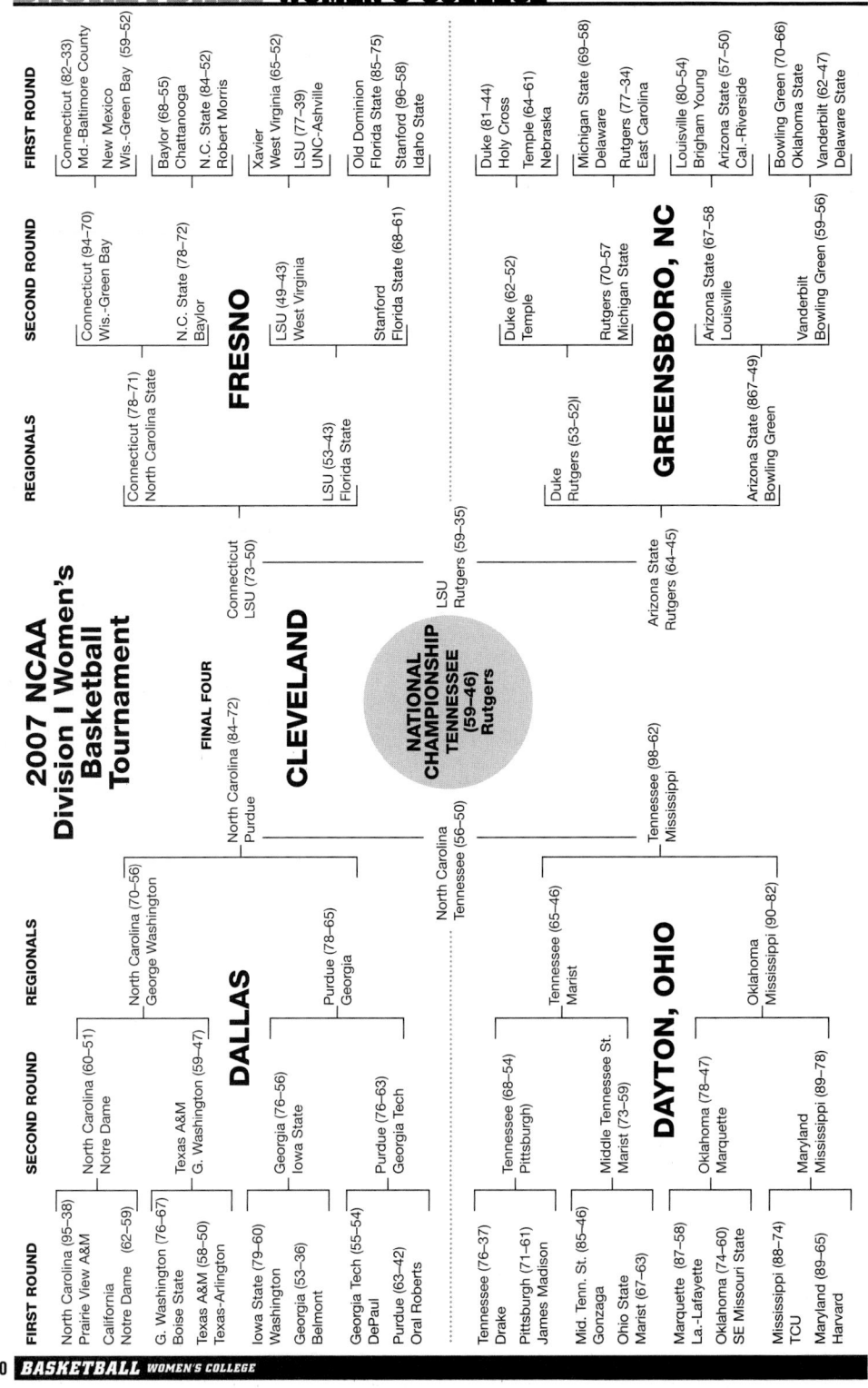

2007 NCAA Division I Women's Basketball Tournament

FIRST ROUND

Connecticut (82–33)
Md.-Baltimore County
New Mexico
Wis.-Green Bay (59–52)

Baylor (68–55)
Chattanooga
N.C. State (84–52)
Robert Morris

Xavier
West Virginia (65–52)
LSU (77–39)
UNC-Ashville

Old Dominion
Florida State (85–75)
Stanford (96–58)
Idaho State

Duke (81–44)
Holy Cross
Temple (64–61)
Nebraska

Michigan State (69–58)
Delaware
Rutgers (77–34)
East Carolina

Louisville (80–54)
Brigham Young
Arizona State (57–50)
Cal.-Riverside

Bowling Green (70–66)
Oklahoma State
Vanderbilt (62–47)
Delaware State

SECOND ROUND

Connecticut (94–70)
Wis.-Green Bay

N.C. State (78–72)
Baylor

LSU (49–43)
West Virginia

Stanford
Florida State (68–61)

Duke (62–52)
Temple

Rutgers (70–57)
Michigan State

Arizona State (67–58)
Louisville

Vanderbilt
Bowling Green (59–56)

REGIONALS

FRESNO

Connecticut (78–71)
North Carolina State

LSU (53–43)
Florida State

Duke
Rutgers (53–52)l

Arizona State (867–49)
Bowling Green

GREENSBORO, NC

FINAL FOUR

Connecticut
LSU (73–50)

CLEVELAND

LSU
Rutgers (59–35)

Arizona State
Rutgers (64–45)

NATIONAL CHAMPIONSHIP (59–46) Rutgers

TENNESSEE

Tennessee (98–62)
Mississippi

North Carolina
Tennessee (56–50)

North Carolina (84–72)
Purdue

DALLAS

Tennessee (65–46)
Marist

Oklahoma
Mississippi (90–82)

DAYTON, OHIO

REGIONALS

North Carolina (70–56)
George Washington

Purdue (78–65)
Georgia

SECOND ROUND

North Carolina (60–51)
Notre Dame

Texas A&M
G. Washington (59–47)

Georgia (76–56)
Iowa State

Purdue (76–63)
Georgia Tech

Tennessee (68–54)
Pittsburgh

Middle Tennessee St.
Marist (73–59)

Oklahoma (78–47)
Marquette

Maryland
Mississippi (89–78)

FIRST ROUND

North Carolina (95–38)
Prairie View A&M
California
Notre Dame (62–59)

G. Washington (76–67)
Boise State
Texas A&M (58–50)
Texas-Arlington

Iowa State (79–60)
Washington
Georgia (53–36)
Belmont

Georgia Tech (55–54)
DePaul
Purdue (63–42)
Oral Roberts

Tennessee (76–37)
Drake
Pittsburgh (71–61)
James Madison

Mid. Tenn. St. (85–46)
Gonzaga
Ohio State
Marist (67–63)

Marquette (87–58)
La.-Lafayette
Oklahoma (74–60)
SE Missouri State

Mississippi (88–74)
TCU
Maryland (89–65)
Harvard

2006-07 NCAA WOMEN'S DIVISION I INDIVIDUAL LEADERS

SCORING

PLAYER	CLASS	GP	FG	3FG	FT	PTS	AVG
Carrie Moore, Western Michigan	Sr.	32	272	52	217	813	25.4
Crystal Kelly, Western Kentucky	Jr.	28	220	7	220	667	23.8
Courtney Paris, Oklahoma	So.	30	289	0	129	707	23.6
Chrissy Givens, Middle Tennessee St.	Sr.	32	285	25	133	728	22.8
Tye Jackson, Houston	Jr.	22	162	54	117	495	22.5
Alisha Dill, Coastal Carolina	Sr.	29	209	62	172	652	22.5
Angel McCoughtry, Louisville	So.	33	274	41	134	723	21.9
Natalie Doma, Idaho State	Jr.	30	248	8	149	653	21.8
Joi Scott, Murray State	Sr.	26	213	6	133	565	21.7
Carmen Guzman, Ala.-Birmingham	Sr.	30	220	64	142	646	21.5
Adrianne Davie, Arkansas State	Sr.	32	250	16	153	669	20.9

KEY GP=games played; FG=field goals; 3FG=3-point field goals; FT=free throws; PTS=points; AVG=average

LEGENDS

Bridgette Gordon was named the Most Outstanding Player of the Final Four in 1989.

PETER READ MILLER

■ **Bridgette Gordon, guard,** b. April 27, 1967, Deland, Florida. A large part of the foundation of Tennessee's college basketball dynasty was laid by Bridgette Gordon. As a Lady Volunteer, the scrappy Gordon was both an offensive and defensive standout, scoring 2,450 career points—second-highest in school history—and grabbing 338 career steals—a school record. A two-time All-America player, she led Tennessee to a record four straight Final Fours in the late 1980s and helped the school win its first two national titles, in 1987 and 1989. In 1988, she became one of only two women's college players on the gold-medal winning U.S. Olympic team. In between professional stints in Europe, Gordon played two seasons in the WNBA with the Sacramento Monarchs. In 2000, Gordon was elected to the Women's Basketball Hall of Fame.

■ **Jennifer Azzi, guard,** b. August 31, 1968, Oak Ridge, Tennessee. Azzi spent four years at Stanford and was a two-time first-team All-America selection. As a senior during the 1989-90 season, Azzi helped propel the Cardinal to their first national championship. That year, she was named the Most Outstanding Player of the NCAA tournament and was honored with the Wade Trophy, which is given annually to the best women's college basketball player in the nation. She went on to play for the gold-medal winning U.S. Olympic team in 1996 and have an eight-year pro career.

■ **Nancy Lieberman, guard,** b. July 1, 1958, Brooklyn, New York. Lieberman was among women's basketball's early pioneers. At Old Dominion, Lieberman helped the Lady Monarchs win back-to-back national championships in 1979 and 1980. During her college career, she was a three-time All-America player and was the first two-time winner of the Wade Trophy. After college, she went on to play in numerous women's professional basketball leagues, and in 1986, she became the first woman ever to play in a men's pro league when she joined the United States Basketball League. In 1996, the 38-year-old Lieberman came out of retirement to play one season with the WNBA's Phoenix Mercury. That same year, she was elected to the Basketball Hall of Fame.

2006-07 NCAA WOMEN'S DIVISION I INDIVIDUAL LEADERS (cont.)

FIELD GOAL PERCENTAGE

PLAYER	CLASS	GP	FGM	FGA	PCT
Crystal Langhorne, Maryland	Jr.	32	202	280	72.1
Crystal Kelly, Western Kentucky	Jr.	28	220	356	61.8
Jackie McFarland, Colorado	Jr.	29	172	285	60.4
Jessica Davenport, Ohio State	Sr.	31	218	364	59.9
Jenna Real, Loyola (Ill.)	Sr.	28	148	250	59.2
Dani Wright, Brigham Young	Sr.	32	162	274	59.1
Tina Charles, Connecticut	Fr.	32	168	286	58.7
Alysha Clark, Belmont	So.	29	168	286	58.7
Joi Scott, Murray State	Sr.	26	213	365	58.4
Marcedes Walker, Pittsburgh	Jr.	30	185	318	58.2

Note: Minimum 5 field goals made per game.

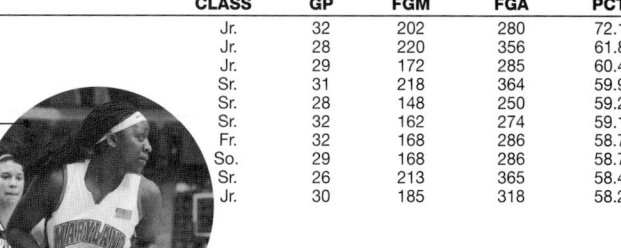

Crystal Langhorne, Maryland

FREE THROW PERCENTAGE

PLAYER	CLASS	GP	FTM	FTA	PCT
Bracey Barker, Maine	Sr.	24	92	100	92.0
Carlynn Savant, Missouri	Sr.	30	104	114	91.2
Chelsea Marandola, Providence	So.	28	87	96	90.6
Stephanie Raymond, Northern Illinois	Sr.	31	163	181	90.1
Jami Montagnino, Tulane	Sr.	31	107	119	89.9
Jordan Sykes, Fairleigh Dickinson	Fr.	29	80	89	89.9
Katie Gearlds, Purdue	Sr.	33	100	112	89.3
Morgan Warburton, Utah	So.	31	129	145	89.0
Julie Briody, New Mexico	Sr.	32	163	184	88.6
Laiken Dollente, Portland	Fr.	30	163	184	88.6

Note: Minimum 2.5 free throws made per game.

REBOUNDING

PLAYER	CLASS	GP	REB	AVG
Lachelle Lyles, Southeast Missouri State	Sr.	30	517	17.2
Courtney Paris, Oklahoma	So.	30	485	16.2
Sylvia Fowles, LSU	Jr.	33	423	12.8
Alysha Clark, Belmont	So.	29	367	12.7
Natalie Doma, Idaho State	Jr.	30	365	12.2
Meredith Alexis, James Madison	Sr.	32	376	11.8
Jillian Roberts, Tulsa	Sr.	30	349	11.6
Stephanie Duda, Cal.-Irvine	Jr.	30	332	11.1
LaJoyce King, Cal-St. Northridge	Sr.	26	284	10.9
Sherell Neal, New Mexico State	Jr.	31	335	10.8

ASSISTS

PLAYER	CLASS	GP	A	APG
Amanda Rego, San Diego	Jr.	29	222	7.7
Kristin Chaney, Southern Miss	Sr.	30	210	7.0
Andrea Benvenuto, James Madison	Sr.	32	217	6.8
Mandy Morales, Montana	So.	30	203	6.8
Kelcey Roegiers-Jensen, Geogia State	Sr.	30	197	6.6
Stephanie Raymond, Northern Illinois	Sr.	31	201	6.5
Mercedes Fox-Griffin, Oregon State	So.	28	180	6.4
Lyndsey Medders, Iowa State	Sr.	31	197	6.4
Ashley Langford, Tulane	So.	31	195	6.3
Brooke Wilhoit, East Tennessee State	Sr.	31	188	6.1

KEY
GP=games played; FGM=field goals made; FGA=field goals attempted; PCT=percentage; FTM=free throws made; FTA=free throws attempted; REB=rebounds; AVG=average; A=assists; APG=assists per game

DID YOU KNOW?

Rutgers' C. Vivian Stringer is the first head coach—male or female—to take teams from three different schools to the NCAA tournament's Final Four. She coached teams from Cheyney State (1982), Iowa (1993), and Rutgers (2000, 2007) to the tourney's semifinals.

3-POINT FIELD GOAL PERCENTAGE

PLAYER	CLASS	GP	3FGM	3FGA	PCT
Brittany Carfora, Columbia	Jr.	27	55	106	51.9
Caroline Williams, Vanderbilt	Sr.	32	89	178	50.0
Kristi Toliver, Maryland	So.	32	66	140	47.1
Kelsey Luna, Indiana State	Fr.	30	79	171	46.2
Candice Wiggins, Stanford	Jr.	27	75	168	44.6
Mel Thomas, Connecticut	Jr.	32	78	181	43.1
Jenna Graber, La Salle	Sr.	30	62	144	43.1
Chandice Cronk, Santa Clara	Jr.	30	94	220	42.7
Ashley Davis, Tennessee State	Sr.	31	74	175	42.3
Leah Phillips, Indiana State	So.	30	65	154	42.2

Note: Minimum 2 3-point field goals made per game.

STEALS

PLAYER	CLASS	GP	STL	SPG
Armintie Price, Mississippi	Sr.	31	118	3.8
Shannon Carlisle, Howard	Sr.	30	111	3.7
Whitney Tossie, Appalachian State	Jr.	31	113	3.6
Amanda Pape, Sacred Heart	Sr.	32	107	3.3
Lele Hardy, Clemson	Fr.	30	98	3.3
Brittany Hollins, Georgia State	So.	30	98	3.3
Jillian Robbins, Tulsa	Sr.	30	98	3.3
Alexis Hornbuckle, Tennessee	Jr.	31	101	3.3

BLOCKS

PLAYER	CLASS	GP	BLK	BPG
Alison Bales, Duke	Sr.	31	140	4.5
Allyssa DeHaan, Michigan State	Fr.	31	138	4.5
Amber Harris, Xavier	Fr.	33	133	4.0
Courtney Paris, Oklahoma	So.	30	105	3.5
Katja Bavendam, St. Francis (N.Y.)	Jr.	31	98	3.2
LaToya Pringle, North Carolina	Jr.	33	104	3.2
Hope Foster, Bucknell	Jr.	30	93	3.1
Lasma Jekabsone, Florida Int'l	Sr.	30	92	3.1
Lacey Cormier', Grambling	Sr.	28	85	3.0
Lindsay Wisdom-Hylton, Purdue	Jr.	33	99	3.0

Alison Bales, Duke

MAX TURNER/ICON SMI

KEY GP=games played; 3FGM=3-point field goals made; 3FGA=3-point field goals attempted; PCT=percentage; STL=steals; SPG=steals per game; BLK=blocks; BPG=blocks per game

NCAA WOMEN'S DIVISION I CHAMPIONSHIP RESULTS

YEAR	WINNER	SCORE	RUNNER-UP	WINNING COACH
2007	Tennessee	59–46	Rutgers	Pat Summitt
2006	Maryland	78–75 (OT)	Duke	Brenda Frese
2005	Baylor	84–62	Michigan State	Kim Mulkey-Robertson
2004	Connecticut	70–61	Tennessee	Geno Auriemma
2003	Connecticut	73–68	Tennessee	Geno Auriemma
2002	Connecticut	82–70	Oklahoma	Geno Auriemma
2001	Notre Dame	68–66	Purdue	Muffet McGraw
2000	Connecticut	71–52	Tennessee	Geno Auriemma
1999	Purdue	62–45	Duke	Carolyn Peck
1998	Tennessee	93–75	Louisiana Tech	Pat Summitt
1997	Tennessee	68–59	Old Dominion	Pat Summitt
1996	Tennessee	83–65	Georgia	Pat Summitt
1995	Connecticut	70–64	Tennessee	Geno Auriemma
1994	North Carolina	60–59	Louisiana Tech	Sylvia Hatchell
1993	Texas Tech	84–82	Ohio State	Marsha Sharp
1992	Stanford	78–62	Western Kentucky	Tara VanDerveer
1991	Tennessee	70–67 (OT)	Virginia	Pat Summitt
1990	Stanford	88–81	Auburn	Tara VanDerveer
1989	Tennessee	76–60	Auburn	Pat Summitt
1988	Louisiana Tech	56–54	Auburn	Leon Barmore
1987	Tennessee	67–44	Louisiana Tech	Pat Summitt
1986	Texas	97–81	USC	Jody Conradt
1985	Old Dominion	70–65	Georgia	Marianne Stanley
1984	USC	72–61	Tennessee	Linda Sharp
1983	USC	69–67	Louisiana Tech	Linda Sharp
1982	Louisiana Tech	76–62	Cheyney State	Sonja Hogg/Leon Barmore

TRIVIA CHALLENGE

1 Only two players in the history of NCAA Division I women's basketball have scored 3,000 points and grabbed 1,500 rebounds during their college careers. Patricia Haskins is one; can you name the other?
a. Chamique Holdsclaw
b. Cheryl Miller
c. Diana Taurasi

2 During the 2005–06 season, freshman Oklahoma center Courtney Paris set the all-time NCAA single-season record in which category?
a. Rebounds
b. Blocks
c. Assists

3 Tennessee has won seven NCAA titles, more than any other school. But how many times have the Lady Volunteers *lost* in a national title game?
a. 1
b. 3
c. 5

4 The three-point line is farther from the hoop in men's college basketball than it is for women's college games.
a. True
b. False

5 In 2003 and again in 2004, the same two schools played each other in the NCAA national championship game. Name both teams.
a. Connecticut and Tennessee
b. Tennessee and Louisiana Tech
c. North Carolina and Duke

6 Which active Division I head coach is the only one to have had two undefeated seasons during their career?
a. Pat Summitt
b. C. Vivian Stringer
c. Geno Auriemma

7 In what year did the NCAA Division I women's basketball tournament expand to 64 teams?
a. 1984
b. 1994
c. 2004

8 In which decade did these milestones in women's basketball take place: Women's hoops made its Olympics debut, the sport's first Top 20 college poll was published, and Ann Meyers tried out with the NBA's Indiana Pacers?
a. The 1970s
b. The 1980s
c. The 1990s

Courtney Paris

AP PHOTO/SUE OGROCKI

Trivia Challenge: 1. b; 2. a; 3. c; 4. b; 5. a; 6. c; 7. b; 8. a.

FAST FACT

Only five women's college basketball head coaches have won multiple titles: Tennessee's Pat Summitt (9), Connecticut's Geno Auriemma (5), Stanford's Tara VanDerVeer (2), USC's Linda Sharp (2), and Louisiana Tech's Leon Barmore (2).

SIKIDS.com

Visit our website for the latest stats and sports info.

NCAA WOMEN'S DIVISION I SINGLE-SEASON LEADERS

POINTS

PLAYER	YEAR	GP	PTS
Jackie Stiles, Southwest Missouri State*	2001	35	1,062
Cindy Brown, Long Beach State	1987	35	974
Genia Miller, California State-Fullerton	1991	33	969
Sheryl Swoopes, Texas Tech	1993	34	955
Andrea Congreaves, Mercer	1992	28	925
Wanda Ford, Drake	1986	30	919
Chamique Holdsclaw, Tennessee	1998	39	915
Barbara Kennedy, Clemson	1982	31	908
Patricia Hoskins, Mississippi Valley State	1989	27	908
LaTaunya Pollard, Long Beach State	1983	31	907

SCORING AVERAGE

PLAYER	YEAR	GP	FG	3FG	FT	PTS	AVG
Patricia Hoskins, Mississippi Valley State	1989	27	345	13	205	908	33.6
Andrea Congreaves, Mercer	1992	28	353	77	142	925	33.0
Deborah Temple, Delta State	1984	28	373	—	127	873	31.2
Andrea Congreaves, Mercer	1993	26	302	51	150	805	31.0
Wanda Ford, Drake	1986	30	390	—	139	919	30.6
Anucha Brown, Northwestern	1985	28	341	—	173	855	30.5
LeChandra LeDay, Grambling	1988	28	334	36	146	850	30.4
Jackie Stiles, Southwest Missouri State*	2001	35	365	65	267	1,062	30.3
Kim Perrot, La.-Lafayette	1990	28	309	95	128	841	30.0

* Now known as Missouri State.

TODAY'S STARS

■ **Sylvia Fowles, center,** b. October 6, 1985, Miami, Florida. Nicknamed "Big Syl," the 6'6" Fowles had already made a name for herself before reaching college when she became the first female player to dunk in a high school game. In her first three seasons at LSU, she continued to dominate inside the paint and scored 1,626 career points. In 2007, Fowles averaged 17.2 points, 12.8 rebounds, and 1.9 blocks per game and helped LSU reach the Final Four. She was a unanimous choice for first-team All-SEC honors and was also named a second-team All-America center.

In 2007, Sylvia Fowles recorded a double-double in all 14 SEC games, a first in conference history.

■ **Crystal Langhorne, forward,** b. October 27, 1986, Willingboro, New Jersey. Langhorne made an immediate impact after coming to Maryland in 2004, and was recognized as the ACC Rookie of the year as a freshman. As a sophomore, Langhorne not only led the nation in shooting percentage (65.7), she also led the Terrapins to their first national title. During the 2006–07 season, Langhorne was again the most accurate shooter in the country and was named an All-America player for the second straight season.

■ **Kia Vaughn, center,** b. January 24, 1987, Bronx, New York. The 6'4" Vaughn had a breakout season in 2006-07, leading her Rutgers team in scoring average (12.8) as well as rebounds (9.3) and blocks (2.6) per game. Thanks to the sophomore's powerful play in the post, the Scarlet Knights rebounded from a rocky 2–4 start and went on to win their first Big East conference tournament title and play their way into the NCAA tournament's national championship game. Although Tennessee beat Rutgers, Vaughn still sparkled, leading her team with 20 points and 10 rebounds in the championship game.

HOCKEY

Brothers Rob (left) and Scott Niedermayer led the Anaheim Ducks to their first Stanley Cup title.

DAVID E. KLUTHO

Even as new players made their presence known, some big-name veterans continued to flex their scoring muscle. Brendan Shanahan and Jaromir Jagr of the Rangers and Joe Sakic of the Avalanche all reached the 600-goal mark in their career. Mats Sundin of the Maple Leafs, Teemu Selanne of the Ducks, Peter Bondra of the Blackhawks, and Mike Modano of the Stars all joined the 500-goal club.

The swift Buffalo Sabres skated circles around their opponents and took home the Presidents' Trophy with the

NHL TEAMS

EASTERN CONFERENCE
Atlanta Thrashers
Boston Bruins
Buffalo Sabres
Carolina Hurricanes
Florida Panthers
Montreal Canadiens
New Jersey Devils
New York Islanders
New York Rangers
Ottawa Senators
Philadelphia Flyers
Pittsburgh Penguins
Tampa Bay Lightning
Toronto Maple Leafs
Washington Capitals

WESTERN CONFERENCE
Anaheim Ducks
Calgary Flames
Chicago Blackhawks
Colorado Avalanche
Columbus Blue Jackets
Dallas Stars
Detroit Red Wings
Edmonton Oilers
Los Angeles Kings
Minnesota Wild
Nashville Predators
Phoenix Coyotes
San Jose Sharks
St. Louis Blues
Vancouver Canucks

The 2006–07 season was the second under new NHL rules designed to increase offense. The league's top teams continued to develop a style of play that was both fast-paced and physical, and no squad evolved more than Anaheim. Before the season, the Ducks dropped the "Mighty" from their name and ditched their cartoonish purple uniforms. Dressed in no-nonsense brown, the Ducks were the NHL's toughest team. They proved to be the league's best, as well, winning the Stanley Cup for the first time.

There were other changes during a busy season on the ice. First the NHL All-Star Game returned after a two-year break and the West defeated the East, 12–9. Daniel Briere of the Buffalo Sabres had a goal and four assists and was named the game's MVP despite playing for the losing team.

Pittsburgh continued to be the center of the NHL's wave of young talent. Evgeni Malkin of the Penguins led all rookies in goals (33) and points (85). Teammate Jordan Staal became the youngest player (18 years, 153 days) to score a hat-trick. But both young Pens took a back seat to 19-year-old Sidney Crosby. The Pittsburgh superstar led the NHL in points (120) and assists (84). He became the first teenager to lead a major North American team sport in scoring for a season.

Ottawa's Daniel Alfredsson (right) powered the Senators to their first Stanley Cup Final appearance.

LOU CAPOZZOLA (2)

Not yet 20 years old, Pittsburgh's Sidney Crosby scored a league-high 120 points and was named the NHL's Most Valuable Player.

league's best record (53 wins, 113 points), ending the Detroit Red Wings' two-year reign. Detroit still finished atop the Western Conference (50, 113), with veteran goalie Dominik Hasek leading the way (2.05 goals-against average).

Grit prevailed over pure skill in the playoffs, however. The Ottawa Senators played tough and shut down the Sabres four games to one in the Eastern Conference finals. The Ducks downed the Red Wings four games to two in the bruising Western Conference finals. That set up a Stanley Cup showdown between Anaheim and Ottawa. The Ducks did what no other team had been able to, by shutting down the Sens' feared top line of Daniel Alfredsson, Jason Spezza, and Dany Heatley. Anaheim won the series and the Cup, four games to one, with Ducks defenseman Scott Niedermayer winning the Conn Smythe trophy as the postseason MVP.

NHL 2006-2007 FINAL STANDINGS

Atlantic Division

	GP	W	L	OTL	GF	GA	PTS
y-New Jersey	82	49	24	9	216	201	107
x-Pittsburgh	82	47	24	11	277	246	105
x-NY Rangers	82	42	30	10	242	216	94
x-NY Islanders	82	40	30	12	248	240	92
Philadelphia	82	22	48	12	214	303	56

Central Division

	GP	W	L	OTL	GF	GA	PTS
yz-Detroit	82	50	19	13	254	199	113
x-Nashville	82	51	23	8	272	212	110
St. Louis	82	34	35	13	214	254	81
Columbus	82	33	42	7	201	249	73
Chicago	82	33	42	7	201	249	71

Northeast Division

	GP	W	L	OTL	GF	GA	PTS
yz-Buffalo	82	53	22	7	308	242	113
x-Ottawa	82	48	25	9	288	222	105
Toronto	82	40	31	11	258	269	91
Montreal	82	42	34	6	245	256	90
Boston	82	35	41	6	219	289	76

Northwest Division

	GP	W	L	OTL	GF	GA	PTS
y-Vancouver	82	49	26	7	222	201	105
x-Minnesota	82	48	26	8	235	191	104
x-Calgary	82	43	29	10	258	226	96
Colorado	82	44	31	7	272	251	95
Edmonton	82	32	43	7	195	248	71

Southeast Division

	GP	W	L	OTL	GF	GA	PTS
y-Atlanta	82	43	28	11	246	245	97
x-Tampa Bay	82	44	33	5	253	261	93
Carolina	82	40	34	8	241	253	88
Florida	82	35	31	16	247	257	86
Washington	82	28	40	14	235	286	70

Pacific Division

	GP	W	L	OTL	GF	GA	PTS
y-Anaheim	82	48	20	14	258	208	110
x-San Jose	82	51	26	5	258	199	107
x-Dallas	82	50	25	7	226	197	107
Los Angeles	82	27	41	14	227	283	68
Phoenix	82	31	46	5	216	284	67

KEY GP=games played; W=win; L=loss; OTL=overtime loss; GF=goals for; GA=goals against; PTS=points; GF/GA include team goals awarded in shootout victories; x=clinched playoff spot; y=clinched division title; z=clinched best record in conference

2007 STANLEY CUP CHAMPIONSHIP

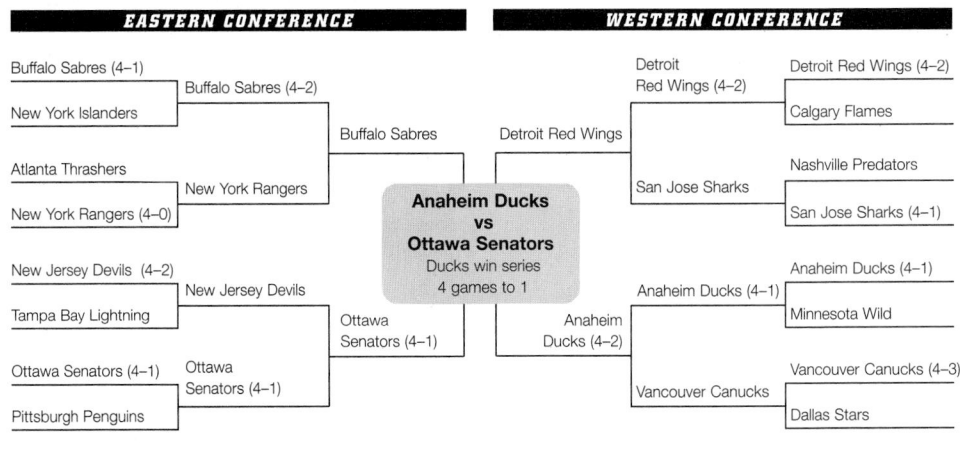

EASTERN CONFERENCE   **WESTERN CONFERENCE**

Buffalo Sabres (4–1)

Buffalo Sabres (4–2)

New York Islanders

Buffalo Sabres   Detroit Red Wings

Atlanta Thrashers

New York Rangers

New York Rangers (4–0)

New Jersey Devils (4–2)

New Jersey Devils

Tampa Bay Lightning

Ottawa Senators (4–1)   Ottawa Senators (4–1)

Ottawa Senators (4–1)   Ottawa Senators (4–1)

Pittsburgh Penguins

Anaheim Ducks
vs
Ottawa Senators
Ducks win series
4 games to 1

Detroit Red Wings (4–2)   Detroit Red Wings (4–2)

Calgary Flames

San Jose Sharks   Nashville Predators

San Jose Sharks (4–1)

Anaheim Ducks (4–1)   Anaheim Ducks (4–1)

Minnesota Wild

Anaheim Ducks (4–2)

Vancouver Canucks   Vancouver Canucks (4–3)

Dallas Stars

QUARTERFINALS   SEMIFINALS   FINALS   STANLEY CUP   FINALS   SEMIFINALS   QUARTERFINALS

2007 STANLEY CUP PLAYOFF RESULTS

Conference Quarterfinals

EASTERN CONFERENCE

Buffalo Sabres vs. New York Islanders
GAME 1. April 12 – Sabres 4, Islanders 1
GAME 2. April 14 – Islanders 3, Sabres 2
GAME 3. April 16 – Sabres 3, Islanders 2
GAME 4. April 18 – Sabres 4, Islanders 2
GAME 5. April 20 – Sabres 4, Isanders 3
Sabres win series 4–1.

New Jersey Devils vs. Tampa Bay Lightning
GAME 1. April 12 – Devils 5, Lightning 3
GAME 2. April 14 – Lightning 3, Devils 2
GAME 3. April 16 – Lightning 3, Devils 2
GAME 4. April 18 – Devils 4, Lightning 3 (OT)
GAME 5. April 20 – Devils 3, Lightning 0
GAME 6. April 22 – Devils 3, Lightning 2
Devils win series 4–2.

Atlanta Thrashers vs. New York Rangers
GAME 1. April 12 – NY Rangers 4, Thrashers 3
GAME 2. April 14 – NY Rangers 2, Thrashers 1
GAME 3. April 17 – NY Rangers 7, Thrashers 0
GAME 4. April 18 – NY Rangers 4, Thrashers 2
Rangers win series 4–0.

Ottawa Senators vs. Pittsburgh Penguins
GAME 1. April 11 – Senators 6, Penguins 3
GAME 2. April 14 – Penguins 4, Senators 3
GAME 3. April 15 – Senators 4, Penguins 2
GAME 4. April 17 – Senators 2, Penguins 1
GAME 5. April 19 – Senators 3, Penguins 0
Senators win series 4–1.

WESTERN CONFERENCE

Detroit Red Wings vs. Calgary Flames
GAME 1. April 12 – Red Wings 4, Flames 1
GAME 2. April 15 – Red Wings 3, Flames 1
GAME 3. April 17 – Flames 3, Red Wings 2
GAME 4. April 19 – Flames 3, Red Wings 2
GAME 5. April 21 – Red Wings 5, Flames 1
GAME 6. April 22– Red Wings 2, Flames 1 (2OT)
Red Wings win series 4–2.

Anaheim Ducks vs. Minnesota Wild
GAME 1. April 11 – Ducks 2, Wild 1
GAME 2. April 13 – Ducks 3, Wild 2
GAME 3. April 15 – Ducks 2, Wild 1
GAME 4. April 17 – Wild 4, Ducks 1
GAME 5. April 19 – Ducks 4, Wild 1
Ducks win series 4–1.

Vancouver Canucks vs. Dallas Stars
GAME 1. April 11 – Canucks 5, Stars 4 (OT)
GAME 2. April 13 – Stars 2, Canucks 0
GAME 3. April 15 – Canucks 2, Stars 1 (OT)
GAME 4. April 17 – Canucks 2, Stars 1
GAME 5. April 19 – Stars 1, Canucks 0 (OT)
GAME 6. April 21 – Stars 2, Canucks 0
GAME 7. April 23 – Canucks 4, Stars 1
Canucks win series 4–3.

Nashville Predators vs. San Jose Sharks
GAME 1. Apr 11 – Sharks 5, Predators 4 (2OT)
GAME 2. Apr 13 – Predators 5, Sharks 2
GAME 3. Apr 16 – Sharks 3, Predators 1
GAME 4. Apr 18 – Sharks 3, Predators 2
GAME 5. Apr 20 – Sharks 3, Predators 2
Sharks win series 4–1.

Conference Semifinals

EASTERN CONFERENCE

Buffalo Sabres vs. New York Rangers
GAME 1. April 25– Sabres 5, Rangers 2
GAME 2. April 27 – Sabres 3, Rangers 2
GAME 3. April 29 – Rangers 2, Sabres 1 (2OT)
GAME 4. May 1 – Rangers 2, Sabres 1
GAME 5. May 4 – Sabres 2, Rangers 1 (OT)
GAME 6. May 6 – Sabres 5, Rangers 4
Sabres win series 4–2.

Ottawa Senators vs. New Jersey Devils
GAME 1. April 26 – Senators 5, Devils 4
GAME 2. April 28 – Devils 3, Senators 2 (2OT)
GAME 3. April 30 – Senators 2, Devils 0
GAME 4. May 2 – Senators 3, Devils 2
GAME 5. May 5 – Senators, 3, Devils 2
Senators win series 4–1.

WESTERN CONFERENCE

San Jose Sharks vs. Detroit Red Wings
GAME 1. April 26 – Sharks 2, Red Wings 0
GAME 2. April 28 – Red Wings 3, Sharks 2
GAME 3. April 30 – Sharks 2, Red Wings 1
GAME 4. May 2 – Red Wings 3, Sharks 2 (OT)
GAME 5. May 5 – Red Wings 4, Sharks 1
GAME 6. May 6 – Red Wings 2, Sharks 0
Red Wings win series 4–2.

Anaheim Ducks vs. Vancouver Canucks
GAME 1. April 25 – Ducks 5, Canucks 1
GAME 2. April 27 – Canucks 2, Ducks 1 (2OT)
GAME 3. April 29 – Ducks 3, Canucks 2
GAME 4. May 1 – Ducks 3, Canucks 2 (OT)
GAME 5. May 3 – Ducks 2, Canucks 1 (2OT)
Ducks win series 4–1.

Conference Finals

EASTERN CONFERENCE

Buffalo Sabres vs. Ottawa Senators
GAME 1. May 10 – Senators 5, Sabres 2
GAME 2. May 12 – Senators 4, Sabres 3 (2OT)
GAME 3. May 14 – Senators 1, Sabres 0
GAME 4. May 16 – Sabres 3, Senators 2
GAME 5. May 19 – Senators 3, Sabres 2 (OT)
Senators win series 4–1.

WESTERN CONFERENCE

Detroit Red Wings vs. Anaheim Ducks
GAME 1. May 11 – Red Wings 2, Ducks 1
GAME 2. May 13 – Ducks 4, Red Wings 3 (OT)
GAME 3. May 15 – Red Wings 5, Ducks 0
GAME 4. May 17 – Ducks 5, Red Wings 3
GAME 5. May 20 – Ducks 2, Red Wings 1 (OT)
GAME 6. May 22 – Ducks 4, Red Wings 3
Ducks win series 4-2.

Stanley Cup Final

Ottawa Senators vs. Anaheim Ducks
GAME 1. May 28 – Ducks 3, Senators 2
GAME 2. May 30 – Ducks 1, Senators 0
GAME 3. June 2 – Senators 5, Ducks 3
GAME 4. June 4 – Ducks 3, Senators 2
GAME 5. June 6 – Ducks 6, Senators 2
Ducks win series 4-1.

STANLEY CUP CHAMPIONSHIP BOX SCORES

Game 1: May 28, 2007 — Anaheim 3, Ottawa 2

	1st	2nd	3rd	Total
Ottawa	1	1	0	2
Anaheim	1	0	2	3

1st Period Scoring
Ottawa 1:38, Mike Fisher (power play)
　(Andrej Meszaros, Mike Comrie)
Anaheim 10:55, Andy McDonald (Teemu Selanne)
2nd Period Scoring
Ottawa 4:36, Wade Redden (power play)
　(Daniel Alfredsson, Jason Spezza)
3rd Period Scoring
Anaheim 5:44, Ryan Getzlaf (Corey Perry, Ric Jackman)
Anaheim 17:09, Travis Moen (Rob Niedermayer, Scott
　Niedermayer)

Game 2: May 30, 2007— Anaheim 1, Ottawa 0

	1st	2nd	3rd	Total
Ottawa	0	0	0	0
Anaheim	0	0	1	1

3rd Period Scoring
Anaheim 14:16, Samuel Pahlsson (unassisted)

Game 3: June 2, 2007 — Ottawa 5, Anaheim 3

	1st	2nd	3rd	Total
Ottawa	1	3	1	5
Anaheim	1	2	0	3

1st Period Scoring
Anaheim 5:39, Andy McDonald (power play) (Teemu Selanne)
Ottawa 16:10, Chris Neil (Chris Kelly, Andrej Meszaros)
2nd Period Scoring
Anaheim 5:20, Corey Perry (Dustin Penner, Ryan Getzlaf)
Ottawa 5:47, Mike Fisher (Anton Volchenkov)
Anaheim 7:38, Ryan Getzlaf (Dustin Penner, Corey Perry)
Ottawa 16:14, Daniel Alfredsson (power play) (Wade Redden,
　Joseph Corvo)
Ottawa 18:34, Dean McAmmond (Oleg Saprykin, Christoph
　Schubert)
3rd Period Scoring
Ottawa 8:22, Anton Volchenkov (Antoine Vermette, Chris
　Kelly)

STANLEY CUP CHAMPIONSHIP BOX SCORES (cont.)

Game 4: June 4, 2007 — Anaheim 3, Ottawa 2

	1st	2nd	3rd	Total
Ottawa	1	1	0	2
Anaheim	0	2	1	3

1st Period Scoring
Ottawa 19:59, Daniel Alfredsson (power play) (Peter Schaefer, Mike Fisher)

2nd Period Scoring
Anaheim 10:06, Andy McDonald (Todd Marchant, Corey Perry)
Anaheim 11:06, Andy McDonald (Rob Niedermayer, Sean O'Donnell)
Ottawa 18:00, Dany Heatley (Patrick Eaves, Jason Spezza)

3rd Period Scoring
Anaheim 4:07, Dustin Penner (Teemu Selanne, Andy McDonald)

Game 5: June 6, 2007 — Anaheim 6, Ottawa 2

	1st	2nd	3rd	Total
Ottawa	0	2	0	2
Anaheim	2	2	2	6

1st Period Scoring
Anaheim 3:41, Andy McDonald (power play) (Ryan Getzlaf, Chris Pronger)
Anaheim 17:41, Rob Niedermayer (Corey Perry)

2nd Period Scoring
Ottawa 11:27, Daniel Alfredsson (Peter Schaefer, Mike Fisher)
Anaheim 15:44, Travis Moen (unassisted)
Ottawa 17:38, Daniel Alfredsson (shorthanded) (unassisted)
Anaheim 18:28, Francois Beauchemin (power play) (Andy McDonald)

3rd Period Scoring
Anaheim 4:01, Travis Moen (Scott Niedermayer, Samuel Pahlsson)
Anaheim 17:00, Corey Perry (unassisted)

DID YOU KNOW?

The original Stanley Cup was purchased by Lord Stanley, the Governor General of Canada, in 1892 for roughly $50. The silver cup was 11½ inches across and only 9½ inches high at the time. Today, the Stanley Cup weighs more than 35 pounds and stands 35¼ inches tall thanks to several additional sections that have been added to the base to accommodate all of the engraved names of the winning teams and their players over the years. Henri Richard holds the record for the player whose name appears the most number of times on the Cup with 11, while Scotty Bowman holds the same record for coaches, with 9.

2006–2007 NHL INDIVIDUAL LEADERS

SCORING

Points

PLAYER	GP	PTS
Sidney Crosby, Penguins	79	120
Joe Thornton, Sharks	82	114
Vincent Lecavalier, Lightning	82	108
Dany Heatley, Senators	82	105
Martin St. Louis, Lightning	82	102
Marian Hossa, Thrashers	82	100
Joe Sakic, Avalanche	82	100
Jaromir Jagr, Rangers	82	96
Marc Savard, Bruins	82	96
Daniel Briere, Sabres	81	95
Teemu Selanne, Ducks	82	94
Jarome Iginla, Flames	70	94
Alexander Ovechkin, Capitals	82	92
Olli Jokinen, Panthers	82	91
Jason Spezza, Senators	67	87
Daniel Alfredsson, Senators	77	87
Pavel Datsyuk, Red Wings	79	87
Evgeni Malkin, Penguins	78	85
Thomas Vanek, Sabres	82	84
Daniel Sedin, Canucks	81	84

Goals

PLAYER	GP	G
Vincent Lecavalier, Lightning	82	52
Dany Heatley, Senators	82	50
Teemu Selanne, Ducks	82	48
Alexander Ovechkin, Capitals	82	46
Martin St. Louis, Lightning	82	43
Marian Hossa, Thrashers	82	43
Thomas Vanek, Sabres	82	43
Ilya Kovalchuk, Thrashers	82	42
Simon Gagne, Penguins	76	41
Jason Blake, Islanders	82	40
Jarome Iginla, Flames	70	39
Olli Jokinen, Panthers	82	39
Alexander Semin, Capitals	77	38
Jonathan Cheechoo, Sharks	76	37
Chris Drury, Sabres	77	37
Sidney Crosby, Penguins	79	36
Joe Sakic, Avalanche	82	36
Daniel Sedin, Canucks	81	36
Ryan Smyth, Islanders	71	36
Bill Guerin, Sharks	77	36

SCORING (cont'd)
Assists

PLAYER	GP	A
Joe Thornton, Sharks	82	92
Sidney Crosby, Penguins	79	84
Marc Savard, Bruins	82	74
Henrik Sedin, Canucks	82	71
Jaromir Jagr, Rangers	82	66
Joe Sakic, Avalanche	82	64
Daniel Briere, Sabres	81	63
Pavel Datsyuk, Red Wings	79	60
Martin St. Louis, Lightning	82	59
Alex Tanguay, Flames	81	59
Daniel Alfredsson, Senators	77	58
Marian Hossa, Thrashers	82	57
Michael Nylander, Rangers	79	57
Vincent Lecavalier, Lightning	82	56
Andrew Brunette, Avalanche	82	56
Rod Brind'Amour, Hurricanes	78	56
Dany Heatley, Senators	82	55
Jarome Iginla, Flames	70	55
Scott Niedermayer, Ducks	79	54
Sergei Gonchar, Penguins	82	54

Plus/Minus

PLAYER	GP	+/-
Thomas Vanek, Sabres	82	47
Daniel Alfredsson, Senators	77	42
Nicklas Lidstrom, Red Wings	80	40
Tom Preissing, Senators	80	40
Derek Roy, Sabres	75	37
Anton Volchenkov, Senators	78	37
Pavel Datsyuk, Red Wings	79	36
Chris Phillips, Senators	82	36
Marek Malik, Rangers	69	32
Dany Heatley, Senators	82	31
Christoph Schubert, Senators	80	30
Brian Campbell, Sabres	82	28
Chris Kelly, Senators	82	28
Chris Pronger, Ducks	66	27
Robyn Regehr, Flames	78	27
Jaromir Jagr, Rangers	82	26
Henrik Zetterberg, Red Wings	63	26
Teemu Selanne, Ducks	82	26
Jason Pominville, Sabres	82	25
Danny Markov, Red Wings	66	25

Note: +/- = plus minus rating (A player is awarded a plus (+1) each time he is on the ice when his team scores an even-strength or shorthanded goal. He receives a minus (-1) each time he is on the ice when the opposing team scores an even-strength or short-handed goal. Power-play goals are not included in the rating.)

KEY
A=assists; G=goals; GP=games played; GA=goals allowed; GAA=goals-against average; OTL=overtime loss; +/-=plus/minus; PTS=points; SA=shots allowed; SV%=save percentage; SO=shutouts

GOAL TENDING
Goals-Against Average

PLAYER	GP	GAA
Niklas Backstrom, Wild	41	1.97
Dominik Hasek, Red Wings	56	2.05
Martin Brodeur, Devils	78	2.18
Marty Turco, Stars	67	2.23
Jean-Sebastien Giguere, Ducks	56	2.26
Roberto Luongo, Canucks	76	2.29
Evgeni Nabokov, Sharks	50	2.29
Henrik Lundqvist, Rangers	70	2.34
Vesa Toskala, Sharks	38	2.35
Chris Mason, Predators	40	2.38
Tomas Vokoun, Predators	44	2.40
Miikka Kiprusoff, Flames	74	2.46
Ray Emery, Senators	58	2.47
Ilja Bryzgalov, Ducks	27	2.47
Manny Fernandez, Wild	44	2.55
Rick Dipietro, Islanders	62	2.58
Manny Legace, Blues	45	2.59
Mathieu Garon, Kings	32	2.66
Peter Budaj, Avalanche	57	2.68
Ryan Miller, Sabres	63	2.73

Shutouts

PLAYER	GP	W	L	OTL	SO
Martin Brodeur, Devils	78	48	23	7	12
Dominik Hasek, Red Wings	56	38	11	6	8
Miikka Kiprusoff, Flames	74	40	24	9	7
Evgeni Nabokov, Sharks	50	25	16	4	7
Marty Turco, Stars	67	38	20	5	6
Roberto Luongo, Canucks	76	47	22	6	5
Marc-Andre Fleury, Penguins	67	40	16	9	5
Henrik Lundqvist, Rangers	70	37	22	8	5
Ray Emery, Senators	58	33	16	6	5
Rick Dipietro, Islanders	62	32	19	9	5

Save Percentage

PLAYER	GP	GA	SA	SV%	W	L	OTL
Niklas Backstrom, Wild	41	73	1,028	.929	23	8	6
Chris Mason, Predators	40	93	1,244	.925	24	11	4
Martin Brodeur, Devils	78	171	2,182	.922	48	23	7
Roberto Luongo, Canucks	76	171	2,169	.921	47	22	6
Tomas Vokoun, Predators	44	104	1,299	.920	27	12	4
Rick Dipietro, Islanders	62	156	1,917	.919	32	19	9
Ray Emery, Senators	58	138	1,691	.918	33	16	6
J. Giguere, Ducks	56	122	1,490	.918	36	10	8
Miikka Kiprusoff, Flames	74	181	2,190	.917	40	24	9
Henrik Lundqvist, Rangers	70	160	1,927	.917	37	22	8

Wins

PLAYER	GP	W	L	OTL
Martin Brodeur, Devils	78	48	23	7
Roberto Luongo, Canucks	76	47	22	6
Marc-Andre Fleury, Penguins	67	40	16	9
Ryan Miller, Sabres	63	40	16	6
Miikka Kiprusoff, Flames	74	40	24	9
Dominik Hasek, Red Wings	56	38	11	6
Marty Turco, Stars	67	38	20	5
Henrik Lundqvist, Rangers	70	37	22	8
Andrew Raycroft, Maple Leafs	72	37	25	9
J. Giguere, Ducks	56	36	10	8

NHL TEAM-BY-TEAM STATS

ANAHEIM DUCKS

PLAYER	GP	G	A	PTS	+/-	PIM
Teemu Selanne	82	48	46	94	26	82
Andy McDonald	82	27	51	78	16	46
Scott Niedermayer	79	15	54	69	6	86
Chris Kunitz	81	25	35	60	23	81
Chris Pronger	66	13	46	59	27	69
Ryan Getzlaf	82	25	33	58	17	66
Dustin Penner	82	29	16	45	-2	58
Corey Perry	82	17	27	44	12	55
Francois Beauchemin	71	7	21	28	7	49
Samuel Pahlsson	82	8	18	26	-4	42
Todd Marchant	56	8	15	23	7	44
Travis Moen	82	11	10	21	-4	101
Sean O'Donnell	79	2	15	17	9	92
Rob Niedermayer	82	5	11	16	-8	77
Shane O'Brien	62	2	12	14	5	140
Ric Jackman	24	1	10	11	3	10
Ryan Shannon	53	2	9	11	-2	10
Shawn Thornton	48	2	7	9	3	88
Joe DiPenta	76	2	6	8	1	48
Todd Fedoruk	10	0	3	3	2	36

GOALTENDER	GP	GA	SA	GAA	SV	SV%	SO
Jean-Sebastien Giguere	56	122	1,490	2.26	1,368	.918	4
Ilya Bryzgalov	27	62	668	2.47	606	.907	1

ATLANTA THRASHERS

PLAYER	GP	G	A	PTS	+/-	PIM
Marian Hossa	82	43	57	100	18	49
Slava Kozlov	81	28	52	80	9	36
Ilya Kovalchuk	82	42	34	76	-2	66
Scott Mellanby	69	12	24	36	-9	63
Bobby Holik	82	11	18	29	-3	86
Jon Sim	77	17	12	29	-1	60
Glen Metropolit	57	12	16	28	9	20
Greg de Vries	82	3	21	24	-3	66
Niclas Havelid	77	3	18	21	-2	52
Steve Rucchin	47	5	16	21	-4	14
Jim Slater	74	5	14	19	8	62
Steve McCarthy	46	4	12	16	4	24
Andy Sutton	55	2	14	16	6	76
Eric Belanger	24	9	6	15	0	12
Keith Tkachuk	18	7	8	15	8	34
Alexei Zhitnik	18	2	12	14	4	14
Brad Larsen	72	7	6	13	-11	39
J.P. Vigier	72	5	8	13	0	27
Niko Kapanen	60	4	9	13	-12	20
Shane Hnidy	72	5	7	12	15	63
Vitaly Vishnevski	52	3	9	12	-5	31
Garnet Exelby	58	2	8	10	2	56

GOALTENDER	GP	GA	SA	GAA	SV	SV%	SO
Kari Lehtonen	68	183	2,075	2.79	1,892	.912	4
Johan Hedberg	21	51	500	2.89	449	.898	0

BOSTON BRUINS

PLAYER	GP	G	A	PTS	+/-	PIM
Marc Savard	82	22	74	96	-19	96
Patrice Bergeron	77	22	48	70	-28	26
Glen Murray	59	28	17	45	-12	44
Marco Sturm	76	27	17	44	-24	46
Zdeno Chara	80	11	32	43	-21	100
Brad Boyes	62	13	21	34	-17	25
Phil Kessel	70	11	18	29	-12	12
P.J. Axelsson	55	11	16	27	-10	52
Brandon Bochenski	31	11	11	22	3	14
Paul Mara	59	3	15	18	-22	95
Shean Donovan	76	6	11	17	-13	56
Mark Mowers	78	5	12	17	-10	26
Brad Stuart	48	7	10	17	-22	26
Wayne Primeau	51	7	8	15	-15	75
Petr Tenkrat	64	9	5	14	-16	34
Stanislav Chistov	60	5	8	13	-8	36
Andrew Alberts	76	0	10	10	-15	124
Jason York	49	1	7	8	-14	32
Petr Kalus	9	4	1	5	0	6

GOALTENDER	GP	GA	SA	GAA	SV	SV%	SO
Tim Thomas	66	189	1,985	3.13	1,796	.905	3
Hannu Toivonen	18	63	502	4.23	439	.875	0
Joey MacDonald	7	16	195	2.68	179	.918	0

BUFFALO SABRES

PLAYER	GP	G	A	PTS	+/-	PIM
Daniel Briere	81	32	63	95	17	89
Thomas Vanek	82	43	41	84	47	40
Chris Drury	77	37	32	69	1	30
Jason Pominville	82	34	34	68	25	30
Derek Roy	75	21	42	63	37	60
Maxim Afinogenov	56	23	38	61	19	66
Jochen Hecht	76	19	37	56	19	39
Brian Campbell	82	6	42	48	28	35
Ales Kotalik	66	16	22	38	-5	46
Dmitri Kalinin	82	7	22	29	19	36
Teppo Numminen	79	2	27	29	17	32
Drew Stafford	41	13	14	27	5	33
Nathan Paetsch	63	2	22	24	10	50
Paul Gaustad	54	9	13	22	11	74
Jaroslav Spacek	65	5	16	21	20	62
Toni Lydman	67	2	17	19	10	55
Henrik Tallinder	47	4	10	14	19	34
Jiri Novotny	50	6	7	13	-2	26
Adam Mair	82	2	9	11	-1	128
Daneil Paille	29	3	8	11	5	18
Dainius Zubrus	19	4	4	8	-3	12
Clarke MacArthur	19	3	4	7	4	4

GOALTENDER	GP	GA	SA	GAA	SV	SV%	SO
Ryan Miller	63	168	1,886	2.73	1,718	.911	2
Martin Biron	19	54	533	3.04	479	.899	0
Ty Conklin	5	13	120	3.43	107	.892	0

CALGARY FLAMES

PLAYER	GP	G	A	PTS	+/-	PIM
Jarome Iginla	70	39	55	94	12	40
Alex Tanguay	81	22	59	81	12	44
Daymond Langkow	81	33	44	77	23	44
Kristian Huselius	81	34	43	77	21	26
Dion Phaneuf	79	17	33	50	10	98
Matthew Lombardi	81	20	26	46	10	48
Roman Hamrlik	75	7	31	38	22	88
Tony Amonte	81	10	20	30	-4	40
Stephane Yelle	56	10	14	24	5	32
Craig Conroy	28	8	13	21	10	18
Robyn Regehr	78	2	19	21	27	75
David Moss	41	10	8	18	5	12
Chuck Kobasew	40	4	13	17	7	37
Marcus Nilson	63	5	10	15	7	27
Mark Giordano	48	7	8	15	7	36
Byron Ritchie	64	8	6	14	3	68
Andrew Ference	54	2	10	12	7	66
Jeff Friesen	72	6	6	12	-2	34
Rhett Warrener	62	4	6	10	6	67
Wayne Primeau	27	3	4	7	-2	36
Andrei Zyuzin	49	1	5	6	-2	30
Brad Stuart	27	0	5	5	12	18

GOALTENDER	GP	GA	SA	GAA	SV	SV%	SO
Miikka Kiprusoff	74	181	2,190	2.46	2,009	.917	7
Jamie McLennan	9	32	304	3.60	272	.895	0

CAROLINA HURRICANES

PLAYER	GP	G	A	PTS	+/-	PIM
Ray Whitney	81	32	51	83	-5	46
Rod Brind'Amour	78	26	56	82	7	46
Eric Staal	82	30	40	70	-6	68
Justin Williams	82	33	34	67	-11	73
Erik Cole	71	29	32	61	2	76
Scott Walker	81	21	30	51	-10	45
Mike Commodore	82	7	22	29	0	113
Cory Stillman	43	5	22	27	-8	24
Andrew Ladd	65	11	10	21	1	46
Eric Belanger	56	8	12	20	-2	14
Chad LaRose	80	6	12	18	-2	10
David Tanabe	60	5	12	17	5	44
Craig Adams	82	7	7	14	-9	54
Anton Babchuk	52	2	12	14	-6	30
Andrew Hutchinson	41	3	11	14	0	30
Glen Wesley	68	1	12	13	11	56
Bret Hedican	50	0	10	10	-8	36
Niclas Wallin	67	2	8	10	-2	48
Josef Vasicek	25	2	7	9	-6	22
Frantisek Kaberle	27	2	6	8	8	20
Trevor Letowski	61	2	6	8	-8	18

GOALTENDER	GP	GA	SA	GAA	SV	SV%	SO
Cam Ward	60	167	1,625	2.93	1,458	.897	2
John Grahame	28	72	702	2.85	630	.897	0

CHICAGO BLACKHAWKS

PLAYER	GP	G	A	PTS	+/-	PIM
Martin Havlat	56	25	32	57	15	28
Radim Vrbata	77	14	27	41	-4	26
Jeff Hamilton	70	18	21	39	-4	22
Tuomo Ruutu	71	17	21	38	4	95
Bryan Smolinski	62	14	23	37	10	29
Patrick Sharp	80	20	15	35	-15	74
Duncan Keith	82	2	29	31	0	76
Denis Arkhipov	79	10	17	27	-13	54
Martin Lapointe	82	13	11	24	-14	98
Brent Seabrook	81	4	20	24	-6	104
Tony Salmelainen	57	6	11	17	-3	26
Rene Bourgue	44	7	10	17	-4	38
Adrian Aucoin	59	4	12	16	-22	50
Peter Bondra	37	5	9	14	2	26
Lasse Kukkonen	54	5	9	14	5	30
Mikael Holmgvist	63	6	7	13	-5	31
James Wisniewski	50	2	8	10	3	39
Michal Handzus	8	3	5	8	4	6
Cam Barker	35	1	7	8	-12	44
Jassen Cullimore	65	1	6	7	-6	64
Jim Vandermeer	46	1	6	7	-3	53

GOALTENDER	GP	GA	SA	GAA	SV	SV%	SO
Nikolai Khabibulin	60	163	1,668	2.86	1,505	.902	1
Brian Boucher	15	45	389	3.27	344	.884	1
Patrick Lalime	12	33	317	3.07	284	.896	1

COLORADO AVALANCHE

PLAYER	GP	G	A	PTS	+/-	PIM
Joe Sakic	82	36	64	100	2	46
Andrew Brunette	82	27	56	83	-8	36
Paul Stastny	82	28	50	78	4	42
Milan Hejduk	80	35	35	70	10	44
Wojtek Wolski	76	22	28	50	2	14
Tyler Arnason	82	16	33	49	-8	26
John-Michael Liles	71	14	30	44	0	24
Brett Clark	82	10	29	39	5	50
Brett McLean	78	15	20	35	8	36
Marek Svatos	66	15	15	30	1	46
Ian Laperriere	81	8	21	29	5	133
Brad Richardson	73	14	8	22	4	28
Ken Klee	81	3	16	19	18	68
Mark Rycroft	66	6	6	12	3	31
Patrice Brisebois	33	1	10	11	-5	22
Karlis Skrastins	68	0	11	11	0	30
Ben Guite	39	3	8	11	-4	16
Ossi Vaananen	74	2	6	8	6	69
Pierre Turgeon	17	4	3	7	-1	10
Kurt Sauer	48	0	6	6	-3	24
Jordan Leopold	15	2	3	5	-4	14
Jeff Finger	22	1	4	5	10	11

GOALTENDER	GP	GA	SA	GAA	SV	SV%	SO
Peter Budaj	57	143	1,499	2.68	1,356	.905	3
Jose Theodore	33	95	870	3.26	775	.891	0

COLUMBUS BLUE JACKETS

PLAYER	GP	G	A	PTS	+/-	PIM
David Vyborny	82	16	48	64	6	60
Rick Nash	75	27	30	57	-8	73
Sergei Fedorov	73	18	24	42	-7	56
Fredrik Modin	79	22	20	42	-3	50
Jason Chimera	82	15	21	36	2	91
Ron Hainsey	80	9	25	34	-19	69
Nikolai Zherdev	71	10	22	32	-19	26
Anson Carter	54	10	17	27	-1	16
Dan Fritsche	59	12	15	27	3	35
Manny Malhotra	82	9	16	25	-8	76
Anders Eriksson	79	0	23	23	12	46
Rostislav Klesla	75	9	13	22	-13	105
Gilbert Brule	78	9	10	19	-21	28
Alexander Svitov	76	7	11	18	-10	145
Adam Foote	59	3	9	12	-17	71
Duvie Westcott	23	4	6	10	-13	18
Aaron Johnson	61	3	7	10	-9	38
Geoff Platt	26	4	5	9	1	10
Ole-Kristian Tollefsen	70	2	3	5	2	123
Marc Methot	20	0	4	4	5	12

GOALTENDER	GP	GA	SA	GAA	SV	SV%	SO
Fredrik Norrena	55	137	1,420	2.78	1,283	.904	3
Pascal Leclaire	24	65	629	2.97	564	.897	1
Ty Conklin	11	27	210	3.30	183	.871	0

DALLAS STARS

PLAYER	GP	G	A	PTS	+/-	PIM
Mike Ribeiro	81	18	41	59	3	22
Sergei Zubov	78	12	42	54	0	26
Philippe Boucher	76	19	32	51	2	104
Jussi Jokinen	82	14	34	48	8	18
Jere Lehtinen	73	26	17	43	5	16
Mike Modano	59	22	21	43	9	34
Brenden Morrow	40	16	15	31	-2	33
Niklas Hagman	82	17	12	29	3	34
Eric Lindros	49	5	21	26	-1	70
Stu Barnes	82	13	12	25	-2	40
Jeff Halpern	76	8	17	25	-7	78
Antti Miettinen	74	11	14	25	-5	38
Darryl Sydor	74	5	16	21	-4	36
Loui Eriksson	59	6	13	19	-3	18
Stephane Robidas	75	0	17	17	-1	86
Ladislav Nagy	25	4	10	14	-3	6
Trevor Daley	74	4	8	12	2	63
Patrik Stefan	41	5	6	11	5	10
Jaroslav Modry	57	1	9	10	10	32
Matthew Barnaby	39	1	6	7	5	127

GOALTENDER	GP	GA	SA	GAA	SV	SV%	SO
Marty Turco	67	140	1,564	2.23	1,424	.910	6
Mike Smith	23	45	511	2.23	466	.912	3

DETROIT RED WINGS

PLAYER	GP	G	A	PTS	+/-	PIM
Pavel Datsyuk	79	27	60	87	36	20
Henrik Zetterberg	63	33	35	68	26	36
Nicklas Lidstrom	80	13	49	62	40	46
Tomas Holmstrom	77	30	22	52	13	58
Robert Lang	81	19	33	52	12	66
Mathieu Schneider	68	11	41	52	12	66
Daniel Cleary	71	20	20	40	6	24
Mikael Samuelsson	53	14	20	34	1	28
Johan Franzen	69	10	20	30	20	37
Kris Draper	81	14	15	29	7	58
Jason Williams	58	11	15	26	7	24
Jiri Hudler	76	15	10	25	16	36
Niklas Kronwall	68	1	21	22	0	54
Brett Lebda	74	5	13	18	16	61
Valtteri Filppula	73	10	7	17	8	20
Danny Markov	66	4	12	16	25	59
Kyle Calder	19	5	9	14	6	22
Chris Chelios	71	0	11	11	11	34
Kirk Maltby	82	6	5	11	-9	50
Andreas Lilja	57	0	5	5	6	54

GOALTENDER	GP	GA	SA	GAA	SV	SV%	SO
Dominik Hasek	56	144	1,309	2.05	1,195	.913	8
Chris Osgood	21	46	496	2.38	450	.907	0
Joey MacDonald	8	27	211	3.46	184	.872	0

EDMONTON OILERS

PLAYER	GP	G	A	PTS	+/-	PIM
Ryan Smyth	53	31	22	53	2	38
Petr Sykora	82	22	31	53	-20	40
Ales Hemsky	64	13	40	53	-7	40
Shawn Horcoff	80	16	35	51	-22	56
Jarret Stoll	51	13	26	39	2	48
Raffi Torres	82	15	19	34	-7	88
Joffrey Lupul	81	16	12	28	-29	45
Fernando Pisani	77	14	14	28	-1	40
Marc-Andre Bergeron	55	8	17	25	-9	28
Marty Reasoner	72	6	14	20	-15	60
Steve Staios	58	2	15	17	-5	97
Patrick Thoresen	68	4	12	16	-1	52
Toby Petersen	64	6	9	15	-18	4
Daniel Tjarnqvist	37	3	12	15	3	30
Jason Smith	82	2	9	11	-13	103
Marc-Antoine Pouliot	46	4	7	11	-2	18
Matt Greene	78	1	9	10	-22	109
Ladislav Smid	77	3	7	10	-16	37
Brad Winchester	59	4	5	9	-10	86
Jan Hejda	39	1	8	9	-6	20

GOALTENDER	GP	GA	SA	GAA	SV	SV%	SO
Dwayne Roloson	68	180	1,969	2.75	1,789	.909	4
Jussi Markkanen	22	52	457	3.14	405	.886	0

HOCKEY

FLORIDA PANTHERS

PLAYER	GP	G	A	PTS	+/-	PIM
Olli Jokinen	82	39	52	91	18	78
Nathan Horton	82	31	31	62	15	61
Jozef Stumpel	73	23	34	57	2	22
Stephen Weiss	74	20	28	48	-1	28
Martin Gelinas	82	14	30	44	7	36
Jay Bouwmeester	82	12	30	42	23	66
Ville Peltonen	72	17	20	37	7	28
Chris Gratton	81	13	22	35	1	94
Ruslan Salei	82	6	26	32	-13	102
Rostislav Olesz	75	11	19	30	2	28
Gary Roberts	50	13	16	29	5	71
Mike Van Ryn	78	4	25	29	-5	64
Juraj Kolnik	64	11	14	25	2	18
Bryan Allen	82	4	21	25	7	112
Joel Kwiatkowski	41	5	5	10	-5	20
David Booth	48	3	7	10	0	12
Steve Montador	72	1	8	9	1	119
Gregory Campbell	79	6	3	9	-10	66
Joe Nieuwendyk	15	5	3	8	-4	4
Todd Bertuzzi	7	1	6	7	-4	13

GOALTENDER	GP	GA	SA	GAA	SV	SV%	SO
Ed Belfour	58	152	1,550	2.77	1,398	.902	1
Alex Auld	27	82	729	3.35	647	.888	1
Craig Anderson	5	8	116	2.21	108	.931	0

LOS ANGELES KINGS

PLAYER	GP	G	A	PTS	+/-	PIM
Michael Cammalleri	81	34	46	80	5	48
Alexander Frolov	82	35	36	71	-8	34
Anze Kopitar	72	20	41	61	-12	24
Lubomir Visnovsky	69	18	40	58	1	26
Dustin Brown	81	17	29	46	-21	54
Derek Armstrong	67	11	33	44	13	62
Rob Blake	72	14	20	34	-26	82
Sean Avery	55	10	18	28	-10	116
Brent Sopel	44	4	19	23	2	14
Tom Kostopoulos	76	7	15	22	-2	73
Brian Willsie	81	11	10	21	-20	49
Patrick O'Sullivan	44	5	14	19	-6	14
Craig Conroy	52	5	11	16	-13	38
Scott Thornton	58	7	6	13	-15	85
Kevin Dallman	53	1	9	10	-13	12
Mattias Norstrom	62	2	7	9	-20	40
Mike Weaver	39	3	6	9	-4	16
Jamie Lundmark	29	7	2	9	-8	25

GOALTENDER	GP	GA	SA	GAA	SV	SV%	SO
Mathieu Garon	32	79	849	2.66	770	.907	2
Dan Cloutier	24	85	608	3.98	523	.860	0
Sean Burke	23	68	687	3.12	619	.901	1
Barry Brust	11	30	245	3.70	215	.878	0

MINNESOTA WILD

PLAYER	GP	G	A	PTS	+/-	PIM
Pavol Demitra	71	25	39	64	0	28
Brian Rolston	78	31	33	64	6	46
Marian Gaborik	48	30	27	57	12	40
Pierre-Marc Bouchard	82	20	37	57	13	14
Mikko Koivu	82	20	34	54	6	58
Todd White	77	13	31	44	8	24
Mark Parrish	76	19	20	39	9	18
Brent Burns	77	7	18	25	16	26
Wes Walz	62	9	15	24	3	30
Branko Radivojevic	82	11	13	24	-9	21
Kurtis Foster	57	3	20	23	-3	52
Kim Johnsson	76	3	19	22	-4	64
Petteri Nummelin	51	3	17	20	-15	22
Stephane Veilleux	75	7	11	18	3	47
Keith Carney	80	4	13	17	22	58
Martin Skoula	81	0	15	15	9	36
Pascal Dupuis	48	10	3	13	-7	38
Nick Schultz	82	2	10	12	0	42
Wyatt Smith	61	3	3	6	-8	16
Adam Hall	23	2	3	5	2	8

GOALTENDER	GP	GA	SA	GAA	SV	SV%	SO
Manny Fernandez	44	103	1,158	2.55	1,055	.911	2
Niklas Backstrom	41	73	1,028	1.97	955	.929	5
Josh Harding	7	7	174	1.16	167	.960	1

MONTREAL CANADIENS

PLAYER	GP	G	A	PTS	+/-	PIM
Saku Koivu	81	22	53	75	-21	74
Sheldon Souray	81	26	38	64	-28	135
Michael Ryder	82	30	28	58	-25	60
Andrei Markov	77	6	43	49	2	56
Alexei Kovalev	73	18	29	47	-19	78
Tomas Plekanec	81	20	27	47	10	36
Christopher Higgins	61	22	16	38	-11	26
Mark Streit	76	10	26	36	-5	14
Mike Johnson	80	11	20	31	6	40
Guillaume Latendresse	80	16	13	29	-20	47
Sergei Samsonov	63	9	17	26	-4	10
Radek Bonk	74	13	10	23	0	54
Mike Komisarek	82	4	15	19	7	96
Craig Rivet	54	6	10	16	-7	57
Alexander Perezhogin	61	6	9	15	11	48
Francis Bouillon	62	3	11	14	-10	52
Maxim Lapierre	46	6	6	12	-7	24
Andrei Kostitsyn	22	1	10	11	3	6
Steve Begin	52	5	5	10	-6	46
Mathieu Dandenault	68	2	6	8	-8	40

GOALTENDER	GP	GA	SA	GAA	SV	SV%	SO
Cristobal Huet	42	107	1,280	2.81	1,173	.916	2
David Aebischer	32	93	929	3.17	836	.900	0
Jaroslav Halak	16	44	469	2.89	425	.906	2

NASHVILLE PREDATORS

PLAYER	GP	G	A	PTS	+/-	PIM
Paul Kariya	82	24	52	76	6	36
J.P. Dumont	82	21	45	66	14	28
David Legwand	78	27	36	63	23	44
Steve Sullivan	57	22	38	60	16	20
Martin Erat	68	16	41	57	13	50
Kimmo Timonen	80	13	42	55	20	42
Jason Arnott	68	27	27	54	15	48
Shea Weber	79	17	23	40	13	60
Scott Hartnell	64	22	17	39	19	96
Alexander Radulov	64	18	19	37	19	26
Marek Zidlicky	79	4	26	30	8	72
Vernon Fiddler	72	11	15	26	11	40
Ryan Suter	82	8	16	24	10	54
Dan Hamhuis	81	6	14	20	8	66
Peter Forsberg	17	2	13	15	5	16
Josef Vasicek	38	4	9	13	1	29
Scott Nichol	59	7	6	13	7	79
Jerred Smithson	64	5	7	12	-8	42
Jordin Tootoo	65	3	6	9	-11	116
Greg Zanon	66	3	5	8	16	32

GOALTENDER	GP	GA	SA	GAA	SV	SV%	SO
Tomas Vokoun	44	104	1,299	2.40	1,195	.920	5
Chris Mason	40	93	1,244	2.38	1,151	.925	5

NEW JERSEY DEVILS

PLAYER	GP	G	A	PTS	+/-	PIM
Patrik Elias	75	21	48	69	1	38
Zach Parise	82	31	31	62	-3	30
Scott Gomez	72	13	47	60	7	42
Jamie Langenbrunner	82	23	37	60	-10	64
Brian Rafalski	82	8	47	55	4	34
Brian Gionta	62	25	20	45	-3	36
Travis Zajac	80	17	25	42	1	16
Sergei Brylin	82	16	24	40	-5	35
John Madden	74	12	20	32	-7	14
Jay Pandolfo	82	13	14	27	-5	8
Paul Martin	82	3	23	26	-9	18
Brad Lukowich	75	4	8	12	1	36
Johnny Oduya	76	2	9	11	-5	61
Erik Rasmussen	71	3	7	10	-2	25
Michael Rupp	76	6	3	9	-10	92
Jim Dowd	66	4	4	8	-5	20
Colin White	69	0	8	8	-8	69
Andy Greene	23	1	5	6	-1	6
David Clarkson	7	3	1	4	-1	6

GOALTENDER	GP	GA	SA	GAA	SV	SV%	SO
Martin Brodeur	78	171	2,182	2.18	2,011	.922	12
Scott Clemmensen	6	16	144	3.14	128	.889	0

NEW YORK ISLANDERS

PLAYER	GP	G	A	PTS	+/-	PIM
Jason Blake	82	40	29	69	1	34
Miroslav Satan	81	27	32	59	-12	46
Mike Sillinger	82	26	33	59	5	46
Viktor Kozlov	81	25	26	51	12	28
Alexei Yashin	58	18	32	50	6	44
Tom Poti	78	6	38	44	-1	74
Trent Hunter	77	20	15	35	5	22
Andy Hilbert	81	8	20	28	10	34
Chris Simon	67	10	17	27	17	75
Richard Park	82	10	16	26	4	33
Sean Hill	81	1	24	25	6	110
Arron Asham	80	11	12	23	3	63
Randy Robitaille	50	6	17	23	-2	22
Marc-Andre Bergeron	23	6	15	21	5	10
Radek Martinek	43	2	15	17	19	40
Ryan Smyth	18	5	10	15	0	14
Brendan Witt	81	1	13	14	14	131
Chris Campoli	51	1	13	14	-3	23
Mike York	32	6	7	13	-9	14
Alexei Zhitnik	30	2	9	11	13	40

GOALTENDER	GP	GA	SA	GAA	SV	SV%	SO
Rick DiPietro	62	156	1,917	2.58	1,761	.919	5
Mike Dunham	19	61	552	3.74	491	.889	0
Wade Dubielewicz	8	13	198	2.06	185	.934	0

NEW YORK RANGERS

PLAYER	GP	G	A	PTS	+/-	PIM
Jaromir Jagr	82	30	66	96	26	78
Michael Nylander	79	26	57	83	12	42
Martin Straka	77	29	41	70	16	24
Brendan Shanahan	67	29	33	62	2	47
Matt Cullen	80	16	25	41	0	52
Michal Rozsival	80	10	30	40	10	52
Petr Prucha	79	22	18	40	-7	30
Karel Rachunek	66	6	20	26	-9	38
Marek Malik	69	2	19	21	32	70
Sean Avery	29	8	12	20	11	58
Marcel Hossa	64	10	8	18	-4	26
Fedor Tyutin	66	2	12	14	-8	44
Aaron Ward	60	3	10	13	-3	57
Blair Betts	82	9	4	13	-4	24
Adam Hall	49	4	8	12	-13	18
Jed Ortmeyer	41	2	9	11	7	22
Jason Ward	46	4	6	10	-3	26
Thomas Pock	44	4	4	8	-4	16
Jarkko Immonen	14	1	5	6	-2	4
Ryan Callahan	14	4	2	6	5	9
Daniel Girardi	34	0	6	6	7	8

GOALTENDER	GP	GA	SA	GAA	SV	SV%	SO
Henrik Lundqvist	70	160	1,927	2.34	1,767	.917	5
Kevin Weekes	14	43	355	3.39	312	.879	0

HOCKEY

OTTAWA SENATORS

PLAYER	GP	G	A	PTS	+/-	PIM
Dany Heatley	82	50	55	105	31	74
Daniel Alfredsson	77	29	58	87	42	42
Jason Spezza	67	34	53	87	19	45
Mike Fisher	68	22	26	48	15	41
Peter Schaefer	77	12	34	46	7	32
Antoine Vermette	77	19	20	39	-2	52
Chris Kelly	82	15	23	38	28	40
Tom Preissing	80	7	31	38	40	18
Joe Corvo	76	8	29	37	8	42
Wade Redden	64	7	29	36	1	50
Andrej Meszaros	82	7	28	35	-15	102
Patrick Eaves	73	14	18	32	1	36
Dean McAmmond	81	14	15	29	11	28
Chris Neil	82	12	16	28	6	177
Chris Phillips	82	8	18	26	36	80
Mike Comrie	41	13	12	25	-1	24
Christoph Schubert	80	8	17	25	30	56
Anton Volchenkov	78	1	18	19	37	67
Denis Hamel	43	4	3	7	4	10
Oleg Saprykin	12	1	1	2	-3	4
Brian McGrattan	45	0	2	2	-1	100

GOALTENDER	GP	GA	SA	GAA	SV	SV%	SO
Ray Emery	58	138	1,691	2.47	1,553	.918	5
Martin Gerber	29	74	784	2.78	710	.906	1

PHILADELPHIA FLYERS

PLAYER	GP	G	A	PTS	+/-	PIM
Simon Gagne	76	41	27	68	2	30
Mike Knuble	64	24	30	54	2	56
Joni Pitkanen	77	4	39	43	-25	88
Peter Forsberg	40	11	29	40	2	72
Jeff Carter	62	14	23	37	-17	48
Mike Richards	59	10	22	32	-12	52
Geoff Sanderson	58	11	18	29	-16	44
R.J. Umberger	81	16	12	28	-32	41
Sami Kapanen	77	11	14	25	-21	22
Randy Jones	66	4	18	22	-14	38
Alexandre Picard	62	3	19	22	-19	17
Kyle Calder	59	9	12	21	-31	36
Randy Robitaille	28	5	12	17	-4	22
Dmitry Afanasenkov	41	8	7	15	-19	12
Alexei Zhitnik	31	3	10	13	-16	38
Scottie Upshall	18	6	7	13	4	8
Stefan Ruzicka	40	3	10	13	-6	18
Ryan Potulny	35	7	5	12	1	22
Todd Fedoruk	48	3	8	11	-11	84
Ben Eager	63	6	5	11	-13	233

GOALTENDER	GP	GA	SA	GAA	SV	SV%	SO
Antero Niittymaki	52	166	1,567	3.38	1,401	.894	0
Robert Esche	18	62	483	4.32	421	.872	1
Martin Biron	16	47	509	3.01	462	.908	0

PHOENIX COYOTES

PLAYER	GP	G	A	PTS	+/-	PIM
Shane Doan	73	27	28	55	-14	73
Ladislav Nagy	55	8	33	41	-2	48
Owen Nolan	76	16	24	40	-2	56
Oleg Saprykin	59	14	20	34	8	54
Yanic Perreault	49	19	14	33	-2	30
Steve Reinprecht	49	9	24	33	-3	28
Ed Jovanovski	54	11	18	29	-6	63
Jeremy Roenick	70	11	17	28	-18	32
Zbynek Michalek	82	4	24	28	-20	34
Keith Ballard	70	5	22	27	-7	59
Derek Morris	82	6	19	25	-18	115
Mike Zigomanis	75	14	9	23	-8	46
Georges Laraque	56	5	17	22	7	52
Mike Comrie	24	7	13	20	1	20
Travis Roche	50	6	13	19	2	22
Fredrik Sjostrom	78	9	9	18	-11	48
Bill Thomas	24	8	6	14	-6	2
Nick Boynton	59	2	9	11	-13	138
Patrick Fischer	27	4	6	10	0	24
Niko Kapanen	19	2	7	9	-11	8
Mathias Tjarnqvist	26	5	4	9	-2	2

GOALTENDER	GP	GA	SA	GAA	SV	SV%	SO
Curtis Joseph	55	159	1,481	3.19	1,322	.893	4
Mikael Tellqvist	30	90	780	3.39	690	.885	2

PITTSBURGH PENGUINS

PLAYER	GP	G	A	PTS	+/-	PIM
Sidney Crosby	79	36	84	120	10	60
Evgeni Malkin	78	33	52	85	2	80
Mark Recchi	82	24	44	68	1	62
Sergei Gonchar	82	13	54	67	-5	72
Ryan Whitney	81	14	45	59	9	77
Michel Ouellet	73	19	29	48	-3	30
Jordan Staal	81	29	13	42	16	24
Colby Armstrong	80	12	22	34	2	67
Erik Christensen	61	18	15	33	-3	26
Ryan Malone	64	16	15	31	4	71
Maxime Talbot	75	13	11	24	-2	53
Jarkko Ruutu	81	7	9	16	0	125
Nils Ekman	34	6	9	15	-14	24
Dominic Moore	59	6	9	15	1	46
Gary Roberts	19	7	6	13	-5	26
Josef Melichar	70	1	11	12	1	44
Robert Scuderi	78	1	10	11	3	28
John LeClair	21	2	5	7	-2	12
Ronald Petrovicky	31	3	3	6	4	28
Brooks Orpik	70	0	6	6	4	82

GOALTENDER	GP	GA	SA	GAA	SV	SV%	SO
Marc-Andre Fleury	67	184	1,954	2.83	1,770	.906	5
Jocelyn Thibault	22	52	572	2.83	520	.909	1

SAN JOSE SHARKS

PLAYER	GP	G	A	PTS	+/-	PIM
Joe Thornton	82	22	92	114	24	44
Patrick Marleau	77	32	46	78	9	33
Jonathan Cheechoo	76	37	32	69	11	69
Milan Michalek	78	26	40	66	17	36
Matt Carle	77	11	31	42	9	30
Ryane Clowe	58	16	18	34	4	78
Mike Grier	81	16	17	33	-5	43
Christian Ehrhoff	82	10	23	33	8	63
Steve Bernier	62	15	16	31	5	29
Joe Pavelski	46	14	14	28	4	18
Marc-Edouard Vlasic	81	3	23	26	13	18
Scott Hannan	79	4	20	24	1	38
Patrick Rissmiller	79	7	15	22	1	22
Mark Bell	71	11	10	21	-9	83
Curtis Brown	78	8	12	20	-2	56
Kyle McLaren	67	5	12	17	10	61
Mark Smith	41	3	10	13	-4	42
Marcel Goc	78	5	8	13	-2	24
Bill Guerin	16	8	1	9	2	14
Craig Rivet	17	1	7	8	8	12

GOALTENDER	GP	GA	SA	GAA	SV	SV%	SO
Evgeni Nabokov	50	106	1,227	2.29	1,121	.914	7
Vesa Toskala	38	84	915	2.35	831	.908	4

ST. LOUIS BLUES

PLAYER	GP	G	A	PTS	+/-	PIM
Doug Weight	82	16	43	59	10	56
Lee Stempniak	82	27	25	52	-2	33
Petr Cajanek	77	15	33	48	9	54
Bill Guerin	61	28	19	47	8	52
Keith Tkachuk	61	20	23	43	3	92
Radek Dvorak	82	10	27	37	-6	48
Jay McClement	81	8	28	36	3	55
Martin Rucinsky	52	12	21	33	-3	48
Eric Brewer	82	6	23	29	-10	69
Barret Jackman	70	3	24	27	20	82
David Backes	49	10	13	23	6	37
Jamal Mayers	80	8	14	22	-19	89
Dennis Wideman	55	5	17	22	-7	44
Christian Backman	61	7	11	18	13	36
Dallas Drake	60	6	6	12	-14	38
Brad Boyes	19	4	8	12	0	4
Ryan Johnson	59	7	4	11	-7	47
Dan Hinote	41	5	5	10	-8	23
Jeff Woywitka	34	1	6	7	4	12
Bryce Salvador	64	2	5	7	-5	55

GOALTENDER	GP	GA	SA	GAA	SV	SV%	SO
Manny Legace	45	109	1,177	2.59	1,068	.907	5
Curtis Sanford	31	79	707	3.18	628	.888	0
Jason Bacashihua	19	47	450	3.16	403	.896	0

TAMPA BAY LIGHTNING

PLAYER	GP	G	A	PTS	+/-	PIM
Vincent Lecavalier	82	52	56	108	2	44
Martin St. Louis	82	43	59	102	7	28
Brad Richards	82	25	45	70	-19	23
Dan Boyle	82	20	43	63	-5	62
Vaclav Prospal	82	14	41	55	-24	36
Filip Kuba	81	15	22	37	-9	36
Eric Perrin	82	13	23	36	-7	30
Ruslan Fedotenko	80	12	20	32	-3	52
Paul Ranger	72	4	24	28	5	42
Ryan Criag	72	14	13	27	-11	55
Nikita Alexeev	63	10	11	21	10	12
Cory Sarich	82	0	15	15	-6	70
Doug Janik	75	2	9	11	-11	53
Andreas Karlsson	53	3	6	9	-4	12
Nick Tarnasky	77	5	4	9	-6	80
Nolan Pratt	81	1	7	8	0	44
Jason Ward	17	4	4	8	-11	10
Tim Taylor	71	1	5	6	-5	16
Dmitry Afanasenkov	33	3	3	6	-6	8

GOALTENDER	GP	GA	SA	GAA	SV	SV%	SO
Johan Holmqvist	48	121	1,134	2.85	1,013	.893	1
Marc Denis	44	125	1,068	3.19	943	.883	1
Karri Ramo	2	4	23	3.45	19	.826	0

TORONTO MAPLE LEAFS

PLAYER	GP	G	A	PTS	+/-	PIM
Mats Sundin	75	27	49	76	-2	62
Tomas Kaberle	74	11	47	58	3	20
Bryan McCabe	82	15	42	57	3	115
Alexei Ponikarovsky	71	21	24	45	8	63
Darcy Tucker	56	24	19	43	-11	81
Jeff O'Neill	74	20	22	42	1	54
Kyle Wellwood	48	12	30	42	3	0
Matthew Stajan	82	10	29	39	3	44
Alexander Steen	82	15	20	35	5	26
Nik Antropov	54	18	15	33	8	44
Bates Battaglia	82	12	19	31	9	45
Johnny Pohl	74	13	16	29	-4	10
Chad Kilger	82	14	14	28	-5	58
Ian White	76	3	23	26	8	40
Pavel Kubina	61	7	14	21	7	48
Hal Gill	82	6	14	20	11	91
Boyd Devereaux	33	8	11	19	4	12
Carlo Colaiacovo	48	8	9	17	5	22
Michael Peca	35	4	11	15	2	60
Yanic Perreault	17	2	3	5	1	4
Brendan Bell	31	1	4	5	-3	19
Kris Newbury	15	2	2	4	4	26

GOALTENDER	GP	GA	SA	GAA	SV	SV%	SO
Andrew Raycroft	72	205	1,931	2.99	1,726	.894	2
Jean-Sebastien Aubin	20	46	371	3.43	325	.876	0

VANCOUVER CANUCKS

PLAYER	GP	G	A	PTS	+/-	PIM
Daniel Sedin	81	36	48	84	19	36
Henrik Sedin	82	10	71	81	19	66
Markus Naslund	82	24	36	60	3	54
Brendan Morrison	82	20	31	51	-9	60
Kevin Bieksa	81	12	30	42	1	134
Taylor Pyatt	76	23	14	37	5	42
Sami Salo	67	14	23	37	21	26
Mattias Ohlund	77	11	20	31	-3	80
Matt Cooke	81	10	20	30	0	64
Trevor Linden	80	12	13	25	-6	34
Jan Bulis	79	12	11	23	-8	70
Lukas Krajicek	78	3	13	16	-4	64
Ryan Kesler	48	6	10	16	1	40
Willie Mitchell	62	1	10	11	1	45
Jeff Cowan	42	7	3	10	4	93
Alex Burrows	81	3	6	9	-7	93
Rory Fitzpatrick	58	1	6	7	12	46
Josh Green	57	2	5	7	0	25
Bryan Smolinski	20	4	3	7	-3	8
Tommi Santala	30	1	5	6	0	24

GOALTENDER	GP	GA	SA	GAA	SV	SV%	SO
Roberto Luongo	76	171	2,169	2.28	1,998	.921	5
Dany Sabourin	9	21	224	2.63	203	.906	0

WASHINGTON CAPITALS

PLAYER	GP	G	A	PTS	+/-	PIM
Alexander Ovechkin	82	46	46	92	-19	52
Alexander Semin	77	38	35	73	-7	90
Chris Clark	74	30	24	54	-10	66
Dainius Zubrus	60	20	32	52	-16	50
Matt Pettinger	64	16	16	32	-13	22
Boyd Gordon	71	7	22	29	10	14
Brian Pothier	72	3	25	28	-11	44
Kris Beech	64	8	18	26	-11	46
Ben Clymer	66	7	13	20	-17	44
Richard Zednik	32	6	12	18	-4	16
Brooks Laich	73	8	10	18	-2	29
Brian Sutherby	69	7	10	17	-9	78
Steve Eminger	68	1	16	17	-14	63
Jamie Heward	52	4	12	16	4	27
Matt Bradley	57	4	9	13	-5	47
Donald Brashear	77	4	9	13	1	156
Shaone Morrisonn	78	3	10	13	3	106
Mike Green	70	2	10	12	-10	36
Jakub Klepis	41	3	7	10	-2	28
Milan Jurcina	30	2	7	9	5	24
Lawrence Nycholat	18	2	6	8	-3	12
Tomas Fleischmann	29	4	4	8	-6	8

GOALTENDER	GP	GA	SA	GAA	SV	SV%	SO
Olaf Kolzig	54	159	1,771	3.00	1,612	.910	1
Brent Johnson	30	99	894	3.61	795	.889	0

LEGENDS

In 2001, after 22 seasons in the NHL, Ray Bourque won his first and only Stanley Cup title.

■ **Ray Bourque, defenseman,** b. December 28, 1960, Montreal, Quebec, Canada. Considered one of the best defensemen in hockey history, Bourque was chosen by the Boston Bruins in the first round of the 1979 draft. He made an immediate impact in his first NHL season, scoring 65 points and winning the league's rookie of the year trophy. Bourque's ability to score was legendary and he finished his career with more goals (410) and more assists (1,169) than any other defenseman in NHL history. In 1988 and again in 1990, he led Boston to the Stanley Cup Final, but both times his teams lost. A perennial All-Star, Bourque was named the NHL's best defenseman five times between 1987 and 1994. After more than 20 years in Boston, Bourque was traded to Colorado in 2000. The next season—Bourque's last—he set an NHL record with his 19th consecutive All-Star game appearance and finally hoisted Lord Stanley's Cup after the Avalanche beat the New Jersey Devils in a thrilling, seven-game series. In 2004, Bourque was inducted into the Hockey Hall of Fame.

■ **Mike Modano, center,** b. June 7, 1970, Livonia, Michigan. Modano was the first overall pick of the 1988 NHL Draft at age 17. He has played his entire 17-year career with the Stars and currently holds eight franchise records. A seven-time All-Star, Modano has averaged 30 goals and 42 assists a season since coming to the NHL. In 1999, Modano scored more than 20 points in the postseason and led the Stars to that franchise's first and only Stanley Cup victory. In March 2007, Modano scored his 503rd career goal, passing hockey legend Joe Mullen for the most goals in NHL history by an American-born player.

■ **Terry Sawchuk, goaltender,** b. December 28, 1929, Winnipeg, Manitoba, Canada. During the 1950–51 season, Sawchuk recorded an impressive 1.99 goals against average with Detroit and was named the league's rookie of the year. Over the next four seasons, Sawchuk won three Vezina Trophies as the league's best goalie (1952, '53, and '55) and helped guide the Red Wings to three Stanley Cup titles (1952, '54, and '55). After a short stint in Boston, he returned to the Red Wings in 1957 for seven more years before being traded to Toronto. As a Maple Leaf, Sawchuk won both his fourth career Vezina Trophy (1965) and Stanley Cup title (1967). By the end of his 21-year career in 1970, Sawchuk had recorded more wins (447) and shutouts (103) than any other goalie in NHL history. He was inducted into the Hockey Hall of Fame in 1971.

THE STANLEY CUP

Awarded annually to the team that wins the NHL's best-of-seven final-round playoffs. The Stanley Cup is the oldest trophy for which professional athletes in North America compete. It was donated in 1893 by Frederick Arthur, Lord Stanley of Preston.

SEASON	CHAMPION	FINALIST	GAMES PLAYED IN FINAL
2006–07	Anaheim Ducks	Ottawa Senators	5
2005–06	Carolina Hurricanes	Edmonton Oilers	7
2003–04	Tampa Bay Lightning	Calgary Flames	7
2002–03	New Jersey Devils	Anaheim Mighty Ducks	7
2001–02	Detroit Red Wings	Carolina Hurricanes	5
2000–01	Colorado Avalanche	New Jersey Devils	7
1999–00	New Jersey Devils	Dallas Stars	6
1998–99	Dallas Stars	Buffalo Sabres	6
1997–98	Detroit Red Wings	Washington Capitals	4
1996–97	Detroit Red Wings	Philadelphia Flyers	4
1995–96	Colorado Avalanche	Florida Panthers	4
1994–95	New Jersey Devils	Detroit Red Wings	4
1993–94	New York Rangers	Vancouver Canucks	7
1992–93	Montreal Canadiens	Los Angeles Kings	5
1991–92	Pittsburgh Penguins	Chicago Blackhawks	4
1990–91	Pittsburgh Penguins	Minnesota North Stars	6
1989–90	Edmonton Oilers	Boston Bruins	5
1988–89	Calgary Flames	Montreal Canadiens	6
1987–88	Edmonton Oilers	Boston Bruins	4
1986–87	Edmonton Oilers	Philadelphia Flyers	7
1985–86	Montreal Canadiens	Calgary Flames	5
1984–85	Edmonton Oilers	Philadelphia Flyers	5
1983–84	Edmonton Oilers	New York Islanders	5
1982–83	New York Islanders	Edmonton Oilers	4
1981–82	New York Islanders	Vancouver Canucks	4
1980–81	New York Islanders	Minnesota North Stars	5
1979–80	New York Islanders	Philadelphia Flyers	6
1978–79	Montreal Canadiens	New York Rangers	5
1977–78	Montreal Canadiens	Boston Bruins	6
1976–77	Montreal Canadiens	Boston Bruins	4
1975–76	Montreal Canadiens	Philadelphia Flyers	4
1974–75	Philadelphia Flyers	Buffalo Sabres	6
1973–74	Philadelphia Flyers	Boston Bruins	6
1972–73	Montreal Canadiens	Chicago Blackhawks	6
1971–72	Boston Bruins	New York Rangers	6
1970–71	Montreal Canadiens	Chicago Blackhawks	7
1969–70	Boston Bruins	St. Louis Blues	4
1968–69	Montreal Canadiens	St. Louis Blues	4
1967–68	Montreal Canadiens	St. Louis Blues	4
1966–67	Toronto Maple Leafs	Montreal Canadiens	6
1965–66	Montreal Canadiens	Detroit Red Wings	6
1964–65	Montreal Canadiens	Chicago Blackhawks	7
1963–64	Toronto Maple Leafs	Detroit Red Wings	7
1962–63	Toronto Maple Leafs	Detroit Red Wings	5
1961–62	Toronto Maple Leafs	Chicago Blackhawks	6
1960–61	Chicago Blackhawks	Detroit Red Wings	6
1959–60	Montreal Canadiens	Toronto Maple Leafs	4
1958–59	Montreal Canadiens	Toronto Maple Leafs	5
1957–58	Montreal Canadiens	Boston Bruins	6
1956–57	Montreal Canadiens	Boston Bruins	5
1955–56	Montreal Canadiens	Detroit Red Wings	5
1954–55	Detroit Red Wings	Montreal Canadiens	7
1953–54	Detroit Red Wings	Montreal Canadiens	7
1952–53	Montreal Canadiens	Boston Bruins	5

Note: The 2004–2005 season was cancelled because of a lockout.

THE STANLEY CUP (cont.)

GAMES PLAYED

SEASON	CHAMPION	FINALIST	IN FINAL
1951–52	Detroit Red Wings	Montreal Canadiens	4
1950–51	Toronto Maple Leafs	Montreal Canadiens	5
1949–50	Detroit Red Wings	New York Rangers	7
1948–49	Toronto Maple Leafs	Detroit Red Wings	4
1947–48	Toronto Maple Leafs	Detroit Red Wings	4
1946–47	Toronto Maple Leafs	Montreal Canadiens	6
1945–46	Montreal Canadiens	Boston Bruins	5
1944–45	Toronto Maple Leafs	Detroit Red Wings	7
1943–44	Montreal Canadiens	Chicago Blackhawks	4
1942–43	Detroit Red Wings	Boston Bruins	4
1941–42	Toronto Maple Leafs	Detroit Red Wings	7
1940–41	Boston Bruins	Detroit Red Wings	4
1939–40	New York Rangers	Toronto Maple Leafs	6
1938–39	Boston Bruins	Toronto Maple Leafs	5
1937–38	Chicago Blackhawks	Toronto Maple Leafs	4
1936–37	Detroit Red Wings	New York Rangers	5
1935–36	Detroit Red Wings	Toronto Maple Leafs	4
1934–35	Montreal Maroons	Toronto Maple Leafs	3
1933–34	Chicago Blackhawks	Detroit Red Wings	4
1932–33	New York Rangers	Toronto Maple Leafs	4
1931–32	Toronto Maple Leafs	New York Rangers	3
1930–31	Montreal Canadiens	Chicago Blackhawks	5
1929–30	Montreal Canadiens	Boston Bruins	2
1928–29	Boston Bruins	New York Rangers	2
1927–28	New York Rangers	Montreal Maroons	5
1926–27	Ottawa Senators	Boston Bruins	4
1925–26	Montreal Maroons	Victoria Cougars	4
1924–25	Victoria Cougars	Montreal Canadiens	4
1923–24	Montreal Canadiens	Vancouver Maroons, Calgary Tigers	2, 2*
1922–23	Ottawa Senators	Edmonton Eskimos, Vancouver Maroons	2, 4*
1921–22	Toronto St. Pats	Vancouver Millionaires	5
1920–21	Ottawa Senators	Vancouver Millionaires	5
1919–20	Ottawa Senators	Seattle Metropolitans	5
1918–19	No decision*	No decision*	5
1917–18	Toronto Arenas	Vancouver Millionaires	5
1916–17	Seattle Metropolitans	—	—
1915–16	Montreal Canadiens	—	—
1914–15	Vancouver Millionaires	—	—
1913–14	Toronto Blueshirts	—	—
1912–13	Quebec Bulldogs	—	—
1911–12	Quebec Bulldogs	—	—
1910–11	Ottawa Senators	—	—
1909–10	Montreal Wanderers	—	—
1908–09	Ottawa Senators	—	—
1907–08	Montreal Wanderers	—	—
1906–07	Montreal Wanderers (Mar.)	—	—
1906–07	Kenora Thistles (Jan.)	—	—
1905–06	Montreal Wanderers (Mar.)	—	—
1905–06	Ottawa Silver Seven (Feb.)	—	—
1904–05	Ottawa Silver Seven	—	—
1903–04	Ottawa Silver Seven	—	—
1902–03	Ottawa Silver Seven (Mar.)	—	—
1902–03	Montreal A.A.A. (Feb.)	—	—
1901–02	Montreal A.A.A. (Mar.)	—	—

*In 1923–24, the Montreal Canadiens beat the Vancouver Maroons in two games and the Calgary Tigers in two games. In 1922–23, the Ottawa Senators beat the Edmonton Eskimos in two games and the Vancouver Maroons in four games. In 1918–19, the Montreal Canadiens traveled to meet the Seattle Metropolitans. After five games had been played — the teams were tied at two wins apiece and one tie — the series was called off by the local Department of Health because of an influenza epidemic and the death of Canadien defenseman Joe Hall from influenza.

THE STANLEY CUP (cont.)

SEASON	CHAMPION	FINALIST	GAMES PLAYED IN FINAL
1901–02	Winnipeg Victorias (Jan.)	—	—
1900–01	Winnipeg Victorias	—	—
1899–00	Montreal Shamrocks	—	—
1898–99	Montreal Shamrocks (Mar.)	—	—
1898–99	Montreal Victorias (Feb.)	—	—
1897–98	Montreal Victorias	—	—
1896–97	Montreal Victorias	—	—
1895–96	Montreal Victorias (Dec.)	—	—
1895–96	Winnipeg Victorias (Feb.)	—	—
1894–95	Montreal Victorias	—	—
1893–94	Montreal A.A.A.	—	—
1892–93	Montreal A.A.A.	—	—

TRIVIA CHALLENGE

1 What part of a hockey rink is also known as "the crease?"
a. The zone between the two blue lines.
b. The four corners of the rink.
c. The box in front of and the trapezoidal area beside and behind the goal.

2 Hall of Fame goalie Patrick Roy was named MVP of the Stanley Cup playoffs more times than any player in NHL history. How many Conn Smythe Trophies did he win?
a. 1
b. 3
c. 5

3 Why does Pittsburgh Penguins phenom Sidney Crosby wear the jersey number 87?
a. It's one less than Pittsburgh legend Mario Lemieux's number 88.
b. That's just the number he was given.
c. His birthday is 8/7/87.

4 An NHL player serving a minor penalty can leave the penalty box if the other team scores a non-penalty shot goal.
a. True
b. False

5 When was the last year that two Canadian teams played in the Stanley Cup Final?
a. 1989
b. 1979
c. 1999

6 Which NHL franchise has won 24 Stanley Cup titles, more than any other team?
a. Detroit Red Wings
b. Toronto Maple Leafs
c. Montreal Canadiens

Patrick Roy

7 Hockey legend Wayne Gretzky played for four teams during his 20-year NHL career. For which team did he play the *least* amount of games?
a. New York Rangers
b. St. Louis Blues
c. Edmonton Oilers

8 In 2006, which Washington Capitals left winger became the first rookie in 15 years to be named a first-team NHL All-Star.
a. Alexander Ovechkin
b. Ilya Kovalchuk
c. Miikka Kiprusoff

AP PHOTO/RYAN REMIORZ

Trivia Challenge: 1. c; 2. b; 3. c; 4. a; 5. a; 6. c; 7. b; 8. a;

CONN SMYTHE TROPHY (PAST 20 SEASONS)

Awarded to the Most Valuable Player of the Stanley Cup playoffs, as selected by the Professional Hockey Writers Association. The trophy was named for the former coach, general manager, president, and owner of the Toronto Maple Leafs.

SEASON	PLAYER	SEASON	PLAYER
2006–07	Scott Niedermayer, Anaheim Ducks	1995–96	Joe Sakic, Colorado Avalanche
2005–06	Cam Ward, Carolina Hurricanes	1994–95	Claude Lemieux, New Jersey Devils
2003–04	Brad Richards, Tampa Bay Lightning	1993–94	Brian Leetch, New York Rangers
2002–03	Jean-Sebastien Giguere, Anaheim Mighty Ducks	1992–93	Patrick Roy, Montreal Canadiens
2001–02	Nicklas Lidstrom, Detroit Red Wings	1991–92	Mario Lemieux, Pittsburgh Penguins
2000–01	Patrick Roy, Colorado Avalanche	1990–91	Mario Lemieux, Pittsburgh Penguins
1999–00	Scott Stevens, New Jersey Devils	1989–90	Bill Ranford, Edmonton Oilers
1998–99	Joe Nieuwendyk, Dallas Stars	1988–89	Al MacInnis, Calgary Flames
1997–98	Steve Yzerman, Detroit Red Wings	1987–88	Wayne Gretzky, Edmonton Oilers
1996–97	Mike Vernon, Detroit Red Wings	1986–87	Ron Hextall, Philadelphia Flyers

HART MEMORIAL TROPHY (PAST 20 SEASONS)

Awarded annually "to the player adjudged to be the most valuable to his team." The original trophy was donated by Dr. David A. Hart, father of Cecil Hart, former manager-coach of the Montreal Canadiens.

SEASON	WINNER	SEASON	WINNER
2006–07	Sidney Crosby, Pittsburgh Penguins	1995–96	Mario Lemieux, Pittsburgh Penguins
2005–06	Joe Thornton, San Jose Sharks	1994–95	Eric Lindros, Philadelphia Flyers
2003–04	Martin St. Louis, Tampa Bay Lightning	1993–94	Sergei Fedorov, Detroit Red Wings
2002–03	Peter Forsberg, Colorado Avalanche	1992–93	Mario Lemieux, Pittsburgh Penguins
2001–02	Jose Theodore, Montreal Canadiens	1991–92	Mark Messier, New York Rangers
2000–01	Joe Sakic, Colorado Avalanche	1990–91	Brett Hull, St. Louis Blues
1999–00	Chris Pronger, St. Louis Blues	1989–90	Mark Messier, Edmonton Oilers
1998–99	Jaromir Jagr, Pittsburgh Penguins	1988–89	Wayne Gretzky, Los Angeles Kings
1997–98	Dominik Hasek, Buffalo Sabres	1987–88	Mario Lemieux, Pittsburgh Penguins
1996–97	Dominik Hasek, Buffalo Sabres	1986–87	Wayne Gretzky, Edmonton Oilers

ART ROSS TROPHY (PAST 20 SEASONS)

Awarded annually "to the player who leads the league in scoring points at the end of the regular season." The trophy was presented to the NHL in 1947 by Arthur Howie Ross, former manager-coach of the Boston Bruins. If two or more players are tied, the tie-breakers, in order, are: (1) player with most goals, (2) player with fewer games played, (3) player who scored the first goal of the season.

SEASON	WINNER	POINTS	SEASON	WINNER	POINTS
2006–07	Sidney Crosby, Pittsburgh Penguins	120	1995–96	Mario Lemieux, Pittsburgh Penguins	161
2005–06	Joe Thornton, San Jose Sharks	125	1994–95	Jaromir Jagr, Pittsburgh Penguins	70
2003–04	Martin St. Louis, Tampa Bay Lightning	94	1993–94	Wayne Gretzky, Los Angeles Kings	130
2002–03	Peter Forsberg, Colorado Avalanche	106	1992–93	Mario Lemieux, Pittsburgh Penguins	160
2001–02	Jarome Iginla, Calgary Flames	96	1991–92	Mario Lemieux, Pittsburgh Penguins	131
2000–01	Jaromir Jagr, Pittsburgh Penguins	121	1990–91	Wayne Gretzky, Los Angeles Kings	163
1999–00	Jaromir Jagr, Pittsburgh Penguins	96	1989–90	Wayne Gretzky, Los Angeles Kings	142
1998–99	Jaromir Jagr, Pittsburgh Penguins	127	1988–89	Mario Lemieux, Pittsburgh Penguins	199
1997–98	Jaromir Jagr, Pittsburgh Penguins	102	1987–88	Mario Lemieux, Pittsburgh Penguins	168
1996–97	Mario Lemieux, Pittsburgh Penguins	122	1986–87	Wayne Gretzky, Edmonton Oilers	183

Note: The 2004–2005 season was cancelled because of a lockout.

HOCKEY

LADY BYNG MEMORIAL TROPHY (PAST 20 SEASONS)

Awarded annually "to the player adjudged to have exhibited the best type of sportsmanship and gentlemanly conduct combined with a high standard of playing ability." Lady Byng, who first presented the trophy in 1925, was the wife of Canada's Governor-General. She donated a second trophy in 1936 because the first one was given permanently to Frank Boucher of the New York Rangers, who had won it seven times in eight seasons.

SEASON	WINNER	SEASON	WINNER
2006–07	Pavel Datsyuk, Detroit Red Wings	1995–96	Paul Kariya, Anaheim Mighty Ducks
2005–06	Pavel Datsyuk, Detroit Red Wings	1994–95	Ron Francis, Pittsburgh Penguins
2003–04	Brad Richards, Tampa Bay Lightning	1993–94	Wayne Gretzky, Los Angeles Kings
2002–03	Alexander Mogilny, Toronto Maple Leafs	1992–93	Pierre Turgeon, New York Islanders
2001–02	Ron Francis, Carolina Hurricanes	1991–92	Wayne Gretzky, Los Angeles Kings
2000–01	Joe Sakic, Colorado Avalanche	1990–91	Wayne Gretzky, Los Angeles Kings
1999–00	Pavol Demitra, St. Louis Blues	1989–90	Brett Hull, St. Louis Blues
1998–99	Wayne Gretzky, New York Rangers	1988–89	Joe Mullen, Calgary Flames
1997–98	Ron Francis, Pittsburgh Penguins	1987–88	Mats Naslund, Montreal Canadiens
1996–97	Paul Kariya, Anaheim Mighty Ducks	1986–87	Joe Mullen, Calgary Flames

JAMES NORRIS MEMORIAL TROPHY (PAST 20 SEASONS)

Awarded annually "to the defense player who demonstrates throughout the season the greatest all-around ability in the position." James Norris was the former owner-president of the Detroit Red Wings.

SEASON	WINNER	SEASON	WINNER
2006–07	Nicklas Lidstrom, Detroit Red Wings	1995–96	Chris Chelios, Chicago Blackhawks
2005–06	Nicklas Lidstrom, Detroit Red Wings	1994–95	Paul Coffey, Detroit Red Wings
2003–04	Scott Niedermayer, New Jersey Devils	1993–94	Ray Bourque, Boston Bruins
2002–03	Nicklas Lidstrom, Detroit Red Wings	1992–93	Chris Chelios, Chicago Blackhawks
2001–02	Nicklas Lidstrom, Detroit Red Wings	1991–92	Brian Leetch, New York Rangers
2000–01	Nicklas Lidstrom, Detroit Red Wings	1990–91	Ray Bourque, Boston Bruins
1999–00	Chris Pronger, St. Louis Blues	1989–90	Ray Bourque, Boston Bruins
1998–99	Al MacInnis, St. Louis Blues	1988–89	Chris Chelios, Montreal Canadiens
1997–98	Rob Blake, Los Angeles Kings	1987–88	Ray Bourque, Boston Bruins
1996–97	Brian Leetch, New York Rangers	1986–87	Ray Bourque, Boston Bruins

CALDER MEMORIAL TROPHY (PAST 20 SEASONS)

Awarded annually "to the player selected as the most proficient in his first year of competition in the National Hockey League." Frank Calder was a former NHL president. Sergei Makarov, who won the award in 1989-90, was the oldest recipient of the trophy, at 31. If a player is 26 or older as of September 15 of a season, he is no longer eligible to win the award.

SEASON	WINNER	SEASON	WINNER
2006–07	Evgeni Malkin, Pittsburgh Penguins	1995–96	Daniel Alfredsson, Ottawa Senators
2005–06	Alexander Ovechkin, Washington Capitals	1994–95	Peter Forsberg, Quebec Nordiques
2003–04	Andrew Raycroft, Boston Bruins	1993–94	Martin Brodeur, New Jersey Devils
2002–03	Barret Jackman, St. Louis Blues	1992–93	Teemu Selanne, Winnipeg Jets
2001–02	Dany Heatley, Atlanta Thrashers	1991–92	Pavel Bure, Vancouver Canucks
2000–01	Evgeni Nabokov, San Jose Sharks	1990–91	Ed Belfour, Chicago Blackhawks
1999–00	Scott Gomez, New Jersey Devils	1989–90	Sergei Makarov, Calgary Flames
1998–99	Chris Drury, Colorado Avalanche	1988–89	Brian Leetch, New York Rangers
1997–98	Sergei Samsonov, Boston Bruins	1987–88	Joe Nieuwendyk, Calgary Flames
1996–97	Bryan Berard, New York Islanders	1986–87	Luc Robitaille, Los Angeles Kings

Awarded annually "to the goalkeeper adjudged to be the best at his position." The trophy was named for Georges Vezina, an outstanding goalie for the Montreal Canadiens who collapsed during a game on November 28, 1925, and died four months later of tuberculosis. The general managers of the NHL teams vote on the award.

SEASON	WINNER	SEASON	WINNER
2006–07	Martin Brodeur, New Jersey Devils	1995–96	Jim Carey, Washington Capitals
2005–06	Miikka Kiprusoff, Calgary Flames	1994–95	Dominik Hasek, Buffalo Sabres
2003–04	Martin Brodeur, New Jersey Devils	1993–94	Dominik Hasek, Buffalo Sabres
2002–03	Martin Brodeur, New Jersey Devils	1992–93	Ed Belfour, Chicago Blackhawks
2001–02	Jose Theodore, Montreal Canadiens	1991–92	Patrick Roy, Montreal Canadiens
2000–01	Dominik Hasek, Buffalo Sabres	1990–91	Ed Belfour, Chicago Blackhawks
1999–00	Olaf Kolzig, Washington Capitals	1989–90	Patrick Roy, Montreal Canadiens
1998–99	Dominik Hasek, Buffalo Sabres	1988–89	Patrick Roy, Montreal Canadiens
1997–98	Dominik Hasek, Buffalo Sabres	1987–88	Grant Fuhr, Edmonton Oilers
1996–97	Dominik Hasek, Buffalo Sabres	1986–87	Ron Hextall, Philadelphia Flyers

SELKE TROPHY (PAST 20 SEASONS)

Awarded annually "to the forward who best excels in the defensive aspects of the game." The trophy was named for Frank J. Selke, the architect of the Montreal Canadiens dynasty that won the Stanley Cup five consecutive times in the late 1950's. The winner is selected by a vote of the Professional Hockey Writers Association.

SEASON	WINNER	SEASON	WINNER
2006–07	Rod Brind'Amour, Carolina Hurricanes	1995–96	Sergei Fedorov, Detroit Red Wings
2005–06	Rod Brind'Amour, Carolina Hurricanes	1994–95	Ron Francis, Pittsburgh Penguins
2003–04	Kris Draper, Detroit Red Wings	1993–94	Sergei Fedorov, Detroit Red Wings
2002–03	Jere Lehtinen, Dallas Stars	1992–93	Doug Gilmour, Toronto Maple Leafs
2001–02	Michael Peca, New York Islanders	1991–92	Guy Carbonneau, Montreal Canadiens
2000–01	John Madden, New Jersey Devils	1990–91	Dirk Graham, Chicago Blackhawks
1999–00	Steve Yzerman, Detroit Red Wings	1989–90	Rick Meagher, St. Louis Blues
1998–99	Jere Lehtinen, Dallas Stars	1988–89	Guy Carbonneau, Montreal Canadiens
1997–98	Jere Lehtinen, Dallas Stars	1987–88	Guy Carbonneau, Montreal Canadiens
1996–97	Michael Peca, Buffalo Sabres	1986–87	Dave Poulin, Philadelphia Flyers

ALL-TIME CAREER RECORDS

Points

PLAYER	YRS	GP	G	A	PTS	PTS/GAME
Wayne Gretzky, Edm, LA, StL, NYR	20	1,487	894	1,963	2,857	1.921
Mark Messier, Edm, Van, NYR	25	1,756	694	1,193	1,887	1.075
Gordie Howe, Det, Hart	26	1,767	801	1,049	1,850	1.047
Ron Francis, Hart, Pitt, Car, Tor	23	1,731	549	1,249	1,798	1.039
Marcel Dionne, Det, LA, NYR	18	1,348	731	1,040	1,771	1.314

Goal-Scoring

PLAYER	YRS	GP	G	G/GAME
Wayne Gretzky, Edm, LA, StL, NYR	20	1,487	894	.601
Gordie Howe, Det, Hart	26	1,767	801	.453
Brett Hull, Cal, StL, Dal, Det	19	1,264	741	.586
Marcel Dionne, Det, LA, NYR	18	1,348	731	.542
Phil Esposito, Chi, Bos, NYR	18	1,282	717	.559

KEY YRS=years; GP=games played; G=goals; A=assists; PTS=points; PTS/GAME=points per game; G/Game=goals per game

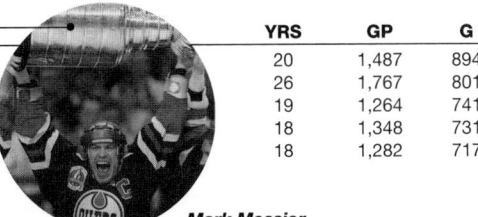

Mark Messier

RICHARD MACKSON

CAREER RECORDS (cont.)

Assists

PLAYER	YRS	GP	A	A/GAME
Wayne Gretzky, Edm, LA, StL, NYR	20	1,487	1,963	1.320
Ron Francis, Hart, Pitt, Car, Tor	23	1,731	1,249	.721
Mark Messier, Edm, NYR, Van	25	1,756	1,193	.679
Ray Bourque, Bos, Col	22	1,612	1,169	.725
Paul Coffey, Edm, Pitt, LA, Det, Hart, Phi, Chi, Car, Bos	21	1,409	1,135	.806

GOALTENDING

Wins

GOALTENDER	W	L	T
Patrick Roy, Mtl, Col	551	315	131
Martin Brodeur, NJ	494	263	105
Ed Belfour, Chi, SJ, Dal, Tor, Fla	484	320	111
Terry Sawchuk, Det, Bos, Tor, LA, NYR	447	330	172
Curtis Joseph, StL, Edm, Tor, Det, Phoe	446	341	90

Martin Brodeur

LOU CAPOZZOLA

Shutouts

GOALTENDER	TEAM	YRS	GP	SO
Terry Sawchuk	Det, Bos, Tor, LA, NYR	21	971	103
George Hainsworth	Mtl, Tor	11	465	94
Martin Brodeur	NJ	14	891	92
Glenn Hall	Det, Chi, StL	18	906	84
Jacques Plante	Mtl, NYR, StL, Tor, Bos	18	837	82

Goals-Against Average (Pre-1950)

GOALTENDER	TEAM	YRS	GP	GA	GAA
George Hainsworth	Mtl, Tor	11	465	937	1.91
Alex Connell	Ott, Det, NYA, Mtl M	12	417	830	1.91
Chuck Gardiner	Chi	7	316	664	2.02
Lorne Chabot	NYR, Tor, Mtl, Chi, Mtl M, NYA	11	411	861	2.04
Tiny Thompson	Bos, Det	12	553	1,183	2.08

Goals-Against Average (Post-1950)

GOALTENDER	TEAM	YRS	GP	GA	GAA
Martin Brodeur	NJ	14	891	1,931	2.20
Dominik Hasek	Chi, Buf, Det, Ott	15	694	1,488	2.21
Ken Dryden	Mtl	8	397	870	2.24
Jacques Plante	Mtl, NYR, StL, Tor, Bos	18	837	1,965	2.38
Chris Osgood	Det, NYI, StL	13	621	1,455	2.45

Note: Minimum 350 games played. Goals-against average equals goals against per 60 minutes played.

KEY YRS=years; GP=games played; A/GAME=assists per game; W=win; L=loss; T=tie; SO=shutout; GA=goals allowed; GAA=goals-against average

TODAY'S STARS

■ **Vincent Lecavalier, center,** b. April 21, 1980, Ile-Bizard, Quebec, Canada. Drafted by the Lightning in 1998 at age 17, Lecavalier was named team captain less than two years later, the youngest player to receive this honor in NHL history. Lecavalier is a talented scorer. Along with teammate Martin St. Louis, he powered Tampa Bay to its first and only Stanley Cup title in 2004. That same year, Lecavalier was named MVP of the Canadian national team after it won gold at the World Cup of Hockey. During the 2006–07 season, Lecavalier earned his second career trip to the All-Star game and scored a league-high 52 goals.

■ **Evgeni Malkin, left wing,** b. July 31, 1986, Magnitogorsk, Russia. After several years of playing professionally in his native country, Malkin dramatically slipped away from his Russian team

Vincent Lecavalier has averaged 40 goals a season since 2003.

ANDY MARLIN/GETTY IMAGES

while on a 2006 road trip to Finland. He quickly made his way to the United States and less than two weeks later, Malkin signed a contract to play in the NHL with the Pittsburgh Penguins. A preseason injury postponed Malkin's 2006–07 season debut, but when he finally did start, he wasted little time proving his worth. He became the first NHL player in 89 years to score a goal in each of his first six games. At the end of his first season, Malkin had 33 goals and 52 assists. He easily won the Calder Trophy, as the NHL's top rookie.

■ **Marty Turco, goaltender,** b. August 13, 1975, Sault Ste. Marie, Ontario, Canada. After winning two NCAA hockey titles at the University of Michigan, Turco came to Dallas in 1999 and played backup to legendary goalie Ed Belfour for two years. In 2001, Turco took over as the Stars' starting goalie and cemented his reputation as one of the stingiest goalies in the league. In his first six NHL seasons, Turco was named an All-Star three-times and won 175 games with 30 shutouts. He has a career goals-against average of 2.11.

DID YOU KNOW?

In the 90-year history of the NHL, only one team has lost the first three games of the Stanley Cup Final and then rallied to win the title in seven games, the 1942 Toronto Maple Leafs.

SOCCER

After relocating from San Jose in 2006, the new Houston Dynamo won the franchise's third MLS Cup.

THOMAS B. SHEA/WIREIMAGE.COM

MLS TEAMS

EASTERN CONFERENCE
Chicago Fire
Columbus Crew
D.C. United
Kansas City Wizards
New York Red Bulls
New England Revolution
Toronto FC

WESTERN CONFERENCE
Club Deportivo Chivas USA
Colorado Rapids
FC Dallas
Los Angeles Galaxy
Real Salt Lake
Houston Dynamo

Houston, we have liftoff. In its first season in a new home, the Houston Dynamo (formerly the San Jose Earthquakes) won the 2006 MLS Cup. After playing to a 1–1 tie through regulation and extra time, Houston defeated the New England Revolution in a penalty kick shootout (4–3). Dynamo forward Bryan Ching scored the tying goal in the game's 114th minute and then punched home the winning kick in the shootout. He was named Cup final MVP.

The Revolution became the second team in MLS history to lose three Cup finals. At least New England had the satisfaction of defeating the league's top team in the playoffs. D.C. United finished the season with the league's best record (15–7–10) but fell to the Revolution in the Eastern Conference finals, 1–0.

In addition to the strong regular season, D.C. United cleaned up in the year-end awards. Midfielder Christian Gomez won the MLS MVP award

after finishing tied for second in the league in goals (14) and assists (11). Bobby Boswell was named Defender of the Year, and Troy Perkins won Goaltender of the Year honors. Seventeen-year-old midfielder Freddy Adu was named to his first MLS All-Star team for D.C. but was traded to Real Salt Lake after the season ended.

Big changes are afoot in MLS for 2007, when a new team and a new superstar will join the league. Toronto will be MLS's first Canadian team, and David Beckham will join the Los Angeles Galaxy. The English superstar signed a five-year deal in January worth up to $250 million in salary and endorsements.

In women's soccer, the U.S. National Team was in good shape despite the recent retirement of stars such as Mia Hamm and Julie Foudy. The team qualified for its fifth consecutive FIFA Women's World Cup, which will be played in China from September 10–30, 2007. This new U.S. team is led by 26-year-old forward Abby Wambach. Through December 4, 2006, Wambach had scored 66 goals in 84 career games with the national team. That's the highest goals-per-game ratio in team history. And the presence of Kristine Lilly means that the U.S. will still have steady veteran leadership at the World Cup.

Dynamo forward Brian Ching drove home the MLS Cup-clinching goal during an overtime shootout.

FAST FACT

Since MLS began in 1996, four of the eleven MLS Cup championships have been decided in overtime.

English soccer superstar David Beckham made the leap to the MLS in 2007.

2006 MLS FINAL STANDINGS

EASTERN CONFERENCE

TEAM	GP	W	L	T	PTS	GF	GA
y-New England	32	17	7	8	59	55	37
x-D.C. United	32	16	10	6	54	58	37
x-Chicago	32	15	13	4	49	49	50
x-New York	32	12	9	11	47	53	49
Kansas City	32	11	9	12	45	52	44
Columbus	32	11	16	5	38	34	45

WESTERN CONFERENCE

TEAM	GP	W	L	T	PTS	GF	GA
y Houston	32	18	4	10	64	53	31
x-FC Dallas	32	13	10	9	48	52	44
x-Colorado	32	13	13	6	45	40	37
x-Los Angeles	32	13	13	6	45	44	45
Real Salt Lake	32	5	22	5	20	30	65
Chivas USA	32	4	22	6	18	31	67

Note: Three points for a win. One point for a tie.
x=clinched playoffs; y=conference champion

KEY GP=games played; W=win; L=loss; T=tie; PTS=points; GF=goals for; GA=goals against

SOCCER

MLS CUP 2006

Pizza Hut Park, Frisco, Texas
November 12, 2006
Attendance: 22,427

	1st Half	2nd Half	Final
Houston Dynamo	0	1	1
New England Revolution	0	1	1

Scoring Summary:

NE: Taylor Twellman 3 (Khano Smith 1) 113
HOU: Brian Ching 3 (Brian Mullan 3) 114

Shootout Summary:

NE: Joseph (goal), Reis (goal), Noonan (miss), Twellman (goal), Heaps (saved)

HOU: Gray (goal), Holden (goal), De Rosario (goal), Davis (saved), Ching (goal)

Dynamo: Pat Onstad, Craig Waibel, Ryan Cochrane, (Kelly Gray 11), Eddie Robinson, Wade Barrett, Brian Mullan, Dwayne De Rosario, Adrian Serioux (Stuart Holden 12), Brad Davis, Brian Ching, Paul Dalglish (Alejandro Moreno 81)

Revolution: Matt Reis, Jay Heaps, Michael Parkhurst, Avery John, Andy Dorman (Clint Dempsey 62), Steve Ralston, Daniel Hernandez (Jeff Larentowicz 12), Shalrie Joseph, Joe Franchino (Khano Smith 53), Pat Noonan, Taylor Twellman

Note: Numbers next to player names indicate time of game.

2006 MLS PLAYOFFS

```
United
        ┐
        ├ United (2–1)                                          Rapids (3–3)*         FC Dallas
Red Bulls ┘                         DYNAMO                               ┐
                 ┐                   1 – 1                                ├         Rapids
Fire             ├ Revolution (1–0)         Dynamo (3–1)                 ┘
  ┐              │                    PK (4–3)                           ┐         Chivas USA
  ├ Revolution (2–2)*                            Dynamo (3–2)            ├
Revolution ┘                                                             ┘         Dynamo
```

*Score tied after 1st and 2nd legs, winner decided by penalty kicks

PLAYOFF LEADERS

GOALS	GP	G
Brian Ching, Dynamo	4	3
Taylor Twellman, Revolution	4	3
Paul Dalglish, Dynamo	4	2
4 players tied with 2		

ASSISTS	GP	A
Brian Mullan, Dynamo	4	3
Brad Davis, Dynamo	4	2
Jovan Kirovski, Rapids	3	1
2 players tied with 1		

SHOTS	GP	SH
Matt Reis, Revolution	4	20
Matthew Pickens, Fire	2	18
Pat Onstad, Dynamo	4	14
Troy Perkins, United	3	8

GOALS-AGAINST AVERAGE	GP	GAA
Matt Reis, Revolution	4	0.64
Troy Perkins, United	3	0.67
Matthew Pickens, Fire	2	0.86
Pat Onstad, Dynamo	4	0.92
Jon Conway, MetroStars	2	1.00
Tony Meola, MetroStars	2	1.50
Pat Onstad, Earthquakes	2	2.00
Nick Rimando, United	2	2.00
Minimum: 75 minutes played		

KEY GP=games played; G=goals; A=assists; SH=shots; GAA=goals-against average

MLS STARS

Joseph (center) of the New England Revolution

■ **Shalrie Joseph, midfielder,** b. May 24, 1978, St. George, Grenada. In three MLS seasons, Joseph has been named to the league's Best XI team twice and its All-Star team every year. As a midfielder for the Revolution, Joseph has developed a reputation as a tough, yet clean, tackler as well as a precise, long-range passer. Joseph's stellar play is a major reason New England has played in the last two MLS Cup finals. Nicknamed "Chaz," Joseph moved to New York City as a teenager, although he still plays on the Grenadian national soccer team.

■ **Matt Reis, goalkeeper,** b. March 28, 1975, Atlanta, Georgia. In 2006, Reis had a 1.13 goals-against average as keeper for the New England Revolution, tied for second-best in the league. A nine-year veteran, Reis first came into his own in 2001 and 2002, when he helped propel the Los Angeles Galaxy to two straight MLS Cup appearances and one MLS title.

■ **Amado Guevara, midfielder,** b. May 2, 1976, Tegucigalpa, Honduras. Guevara, whose nickname is "El Lobo" (The Wolf), played in soccer leagues in South America and Europe for ten years before joining the MLS's MetroStars in 2003. Only a year later, Guevara led the MLS in scoring and was named league MVP as well as MVP of the All-Star game. Following the 2006 season, Guevara was traded to Chivas USA.

2006 MLS STATISTICAL LEADERS

SCORING	GP	G	A
Taylor Twellman, Revolution	29	17	8
Landon Donovan, Galaxy	26	16	11
Jaime Moreno, United	31	16	7
Carlos Ruiz, Dallas	21	13	2
Jeff Cunningham, Rapids	29	13	3
Herculez Gomez, Galaxy	26	12	2
Amado Guevara, MetroStars	28	12	11
Clint Dempsey, Revolution	30	11	10
Christian Gomez, United	33	11	9
Youri Djorkaeff, MetroStars	26	11	8
Josh Wolff, Wizards	22	10	10

GOALS	GP	G
Taylor Twellman, Revolution	25	17
Jaime Moreno, United	29	16
Jeff Cunningham, Rapids	26	12
Landon Donovan, Galaxy	22	12
Christian Gomez, United	31	11
Herculez Gomez, Galaxy	22	11
Amado Guevara, MetroStars	26	11
Carlos Ruiz, Dallas	19	11
Clint Dempsey, Revolution	26	10
Youri Djorkaeff, MetroStars	24	10
Josh Wolff, Wizards	22	10

ASSISTS	GP	A
Dwayne De Rosario, Earthquakes	28	13
Ronnie O'Brien, Dallas	28	12
Simon Elliott, Crew	32	11
Amado Guevara, MetroStars	26	11
Landon Donovan, Galaxy	22	10
Josh Wolff, Wizards	22	10
Ronald Cerritos, Earthquakes	30	9
Clint Dempsey, Revolution	26	9
Christian Gomez, United	31	9
Chris Klein, Wizards	31	9

GOALS-AGAINST AVERAGE	G
Pat Onstad, Earthquakes	0.97
Jonny Walker, Crew	1.13
Matt Reis, Revolution	1.13
Nick Rimando, United	1.17
Joe Cannon, Rapids	1.20
Zach Wells, MetroStars	1.24
Scott Garlick, Dallas	1.36
Bo Oshoniyi, Wizards	1.38
Kevin Hartman, Galaxy	1.39
Zach Thornton, Fire	1.64
Tony Meola, MetroStars	1.87
Brad Guzan, Chivas	1.99
D.J. Countess, Real Salt Lake	2.01

KEY GP=games played; G=goals; A=assists; PTS=points; GAA=goals-against average; W=win; L=loss; T=tie

TEAM-BY-TEAM STATS

CHICAGO FIRE

PLAYER	GP	MIN	G	A	C	SHOTS	SOG
Andy Herron	20	1,449	9	1	3	37	25
Nate Jaqua	28	2,037	8	2	4	48	17
Chris Rolfe	21	1,636	7	1	1	39	19
Chad Barrett	16	780	5	1	2	26	14
Thiago	27	2,229	3	2	0	39	19
Diego Gutierrez	25	1,879	2	3	6	18	8
Justin Mapp	26	1,866	2	8	0	36	10
Chris Armas	27	2,366	1	5	5	20	6
C.J. Brown	28	2,429	1	2	3	7	3
Calen Carr	22	500	1	1	3	12	8
Jim Curtin	11	660	1	0	1	1	1
Brian Plotkin	14	529	1	1	2	14	4
Dasan Robinson	23	2,054	1	0	5	8	1
Gonzalo Segares	25	1,984	1	1	8	7	2
Pascal Bedrossian	1	29	0	0	0	0	0
Floyd Franks	9	151	0	0	0	4	2
Leonard Griffin	6	343	0	0	2	0	0
Ivan Guerrero	29	2,526	0	9	2	20	12
Ryan Johnson	3	46	0	0	0	3	2
Jared Montz	1	13	0	1	0	0	0
Logan Pause	25	1,782	0	1	5	4	1
Tony Sanneh	19	1,296	0	1	0	4	1
*Jack Stewart	5	139	0	0	1	1	1
John Thorrington	2	11	0	0	0	0	0
FIRE	**32**	**2,880**	**43**	**41**	**53**	**345**	**155**
OPPONENTS	**32**	**2,880**	**41**	**42**	**66**	**399**	**175**

GOALKEEPER	GP	MIN	SHOTS	SVS	SHO	GA	GAA
Zach Thornton	24	2,160	118	86	7	30	1.25
Matt Pickens	8	720	57	47	1	11	1.38
TOTALS	**32**	**2,880**	**155**	**133**	**8**	**41**	**1.28**

CHIVAS USA

PLAYER	GP	MIN	G	A	C	SHOTS	SOG
Ante Razov	28	2,485	14	8	6	98	40
Juan Pablo Garcia	29	2,438	8	6	5	51	29
Jonathan Bornstein	32	2,878	6	4	2	38	21
Claudio Suarez	20	1,778	6	1	1	10	6
Juan Francisco Palencia	23	1,914	4	4	0	46	23
Francisco Mendoza	31	2,652	3	6	6	40	22
Jesse Marsch	30	2,604	2	3	7	13	7
Brent Whitfield	11	363	1	1	0	4	3
Esteban Arias	4	40	0	0	0	0	0
Rene Corona	1	14	0	0	3	16	5
Johnnie Garcia	2	84	0	0	0	2	0
Drew Helm	8	123	0	0	0	2	1
Jason Hernandez	29	2,243	0	0	4	3	2
Sacha Kljestan	32	2,676	0	7	5	22	8
Carlos Llamosa	13	921	0	1	6	2	0
Rodrigo Lopez	2	21	0	0	0	1	1
Jesus Morales	7	356	0	1	3	11	4
John O'Brien	1	5	0	0	0	0	0
Orlando Perez	23	1,173	0	0	2	3	3
Tim Regan	30	2,618	0	0	5	10	2
Matt Taylor	15	323	0	1	0	6	2
Lawson Vaughn	17	1,046	0	1	3	0	0
CHIVAS USA	**32**	**2,880**	**45**	**44**	**56**	**363**	**174**
OPPONENTS	**32**	**2,880**	**42**	**44**	**48**	**364**	**157**

GOALKEEPER	GP	MIN	SHOTS	SVS	SHO	GA	GAA
Preston Burpo	19	1,710	87	58	5	23	1.21
Brad Guzan	13	1,170	70	49	5	19	1.46
TOTALS	**32**	**2,880**	**174**	**107**	**10**	**42**	**1.31**

*Player no longer with team

KEY GP=games played; MIN=minutes played; G=goals; A=assists; C=corner kick; SOG=shots on goal; SHO=shutouts; SVS=saves; GA=goals allowed; GAA=goals-against average

COLORADO RAPIDS

PLAYER	GP	MIN	G	A	C	SHOTS	SOG
Kyle Beckerman	31	2,270	7	2	8	57	27
Nicolas Hernandez	30	2,524	7	6	3	37	18
Jovan Kirovski	26	1,865	5	2	3	40	16
*Dedi Ben Dayan	16	927	4	2	1	26	11
Jacob Peterson	28	1,548	4	3	1	16	8
Thiago Martins	25	1,393	3	4	6	46	19
Clint Mathis	25	1,346	2	1	3	31	9
Fabrice Noel	9	371	1	0	0	11	7
Daniel Wasson	17	714	1	0	1	12	6
Colin Clark	7	298	0	0	2	4	1
Terry Cooke	23	1,997	0	12	0	31	13
Matt Crawford	2	138	0	0	0	0	0
Eric Denton	22	1,890	0	2	2	10	1
Hunter Freeman	27	2,131	0	1	7	8	2
Dan Gargan	22	1,482	0	1	6	7	3
*Cornell Glen	1	13	0	0	0	0	0
Luchi Gonzalez	2	8	0	0	0	0	0
Aitor Karanka	27	2,414	0	1	3	11	4
Pablo Mastroeni	20	1,779	0	0	6	2	0
Alian Nkong	5	199	0	0	0	2	0
*Jean Philippe Peguero	2	168	0	1	0	3	0
Mike Petke	26	2,256	0	0	10	7	1
Melvin Tarley	3	34	0	0	0	3	3
Chris Wingert	10	446	0	0	1	0	0
RAPIDS	**32**	**2,880**	**36**	**38**	**65**	**364**	**149**
OPPONENTS	**32**	**2,880**	**49**	**45**	**51**	**336**	**168**

GOALKEEPER	GP	MIN	SHOTS	SVS	SHO	GA	GAA
Joe Cannon	28	2440	146	99	7	42	1.55
Bouna Coundoul	5	440	22	15	2	7	1.43
TOTALS	**32**	**2,880**	**149**	**114**	**9**	**49**	**1.53**

COLUMBUS CREW

PLAYER	GP	MIN	G	A	C	SHOTS	SOG
Jason Garey	25	1,712	5	2	2	31	17
Joseph Ngwenya	20	804	5	2	5	27	13
Eddie Gaven	30	2,560	4	4	3	57	27
Kei Kamara	19	930	3	0	1	26	9
Sebastian Rozental	20	1,231	3	1	1	29	12
*Leonard Bisaku	7	336	1	0	2	6	3
Ned Grabavoy	10	388	1	1	1	7	3
Ezra Hendrickson	24	1,869	1	2	1	15	5
Ritchie Kotschau	26	2,109	1	2	4	6	1
Chad Marshall	26	2,255	1	1	1	11	3
*Kyle Martino	6	400	1	0	1	10	4
Jose Retiz	22	1,732	1	1	7	22	7
Jacob Thomas	19	1,074	1	2	1	21	9
Eric Vasquez	12	504	1	0	0	9	2
Ricado Virtuoso	10	571	1	0	1	15	8
Marc Burch	7	479	0	1	0	2	0
Knox Cameron	10	355	0	0	0	3	1
Ryan Coiner	6	282	0	1	0	8	4
Marcos Gonzalez	21	1,660	0	0	5	12	2
Frankie Hejduk	4	360	0	0	2	5	1
*Joel Kitamirike	1	19	0	0	1	0	0
Chris Leitch	24	1,662	0	1	2	4	2
Brandon Moss	20	1,610	0	0	5	8	2
Duncon Oughton	9	776	0	2	1	8	3
Rusty Pierce	18	1,524	0	0	5	8	2
Danny Szetela	4	237	0	1	0	4	3
Tim Ward	11	605	0	0	1	2	1
CREW	**32**	**2,880**	**30**	**24**	**56**	**358**	**145**
OPPONENTS	**32**	**2,880**	**42**	**40**	**56**	**457**	**186**

GOALKEEPER	GP	MIN	SHOTS	SVS	SHO	GA	GAA
Bill Gaudette	11	990	60	45	3	13	1.18
Noah Palmer	10	900	56	40	1	13	1.30
Jon Busch	8	715	45	34	3	9	1.13
Andy Gruenebaum	3	185	14	12	0	2	0.97
*Dan Popik	1	90	11	7	0	5	5.00
TOTALS	**32**	**2,880**	**145**	**138**	**7**	**42**	**1.31**

D.C. UNITED

PLAYER	GP	MIN	G	A	C	SHOTS	SOG
Christian Gomez	30	2,367	14	11	7	63	35
Jaime Moreno	32	2,700	11	10	3	51	31
Alecko Eskandarian	22	1,478	7	2	6	57	30
Facundo Erpen	30	2,626	3	2	2	29	9
Joshua Gros	29	2,576	3	5	5	33	18
*Freddy Adu	32	2,521	2	8	0	55	25
Ben Olsen	20	1,535	2	3	7	21	10
Bobby Boswell	30	2,700	1	1	8	5	4
Brian Carroll	31	2,779	1	3	6	12	4
Matias Donnet	8	521	1	0	1	5	3
*Lucio Filomeno	11	437	1	1	2	11	5
Clyde Simms	24	1,351	1	1	0	8	5
Jamil Walker	19	412	1	1	0	7	5
Jeff Carroll	2	101	0	0	0	0	0
Stephen deRoux	4	228	0	0	1	3	0
Rod Dyachenko	9	298	0	0	2	7	2
Devon McTavish	5	265	0	0	0	1	1
Domenic Mediate	8	243	0	0	0	1	1
Justin Moose	1	1	0	0	0	0	0
Bryan Namoff	26	2,241	0	1	6	5	2
Matt Nickell	3	14	0	0	1	2	1
Brandon Prideaux	9	784	0	0	3	0	0
*Santino Quaranta	4	65	0	0	0	1	1
Robert Ssejjemba	1	25	0	0	0	1	1
David Stokes	3	52	0	0	0	0	0
John Wilson	11	407	0	0	1	1	1
D.C. UNITED	**32**	**2,880**	**52**	**49**	**63**	**379**	**194**
OPPONENTS	**32**	**2,880**	**38**	**30**	**67**	**330**	**150**

GOALKEEPER	GP	MIN	SHOTS	SVS	SHO	GA	GAA
Troy Perkins	30	2,700	140	100	8	34	1.13
Nick Rimando	2	180	10	6	0	4	2.00
TOTALS	**32**	**2,880**	**150**	**106**	**8**	**38**	**1.19**

FC DALLAS

PLAYER	GP	MIN	G	A	C	SHOTS	SOG
Carlos Ruiz	27	2,113	13	5	6	54	29
Kenny Cooper	31	2,453	11	4	3	65	30
Ramon Nunez	25	1,661	6	4	4	51	15
Arturo Alvarez	19	578	3	1	2	17	11
Roberto Mina	16	883	3	1	2	26	14
Bobby Rhime	30	2,593	2	2	7	13	5
Abe Thompson	14	674	2	6	2	10	5
Drew Moor	27	2,280	1	1	6	12	5
Richard Mulrooney	25	2,075	1	9	1	12	5
Ronnie O'Brien	27	2,331	1	11	4	69	24
Dominic Oduro	16	413	1	0	0	9	3
Aaron Pitchkolan	10	94	1	0	1	2	1
Greg Vanney	28	2,510	1	2	3	9	3
David Wagnefuhr	13	495	1	0	0	6	2
*Mark Wilson	12	582	1	1	0	7	2
Chris Gbandi	28	2,393	0	2	3	14	7
Clarence Goodson	13	866	0	0	3	8	3
Dax McCarty	2	12	0	0	0	0	0
Justin Moore	2	159	0	0	0	0	0
Marcelo Saragosa	7	291	0	0	0	2	0
Simo Valakari	31	2,608	0	1	6	10	3
Alex Yi	11	667	0	0	2	2	1
DALLAS	**32**	**2,880**	**48**	**51**	**58**	**398**	**168**
OPPONENTS	**32**	**2,880**	**44**	**43**	**43**	**379**	**157**

GOALKEEPER	GP	MIN	SHOTS	SVS	SHO	GA	GAA
Dario Sala	28	2,457	129	93	5	34	1.24
Shaka Hislop	4	360	25	13	0	10	2.50
Jeff Cassar	1	45	3	3	0	0	0.00
TOTALS	**32**	**2,880**	**157**	**109**	**5**	**44**	**1.38**

*Player no longer with team

HOUSTON DYNAMO

PLAYER	GP	MIN	G	A	C	SHOTS	SOG
Brian Ching	21	1,822	11	2	1	64	30
Dwayne De Rosario	30	2,534	11	5	2	55	26
Craig Waibel	28	2,401	5	1	3	12	7
Alejandro Moreno	30	2,620	3	6	2	36	21
Ricardo Clark	31	2,728	2	3	4	37	14
Paul Dalglish	6	313	2	1	3	13	7
Brian Mullan	31	2,744	2	4	6	27	10
Eddie Robinson	25	2,084	2	3	11	8	3
Ryan Cochrane	27	2,172	1	0	4	3	2
Brad Davis	28	2,036	1	11	4	42	19
Stuart Holden	13	344	1	0	0	6	3
Adrian Serioux	20	1,412	1	0	4	6	3
Chris Wondolowski	6	198	1	0	0	4	2
Wade Barrett	31	2,756	0	3	1	14	5
*Ronald Cerritos	15	654	0	1	0	10	3
Kevin Goldthwaite	20	821	0	1	2	5	3
Kelly Gray	18	868	0	0	2	4	0
Patrick Ianni	2	2	0	0	0	0	0
Julian Nash	6	95	0	0	0	2	0
EARTHQUAKES	**32**	**2,880**	**44**	**41**	**51**	**348**	**158**
OPPONENTS	**32**	**2,880**	**40**	**33**	**67**	**289**	**132**
GOALKEEPER	**GP**	**MIN**	**SHOTS**	**SVS**	**SHO**	**GA**	**GAA**
Pat Onstad	32	2,880	132	85	5	40	1.25
TOTALS	**32**	**2,880**	**158**	**85**	**5**	**40**	**1.25**

KANSAS CITY WIZARDS

PLAYER	GP	MIN	G	A	C	SHOTS	SOG
Scott Sealy	29	1,762	10	1	3	41	23
Jose Burciaga Jr.	30	2,590	8	8	3	50	22
Josh Wolff	19	1,587	5	2	1	41	19
Davy Arnaud	32	2,785	4	4	6	57	24
Dave van de Bergh	13	991	3	2	0	22	12
Sasha Victorine	31	2,701	3	8	3	31	9
Jimmy Conrad	15	1,252	2	0	3	7	5
Eddie Johnson	19	1,480	2	1	2	47	21
Ryan Pore	19	563	2	0	0	14	7
Nick Garcia	29	2,519	1	0	6	4	3
Jack Jewsbury	28	1,817	1	3	4	28	12
Shavar Thomas	26	2,147	1	1	5	7	3
Alex Zotinca	24	1,303	1	1	3	23	7
Matt Groenwald	19	1,221	0	2	0	1	1
*Jermaine Hue	2	51	0	0	0	1	1
Will John	1	3	0	0	0	0	0
Yura Movsisyan	10	221	0	0	1	15	5
Sergei Raad	1	22	0	0	0	0	0
Ryan Raybould	8	583	0	1	2	1	0
Brian Roberts	1	17	0	0	0	1	0
Tyson Wahl	10	607	0	0	0	5	2
Lance Watson	11	450	0	0	2	4	2
Kerry Zavagnin	25	2,069	0	1	4	8	2
WIZARDS	**32**	**2,880**	**43**	**35**	**51**	**408**	**180**
OPPONENTS	**32**	**2,880**	**45**	**43**	**52**	**348**	**150**
GOALKEEPER	**GP**	**MIN**	**SHOTS**	**SVS**	**SHO**	**GA**	**GAA**
Bo Oshoniyi	29	2,610	138	95	5	41	1.41
Will Hesmer	3	270	12	9	1	4	1.33
TOTALS	**32**	**2,880**	**150**	**104**	**6**	**44**	**1.41**

SOCCER

LOS ANGELES GALAXY

PLAYER	GP	MIN	G	A	C	SHOTS	SOG
Landon Donovan	24	2,147	12	8	3	44	28
Herculez Gomez	30	1,802	5	3	5	55	26
Alan Gordon	17	1,021	4	2	1	38	20
Cobi Jones	27	1,710	4	4	0	14	6
Santino Quaranta	12	772	3	0	2	14	4
Chris Albright	23	2,036	2	5	5	18	5
Cornell Glen	4	235	2	0	2	7	5
Peter Vagenas	25	2,046	2	5	3	15	5
Josh Gardner	18	1,058	1	3	3	13	5
*John Wolyniec	10	651	1	0	1	17	9
*Benjamin Benditson	1	85	0	0	0	0	0
*Marc Burch	3	27	0	0	0	0	0
*Ednaldo da Conceicao	1	19	0	0	0	1	0
*Todd Dunivant	13	1,133	0	1	2	6	5
Michael Enfield	5	126	0	0	0	2	0
Gavin Glinton	1	26	0	0	0	1	1
*Ned Grabavoy	7	350	0	0	0	7	2
Ugo Ihemelu	29	2,610	0	0	8	0	0
Ante Jazic	11	990	0	0	1	3	0
Quavas Kirk	22	993	0	2	0	10	2
Tyrone Marshall	25	2,149	0	0	7	13	3
Kyle Martino	9	555	0	1	1	7	4
Stefani Miglioranzi	3	25	0	0	0	0	0
Paulo Nagamura	29	2,372	0	4	5	30	9
*Joseph Ngwenya	2	123	0	0	0	2	0
Troy Roberts	14	892	0	1	2	3	1
*Marcelo Saragosa	10	822	0	0	4	5	2
Nathan Sturgis	15	1,247	0	0	0	1	0
Kyle Veris	10	732	0	0	1	7	1
GALAXY	**32**	**2,880**	**37**	**39**	**57**	**335**	**144**
OPPONENTS	**32**	**2,880**	**37**	**42**	**68**	**332**	**136**

GOALKEEPER	GP	MIN	SHOTS	SVS	SHO	GA	GAA
Kevin Hartman	28	2,520	120	88	9	32	1.14
Steve Cronin	4	360	16	11	0	5	1.25
TOTALS	**32**	**2,880**	**136**	**99**	**9**	**37**	**1.16**

NEW YORK RED BULLS

PLAYER	GP	MIN	G	A	C	SHOTS	SOG
Amado Guevara	28	2,346	8	5	6	56	23
Edson Buddle	28	2,112	6	3	1	65	29
*Jean Philippe Peguero	12	1,080	6	2	2	24	12
Josmer Altidore	7	330	3	0	1	7	5
Chris Henderson	32	2,188	3	1	0	30	14
Mike Magee	17	938	3	1	4	23	12
Seth Stammler	29	2,374	3	5	7	16	14
John Wolyniec	11	747	3	2	1	19	7
Youri Djorkaef	21	1,824	2	4	2	59	20
Todd Dunivant	9	725	2	1	1	8	4
Jordan Cila	4	78	1	0	0	3	3
Jerrod Laventure	5	70	1	1	0	2	1
Blake Camp	3	36	0	0	0	2	1
Peter Canero	9	278	0	0	1	2	1
Taylor Graham	10	568	0	0	1	2	0
Elie Ikangu	2	22	0	0	0	0	0
Steve Jolley	16	851	0	0	1	2	1
Dema Kovalenko	12	1,080	0	1	4	19	9
Mark Lisi	9	506	0	1	2	3	2
*Thiago Martins	1	11	0	0	0	1	1
Carlos Mendes	31	2,751	0	1	6	0	0
Danny O'Rourke	28	2,400	0	2	7	7	1
Jeff Parke	31	2,771	0	0	5	6	2
Markus Schopp	5	199	0	0	3	6	3
Joe Vide	7	282	0	0	2	4	0
Marvell Wynne	28	2,170	0	3	4	10	5
RED BULLS	**32**	**2,880**	**41**	**38**	**63**	**392**	**170**
OPPONENTS	**32**	**2,880**	**41**	**40**	**48**	**411**	**187**

GOALKEEPER	GP	MIN	SHOTS	SVS	SHO	GA	GAA
Tony Meola	20	1800	120	91	5	29	1.45
Jon Conway	12	1080	67	54	5	12	1.00
TOTALS	**32**	**2,880**	**187**	**145**	**10**	**41**	**1.28**

*Player no longer with team

NEW ENGLAND REVOLUTION

PLAYER	GP	MIN	G	A	C	SHOTS	SOG
Taylor Twellman	32	2,856	11	5	3	86	42
Clint Dempsey	21	1,865	8	4	5	67	31
Andy Dorman	32	2,834	6	10	5	60	33
Steve Ralston	30	2,683	6	5	0	23	14
Shalrie Joseph	26	2,331	3	1	6	27	7
Jose Manuel Abundis	2	140	1	0	0	4	2
Jeff Larentowicz	26	1,974	1	1	4	20	5
Pat Noonan	14	851	1	3	1	16	5
Khano Smith	10	342	1	0	4	10	4
Kyle Brown	12	291	0	1	0	3	1
Jose Cancela	21	1,387	0	5	0	28	15
Joe Franchino	21	1,521	0	1	9	18	3
Jani Galik	2	46	0	0	0	0	0
Jay Heaps	31	2,790	0	4	7	11	2
Daniel Hernandez	7	429	0	0	3	1	0
Avery John	10	893	0	0	3	0	0
Marshall Leonard	1	76	0	0	0	0	0
Tony Lochhead	16	797	0	2	1	0	0
Michael Parkhurst	30	2,700	0	0	1	0	0
James Riley	20	1,706	0	0	5	3	2
Willie Sims	9	219	0	0	0	5	1
Danny Wynn	2	62	0	0	0	0	0
REVOLUTION	**32**	**2,880**	**39**	**42**	**58**	**382**	**167**
OPPONENTS	**32**	**2,880**	**35**	**31**	**71**	**399**	**182**

GOALKEEPER	GP	MIN	SHOTS	SVS	SHO	GA	GAA
Matt Reis	32	2,880	182	141	10	35	1.09
TOTALS	**32**	**2,880**	**182**	**141**	**10**	**35**	**1.09**

REAL SALT LAKE

PLAYER	GP	MIN	G	A	C	SHOTS	SOG
Jeff Cunningham	31	2,404	16	11	6	83	45
Jason Kreis	30	2,434	8	5	3	56	22
Chris Klein	32	2,842	7	8	0	70	27
Atiba Harris	22	1,146	4	1	8	24	15
Mehdi Ballouchy	32	2,162	2	2	4	19	5
Carey Talley	30	2,618	2	8	7	19	6
Andy Williams	29	1,943	2	6	5	37	14
Chris Brown	9	297	1	0	0	1	1
Douglas Sequeira	18	1,246	1	0	3	16	4
Jafet Soto	8	192	1	0	0	2	2
Nelson Akwari	18	1,308	1	0	2	4	1
Nikolas Besagno	4	263	0	0	1	0	0
Kenny Cutler	15	918	0	0	2	5	1
Willis Forko	26	2,254	0	1	2	0	0
Christian Jimenez	1	6	0	0	0	0	0
*Ryan Johnson	7	154	0	0	0	1	1
Kevin Novak	26	2,029	0	0	3	3	1
Eddie Pope	22	1,926	0	0	4	5	1
Jack Stewart	12	987	0	0	1	4	0
Daniel Torres	16	1,363	0	0	1	1	0
Jamie Watson	10	104	0	0	1	4	1
Joey Worthen	3	29	0	0	0	1	0
REAL SALT LAKE	**32**	**2,880**	**45**	**23**	**59**	**355**	**147**
OPPONENTS	**32**	**2,880**	**49**	**60**	**53**	**383**	**171**

GOALKEEPER	GP	MIN	SHOTS	SVS	SHO	GA	GAA
Scott Garlick	31	2,745	158	108	4	43	1.41
Jay Nolly	2	135	13	7	0	6	4.00
TOTALS	**32**	**2,880**	**147**	**115**	**4**	**49**	**1.53**

ALL-TIME MLS CUP RESULTS

YEAR	CHAMPION	SCORE	RUNNER-UP
2006	Houston Dynamo	1–1 (OT)	New England Revolution
2005	Los Angeles Galaxy	1–0	New England Revolution
2004	D.C. United	3–2	Kansas City Wizards
2003	San Jose Earthquakes	4–2	Chicago Fire
2002	Los Angeles Galaxy	1–0 (OT)	New England Revolution
2001	San Jose Earthquakes	2–1 (OT)	Los Angeles Galaxy
2000	Kansas City Wizards	1–0	Chicago Fire
1999	D.C. United	2–0	Los Angeles Galaxy
1998	Chicago Fire	2–0	D.C. United
1997	D.C. United	2–1	Colorado Rapids
1996	D.C. United	3–2 (OT)	Los Angeles Galaxy

FAST FACT

The largest crowd to attend an MLS Cup was in 2002, when 61,316 fans watched the Los Angeles Galaxy beat the hometown favorite New England Revolution in overtime at Gillette Stadium in Foxboro, Massachusetts.

MLS AWARD WINNERS

YEAR	MVP	TOP GOAL SCORER*	GOAL OF THE YEAR	COACH
2006	Christian Gomez, United	Jeff Cunningham, Real Salt Lake	Brian Ching, Real Salt Lake	Bob Bradley, Chivas
2005	Taylor Twellman, Revolution	Taylor Twellman, Revolution	Dwayne De Rosario, Earthquakes	Dominic Kinnear, Earthquakes
2004	Amado Guevara, MetroStars	Amado Guevara, MetroStars	Dwayne De Rosario, Earthquakes	Greg Andrulis, Crew
2003	Preki, Wizards	Preki, Wizards	Damani Ralph, Fire	Dave Sarachan, Fire
2002	Carlos Ruiz, Galaxy	Taylor Twellman, Revolution	Carlos Ruiz, Galaxy	Steve Nicol, Revolution
2001	Alex Pineda Chacon, Fusion	Alex Pineda Chacon, Fusion	Clint Mathis, MetroStars	Frank Yallop, Earthquakes
2000	Tony Meola, Wizards	Mamadou Diallo, Mutiny	Marcelo Balboa, Rapids	Bob Gansler, Wizards
1999	Jason Kreis, Burn	Jason Kreis, Burn	Marco Etcheverry, United	Sigi Schmid, Galaxy
1998	Marco Etcheverry, United	Stern John, Crew	Brian McBride, Crew	Bob Bradley, Fire
1997	Preki, Wizards	Preki, Wizards	Marco Etcheverry, United	Bruce Arena, United
1996	Carlos Valderrama, Mutiny	Roy Lassiter, Mutiny	Eric Wynalda, Clash	Thomas Rongen, Mutiny

YEAR	GOALKEEPER	DEFENDER	ROOKIE	COMEBACK PLAYER
2006	Troy Perkins, United	Bobby Boswell, United	Jonathan Bornstein, Chivas	Richard Mulrooney, FC Dallas
2005	Pat Onstad, Earthquakes	Jimmy Conrad, Wizards	Michael Parkhurst, Revolution	Chris Klein, Wizards
2004	Joe Cannon, Rapids	Robin Fraser, Crew	Clint Dempsey, Revolution	Brian Ching, Earthquakes
2003	Pat Onstad, Earthquakes	Carlos Bocanegra, Fire	Damani Ralph, Fire	Chris Armas, Fire
2002	Joe Cannon, Earthquakes	Carlos Bocanegra, Fire	Kyle Martino, Crew	Chris Klein, Wizards
2001	Tim Howard, MetroStars	Jeff Agoos, Earthquakes	Rodrigo Faria, MetroStars	Troy Dayak, Earthquakes
2000	Tony Meola, Wizards	Peter Vermes, Wizards	Carlos Bocanegra, Fire	Tony Meola, Wizards
1999	Kevin Hartman, Galaxy	Robin Fraser, Galaxy	Jay Heaps, Fusion	Not awarded
1998	Zach Thornton, Fire	Lubos Kubik, Fire	Ben Olsen, United	Not awarded
1997	Brad Friedel, Crew	Eddie Pope, United	Mike Duhaney, Mutiny	Not awarded
1996	Mark Dodd, Burn	John Doyle, Clash	Steve Ralston, Mutiny	Not awarded

LEGENDS

■ Landon Donovan, forward,

b. March 2, 1982, Redlands, California. At age 24, Donovan was named to his sixth career All-Star team in 2006. During his career, he has won three MLS titles (with San Jose in 2001 and 2003 and with Los Angeles in 2005) and set the league record for most career goals in the postseason (14). Donovan played on the U.S. men's national soccer team in the 2000 and 2004 Olympics as well as in the 2002 and 2006 FIFA World Cups. He was also the first man to be named U.S. Player of the Year two years in a row.

■ Cobi Jones, midfielder,

b. June 16, 1970, Detroit, Michigan. Jones, a nine-time All-Star, has played for Los Angeles since the MLS's first season in 1996. He won titles with the Galaxy in 2002 and 2005. He also played on three U.S. World Cup teams (1994, 1998, and 2002) and now holds the all-time record for most U.S. national team appearances.

■ Alexi Lalas, defender/executive,

b. June 1, 1970, Birmingham, Michigan. With his wild red hair and colorful personality, Lalas burst onto the soccer scene with the U.S. national team in 1990. In 2003, after a seven-year MLS career, the 33-year old Lalas retired to become general manager of the San Jose Earthquakes. He is currently the president and GM of the Los Angeles Galaxy.

Donovan (left) has won three MLS titles during his six-year career.

AP PHOTO/DANNY MOLOSHOK

MLS ALL-STAR GAME RESULTS

YEAR	RESULT	SITE	MVP
2006	MLS 1, Chelsea FC 0	Bridgeview, Ill	Dwayne De Rosario, Houston Dynamo
2005	MLS 4, Fulham FC 1	Columbus, Ohio	Taylor Twellman, New England Revolution
2004	East 3, West 2	Washington, D.C.	Amado Guevara, MetroStars
2003	MLS 3, Guadalajara Chivas 1	Carson, California	Carlos Ruiz, Los Angeles Galaxy
2002	MLS 3, USA 2	Washington, D.C.	Marco Etcheverry, D.C. United
2001	East 6, West 6	San Jose, California	Landon Donovan, San Jose Earthquakes
2000	East 9, West 4	Columbus, Ohio	Mamadou Diallo, Tampa Bay Mutiny
1999	West 6, East 4	San Diego, California	Preki, Kansas City Wizards
1998	MLS USA 6, World 1	Orlando, Florida	Brian McBride, Columbus Crew
1997	East 5, West 4	East Rutherford, New Jersey	Carlos Valderrama, Tampa Bay Mutiny
1996	East 3, West 2	East Rutherford, New Jersey	Carlos Valderrama, Tampa Bay Mutiny

SOCCER

UNITED SOCCER LEAGUE FIRST DIVISION* CHAMPIONS

YEAR	CHAMPION	SCORE	RUNNER-UP
2006	Vancouver Whitecaps	3-0	Rochester Raging Rhinos
2005	Seattle Sounders	1-1 (4-3 on PKs)	Richmond Kickers
2004	Montreal Impact	2-0	Seattle Sounders
2003	Charleston Battery	3-0	Minnesota Thunder
2002	Milwaukee Rampage	2-1 (2 OT)	Richmond Kickers
2001	Rochester Raging Rhinos	2-0	Hershey Wildcats
2000	Rochester Raging Rhinos	3-1	Minnesota Thunder
1999	Minnesota Thunder	2-1	Rochester Raging Rhinos
1998	Rochester Raging Rhinos	3-1	Minnesota Thunder
1997	Milwaukee Rampage	2-1 (SO)	Carolina Dynamo
1996	Seattle Sounders	2-0	Rochester Raging Rhinos
1995	Seattle Sounders	1-2 (SO), 3-0, 2-1 (SO)	Atlanta Ruckus
1994	Montreal Impact	1-0	Colorado Foxes
1993	Colorado Foxes	3-1 (OT)	Los Angeles Salsa
1992	Colorado Foxes	1-0	Tampa Bay Rowdies
1991	San Francisco Bay Blackhawks	1-3, 2-0 (1-0 on PKs)	Albany Capitals

*United Soccer League is a minor league system for Major League Soccer.

UNITED SOCCER LEAGUE RESULTS

2006 FIRST DIVISION FINAL STANDINGS

Team	GP	W	L	T
Montreal Impact	28	14	5	9
Rochester Raging Rhinos	28	13	4	11
Charleston Battery	28	13	8	7
Vancouver Whitecaps	28	12	6	10
Miami FC	28	11	11	6
Puerto Rico Islanders	28	10	10	8
Seattle Sounders	28	11	13	4
Atlanta Silverbacks	28	10	13	5
Virginia Beach Mariners	28	8	12	8
Toronto Lynx	28	8	12	8
Portland Timbers	28	7	15	6
Minnesota Thunder	28	7	15	6

2006 FIRST DIVISION CHAMPIONSHIP

PAETEC Park Rochester, New York
Saturday, September 30, 2006

Vancouver Whitecaps 3, Rochester Raging Rhinos 0

Scoring Summary

Vancouver: Own Goal 45
Vancouver: Tony Donatelli (Joey Gjertsen) 55
Vancouver: Sita-Taty Matondo (David Testo) 86

DID YOU KNOW?

Although more well known for founding the American Football League, Lamar Hunt was also a pioneer in bringing pro soccer to the United States. Until his death in 2006, he owned MLS franchises in Columbus and Dallas.

2006 LAMAR HUNT U.S. OPEN CUP RESULTS

The annual Lamar Hunt U.S. Open Cup is open to all amateur and professional soccer teams in the United States. The tournament is a single-elimination event running at the same time as the MLS season. The winner advances to the CONCACAF (Confederation of North, Central American, and Caribbean Association Football) Cup, a tournament of the top club teams from North and Central America and the Caribbean.

QUARTERFINALS
D.C. United 3, New York Red Bulls 1
Chicago Fire 2, New England Revolution 1
Houston Dynamo 3, FC Dallas 0
Los Angeles Galaxy 3, Colorado Rapids 1

SEMI-FINALS
Chicago Fire 3, D.C. United 0
Los Angeles Galaxy 3, Houston Dynamo 1

2006 LAMAR HUNT
U.S. OPEN CUP FINAL RESULTS
September 27, 2006, Bridgeview, Illinois
Chicago Fire 3, Los Angeles Galaxy 1
Scoring summary: Chicago–Nate Jaqua (Andy Herron) 9th minute. Chicago–Andy Herron (Justin Mapp) 16. Los Angeles–Alan Gordon (unassisted) 52. Chicago–Thiago (Tony Sanneh) 88.

LAMAR HUNT U.S. OPEN CUP RESULTS

YEAR	CHAMPION	YEAR	CHAMPION
2006	Chicago Fire (MLS)	1959	McIlvaine Canvasbacks (Los Angeles, CA)
2005	Los Angeles Galaxy (MLS)	1958	Los Angeles Kickers (CA)
2004	Kansas City Wizards (MLS)	1957	Kutis SC (St. Louis, MO)
2003	Chicago Fire (MLS)	1956	Harmarville SC (PA)
2002	Columbus Crew (MLS)	1955	Eintracht Sport Club (New York City)
2001	Los Angeles Galaxy (MLS)	1954	New York Americans (New York City)
2000	Chicago Fire (MLS)	1953	Falcons SC (Chicago, IL)
1999	Rochester Raging Rhinos (A-League)	1952	Harmarville SC (PA)
1998	Chicago Fire (MLS)	1951	German Hungarian SC (New York City)
1997	Dallas Burn (MLS)	1950	Simpkins-Ford SC (St. Louis, MO)
1996	D.C. United (MLS)	1949	Morgan SC (PA)
1995	Richmond Kickers (VA)	1948	Simpkins-Ford SC (St. Louis, MO)
1994	Greek American AC (San Francisco, CA)	1947	Ponta Delgada SC (Fall River, MA)
1993	Club Deportivo Mexico (San Francisco, CA)	1946	Chicago Viking FC (IL)
1992	San Jose Oaks (CA)	1945	Brookhattan FC (New York City)
1991	Brooklyn Italians SC (East New York, NY)	1944	Brooklyn Hispano SC (New York City)
1990	AAC Eagles (Chicago, IL)	1943	Brooklyn Hispano SC (New York City)
1989	HRC Kickers (St. Petersburg, FL)	1942	Gallatin SC (PA)
1988	Busch SC (St. Louis, MO)	1941	Pawtucket FC (RI)
1987	Club Espana (Washington, D.C.)	1940	No winner
1986	Kutis SC (St. Louis, MO)	1939	St. Mary's Celtic SC (Brooklyn, NY)
1985	Greek American AC (San Francisco, CA)	1938	Sparta A and BA (Chicago, IL)
1984	AO Krete (New York City)	1937	New York American FC (New York City)
1983	NY Pancyprian-Freedoms (New York City)	1936	German-Americans (Philadelphia, PA)
1982	NY Pancyprian-Freedoms (New York City)	1935	Central Breweries FC (Chicago, IL)
1981	Maccabee SC (Los Angeles, CA)	1934	Stix, Baer and Fuller FC (St. Louis, MO)
1980	NY Pancyprian-Freedoms (New York City)	1933	Stix, Baer and Fuller FC (St. Louis, MO)
1979	Brooklyn Dodgers SC (New York City)	1932	New Bedford FC (MA)
1978	Maccabee SC (Los Angeles, CA)	1931	Fall River FC (MA)
1977	Maccabee SC (Los Angeles, CA)	1930	Fall River FC (MA)
1976	San Francisco AC (CA)	1929	Hakoah All Stars SC (New York City)
1975	Maccabee SC (Los Angeles, CA)	1928	New York National FC (New York City)
1974	Greek American AA (New York City)	1927	Fall River FC (MA)
1973	Maccabee SC (Los Angeles, CA)	1926	Bethlehem Steel FC (PA)
1972	Elizabeth SC (Union, NJ)	1925	Shawsheen FC (Andover, MA)
1971	Hota SC (New York City)	1924	Fall River FC (MA)
1970	Elizabeth SC (Union, NJ)	1923	Paterson FC (NJ)
1969	Greek American AA (New York City)	1922	Scullin Steel FC (St. Louis, MO)
1968	Greek American AA (New York City)	1921	Robbins Dry Dock FC (Brooklyn, NY)
1967	Greek American AA (New York City)	1920	Ben Miller FC (St. Louis, MO)
1966	Ukrainian Nationals (Philadelphia, PA)	1919	Bethlehem Steel FC (PA)
1965	New York Hungaria (New York City)	1918	Bethlehem Steel FC (PA)
1964	Los Angeles Kickers (CA)	1917	Fall River Rovers (MA)
1963	Ukrainian Nationals (Philadelphia, PA)	1916	Bethlehem Steel FC (PA)
1962	New York Hungaria (New York City)	1915	Bethlehem Steel FC (PA)
1961	Ukrainian Nationals (Philadelphia, PA)	1914	Brooklyn Field Club (New York City)
1960	Ukrainian Nationals (Philadelphia, PA)		

2006 WORLD CUP GROUP STANDINGS

GROUP A

Country	GP	W	L	T	GF	GA	Pts
*Germany	3	3	0	0	8	2	9
*Ecuador	3	2	1	0	5	3	6
Poland	3	1	2	0	2	4	3
Costa Rica	3	0	3	0	3	9	0

GROUP B

Country	GP	W	L	T	GF	GA	Pts
*England	3	2	0	1	5	2	7
*Sweden	3	1	0	2	3	2	5
Paraguay	3	1	2	0	2	2	3
Trinidad-Tobago	3	0	2	1	0	4	1

GROUP C

Country	GP	W	L	T	GF	GA	Pts
*Argentina	3	2	0	1	8	1	7
*Netherlands	3	2	0	1	3	1	7
Cote D'Ivoire	3	1	2	0	5	6	3
Serbia-Montenegro	3	0	3	0	2	10	0

GROUP D

Country	GP	W	L	T	GF	GA	Pts
*Portugal	3	3	0	0	5	1	9
*Mexico	3	1	1	1	4	3	4
Angola	3	0	1	2	1	2	2
Iran	3	0	2	1	2	6	1

GROUP E

Country	GP	W	L	T	GF	GA	Pts
*Italy	3	2	0	1	5	1	7
*Ghana	3	2	1	0	4	3	6
Czech Republic	3	1	2	0	3	4	3
United States	3	0	2	1	2	6	1

2006 WORLD CUP FINAL

	1st half	2nd half	Total	OT	PK
ITALY	1	0	1	0	5
FRANCE	1	0	1	0	3

First-half Scoring: 1, France, Zidane (6:05 on penalty kick); 1, Italy, Materazzi (18:44)

Penalty Kicks: 5, Italy: Pirlo, Materazzi, De Rossi, Del Piero, Grosso; 3, France: Wiltford, Abidal, Sagnol

KEY: OT=overtime; PK=penalty kicks

GROUP F

Country	GP	W	L	T	GF	GA	Pts
*Brazil	3	3	0	0	7	1	9
*Australia	3	1	1	1	5	5	4
Croatia	3	0	1	2	2	3	2
Japan	3	0	2	1	2	7	1

GROUP G

Country	GP	W	L	T	GF	GA	Pts
*Switzerland	3	2	0	1	4	0	7
*France	3	1	0	2	3	1	5
South Korea	3	1	1	1	3	4	4
Togo	3	0	3	0	1	6	0

GROUP H

Country	GP	W	L	T	GF	GA	Pts
*Spain	3	3	0	0	8	1	9
*Ukraine	3	2	1	0	5	4	6
Tunisia	3	0	2	1	3	6	1
Saudi Arabia	3	0	2	1	2	7	1

*Advanced to second round.

Note: In group play, teams are awarded three points for a victory, one for a tie. The top two in each group advance to the Round of 16.

2006 WORLD CUP FINAL BRACKET

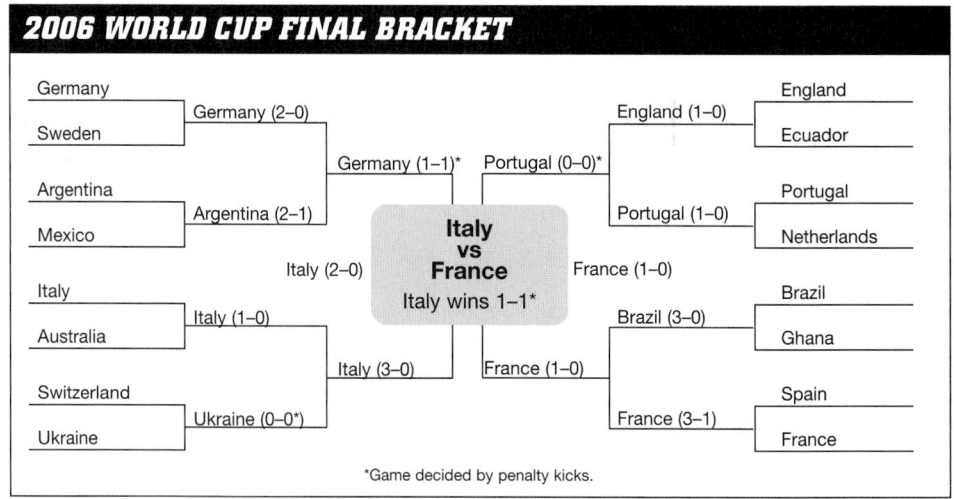

```
Germany
            Germany (2–0)                                          England (1–0)
Sweden                                                                              Ecuador
                        Germany (1–1)*  Portugal (0–0)*
Argentina                                                                           Portugal
            Argentina (2–1)                                        Portugal (1–0)
Mexico                                                                              Netherlands
                        Italy (2–0)          Italy          France (1–0)
Italy                                         vs                                    Brazil
            Italy (1–0)                     France                 Brazil (3–0)
Australia                               Italy wins 1–1*                             Ghana
                        Italy (3–0)      France (1–0)
Switzerland                                                                         Spain
            Ukraine (0–0*)                                         France (3–1)
Ukraine                                                                             France
```

England
Ecuador
Portugal
Netherlands
Brazil
Ghana
Spain
France

*Game decided by penalty kicks.

WORLD CUP STARS

Ronaldo

■ **Ronaldo, forward,** b. September 22, 1976, Rio de Janeiro, Brazil. A soccer prodigy, Ronaldo Luis Nazária de Lima was first recruited for the Brazilian national youth team at age 14, and began his professional career a mere three years later. He has been a member of the last four Brazilian World Cup teams and in 2002, he earned the tournament's Golden Boot award for scoring eight goals, two of which came in Brazil's victorious final match against Germany. In the 2006 World Cup, Ronaldo notched his 15th career World Cup goal—breaking the all-time record previously held by Gërd Muller—during a Round of 16 match against Ghana. He is only the second player in World Cup history to have scored at least three goals in three different World Cups.

■ **Hernan Crespo, forward,** b. July 5, 1975, Florida, Argentina. Crespo played on his third straight World Cup team in 2006, scoring three goals in four matches and helping Argentina reach the quarterfinals in Germany. After playing in the shadow of legendary Argentinian forward Gabriel Batistuta during the 1998 and 2002 World Cups, Crespo was finally able to unleash the long-range scoring strikes that he has become known for while playing for professional soccer clubs like Chelsea and AC Milan.

Kristine Lilly (right)

■ **Kristine Lilly, midfielder,** b. July 22, 1971, Wilton, Connecticut. Lilly is the "iron woman" of the U.S. women's national team. She has played in more than 300 international soccer matches, more than any other man or woman in the sport. She first joined the U.S. team in 1987 and was a key part of the team's successful title runs in 1991 and 1999. Now captain of the U.S. women's team, Lilly looks to bring the trophy back to the United States once again after the 2007 Women's World Cup in China.

ALL-TIME WORLD CUP SCORING LEADERS

PLAYER, NATION	TOURNAMENTS	GOALS
Ronaldo, Brazil	1998, 2002, 2006	15
Gerd Müller, West Germany	1970, 1974	14
Just Fontaine, France	1958	13
Pelé, Brazil	1958, 1962, 1966, 1970	12
Jürgen Klinsman, Germany	1990, 1994, 1998	11
Sandor Kocsis, Hungary	1954	11
Teofilo Cubillas, Peru	1970, 1978	10
Miroslav Klose, Germany	2002, 2006	10
Gregorz Lato, Poland	1974, 1978, 1982	10
Helmut Rahn, West Germany	1954, 1958	10
Gary Lineker, England	1986, 1990	10

WORLD CUP LEGENDS

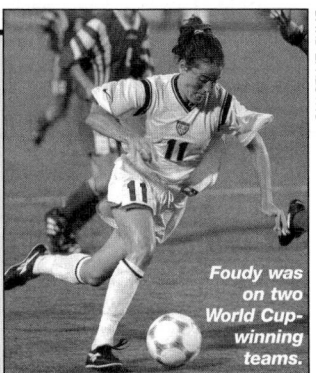

Foudy was on two World Cup-winning teams.

■ **Julie Foudy, midfielder,** b. January 23, 1971, San Diego, California. For nearly two decades, Foudy, along with teammates Mia Hamm, Joy Fawcett, and Brandi Chastain, were the faces of women's soccer in the United States. In 1991, the 20-year-old Foudy was a key part of the U.S. national team's first World Cup title. Foudy enjoyed a successful World Cup and Olympic career during the 1990s, winning Olympic gold in 1996 and another World Cup title in 1999. She became captain of the U.S. team in 2000. After a final trip to the World Cup in 2003 and a second Olympic gold medal at Athens in 2004, Foudy retired, having made a remarkable 271 career appearances in international play.

■ **Bobby Moore, defender,** b. April 12, 1941, Barking, England. Although Moore never scored a goal in the World Cup, his presence on the pitch was always felt: He is considered one of the best defenders in World Cup history. He played on three of England's World Cup teams, but it was his heroic performance as captain in 1966 that secured his place in soccer lore. Playing in front of his home country's fans in London's Wembley Stadium, Moore led England to its only World Cup title.

■ **Roberto Baggio, forward,** b. February 18, 1967, Caldogno, Italy. Nicknamed "Il Divino Codino" (The Divine Ponytail) because of his habit of wearing his long, flowing hair tied back during soccer matches, Baggio was a force for Italian national teams throughout the 1990s. Used sparingly in his first World Cup in 1990, Baggio had a breakout performance four years later when he scored five goals—second-most in the tournament—and propelled Italy to the World Cup final match against Brazil. In 1998, playing off the bench, Baggio again inspired his teammates and scored two goals. He was the first player in Italian soccer history to score a goal in three different World Cup tournaments.

ALL-TIME WORLD CUP RESULTS

YEAR	CHAMPION	SCORE	RUNNER-UP	WINNING COACH
2006	Italy	1–1 (5–3)	France	Marcello Lippi
2002	Brazil	2–0	Germany	Luiz Felipe Scolari
1998	France	3–0	Brazil	Aime Jacquet
1994	Brazil	0–0 (3–2)	Italy	Carlos Alberto Parreira
1990	West Germany	1–0	Argentina	Franz Beckenbauer
1986	Argentina	3–2	West Germany	Carlos Bilardo
1982	Italy	3–1	West Germany	Enzo Bearzot
1978	Argentina	3–1	Netherlands	César Menotti
1974	West Germany	2–1	Netherlands	Helmut Schön
1970	Brazil	4–1	Italy	Mario Zagallo
1966	England	4–2	West Germany	Alf Ramsey
1962	Brazil	3–1	Czechoslovakia	Aymore Moreira
1958	Brazil	5–2	Sweden	Vicente Feola
1954	West Germany	3–2	Hungary	Sepp Herberger
1950	Uruguay	2–1	Brazil	Juan Lopez
1938	Italy	4–2	Hungary	Vittorio Pozzo
1934	Italy	2–1	Czechoslovakia	Vittorio Pozzo
1930	Uruguay	4–2	Argentina	Alberto Supicci

SIMON BRUTY/SPORTS ILLUSTRATED

SOCCER TRIVIA

1 Germany's Miroslav Klose scored more goals (five) than any other player in the 2006 World Cup. How many total World Cup goals does he have in his career?
a. 5
b. 8
c. 10

Miroslav Klose (right)

2 In which of the following game situations can a soccer player NEVER be called offsides?
a. Throw in
b. Free kick
c. Penalty shot

3 Which team won the MLS Cup championship in three of the league's first four years?
a. Los Angeles Galaxy
b. D.C. United
c. Dallas Burn

4 Which U.S. women's soccer player drew worldwide attention for removing her jersey while celebrating the U.S. national team's victory over China in the 1999 women's World Cup?
a. Brandi Chastain
b. Julie Foudy
c. Mia Hamm

5 What color do both the French and Italian national soccer teams use as their nickname?
a. Red
b. Blue
c. Yellow

6 Barring any time added for penalties, all MLS and World Cup soccer matches are played as two 45-minute halves.
a. True
b. False

7 What is another name for the field on which a soccer match is played?
a. Pitch
b. Diamond
c. Gridiron

8 In 2010, for the first time in history, the World Cup will be held in an African country. Name that nation.
a. South Africa
b. Kenya
c. Nigeria

9 Which country won the men's World Cup in 1994, in the first tournament hosted by the United States?
a. England
b. United States
c. Brazil

10 The largest crowd to ever witness a women's sporting event occurred when more than 90,000 fans attended the final match of the 1999 women's World Cup. In what stadium was this match held?
a. Rose Bowl (Pasadena, California)
b. Wembley Stadium (London, England)
c. Tokyo Dome (Tokyo, Japan)

Trivia Challenge: 1. c; 2. a; 3. b; 4. a; 5. b; 6. a.; 7. c; 8. a; 9. c; 10. a.

SIKIDS.COM
Visit our website for the latest stats and sports info.

ACTION SPORTS

Travis Pastrana flipped out at the 2006 X Games in Los Angeles, California, in August. In front of a loud crowd at the Staples Center, the freestyle motocross rider became the first person ever to pull off a double backflip in competition. The maneuver earned Pastrana the gold medal in Moto X best trick at X Games 12. It was one of three golds that Pastrana took home from the event. He also won Moto X freestyle and the first-ever rally car competition.

BMX big air also made its X Games debut. Kevin Robinson finished in first place after speeding down the mega ramp and boosting a backflip tuck no-hander across the gap before launching into a no-handed flair on the quarterpipe. Robinson also struck gold in the BMX vert best trick competition, finishing first after landing an amazing double flair.

In skateboarding, Shaun White failed to land the first 1080 in the vert best trick event at the X Games. That opened the door for Bucky Lasek to take home the gold with a frontside cab varial heelflip. Danny Way continued his big air dominance, winning his third consecutive gold medal in the event by landing a rocket air backflip across the mega ramp's 70-foot gap.

The Dew Action Sports tour also rolled through its second season with many of the same results. Lasek repeated as vert skating champ, Ryan Sheckler doubled up in street skating, and Jamie Bestwick won his second BMX vert title. But there were also a few new faces hoisting Dew Cup trophies

At the 2006 Summer X Games, Travis Pastrana landed the first double backflip in freestyle motocross history.

when the tour finished its fifth and final event. Daniel Dhers and Anthony Napolitan won the BMX park and BMX dirt championships, respectively, and Nate Adams was crowned freestyle motocross champ.

Winter brought not only a change of season, but a possible changing of the guard. Shaun White, who won every event in which he competed in 2005–06, failed to win gold in either superpipe or slopestyle at the Winter X Games. Steve Fisher's huge airs forced White to settle for the silver in the super-pipe. And Andreas Wiig and Jussi Oksanen's performances in slopestyle meant White had to go home with a bronze medal. In women's superpipe, two-time champ Gretchen Bleiler was dethroned by Torah Bright. The 20-year-old Australian won her first Winter

X gold medal with a stylish mix of technical tricks. Another change was the addition of snowmobile freestyle to the lineup of events. Chris Burandt launched his sled off the snowy jumps into numerous backflips to finish first. Not everything changed, though. Skier Tanner Hall repeated as ski superpipe gold medalist, barely squeaking by his friend Simon Dumont.

In warmer climates, Kelly Slater once again reigned over the surfing world, winning his eighth world title. Slater won two events on the ASP World Championship Tour and never finished lower than fifth. A familiar name also reigned on the women's tour. Layne Beachley, who was world champ from 1998 through 2003, returned to the top and won her seventh title.

WINTER X GAMES RESULTS

MONO X

YEAR	EVENT	GOLD	SILVER	BRONZE
2007	Skier X	Tyler Walker, U.S.	Kevin Connolly U.S.	Kees-Jan van der Klooster, Netherlands

MOTO X

YEAR	EVENT	GOLD	SILVER	BRONZE
2006	Best Trick	Jeremy Stenberg, U.S.	Mat Rebeaud, U.S.	Ronnie Faisst, U.S.
2005	Best Trick	Brian Deegan, U.S.	Jeff Kargola, U.S.	Dustin Miller, U.S.
2004	Best Trick	Caleb Wyatt, U.S.	Mike Metzger, U.S.	Nate Adams, U.S.
2003	Big Air	Mike Metzger, U.S.	Dane Kinnaird, Australia	Caleb Wyatt, U.S.
2002	Big Air	Brian Deegan, U.S.	Mike Jones, U.S.	Tommy Clowers, U.S.
2001	Big Air	Mike Jones, U.S.	Tommy Clowers, U.S.	Clifford Adoptante, U.S.

SKIING — MEN

YEAR	EVENT	GOLD	SILVER	BRONZE
2007	Skier X	Casey Puckett, U.S.	Jake Fiala, U.S.	Enak Gavaggio, France
2006	Skier X	Lars Lewen, Sweden	Reggie Crist, U.S.	Chris Del Bosco, U.S.
2005	Skier X	Reggie Crist, U.S.	Zach Crist, U.S.	Enak Gavaggio, France
2004	Skier X	Casey Puckett, U.S.	Lars Lewen, Sweden	Reggie Crist, U.S.
2003	Skier X	Lars Lewen, Sweden	Reggie Crist, U.S.	Enak Gavaggio, France
2002	Skier X	Reggie Crist, U.S.	Peter Lind, Sweden	Enak Gavaggio, France
2001	Skier X	Zach Crist, U.S.	Tomas Andersson, Sweden	Enak Gavaggio, France
2000	Skier X	Shaun Palmer, U.S.	Bill Hudson, U.S.	Zach Crist, U.S.
1999	Skier X	Enak Gavaggio, France	Shane McConkey, U.S.	Jeremy Nobis, U.S.
1998	Skier X	Denis Rey, France	Kent Kreitler, U.S.	Chris Davenport, U.S.
2007	Slopestyle	Candide Thovex, France	Sammy Carlson, U.S.	Cobly West, U.S.
2006*	Best Trick	T.J. Schiller, Canada	Charles Gagnier, Canada	Andrea Hatveit, Norway
2005	Slopestyle	Charles Gagnier, Canada	Tanner Hall, U.S.	Jon Olsson, Sweden
2004	Slopestyle	Tanner Hall, U.S.	Peter Olenick, U.S.	Jon Olsson, Sweden
2003	Slopestyle	Tanner Hall, U.S.	Pep Fujas, U.S.	Jon Olsson, Sweden
2002	Slopestyle	Tanner Hall, U.S.	C.R. Johnson, U.S.	Jon Olsson, Sweden
2007	Superpipe	Tanner Hall, U.S.	Simon Dumont, U.S.	Peter Olenick, U.S.
2006	Superpipe	Tanner Hall, U.S.	Laurent Favre, France	Simon Dumont, U.S.
2005	Superpipe	Simon Dumont, U.S.	Tanner Hall, U.S.	Jon Olsson, Sweden
2004	Superpipe	Simon Dumont, U.S.	Jon Olsson, Sweden	Peter Olenick, U.S.
2003	Superpipe	Candide Thovex, France	Tanner Hall, U.S.	Jon Olsson, Sweden
2002	Superpipe	Jon Olsson, Sweden	Philippe Larose, Canada	Philippe Poirier, Canada
2001	Big Air	Tanner Hall, U.S.	Evan Raps, U.S.	C.R. Johnson, U.S.
2000	Big Air	Candide Thovex, France	Skogen Sprang, U.S.	Evan Raps, U.S.
1999	Big Air	J.F. Cusson, Canada	Jonny Moseley, U.S.	Vincent Dorion, Canada

SKIING — WOMEN

YEAR	EVENT	GOLD	SILVER	BRONZE
2007	Skier X	Ophelie David, France	Valentine Scuotto, France	Meryll Boulangeat, France
2006	Skier X	Karin Huttary, Austria	Gro Kvinlog, Norway	Ophelie David, France
2005	Skier X	Sanna Tidstrand, Sweden	Karin Huttary, Austria	Magdalena Jonsson, Sweden
2004	Skier X	Karin Huttary, Austria	Aleisha Cline, Canada	Sanna Tidstrand, Sweden
2003	Skier X	Aleisha Cline, Canada	Karin Huttary, Austria	Cecilie Larsen, Norway
2002	Skier X	Aleisha Cline, Canada	Magdalena Jonsson, Sweden	Patti Sherman-Kauf, U.S.
2001	Skier X	Aleisha Cline, Canada	Magdalena Jonsson, Sweden	Chiara Lawrence, U.S.
2000	Skier X	Anik Demers, Canada	Chiara Lawrence, U.S.	Patti Sherman-Kauf, U.S.
1999	Skier X	Aleisha Cline, Canada	Darian Boyle, U.S.	Patti Sherman-Kauf, U.S.
2007	Superpipe	Sarah Burke, Canada	Grete Eliassen, Norway	Jen Hudak, U.S.
2006	Superpipe	Grete Eliassen, Norway	Sarah Burke, Canada	Marie Martinod-Routin, France
2005	Superpipe	Grete Eliassen, Norway	Sarah Burke, Canada	Kristi Leskinen, U.S.

* Ski Slopestyle was turned into Ski Best Trick due to time considerations.

WINTER X GAMES RESULTS (cont.)

SNOWBOARDING — MEN

YEAR	EVENT	GOLD	SILVER	BRONZE
2007	Slopestyle	Andreas Wiig, Norway	Jussi Oksanen, Finland	Shaun White, U.S.
2006	Slopestyle	Shaun White, U.S.	Andreas Wiig, Norway	Danny Kass, U.S.
2005	Slopestyle	Shaun White, U.S.	Danny Kass, U.S.	Travis Rice, U.S.
2004	Slopestyle	Shaun White, U.S.	Danny Kass, U.S.	Andreas Wiig, Norway
2003	Slopestyle	Shaun White, U.S.	Jussi Oksanen, Finland	Jimi Tomer, U.S.
2002	Slopestyle	Travis Rice, U.S.	Shaun White, U.S.	Todd Richards, U.S.
2001	Slopestyle	Kevin Jones, U.S.	Todd Richards, U.S.	Jussi Oksanen, Finland
2000	Slopestyle	Kevin Jones, U.S.	Todd Richards, U.S.	Peter Line, U.S.
1999	Slopestyle	Peter Line, U.S.	Kevin Jones, U.S.	Jimmy Halopoff, U.S.
1998	Slopestyle	Ross Powers, U.S.	Kevin Jones, U.S.	Rob Kingwill, U.S.
1997	Slopestyle	Daniel Franck, Norway	Jimmy Halopoff, U.S.	Bryan Iguchi, U.S.
2007	Snowboarder X	Nate Holland, U.S.	Xavier de le Rue, France	Seth Wescott, U.S.
2006	Snowboarder X	Nate Holland, U.S.	Marco Huser, Switzerland	Jayson Hale, U.S.
2005	Snowboarder X	Xavier de le Rue, France	Seth Wescott, U.S.	Marco Huser, Switzerland
2004	Snowboarder X	Ueli Kestenholz, Switzerland	Seth Wescott, U.S.	Xavier de le Rue, France
2003	Snowboarder X	Ueli Kestenholz, Switzerland	Xavier de le Rue, France	Michael Rosengren, U.S.
2002	Snowboarder X	Philippe Conte, Switzerland	Seth Wescott, U.S.	Berti Denervaud, Switzerland
2001	Snowboarder X	Scott Gaffney, Canada	Mark Schulz, U.S.	Seth Wescott, U.S.
2000	Snowboarder X	Drew Neilson, Canada	Scott Gaffney, Canada	Jason Ford, U.S.
1999	Snowboarder X	Shaun Palmer, U.S.	Drew Neilson, Canada	Scott Gaffney, Canada
1998	Snowboarder X	Shaun Palmer, U.S.	Jason Brown, U.S.	Seth Wescott, U.S.
1997	Snowboarder X	Shaun Palmer, U.S.	Berti Denervaud, Switzerland	Mike Basich, U.S.
2007	Superpipe	Steve Fisher, U.S.	Shaun White, U.S.	Mason Aguirre, U.S.
2006	Superpipe	Shaun White, U.S.	Mason Aguirre, U.S.	Scotty Lago, U.S.
2005	Superpipe	Antti Autti, Finland	Andy Finch, U.S.	Danny Kass, U.S.
2004	Superpipe	Steve Fisher, U.S.	Danny Kass, U.S.	Keir Dillon, U.S.
2003	Superpipe	Shaun White, U.S.	Danny Kass, U.S.	Markku Koski, Finland
2002	Superpipe	J.J. Thomas, U.S.	Shaun White, U.S.	Keir Dillon, U.S.
2001	Superpipe	Danny Kass, U.S.	Tommy Czeschin, U.S.	Ross Powers, U.S.
2000	Superpipe	Todd Richards, U.S.	Ross Powers, U.S.	Tommy Czeschin, U.S.
1999	Halfpipe	Jimi Scott, U.S.	Mike Michalchuk, Canada	Luke Wynen, U.S.
1998	Halfpipe	Ross Powers, U.S.	Guillaume Chastagnol, France	Todd Richards, U.S.
1997	Halfpipe	Todd Richards, U.S.	Daniel Franck, Norway	Fabien Rohrer, Switzerland
2001	Big Air	Jussi Oksanen, Finland	Todd Richards, U.S.	Josh Dirksen, U.S.
2000	Big Air	Peter Line, U.S.	Jason Borgstede, U.S.	Kevin Jones, U.S.
1999	Big Air	Kevin Sansalone, Canada	Peter Line, U.S.	Kevin Jones, U.S.
1998	Big Air	Jason Borgstede, U.S.	Ryan W. Williams, U.S.	Kevin Jones, U.S.
1997	Big Air	Jimmy Halopoff, U.S.	Steve Adkins, U.S.	Bjorn Leines, U.S.

SNOWBOARDING — WOMEN

YEAR	EVENT	GOLD	SILVER	BRONZE
2007	Slopestyle	Jamie Anderson, U.S.	Hana Beaman, U.S.	Chanelle Sladics, U.S.
2006	Slopestyle	Janna Meyen, U.S.	Hana Beaman, U.S.	Jamie Anderson, U.S.
2005	Slopestyle	Janna Meyen, U.S.	Silvia Mittermueller, Germany	Natasza Zurek, Canada
2004	Slopestyle	Janna Meyen, U.S.	Tara Dakides, U.S.	Jessica Dalpiaz, U.S.
2003	Slopestyle	Janna Meyen, U.S.	Hana Beaman, U.S.	Lindsey Jacobellis, U.S.
2002	Slopestyle	Tara Dakides, U.S.	Janna Meyen, U.S.	Barrett Christy, U.S.
2001	Slopestyle	Jaime MacLeod, U.S.	Shannon Dunn, U.S.	Marni Yamada, U.S.
2000	Slopestyle	Tara Dakides, U.S.	Jaime MacLeod, U.S.	Barrett Christy, U.S.
1999	Slopestyle	Tara Dakides, U.S.	Barrett Christy, U.S.	Jaime MacLeod, U.S.
1998	Slopestyle	Jennie Waara, Sweden	Barrett Christy, U.S.	Aurelie Sayres, U.S.
1997	Slopestyle	Barrett Christy, U.S.	Cara-Beth Burnside, U.S.	Jennie Waara, Sweden
2007	Snowboarder X	Joanie Anderson, U.S.	Lindsey Jacobellis, U.S.	Maelie Ricker, Canada
2006	Snowboarder X	Maelle Ricker, Canada	Joanie Anderson, U.S.	Claudia Haeusermann, Switzerland
2005	Snowboarder X	Lindsey Jacobellis, U.S.	Erin Simmons, Canada	Karine Ruby, France
2004	Snowboarder X	Lindsey Jacobellis, U.S.	Karine Ruby, France	Yvonne Mueller, Switzerland

SNOWBOARDING — WOMEN (cont.)

YEAR	EVENT	GOLD	SILVER	BRONZE
2003	Snowboarder X	Lindsey Jacobellis, U.S.	Tanja Frieden, Switzerland	Yvonne Mueller, Switzerland
2002	Snowboarder X	Ine Poetzl, Austria	Erin Simmons, Canada	Tanja Frieden, Switzerland
2001	Snowboarder X	Line Oestvold, Norway	Erin Simmons, Canada	Amy Johnson, U.S.
2000	Snowboarder X	Leslee Olson, U.S.	Carlee Baker, Canada	Line Oestvold, Norway
1999	Snowboarder X	Maelle Ricker, Canada	Leslee Olson, U.S.	Candice Drouin, Canada
1998	Snowboarder X	Tina Dixon, U.S.	Corrie Rudishauser, U.S.	Katrina Warnick, U.S.
1997	Snowboarder X	Jennie Waara, Sweden	Hillary Maybery, U.S.	Aurelie Sayres, U.S.
2007	Superpipe	Torah Bright, Australia	Gretchen Bleiler, U.S.	Elena Hight, U.S.
2006	Superpipe	Kelly Clark, U.S.	Torah Bright, Australia	Soko Yamaoka, Japan
2005	Superpipe	Gretchen Bleiler, U.S.	Doriane Vidal, France	Hannah Teter, U.S.
2004	Superpipe	Hannah Teter, U.S.	Kelly Clark, U.S.	Doriane Vidal, France
2003	Superpipe	Gretchen Bleiler, U.S.	Kelly Clark, U.S.	Hannah Teter, U.S.
2002	Superpipe	Kelly Clark, U.S.	Stine Brun Kjeldaas, Norway	Natasza Zurek, Canada
2001	Superpipe	Shannon Dunn, U.S.	Natasza Zurek, Canada	Fabienne Reuteler, Switzerland
2000	Superpipe	Stine Brun Kjeldaas, Norway	Barrett Christy, U.S.	Natasza Zurek, Canada
1999	Halfpipe	Michelle Taggart, U.S.	Shannon Dunn, U.S.	Cara-Beth Burnside, U.S.
1998	Halfpipe	Cara-Beth Burnside, U.S.	Michelle Taggart, U.S.	Nicola Thost, Germany
1997	Halfpipe	Shannon Dunn, U.S.	Jennie Waara, Sweden	Nicole Angelrath, Switzerland
2001	Big Air	Tara Dakides, U.S.	Barrett Christy, U.S.	Jenna Murano, U.S.
2000	Big Air	Tara Dakides, U.S.	Leah Wagner, Canada	Jessica Dalpiaz, U.S.
1999	Big Air	Barrett Christy, U.S.	Tara Dakides, U.S.	Janet Matthews, Canada
1998	Big Air	Tina Basich, U.S.	Barrett Christy, U.S.	Tara Zwink, U.S.
1997	Big Air	Barrett Christy, U.S.	Tara Zwink, U.S.	Tina Basich, U.S.

SNOWMOBILING

YEAR	EVENT	GOLD	SILVER	BRONZE
2007	SnoCross	Tucker Hibbert, U.S.	Ryan Simons, Canada	T.J. Gulla, U.S.
2006	SnoCross	Blair Morgan, Canada	Levi LaVallee, U.S.	Ross Martin, U.S.
2005	SnoCross	Blair Morgan, Canada	Tucker Hibbert, U.S.	Steve Martin, Canada
2004	SnoCross	Michael Island, Canada	Tucker Hibbert, U.S.	Blair Morgan, Canada
2003	SnoCross	Blair Morgan, Canada	D.J. Eckstrom, U.S.	Tucker Hibbert, U.S.
2002	SnoCross	Blair Morgan, Canada	Tucker Hibbert, U.S.	Tomi Ahmasalo, Finland
2001	SnoCross	Blair Morgan, Canada	Kent Ipsen, U.S.	D.J. Eckstrom, U.S.
2000	SnoCross	Tucker Hibbert, U.S.	Blair Morgan, Canada	T.J. Gulla, U.S.
1999	SnoCross	Chris Vincent, U.S.	Blair Morgan, Canada	Trevor John, U.S.
1998	SnoCross	Toni Haikonen, Finland	Dennis Burks, U.S.	Per Berggren, Sweden
2004	HillCross	Levi LaVallee, U.S.	Justin Tate, U.S.	Carl Kuster, Canada
2003	HillCross	T.J. Gulla, U.S.	Carl Kuster, Canada	Steve Martin, Canada
2002	HillCross	Carl Kuster, Canada	Steve Martin, Canada	Rick Ward, U.S.
2001	HillCross	Carl Kuster, Canada	Vinny Clark, Canada	Matt Luczynski, U.S.

ULTRACROSS*

YEAR	GOLD	SILVER	BRONZE
2005	Marco Huser, Switzerland	Xavier de le Rue, France	Nate Holland, U.S.
	Eric Andersson, Sweden	Davey Barr, Canada	Eric Archer, U.S.
2004	Nate Holland, U.S.	Lars Lewen, Sweden	Xavier Kuhn, France
	Reggie Crist, U.S.	Xavier de le Rue, France	Drew Neilson, Canada
2003	Xavier de le Rue, France	Seth Wescott, U.S.	Ben Jacobellis, U.S.
	Kaj Zackrisson, Sweden	Peter Lind, Sweden	Lars Lewen, Sweden
2002	Seth Wescott, U.S.	Scott Gaffney, Canada	Rob Fagan, Canada
	Peter Lind, Sweden	Eric Archer, U.S.	Enak Gavaggio, France
2001	Shaun Palmer, U.S.	Jason Evans, U.S.	Pontus Staahlkloo, Sweden
	Hiroomi Takizawa, Japan	Isidor Gruener, Austria	Matt Murphy, U.S.
2000	Travis McLain, U.S.	Scott Gaffney, Canada	Terry Plum, U.S.
	Peter Lind, Sweden	Sverre Liliequist, Sweden	Mike Dill, U.S.

*First athlete listed is a snowboarder; the second athlete is a skier.

U.S. OPEN SNOWBOARDING CHAMPIONSHIPS RESULTS

HALFPIPE — MEN

YEAR	GOLD	SILVER	BRONZE
2007	Shaun White, U.S.	Danny Davis, U.S.	Markus Malin, Finland
2006	Shaun White, U.S.	Danny Davis, U.S.	Mason Aguirre, U.S.
2005	Danny Kass, U.S.	Steve Fisher, U.S.	Antti Autti, Finland
2004	Danny Kass, U.S.	Steve Fisher, U.S.	Keir Dillon, U.S.
2003	Ross Powers, U.S.	Kazuhiro Kokubo, Japan	Daniel Franck, Norway
2002	Danny Kass, U.S.	Markku Koski, Finland	Keir Dillon, U.S.
2001	Danny Kass, U.S.	Abe Teter, U.S.	Daniel Franck, Norway
2000	Guillaume Morisset, Canada	Ross Powers, U.S.	Xavier Hoffman, Germany
1999	Ross Powers, U.S.	Xavier Hoffman, Germany	Tommy Czeschin, U.S.
1998	Rob Kingwill, U.S.	Terje Haakonsen, Norway	Todd Richards, U.S.
1997	Todd Richards, U.S.	Terje Haakonsen, Norway	Sebu Kuhlberg, Finland
1996	Jimi Scott, U.S.	Sami Hyry, Finland	Max Ploetzender, Austria
1995	Terje Haakonsen, Norway	Jason Evans, U.S.	J.J. Collier, U.S.
1994	Todd Richards, U.S.	Lael Gregory, U.S.	Jason Evans, U.S.
1993	Terje Haakonsen, Norway	Keith Wallace, U.S.	Sebu Kuhlberg, Finland
1992	Terje Haakonsen, Norway	Jeff Brushie, U.S.	Todd Richards, U.S.
1991	Jimi Scott, U.S.	Craig Kelly, U.S.	Shaun Palmer, U.S.
1990	Craig Kelly, U.S.	Shaun Palmer, U.S.	Jeff Brushie, U.S.
1989	Craig Kelly, U.S.	Bert Lamar, U.S.	Terry Kidwell, U.S.
1988	Terry Kidwell, U.S.	Bert Lamar, U.S.	Craig Kelly, U.S.

HALFPIPE — WOMEN

YEAR	GOLD	SILVER	BRONZE
2007	Kelly Clark, U.S.	Gretchen Bleiler, U.S.	Torah Bright, Australia
2006	Torah Bright, Australia	Gretchen Bleiler, U.S.	Elena Hight, U.S.
2005	Gretchen Bleiler, U.S.	Torah Bright, Australia	Hannah Teter, U.S.
2004	Kelly Clark, U.S.	Tricia Byrnes, U.S.	Stine Brun Kjeldaas, Norway
2003	Gretchen Bleiler, U.S.	Natasza Zurek, Canada	Hannah Teter, U.S.
2002	Kelly Clark, U.S.	Tricia Byrnes, U.S.	Stine Brun Kjeldaas, Norway
2001	Natasza Zurek, Canada	Shannon Dunn, U.S.	Gretchen Bleiler, U.S.
2000	Natasza Zurek, Canada	Shannon Dunn, U.S.	Barrett Christy, U.S.
1999	Nicola Thost, Germany	Tricia Byrnes, U.S.	Shannon Dunn, U.S.
1998	Nicola Thost, Germany	Tricia Byrnes, U.S.	Tara Teigen, Canada
1997	Barrett Christy, U.S.	Tricia Byrnes, U.S.	Michelle Taggart, U.S.
1996	Satu Jarvela, Finland	Michelle Taggart, U.S.	Jennie Waara, Sweden
1995	Satu Jarvela, Finland	Nicole Angelrath, Switzerland	Jennie Waara, Sweden
1994	Shannon Dunn, U.S	Tina Basich, U.S.	Sandra Farmand, Germany
1993	Shannon Dunn, U.S.	Janna Meyen, U.S.	Tricia Byrnes, U.S.
1992	Tricia Byrnes, U.S.	Nicole Angelrath, Switzerland	Tina Basich, U.S.
1991	Janna Meyen, U.S.	Tina Basich, U.S.	Michelle Taggart, U.S.
1990	Tina Basich, U.S.	Lisa Vinciguerra, U.S.	Jean Higgins, U.S.
1989	Jean Higgins, U.S.	Tara Eberhard, U.S.	Ashild Lofthus, Norway
1988	Petra Mussig, Germany	Jean Higgins, U.S.	Gayle Guerin, U.S.

QUARTERPIPE — MEN

YEAR	GOLD	SILVER	BRONZE
2005	Danny Davis, U.S.	Risto Matilla, Finland	Kevin Pierce, U.S.

QUARTERPIPE — WOMEN

YEAR	GOLD	SILVER	BRONZE
2005	Hana Beaman, U.S.	Junko Asazuma, Japan	Molly Aguirre, U.S.

RAIL JAM — MEN

YEAR	GOLD	SILVER	BRONZE
2005	Eddie Wall, U.S.	Yale Cousino, U.S.	Jed Anderson, U.S.
2004	Rahm Klampert, U.S.	Travis Rice, U.S.	Chris Rotax, U.S.
2003	Travis Rice, U.S.	Shaun White, U.S.	Zach Leach, U.S.

U.S. OPEN SNOWBOARDING CHAMPIONSHIPS RESULTS (cont.)

RAIL JAM — WOMEN

YEAR	GOLD	SILVER	BRONZE
2005	Leanne Pelosi, Canada	Hana Beaman, U.S.	Spencer O'Brien, Canada
2004	Leanne Pelosi, Canada	Erin Comstock, U.S.	Natasza Zurek, Canada

SLOPESTYLE — MEN

Travis Rice

YEAR	GOLD	SILVER	BRONZE
2007	Travis Rice, U.S.	Janne Korpi, Finland	Shaun White, U.S.
2006	Shaun White, U.S.	Chas Guidemond, U.S.	Jussi Oksanen, Finland
2005	Risto Mattila, Finland	Jussi Oksanen, Finland	Andreas Wiig, Norway
2004	Jake Blauvelt, U.S.	Travis Rice, U.S.	Christopher Schmidt, Germany
2003	Shaun White, U.S.	Travis Rice, U.S.	Nate Sheehan, U.S.
2002	Rahm Klampert, U.S.	Travis Rice, U.S.	Ryan Paris, U.S.

SLOPESTYLE — WOMEN

YEAR	GOLD	SILVER	BRONZE
2007	Jamie Anderson, U.S.	Torah Bright, Australia	Jenny Jones, U.K.
2006	Hana Beaman, U.S.	Spencer O'Brien, U.S.	Jamie Anderson, U.S.
2005	Janna Meyen, U.S.	Leanne Pelosi, Canada	Natasza Zurek, Canada
2004	Priscilla Levac, Canada	Kelly Clark, U.S.	Hana Beaman, U.S.
2003	Hana Beaman, U.S.	Priscilla Levac, Canada	Hannah Teter, U.S.
2002	Annie Boulanger, Canada	Hannah Teter, U.S.	Jaime MacLeod, U.S.

SUMMER X GAMES RESULTS

AGGRESSIVE IN-LINE — MEN

YEAR	EVENT	GOLD	SILVER	BRONZE
2003	Park	Bruno Lowe, Germany	Stephane Alfano, France	Sven Boekhorst, Netherlands
2002	Park	Jaren Grob, U.S.	Bruno Lowe, Germany	Blake Dennis, Australia
2001	Park	Jaren Grob, U.S.	Louie Zamora, U.S.	Franky Morales, U.S.
2000	Park	Sven Boekhorst, Netherlands	Jaren Grob, U.S.	Sam Fogarty, Australia
1999	Street	Nicky Adams, Canada	Blake Dennis, Australia	Aaron Feinberg, U.S.
1998	Street	Jonathan Bergeron, Canada	Marco Hintze, Mexico	Aaron Feinberg, U.S.
1997	Street	Aaron Feinberg, U.S.	Tim Ward, Australia	Chris Edwards, U.S.
1996	Street	Arlo Eisenberg, U.S.	Matt Mantz, U.S.	Chris Edwards, U.S.
1995	Street	Matt Salerno, Australia	Scott Bentley, New Zealand	Ryan Jacklone, U.S.
2004	Vert	Takeshi Yasutoko, Japan	Marco De Santi, Brazil	Eito Yasutoko, Japan
2003	Vert	Eito Yasutoko, Japan	Takeshi Yasutoko, Japan	Nel Martin, Spain
2002	Vert	Takeshi Yasutoko, Japan	Eito Yasutoko, Japan	Marc Englehart, U.S.
2001	Vert	Taig Khris, France	Takeshi Yasutoko, Japan	Shane Yost, Australia
2000	Vert	Eito Yasutoko, Japan	Takeshi Yasutoko, Japan	Cesar Mora, Australia
1999	Vert	Eito Yasutoko, Japan	Cesar Mora, Australia	Matt Salerno, Australia
1998	Vert	Cesar Mora, Australia	Matt Salerno, Australia	Taig Khris, France
1997	Vert	Tim Ward, Australia	Taig Khris, France	Chris Edwards, U.S.
1996	Vert	Rene Hulgreen, Denmark	Tom Fry, Australia	Chris Edwards, U.S.
1995	Vert	Tom Fry, Australia	Cesar Mora, Australia	Manuel Billiris, Australia
1999	Vert Triples	Sven Boekhorst, Netherlands	Mike Budnik, U.S.	Maki Komori, Japan
		Javier Bujanda, Spain	Cesar Mora, Australia	Eito Yasutoko, Japan
		Taig Khris, France	Matt Salerno, Australia	Takeshi Yasutoko, Japan
1998	Vert Triples	Paul Malina, Australia	Mike Budnik, U.S.	Sven Boekhorst, Netherlands
		Viorel Popa, U.S.	Cesar Mora, Australia	Javier Bujanda, Spain
		Sam Fogarty, Australia	Matt Salerno, Australia	Taig Khris, France
1996	Best Trick	Dion Antony, Australia	Ryan Jacklone, U.S.	Eric Schrijn, U.S.
1995	Best Trick	B. Hardin, U.S.	Ryan Jacklone, U.S.	Brooke Howard-Smith, New Zealand
1995	High Air	Chris Edwards, U.S.	Manuel Billiris, Australia	Ichi Komori, Japan

SUMMER X GAMES RESULTS (cont.)

AGGRESSIVE IN-LINE — WOMEN

YEAR	EVENT	GOLD	SILVER	BRONZE
2003	Park	Fabiola da Silva, Brazil	Jenny Logue, United Kingdom	Martina Svobodova, Slovakia
2002	Park	Martina Svobodova, Slovakia	Jenna Downing, United Kingdom	Fallon Heffernan, U.S.
2001	Park	Martina Svobodova, Slovakia	Fallon Heffernan, U.S.	Anneke Winter, Germany
2000	Park	Fabiola da Silva, Brazil	Martina Svobodova, Slovakia	Kelly Matthews, U.S.
1999	Street	Sayaka Yabe, Japan	Kelly Matthews, U.S.	Jenny Curry, U.S.
1998	Street	Jenny Curry, U.S.	Salima Sanga, Switzerland	Sayaka Yabe, Japan
1997	Street	Sayaka Yabe, Japan	Katie Brown, U.S.	True Otis, U.S.
2001	Vert	Fabiola da Silva, Brazil	Ayumi Kawasaki, Japan	N/A
2000	Vert	Fabiola da Silva, Brazil	Ayumi Kawasaki, Japan	Merce Borrull, Spain
1999	Vert	Ayumi Kawasaki, Japan	Fabiola da Silva, Brazil	Maki Komori, Japan
1998	Vert	Fabiola da Silva, Brazil	Ayumi Kawasaki, Japan	Maki Komori, Japan
1997	Vert	Fabiola da Silva, Brazil	Claudia Trachsel, Switzerland	Ayumi Kawasaki, Japan
1996	Vert	Fabiola da Silva, Brazil	Jodie Tyler, Australia	Tasha Hodgson, Australia
1995	Vert	Tasha Hodgson, Australia	Angie Walton, New Zealand	Laura Connery, U.S.

BAREFOOT JUMPING

YEAR	GOLD	SILVER	BRONZE
1998	Peter Fleck, U.S.	Ron Scarpa, U.S.	Massimiliano Colosio, Italy
1997	Peter Fleck, U.S.	Evan Berger, South Africa	Warren Fine, South Africa
1996	Ron Scarpa, U.S.	Jon Kretchman, U.S.	Rael Nurick, South Africa
1995	Justin Seers, Australia	Ron Scarpa, U.S.	Rael Nurick, South Africa

Anthony Napolitan

FAST FACT

In 2006, Corey Bohan from Australia and Anthony Napolitan from the United States finished in the top three in the BMX dirt event at both the Summer X Games and on the Dew Action Sports Tour. At the X Games, Bohan won gold and Napolitan took bronze, but on the Dew Tour, it was Napolitan who came in first and Bohan who came in third.

BIKE STUNT

YEAR	EVENT	GOLD	SILVER	BRONZE
2006	Dirt	Corey Bohan, Australia	Ryan Nyquist, U.S.	Anthony Napolitan, U.S.
2005	Dirt	Corey Bohan, Australia	Chris Doyle, U.S.	Ryan Guettler, U.S.
2004	Dirt	Corey Bohan, Australia	Chris Doyle, U.S.	T.J. Lavin, U.S.
2003	Dirt	Ryan Nyquist, U.S.	Corey Bohan, Australia	Chris Doyle, U.S.
2002	Dirt	Allan Cooke, U.S.	Ryan Nyquist, U.S.	Chris Doyle, U.S.
2001	Dirt	Stephen Murray, United Kingdom	Ryan Nyquist, U.S.	T.J. Lavin, U.S.
2000	Dirt	Ryan Nyquist, U.S.	Cory Nastazio, U.S.	T.J. Lavin, U.S.
1999	Dirt	T.J. Lavin, U.S.	Brian Foster, U.S.	Ryan Nyquist, U.S.
1998	Dirt	Brian Foster, U.S.	Ryan Nyquist, U.S.	Joey Garcia, U.S.
1997	Dirt	T.J. Lavin, U.S.	Brian Foster, U.S.	Ryan Nyquist, U.S.
1996	Dirt	Joey Garcia, U.S.	T.J. Lavin, U.S.	Brian Foster, U.S.
1995	Dirt	Jay Miron, Canada	Taj Mihelich, U.S.	Joey Garcia, U.S.

TODAY'S STARS

■ **Steve Fisher, snowboarding,** b. September 21, 1982, Olathe, Kansas. Growing up in Minnesota, Fisher first learned to snowboard on a halfpipe built on top of a former garbage dump when he was eight years old. Nicknamed "Fish," he had a break-out season in 2004, coming in second at the U.S. Open snowboarding championships, claiming two Vans Triple Crown pipe victories, and taking gold in the superpipe event at the Winter X Games. Although he again came in second in the halfpipe at the 2005 U.S. Open, he just missed making the 2006 U.S. Winter Olympic team. In 2007, Fisher charged back, and repeated as superpipe champion at the 2007 Winter X Games.

■ **Reggie Crist, skier,** b. July 12, 1968, Okinawa, Japan. Crist grew up in Ketchum, Idaho, and started his professional career as a World Cup downhill skier, but turned to freeskiing in the late 1990s. He medaled in five straight Winter X Games from 2002 to 2006 and won gold in the skier X event in 2002 and 2005. In 2005, Crist's brother Zach, who came in second in the skier X event joined him on the medal stand. In addition to skiing, Crist has become a well-known film producer of ski movies.

■ **Elissa Steamer, skateboarding,** b. July 31, 1975, Fort Myers, Florida. At age 23, Steamer burst onto the pro skateboarding scene by winning the first women's street event at the 1998 Slam City Jam. Since then, she has captured first place at the 2004 Summer Gravity Games, as well as won gold medals at the last three Summer X Games. Steamer, who was voted the best female skateboarder in the world in 2003, was also the first female skateboarder to be featured in a Tony Hawk video game.

Steve Fisher

SUMMER X GAMES RESULTS (cont.)

BIKE STUNT (cont.)

YEAR	EVENT	GOLD	SILVER	BRONZE
2003	Flatland	Simon O'Brien, Australia	Nathan Penonzek, Canada	Trevor Meyer, U.S.
2002	Flatland	Martti Kuoppa, Finland	Michael Steingraeber, Germany	Phil Dolan, United Kingdom
2001	Flatland	Martti Kuoppa, Finland	Phil Dolan, United Kingdom	Matt Wilhelm, U.S.
2000	Flatland	Martti Kuoppa, Finland	Michael Steingraeber, Germany	Phil Dolan, United Kingdom
1999	Flatland	Trevor Meyer, U.S.	Phil Dolan, United Kingdom	Nathan Penonzek, Canada
1998	Flatland	Trevor Meyer, U.S.	Andrew Faris, Canada	Martti Kuoppa, Finland
1997	Flatland	Trevor Meyer, U.S.	Nate Hanson, U.S.	Andrew Faris, Canada
2006	Park	Scotty Cranmer, U.S.	Morgan Wade, U.S.	Daniel Dhers, U.S.
2005	Park	Dave Mirra, U.S.	Scotty Cranmer, U.S.	Ryan Nyquist, U.S.
2004	Park	Dave Mirra, U.S.	Ryan Nyquist, U.S.	Ryan Guettler, Australia
2003	Park	Ryan Nyquist, U.S.	Gary Young, U.S.	Dave Mirra, U.S.
2002	Park	Ryan Nyquist, U.S.	Alistair Whitton, United Kingdom	Chad Kagy, U.S.
2001	Park	Bruce Crisman, U.S.	Alistair Whitton, United Kingdom	Jay Miron, Canada
2000	Park	Dave Mirra, U.S.	Markus Wilke, Germany	Ryan Nyquist, U.S.

SUMMER X GAMES RESULTS (cont.)

BIKE STUNT (cont.)

YEAR	EVENT	GOLD	SILVER	BRONZE
1999	Street	Dave Mirra, U.S.	Jay Miron, Canada	Chad Kagy, U.S.
1998	Street	Dave Mirra, U.S.	Jay Miron, Canada	Dennis McCoy, U.S.
1997	Street	Dave Mirra, U.S.	Dennis McCoy, U.S.	Dave Voelker, U.S.
1996	Street	Dave Mirra, U.S.	Jay Miron, Canada	Rob Nolli, U.S.
2006	Vert	Chad Kagy, U.S.	Jamie Bestwick, U.K.	Simon Tabron, U.K.
2005	Vert	Jamie Bestwick, U.K.	Chad Kagy, U.S.	Kevin Robinson, U.S.
2004	Vert	Dave Mirra, U.S.	Simon Tabron, U.K.	Kevin Robinson, U.S.
2003	Vert	Jamie Bestwick, U.K.	Dave Mirra, U.S.	Kevin Robinson, U.S.
2002	Vert	Dave Mirra, U.S.	Mat Hoffman, U.S.	Simon Tabron, U.K.
2001	Vert	Dave Mirra, U.S.	Jay Miron, Canada	Mat Hoffman, U.S.
2000	Vert	Jamie Bestwick, U.K.	Dave Mirra, U.S.	Mat Hoffman, U.S.
1999	Vert	Dave Mirra, U.S.	Jay Miron, Canada	Simon Tabron, U.K.
1998	Vert	Dave Mirra, U.S.	Dennis McCoy, U.S.	Simon Tabron, U.K.
1997	Vert	Dave Mirra, U.S.	Dennis McCoy, U.S.	Mat Hoffman, U.S.
1996	Vert	Mat Hoffman, U.S.	Dave Mirra, U.S.	Jamie Bestwick, U.K
1995	Vert	Mat Hoffman, U.S.	Dave Mirra, U.S.	Jay Miron, Canada
1998	Vert Doubles	Dave Mirra, U.S. Dennis McCoy, U.S.	Jay Miron, Canada Dave Osato, Canada	Jason Davies, United Kingdom John Parker, U.S.

BUNGY

YEAR	GOLD	SILVER	BRONZE
1996	Peter Bihun, Canada	Doug Anderson, Canada	Carolyn Anderson, Canada
1995	Doug Anderson, Canada	Mark Baldwin, U.S.	Todd Watkins, U.S.

DOWNHILL BMX

YEAR	GOLD	SILVER	BRONZE
2003	Brandon Meadows, U.S.	Kyle Bennett, U.S.	Michael Day, U.S.
2002	Robbie Miranda, U.S.	Kyle Bennett, U.S.	Robert de Wilde, Netherlands
2001	Brandon Meadows, U.S.	Brian Foster, U.S.	John Whipperman, U.S.

DOWNHILL IN-LINE — MEN

YEAR	EVENT	GOLD	SILVER	BRONZE
1998		Patrick Naylor, U.S.	Jeremy Anderson, U.S.	Dane Lewis, U.S.
1997		Derek Downing, U.S.	Keith Turner, U.S.	B.J. Steketee, U.S.
1996		Dante Muse, U.S.	Derek Parra, U.S.	Jim Wiederhold, U.S.
1995	Combined	Derek Downing, U.S.	Jim Wiederhold, U.S.	Jondon Trevena, U.S.

DOWNHILL IN-LINE — WOMEN

YEAR	GOLD	SILVER	BRONZE
1998	Julie Brandt, U.S.	Aimee Sanderson, U.S.	Theresa Cliff, U.S.
1997	Gypsy Tidwell, U.S.	Julie Brandt, U.S.	Jessica Apgar, U.S.
1996	Gypsy Tidwell, U.S.	Jennifer Jones, U.S.	Desly Hill, Australia

KITESKIING

YEAR	GOLD	SILVER	BRONZE
1995	Cory Roessler, U.S.	Clarin Mustad, Norway	Thomas Jeltsch, Germany

MOUNTAIN BIKING — MEN

YEAR	EVENT	GOLD	SILVER	BRONZE
1995	Dual Downhill	Robert Naughton, U.S.	Jurgen Beneke, Germany	Todd Tanner, U.S.
1995	Dual Slalom	Jimmy Knight, U.S.	Myles Rockwell, U.S.	Mike King, U.S.
1995	Observed Trials	Libor Karas, Czech Republic	Hans Rey, Germany	Marc Brooks, U.S.

MOUNTAIN BIKING — WOMEN

YEAR	EVENT	GOLD	SILVER	BRONZE
1995	Dual Downhill	Cheri Elliott, U.S.	Kim Sonier, U.S.	Leigh Donovan, U.S.
1995	Dual Slalom	Leigh Donovan, U.S.	Cheri Elliott, U.S.	Giovanna Bonazzi, Italy

MOTO X

YEAR	EVENT	GOLD	SILVER	BRONZE
2003	Big Air	Brian Deegan, U.S.	Nate Adams, U.S.	Kenny Bartram, U.S.
2002	Big Air	Mike Metzger, U.S.	Carey Hart, U.S.	Brian Deegan, U.S.
2001	Big Air	Kenny Bartram, U.S.	Dustin Miller, U.S.	Brian Deegan, U.S.
2006	Freestyle	Travis Pastrana, U.S.	Adam Jones, U.S.	Mike Mason, U.S.
2005	Freestyle	Travis Pastrana, U.S.	Kenny Bartram, U.S.	Nate Adams, U.S.
2004	Freestyle	Nate Adams, U.S.	Travis Pastrana, U.S.	Adam Jones, U.S.
2003	Freestyle	Travis Pastrana, U.S.	Nate Adams, U.S.	Brian Deegan, U.S.
2002	Freestyle	Mike Metzger, U.S.	Kenny Bartram, U.S.	Drake McElroy, U.S.
2001	Freestyle	Travis Pastrana, U.S.	Clifford Adoptante, U.S.	Jake Windham, U.S.
2000	Freestyle	Travis Pastrana, U.S.	Tommy Clowers, U.S.	Brian Deegan, U.S.
1999	Freestyle	Travis Pastrana, U.S.	Mike Cinqmars, U.S.	Brian Deegan, U.S.
2006	Step Up	Matt Buyten, U.S.	Jeremy McGrath, U.S.	Brian Deegan, U.S.
2005	Step Up	Tommy Clowers, U.S.	Matt Buyten, U.S.	Jeremy McGrath, U.S.
2004	Step Up	Jeremy McGrath, U.S.	Matt Buyten, U.S.	Tommy Clowers, U.S.
2003	Step Up	Matt Buyten, U.S.	Tommy Clowers, U.S.	Ronnie Renner, U.S.
2002	Step Up	Tommy Clowers, U.S.	Mike Metzger, U.S.	Brian Deegan, U.S.
2001	Step Up	Tommy Clowers, U.S.	Travis Pastrana, U.S.	Colin Morrison, U.S. (tie) Ronnie Renner, U.S. Kris Rourke, U.S. Jeremy Stenberg, U.S.
2000	Step Up	Tommy Clowers, U.S.	Kris Rourke, U.S.	Brian Deegan, U.S.
2006	Super Moto	Jeff Ward, U.S.	Mark Burkhart, U.S.	Doug Henry, U.S.
2005	Super Moto	Doug Henry, U.S.	Jeremy McGrath, U.S.	Chad Reed, Australia
2004	Super Moto	Ben Bostrom, U.S.	Eddy Seel, Belgium	Jeremy McGrath, U.S.
2005	Best Trick	Jeremy Stenberg, U.S.	Travis Pastrana, U.S.	Nate Adams, U.S.
2004	Best Trick	Chuck Carothers, U.S.	Nate Adams, U.S.	Travis Pastrana, U.S.

Nate
Adams

SUMMER X GAMES RESULTS (cont.)

SKATEBOARDING — MEN

YEAR	EVENT	GOLD	SILVER	BRONZE
2003	Park	Ryan Sheckler, U.S.	Rodil de Araujo, Jr., Brazil	Chad Bartie, Australia
2002	Park	Rodil de Araujo, Jr., Brazil	Wagner Ramos, Brazil	Eric Koston, U.S.
2001	Park	Rodil de Araujo, Jr., Brazil	Kerry Getz, U.S.	Caine Gayle, U.S.
2000	Park	Eric Koston, U.S.	Rodil de Araujo, Jr., Brazil	Kerry Getz, U.S.
2006	Street	Chris Cole, U.S.	Ryan Sheckler, U.S.	Andrew Reynolds, U.S.
2005	Street	Paul Rodriguez, U.S.	Greg Lutzka, U.S.	Chris Cole, U.S.
2004	Street	Paul Rodriguez, U.S.	Andrew Reynolds, U.S.	Bastien Salabanzi, France
2003	Street	Eric Koston, U.S.	Rodil de Araujo, Jr., Brazil	Paul Rodriguez, U.S.
2002	Street	Rodil de Araujo, Jr., Brazil	Wagner Ramos, Brazil	Kyle Berard, U.S.
2001	Street	Kerry Getz, U.S.	Eric Koston, U.S.	Chris Senn, U.S.
1999	Street	Chris Senn, U.S.	Pat Channita, U.S.	Chad Fernandez, U.S.
1998	Street	Rodil de Araujo, Jr., Brazil	Andy Macdonald, U.S.	Chris Senn, U.S.
1997	Street	Chris Senn, U.S.	Andy Macdonald, U.S.	Brian Patch, U.S.
1996	Street	Rodil de Araujo, Jr., Brazil	Chris Senn, U.S.	Brian Patch, U.S.
1995	Street	Chris Senn, U.S.	Tony Hawk, U.S.	Willy Santos, U.S.
2003	Street Best Trick	Chad Muska, U.S.	Rodil de Araujo, Jr., Brazil	Wagner Ramos, Brazil
2002	Street Best Trick	Rodil de Araujo, Jr., Brazil	Wagner Ramos, Brazil	Dayne Brummet, U.S.
2001	Street Best Trick	Rick McCrank, Canada	Kerry Getz, U.S.	Eric Koston, U.S.
1996	Street Best Trick	Gershon Mosley, U.S.	Chris Senn, U.S.	Brian Patch, U.S.
1995	Street Best Trick	Jamie Thomas, U.S.	Gershon Mosley, U.S.	Kareem Campbell, U.S.
2005	Vert	Pierre-Luc Gagnon, Canada	Shaun White, U.S.	Sandro Dias, Brazil
2004	Vert	Bucky Lasek, U.S.	Pierre-Luc Gagnon, Canada	Rune Glifberg, Denmark
2003	Vert	Bucky Lasek, U.S.	Andy Macdonald, U.S.	Rune Glifberg, Denmark
2002	Vert	Pierre-Luc Gagnon, Canada	Bob Burnquist, Brazil	Rune Glifberg, Denmark
2001	Vert	Bob Burnquist, Brazil	Bucky Lasek, U.S.	Tas Pappas, Australia
2000	Vert	Bucky Lasek, U.S.	Pierre-Luc Gagnon, Canada	Colin McKay, Canada
1999	Vert	Bucky Lasek, U.S.	Andy Macdonald, U.S.	Tony Hawk, U.S.
1998	Vert	Andy Macdonald, U.S.	Giorgio Zattoni, Italy	Tony Hawk, U.S.
1997	Vert	Tony Hawk, U.S.	Rune Glifberg, Denmark	Bob Burnquist, Brazil
1996	Vert	Andy Macdonald, U.S.	Tony Hawk, U.S.	Tas Pappas, Australia
1995	Vert	Tony Hawk, U.S.	Neal Hendrix, U.S.	Rune Glifberg, Denmark
2006	Vert Best Trick	Bucky Lasek, U.S.	Max Dufour, Canada	Bob Burnquist, Brazil
2005	Vert Best Trick	Bob Burnquist, Brazil	Colin McKay, Canada	Pierre-Luc Gagnon, Canada
2004	Vert Best Trick	Sandro Dias, Brazil	Pierre-Luc Gagnon, Canada	Danny Mayer, U.S.
2003	Vert Best Trick	Tony Hawk, U.S.	Sandro Dias, Brazil	Andy Macdonald, U.S.
2002	Vert Best Trick	Pierre-Luc Gagnon, Canada	Sandro Dias, Brazil	Tony Hawk, U.S.
2001	Vert Best Trick	Matt Dove, U.S.	Tony Hawk, U.S.	Bob Burnquist, Brazil
2000	Vert Best Trick	Bob Burnquist, Brazil	Colin McKay, Canada	Andy Macdonald, U.S.
1999	Vert Best Trick	Tony Hawk, U.S.	Colin McKay, Canada	Bob Burnquist, Brazil
2005	Big Air	Danny Way, U.S.	Pierre-Luc Gagnon, Canada	Andy Macdonald, U.S.
2004	Big Air	Danny Way, U.S.	Pierre-Luc Gagnon, Canada	Andy Macdonald, U.S.

Danny Way

SKATEBOARDING — MEN (cont.)

YEAR	EVENT	GOLD	SILVER	BRONZE
2003	Vert Doubles	Bucky Lasek, U.S.	Rune Glifberg, Denmark	Neal Hendrix, U.S.
		Bob Burnquist, Brazil	Mike Crum, U.S.	Buster Halterman, U.S.
2002	Vert Doubles	Tony Hawk, U.S.	Bob Burnquist, Brazil	Mike Crum, U.S.
		Andy Macdonald, U.S.	Bucky Lasek, U.S.	Rune Glifberg, Denmark
2001	Vert Doubles	Tony Hawk, U.S.	Mike Crum, U.S.	Mike Frazier, U.S.
		Andy Macdonald, U.S.	Chris Gentry, U.S.	Neal Hendrix, U.S.
2000	Vert Doubles	Tony Hawk, U.S.	Pierre-Luc Gagnon, Canada	Sandro Dias, Brazil
		Andy Macdonald, U.S.	Max Dufour, Canada	Cristiano Mateus, Brazil
1999	Vert Doubles	Tony Hawk, U.S.	Bucky Lasek, U.S.	Mike Crum, U.S.
		Andy Macdonald, U.S.	Brian Patch, U.S.	Rune Glifberg, Denmark
1998	Vert Doubles	Tony Hawk, U.S.	Bucky Lasek, U.S.	Bob Burnquist, Brazil
		Andy Macdonald, U.S.	Brian Patch, U.S.	Lincoln Ueda, Brazil
1997	Vert Doubles	Tony Hawk, U.S.	Mike Frazier, U.S.	Max Dufour, Canada
		Andy Macdonald, U.S.	Neal Hendrix, U.S.	Mathias Ringstrom, Sweden
1995	High Air	Danny Way, U.S.	Neal Hendrix, U.S.	Tas Pappas, Australia

SKATEBOARDING — WOMEN

YEAR	EVENT	GOLD	SILVER	BRONZE
2006	Street	Elissa Steamer, U.S.	Lauren Perkins, U.S.	Lacey Baker, U.S.
2005	Street	Elissa Steamer, U.S.	Evelien Bouilliart, Belgium	Marissa Del Santo, U.S.
2004	Street	Elissa Steamer, U.S.	Vanessa Torres, U.S.	Lauren Perkins, U.S.
2006	Vert	Cara-Beth Burnside, U.S.	Mimi Koop, U.S.	Karen Jones, U.S.
2005	Vert	Cara-Beth Burnside, U.S.	Lyn-Z Adams Hawkins, U.S.	Mimi Knoop, U.S.
2004	Vert	Lyn-Z Adams Hawkins, U.S.	Cara-Beth Burnside, U.S.	Mimi Knoop, U.S.

SPORT CLIMBING — MEN

YEAR	EVENT	GOLD	SILVER	BRONZE
2002	Speed	Maxim Stenkovoy, Ukraine	Alexandre Pechekhonov, Russia	Serguei Sinitsyn, Russia
2001	Speed	Maxim Stenkovoy, Ukraine	Vladimir Zakharov, Ukraine	Chris Bloch, U.S.
2000	Speed	Vladimir Zakharov, Ukraine	Chris Bloch, U.S.	Tomasz Oleksy, Poland
1999	Speed	Aaron Shamy, U.S.	Chris Bloch, U.S.	Vladimir Netsvetaev, Russia
1998	Speed	Vladimir Netsvetaev, Russia	Aaron Shamy, U.S.	Chris Bloch, U.S.
1997	Speed	Hans Florine, U.S.	Chris Bloch, U.S.	Jason Campbell, U.S.
1996	Speed	Hans Florine, U.S.	Chris Bloch, U.S.	Tim Fairfield, U.S.
1995	Speed	Hans Florine, U.S.	Salavat Rakhmetov, Russia	Yuji Hirayama, Japan
1999	Bouldering	Chris Sharma, U.S.	Francois Petit, France	Stephane Julien, France
1998	Difficulty	Christian Core, Italy	Francois Legrand, France	Vadim Vinokur, U.S.
1997	Difficulty	Francois Legrand, France	Yuji Hirayama, Japan	Chris Sharma, U.S.
1996	Difficulty	Arnaud Petit, France	Francois Lombard, France	Cristian Brenna, Italy
1995	Difficulty	Ian Vickers, United Kingdom	Arnaud Petit, France	Francois Petit, France

SPORT CLIMBING — WOMEN

YEAR	EVENT	GOLD	SILVER	BRONZE
2002	Speed	Tori Allen, U.S.	Olga Zakharova, Ukraine	Etti Hendrawati, Indonesia
2001	Speed	Elena Repko, Ukraine	Olga Zakharova, Ukraine	Alena Ostapenko, Ukraine
2000	Speed	Etti Hendrawati, Indonesia	Elena Repko, Ukraine	Olga Zakharova, Ukraine
1999	Speed	Renata Piszczek, Poland	Olga Zakharova, Ukraine	Etti Hendrawati, Indonesia
1998	Speed	Elena Ovchinnikova, U.S.	Yuyun Yuniar, Indonesia	Venera Tchereshneva, Russia
1997	Speed	Elena Ovchinnikova, U.S.	Abby Watkins, Australia	Mi Sun Go, South Korea
1996	Speed	Cecile Le Flem, France	Elena Choumilova, Russia	Natalie Richer, France
1995	Speed	Elena Ovchinnikova, Russia	Diane Russell, U.S.	Georgia Phipps-Franklin, U.S.
1999	Bouldering	Stephanie Bodet, France	Liv Sansoz, France	Elena Choumilova, Russia
1998	Difficulty	Katie Brown, U.S.	Mi Sun Go, South Korea	Elena Choumilova, Russia
1997	Difficulty	Katie Brown, U.S.	Liv Sansoz, France	Muriel Sarkany, Belgium
1996	Difficulty	Katie Brown, U.S.	Laurence Guyon, France	Liv Sansoz, France
1995	Difficulty	Robyn Erbesfield, U.S.	Elena Ovchinnikova, Russia	Mia Axon, U.S.

TRIVIA CHALLENGE

1 Of the following trick names, which one is NOT a real skateboarding stunt?
a. frontside nollie nose manual
b. sideways realie whiplash
c. goofy 360 heelflip

2 How many athletes competed in both the 2006 Winter X Games and the 2006 Winter Olympics?
a. 28
b. 14
c. 7

3 What Winter X Games event combines elements of dirt-track motorcycle racing, downhill skiing, and snowboarding?
a. Halfpipe
b. Slopestyle
c. Snowboardcross

4 Which motocross rider holds the all-time record for most combined championships?
a. Ricky Carmichael
b. Jeremy McGrath
c. Jeff Stanton

5 Which legendary BMX rider invented both the "tailwhip-nosepick" and "lookback" tricks?
a. Dave Mirra
b. Jamie Bestwick
c. Dave Voelker

Lindsey Jacobellis

6 Three-time Winter X Games gold medalist Lindsey Jacobellis was the first American rider to accomplish what snowboarding feat?
a. Win snowboardcross and halfpipe events at the same World Cup
b. Land a 900-degree flip
c. Medal in back-to-back X Games

Trivia Challenge: 1. b; 2. a; 3. c; 4. a; 5. c; 6. a.

BEN LIEBENBERG/WIREIMAGE.COM

SUMMER X GAMES RESULTS (cont.)

STREET LUGE

YEAR	EVENT	GOLD	SILVER	BRONZE
2001	Super Mass	Brent DeKeyser, U.S.	David Rogers, U.S.	Dave Auld, U.S.
2000	Super Mass	Bob Pereyra, U.S.	Lee Dansie, United Kingdom	John Rogers, U.S.
1999	Super Mass	David Rogers, U.S.	Biker Sherlock, U.S.	Sean Slate, U.S.
1998	Super Mass	Rat Sult, U.S.	Bob Pereyra, U.S.	Todd Lehr, U.S.
1997	Super Mass	Chris Ponseti, U.S.	Biker Sherlock, U.S.	Rat Sult, U.S.
2000	Dual	Bob Ozman, U.S.	Wade Sokol, U.S.	Bob Pereyra, U.S.
1999	Dual	Dennis Derammelaere, U.S.	Lee Dansie, United Kingdom	Biker Sherlock, U.S.
1998	Dual	Biker Sherlock, U.S.	Stefan Wagner, Germany	Dave Auld, U.S.
1997	Dual	Biker Sherlock, U.S.	Dennis Derammelaere, U.S.	Darren Lott, U.S.
1996	Dual	Shawn Goulart, U.S.	Stefan Wagner, Germany	Dennis Derammelaere, U.S.
1995	Dual	Bob Pereyra, U.S.	Stefan Wagner, Germany	Shawn Goulart, U.S.
1998	Mass	Rat Sult, U.S.	Sean Slate, U.S.	Steve Fernando, U.S.
1997	Mass	Biker Sherlock, U.S.	Dennis Derammelaere, U.S.	Lee Dansie, United Kingdom
1996	Mass	Biker Sherlock, U.S.	Daryl Thompson, U.S.	Dennis Derammelaere, U.S.
1995	Mass	Shawn Goulart, U.S.	Lee Dansie, United Kingdom	Stefan Wagner, Germany

SURFING — MEN

YEAR	GOLD	SILVER	BRONZE
2005	East Coast	West Coast	N/A
2004	East Coast	West Coast	N/A
2003	East Coast	West Coast	N/A

WAKEBOARDING — MEN

YEAR	GOLD	SILVER	BRONZE
2005	Danny Harf, U.S.	Phillip Soven, U.S.	Josh Sanders, Australia
2004	Phillip Soven, U.S.	Chad Sharpe, Canada	Parks Bonifay, U.S.
2003	Danny Harf, U.S.	Parks Bonifay, U.S.	Daniel Watkins, U.S.
2002	Danny Harf, U.S.	Darin Shapiro, U.S.	Shaun Murray, U.S.
2001	Danny Harf, U.S.	Darin Shapiro, U.S.	Erik Ruck, U.S.
2000	Darin Shapiro, U.S.	Shaun Murray, U.S.	Shane Bonifay, U.S.
1999	Parks Bonifay, U.S.	Darin Shapiro, U.S.	Brannan Johnson, U.S.
1998	Darin Shapiro, U.S.	Shaun Murray, U.S.	Zane Schwenk, U.S.
1997	Jeremy Kovak, Canada	Darin Shapiro, U.S.	Parks Bonifay, U.S.
1996	Parks Bonifay, U.S.	Jeremy Kovak, Canada	Scott Byerly, U.S.

WAKEBOARDING — WOMEN

YEAR	GOLD	SILVER	BRONZE
2005	Dallas Friday, U.S.	Emily Copeland, U.S.	Tara Hamilton, U.S.
2004	Dallas Friday, U.S.	Tara Hamilton, U.S.	Maeghan Major, U.S.
2003	Dallas Friday, U.S.	Melissa Marquardt, U.S.	Emily Copeland, U.S.
2002	Emily Copeland, U.S.	Dallas Friday, U.S.	Leslie Kent, U.S.
2001	Dallas Friday, U.S.	Emily Copeland, U.S.	Tara Hamilton, U.S.
2000	Tara Hamilton, U.S.	Dallas Friday, U.S.	Maeghan Major, U.S.
1999	Maeghan Major, U.S.	Emily Copeland, U.S.	Andrea Gaytan, Mexico
1998	Andrea Gaytan, Mexico	Dana Preble, U.S.	Tara Hamilton, U.S.
1997	Tara Hamilton, U.S.	Andrea Gaytan, Mexico	Jaime Necrason, U.S.

WINDSURFING — MEN

YEAR	GOLD	SILVER	BRONZE
1995	Bjorn Dunkerbeck, Spain	Micah Buzianis, U.S.	Al Aguera, U.S.

WINDSURFING — WOMEN

YEAR	GOLD	SILVER	BRONZE
1995	Angela Cochran, U.S.	Jayne Fenner-Benedict, U.S.	Jutta Mueller, Germany

X VENTURE RACE

YEAR	GOLD	SILVER	BRONZE
1997	Team Presidio	Team Endeavour	Team Red Hot
	Ian Adamson, Australia	Louise Cooper-Lovelace, U.S.	Sharyn Davis, Australia
	John Howard, New Zealand	Neil Jones, New Zealand	John Jacoby, Australia
	Andrea Spitzer, Germany	Jeff Mitchell, New Zealand	Tim Smallwood, Australia
1996	Team Kobeer	Team Eco-Internet	Team Mirage
	Angelika Castaneda, U.S.	Ian Adamson, Australia	Kirk Boylston, U.S.
	John Howard, New Zealand	Robert Nagle, Ireland	Nancy Bristow, U.S.
	Keith Murray, New Zealand	Vivienne Prince, U.S.	Steve Gurney, New Zealand
1995	Team Thredbo	Twin Team	Team Eco-Internet
	Jane Hall, Australia	Angelika Castaneda, U.S.	Ian Adamson, Australia
	Andrew Hislop, Australia	Adrian Crane, U.S.	John Howard, New Zealand
	Rod Hislop, Australia	Tom Possert, U.S.	Keith Murray, New Zealand
	John Jacoby, Australia	Robert Rambach, U.S.	Robert Nagle, Ireland
	Novak Thompson, Australia	Marshall Ulrich, U.S.	Cathy Sassin-Smith, U.S.

ACTION SPORTS

DEW ACTION SPORTS TOUR CHAMPIONS

SKATEBOARDING — MEN

YEAR	EVENT	FIRST	SECOND	THIRD
2006	Skate Park	Ryan Sheckler, U.S.	Jereme Rogers, U.S.	Rodolfo Ramos, Brazil
2005	Skate Park	Ryan Sheckler, U.S.	Chad Fernandez, U.S.	Greg Lutzka, U.S.
2006	Skate Vert	Bucky Lasek, U.S.	Sandro Dias, Brazil	Bob Burnquist, Brazil
2005	Skate Vert	Bucky Lasek, U.S.	Pierre-Luc Gagnon, Canada	Andy Macdonald, U.S.

Ryan Sheckler has won back-to-back skate park titles on the Dew Action Sports Tour.

SOREN MCCARTY/WIREIMAGE.COM

BIKE STUNT — MEN

YEAR	EVENT	FIRST	SECOND	THIRD
2006	BMX Park	Daniel Dhers, Venezuela	Scotty Cranmer, U.S.	Ryan Nyquist, U.S.
2005	BMX Park	Ryan Guettler, Australia	Scotty Cranmer, U.S.	Ryan Nyquist, U.S.
2006	BMX Vert	Jamie Bestwick, U.K.	Chad Kagy, U.S.	Kevin Robinson, U.S.
2005	BMX Vert	Jamie Bestwick, U.K.	Kevin Robinson, U.S.	Chad Kagy, U.S.
2006	BMX Dirt	Anthony Napolitan, U.S.	Luke Parslow, Australia	Corey Bohan, Australia
2005	BMX Dirt	Ryan Guettler, Australia	Corey Bohan, Australia	Cameron White, Australia

MOTO X— MEN

YEAR	EVENT	FIRST	SECOND	THIRD
2006	FMX Park	Nate Adams, U.S.	Mike Mason, U.S.	Travis Pastrana, U.S.
2005	FMX Park	Kenny Bartram, U.S.	Jeremy Stenberg, U.S.	Mike Mason, U.S.

WINTER GRAVITY GAMES RESULTS

SNOWBOARDING — MEN

YEAR	EVENT	GOLD	SILVER	BRONZE
2005	Snowboardcross	Xavier de le Rue, France	Jason Smith, U.S.	Mike Rosengren, U.S.
2005	Slopestyle	Chad Otterstrom, U.S.	Antti Autti, Finland	Wyatt Caldwell, U.S.
2005	Superpipe	Crispin Lipscomb, Canada	Danny Davis, U.S.	Risto Mattila, Finland
2005	Rail Jam	Chad Otterstrom, U.S.	N/A	N/A

SNOWBOARDING — WOMEN

YEAR	EVENT	GOLD	SILVER	BRONZE
2005	Snowboardcross	Leslee Olson, U.S.	Marni Yamada, U.S.	Jordan Karlinski, U.S.
2005	Slopestyle	Janna Meyen, U.S.	Silvia Mittermueller, Germany	Izumi Amaike, Japan
2005	Superpipe	Gretchen Bleiler, U.S.	Hannah Teter, U.S.	Elena Hight, U.S.
2005	Rail Jam	Leanne Pelosi, Canada	N/A	N/A

Note: Winter Gravity Games were not held in 2006 because of the Winter Olympics.

LEGENDS

■ **Kelly Slater, surfing,** b. February 11, 1972, Cocoa Beach, Florida. Slater has won 36 tournaments and eight world titles during his career, more than anyone else in the sport. In 2005, at a tournament in Tahiti, he became the first surfer to earn two perfect 10s in the ASP's two-wave scoring system. Outside the water, Slater has acted on the TV show *Baywatch*, appeared in music videos, and sung with his rock band, The Surfers.

Kelly Slater won five straight ASP surfing titles between 1994 and 1998.

AP PHOTO/KAREN WILSON, ASP

■ **Ricky Carmichael, motocross,** b. November 27, 1979, Clearwater, Florida. Carmichael began motorcycle racing as an amateur at age three and turned pro just before his 17th birthday in 1996. He has dominated the sport for the past decade, winning more than 100 AMA events in the 125cc and 250cc divisions. Since Carmichael moved up to the larger engine in 1999, he has won five Supercross titles and five National championships. In 2002, he recorded the first-ever perfect season in AMA 250 history, a feat he repeated two years later. Carmichael ended his motocross career on a high note in 2006 by winning his fifth Supercross title at the last event of the season.

■ **Dallas Friday, wakeboarding,** b. September 6, 1986, Orlando, Florida. Friday has been at the top of the wakeboarding pro circuit since her rookie year in 2000, when she was 14 years old. That year, she came in second in her debut at the Summer X Games and just missed a medal at the Gravity Games. Since then, Friday has won two golds and a bronze at the Gravity Games and come in first in four out of the last five wakeboarding events at the X Games. For the past six years, Friday has been voted the number one female wakeboarder in the world. In 2004 and again in 2006, she won the ESPY award for "best female action sports athlete."

WINTER GRAVITY GAMES RESULTS

SKIING — MEN

YEAR	EVENT	GOLD	SILVER	BRONZE
2005	Skiercross	Casey Puckett, U.S.	Zach Crist, U.S.	Jakub Fiala, U.S.
2005	Slopestyle	T.J. Schiller, Canada	Simon Dumont, U.S.	Charles Gagnier, Canada
2005	Superpipe	Corey Vanular, U.S.	Andrew Woods, U.S.	Simon Dumont, U.S.
2005	Rail Jam	Tim Russell, U.S.	N/A	N/A

SKIING — WOMEN

YEAR	EVENT	GOLD	SILVER	BRONZE
2005	Skiercross	Brett Buckles, U.S.	Valentine Scuotto, France	Sara-Maude Boucher, Canada
2005	Superpipe	Kristi Leskinen, U.S.	Sarah Burke, Canada	Grete Eliassen, Norway
2005	Rail Jam	Grete Eliassen, Norway	N/A	N/A

SUMMER GRAVITY GAMES RESULTS

BIKE

YEAR	EVENT	GOLD	SILVER	BRONZE
2004	Street	Morgan Wade, U.S.	Ryan Nyquist, U.S.	Steven McCann, Australia
2003	Street	Dave Mirra, U.S.	Ryan Nyquist, U.S.	Steven McCann, Australia
2002	Street	Dave Mirra, U.S.	Ryan Nyquist, U.S.	Tom Haugen, U.S.
2001	Street	Ryan Nyquist, U.S.	Dave Osato, Canada	Chad Kagy, U.S.
2000	Street	Dave Osato, Canada	Ryan Nyquist, U.S.	Mike Laird, U.S.
1999	Street	Dave Mirra, U.S.	Ryan Nyquist, U.S.	Jay Miron, Canada
2005	Dirt	Ryan Guettler, U.S.	Luke Parslow, U.S.	Joey Marks, U.S.
2004	Dirt	Ryan Nyquist, U.S.	Steven McCann, Australia	Stephen Murray, U.K.
2003	Dirt	Ryan Nyquist, U.S.	Chris Doyle, U.S.	Steven McCann, Australia
2002	Dirt	Stephen Murray, U.K.	Allan Cooke, U.S.	Chris Doyle, U.S.
2001	Dirt	Stephen Murray, U.K.	Todd Walkowiak, U.S.	Chris Doyle, U.S.
2000	Dirt	T.J. Lavin, U.S.	Chris Doyle, U.S.	Ryan Jordan, U.S.
1999	Dirt	Ryan Nyquist, U.S.	Todd Walkowiak, U.S.	T.J. Lavin, U.S.

Ryan Nyquist

2005	Vert	Jamie Bestwick, U.K.	Dennis McCoy, U.S.	Kevin Robinson, U.S.
2004	Vert	Jamie Bestwick, U.K.	Chad Kagy, U.S.	Kevin Robinson, U.S.
2003	Vert	Dave Mirra, U.S.	Kevin Robinson, U.S.	Simon Tabron, U.K.
2002	Vert	Simon Tabron, U.K.	Dave Mirra, U.S.	Jay Miron, Canada
2001	Vert	Jamie Bestwick, U.K.	Kevin Robinson, U.S.	Simon Tabron, U.K.
2000	Vert	Dave Mirra, U.S.	Jamie Bestwick, U.K.	Jay Miron, Canada
1999	Vert	Jamie Bestwick, U.K.	Jay Miron, Canada	John Parker, U.S.

FREESTYLE MOTOCROSS

YEAR	GOLD	SILVER	BRONZE
2005	Kenny Bartram, U.S.	Jeremy Stenberg, U.S.	Ronnie Renner, U.S.
2004	Nate Adams, U.S.	Jeremy Stenberg, U.S.	Ronnie Faisst, U.S.
2003	Nate Adams, U.S.	Travis Pastrana, U.S.	Ronnie Renner, U.S.
2002	Travis Pastrana, U.S.	Mike Metzger, U.S.	Kenny Bartram, U.S.
2001	Travis Pastrana, U.S.	Clifford Adoptante, U.S.	Tommy Clowers, U.S.
2000	Brian Deegan, U.S.	Mike Metzger, U.S.	Kenny Bartram, U.S.
1999	Travis Pastrana, U.S.	Brian Deegan, U.S.	Carey Hart, U.S.

Note: Summer Gravity Games were not held in 2006 due to scheduling conflicts.

Bucky Lasek

TRIVIA CHALLENGE

How many medals has skateboarder Bucky Lasek won at the Summer X Games and Summer Gravity Games combined?

15 (Ten X Games medals: six gold, four silver, five Gravity Games medals: three gold, two silver)

FAST FACT

Women's skateboarding debuted as a medal event at the 2004 Summer Gravity Games in Cleveland, Ohio.

SKATEBOARDING — MEN

YEAR	EVENT	GOLD	SILVER	BRONZE
2005	Vert	Bucky Lasek, U.S	Andy Macdonald, U.S.	Sandro Dias, Brazil
2004	Vert	Rune Glifberg, Denmark	Andy Macdonald, U.S.	Pierre-Luc Gagnon, Canada
2003	Vert	Bucky Lasek, U.S.	Andy Macdonald, U.S.	Rune Glifberg, Denmark
2002	Vert	Bucky Lasek, U.S.	Bob Burnquist, Brazil	Pierre-Luc Gagnon, Canada
2001	Vert	Rune Glifberg, Denmark	Bucky Lasek, U.S.	Andy Macdonald, U.S.
2000	Vert	Andy Macdonald, U.S.	Bob Burnquist, Brazil	Pierre-Luc Gagnon, Canada
1999	Vert	Bob Burnquist, Brazil	Bucky Lasek, U.S.	Andy Macdonald, U.S.
2004	Vert Best Trick	Sandro Diaz, Brazil	Danny Mayer, U.S.	Pierre-Luc Gagnon, Canada
2003	Vert Best Trick	Mathias Ringstrom, Sweden	Danny Mayer, U.S.	Sandro Diaz, Brazil
2002	Vert Best Trick	Pierre-Luc Gagnon, Canada	Bob Burnquist, Brazil	Sandro Diaz, Brazil
2005	Street	Chris Cole, U.S.	Wagner Ramos, Brazil	Andre Genovesi, Brazil
2004	Street	Rodil de Araujo, Jr., Brazil	Greg Lutzka, U.S.	Ryan Sheckler, U.S.
2003	Street	Ryan Sheckler, U.S.	Rick McCrank, Canada	Chris Senn, U.S.
2002	Street	Eric Koston, U.S.	Pat Channita, U.S.	Kerry Getz, U.S.
2001	Street	Eric Koston, U.S.	Rick McCrank, Canada	Kyle Berard, U.S.
2000	Street	Eric Koston, U.S.	Brian Anderson, U.S.	Kerry Getz, U.S.
1999	Street	Brian Anderson, U.S.	Rodil de Araujo, Jr., Brazil	Eric Koston, U.S.
2004	Street Best Trick	Paul Machnau, Canada	Nilton Neves, Brazil	Josh Evin, Canada
2003	Street Best Trick	Chris Haslam, Canada	Daniel Vieira, Brazil	Chad Bartie, Australia
2002	Downhill, 2-person	Mark Golter, U.S.	Dane Van Bommel, U.S.	Alex Wenk, Switzerland
2001	Downhill, 2-person	Dane Van Bommel, U.S.	Gary Hardwick, U.S.	Mark Golter, U.S.
2000	Downhill, 2-person	Dane Van Bommel, U.S.	John Gwiazdowski, U.S.	Alex Wenk, Switzerland
1999	Downhill, 2-person	Lee Dansie, United Kingdom	Biker Sherlock, U.S.	Dane Van Bommel, U.S.
2002	Downhill, 4-person	Darryl Freeman, U.S.	Mark Golter, U.S.	Dane Van Bommel, U.S.
2001	Downhill, 4-person	Dane Van Bommel, U.S.	Alex Wenk, Switzerland	Lee Dansie, United Kingdom
2000	Downhill, 4-person	Dane Van Bommel, U.S.	John Gwiazdowski, U.S.	Alex Wenk, Switzerland
1999	Downhill, 4-person	Biker Sherlock, U.S.	Dane Van Bommel, U.S.	Emanuel Antuna, France

SUMMER GRAVITY GAMES RESULTS (cont.)

SKATEBOARDING — WOMEN

YEAR	EVENT	GOLD	SILVER	BRONZE
2004	Street	Elissa Steamer, U.S.	Lauren Perkins, U.S.	Lyn-Z Adams Hawkins, U.S.

AGGRESSIVE IN-LINE — MEN

YEAR	EVENT	GOLD	SILVER	BRONZE
2001	Street	Blake Dennis, Australia	Louie Zamora, U.S.	Aaron Feinberg, U.S.
2000	Street	Sven Boekhorst, Netherlands	Blake Dennis, Australia	Wilfried Rossignol, France
1999	Street	Sven Boekhorst, Netherlands	Den Bosch, Netherlands	Louie Zamora, U.S.
2003	Street Best Trick	Richie Velasquez, U.S.	Stephane Alfano, France	Brian Aragon, U.S.
2003	Vert	Eito Yasutoko, Japan	Marco de Santi, Brazil	Marc Englehart, U.S.
2002	Vert	Marc Englehart, U.S.	Takeshi Yasutoko, Japan	Shane Yost, Tasmania
2001	Vert	Taig Khris, France	Takeshi Yasutoko, Japan	Matt Lindenmuth, U.S.
2000	Vert	Matt Salerno, Australia	Taig Khris, France	Eito Yasutoko, Japan
1999	Vert	Taig Khris, France	Shane Yost, Australia	Cesar Mora, Australia

AGGRESSIVE IN-LINE — WOMEN

YEAR	EVENT	GOLD	SILVER	BRONZE
2001	Street	Martina Svobodova, Slovakia	Fabiola da Silva, Brazil	Deborah West, U.S.
2000	Street	Martina Svobodova, Slovakia	Fabiola da Silva, Brazil	Kelly Matthews, U.S.
1999	Street	Fabiola da Silva, Brazil	Anneke Winter, Germany	Kelly Matthews, U.S.
2001	Vert	Ayumi Kawasaki, Japan	Fabiola da Silva, Brazil	N/A
2000	Vert	Fabiola da Silva, Brazil	Ayumi Kawasaki, Japan	Merce Borrull, Spain
1999	Vert	Fabiola da Silva, Brazil	Merce Borrull, Spain	Maki Komori, Japan

WAKEBOARDING — MEN

YEAR	GOLD	SILVER	BRONZE
2005	Phillip Sloven, U.S.	Daniel Watkins, U.S.	Rusty Malinoski, Canada
2004	Trevor Hansen, U.S.	Andrew Adkinson, U.S.	Brett Eisenhauer, Australia
2003	Parks Bonifay, U.S.	Shane Bonifay, U.S.	Brett Eisenhauer, Australia
2002	Mark Kenney, U.S.	Danny Harf, U.S.	Darin Shapiro, U.S.
2001	Darin Shapiro, U.S.	Parks Bonifay, U.S.	Daniel Watkins, Australia
2000	Parks Bonifay, U.S.	Darin Shapiro, U.S.	Ryan Wynne, U.S.
1999	Shaun Murray, U.S.	Parks Bonifay, U.S.	Rob Struharik, U.S.

WAKEBOARDING — WOMEN

YEAR	GOLD	SILVER	BRONZE
2005	Emily Copeland, U.S.	Lauren Loe, U.S.	Dallas Friday, U.S.
2004	Dallas Friday, U.S.	Emily Copeland, U.S.	Lauren Loe, U.S.
2003	Emily Copeland, U.S.	Tara Hamilton, U.S.	Leslie Kent, U.S.
2002	Emily Copeland, U.S.	Melissa Marquardt, U.S.	Dallas Friday, U.S.
2001	Dallas Friday, U.S.	Tara Hamilton, U.S.	Christy Smith, U.S.
2000	Maeghan Major, U.S.	Tara Hamilton, U.S.	Lauren Loe, U.S.
1999	Andrea Gaytan, Mexico	Tara Hamilton, U.S.	Christy Smith, U.S.

STREET LUGE

YEAR	EVENT	GOLD	SILVER	BRONZE
2002	4-person	Mike McIntyre, U.S.	John Rogers, U.S.	Dave Rogers, U.S.
2001	4-person	Rat Sult, U.S.	Biker Sherlock, U.S.	John Fryer, U.S.
1999	4-person	Sean Mallard, U.S.	Biker Sherlock, U.S.	George Orton, U.S.
2002	6-person	Dave Rogers, U.S.	Mike McIntyre, U.S.	John Rogers, U.S.
2001	6-person	Rat Sult, U.S.	Kurtis Head, U.S.	David Kelly, U.S.
1999	6-person	Biker Sherlock, U.S.	Sean Slate, U.S.	Wade Sokol, U.S.

SURFING — ALL-TIME RESULTS

Bobby Martinez,
2006 ASP Rookie of the Year

AFP PHOTO / RAFA RIVAS

YEAR	MEN	YEAR	LONGBOARD
2006	Kelly Slater, U.S.	2005	*Longboard cancelled in 2005*
2005	Kelly Slater, U.S.	2004	Joel Tudor, U.S.
2004	Andy Irons, U.S.	2003	Beau Young, Australia
2003	Andy Irons, U.S.	2002	Colin McPhillips, U.S.
2002	Andy Irons, U.S.	2001	Colin McPhillips, U.S.
2001	C.J. Hobgood, U.S.	2000	Beau Young, Australia
2000	Sunny Garcia, U.S.	1999	Colin McPhillips, U.S.
1999	Mark Occhilupo, Australia	1998	Joel Tudor, U.S.
1998	Kelly Slater, U.S.	1997	Dino Miranda, U.S.
1997	Kelly Slater, U.S.	1996	Bonga Perkins, U.S.
1996	Kelly Slater, U.S.	1995	Rusty Keaulana, U.S.
1995	Kelly Slater, U.S.	1994	Rusty Keaulana, U.S.
1994	Kelly Slater, U.S.	1993	Rusty Keaulana, U.S.
1993	Derek Ho, U.S.	1992	Joey Hawkins, U.S.
1992	Kelly Slater, U.S.	1991	Martin McMillan, Australia
1991	Damien Hardman, Australia	1990	Nat Young, Australia
1990	Tom Curren, U.S.	1989	Nat Young, Australia
1989	Martin Potter, United Kingdom	1988	Nat Young, Australia
1988	Barton Lynch, Australia	1987	Stuart Entwistle, Australia
1987	Damien Hardman, Australia	1986	Nat Young, Australia
1986	Tom Curren, U.S.		
1985	Tom Curren, U.S.		
1984	Tom Carroll, Australia		
1983	Tom Carroll, Australia		
1982	Mark Richards, Australia		
1981	Mark Richards, Australia		
1980	Mark Richards, Australia		
1979	Mark Richards, Australia		
1978	Wayne Bartholomew, Australia		
1977	Shaun Tomson, South Africa		
1976	Peter Townend, Australia		

SURFING — ALL-TIME RESULTS (cont.)

ASSOCIATION OF SURFING PROFESSIONALS (ASP) WORLD CHAMPIONS (cont.)

YEAR	WOMEN
2006	Layne Beachley, Australia
2005	Chelsea Georgeson, Australia
2004	Sofia Mulanovich, Peru
2003	Layne Beachley, Australia
2002	Layne Beachley, Australia
2001	Layne Beachley, Australia
2000	Layne Beachley, Australia
1999	Layne Beachley, Australia
1998	Layne Beachley, Australia
1997	Lisa Andersen, U.S.
1996	Lisa Andersen, U.S.
1995	Lisa Andersen, U.S.
1994	Lisa Andersen, U.S.
1993	Pauline Menczer, Australia
1992	Wendy Botha, Australia
1991	Wendy Botha, Australia
1990	Pam Burridge, Australia
1989	Wendy Botha, Australia
1988	Freida Zamba, U.S.
1987	Wendy Botha, South Africa
1986	Freida Zamba, U.S.
1985	Freida Zamba, U.S.
1984	Freida Zamba, U.S.
1983	Kim Mearig, U.S.

Layne Beachley

YEAR	WOMEN
1982	Debbie Beacham, U.S.
1981	Margo Oberg, U.S.
1980	Margo Oberg, U.S.
1979	Lynne Boyer, U.S.
1978	Lynne Boyer, U.S.
1977	Margo Oberg, U.S

MOTOCROSS — ALL-TIME RESULTS

250CC SUPERCROSS

YEAR	CHAMPION	HOMETOWN
2006	Ricky Carmichael	Havana, Florida
2005	Ricky Carmichael	Havana, Florida
2004	Chad Reed	Kurri Kurri, Australia
2003	Ricky Carmichael	Havana, Florida
2002	Ricky Carmichael	Havana, Florida
2001	Ricky Carmichael	Havana, Florida
2000	Jeremy McGrath	Menifee, California
1999	Jeremy McGrath	Menifee, California
1998	Jeremy McGrath	Menifee, California
1997	Jeff Emig	Riverside, California
1996	Jeremy McGrath	Menifee, California
1995	Jeremy McGrath	Murrieta, California
1994	Jeremy McGrath	Murrieta, California
1993	Jeremy McGrath	Murrieta, California
1992	Jeff Stanton	Sherwood, Michigan
1991	Jean-Michel Bayle	Manosque, France

YEAR	CHAMPION	HOMETOWN
1990	Jeff Stanton	Sherwood, Michigan
1989	Jeff Stanton	Sherwood, Michigan
1988	Rick Johnson	El Cajon, California
1987	Jeff Ward	Mission Viejo, California
1986	Rick Johnson	El Cajon, California
1985	Jeff Ward	Mission Viejo, California
1984	Johnny O'Mara	Simi Valley, California
1983	David Bailey	Axton, Virginia
1982	Donnie Hansen	Canyon Country, California
1981	Mark Barnett	Bridgeview, Illinois
1980	Mike Bell	Lakewood, California
1979	Bob Hannah	Carson, Nevada
1978	Bob Hannah	Whittier, California
1977	Bob Hannah	Whittier, California
1976	Jim Weinert	Laguna Beach, California
1975	Jim Ellis	Cobalt, Connecticut
1974	Pierre Karsmakers	Netherlands

250CC MOTOCROSS

YEAR	CHAMPION	HOMETOWN
2006	Ricky Carmichael	Havana, Florida
2005	Ricky Carmichael	Havana, Florida
2004	Ricky Carmichael	Havana, Florida
2003	Ricky Carmichael	Havana, Florida
2002	Ricky Carmichael	Havana, Florida
2001	Ricky Carmichael	Havana, Florida
2000	Ricky Carmichael	Havana, Florida
1999	Greg Albertyn	Johannesburg, South Africa
1998	Doug Henry	Oxford, Connecticut
1997	Jeff Emig	Riverside, California
1996	Jeff Emig	Riverside, California
1995	Jeremy McGrath	Murrieta, California
1994	Mike LaRocco	South Bend, Indiana
1993	Mike Kiedrowski	Acton, California

YEAR	CHAMPION	HOMETOWN
1992	Jeff Stanton	Sherwood, Michigan
1991	Jean-Michel Bayle	Manosque, France
1990	Jeff Stanton	Sherwood, Michigan
1989	Jeff Stanton	Sherwood, Michigan
1988	Jeff Ward	Mission Viejo, California
1987	Rick Johnson	El Cajon, California
1986	Rick Johnson	El Cajon, California
1985	Jeff Ward	Mission Viejo, California
1984	Rick Johnson	El Cajon, California
1983	David Bailey	Axton, Virginia
1982	Donnie Hansen	Canyon Country, California
1981	Kent Howerton	San Antonio, Texas
1980	Kent Howerton	San Antonio, Texas
1979	Bob Hannah	Carson City, Nevada
1978	Bob Hannah	Whittier, California
1977	Tony DiStefano	Morrisville, Pennsylvania
1976	Tony DiStefano	Morrisville, Pennsylvania
1975	Tony DiStefano	Morrisville, Pennsylvania
1974	Gary Jones	Hacienda Heights, California
1973	Gary Jones	Hacienda Heights, California
1972	Gary Jones	Hacienda Heights, California

Ryan Villopoto

JEFF KARDAS/WIREIMAGE.COM

125CC MOTOCROSS

YEAR	CHAMPION	HOMETOWN
2006	Ryan Villopoto	Poulsbo, Washington
2005	Ivan Tedesco	Temecula, California
2004	James Stewart, Jr.	Haines City, Florida
2003	Grant Langston	Durban, South Africa
2002	James Stewart, Jr.	Haines City, Florida
2001	Michael Brown	Piney Flats, Tennessee
2000	Travis Pastrana	Annapolis, Maryland
1999	Ricky Carmichael	Havana, Florida
1998	Ricky Carmichael	Havana, Florida
1997	Ricky Carmichael	Havana, Florida
1996	Steve Lamson	Pollock Pines, California
1995	Steve Lamson	Pollock Pines, California
1994	Doug Henry	Oxford, Connecticut
1993	Doug Henry	Oxford, Connecticut
1992	Jeff Emig	Highland, California
1991	Mike Kiedrowski	Canyon Country, California
1990	Guy Cooper	Stillwater, Oklahoma

YEAR	CHAMPION	HOMETOWN
1989	Mike Kiedrowski	Canyon Country, California
1988	George Holland	Kerman, California
1987	Micky Dymond	Yorba Linda, California
1986	Micky Dymond	Yorba Linda, California
1985	Ron Lechien	El Cajon, California
1984	Jeff Ward	Mission Viejo, California
1983	Johnny O'Mara	Simi Valley, California
1982	Mark Barnett	Bridgeview, Illinois
1981	Mark Barnett	Bridgeview, Illinois
1980	Mark Barnett	Bridgeview, Illinois
1979	Broc Glover	El Cajon, California
1978	Broc Glover	El Cajon, California
1977	Broc Glover	El Cajon, California
1976	Bob Hannah	Whittier, California
1975	Marty Smith	San Diego, California
1974	Marty Smith	San Diego, California

GOLF

Tiger Woods won the last two majors in 2006 and finished a close second at the first two majors of 2007.

ROBERT BECK

Tiger Woods had a bittersweet year in 2006–07. The No. 1 player in the world began 2006 with wins at the Buick Invitational and the Ford Championship at Doral. He came up just short in his attempt to defend his title at the Masters, tying for third behind champion Phil Mickelson.

But on May 3, Tiger's father, Earl Woods, died after a long battle with cancer. Woods took the loss hard. He didn't play in another event until the U.S. Open in mid-June, where he missed the cut. It was the first time he'd missed the cut at a major in his pro career.

Tiger bounced back, though. He finished as runner-up at the Western Open in July and he completed the season with six-consecutive Tour victories. His impressive winning streak included the final two majors

of the season, the British Open and the PGA Championship. He began 2007 by defending his Buick title, giving him seven consecutive victories. It was the second-longest streak in the history of the PGA Tour.

While golf's biggest superstar continued to make the biggest headlines, Tiger wasn't the only tale on tour. Australian star Geoff Ogilvy made a splash in 2006 when he won the WGC-Accenture Match Play Championship and followed that up with his first-ever major victory at the U.S. Open. Ogilvy chipped in to save par on the 71st hole of the U.S. Open. He was watching from the clubhouse as Phil Mickelson made a disastrous double bogey on the final hole to give him the title.

Zach Johnson and Angel Cabrera also became first-time major winners when they

claimed the 2007 Masters and U.S. Open, respectively. Johnson and Cabrera managed to hold off Woods, who placed second in both tournaments.

On the LPGA tour, Lorena Ochoa unseated perennial Number 1 Annika Sorenstam as the top-ranked player in the world in April 2007. Ochoa won a tour-leading six tournaments in 2006 and maintained her high level of play into '07. She became the first Mexican-born player on either the men's or women's tour to be ranked Number 1 in the world. She also took home Player of the Year honors in 2006, snapping Sorenstam's five-year hold on the award.

Sorenstam didn't go home entirely empty-handed, of course. The Swedish superstar won her 10th career major championship at the 2006 U.S. Women's Open. She won only one tournament the rest of the year, but placed in the Top 5 in 11 of her 20 starts.

Morgan Pressel became the youngest golfer to win an LPGA major (18 years, 313 days) by capturing the 2007 Kraft Nabisco Championship. Pressel shot a 3-under 69 on the final day of the tournament then waited and watched. Brittany Lincicome, Suzann Pettersen, and Catriona Matthew all dropped strokes down the stretch, giving the talented teen a one-shot victory.

Two months later, Pettersen redeemed herself at the LPGA Championship. Her 5-under 67 in the final round held off a charging Karrie Webb and earned Pettersen her first career victory at a major.

In 2006, Lorena Ochoa led the LPGA Tour with six victories and more than $2.5 million in winnings.

TODD BIGELOW/AURORA

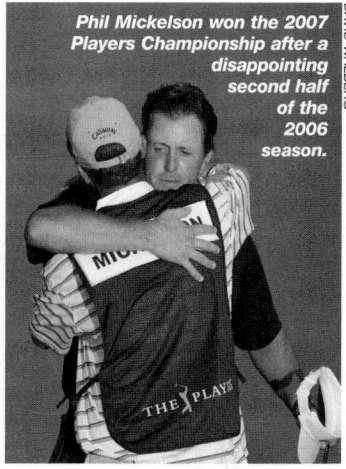

DAVID WALBERG

Phil Mickelson won the 2007 Players Championship after a disappointing second half of the 2006 season.

FAST FACT

Only four active players have more than 30 career PGA tournament victories as of June 2007: Tiger Woods (57), Tom Watson (39), Vijay Singh (32), and Phil Mickelson (31).

ALL-TIME CHAMPIONS – MEN

THE MASTERS

YEAR	WINNER	YEAR	WINNER	YEAR	WINNER
2007	Zach Johnson	1983	Seve Ballesteros	1959	Art Wall, Jr.
2006	Phil Mickelson	1982	*Craig Stadler	1958	Arnold Palmer
2005	*Tiger Woods	1981	Tom Watson	1957	Doug Ford
2004	Phil Mickelson	1980	Seve Ballesteros	1956	Jack Burke, Jr.
2003	*Mike Weir	1979†	*Fuzzy Zoeller	1955	Cary Middlecoff
2002	Tiger Woods	1978	Gary Player	1954	*Sam Snead
2001	Tiger Woods	1977	Tom Watson	1953	Ben Hogan
2000	Vijay Singh	1976	Ray Floyd	1952	Sam Snead
1999	Jose Maria Olazabal	1975	Jack Nicklaus	1951	Ben Hogan
1998	Mark O'Meara	1974	Gary Player	1950	Jimmy Demaret
1997	Tiger Woods	1973	Tommy Aaron	1949	Sam Snead
1996	Nick Faldo	1972	Jack Nicklaus	1948	Claude Harmon
1995	Ben Crenshaw	1971	Charles Coody	1947	Jimmy Demaret
1994	Jose Maria Olazabal	1970	*Billy Casper	1946	Herman Keiser
1993	Bernhard Langer	1969	George Archer	1943–45	No tournament
1992	Fred Couples	1968	Bob Goalby	1942	*Byron Nelson
1991	Ian Woosnam	1967	Gay Brewer, Jr.	1941	Craig Wood
1990	*Nick Faldo	1966	*Jack Nicklaus	1940	Jimmy Demaret
1989	*Nick Faldo	1965	Jack Nicklaus	1939	Ralph Guldahl
1988	Sandy Lyle	1964	Arnold Palmer	1938	Henry Picard
1987	*Larry Mize	1963	Jack Nicklaus	1937	Byron Nelson
1986	Jack Nicklaus	1962	Arnold Palmer	1936	Horton Smith
1985	Bernhard Langer	1961	Gary Player	1935	*Gene Sarazen
1984	Ben Crenshaw	1960	Arnold Palmer	1934	Horton Smith

*Winner in playoff. †Playoff cut from 18 holes to sudden death. Note: Played at Augusta National Golf Club, Augusta, Georgia.

ALL-TIME CHAMPIONS — MEN (cont.)

U.S. OPEN

YEAR	WINNER	YEAR	WINNER	YEAR	WINNER
2007	Angel Cabrera	1970	Tony Jacklin	1931	*Billy Burke
2006	Geoff Ogilvy	1969	Orville Moody	1930	Bobby Jones
2005	Michael Campbell	1968	Lee Trevino	1929	*Bobby Jones
2004	Retief Goosen	1967	Jack Nicklaus	1928	*Johnny Farrell
2003	Jim Furyk	1966	*Billy Casper	1927	*Tommy Armour
2002	Tiger Woods	1965	*Gary Player	1926	Bobby Jones
2001	*Retief Goosen	1964	Ken Venturi	1925	*Willie MacFarlane
2000	Tiger Woods	1963	*Julius Boros	1924	Cyril Walker
1999	Payne Stewart	1962	*Jack Nicklaus	1923	*Bobby Jones
1998	Lee Janzen	1961	Gene Littler	1922	Gene Sarazen
1997	Ernie Els	1960	Arnold Palmer	1921	Jim Barnes
1996	Steve Jones	1959	Billy Casper	1920	Edward Ray
1995	Corey Pavin	1958	Tommy Bolt	1919	*Walter Hagen
1994	*Ernie Els	1957	*Dick Mayer	1917–18	No tournament
1993	Lee Janzen	1956	Cary Middlecoff	1916	Chick Evans
1992	Tom Kite	1955	*Jack Fleck	1915	Jerry Travers
1991	*Payne Stewart	1954	Ed Furgol	1914	Walter Hagen
1990	*Hale Irwin	1953	Ben Hogan	1913	*Francis Ouimet
1989	Curtis Strange	1952	Julius Boros	1912	John McDermott
1988	*Curtis Strange	1951	Ben Hogan	1911	*John McDermott
1987	Scott Simpson	1950	*Ben Hogan	1910	*Alex Smith
1986	Ray Floyd	1949	Cary Middlecoff	1909	George Sargent
1985	Andy North	1948	Ben Hogan	1908	*Fred McLeod
1984	*Fuzzy Zoeller	1947	*Lew Worsham	1907	Alex Ross
1983	Larry Nelson	1946	*Lloyd Mangrum	1906	Alex Smith
1982	Tom Watson	1942–45	No tournament	1905	Willie Anderson
1981	David Graham	1941	Craig Wood	1904	Willie Anderson
1980	Jack Nicklaus	1940	*Lawson Little	1903	*Willie Anderson
1979	Hale Irwin	1939	*Byron Nelson	1902	Laurie Auchterlonie
1978	Andy North	1938	Ralph Guldahl	1901	*Willie Anderson
1977	Hubert Green	1937	Ralph Guldahl	1900	Harry Vardon
1976	Jerry Pate	1936	Tony Manero	1899	Willie Smith
1975	*Lou Graham	1935	Sam Parks, Jr.	1898	Fred Herd
1974	Hale Irwin	1934	Olin Dutra	1897†	Joe Lloyd
1973	Johnny Miller	1933	Johnny Goodman	1896†	James Foulis
1972	Jack Nicklaus	1932	Gene Sarazen	1895†	Horace Rawlins
1971	*Lee Trevino				

*Winner in playoff. The 1990 playoff went to one hole of sudden death after an 18-hole playoff.
In the 1994 playoff, Montgomerie was eliminated after 18 playoff holes, and Els beat Roberts on the 20th. †Before 1898, 36 holes; from 1898 on, 72 holes.

BRITISH OPEN

YEAR	WINNER	YEAR	WINNER	YEAR	WINNER
2007	*Padraig Harrington	1985	Sandy Lyle	1964	Tony Lema
2006	Tiger Woods	1984	Seve Ballesteros	1963	*Bob Charles
2005	Tiger Woods	1983	Tom Watson	1962	Arnold Palmer
2004	*Todd Hamilton	1982	Tom Watson	1961	Arnold Palmer
2003	Ben Curtis	1981	Bill Rogers	1960	Kel Nagle
2002	*Ernie Els	1980	Tom Watson	1959	Gary Player
2001	David Duval	1979	Seve Ballesteros	1958	*Peter Thomson
2000	Tiger Woods	1978	Jack Nicklaus	1957	Bobby Locke
1999	*Paul Lawrie	1977	Tom Watson	1956	Peter Thomson
1998	*Mark O'Meara	1976	Johnny Miller	1955	Peter Thomson
1997	Justin Leonard	1975	*Tom Watson	1954	Peter Thomson
1996	Tom Lehman	1974	Gary Player	1953	Ben Hogan
1995	*John Daly	1973	Tom Weiskopf	1952	Bobby Locke
1994	Nick Price	1972	Lee Trevino	1951	Max Faulkner
1993	Greg Norman	1971	Lee Trevino	1950	Bobby Locke
1992	Nick Faldo	1970	*Jack Nicklaus	1949	*Bobby Locke
1991	Ian Baker-Finch	1969	Tony Jacklin	1948	Henry Cotton
1990	Nick Faldo	1968	Gary Player	1947	Fred Daly
1989††	*Mark Calcavecchia	1967	Robert DeVicenzo	1946	Sam Snead
1988	Seve Ballesteros	1966	Jack Nicklaus	1940–45	No tournament
1987	Nick Faldo	1965	Peter Thomson	1939	Richard Burton
1986	Greg Norman				

*Winner in playoff. †† Playoff cut from 18 holes to 4 holes.

BRITISH OPEN (cont.)

YEAR	WINNER	YEAR	WINNER	YEAR	WINNER
1938	Reginald A. Whitcombe	1920	George Duncan	1898	Harry Vardon
1937	Henry Cotton	1915–19	No tournament	1897	Harold Hilton
1936	Alfred Padgham	1914	Harry Vardon	1896	*Harry Vardon
1935	Alfred Perry	1913	John H. Taylor	1895	John H. Taylor
1934	Henry Cotton	1912	Ted Ray	1894	John H. Taylor
1933	*Denny Shute	1911	Harry Vardon	1893	William Auchterlonie
1932	Gene Sarazen	1910	James Braid	1892**	Harold Hilton
1931	Tommy Armour	1909	John H. Taylor	1891	Hugh Kirkaldy
1930	Bobby Jones	1908	James Braid	1890	John Ball
1929	Walter Hagen	1907	Arnaud Massy	1889	*Willie Park, Jr.
1928	Walter Hagen	1906	James Braid	1888	Jack Burns
1927	Bobby Jones	1905	James Braid	1887	Willie Park, Jr.
1926	Bobby Jones	1904	Jack White	1886	David Brown
1925	Jim Barnes	1903	Harry Vardon	1885	Bob Martin
1924	Walter Hagen	1902	Alexander Herd	1884	Jack Simpson
1923	Arthur G. Havers	1901	James Braid	1883	*Willie Fernie
1922	Walter Hagen	1900	John H. Taylor	1882	Robert Ferguson
1921	*Jock Hutchison	1899	Harry Vardon		

*Winner in playoff.
**Championship extended from 36 to 72 holes.

LEGENDS

Lee Trevino won a total of nine career majors on the PGA and Senior Tours.

WALTER IOOSS JR.

■ **Lee Trevino,** b. December 1, 1939, Dallas, Texas. The son of Mexican immigrants, Trevino grew up next to a golf course and taught himself the game by working as a caddie. After several years as an assistant golf pro, he joined the PGA Tour in 1967. Known for his playful, laid-back style on the golf course, Trevino quickly earned the nickname "The Merry Mex." Just one year after his PGA Tour debut, he won the first of his 29 career victories at the 1968 U.S. Open. In 1971, he won an impressive six PGA tournaments, including the British Open and his second U.S. Open title, where he defeated Jack Nicklaus in a thrilling 18-hole playoff. After being struck by lightning at the 1975 Western Open, his game suffered, but he rallied late in his career and pulled off a surprise victory at the 1984 PGA Championship at the age of 44. Trevino was elected to the World Golf Hall of Fame in 1981.

■ **Billy Casper,** b. June 24, 1931, San Diego, California. Casper was introduced to the game by his father at the age of five and went on to become one of the most successful golfers in PGA Tour history. In all, he won 51 times on the PGA Tour, including two victories at the U.S. Open (1959, '66) and one at The Masters (1970). Casper led the Tour in lowest scoring average five times between 1960 and 1968 and was inducted into the World Golf Hall of Fame in 1978. In addition, Casper also played on eight Ryder Cup teams during his career and holds the all-time record for most points scored by an American (23.5).

■ **Greg Norman,** b. February 10, 1955, Mount Isa, Australia. After playing primarily in his native Australia for several years, "The Shark," as he came to be known, won his first PGA tournament in 1984. Over the next 13 years, Norman notched 19 more victories and finished the season ranked Number 1 in the world seven times. Despite this, he often struggled or suffered bad luck at major tournaments, winning only two (the 1986 and '93 British Opens) during his career. In 2001, he was elected to the World Golf Hall of Fame.

ALL-TIME CHAMPIONS – MEN (cont.)

BRITISH OPEN (cont.)

YEAR	WINNER	YEAR	WINNER	YEAR	WINNER
1881	Robert Ferguson	1873	Tom Kidd	1865	Andrew Strath
1880	Robert Ferguson	1872	Tom Morris, Jr.	1864	Tom Morris, Sr.
1879	Jamie Anderson	1871	No tournament	1863	Willie Park
1878	Jamie Anderson	1870	Tom Morris, Jr.	1862	Tom Morris, Sr.
1877	Jamie Anderson	1869	Tom Morris, Jr.	1861‡	Tom Morris, Sr.
1876	*Bob Martin	1868	Tom Morris, Jr.	1860†	Willie Park
1875	Willie Park	1867	Tom Morris, Sr.		
1874	Mungo Park	1866	Willie Park		

*Tied, but opponent refused playoff. ‡The second annual Open was open to amateurs and pros. †The first event was open only to pro golfers.

TODAY'S STARS

Before his victory at the 2007 Masters, Zach Johnson had only won one other PGA Tour event, the 2004 BellSouth Classic.

JOHN BIEVER/SPORTS ILLUSTRATED

■ **Zach Johnson,** b. February 24, 1976, Iowa City, Iowa. Johnson burst onto the PGA Tour in 2004 by becoming just the second golfer in history to earn more than $2 million in winnings in his rookie season. That year, he made 24 of 30 cuts and earned his first Tour win in just his 13th career tournament. In 2005, he continued his steady play, again posting five top-10 finishes. Johnson had an up and down 2006, but still played well enough to earn a spot on the U.S. Ryder Cup team. Then, in 2007, a final-round 69 at a cold and windy Masters pushed him past Tiger Woods to give him a two-shot victory and his first green jacket. Six weeks later, Johnson's playoff victory at the AT&T Classic pushed his world ranking into the top 15 and cemented his reputation as one of the best young golfers on the Tour.

■ **Charles Howell III,** b. June 20, 1979, Augusta, Georgia. Growing up near the home of the Masters, Howell began playing golf at age seven and won five tournaments by age 11. After a distinguished college career at Oklahoma State, where he was the 2000 NCAA individual champion, Howell turned pro and played well enough to be named the 2001 PGA Tour rookie of the year. The next season, he won his first tournament and finished ninth on the money list. But over the next four seasons, Howell couldn't seem to win, and had a string of nine runner-up finishes without a victory. In 2007, though, Howell won in a playoff at the 2007 Nissan Open for his second career victory. He now ranks in the top 15 in the official world rankings.

■ **Rory Sabbatini,** b. April 2, 1976, Durban, South Africa. Sabbatini left South Africa in 1996 to play golf at the University of Arizona, where he earned three-time All-America honors. When he turned pro in 1999 at age 22, he was the youngest player on the PGA Tour. Known as a fiery and outspoken competitor, Sabbatini possesses a great short game around the green. He has won four times on Tour and finished in the top 20 on the annual money list in 2004 and 2006. In 2007, Sabbatini had the best finish of his career at a major tournament when he tied Tiger Woods for second place at the Masters.

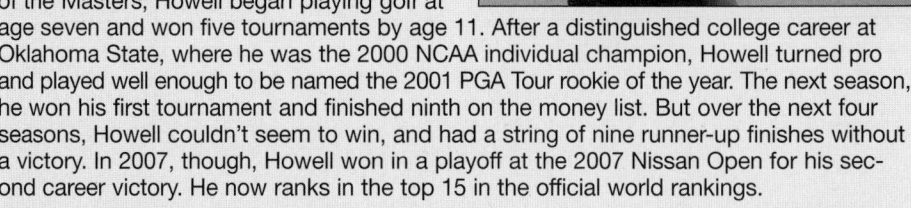

TRIVIA CHALLENGE

1 In 1997, Tiger Woods won his first Masters by finishing 18-under-par and setting a new major championship record for margin of victory. How many strokes did he win by?
a. 12
b. 9
c. 6

2 Which South African golf star has earned the nickname "The Big Easy" for his fluid, seemingly effortless swing?
a. Retief Goosen
b. Rory Sabbatini
c. Ernie Els

3 In golf, what is the penalty for jumping up and down on the green and causing a stopped ball overhanging the hole to fall in without it being struck by a club?
a. No penalty
b. One stroke
c. Two strokes

4 When was the last time the U.S. team won golf's Ryder Cup?
a. 1993
b. 1999
c. 2006

5 During his career, Hall-of-Famer Vijay Singh has never finished higher than 6th place at which one of these major tournaments?
a. Masters
b. British Open
c. U.S. Open

6 Dimples were added to give golf balls less air resistance, allowing them to be hit up to four times farther than if they were smooth.
a. True
b. False

7 Which active PGA Tour player has won more career victories than any other left-handed golfer in history?
a. Greg Chalmers
b. Phil Mickelson
c. Mike Weir

Vijay Singh

FRED VUICH

Trivia Challenge: 1. a; 2. c; 3. b; 4. b; 5. c; 6. a; 7. b.

ALL-TIME CHAMPIONS – MEN (cont.)

PGA CHAMPIONSHIP

YEAR	WINNER	YEAR	WINNER	YEAR	WINNER
2006	Tiger Woods	1988	Jeff Sluman	1970	Dave Stockton
2005	Phil Mickelson	1987	*Larry Nelson	1969	Ray Floyd
2004	Vijay Singh	1986	Bob Tway	1968	Julius Boros
2003	Shaun Micheel	1985	Hubert Green	1967	*Don January
2002	Rich Beem	1984	Lee Trevino	1966	Al Geiberger
2001	David Toms	1983	Hal Sutton	1965	Dave Marr
2000	*Tiger Woods	1982	Raymond Floyd	1964	Bobby Nichols
1999	Tiger Woods	1981	Larry Nelson	1963	Jack Nicklaus
1998	Vijay Singh	1980	Jack Nicklaus	1962	Gary Player
1997	Davis Love III	1979	*David Graham	1961	*Jerry Barber
1996	*Mark Brooks	1978	*John Mahaffey	1960	Jay Hebert
1995	*Steve Elkington	1977†	*Lanny Wadkins	1959	Bob Rosburg
1994	Nick Price	1976	Dave Stockton	1958	Dow Finsterwald
1993	*Paul Azinger	1975	Jack Nicklaus	1957	Lionel Hebert
1992	Nick Price	1974	Lee Trevino	1956	Jack Burke
1991	John Daly	1973	Jack Nicklaus	1955	Doug Ford
1990	Wayne Grady	1972	Gary Player	1954	Chick Harbert
1989	Payne Stewart	1971	Jack Nicklaus	1953	Walter Burkemo

*Winner in playoff. †Playoff changed from 18 holes to sudden death.

GOLF

ALL-TIME CHAMPIONS — MEN (cont.)

PGA CHAMPIONSHIP (cont.)

YEAR	WINNER	YEAR	WINNER	YEAR	WINNER
1952	Jim Turnesa	1940	Byron Nelson	1928	Leo Diegel
1951	Sam Snead	1939	Henry Picard	1927	Walter Hagen
1950	Chandler Harper	1938	Paul Runyan	1926	Walter Hagen
1949	Sam Snead	1937	Denny Shute	1925	Walter Hagen
1948	Ben Hogan	1936	Denny Shute	1924	Walter Hagen
1947	Jim Ferrier	1935	Johnny Revolta	1923	Gene Sarazen
1946	Ben Hogan	1934	Paul Runyan	1922	Gene Sarazen
1945	Byron Nelson	1933	Gene Sarazen	1921	Walter Hagen
1944	Bob Hamilton	1932	Olin Dutra	1920	Jock Hutchison
1943	No tournament	1931	Tom Creavy	1919	Jim Barnes
1942	Sam Snead	1930	Tommy Armour	1917–18	No tournament
1941	Vic Ghezzi	1929	Leo Diegel	1916	Jim Barnes

ALL-TIME CHAMPIONS — WOMEN

LPGA CHAMPIONSHIP

YEAR	WINNER	YEAR	WINNER	YEAR	WINNER
2007	Suzann Pettersen	1989	Nancy Lopez	1971	Kathy Whitworth
2006	Se Ri Pak	1988	Sherri Turner	1970	*Shirley Englehorn
2005	Annika Sorenstam	1987	Jane Geddes	1969	Betsy Rawls
2004	Annika Sorenstam	1986	Pat Bradley	1968	*Sandra Post
2003	Annika Sorenstam	1985	Nancy Lopez	1967	Kathy Whitworth
2002	Se Ri Pak	1984	Patty Sheehan	1966	Gloria Ehret
2001	Karrie Webb	1983	Patty Sheehan	1965	Sandra Haynie
2000	*Juli Inkster	1982	Jan Stephenson	1964	Mary Mills
1999	Juli Inkster	1981	Donna Caponi	1963	Mickey Wright
1998	Se Ri Pak	1980	Sally Little	1962	Judy Kimball
1997	*Chris Johnson	1979	Donna Caponi	1961	Mickey Wright
1996	Laura Davies	1978	Nancy Lopez	1960	Mickey Wright
1995	Kelly Robbins	1977	Chako Higuchi	1959	Betsy Rawls
1994	Laura Davies	1976	Betty Burfeindt	1958	Mickey Wright
1993	Patty Sheehan	1975	Kathy Whitworth	1957	Louise Suggs
1992	Betsy King	1974	Sandra Haynie	1956	*Marlene Hagge
1991	Meg Mallon	1973	Mary Mills	1955	†Beverly Hanson
1990	Beth Daniel	1972	Kathy Ahern		

*Won in playoff. The 1956 and 1997 titles were decided in sudden death; 1968 and 1970 were 18-hole playoffs. †Won match-play final.

U.S. WOMEN'S OPEN

YEAR	WINNER	YEAR	WINNER	YEAR	WINNER
2007	Cristie Kerr	1986	*Jane Geddes	1965	Carol Mann
2006	Annika Sorenstam	1985	Kathy Baker	1964	*Mickey Wright
2005	Birdie Kim	1984	Hollis Stacy	1963	Mary Mills
2004	Meg Mallon	1983	Jan Stephenson	1962	Murle Breer
2003	*Hilary Lunke	1982	Janet Anderson	1961	Mickey Wright
2002	Juli Inkster	1981	Pat Bradley	1960	Betsy Rawls
2001	Karrie Webb	1980	Amy Alcott	1959	Mickey Wright
2000	Karrie Webb	1979	Jerilyn Britz	1958	Mickey Wright
1999	Juli Inkster	1978	Hollis Stacy	1957	Betsy Rawls
1998	†Se Ri Pak	1977	Hollis Stacy	1956	*Kathy Cornelius
1997	Alison Nicholas	1976	*JoAnne Carner	1955	Fay Crocker
1996	Annika Sorenstam	1975	Sandra Palmer	1954	Babe Zaharias
1995	Annika Sorenstam	1974	Sandra Haynie	1953	*Betsy Rawls
1994	Patty Sheehan	1973	Susie Berning	1952	Louise Suggs
1993	Lauri Merten	1972	Susie Berning	1951	Betsy Rawls
1992	*Patty Sheehan	1971	JoAnne Carner	1950	Babe Zaharias
1991	Meg Mallon	1970	Donna Caponi	1949	Louise Suggs
1990	Betsy King	1969	Donna Caponi	1948	Babe Zaharias
1989	Betsy King	1968	Susie Berning	1947	Betty Jameson
1988	Liselotte Neumann	1967	Catherine LaCoste	1946	Patty Berg
1987	*Laura Davies	1966	Sandra Spuzich		

*Winner in playoff. †Winner on second hole of sudden death after 18-hole playoff ended in a tie.

LEGENDS

Karrie Webb ranks second all-time in LPGA career earnings.

ROBERT BECK

■ **Karrie Webb,** b. December 21, 1974, Ayr, Australia. Webb first qualified for the LPGA Tour in late 1995 in dramatic fashion when she placed second at the Tour's qualifying tournament while playing with a broken wrist. The next year, at just her second LPGA event, Webb secured her first Tour victory by defeating two veterans in a four-hole, sudden-death playoff. Since then, Webb has won 34 more times on the LPGA Tour, including seven major victories. In 2001, she completed the LPGA career Grand Slam with her first LPGA championship title, making her one of only six women—and the youngest ever—to have won all four of the major women's tournaments. Her most recent major victory came in 2006, when she eagled the 72nd hole of the Kraft Nabisco Championship from 116 yards out and then beat Lorena Ochoa in a sudden death playoff with a birdie on the same hole. Webb was inducted into the World Golf Hall of Fame in 2005.

■ **Jan Stephenson,** b. December 22, 1951, Sydney, Australia. After a successful amateur and professional career in Australia, Stephenson joined the LPGA Tour in 1974 and, thanks to an impressive debut season, was named Rookie of the Year. Stephenson was a charismatic star with a great golf game, and she often encouraged the LPGA to be more aggressive in marketing the Tour's players to the public. Between 1976 and 1987, Stephenson was among the best of the players on the LPGA Tour, winning 16 tournaments, including three majors victories at the 1981 Peter Jackson Classic (the forerunner to the duMaurier Classic), the 1982 LPGA Championship, and the 1983 U.S. Open. Stephenson, who has earned more than $3 million in career earnings, now works with charities and as a golf course designer.

■ **JoAnne Carner,** b. April 4, 1939, Palm Beach, Florida. After an extended amateur career where she won five U.S. Women's Amateur Championships as well as one LPGA tournament, Carner turned pro in 1970 at age 30. She quickly came to dominate the Tour and won 42 LPGA events over the next 16 years. Carner was named Player of the Year three times during that span. Although she only won two majors (the 1971 and '76 U.S. Opens) during her career, she always played well in the biggest tournaments and finished as runner-up at a major 10 different times. In 1982, she became the 10th woman inducted into the World Golf Hall of Fame. Four years later, she became the second player in LPGA Tour history to reach $2 million in career earnings.

DID YOU KNOW?

In 1979, the LPGA designated the Peter Jackson Classic as the Tour's third major. Then, in 1983, the Nabisco Dinah Shore (now know as the Kraft Nabisco Championship) was designated the fourth major. In 1984, the Peter Jackson Classic was renamed the du Maurier Classic. After the 2000 season, the du Maurier Classic tournament was discontinued and the Weetabix Women's British Open became the fourth major on the Tour in 2001.

Visit our website for the latest stats and sports info.

TODAY'S STARS

In 2007, Morgan Pressel became the youngest winner of a major tournament in LPGA history.

TODD BIGELOW/AURORA

■ **Morgan Pressel,** b. May 23, 1988, Tampa, Florida. In 2001, only four years after she took up the game, the 12-year-old Pressel became, at the time, the youngest player ever to qualify for the U.S. Women's Open. After her mother died in 2003, Pressel moved in with her grandparents, who are also the parents of her uncle Aaron Krickstein, a former Top-10 tennis star. During her successful amateur career, Pressel won a total of 11 American Junior Golf Association titles as well as the 2006 U.S. Women's Amateur Championship. That same year, she was co-leader on the final hole of the U.S. Women's Open before bogeying the 18th to finish tied for second—the highest finish for an amateur at the tournament. After successfuly petitioning the LPGA to turn pro, the 17-year-old Pressel finished 24th on the money list in 2006, her rookie year. She won her first major in 2007 at the Kraft Nabisco Championship—52 days before her 19th birthday.

■ **Lorena Ochoa,** b. November 15, 1981, Guadalajara, Mexico. Only four years after winning LPGA Rookie of the Year honors in 2003, Ochoa proved she had become the best player on Tour in 2006 by winning six tournaments and earning the Player of the Year award. Although she has yet to win a major, Ochoa was one of only two players to finish in the top 20 in all four majors in 2006. Her nearly $2.6 million in winnings also led the Tour that year as she set new records for the fastest player in LPGA history to reach the $4-, $5-, and $6-million marks in career earnings. In 2007, she won two events in the spring, bringing her career LPGA victory total to 11 wins in just five years.

■ **Brittany Lincicome** b. September 19, 1985, St. Petersburg, Florida. Consistently among the LPGA Tour's longest hitters, Lincicome's drives off the tee have averaged more than 270 yards since her rookie year in 2005. In 2006, she took home the trophy at the World Match Play Championships after defeating Michelle Wie, Lorena Ochoa, and Juli Inkster in her final three matches. Her best finish at a major came at the 2007 Kraft Nabisco Championship where she finished in a three-way tie for second.

ALL-TIME CHAMPIONS — WOMEN (cont.)

KRAFT NABISCO CHAMPIONSHIP

YEAR	WINNER	YEAR	WINNER	YEAR	WINNER
2007	Morgan Pressel	1995	Nanci Bowen	1983	Amy Alcott
2006	Karrie Webb	1994	Donna Andrews	1982	Sally Little
2005	Annika Sorenstam	1993	Helen Alfredsson	1981	Nancy Lopez
2004	Grace Park	1992	*Dottie Mochrie	1980	Donna Caponi
2003	Patricia Meunier-Lebouc	1991	Amy Alcott	1979	Sandra Post
2002	Annika Sorenstam	1990	Betsy King	1978	*Sandra Post
2001	Annika Sorenstam	1989	Juli Inkster	1977	Kathy Whitworth
2000	Karrie Webb	1988	Amy Alcott	1976	Judy Rankin
1999	Dottie Pepper	1987	*Betsy King	1975	Sandra Palmer
1998	Pat Hurst	1986	Pat Bradley	1974	*Jo Ann Prentice
1997	Betsy King	1985	Alice Miller	1973	Mickey Wright
1996	Patti Sheehan	1984	*Juli Inkster	1972	Jane Blalock

*Winner in sudden-death playoff. Note: Designated fourth major in 1983; played at Mission Hills Country Club, Rancho Mirage, California.

ALL-TIME CHAMPIONS — WOMEN (cont.)

DU MAURIER CLASSIC

YEAR	WINNER	YEAR	WINNER	YEAR	WINNER
2000	Meg Mallon	1991	Nancy Scranton	1982	Sandra Haynie
1999	Karrie Webb	1990	Cathy Johnston	1981	Jan Stephenson
1998	Brandie Burton	1989	Tammie Green	1980	Pat Bradley
1997	Colleen Walker	1988	Sally Little	1979	Amy Alcott
1996	Laura Davies	1987	Jody Rosenthal	1978	JoAnne Carner
1995	Jenny Lidback	1986	*Pat Bradley	1977	Judy Rankin
1994	Martha Nause	1985	Pat Bradley	1976	*Donna Caponi
1993	Brandie Burton	1984	Juli Inkster	1975	*JoAnne Carner
1992	Sherri Steinhauer	1983	Hollis Stacy	1974	Carole Jo Callison
				1973	*Jocelyne Bourassa

*Winner in sudden-death playoff. Note: Designated third major in 1979; discontinued in 2001.

WOMEN'S BRITISH OPEN

YEAR	WINNER
2006	Sherri Steinhauer
2005	Jeong Jang
2004	Karen Stupples
2003	Annika Sorenstam
2002	Karrie Webb
2001	Se Ri Pak

Note: Designated fourth major in 2001.

FAST FACT

There were 117 international players from 26 different countries on the LPGA Tour in 2007. South Korea had the most with 45 players, while Chile, Colombia, Finland, India, Norway, Malaysia, the Philippines, South Africa, Spain, Thailand, Venezuela, and Wales were tied for the fewest with one player each.

TRIVIA CHALLENGE

1 How does the tournament winner traditionally celebrate her victory at the Kraft Nabisco Championship?
a. Jumping in the lake by the 18th green.
b. Tossing her ball into the gallery.
c. Dancing a jig.

2 How many LPGA Player of the Year titles has Annika Sorenstam won during her career?
a. 4
b. 6
c. 8

3 According to the Rules of Golf, what is the maximum number of clubs a player can carry in his or her bag?
a. 11
b. 14
c. No limit

4 In golf, the player who is farthest away from the hole typcially plays first.
a. True
b. False

5 Suzann Pettersen's 2007 LPGA Championship victory marked the first time that a female player from which European country had won one of golf's majors?
a. Norway
b. Denmark
c. Germany

Suzann Pettersen

6 If a player holes out on their second shot on a par-5 hole, what is the golf term for their score on that hole?
a. Eagle
b. Double Eagle
c. Double Bogey

7 At the 2006 Kraft Nabisco Championship, Lorena Ochoa tied the LPGA record for the lowest 18-hole score at a major championship. What score did she shoot?
a. 60
b. 62
c. 64

TODD BIGELOW/AURORA

Trivia Challenge: 1. a; 2. c; 3. b; 4. a; 5. a; 6. b; 7. a.

MOTOR SPORTS

One team ran laps around the competition in 2006–07: Hendrick Motorsports established itself as the team to beat in the NASCAR Nextel Cup Series. Jimmie Johnson won his first Nextel Cup championship after finishing in the Top 10 in 24 of 36 races in 2006. Two of his Hendrick teammates also had strong years, with Jeff Gordon finishing in sixth place and Kyle Busch finishing 10th.

That was nothing compared to what the team did to start 2007. Hendrick drivers won 10 of the first 14 Nextel Cup races, with Gordon and Johnson winning four apiece and Busch and Casey Mears each winning one.

The biggest news of the NASCAR season came off the track, however. On May 10, Dale Earnhardt Jr. announced that he would be leaving Dale Earnhardt Incorporated (DEI) at the end of the '07 season. The news that the sport's most popular driver was planning to leave the company that his legendary father built made headlines. It also made Junior the most prized free agent in NASCAR history. On June 13, the season's two big storylines met when Junior announced that he would join Hendrick Motorsports in 2008.

With Earnhardt Jr. leaving DEI and Casey Mears picking up his first NASCAR win, it was an upside-down year in motor sports. Casey's uncle Rick Mears is a four-time Indianapolis 500-winner, the most famous event in Indy car racing.

The '07 running of the Indy 500 was also a little unusual as a three-hour rain delay led to a wild finish. Two-time 500 champion Helio Castroneves stormed back to finish in third place after dropping to 29th because of a fueling problem. Marco Andretti, who was passed just before the finish line at the '06 race, ended this one in a dramatic, airborne crash that—luckily—left him unhurt. Once the smoke and rain cleared, Dario Franchitti had picked up his first Indy 500 win.

In June, Dale Earnhardt Jr. announced he would join Hendrick Motorsports after the 2007 racing season.

Kevin Harvick drives in all three NASCAR series—Busch, Truck, and Nextel Cup.

RUSTY JARRETT//GETTY IMAGES FOR NASCAR (LEFT); AP PHOTO/CHUCK BURTON (RIGHT)

Franchitti's teammate, Danica Patrick, also made a strong showing. One of a record three female drivers to start the race, Patrick ran as high as second before finishing eighth.

Sam Hornish Jr. finished fourth at the 2007 Indy 500 after a fantastic 2006 season. Hornish won the 2006 Indy 500 and shared the 2006 IRL Championship with driver Dan Wheldon.

Dan Wheldon (left) and Sam Hornish Jr., who have won four out of the last six IRL season titles, finished as IRL co-champions in 2006.

INDY RACING LEAGUE (IRL) ALL-TIME RESULTS

INDIANAPOLIS 500 WINNERS

Dario Franchitti

YEAR	DRIVER	MILES PER HOUR (M.P.H.)
2007	Dario Franchitti (415*)	151.774
2006	Sam Hornish Jr.	157.085
2005	Dan Wheldon	157.603
2004	Buddy Rice (450*)	138.518
2003	Gil de Ferran	156.291
2002	Helio Castroneves	166.499
2001	Helio Castroneves	141.574
2000	Juan Montoya	167.607
1999	Kenny Brack	153.176
1998	Eddie Cheever Jr.	145.155
1997	Arie Luyendyk	145.827
1996	Buddy Lazier	147.956
1995	Jacques Villeneuve	153.616
1994	Al Unser Jr.	160.872
1993	Emerson Fittipaldi	157.207
1992	Al Unser Jr.	134.477
1991	Rick Mears	176.457
1990	Arie Luyendyk	185.981
1989	Emerson Fittipaldi	167.581
1988	Rick Mears	144.809
1987	Al Unser	162.175
1986	Bobby Rahal	170.722
1985	Danny Sullivan	152.982
1984	Rick Mears	163.612
1983	Tom Sneva	162.117
1982	Gordon Johncock	162.029
1981	Bobby Unser	139.084

YEAR	DRIVER	M.P.H.
1980	Johnny Rutherford	142.862
1979	Rick Mears	158.899
1978	Al Unser	161.363
1977	A.J. Foyt Jr.	161.331
1976	Johnny Rutherford (255*)	148.725
1975	Bobby Unser (435*)	149.213
1974	Johnny Rutherford	158.589
1973	Gordon Johncock (332.5*)	159.036
1972	Mark Donohue	162.962
1971	Al Unser	157.735
1970	Al Unser	155.749
1969	Mario Andretti	156.867
1968	Bobby Unser	152.882
1967	A.J. Foyt Jr.	151.207
1966	Graham Hill	144.317
1965	Jim Clark	150.686
1964	A.J. Foyt Jr.	147.350
1963	Parnelli Jones	143.137
1962	Rodger Ward	140.293
1961	A.J. Foyt Jr.	139.130
1960	Jim Rathmann	138.767
1959	Rodger Ward	135.857
1958	Jimmy Bryan	133.791
1957	Sam Hanks	135.601
1956	Pat Flaherty	128.490
1955	Bob Sweikert	128.213
1954	Bill Vukovich	130.840
1953	Bill Vukovich	128.740
1952	Troy Ruttman	128.922
1951	Lee Wallard	126.244
1950	Johnnie Parsons (345*)	124.002
1949	Bill Holland	121.327
1948	Mauri Rose	119.814
1947	Mauri Rose	116.338
1946	George Robson	114.820
1942–45	No races held during World War II	
1941	Floyd Davis/Mauri Rose	115.117
1940	Wilbur Shaw	114.277

Note: Miles per hour (M.P.H.) denotes average race speed. *Miles completed before race was called because of rain.

INDY RACING LEAGUE ALL-TIME RESULTS (cont.)

INDIANAPOLIS 500 WINNERS (cont.)

YEAR	DRIVER	MILES PER HOUR (M.P.H.)	YEAR	DRIVER	M.P.H.
1939	Wilbur Shaw	115.035	1925	Peter DePaolo	101.127
1938	Floyd Roberts	117.200	1924	L.L. Corum/Joe Boyer	98.234
1937	Wilbur Shaw	113.580	1923	Tommy Milton	90.954
1936	Louis Meyer	109.069	1922	Jimmy Murphy	94.484
1935	Kelly Petillo	106.240	1921	Tommy Milton	89.621
1934	Bill Cummings	104.863	1920	Gaston Chevrolet	88.618
1933	Louis Meyer	104.162	1919	Howdy Wilcox	88.050
1932	Fred Fame	104.144	1917–18	No races held during World War I	
1931	Louis Schneider	96.629	1916	Dario Resta (scheduled for 300 miles)	84.001
1930	Billy Arnold	100.448	1915	Ralph DePalma	89.840
1929	Ray Keech	97.585	1914	Rene Thomas	82.474
1928	Louis Meyer	99.482	1913	Jules Goux	75.933
1927	George Souders	97.545	1912	Joe Dawson	78.719
1926	Frank Lockhart (400*)	95.904	1911	Ray Harroun	74.602

*Miles completed before race was called because of rain.

IRL CHAMPIONS

YEAR	DRIVER
2006 (tie)	Dan Wheldon and Sam Hornish Jr.
2005	Dan Wheldon
2004	Tony Kanaan
2003	Scott Dixon
2002	Sam Hornish Jr.
2001	Sam Hornish Jr.
2000	Buddy Lazier
1999	Greg Ray
1998	Kenny Brack
1996–97*	Tony Stewart
1996 (tie)	Buzz Calkins and Scott Sharp

Marco Andretti

IRL ROOKIES OF THE YEAR

YEAR	DRIVER
2006	Marco Andretti
2005	Danica Patrick
2004	Kosuke Matsuura
2003	Dan Wheldon
2002	Laurent Redon
2001	Felipe Giaffone
2000	Airton Dare
1999	Scott Harrington
1998	Robby Unser
1996–97*	Jim Guthrie
1996 (Series' first year)	No award

*This season started in 1996 and ended in 1997.

CHAMP CAR WORLD SERIES

ALL-TIME CHAMP CAR WORLD SERIES CHAMPIONS (FORMERLY CART)

YEAR	DRIVER	YEAR	DRIVER	YEAR	DRIVER
2006	Sebastien Bourdais	1986	Bobby Rahal	1982	Rick Mears
2005	Sebastien Bourdais	1985	Al Unser	1981	Rick Mears
2004	Sebastien Bourdais	1984	Mario Andretti	1980	Johnny Rutherford
2003	Paul Tracy	1983	Al Unser	1979	Rick Mears
2002	Cristiano da Matta				
2001	Gil de Ferran				
2000	Gil de Ferran				
1999	Juan Montoya				
1998	Alex Zanardi				
1997	Alex Zanardi				
1996	Jimmy Vasser				
1995	Jacques Villeneuve				
1994	Al Unser Jr.				
1993	Nigel Mansell				
1992	Bobby Rahal				
1991	Michael Andretti				
1990	Al Unser Jr.				
1989	Emerson Fittipaldi				
1988	Danny Sullivan				
1987	Bobby Rahal				

Sebastien Bourdais

TODAY'S STARS

RONALD MARTINEZ/GETTY IMAGES

■ Matt Kenseth, b. March 10, 1972, Cambridge, Wisconsin. After winning three races with Robbie Reiser's NASCAR Busch Series team, Kenseth made his NEXTEL Cup debut by finishing sixth at Dover Downs in 1998. Kenseth was named the 2000 Winston Cup Raybestos Rookie of the year. His career really took off in 2003, when he became the Winston Cup champion with 11 Top 5 finishes and 25 Top 10s. Kenseth ended the 2006 season with a career-best 15 Top 5 finishes, 1,132 laps led, and a 9.8 average finish.

In 2006, Matt Kenseth was runner-up to Jimmie Johnson in NASCAR's Chase for the Nextel Cup.

■ Marco Andretti, b. March 13, 1987, Nazareth, Pennsylvania. Son of Michael and grandson of Mario, Marco Andretti finished second in the 2006 Indy 500. Sam Hornish Jr. beat him by 0.0635 seconds. It was the second-closest finish in the race's 90-year history (Al Unser Jr. beat Scott Goodyear by 0.043 seconds in 1992). Andretti won the 2006 Indy Grand Prix of Sonoma and was named the Bombardier Rookie of the Year.

■ Sebastien Bourdais, b. February 28, 1979, Le Mans, France. Bourdais began his Champ Car career with Newman-Haas Racing in 2003 after years of success in France's Formula 3 and Formula Renault. In his first race for Newman-Hass, in St. Petersburg, Florida, Bourdais claimed pole position. His first victory for Newman-Haas came at Brands Hatch, in only his fourth Champ Car race. Bourdais dominated the Champ Car series in 2004 with seven wins and eight poles. History repeated in 2005 and 2006 as Bourdais defended his Champ Car title both years. No driver had won three consecutive titles since Ted Horn in 1948.

FAST FACT

TRIVIA CHALLENGE

The field at the 2007 Indianapolis 500 included a record three female drivers. Can you name them all?.

Danica Patrick (8th Place), Sarah Fisher (18th Place), and Milka Duno (31st Place).

Visit our website for the latest stats and sports info.

TRIVIA CHALLENGE

1 Only one driver has won the Indianapolis 500, Daytona 500, and the 24 Hours of Le Mans. Can you name him?
a. **Mario Andretti**
b. **A.J. Foyt**
c. **Al Unser**

2 What state has earned the nickname NASCAR Valley because so many drivers, teams, and racing employees reside there?
a. **North Carolina**
b. **Texas**
c. **Michigan**

3 In May 2005, Danica Patrick qualified for the Indianapolis 500. Before Patrick, how many other women had qualified for the race?
a. **0**
b. **1**
c. **3**

4 Tony Stewart has competed in the Indianapolis 500, Brickyard 400, and U.S. Grand Prix at Indianapolis during his career.
a. **True**
b. **False**

Tony Stewart

5 How many cars were in the inaugural Indianapolis 500 in 1911?
a. **5**
b. **15**
c. **40**

6 In what year was NASCAR founded?
a. **1938**
b. **1948**
c. **1958**

7 How many NASCAR crew members are allowed over the wall at a pit stop?
a. **5**
b. **6**
c. **7**

Trivia Challenge: 1: b; 2: a; 3: c; 4: b; 5: c; 6: b; 7: c.

NASCAR ALL-TIME RESULTS

NASCAR CHAMPIONS

YEAR	DRIVER	YEAR	DRIVER	YEAR	DRIVER
2006	Jimmie Johnson	1987	Dale Earnhardt	1968	David Pearson
2005	Tony Stewart	1986	Dale Earnhardt	1967	Richard Petty
2004	Kurt Busch	1985	Darrell Waltrip	1966	David Pearson
2003	Matt Kenseth	1984	Terry Labonte	1965	Ned Jarrett
2002	Tony Stewart	1983	Bobby Allison	1964	Richard Petty
2001	Jeff Gordon	1982	Darrell Waltrip	1963	Joe Weatherly
2000	Bobby Labonte	1981	Darrell Waltrip	1962	Joe Weatherly
1999	Dale Jarrett	1980	Dale Earnhardt	1961	Ned Jarrett
1998	Jeff Gordon	1979	Richard Petty	1960	Rex White
1997	Jeff Gordon	1978	Cale Yarborough	1959	Lee Petty
1996	Terry Labonte	1977	Cale Yarborough	1958	Lee Petty
1995	Jeff Gordon	1976	Cale Yarborough	1957	Buck Baker
1994	Dale Earnhardt	1975	Richard Petty	1956	Buck Baker
1993	Dale Earnhardt	1974	Richard Petty	1955	Tim Flock
1992	Alan Kulwicki	1973	Benny Parsons	1954	Lee Petty
1991	Dale Earnhardt	1972	Richard Petty	1953	Herb Thomas
1990	Dale Earnhardt	1971	Richard Petty	1952	Tim Flock
1989	Rusty Wallace	1970	Bobby Isaac	1951	Herb Thomas
1988	Bill Elliott	1969	David Pearson	1950	Bill Rexford
				1949	Red Byron

WINS LEADERS*

RANK	DRIVER
1.	Richard Petty (200)
2.	David Pearson (105)
3.	Bobby Allison** (84)
	Darrell Waltrip** (84)
5.	Cale Yarborough (83)
6.	Jeff Gordon (78)
7.	Dale Earnhardt (76)
8.	Rusty Wallace (55)
9.	Lee Petty (54)
10.	Ned Jarrett** (50)
	Junior Johnson** (50)
12.	Herb Thomas (48)
13.	Buck Baker (46)
14.	Bill Elliott (44)
15.	Tim Flock (39)
16.	Bobby Isaac (37)
17.	Mark Martin (35)
18.	Fireball Roberts (33)
19.	Dale Jarrett (32)
20.	Tony Stewart (29)
21.	Rex White (28)

*Through June 2007
**Tie

Denny Hamlin

ROOKIES OF THE YEAR

YEAR	DRIVER	YEAR	DRIVER
2006	Denny Hamlin	1981	Ron Bouchard
2005	Kyle Busch	1980	Jody Ridley
2004	Kasey Kahne	1979	Dale Earnhardt
2003	Jamie McMurray	1978	Ronnie Thomas
2002	Ryan Newman	1977	Ricky Rudd
2001	Kevin Harvick	1976	Skip Manning
2000	Matt Kenseth	1975	Bruce Hill
1999	Tony Stewart	1974	Earl Ross
1998	Kenny Irwin	1973	Lennie Pond
1997	Mike Skinner	1972	Larry Smith
1996	Johnny Benson	1971	Walter Ballard
1995	Ricky Craven	1970	Bill Dennis
1994	Jeff Burton	1969	Dick Brooks
1993	Jeff Gordon	1968	Pete Hamilton
1992	Jimmy Hensley	1967	Donnie Allison
1991	Bobby Hamilton	1966	James Hylton
1990	Rob Moroso	1965	Sam McQuagg
1989	Dick Trickle	1964	Doug Cooper
1988	Ken Bouchard	1963	Billy Wade
1987	Davey Allison	1962	Tom Cox
1986	Alan Kulwicki	1961	Woodie Wilson
1985	Ken Schrader	1960	David Pearson
1984	Rusty Wallace	1959	Richard Petty
1983	Sterling Marlin	1958	Shorty Rollins
1982	Geoffrey Bodine		

DAYTONA 500 WINNERS

YEAR	DRIVER	M.P.H.	YEAR	DRIVER	M.P.H.	YEAR	DRIVER	M.P.H.
2007	Kevin Harvick	149.335	1990	Derrike Cope	165.761	1973	Richard Petty	157.205
2006	Jimmie Johnson	142.667	1989	Darrell Waltrip	148.466	1972	A.J. Foyt Jr.	161.550
2005	Jeff Gordon	135.173	1988	Bobby Allison	137.531	1971	Richard Petty	144.462
2004	Dale Earnhardt Jr.	156.345	1987	Bill Elliott	176.263	1970	Pete Hamilton	149.601
2003	Michael Waltrip	133.870	1986	Geoffrey Bodine	148.124	1969	Lee Roy Yarbrough	157.950
2002	Ward Burton	142.971	1985	Bill Elliott	172.265	1968	Cale Yarborough	143.251
2001	Michael Waltrip	161.783	1984	Cale Yarborough	150.994	1967	Mario Andretti	146.926
2000	Dale Jarrett	155.669	1983	Cale Yarborough	155.979	1966	Richard Petty	160.627
1999	Jeff Gordon	161.551	1982	Bobby Allison	153.991	1965	Fred Lorenzen	141.539
1998	Dale Earnhardt	172.712	1981	Richard Petty	169.651	1964	Richard Petty	154.334
1997	Jeff Gordon	148.295	1980	Buddy Baker	177.602	1963	Tiny Lund	151.566
1996	Dale Jarrett	154.308	1979	Richard Petty	143.977	1962	Fireball Roberts	152.529
1995	Sterling Marlin	141.710	1978	Bobby Allison	159.730	1961	Marvin Panch	149.601
1994	Sterling Marlin	156.931	1977	Cale Yarborough	153.218	1960	Junior Johnson	124.740
1993	Dale Jarrett	154.972	1976	David Pearson	152.181	1959	Lee Petty	135.521
1992	Davey Allison	168.256	1975	Benny Parsons	153.649			
1991	Ernie Irvan	148.148	1974	Richard Petty	140.894			

TALLADEGA 500* WINNERS

YEAR	DRIVER	M.P.H.	YEAR	DRIVER	M.P.H.	YEAR	DRIVER	M.P.H.
2007	Jeff Gordon	154.167	1994	Jimmy Spencer	163.217	1981	Ron Bouchard	156.737
2006	Jimmie Johnson	142.880	1993	Dale Earnhardt	153.858	1980	Neil Bonnett	166.894
2005	Jeff Gordon	146.904	1992	Ernie Irvan	176.309	1979	Darrell Waltrip	161.229
2004	Jeff Gordon	129.396	1991	Dale Earnhardt	147.383	1978	Lennie Pond	174.700
2003	Dale Earnhardt Jr.	144.625	1990	Dale Earnhardt	174.430	1977	Donnie Allison	162.524
2002	Dale Earnhardt Jr.	159.022	1989	Terry Labonte	157.354	1976	Dave Marcis	157.547
2001	Bobby Hamilton	184.003	1988	Ken Schrader	154.505	1975	Buddy Baker	130.892
2000	Jeff Gordon	161.157	1987	Bill Elliott	171.293	1974	Richard Petty	148.637
1999	Dale Earnhardt	163.395	1986	Bobby Hillin	151.552	1973	Dick Brooks	145.454
1998	Bobby Labonte	163.439	1985	Cale Yarborough	148.772	1972	James Hylton	148.728
1997	Terry Labonte	156.601	1984	Dale Earnhardt	155.485	1971	Bobby Allison	145.945
1996	Jeff Gordon	133.387	1983	Dale Earnhardt	170.611	1970	Pete Hamilton	158.517
1995	Sterling Marlin	173.188	1982	Darrell Waltrip	168.157	1969	Richard Brickhouse	153.778

*From 1969 through 1988, the race was known as the Talladega 500. From 1989 through 2001, it was known as the Die Hard 500. In 2001, it was again called the Talladega 500. (Since 2002, the race has been called the Aaron's 499.)

NASCAR (cont.)

COCA-COLA 600 WINNERS

YEAR	DRIVER	M.P.H.	YEAR	DRIVER	M.P.H.	YEAR	DRIVER	M.P.H.
2007	Casey Mears	130.222	1991	Davey Allison	138.951	1975	Richard Petty	145.327
2006	Kasey Kahne	128.840	1990	Rusty Wallace	137.650	1974	David Pearson	135.720
2005	Jimmie Johnson	114.698	1989	Darrell Waltrip	144.077	1973	Buddy Baker	134.890
2004	Jimmie Johnson	142.763	1988	Darrell Waltrip	124.460	1972	Buddy Baker	142.255
2003	Jimmie Johnson	126.198	1987	Kyle Petty	131.483	1971	Bobby Allison	140.442
2002	Mark Martin	137.729	1986	Dale Earnhardt	140.406	1970	Donnie Allison	129.680
2001	Jeff Burton	138.107	1985	Darrell Waltrip	141.807	1969	Lee Roy Yarbrough	134.361
2000	Matt Kenseth	142.640	1984	Bobby Allison	129.233	1968	Buddy Baker	104.207
1999	Jeff Burton	151.367	1983	Neil Bonnett	140.707	1967	Jim Paschal	135.832
1998	Jeff Gordon	136.424	1982	Neil Bonnett	130.058	1966	Marvin Panch	135.042
1997	Jeff Gordon	136.745	1981	Bobby Allison	129.326	1965	Fred Lorenzen	121.772
1996	Dale Jarrett	147.581	1980	Benny Parsons	119.265	1964	Jim Paschal	125.772
1995	Bobby Labonte	151.952	1979	Darrell Waltrip	136.674	1963	Fred Lorenzen	132.418
1994	Jeff Gordon	139.445	1978	Darrell Waltrip	138.355	1962	Nelson Stacy	125.552
1993	Dale Earnhardt	145.504	1977	Richard Petty	137.676	1961	David Pearson	111.633
1992	Dale Earnhardt	132.980	1976	David Pearson	137.352	1960	Joe Lee Johnson	107.735

BRICKYARD 400* WINNERS

YEAR	DRIVER	M.P.H.	YEAR	DRIVER	M.P.H.
2006	Jimmie Johnson	137.182	1999	Dale Jarrett	148.194
2005	Tony Stewart	118.782	1998	Jeff Gordon	126.772
2004	Jeff Gordon	115.037	1997	Ricky Rudd	130.814
2003	Kevin Harvick	134.554	1996	Dale Jarrett	139.508
2002	Bill Elliott	125.033	1995	Dale Earnhardt	155.206
2001	Jeff Gordon	130.790	1994	Jeff Gordon	131.977
2000	Bobby Labonte	155.912			

FAST FACT

Jeff Gordon has recorded more wins than any other active NASCAR driver, with 78 career Cup victories through June 15, 2007.

SOUTHERN 500** WINNERS

YEAR	DRIVER	M.P.H.
2007	Jeff Gordon	124.372
2006	Greg Biffle	135.127
2005	Greg Biffle	123.031
2004	Jimmie Johnson	125.044
2003	Terry Labonte	120.744
2002	Jeff Gordon	118.617
2001	Ward Burton	122.773
2000	Bobby Labonte	108.273
1999	Jeff Burton	107.816
1998	Jeff Gordon	139.031
1997	Jeff Gordon	121.149
1996	Jeff Gordon	135.757
1995	Jeff Gordon	121.231
1994	Bill Elliott	127.952
1993	Mark Martin	137.932
1992	Darrell Waltrip	129.114
1991	Harry Gant	133.508
1990	Dale Earnhardt	123.141
1989	Dale Earnhardt	135.462
1988	Bill Elliott	128.297
1987	Dale Earnhardt	115.520
1986	Tim Richmond	121.068
1985	Bill Elliott	121.254
1984	Harry Gant	128.270
1983	Bobby Allison	123.343
1982	Cale Yarborough	115.224
1981	Neil Bonnett	126.410
1980	Terry Labonte	115.210

Jeff Gordon won his 78th career race on NASCAR's top circuit at the 2007 Southern/Dodge Avenger 500.

*The race is now know as the Allstate 400 at the Brickyard.
**The race is now known as the Dodge Avenger 500.

SOUTHERN 500 WINNERS (cont.)

YEAR	DRIVER	M.P.H.	YEAR	DRIVER	M.P.H.	YEAR	DRIVER	M.P.H.
1979	David Pearson	126.259	1969	Lee Roy Yarborough	105.612	1959	Jim Reed	111.840
1978	Cale Yarborough	116.828	1968	Cale Yarborough	126.132	1958	Fireball Roberts	102.590
1977	David Pearson	106.797	1967	Richard Petty	130.423	1957	Speedy Thompson	100.094
1976	David Pearson	120.534	1966	Darel Dieringer	114.830	1956	Curtis Turner	95.067
1975	Bobby Allison	116.825	1965	Ned Jarrett	115.924	1955	Herb Thomas	93.281
1974	Cale Yarborough	111.075	1964	Buck Baker	117.757	1954	Herb Thomas	94.930
1973	Cale Yarborough	134.033	1963	Fireball Roberts	129.784	1953	Buck Baker	92.780
1972	Bobby Allison	128.124	1962	Larry Frank	117.965	1952	Fonty Flock	74.510
1971	Bobby Allison	131.398	1961	Nelson Stacy	117.787	1951	Herb Thomas	76.900
1970	Buddy Baker	128.817	1960	Buck Baker	105.901	1950	Johnny Mantz	76.260

TRIVIA CHALLENGE

Who is the youngest NASCAR champion in history?

Jeff Gordon was 24 years and 3 months old when he won the NASCAR championship in 1995.

LEGENDS

■ **Michael Schumacher,** b. January 3, 1969, Hurth Hermulheim, Germany. Widely considered to be the greatest Formula One driver of all time, Schumacher won a record seven F1 championships before retiring in 2006. "Schuey" also holds the records for consecutive championships (5), race victories (91), consecutive wins (7), and wins with one team (72 with Ferrari), along with nearly every other Formula One record. The first German to win an F1 championship, Schumacher is credited with popularizing the sport in his home country.

Michael Schumacher had 91 career wins during his Formula One racing career.

AFP PHOTO/MARK RALSTON

■ **Richard Petty,** b. July 2, 1937, Level Cross, North Carolina. "The King" of NASCAR began as 1959's Rookie of The Year. Petty would go on to win 200 NASCAR races, including seven Daytona 500 titles. The legendary driver of "Ol' 43" also won the Winston Cup championship seven times, a record he now shares with the late Dale Earnhardt. Petty was named to the International Motorsports Hall of Fame in 1997. When he retired, he was awarded the Presidential Medal of Freedom, the nation's highest civilian honor.

■ **Rick Mears,** b. December 3, 1951, Wichita, Kansas. One of only three drivers (A.J. Foyt and Al Unser are the other two) to win the Indianapolis 500 four times, Mears also holds the record for Indy 500 pole positions with six. When he wasn't racing with the IRL, Mears earned three national championsips in the Champ Car World Series (formerly CART). Mears retired in 1992 but continues to work as a consultant for Penske Racing, his former Champ Car team.

TENNIS

Two legends stepped off the court this year, but new superstars emerged to take their place.

Through it all, Roger Federer continued his reign as the most dominant player in the sport. In 2006, Federer won his fourth straight Wimbledon title and his third consecutive U.S. Open. He began 2007 with a second straight championship at the Australian Open and then won Wimbledon for a record-tying fifth straight time in July. That win was Federer's 11th career Grand Slam singles title, just three shy of Pete Sampras's all-time men's record.

Federer was firmly Number 1, but Rafael Nadal emerged as a true star, extending his winning streak on clay to a record 81 straight matches. Federer broke the streak with a victory over Nadal at a French Open tune-up event, but the Spaniard had the last laugh. He beat Federer in the French Open final for the second straight year.

Federer also had to share the spotlight at the 2006 U.S. Open, where his victory was overshadowed by Andre Agassi's retirement. Agassi called it quits after more than 20 years on the ATP circuit and eight Grand Slam singles titles.

On the women's side, Amelie Mauresmo won the first two majors of her career in 2006. The French star beat Belgium's Justine Henin at the Australian Open and Wimbledon.

Henin got her share of glory, though. She won the French Open in 2006 and 2007, giving her three straight titles at Roland Garros and four overall.

Maria Sharapova went a year without a title, but got back on track with a victory at Indian Wells. Later in 2006, she won her second career Grand Slam at the U.S. Open. Sharapova made a bid for two straight Grand Slam titles, advancing to the finals at the 2007 Australian Open. But she fell short against Serena Williams, who won in straight sets.

Meanwhile, Hall of Famer Martina Navratilova retired just shy of her 50th birthday. She went out with one last hurrah, teaming up with Bob Bryan to win the U.S. Open mixed doubles title. It was the 10th Grand Slam title for Navratilova in mixed doubles, to go along with her incredible 18 Grand Slam titles in singles and 31 in women's doubles.

Roger Federer won his 11th Grand Slam title in 2007.

DAVID CALLOW

GRAND SLAM TOURNAMENTS: ALL-TIME MEN'S CHAMPIONS

AUSTRALIAN CHAMPIONSHIPS

Year	Winner	Year	Winner	Year	Winner
2007	Roger Federer	1992	Jim Courier	1976	Mark Edmondson
2006	Roger Federer	1991	Boris Becker	1975	John Newcombe
2005	Marat Safin	1990	Ivan Lendl	1974	Jimmy Connors
2004	Roger Federer	1989	Ivan Lendl	1973	John Newcombe
2003	Andre Agassi	1988	Mats Wilander	1972	Ken Rosewall
2002	Thomas Johansson	1987	Stefan Edberg	1971	Ken Rosewall
2001	Andre Agassi	1986	no tournament	1970	Arthur Ashe
2000	Andre Agassi	1985	Stefan Edberg	*1969	Rod Laver
1999	Yevgeny Kafelnikov	1984	Mats Wilander	1968	Bill Bowrey
1998	Petr Korda	1983	Mats Wilander	1967	Roy Emerson
1997	Pete Sampras	1982	Johan Kriek	1966	Roy Emerson
1996	Boris Becker	1981	Johan Kriek	1965	Roy Emerson
1995	Andre Agassi	1980	Brian Teacher	1964	Roy Emerson
1994	Pete Sampras	1979	Guillermo Vilas	1963	Roy Emerson
1993	Jim Courier	1978	Guillermo Vilas	1962	Rod Laver
		1977 (Dec.)	Vitas Gerulaitis	1961	Roy Emerson
		1977 (Jan.)	Roscoe Tanner	1960	Rod Laver

* Became Open (amateur and professional) in 1969.
Note: Traditionally, the Australian Open was held in January. In 1977, it was moved to December, so there were two tournaments that year. It returned to January in 1987.

AUSTRALIAN CHAMPIONSHIPS (cont.)

Year	Winner
1959	Alex Olmedo
1958	Ashley Cooper
1957	Ashley Cooper
1956	Lew Hoad
1955	Ken Rosewall
1954	Mervyn Rose
1953	Ken Rosewall
1952	Ken McGregor
1951	Richard Savitt
1950	Frank Sedgman
1949	Frank Sedgman
1948	Adrian Quist
1947	Dinny Pails
1946	John Bromwich
1941-45	No tournament
1940	Adrian Quist
1939	John Bromwich
1938	Don Budge
1937	Vivian B. McGrath
1936	Adrian Quist
1935	Jack Crawford
1934	Fred Perry
1933	Jack Crawford
1932	Jack Crawford
1931	Jack Crawford
1930	Gar Moon
1929	John C. Gregory
1928	Jean Borotra
1927	Gerald Patterson
1926	John Hawkes
1925	James Anderson
1924	James Anderson
1923	Pat O'Hara Wood
1922	James Anderson
1921	Rhys H. Gemmell
1920	Pat O'Hara Wood
1919	A.R.F. Kingscote
1916-18	No tournament
1915	Francis G. Lowe
1914	Arthur Wood
1913	E. F. Parker
1912	J. Cecil Parke
1911	Norman Brookes
1910	Rodney Heath
1909	Tony Wilding
1908	Fred Alexander
1907	Horace M. Rice
1906	Tony Wilding
1905	Rodney Heath

FRENCH CHAMPIONSHIPS

Year	Winner
2007	Rafael Nadal
2006	Rafael Nadal
2005	Rafael Nadal
2004	Gaston Gaudio
2003	Juan Carlos Ferrero
2002	Albert Costa
2001	Gustavo Kuerten
2000	Gustavo Kuerten

Year	Winner
1999	Andre Agassi
1998	Carlos Moya
1997	Gustavo Kuerten
1996	Yevgeny Kafelnikov
1995	Thomas Muster
1994	Sergi Bruguera
1993	Sergi Bruguera
1992	Jim Courier
1991	Jim Courier
1990	Andres Gomez
1989	Michael Chang
1988	Mats Wilander
1987	Ivan Lendl
1986	Ivan Lendl
1985	Mats Wilander
1984	Ivan Lendl
1983	Yannick Noah
1982	Mats Wilander
1981	Bjorn Borg
1980	Bjorn Borg
1979	Bjorn Borg
1978	Bjorn Borg
1977	Guillermo Vilas
1976	Adriano Panatta
1975	Bjorn Borg
1974	Bjorn Borg
1973	Ilie Nastase
1972	Andres Gimeno
1971	Jan Kodes
1970	Jan Kodes
1969	Rod Laver
*1968	Ken Rosewall
1967	Roy Emerson
1966	Tony Roche
1965	Fred Stolle
1964	Manuel Santana
1963	Roy Emerson
1962	Rod Laver
1961	Manuel Santana
1960	Nicola Pietrangeli
1959	Nicola Pietrangeli
1958	Mervyn Rose
1957	Sven Davidson
1956	Lew Hoad
1955	Tony Trabert
1954	Tony Trabert
1953	Ken Rosewall
1952	Jaroslav Drobny
1951	Jaroslav Drobny
1950	Budge Patty
1949	Frank Parker
1948	Frank Parker
1947	Jozsef Asboth
1946	Marcel Bernard
1940-45	No tournament
1939	William McNeill
1938	Don Budge
1937	Henner Henkel
1936	Gottfried von Cramm
1935	Fred Perry
1934	Gottfried von Cramm
1933	Jack Crawford

Year	Winner
1932	Henri Cochet
1931	Jean Borotra
1930	Henri Cochet
1929	Rene Lacoste
1928	Henri Cochet
1927	Rene Lacoste
1926	Henri Cochet
†1925	Rene Lacoste

WIMBLEDON CHAMPIONSHIPS

Year	Winner
2007	Roger Federer
2006	Roger Federer
2005	Roger Federer
2004	Roger Federer
2003	Roger Federer
2002	Lleyton Hewitt
2001	Goran Ivanisevic
2000	Pete Sampras
1999	Pete Sampras
1998	Pete Sampras
1997	Pete Sampras
1996	Richard Krajicek
1995	Pete Sampras
1994	Pete Sampras
1993	Pete Sampras
1992	Andre Agassi
1991	Michael Stich
1990	Stefan Edberg
1989	Boris Becker
1988	Stefan Edberg
1987	Pat Cash
1986	Boris Becker
1985	Boris Becker
1984	John McEnroe
1983	John McEnroe
1982	Jimmy Connors
1981	John McEnroe
1980	Bjorn Borg
1979	Bjorn Borg
1978	Bjorn Borg
1977	Bjorn Borg
1976	Bjorn Borg
1975	Arthur Ashe
1974	Jimmy Connors
1973	Jan Kodes
1972	Stan Smith
1971	John Newcombe
1970	John Newcombe
1969	Rod Laver
*1968	Rod Laver
1967	John Newcombe
1966	Manuel Santana
1965	Roy Emerson
1964	Roy Emerson
1963	Chuck McKinley
1962	Rod Laver
1961	Rod Laver
1960	Neale Fraser
1959	Alex Olmedo
1958	Ashley Cooper

* Became Open (amateur and professional) in 1968.
† 1925 was the first year in which players from all countries were allowed to compete.

TODAY'S STARS

■ **Novak Djokovic,** b. May 22, 1987, Belgrade, Serbia. Along with Rafael Nadal and Andy Murray, Djokovic is leading a group of young players to the top of the rankings. The 20-year-old Serb broke into the Top 5 in 2007 after winning his first Masters Series title in Miami. Djokovic also made his deepest run yet at a Grand Slam event in 2007, reaching the semifinals of the French Open, where he lost to good friend and eventual champion Rafael Nadal in straight sets.

Djokovic broke into the Top 5 in the ATP rankings in 2007.

■ **Andy Murray,** b. May 15, 1987, Glasgow, Scotland. At age 20, Murray has been tabbed as the future of British tennis, thanks in large part to his straight-sets dismissal of two-time finalist Andy Roddick in the third round of Wimbledon in 2006. Murray turned pro in 2005—a year which saw him rise from 374 to 63 in the ATP rankings—and won his first title at the 2006 SAP Open in San Jose, California, defeating Roddick and former World Number 1 Lleyton Hewitt along the way. Murray hired famed coach Brad Gilbert in 2006 and entered the Top 10 for the first time in April 2007.

■ **Guillermo Canas,** b. November 25, 1977, Buenos Aires, Argentina. After serving a 13-month suspension for doping, Canas, a former Top 10 player, returned to the ATP Tour in 2007. He defeated World Number 1 Roger Federer in back-to-back Masters events in Indian Wells and Miami. Federer had been the defending champion at both. Canas also made it to the quarterfinals of the 2007 French Open. As a result, his ranking jumped more than 100 positions to put him back in the Top 20.

GRAND SLAM TOURNAMENTS: ALL-TIME MEN'S CHAMPIONS (cont.)

WIMBLEDON CHAMPIONSHIPS (cont.)

Year	Winner	Year	Winner	Year	Winner
1957	Lew Hoad	1932	Ellsworth Vines	1907	Norman E. Brookes
1956	Lew Hoad	1931	Sidney B. Wood, Jr.	1906	H. Laurie Doherty
1955	Tony Trabert	1930	Bill Tilden	1905	H. Laurie Doherty
1954	Jaroslav Drobny	1929	Henri Cochet	1904	H. Laurie Doherty
1953	Vic Seixas	1928	Rene Lacoste	1903	H. Laurie Doherty
1952	Frank Sedgman	1927	Henri Cochet	1902	H. Laurie Doherty
1951	Dick Savitt	1926	Jean Borotra	1901	Arthur W. Gore
1950	Budge Patty	1925	Rene Lacoste	1900	Reggie F. Doherty
1949	Fred Schroeder, Jr.	1924	Jean Borotra	1899	Reggie F. Doherty
1948	Bob Falkenburg	1923	Bill Johnston	1898	Reggie F. Doherty
1947	Jack Kramer	1922	Gerald L. Patterson	1897	Reggie F. Doherty
1946	Yvon Petra	1921	Bill Tilden	1896	Harold S. Mahoney
1940-45	No tournament	1920	Bill Tilden	1895	Wilfred Baddeley
1939	Bobby Riggs	1919	Gerald L. Patterson	1894	Joshua Pim
1938	Don Budge	1915-18	No tournament	1893	Joshua Pim
1937	Don Budge	1914	Norman E. Brookes	1892	Wilfred Baddeley
1936	Fred Perry	1913	Anthony F. Wilding	1891	Wilfred Baddeley
1935	Fred Perry	1912	Anthony F. Wilding	1890	William J. Hamilton
1934	Fred Perry	1911	Anthony F. Wilding	1889	William Renshaw
1933	Jack Crawford	1910	Anthony F. Wilding	1888	Ernest Renshaw
		1909	Arthur W. Gore	1887	Herbert F. Lawford
		1908	Arthur W. Gore	1886	William Renshaw

WIMBLEDON CHAMPIONSHIPS (cont.)

Year	Winner
1885	William Renshaw
1884	William Renshaw
1883	William Renshaw
1882	William Renshaw
1881	William Renshaw
1880	John T. Hartley
1879	John T. Hartley
1878	P. Frank Hadow
1877	Spencer W. Gore

UNITED STATES CHAMPIONSHIPS

Year	Winner
2006	Roger Federer
2005	Roger Federer
2004	Roger Federer
2003	Andy Roddick
2002	Pete Sampras
2001	Lleyton Hewitt
2000	Marat Safin
1999	Andre Agassi

* Became Open (amateur and professional) in 1968.
** Separate amateur event held.

Year	Winner	Year	Winner
1998	Patrick Rafter	1973	John Newcombe
1997	Patrick Rafter	1972	Ilie Nastase
1996	Pete Sampras	1971	Stan Smith
1995	Pete Sampras	1970	Ken Rosewall
1994	Andre Agassi	**1969	Stan Smith
1993	Pete Sampras	1969	Rod Laver
1992	Stefan Edberg	*1968	Arthur Ashe
1991	Stefan Edberg	**1968	Arthur Ashe
1990	Pete Sampras	1967	John Newcombe
1989	Boris Becker	1966	Fred Stolle
1988	Mats Wilander	1965	Manuel Santana
1987	Ivan Lendl	1964	Roy Emerson
1986	Ivan Lendl	1963	Rafael Osuna
1985	Ivan Lendl	1962	Rod Laver
1984	John McEnroe	1961	Roy Emerson
1983	Jimmy Connors	1960	Neale Fraser
1982	Jimmy Connors	1959	Neale Fraser
1981	John McEnroe	1958	Ashley Cooper
1980	John McEnroe	1957	Mal Anderson
1979	John McEnroe	1956	Ken Rosewall
1978	Jimmy Connors	1955	Tony Trabert
1977	Guillermo Vilas	1954	Vic Seixas
1976	Jimmy Connors	1953	Tony Trabert
1975	Manuel Orantes	1952	Frank Sedgman
1974	Jimmy Connors	1951	Frank Sedgman

TRIVIA CHALLENGE

1 In 2007, clay court ace Rafael Nadal broke John McEnroe's record of 75 straight wins on a single surface. On what type of court did McEnroe make his record run?
a. Grass
b. Indoor carpet
c. Hard court

2 What man holds the record for the most non-consecutive weeks as the top-ranked player in the world?
a. Pete Sampras
b. Roger Federer
c. Andre Agassi

3 In which New York City borough is the U.S. Open held?
a. Manhattan
b. The Bronx
c. Queens

4 What is the technical name for the lefthand side of a tennis court?
a. The ad court
b. The deuce court
c. The love court

Rafael Nadal

5 Who is the youngest male tennis player ever to be ranked Number 1, reaching the top spot at 20 years and eight months old?
a. Lleyton Hewitt
b. Andy Roddick
c. Marat Safin

6 The French Open is the only major tournament Pete Sampras didn't win during his career. What was his best result at the clay court Grand Slam?
a. Runner-up
b. Quarterfinalist
c. Semifinalist

Trivia Challenge: 1. b; 2. a; 3. c; 4. a; 5. a; 6. c.

GRAND SLAM TOURNAMENTS: ALL-TIME MEN'S CHAMPIONS (cont.)

UNITED STATES CHAMPIONSHIPS (cont.)		Year	Winner	Year	Winner
		1928	Henri Cochet	1904	Holcombe Ward
Year	**Winner**	1927	Rene Lacoste	1903	H. Laurie Doherty
1950	Arthur Larsen	1926	Rene Lacoste	1902	William A. Larned
1949	Pancho Gonzales	1925	Bill Tilden	1901	William A. Larned
1948	Pancho Gonzales	1924	Bill Tilden	1900	Malcolm D. Whitman
1947	Jack Kramer	1923	Bill Tilden	1899	Malcolm D. Whitman
1946	Jack Kramer	1922	Bill Tilden	1898	Malcolm D. Whitman
1945	Frank Parker	1921	Bill Tilden	1897	Robert D. Wrenn
1944	Frank Parker	1920	Bill Tilden	1896	Robert D. Wrenn
1943	Joseph R. Hunt	1919	Bill Johnston	1895	Frederick H. Hovey
1942	Fred R. Schroeder, Jr.	1918	R.L. Murray	1894	Robert D. Wrenn
1941	Bobby Riggs	1917	R.L. Murray	1893	Robert D. Wrenn
1940	Don McNeill	1916	Richard N. Williams	1892	Oliver S. Campbell
1939	Bobby Riggs	1915	Bill Johnston	1891	Oliver S. Campbell
1938	Don Budge	1914	Richard N. Williams	1890	Oliver S. Campbell
1937	Don Budge	1913	Maurice E. McLoughlin	1889	H. W. Slocum, Jr.
1936	Fred Perry	1912	Maurice E. McLoughlin	1888	H. W. Slocum, Jr.
1935	Wilmer L. Allison	1911	William A. Larned	1887	Richard D. Sears
1934	Fred Perry	1910	William A. Larned	1886	Richard D. Sears
1933	Fred Perry	1909	William A. Larned	1885	Richard D. Sears
1932	Ellsworth Vines	1908	William A. Larned	1884	Richard D. Sears
1931	Ellsworth Vines	1907	William A. Larned	1883	Richard D. Sears
1930	John H. Doeg	1906	William J. Clothier	1882	Richard D. Sears
1929	Bill Tilden	1905	Beals C. Wright	1881	Richard D. Sears

LEGENDS

Bjorn Borg won 89.8% of the Grand Slam matches he played in during his career.

AP PHOTO/ADAM STOLTMAN

■ **Bjorn Borg,** b. June 6, 1956, Stockholm, Sweden. During his nine-year career, Borg won 41 percent of the Grand Slam tournaments he entered, including a record six French Open titles and five consecutive Wimbledon titles. He is the only player to have won in three consecutive years at both tournaments. Borg was inducted into the International Tennis Hall of Fame in 1987. He attempted a comeback in the early 1990's, but failed to win a match.

■ **Andre Agassi,** b. April 29, 1970, Las Vegas, Nevada. After 20 years and eight Grand Slam championships, Agassi retired from tennis in 2006, playing his final match at the U.S. Open. He completed the career Grand Slam in 1999 by winning the French Open and was a four-time champion at the Australian Open. Agassi's thirteen-year rivalry with Pete Sampras was one of the most memorable in the tennis history.

■ **Jimmy Connors,** b. September 2, 1952, East St. Louis, Illinois. Connors won eight Grand Slam titles in his career, including five U.S. Open titles, and was ranked Number 1 in the world for 160 consecutive weeks from July 1974 to August 1977. Connors also holds the record for the most ATP career match wins, with 1,225. In July 2006, Connors signed on to coach top-ranked American Andy Roddick.

GRAND SLAM TOURNAMENTS: ALL-TIME WOMEN'S CHAMPIONS

AUSTRALIAN CHAMPIONSHIPS

Year	Winner
2007	Serena Williams
2006	Amelie Mauresmo
2005	Serena Williams
2004	Justine Henin-Hardenne
2003	Serena Williams
2002	Jennifer Capriati
2001	Jennifer Capriati
2000	Lindsay Davenport
1999	Martina Hingis
1998	Martina Hingis
1997	Martina Hingis
1996	Monica Seles
1995	Mary Pierce
1994	Steffi Graf
1993	Monica Seles
1992	Monica Seles
1991	Monica Seles
1990	Steffi Graf
1989	Steffi Graf
1988	Steffi Graf
1987 (Jan.)	Hana Mandlikova
1985 (Dec.)	Martina Navratilova
1984	Chris Evert Lloyd
1983	Martina Navratilova
1982	Chris Evert Lloyd
1981	Martina Navratilova
1980	Hana Mandlikova
1979	Barbara Jordan
1978	Chris O'Neil
1977 (Dec.)	Evonne Goolagong Cawley
1977 (Jan.)	Kerry Melville Reid
1976	Evonne Goolagong Cawley
1975	Evonne Goolagong Cawley
1974	Evonne Goolagong Cawley
1973	Margaret Smith Court
1972	Virginia Wade
1971	Margaret Smith Court
1970	Margaret Smith Court
*1969	Margaret Smith Court
1968	Billie Jean King
1967	Nancy Richey
1966	Margaret Smith Court
1965	Margaret Smith Court
1964	Margaret Smith Court
1963	Margaret Smith Court
1962	Margaret Smith Court
1961	Margaret Smith Court
1960	Margaret Smith Court
1959	Mary Carter-Reitano
1958	Angela Mortimer
1957	Shirley Fry
1956	Mary Carter
1955	Beryl Penrose
1954	Thelma Long
1953	Maureen Connolly
1952	Thelma Long
1951	Nancye Wynne Bolton
1950	Louise Brough
1949	Doris Hart
1948	Nancye Wynne Bolton
1947	Nancye Wynne Bolton
1946	Nancye Wynne Bolton
1941-45	No tournament

Year	Winner
1940	Nancye Wynne Bolton
1939	Emily Westacott
1938	Dorothy Bundy
1937	Nancye Wynne Bolton
1936	Joan Hartigan
1935	Dorothy Round
1934	Joan Hartigan
1933	Joan Hartigan
1932	Coral Buttsworth
1931	Coral Buttsworth
1930	Daphne Akhurst
1929	Daphne Akhurst
1928	Daphne Akhurst
1927	Esna Boyd
1926	Daphne Akhurst
1925	Daphne Akhurst
1924	Sylvia Lance
1923	Margaret Molesworth
1922	Margaret Molesworth

FRENCH CHAMPIONSHIPS

Year	Winner
2007	Justine Henin
2006	Justine Henin-Hardenne
2005	Justine Henin-Hardenne
2004	Anastasia Myskina
2003	Justine Henin-Hardenne
2002	Serena Williams
2001	Jennifer Capriati
2000	Mary Pierce
1999	Steffi Graf
1998	Arantxa Sánchez-Vicario
1997	Iva Majoli
1996	Steffi Graf
1995	Steffi Graf
1994	Arantxa Sánchez-Vicario
1993	Steffi Graf
1992	Monica Seles
1991	Monica Seles
1990	Monica Seles
1989	Arantxa Sánchez-Vicario
1988	Steffi Graf
1987	Steffi Graf
1986	Chris Evert Lloyd
1985	Chris Evert Lloyd
1984	Martina Navratilova
1983	Chris Evert Lloyd
1982	Martina Navratilova
1981	Hana Mandlikova
1980	Chris Evert Lloyd
1979	Chris Evert Lloyd
1978	Virginia Ruzici
1977	Mima Jausovec
1976	Sue Barker
1975	Chris Evert Lloyd
1974	Chris Evert Lloyd
1973	Margaret Smith Court
1972	Billie Jean King
1971	Evonne Goolagong Cawley
1970	Margaret Smith Court
1969	Margaret Smith Court
**1968	Nancy Richey
1967	Francoise Durr
1966	Ann Jones

Year	Winner
1965	Lesley Turner
1964	Margaret Smith Court
1963	Lesley Turner
1962	Margaret Smith Court
1961	Ann Haydon
1960	Darlene Hard
1959	Christine Truman
1958	Zsuzsi Kormoczy
1957	Shirley Bloomer
1956	Althea Gibson
1955	Angela Mortimer
1954	Maureen Connolly
1953	Maureen Connolly
1952	Doris Hart
1951	Shirley Fry
1950	Doris Hart
1949	Margaret Osborne duPont
1948	Nelly Landry
1947	Patricia Todd
1946	Margaret Osborne
1940-45	No tournament
1939	Simone Mathieu
1938	Simone Mathieu
1937	Hilde Sperling
1936	Hilde Sperling
1935	Hilde Sperling
1934	Margaret Scriven
1933	Margaret Scriven
1932	Helen Wills Moody
1931	Cilly Aussem
1930	Helen Wills Moody
1929	Helen Wills Moody
1928	Helen Wills Moody
1927	Kea Bouman
1926	Suzanne Lenglen
†1925	Suzanne Lenglen

WIMBLEDON CHAMPIONSHIPS

Year	Winner
2007	Venus Williams
2006	Amelie Mauresmo
2005	Venus Williams
2004	Maria Sharapova
2003	Serena Williams
2002	Serena Williams
2001	Venus Williams
2000	Venus Williams
1999	Lindsay Davenport
1998	Jana Novotna
1997	Martina Hingis
1996	Steffi Graf
1995	Steffi Graf
1994	Conchita Martinez
1993	Steffi Graf
1992	Steffi Graf
1991	Steffi Graf
1990	Martina Navratilova
1989	Steffi Graf
1988	Steffi Graf
1987	Martina Navratilova
1986	Martina Navratilova
1985	Martina Navratilova
1984	Martina Navratilova
1983	Martina Navratilova
1982	Martina Navratilova
1981	Chris Evert Lloyd

* Became Open (amateur and professional) in 1969.
** Became Open (amateur and professional) in 1968.
† 1925 was the first year in which players from all countries were allowed to compete.

TODAY'S STARS

Jelena Jankovic is one of several top-ranked Serbian players.

BOB MARTIN/SPORTS ILLUSTRATED

■ **Jelena Jankovic,** b. February 28, 1985, Belgrade, Serbia. Jankovic turned pro in 2000. Her Grand Slam breakthrough came with a semifinal showing at the 2006 U.S. Open. The result helped Jankovic finish the year at Number 12 in the WTA world rankings. In 2007, Jankovic reached the fourth round of the Australian Open, losing to eventual champion Serena Williams. After the tournament, she entered the WTA's Top 10 for the first time in her career. A semifinal loss to three-time champion Justine Henin at the 2007 French Open catapulted Jankovic to Number 3 in the world.

■ **Svetlana Kuznetsova,** b. June 27, 1985, Saint Petersburg, Russia. While Kuznetsova's only Grand Slam title came at the 2004 U.S. Open, she has been among the final eight at every other Slam event at least once. Kuznetsova was the runner-up at the 2006 French Open. Another runner-up finish at the 2007 Pacific Life Open in Indian Wells, California, improved her ranking to Number 3 in the world, matching the best ranking of her career.

■ **Ana Ivanovic,** b. November 6, 1987, Belgrade, Serbia. The second-highest ranked Serbian player in the world (behind Jankovic), Ivanovic is Number 6 overall in the WTA rankings. Ivanovic cemented her reputation as a major talent when she defeated Martina Hingis in the final of the 2006 Canada Masters. But she spent nearly two years hovering just outside the Top 10 before a victory at the 2007 German Open gave her the break she needed. She improved to her career-high Number 6 position after finishing as the runner up at the 2007 French Open.

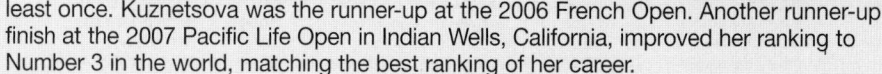

GRAND SLAM TOURNAMENTS: ALL-TIME WOMEN'S CHAMPIONS (cont.)

WIMBLEDON CHAMPIONSHIPS (cont.)

Year	Winner	Year	Winner	Year	Winner
1980	Evonne Goolagong Cawley	1959	Maria Bueno	1931	Cilly Aussem
1979	Martina Navratilova	1958	Althea Gibson	1930	Helen Wills Moody
1978	Martina Navratilova	1957	Althea Gibson	1929	Helen Wills Moody
1977	Virginia Wade	1956	Shirley Fry	1928	Helen Wills Moody
1976	Chris Evert Lloyd	1955	Louise Brough	1927	Helen Wills Moody
1975	Billie Jean King	1954	Maureen Connolly	1926	Kathleen McKane Godfree
1974	Chris Evert Lloyd	1953	Maureen Connolly	1925	Suzanne Lenglen
1973	Billie Jean King	1952	Maureen Connolly	1924	Kathleen McKane
1972	Billie Jean King	1951	Doris Hart	1923	Suzanne Lenglen
1971	Evonne Goolagong Cawley	1950	Louise Brough	1922	Suzanne Lenglen
1970	Margaret Smith Court	1949	Louise Brough	1921	Suzanne Lenglen
1969	Ann Haydon Jones	1948	Louise Brough	1920	Suzanne Lenglen
**1968	Billie Jean King	1947	Margaret Osborne	1919	Suzanne Lenglen
1967	Billie Jean King	1946	Pauline Betz	1915-18	No tournament
1966	Billie Jean King	1940-45	No tournament	1914	Dorothea Lambert Chambers
1965	Margaret Smith Court	1939	Alice Marble	1913	Dorothea Lambert Chambers
1964	Maria Bueno	1938	Helen Wills Moody	1912	Ethel Larcombe
1963	Margaret Smith Court	1937	Dorothy Round	1911	Dorothea Lambert Chambers
1962	Karen Hantze Susman	1936	Helen Jacobs	1910	Dorothea Lambert Chambers
1961	Angela Mortimer	1935	Helen Wills Moody	1909	Dora Boothby
1960	Maria Bueno	1934	Dorothy Round	1908	Charlotte Cooper Sterry
		1933	Helen Wills Moody		
		1932	Helen Wills Moody		

**Became Open (amateur and professional) in 1968.

WIMBLEDON CHAMPIONSHIPS (cont.)		UNITED STATES CHAMPIONSHIPS		Year	Winner
Year	Winner	Year	Winner	1980	Chris Evert Lloyd
1907	May Sutton	2006	Maria Sharapova	1979	Tracy Austin
1906	Dorothea Douglass	2005	Kim Clijsters	1978	Chris Evert Lloyd
1905	May Sutton	2004	Svetlana Kuznetsova	1977	Chris Evert Lloyd
1904	Dorothea Douglass	2003	Justine Henin-Hardenne	1976	Chris Evert Lloyd
1903	Dorothea Douglass	2002	Serena Williams	1975	Chris Evert Lloyd
1902	Muriel Robb	2001	Venus Williams	1974	Billie Jean King
1901	Charlotte Cooper Sterry	2000	Venus Williams	1973	Margaret Smith Court
1900	Blanche Bingley Hillyard	1999	Serena Williams	1972	Billie Jean King
1899	Blanche Bingley Hillyard	1998	Lindsay Davenport	1971	Billie Jean King
1898	Charlotte Cooper	1997	Martina Hingis	1970	Margaret Smith Court
1897	Blanche Bingley Hillyard	1996	Steffi Graf	1969	Margaret Smith Court
1896	Charlotte Cooper	1995	Steffi Graf	*1968	Virginia Wade
1895	Charlotte Cooper	1994	Arantxa Sánchez-Vicario	1967	Billie Jean King
1894	Blanche Bingley Hillyard	1993	Steffi Graf	1966	Maria Bueno
1893	Charlotte Dod	1992	Monica Seles	1965	Margaret Smith
1892	Charlotte Dod	1991	Monica Seles	1964	Maria Bueno
1891	Charlotte Dod	1990	Gabriela Sabatini	1963	Maria Bueno
1890	Lena Rice	1989	Steffi Graf	1962	Margaret Smith
1889	Blanche Bingley Hillyard	1988	Steffi Graf	1961	Darlene Hard
1888	Charlotte Dod	1987	Martina Navratilova	1960	Darlene Hard
1887	Charlotte Dod	1986	Martina Navratilova	1959	Maria Bueno
1886	Blanche Bingley	1985	Hana Mandlikova	1958	Althea Gibson
1885	Maud Watson	1984	Martina Navratilova	1957	Althea Gibson
1884	Maud Watson	1983	Martina Navratilova	1956	Shirley Fry
		1982	Chris Evert Lloyd	1955	Doris Hart
		1981	Tracy Austin	1954	Doris Hart
				1953	Maureen Connolly

* Became Open (amateur and professional) in 1968.

TRIVIA CHALLENGE

1 Who was the highest paid woman in tennis—or any other sport—at the end of 2006?
a. Serena Williams
b. Maria Sharapova
c. Martina Hingis

2 Men's championships were first held at Wimbledon in 1877. In what year was a women's tournament added?
a. 1877
b. 1884
c. 1900

3 What woman holds the record for most weeks spent as the top-ranked player in the world, male or female, with 377?
a. Steffi Graf
b. Monica Seles
c. Margaret Court

4 In 2004, which female player won the inaugural North American hard court season known as the U.S. Open series?
a. Kim Clijsters
b. Maria Sharapova
c. Lindsay Davenport

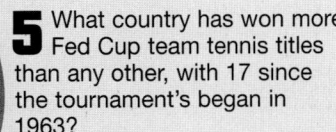
Maria Sharapova

5 What country has won more Fed Cup team tennis titles than any other, with 17 since the tournament's began in 1963?
a. Spain
b. United States
c. Russia

6 What male tennis player did Billie Jean King defeat in 1973's famous "Battle of the Sexes" match?
a. John McEnroe
b. Rod Laver
c. Bobby Riggs

BOB MARTIN

Trivia Challenge: 1. b; 2. b; 3. a; 4. c; 5. b; 6. c.

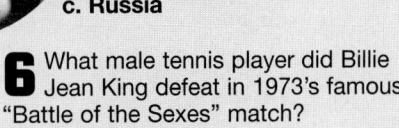

GRAND SLAM TOURNAMENTS: ALL-TIME WOMEN'S CHAMPIONS (cont.)

UNITED STATES CHAMPIONSHIPS (cont.)		Year	Winner	Year	Winner
Year	**Winner**	1931	Helen Wills Moody	1910	Hazel Hotchkiss
1952	Maureen Connolly	1930	Betty Nuthall	1909	Hazel Hotchkiss
1951	Maureen Connolly	1929	Helen Wills Moody	1908	Maud Barger–Wallach
1950	Margaret Osborne duPont	1928	Helen Wills Moody	1907	Evelyn Sears
1949	Margaret Osborne duPont	1927	Helen Wills Moody	1906	Helen Homans
1948	Margaret Osborne duPont	1926	Molla Bjurstedt Mallory	1905	Elisabeth Moore
1947	Louise Brough	1925	Helen Wills Moody	1904	May Sutton
1946	Pauline Betz	1924	Helen Wills Moody	1903	Elisabeth Moore
1945	Sarah Palfrey Cooke	1923	Helen Wills Moody	**1902	Marion Jones
1944	Pauline Betz	1922	Molla Bjurstedt Mallory	1901	Elisabeth Moore
1943	Pauline Betz	1921	Molla Bjurstedt Mallory	1900	Myrtle McAteer
1942	Pauline Betz	1920	Molla Bjurstedt Mallory	1899	Marion Jones
1941	Sarah Palfrey Cooke	1919	Hazel Hotchkiss Wightman	1898	Juliette Atkinson
1940	Alice Marble	1918	Molla Bjurstedt	1897	Juliette Atkinson
1939	Alice Marble	1917	Molla Bjurstedt	1896	Elisabeth Moore
1938	Alice Marble	1916	Molla Bjurstedt	1895	Juliette Atkinson
1937	Anita Lizane	1915	Molla Bjurstedt	1894	Helen Hellwig
1936	Alice Marble	1914	Mary K. Browne	1893	Aline Terry
1935	Helen Jacobs	1913	Mary K. Browne	1892	Mabel Cahill
1934	Helen Jacobs	1912	Mary K. Browne	1891	Mabel Cahill
1933	Helen Jacobs	1911	Hazel Hotchkiss	1890	Ellen C. Roosevelt
1932	Helen Jacobs			1889	Bertha L. Townsend
				1888	Bertha L. Townsend
				1887	Ellen Hansell

** Five-set final abolished.

DID YOU KNOW?

Pete Sampras's 31-match winning streak at Wimbledon was ended by Roger Federer in 2001.

LEGENDS

Margaret Smith Court was ranked Number 1 in the world six times during her career.

■ **Margaret Smith Court,** b. July 16, 1942, Albury, New South Wales, Australia. In 1970, Court became the first woman in the Open era to win all four Grand Slam titles in the same calendar year. But Court's 24 Grand Slam singles titles—more than any other tennis player, male of female— only tell part of her story. Court also won 19 doubles titles and 19 mixed doubles titles. In 1963, Court became the first Australian woman to win Wimbledon. In 2003, Australia's postal system honored Court and her fellow Australian Rod Laver by putting their portraits on postage stamps.

■ **Martina Navratilova,** b. October 18, 1956, Prague, Czech Republic. Winner of 18 Grand Slam singles titles and 41 Grand Slam mixed and women's doubles titles, Navratilova was named the greatest female tennis player of 1965-2005 by *Tennis Magazine.* In addition to her 59 Grand Slam championships, Navratilova owns the record for the longest winning streak in the Open era, with 74 consecutive match wins. Navratilova won a total of 167 singles titles and 177 doubles titles over the course of her career. Both are Open era records. Navratilova ended her career by winning the mixed doubles title at the 2006 U.S. Open.

■ **Chris Evert,** b. December 21, 1954, Fort Lauderdale, Florida. Among Evert's 18 Grand Slam singles titles were a record seven French Open championships. Evert's career match win-loss record, 1,309-146 (.900) is the best of any player in tennis history. At 15, Evert defeated World Number 1 Margaret Court in straight sets at an eight-woman clay court tournament in Charlotte, North Carolina. Evert's 125-match winning streak on clay still stands as the record for both men and women, though Rafael Nadal came close in 2007, winning 81 consecutive matches on clay.

Serena Williams won her third Australian Open title in 2007.

DAVID CALLOW

Justine Henin advanced to all four Grand Slam finals in 2006.

BOB MARTIN

ALL-TIME GRAND SLAM SINGLES CHAMPIONS

MEN

PLAYER	AUS.	FR.	WIM.	U.S.	TOTAL
Pete Sampras	2	0	7	5	14
Roy Emerson	6	2	2	2	12
Bjorn Borg	0	6	5	0	11
*Roger Federer	3	0	5	3	11
Rod Laver	3	2	4	2	11
Bill Tilden	†	0	3	7	10
Jimmy Connors	1	0	2	5	8
Ivan Lendl	2	3	0	3	8
Fred Perry	1	1	3	3	8
Ken Rosewall	4	2	0	2	8
Andre Agassi	4	1	1	2	8
Henri Cochet	†	4	2	1	7
Rene Lacoste	†	3	2	2	7
Bill Larned	†	†	0	7	7
John McEnroe	0	0	3	4	7
John Newcombe	2	0	3	2	7
Willie Renshaw	†	†	7	†	7
Dick Sears	†	†	0	7	7
Mats Wilander	3	3	0	1	7

*Active player. †Did not compete.

WOMEN

PLAYER	AUS.	FR.	WIM.	U.S.	TOTAL
Margaret Smith Court	11	5	3	5	24
Steffi Graf	4	6	7	5	22
Helen Wills Moody	†	4	8	7	19
Chris Evert Lloyd	2	7	3	6	18
Martina Navratilova	3	2	9	4	18
Billie Jean King	1	1	6	4	12
Maureen Connolly	1	2	3	3	9
Monica Seles	4	3	0	2	9
Suzanne Lenglen	†	#2	6	0	8
Molla Bjurstedt Mallory	†	†	0	8	8
*Serena Williams	3	1	2	2	8
Maria Bueno	0	0	3	4	7
Evonne Goolagong	4	1	2	0	7
Dorothea L. Chambers	†	†	7	0	7
Nancye Wynne Bolton	6	0	0	0	6
Louise Brough	1	0	4	1	6
Margaret Osborne duPont	†	2	1	3	6
Doris Hart	1	2	1	2	6
*Justine Henin	1	4	0	1	6
Blanche Bingley Hillyard	†	†	6	†	6
Venus Williams	0	0	4	2	6

*Active player. †Did not compete.
#Suzanne Lenglen also won four singles titles at the French Championships before 1925, when the tournament was first opened to players from all nations.

TRIVIA CHALLENGE

How many British players have won a singles title at Wimbledon in the Open era?

One: Virginia Wade in 1977.

SWIMMING

Michael Phelps broke four world records and won seven gold medals at the 2007 Worlds.

Another year, another earth-shattering performance from Michael Phelps. The American superstar solidified his place as the greatest swimmer of alltime by winning seven gold medals at the 2007 FINA World Championships in Melbourne, Australia. Along the way, he broke five world records. Phelps now holds four individual world records (200-meter freestyle, 200 butterfly, and the 200 and 400 individual medleys), and two relay records (4 x 100 and 4 x 200 freestyle).

The rest of the U.S. team was dominant in Melbourne as well. The Americans took home 40 medals, including 21 golds, in a performance that could carry over to the 2008 Summer Olympics in Beijing, China. Along with Phelps, backstrokers Aaron Peirsol (100 meters) and Ryan Lochte (200) also broke world marks at the Worlds.

On the women's side, 17-year-old Katie Hoff set world records in the 400-meter individual medley and as part of the 800-meter freestyle relay. She is on track to be one of the stars of Beijing. Natalie Coughlin continued her dominance. The veteran swimmer set the world record in the 100-meter backstroke and was also part of the record-setting 800 relay team. Newcomer Leila Vaziri, an NCAA star at Indiana, set the world record in the 50-meter backstroke.

There were plenty of challenges to U.S. swimmers on the women's side, though. In almost any other year, Australian Libby Lenton would have been the star of the Worlds with her five-gold medal performance. French superstar Laure Manaudou broke the world record in the 200-meter freestyle, just a few months after setting the 400-meter freestyle mark at the 2006 European Championships in August. Australia's 4 x 100 medley relay team also set a world record.

But record-setting races weren't confined to the Worlds. At the 2006 U.S. Championships in August, Brendan Hansen set world marks in the 100- and 200-meter breaststroke. He was named the USA Swimming Athlete of the Year.

The record-setting Australian women's medley relay team included two swimmers who set world records in 2006. Leisel Jones established a new 100-meter breaststroke mark at the Australian Championships in March, and Jessica Schipper set the world record in the 200-meter butterfly at the Pan Pacific Championships in August. And Germany's Britta Steffen has become a star as well. Steffen set records in the 100-meter freestyle and as part of the 4 x 100 freestyle relay team at the European Championships.

With the 2008 Olympics on the horizon, a boatload of big-name swimmers seem ready to make waves in Beijing.

2006–07 MAJOR COMPETITIONS – MEN

WORLD CHAMPIONSHIPS
Melbourne, Australia, March 25–April 1, 2007

EVENT	SWIMMER, TEAM	TIME
50-meter freestyle	Benjamin Wildman-Tobriner, United States	21.88
100-meter freestyle	Filippo Magnini, Italy	48.43
200-meter freestyle	Michael Phelps, United States	1:43.86
400-meter freestyle	Tae Hwan Park, Korea	3:44.30
800-meter freestyle	Oussama Mellouli, Tunisia	7:46.95
1,500-meter freestyle	Mateusz Sawrymowicz, Poland	14:45.94
50-meter backstroke	Gerhard Zandberg, South Africa	24.98
100-meter backstroke	Aaron Peirsol, United States	52.98
200-meter backstroke	Ryan Lochte, United States	1:54.32
50-meter breaststroke	Oleg Lisogor, Ukraine	27.66
100-meter breaststroke	Brendan Hansen, United States	59.80
200-meter breaststroke	Kosuke Kitajima, Japan	2:09.80
50-meter butterfly	Roland Schoeman, South Africa	23.18
100-meter butterfly	Michael Phelps, United States	50.77
200-meter butterfly	Michael Phelps, United States	1:52.09
200-meter individual medley	Michael Phelps, United States	1:54.98
400-meter individual medley	Michael Phelps, United States	4:06.22
4x100-meter medley relay	Australia (Matt Welsh, Brenton Rickard, Andrew Lauterstein, Eamon Sullivan)	3:34.93
4x100-meter freestyle relay	United States (Michael Phelps, Neil Walker, Cullen Jones, Jason Lezak)	3:12.72
4x200-meter freestyle relay	United States (Michael Phelps, Ryan Lochte, Klete Keller, Peter Vanderkaay)	7:03.24

U.S. NATIONAL CHAMPIONSHIPS (SUMMER)
Irvine, California, August 1-5, 2006

EVENT	SWIMMER, TEAM	TIME
50-meter freestyle	Cullen Jones, N.C. State Aquatics (North Carolina)	21.94
100-meter freestyle	Jason Lezak, Irvine Novaquatic (California)	48.63
200-meter freestyle	Michael Phelps, Club Wolverine (Michigan)	1:45.63
400-meter freestyle	Klete Keller, Club Wolverine (Michigan)	3:44.27
1,500-meter freestyle	Erik Vendt, Club Wolverine (Michigan)	15:05.41
100-meter backstroke	Aaron Peirsol, Langhorn Aquatics (Texas)	53.38
200-meter backstroke	Aaron Peirsol, Langhorn Aquatics (Texas)	1:56.36
100-meter breaststroke	Brendan Hansen, Longhorn Aquatics (Texas)	59.13
200-meter breaststroke	Brendan Hansen, Longhorn Aquatics (Texas)	2:08.74
100-meter butterfly	Michael Phelps, Club Wolverine (Michigan)	51.51
200-meter butterfly	Michael Phelps, Club Wolverine (Michigan)	1:54.32
200-meter individual medley	Michael Phelps, Club Wolverine (Michigan)	1:56.50
400-meter individual medley	Michael Phelps, Club Wolverine (Michigan)	4:10.16
4x100-meter medley relay	Club Wolverine A (Michigan)	3:41.96
4x100-meter freestyle relay	Longhorn Aquatics (Texas)	3:24.14
4x200-meter freestyle relay	Club Wolverine A (Michigan)	7:26.35

2006–07 MAJOR COMPETITIONS – WOMEN

WORLD CHAMPIONSHIPS
Melbourne, Australia, March 25–April 1, 2007

EVENT	SWIMMER, TEAM	TIME
50-meter freestyle	Lisbeth Lenton, Australia	24.53
100-meter freestyle	Lisbeth Lenton, Australia	53.40
200-meter freestyle	Laure Manaudou, France	1:55.52
400-meter freestyle	Laure Manaudou, France	4:02.61
800-meter freestyle	Kate Ziegler, United States	8:18.52
1,500-meter freestyle	Kate Ziegler, United States	15:53.05
50-meter backstroke	Leila Vaziri, United States	28.16
100-meter backstroke	Natalie Coughlin, United States	59.44
200-meter backstroke	Margaret Hoelzer, United States	2:07.16
50-meter breaststroke	Jessica Hardy, United States	30.63
100-meter breaststroke	Leisel Jones, Australia	1:05.72
200-meter breaststroke	Leisel Jones, Australia	2:21.84
50-meter butterfly	Therese Alshammar, Sweden	25.91
100-meter butterfly	Lisbeth Lenton, Australia	57.15
200-meter butterfly	Jessicah Schipper, Australia	2:06.39
200-meter individual medley	Katie Hoff, United States	2:10.13
400-meter individual medley	Katie Hoff, United States	4:32.89
4x100-meter medley relay	Australia (Emily Seebohm, Leisel Jones, Jessicah Schipper, Lisbeth Lenton)	3:55.74
4x100-meter freestyle relay	Australia (Lisbeth Lenton, Melanie Schlanger, Shayne Reese, Jodie Henry)	3:35.48
4x200-meter freestyle relay	United States (Natalie Coughlin, Dana Vollmer, Lacey Nymeyer, Katie Hoff)	7:50.09

2006-07 MAJOR COMPETITIONS – WOMEN (cont.)

U.S. NATIONAL CHAMPIONSHIPS
Irvine, California, August 1-5, 2006

EVENT	SWIMMER, TEAM	TIME
50-meter freestyle	Kara Lynn Joyce, Athens Bulldogs (Georgia)	24.97
100-meter freestyle	Amanda Weir, Swim Atlanta (Georgia)	53.58
200-meter freestyle	Natalie Coughlin, California Aquatics (California)	1:58.11
400-meter freestyle	Kate Ziegler, The Fish (Virginia)	4:05.75
800-meter freestyle	Haley Peirsol, Club Wolverine (Michigan)	8:26.45
100-meter backstroke	Leyla Vaziri, Coral Springs (Florida)	1:02.64
200-meter backstroke	Margaret Hoelzer, Auburn Aquatic (Alabama)	2:10.71
100-meter breaststroke	Megan Jendrick, King Aquatic Club (Washington)	1:07.54
200-meter breaststroke	Tara Kirk, Stanford Swim (California)	2:28.46
100-meter butterfly	Natalie Coughlin, California Aquatics (California)	57.78
200-meter butterfly	Kim Vanderberg, UCLA (California)	2:08.51
200-meter individual medley	Katie Hoff, North Baltimore (Maryland)	2:10.05
400-meter individual medley	Katie Hoff, North Baltimore (Maryland)	4:35.82
4x100-meter medley relay	California Aquatics A	4:03.32
4x100-meter freestyle relay	Tuscan Ford, (Arizona)	3:42.90
4x200-meter freestyle relay	California Aquatics A	8:08.16

TRIVIA CHALLENGE

1 Which female American swimmer became the first woman to win back-to-back Olympic and World Championship titles in the same event?
a. Summer Sanders
b. Janet Evans
c. Natalie Coughlin

2 Amanda Beard has won seven Olympic medals during her swimming career. How old was she when she won her first gold medal at the 1996 Summer Games?
a. 14
b. 15
c. 16

3 Of the 15 new world records set at the 2007 World Championships, how many were set by Michael Phelps?
a. 1
b. 2
c. 4

Amanda Beard

4 For all races that begin with a dive into the pool, a swimmer's hands must touch the platform at the start of the event or else they will be disqualified.
a. True
b. False

5 Which country has won the most all-time Olympic gold medals in swimming events?
a. Australia
b. United States
c. Russia

6 What nickname was given to nine-time Olympic medalist and Australian swim champ Ian Thorpe?
a. Aussie Posse
b. Amphib-Ian
c. Thorpedo

7 In the freestyle event, a swimmer can use any type of stroke they choose.
a. True
b. False

Trivia Challenge: 1. b; 2. a; 3. c; 4. b; 5. b; 6. c; 7. a.

WORLD AND AMERICAN RECORDS — MEN

FREESTYLE

EVENT	TIME	RECORD HOLDER	DATE	SITE
50 meters	21.64	Alexander Popov, Russia (W)	6-16-00	Moscow, Russia
	21.76	Gary Hall, Jr. (A)	8-15-00	Indianapolis, Indiana
100 meters	47.84	Pieter van den Hoogenband, Netherlands (W)	9-19-00	Sydney, Australia
	48.17	Jason Lezak (A)	7-10-04	Long Beach, California
200 meters	1:43.86	Michael Phelps (W, A)	3-27-07	Melbourne, Australia
400 meters	3:40.08	Ian Thorpe, Australia (W)	7-30-02	Manchester, England
	3:44.11	Klete Keller (A)	8-14-04	Athens, Greece
800 meters	7:38.65	Grant Hackett, Australia (W)	7-27-05	Montreal, Canada
	7:45.63	Larsen Jensen (A)	7-27-05	Montreal, Canada
1,500 meters	14:34.56	Grant Hackett, Australia (W)	7-29-01	Fukuoka, Japan
	14:45.29	Larsen Jensen (A)	8-21-04	Athens, Greece

BACKSTROKE

EVENT	TIME	RECORD HOLDER	DATE	SITE
50 meters	24.80	Thomas Rupprath, Germany (W)	7-27-03	Barcelona, Spain
	24.99	Lenny Krayzelburg (A)	8-28-99	Sydney, Australia
100 meters	52.98	Aaron Peirsol (W, A)	3-27-07	Melbourne, Australia
200 meters	1:54.32	Ryan Lochte (W, A)	3-30-07	Melbourne, Australia

Brendan Hansen,
United States

HEINZ KLUETMEIER

BREASTSTROKE

EVENT	TIME	RECORD HOLDER	DATE	SITE
50 meters	27.18	Oleg Lisogor, Ukraine (W)	8-02-02	Berlin, Germany
	27.39	Ed Moses (A)	3-31-01	Austin, Texas
100 meters	59.13	Brendan Hansen (W, A)	8-01-06	Irvine, California
200 meters	2:08.50	Brendan Hansen (W, A)	8-20-06	Victoria, Canada

BUTTERFLY

EVENT	TIME	RECORD HOLDER	DATE	SITE
50 meters	22.96	Roland Schoeman, South Africa (W)	7-25-05	Montreal, Canada
	23.21	Ian Crocker (A)	7-25-05	Montreal, Canada
100 meters	50.40	Ian Crocker (W, A)	7-30-05	Montreal, Canada
200 meters	1:52.09	Michael Phelps (W, A)	3-28-07	Melbourne, Australia

HEINZ KLUETMEIER

INDIVIDUAL MEDLEY

EVENT	TIME	RECORD HOLDER	DATE	SITE
200 meters	1:54.98	Michael Phelps (W, A)	3-29-07	Melbourne, Australia
400 meters	4:06.22	Michael Phelps (W, A)	4-01-07	Melbourne, Australia

RELAYS

EVENT	TIME	RECORD HOLDER	DATE	SITE
400-meter medley	3:30.68	United States (W, A) (Aaron Peirsol, Brendan Hansen, Ian Crocker, Jason Lezak)	8-21-04	Athens, Greece
400-meter freestyle	3:12.46	United States (W, A) (Michael Phelps, Neil Walker, Cullen Jones, Jason Lezak)	8-19-06	Victoria, Canada
800-meter freestyle	7:03.24	United States (W, A) (Michael Phelps, Ryan Lochte, Klete Keller, Peter Vanderkaay)	3-30-07	Melbourne, Australia

KEY (A)=American Record; (W)=World Record

DID YOU KNOW?

The backstroke and medley relay are the only events where the swimmers are already in the pool at the start of the race.

SWIMMING

WORLD AND AMERICAN RECORDS — WOMEN

FREESTYLE

EVENT	TIME	RECORD HOLDER	DATE	SITE
50 meters	24.13	Inge de Bruijn, Netherlands (W)	9-22-00	Sydney, Australia
	24.63	Dara Torres (A)	9-23-00	Sydney, Australia
100 meters	53.30	Britta Steffen, Germany (W)	8-02-06	Budapest, Hungary
	53.40	Natalie Coughlin (A)	3-29-07	Melbourne, Australia
200 meters	1:55.52	Laure Manaudou, France (W)	3-28-07	Melbourne, Australia
	1:56.43	Natalie Coughlin (A)	3-29-07	Melbourne, Australia
400 meters	4:02.13	Laure Manaudou, France (W)	8-06-06	Budapest, Hungary
	4:03.85	Janet Evans (A)	9-22-88	Seoul, Korea
800 meters	8:16.22	Janet Evans (W, A)	8-20-89	Tokyo, Japan
1,500 meters	15:42.54	Kate Ziegler (W, A)	6-17-07	Mission Viejo, California

BACKSTROKE

EVENT	TIME	RECORD HOLDER	DATE	SITE
50 meters	28.16	Leila Vaziri, United States (W, A)	3-29-07	Melbourne, Australia
100 meters	59.44	Natalie Coughlin (W, A)	3-27-07	Melbourne, Australia
200 meters	2:06.62	Krisztina Egerszegi, Hungary (W)	8-25-91	Athens, Greece
	2:07.16	Margaret Hoelzer (A)	3-31-07	Melbourne, Australia

Leila Vaziri,
United States

BREASTSTROKE

EVENT	TIME	RECORD HOLDER	DATE	SITE
50 meters	30.31	Jade Edmistone, Australia (W)	1-30-06	Melbourne, Australia
	30.85	Jessica Hardy (A)	7-31-05	Montreal, Canada
100 meters	1:05.09	Leisel Jones, Australia (W)	3-20-06	Melbourne, Australia
	1:06.20	Jessica Hardy (A)	7-25-05	Montreal, Canada
200 meters	2:20.54	Leisel Jones, Australia (W)	2-01-06	Melbourne, Australia
	2:22.44	Amanda Beard (A)	7-12-04	Long Beach, California

BUTTERFLY

EVENT	TIME	RECORD HOLDER	DATE	SITE
50 meters	25.57	Anna-Karin Kammerling, Sweden (W)	7-30-02	Berlin, Germany
	26.00	Jenny Thompson (A)	7-26-03	Barcelona, Spain
100 meters	56.61	Inge de Bruijn, Netherlands (W)	9-17-00	Sydney, Australia
	57.34	Natalie Coughlin (A)	3-26-07	Melbourne, Australia
200 meters	2:05.40	Jessicah Schipper, (W)	8-17-06	Victoria, Canada
	2:05.88	Misty Hyman (A)	9-20-00	Sydney, Australia

INDIVIDUAL MEDLEY

EVENT	TIME	RECORD HOLDER	DATE	SITE
200 meters	2:09.72	Yanyan Wu, China (W)	10-17-97	Shanghai, China
	2:10.05	Katie Hoff (A)	8-01-06	Irvine, California
400 meters	4:32.89	Katie Hoff (W, A)	4-01-07	Melbourne, Australia

RELAYS

EVENT	TIME	RECORD HOLDER	DATE	SITE
400-meter medley	3:55.74	Australia (W) (Emily Seebohm, Leisel Jones, Jessicah Schipper, Lisbeth Lenton)	3-31-07	Melbourne, Australia
	3:58.30	United States (A) (B.J. Bedford, Megan Quann, Jenny Thompson, Dara Torres)	9-23-00	Sydney, Australia
400-meter freestyle	3:35.22	Germany (W) (Petra Dallman, Daniela Goetz, Britta Steffen, Annika Liebs)	7-31-06	Budapest, Hungary
	3:35.68	United States (A) (Natalie Coughlin, Lacey Nymeyer, Amanda Weir, Kara Lynn Joyce)	3-25-07	Melbourne, Australia
800-meter freestyle	7:50.09	United States (W, A) (Natalie Coughlin, Dana Vollmer, Lacey Nymeyer, Katie Hoff)	3-29-07	Melbourne, Australia

KEY (A)=American Record; (W)=World Record

LEGENDS

HEINZ KLUETMEIER

■ **Jenny Thompson,** b. February 26, 1973, Dover, New Hampshire. The most decorated American Olympian of all time, Thompson began her swimming career at Stanford. While there, she led her team to four straight undefeated seasons. During her Olympic swimming career, which spanned from the 1992 to 2004 Summer Games, Thompson won a total of 12 medals—eight golds, three silvers, and a bronze. In 2001, while continuing to swim competitively, Thompson began attending medical school. In 2006, two years after retiring from the pool, she began her second career as a doctor.

In 1999, Sports Illustrated ranked Jenny Thompson among the 100 greatest female athletes of all time.

■ **Matt Biondi,** b. October 8, 1965, Palo Alto, California. Biondi is one of only three swimmers who have won seven or more medals in a single Olympics. At the 1988 Summer Games in Seoul, South Korea, Biondi took home five golds, a silver, and a bronze, equalling Mark Spitz's total from 1972. (Michael Phelps won a record eight medals in 2004.) In all, Biondi won eleven career Olympic medals, including eight golds.

■ **Shane Gould,** b. November 23, 1956, Sydney, Australia. The 15-year-old Gould made a splash at the 1972 Summer Games by becoming the first female swimmer to win three Olympic gold medals in world record time. She was also the first swimmer to simultaneously hold world records in every freestyle event, from the 100-meter up to the 1,500-meter. But less than a year after her noteworthy performance in Munich, Gould retired from swimming because she was overwhelmed by all the attention.

ALL-TIME WORLD CHAMPIONSHIP RESULTS – MEN

50-METER FREESTYLE

1973-82	Event not held	
1986	Tom Jager, United States	22.49
1991	Tom Jager, United States	22.16
1994	Alexander Popov, Russia	22.17
1998	Bill Pilczuk, United States	22.29
2001	Anthony Ervin, United States	22.09
2003	Alexander Popov, Russia	21.92
2005	Roland Schoeman, South Africa	21.69
2007	Benjamin Wildman-Tobriner, United States	21.88

100-METER FREESTYLE

1973	Jim Montgomery, United States	51.70
1975	Andy Coan, United States	51.25
1978	David McCagg, United States	50.24
1982	Jorg Woithe, East Germany	50.18
1986	Matt Biondi, United States	48.94
1991	Matt Biondi, United States	49.18
1994	Alexander Popov, Russia	49.12
1998	Alexander Popov, Russia	48.93
2001	Anthony Ervin, United States	48.33
2003	Alexander Popov, Russia	48.42
2005	Filippo Magnini, Italy	48.12
2007	Filippo Magnini, Italy	48.43

200-METER FREESTYLE

1973	Jim Montgomery, United States	1:53.02
1975	Tim Shaw, United States	1:51.04
1978	Billy Forrester, United States	1:51.02
1982	Michael Gross, West Germany	1:49.84

200-METER FREESTYLE (CONT'D)

1986	Michael Gross, West Germany	1:47.92
1991	Giorgio Lamberti, Italy	1:47.27
1994	Antti Kasvio, Finland	1:47.32
1998	Michael Klim, Australia	1:47.41
2001	Ian Thorpe, Australia	1:44.06
2003	Ian Thorpe, Australia	1:45.14
2005	Michael Phelps, United States	1:45.20
2007	Michael Phelps, United States	1:43.86

400-METER FREESTYLE

1973	Rick DeMont, United States	3:58.18
1975	Tim Shaw, United States	3:54.88
1978	Vladimir Salnikov, U.S.S.R.	3:51.94
1982	Vladimir Salnikov, U.S.S.R.	3:51.30
1986	Rainer Henkel, West Germany	3:50.05
1991	Joerg Hoffman, Germany	3:48.04
1994	Kieran Perkins, Australia	3:43.80
1998	Ian Thorpe, Australia	3:46.29
2001	Ian Thorpe, Australia	3:40.17
2003	Ian Thorpe, Australia	3:42.58
2005	Grant Hackett, Australia	3:42.91
2007	Tae Hwan Park, Korea	3:44.30

800-METER FREESTYLE

1973-98	Event not held	
2001	Ian Thorpe, Australia	7:39.16
2003	Grant Hackett, Australia	7:43.82
2005	Grant Hackett, Australia	7:38.65
2007	Oussama Mellouli, Tunisia	7:46.95

SWIMMING

ALL-TIME WORLD CHAMPIONSHIP RESULTS — MEN (cont.)

1,500-METER FREESTYLE

1973	Stephen Holland, Australia	15:31.85
1975	Tim Shaw, United States	15:28.92
1978	Vladimir Salnikov, U.S.S.R.	15:03.99
1982	Vladimir Salnikov, U.S.S.R.	15:01.77
1986	Rainer Henkel, West Germany	15:05.31
1991	Joerg Hoffman, Germany	14:50.36
1994	Kieran Perkins, Australia	14:50.52
1998	Grant Hackett, Australia	14:51.70
2001	Grant Hackett, Australia	14:34.56
2003	Grant Hackett, Australia	14:43.14
2005	Grant Hackett, Australia	14:42.58
2007	Mateusz Sawrymowicz, Poland	14:45.94

50-METER BACKSTROKE

1973-98	Event not held	
2001	Randall Bal, United States	25.34
2003	Thomas Rupprath, Germany	24.80
2005	Aristeidis Grigoriadis, Greece	24.95
2007	Gerhard Zandberg, South Africa	24.98

100-METER BACKSTROKE

1973	Roland Matthes, East Germany	57.47
1975	Roland Matthes, East Germany	58.15
1978	Bob Jackson, United States	56.36
1982	Dirk Richter, East Germany	55.95
1986	Igor Polianski, U.S.S.R.	55.58
1991	Jeff Rouse, United States	55.23
1994	Martin Zubero, Spain	55.17
1998	Lenny Krayzelburg, United States	55.00
2001	Matt Welsh, Australia	54.31
2003	Aaron Peirsol, United States	53.61
2005	Aaron Peirsol, United States	53.62
2007	Aaron Peirsol, United States	52.98

200-METER BACKSTROKE

1973	Roland Matthes, East Germany	2:01.87
1975	Zoltan Varraszto, Hungary	2:05.05
1978	Jesse Vassallo, United States	2:02.16
1982	Rick Carey, United States	2:00.82
1986	Igor Polianski, U.S.S.R.	1:58.78
1991	Martin Zubero, Spain	1:59.52
1994	Vladimir Selkov, Russia	1:57.42
1998	Lenny Krayzelburg, United States	1:58.84
2001	Aaron Peirsol, United States	1:57.13
2003	Aaron Peirsol, United States	1:55.92
2005	Aaron Peirsol, United States	1:54.66
2007	Ryan Lochte, United States	1:54.32

50-METER BREASTSTROKE

1973-98	Event not held	
2001	Oleg Lisogor, Ukraine	27.52
2003	James Gibson, Great Britain	27.56
2005	Mark Warnecke, Germany	27.63
2007	Oleg Lisogor, Ukraine	27.66

100-METER BREASTSTROKE

1973	John Hencken, United States	1:04.02
1975	David Wilkie, Great Britain	1:04.26
1978	Walter Kusch, West Germany	1:03.56
1982	Steve Lundquist, United States	1:02.75
1986	Victor Davis, Canada	1:02.71
1991	Norbert Rozsa, Hungary	1:01.45
1994	Norbert Rozsa, Hungary	1:01.24
1998	Frederik Deburghgraeve, Belgium	1:01.34
2001	Roman Sloudnov, Russia	1:00.16
2003	Kosuke Kitajima, Japan	59.78
2005	Brendan Hansen, United States	59.37
2007	Brendan Hansen, United States	59.80

200-METER BREASTSTROKE

1973	David Wilkie, Great Britain	2:19.28
1975	David Wilkie, Great Britain	2:18.23
1978	Nick Nevid, United States	2:18.37
1982	Victor Davis, Canada	2:14.77
1986	Jozsef Szabo, Hungary	2:14.27
1991	Mike Barrowman, United States	2:11.23
1994	Norbert Rozsa, Hungary	2:12.81
1998	Kurt Grote, United States	2:13.40
2001	Brendan Hansen, United States	2:10.69

200-METER BREASTSTROKE (CONT'D)

2003	Kosuke Kitajima, Japan	2:09.42
2005	Brendan Hansen, United States	2:09.85
2007	Kosuke Kitajima, Japan	2:09.80

50-METER BUTTERFLY

1973-98	Event not held	
2001	Geoff Huegill, Australia	23.50
2003	Matt Welsh, Australia	23.43
2005	Roland Schoeman, South Africa	22.96
2007	Roland Schoeman, South Africa	23.18

100-METER BUTTERFLY

1973	Bruce Robertson, Canada	55.69
1975	Greg Jagenburg, United States	55.63
1978	Joe Bottom, United States	54.30
1982	Matt Gribble, United States	53.88
1986	Pablo Morales, United States	53.54
1991	Anthony Nesty, Suriname	53.29
1994	Rafal Szukala, Poland	53.51
1998	Michael Klim, Australia	52.25
2001	Lars Frolander, Sweden	52.10
2003	Ian Crocker, United States	50.98
2005	Ian Crocker, United States	50.40
2007	Michael Phelps, United States	50.77

200-METER BUTTERFLY

1973	Robin Backhaus, United States	2:03.32
1975	Bill Forrester, United States	2:01.95
1978	Mike Bruner, United States	1:59.38
1982	Michael Gross, West Germany	1:58.85
1986	Michael Gross, West Germany	1:56.53
1991	Melvin Stewart, United States	1:55.69
1994	Denis Pankratov, Russia	1:56.54
1998	Denys Sylantyev, Ukraine	1:56.61
2001	Michael Phelps, United States	1:54.58
2003	Michael Phelps, United States	1:54.35
2005	Pawel Korzeniowski, Poland	1:55.02
2007	Michael Phelps, United States	1:52.09

200-METER INDIVIDUAL MEDLEY

1973	Gunnar Larsson, Sweden	2:08.36
1975	Andras Hargitay, Hungary	2:07.72
1978	Graham Smith, Canada	2:03.65
1982	Aleksandr Sidorenko, U.S.S.R.	2:03.30
1986	Tamás Darnyi, Hungary	2:01.57
1991	Tamás Darnyi, Hungary	1:59.36
1994	Jani Sievin, Finland	1:58.16
1998	Marcel Wouda, Netherlands	2:01.18
2001	Massimiliano Rosolino, Italy	1:59.71
2003	Michael Phelps, United States	1:56.04
2005	Michael Phelps, United States	1:56.68
2007	Michael Phelps, United States	1:54.98

400-METER INDIVIDUAL MEDLEY

1973	Andras Hargitay, Hungary	4:31.11
1975	Andras Hargitay, Hungary	4:32.57
1978	Jesse Vassallo, United States	4:20.05
1982	Ricardo Prado, Brazil	4:19.78
1986	Tamás Darnyi, Hungary	4:18.98
1991	Tamás Darnyi, Hungary	4:12.36
1994	Tom Dolan, United States	4:12.30
1998	Tom Dolan, United States	4:14.95
2001	Alessio Boggiatto, Italy	4:13.15
2003	Michael Phelps, United States	4:09.09
2005	Laszlo Cseh, Hungary	4:09.63
2007	Michael Phelps, United States	4:06.22

400-METER MEDLEY RELAY

1973	United States (Mike Stamm, John Hencken, Joe Bottom, Jim Montgomery)	3:49.49
1975	United States (John Murphy, Rick Colella, Greg Jagenburg, Andy Coan)	3:49.00
1978	United States (Robert Jackson, Nick Nevid, Joe Bottom, David McCagg)	3:44.63
1982	United States (Rick Carey, Steve Lundquist, Matt Gribble, Rowdy Gaines)	3:40.84
1986	United States (Dan Veatch, David Lundberg, Pablo Morales, Matt Biondi)	3:41.25
1991	United States (Jeff Rouse, Eric Wunderlich, Mark Henderson, Matt Biondi)	3:39.66

400-METER MEDLEY RELAY (CONT'D)

1994	United States (Jeff Rouse, Eric Wunderlich, Mark Henderson, Gary Hall, Jr.)	3:37.74
1998	Australia (Matt Welsh, Phil Rogers, Michael Klim, Chris Fydler)	3:37.98
2001	Australia (Matt Welsh, Ian Thorpe, Geoff Huegill, Regan Harrison)	3:35.35
2003	United States (Aaron Peirsol, Brendan Hansen, Ian Crocker, Jason Lezak)	3:31.54
2005	United States (Aaron Peirsol, Brendan Hansen, Ian Crocker, Jason Lezak)	3:31.85
2007	Australia (Matt Welsh, Brenton Rickard, Andrew Lauterstein, Eamon Sullivan)	3:35.93

400-METER FREESTYLE RELAY

1973	United States (Mel Nash, Joe Bottom, Jim Montgomery, John Murphy)	3:27.18
1975	United States (Bruce Furniss, Jim Montgomery, Andy Coan, John Murphy)	3:24.85
1978	United States (Jack Babashoff, Rowdy Gaines, Jim Montgomery, David McCagg)	3:19.74
1982	United States (Chris Cavanaugh, Robin Leamy, David McCagg, Rowdy Gaines)	3:19.26
1986	United States (Tom Jager, Mike Heath, Paul Wallace, Matt Biondi)	3:19.59
1991	United States (Tom Jager, Brent Lang, Doug Gjertsen, Matt Biondi)	3:17.15
1994	United States (Jon Olsen, Josh Davis, Ugur Taner, Gary Hall)	3:16.90
1998	United States (Scott Tucker, Jon Olsen, Neil Walker, Gary Hall)	3:16.69
2001	Australia (Michael Klim, Ian Thorpe, Todd Pearson, Ashley Callus)	3:14.10
2003	Russia (Andrei Kapralov, Ivan Usov, Denis Pimankov, Alexander Popov)	3:14.06

400-METER FREESTYLE RELAY (CONT'D)

2005	United States (Michael Phelps, Neil Walker, Nate Dusing, Jason Lezak)	3:13.77
2007	United States (Michael Phelps, Neil Walker, Cullen Jones, Jason Lezak)	3:12.72

800-METER FREESTYLE RELAY

1973	United States (Kurt Krumpholz, Robin Backhaus, Rick Klatt, Jim Montgomery)	7:33.22
1975	West Germany (Klaus Steinbach, Werner Lampe, Hans Joachim Geisler, Peter Nocke)	7:39.44
1978	United States (Bruce Furniss, Billy Forrester, Bobby Hackett, Rowdy Gaines)	7:20.82
1982	United States (Rich Saeger, Jeff Float, Kyle Miller, Rowdy Gaines)	7:21.09
1986	East Germany (Lars Hinneburg, Thomas Flemming, Dirk Richter, Sven Lodziewski)	7:15.91
1991	Germany (Peter Sitt, Steffen Zesner, Stefan Pfeiffer, Michael Gross)	7:13.50
1994	Sweden (Christer Waller, Tommy Werner, Lars Frolander, Anders Holmertz)	7:17.74
1998	Australia (Daniel Kowalski, Grant Hackett, Ian Thorpe, Michael Klim)	7:12.48
2001	Australia (Michael Klim, Ian Thorpe, William Kirby, Grant Hackett)	7:04.66
2003	Australia (Grant Hackett, Craig Stevens, Nicholas Sprenger, Ian Thorpe)	7:08.58
2005	United States (Michael Phelps, Ryan Lochte, Peter Vanderkaay, Klete Keller)	7:06.58
2007	United States (Michael Phelps, Ryan Lochte, Klete Keller, Peter Vanderkaay)	7:03.24

TODAY'S STARS

In 2007, Lenton anchored Australia's world-record setting 4x100-meter freestyle relay team

■ **Lisbeth Lenton,** b. January 25, 1985, Townsville, Australia. Nicknamed "Libby," Lenton burst onto the world swimming scene at the 2004 Summer Olympics. Only 19 years old, she won an Olympic bronze medal in the 50-meter freestyle and gold in the 400-meter freestyle relay. Lenton has set numerous freestyle world records since then. Most recently, she wowed fans from her native Australia by winning five gold medals at the 2007 World Championships in Melbourne.

■ **Kosuke Kitajima,** b. September 22, 1982, Tokyo, Japan. A breaststroke specialist, Kitajima has twice swept gold medals in both the 100-meter and 200-meter events during the same meet. Once was at the 2003 World Championships, the second time was at the 2004 Summer Games. Kitajima's frequent duels with American breaststroke champion Brendan Hansen have developed into one of most intense rivalries in swimming. At the 2007 World Championships, the pair raced to an even draw, with Hansen winning the 100-meter breaststroke and Kitajima taking gold in the 200-meter.

■ **Kate Ziegler,** b. June 27, 1988, Fairfax, Virginia. The 19-year-old Ziegler has become the premier long distance swimmer in the world. She has won gold medals in the 800-meter and 1,500-meter freestyle at both the 2005 and 2007 World Championships. As only the second woman in history to break the 16-minute barrier in the 1,500-meter freestyle, Ziegler looks poised to break Janet Evans's 20-year-old world record when she competes at the upcoming 2008 Summer Games in Beijing, China.

SWIMMING

ALL-TIME WORLD CHAMPIONSHIPS RESULTS – WOMEN

50-METER FREESTYLE

1973-82	Event not held	
1986	Tamara Costache, Romania	25.28
1991	Zhuang Yong, China	25.47
1994	Le Jingyi, China	24.51
1998	Amy Van Dyken, United States	25.15
2001	Inge de Bruijn, Netherlands	24.47
2003	Inge de Bruijn, Netherlands	24.47
2005	Lisbeth Lenton, Australia	24.59
2007	Lisbeth Lenton, Australia	24.53

100-METER FREESTYLE

1973	Kornelia Ender, East Germany	57.54
1975	Kornelia Ender, East Germany	56.50
1978	Barbara Krause, East Germany	55.68
1982	Birgit Meineke, East Germany	55.79
1986	Kristin Otto, East Germany	55.05
1991	Nicole Haislett, United States	55.17
1994	Le Jingyi, China	54.01
1998	Jenny Thompson, United States	54.95
2001	Inge de Bruijn, Netherlands	54.18
2003	Hanna-Maria Seppala, Finland	54.37
2005	Jodie Henry, Australia	54.18
2007	Lisbeth Lenton, Australia	53.40

200-METER FREESTYLE

1973	Keena Rothhammer, United States	2:04.99
1975	Shirley Babashoff, United States	2:02.50
1978	Cynthia Woodhead, United States	1:58.53
1982	Annemarie Verstappen, Netherlands	1:59.53
1986	Heike Friedrich, East Germany	1:58.26
1991	Hayley Lewis, Australia	2:00.48
1994	Franziska Van Almsick, Germany	1:56.78
1998	Claudia Poll, Costa Rica	1:58.90
2001	Giaan Rooney, Australia	1:58.57
2003	Alena Popchanka, Belarus	1:58.32
2005	Solenne Figues, France	1:58.60
2007	Laure Manaudou, France	1:55.52

400-METER FREESTYLE

1973	Heather Greenwood, United States	4:20.28
1975	Shirley Babashoff, United States	4:16.87
1978	Tracey Wickham, Australia	4:06.28
1982	Carmela Schmidt, East Germany	4:08.98
1986	Heike Friedrich, East Germany	4:07.45
1991	Janet Evans, United States	4:08.63
1994	Yang Aihua, China	4:09.64
1998	Chen Yan, China	4:06.72
2001	Yana Klochkova, Ukraine	4:07.30
2003	Hannah Stockbauer, Germany	4:06.75
2005	Laure Manaudou, France	4:06.44
2007	Laure Manaudou, France	4:02.61

800-METER FREESTYLE

1973	Novella Calligaris, Italy	8:52.97
1975	Jenny Turrall, Australia	8:44.75
1978	Tracey Wickham, Australia	8:24.94
1982	Kim Linehan, United States	8:27.48
1986	Astrid Strauss, East Germany	8:28.24
1991	Janet Evans, United States	8:24.05
1994	Janet Evans, United States	8:29.85
1998	Brooke Bennett, United States	8:28.71
2001	Hannah Stockbauer, Germany	8:24.66
2003	Hannah Stockbauer, Germany	8:23.66
2005	Kate Ziegler, United States	8:25.31
2007	Kate Ziegler, United States	8:18.52

1,500-METER FREESTYLE

1973-98	Event not held	
2001	Hannah Stockbauer, Germany	16:01.02
2003	Hannah Stockbauer, Germany	16:00.18
2005	Kate Ziegler, United States	16:00.41
2007	Kate Ziegler, United States	15:53.05

50-METER BACKSTROKE

1973-98	Event not held	
2001	Haley Cope, United States	28.51
2003	Nina Zhivanevskaya, Spain	28.48

50-METER BACKSTROKE (CONT'D)

2005	Giann Rooney, Australia	28.63
2007	Leila Vaziri, United States	28.16

100-METER BACKSTROKE

1973	Ulrike Richter, East Germany	1:05.42
1975	Ulrike Richter, East Germany	1:03.30
1978	Linda Jezek, United States	1:02.55
1982	Kristin Otto, East Germany	1:01.30
1986	Betsy Mitchell, United States	1:01.74
1991	Krisztina Egerszegi, Hungary	1:01.78
1994	He Cihong, China	1:00.57
1998	Lea Maurer, United States	1:01.16
2001	Natalie Coughlin, United States	1:00.37
2003	Antje Buschschulte, Germany	1:00.50
2005	Kirsty Coventry, Zimbabwe	1:00.24
2007	Natalie Coughlin, United States	59.44

200-METER BACKSTROKE

1973	Melissa Belote, United States	2:20.52
1975	Birgit Treiber, East Germany	2:15.46
1978	Linda Jezek, United States	2:11.93
1982	Cornelia Sirch, East Germany	2:09.91
1986	Cornelia Sirch, East Germany	2:11.37
1991	Krisztina Egerszegi, Hungary	2:09.15
1994	He Cihong, China	2:07.40
1998	Roxanna Maracineanu, France	2:11.26
2001	Diana Mocanu, Romania	2:09.94
2003	Katy Sexton, Great Britain	2:08.74
2005	Kirsty Coventry, Zimbabwe	2:08.52
2007	Margaret Hoelzer, United States	2:07.16

50-METER BREASTSTROKE

1973-98	Event not held	
2001	Xuejuan Luo, China	30.84
2003	Xuejuan Luo, China	30.67
2005	Jade Edmistone, Australia	30.45
2007	Jessica Hardy, United States	30.63

100-METER BREASTSTROKE

1973	Renate Vogel, East Germany	1:13.74
1975	Hannalore Anke, East Germany	1:12.72
1978	Julia Bogdanova, U.S.S.R.	1:10.31
1982	Ute Geweniger, East Germany	1:09.14
1986	Sylvia Gerasch, East Germany	1:08.11
1991	Linley Frame, Australia	1:08.81
1994	Samantha Riley, Australia	1:07.96
1998	Kristy Kowal, United States	1:08.42
2001	Xuejuan Luo, China	1:07.18
2003	Xuejuan Luo, China	1:06.80
2005	Leisel Jones, Australia	1:06.25
2007	Leisel Jones, Australia	1:05.72

200-METER BREASTSTROKE

1973	Renate Vogel, East Germany	2:40.01
1975	Hannalore Anke, East Germany	2:37.25
1978	Lina Kachushite, U.S.S.R.	2:31.42
1982	Svetlana Varganova, U.S.S.R.	2:28.82
1986	Silke Hoerner, East Germany	2:27.40
1991	Elena Volkova, U.S.S.R.	2:29.53
1994	Samantha Riley, Australia	2:26.87
1998	Agnes Kovacs, Hungary	2:25.45
2001	Agnes Kovacs, Hungary	2:24.90
2003	Amanda Beard, United States	2:22.99
2005	Leisel Jones, Australia	2:21.72
2007	Leisel Jones, Australia	2:21.84

50-METER BUTTERFLY

1973-98	Event not held	
2001	Inge de Bruijn, Netherlands	25.90
2003	Inge de Bruijn, Netherlands	25.84
2005	Danni Miatke, Australia	26.11
2007	Therese Alshammar, Sweden	25.91

100-METER BUTTERFLY

1973	Kornelia Ender, East Germany	1:02.53
1975	Kornelia Ender, East Germany	1:01.24

ALL-TIME WORLD CHAMPIONSHIPS RESULTS — WOMEN (CONT.)

100-METER BUTTERFLY (CONT'D)

1978	Joan Pennington, United States	1:00.20
1982	Mary T. Meagher, United States	59.41
1986	Kornelia Gressler, East Germany	59.51
1991	Qian Hong, China	59.68
1994	Liu Limin, China	58.98
1998	Jenny Thompson, United States	58.46
2001	Petria Thomas, Australia	58.27
2003	Jenny Thompson, United States	57.96
2005	Jessica Schipper, Australia	57.23
2007	Lisbeth Lenton, Australia	57.15

200-METER BUTTERFLY

1973	Rosemarie Kother, East Germany	2:13.76
1975	Rosemarie Kother, East Germany	2:13.82
1978	Tracy Caulkins, United States	2:09.87
1982	Ines Geissler, East Germany	2:08.66
1986	Mary T. Meagher, United States	2:08.41
1991	Summer Sanders, United States	2:09.24
1994	Liu Limin, China	2:07.25
1998	Susie O'Neill, Australia	2:07.93
2001	Petria Thomas, Australia	2:06.73
2003	Otylia Jedrzejczak, Poland	2:07.56
2005	Otylia Jedrzejczak, Poland	2:05.61
2007	Jessicah Schipper, Australia	2:06.39

200-METER INDIVIDUAL MEDLEY

1973	Andrea Huebner, East Germany	2:20.51
1975	Kathy Heddy, United States	2:19.80
1978	Tracy Caulkins, United States	2:14.07
1982	Petra Schneider, East Germany	2:11.79
1986	Kristin Otto, East Germany	2:15.56
1991	Li Lin, China	2:13.40
1994	Lu Bin, China	2:12.34
1998	Wu Yanyan, China	2:10.88
2001	Martha Bowen, United States	2:11.93
2003	Yana Klochkova, Ukraine	2:10.75
2005	Katie Hoff, United States	2:10.41
2007	Katie Hoff, United States	2:10.13

400-METER INDIVIDUAL MEDLEY

1973	Gudrun Wegner, East Germany	4:57.71
1975	Ulrike Tauber, East Germany	4:52.76
1978	Tracy Caulkins, United States	4:40.83
1982	Petra Schneider, East Germany	4:36.10
1986	Kathleen Nord, East Germany	4:43.75
1991	Li Lin, China	4:41.45
1994	Dai Guohong, China	4:39.14
1998	Chen Yan, China	4:36.66
2001	Yana Klochkova, Ukraine	4:36.98
2003	Yana Klochkova, Ukraine	4:36.74
2005	Katie Hoff, United States	4:36.07
2007	Katie Hoff, United States	4:32.89

400-METER MEDLEY RELAY

1973	East Germany (Ulrike Richter, Renate Vogel, Rosemarie Kother, Kornelia Ender)	4:16.84
1975	East Germany (Ulrike Richter, Hannelore Anke, Rosemarie Kother, Kornelia Ender)	4:14.74
1978	United States (Linda Jezek, Tracy Caulkins, Joan Pennington, Cynthia Woodhead)	4:08.21
1982	East Germany (Kristin Otto, Ute Gewinger, Ines Geissler, Birgit Meineke)	4:05.80
1986	East Germany (Kathrin Zimmermann, Sylvia Gerasch, Kornelia Gressler, Kristin Otto)	4:04.82
1991	United States (Janie Wagstaff, Tracey McFarlane, Crissy Ahmann-Leighton, Nicole Haislett)	4:06.51

400-METER MEDLEY RELAY (CONT'D)

1994	China (He Cihong, Dai Guohong, Liu Limin, Lu Bin)	4:01.67
1998	United States (Kristy Kowal, Lea Maurer, Jenny Thompson, Amy Van Dyken)	4:01.93
2001	Australia (Dyana Calub, Sarah Ryan, Petria Thomas, Leisel Jones)	4:01.50
2003	China (Shu Zhan, Xuejuan Luo, Yafei Zhou, Yu Yang)	3:59.89
2005	Australia (Sophie Edington, Leisel Jones, Jessicah Schipper, Lisbeth Lenton)	3:57.47
2007	Australia (Emily Seebohm, Leisel Jones, Jessicah Schipper, Lisbeth Lenton)	3:55.74

400-METER FREESTYLE RELAY

1973	East Germany (Kornelia Ender, Andrea Eife, Andrea Huebner, Sylvia Eichner)	3:52.45
1975	East Germany (Kornelia Ender, Barbara Krause, Claudia Hempel, Ute Bruckner)	3:49.37
1978	United States (Tracy Caulkins, Stephanie Elkins, Jill Sterkel, Cynthia Woodhead)	3:43.43
1982	East Germany (Birgit Meineke, Susanne Link, Kristin Otto, Caren Metschuk)	3:43.97
1986	East Germany (Kristin Otto, Manuela Stellmach, Sabine Schulze, Heike Friedrich)	3:40.57
1991	United States (Nicole Haislett, Julie Cooper, Whitney Hedgepeth, Jenny Thompson)	3:43.26
1994	China (Le Jingyi, Ying Shan, Le Ying, Lu Bin)	3:37.91
1998	United States (Catherine Fox, Lindsey Farella, Melanie Valerio, B.J. Bedford)	3:42.11
2001	Germany (Petra Dallman, Antje Buschschulter, Katrin Meissner, Sandra Volker)	3:39.58
2003	United States (Natalie Coughlin, Lindsay Benko, Rhi Jeffrey, Jenny Thompson)	3:38.09
2005	Australia (Jodie Henry, Alice Mills, Shayne Reese, Lisbeth Lenton)	3:37.32
2007	Australia (Lisbeth Lenton, Melanie Schlanger Shayne Reese, Jodie Henry)	3:35.48

800-METER FREESTYLE RELAY

1973-82	Event not held	
1986	East Germany (Manuela Stellmach, Astrid Strauss, Nadja Bergknecht, Heike Friedrich)	7:59.33
1991	Germany (Kerstin Kielgass, Manuela Stellmach, Dagmar Hase, Stephanie Ortwig)	8:02.56
1994	China (Le Ying, Yang Alhua, Zhou Guabin, Lu Bin)	7:57.96
1998	Germany (Silvia Szalai, Antje Buschschulte, Janina Goetz, Franziska Van Almsick)	8:01.46
2001*	Great Britain (Nicola Jackson, Janine Belton, Karen Legg, Karen Pickering) / United States (Natalie Coughlin, Cristina Teuscher, Julie Hardt, Diana Munz)*	7:56.53
2003	United States (Lindsay Benko, Rachel Komisarz, Rhi Jeffrey, Diana Munz)	7:55.70
2005	United States (Natalie Coughlin, Katie Hoff, Whitney Myers, Kaitlin Sandeno)	7:53.70
2007	United States (Natalie Coughlin, Dana Vollmer, Lacey Nymeter, Katie Hoff)	7:.:50.09

*Because of timing malfunctions and an overturned disqualification of the United States, gold medals were awarded to Great Britain and the U.S.

TRACK and FIELD

Jamaican Asafa Powell tied his own 100-meter world record with a 9.77-second dash in June 2006.

AP PHOTO/SCOTT HEPPELL

Track and Field had plenty of highs and lows in 2006. There were many inspiring efforts and record-setting performances, but steroids scandals featuring some of the sport's biggest names also made news.

Good news first: Jamaican sprinter Asafa Powell and U.S. middle-distance runner Sanya Richards were named World Athletes of the Year at the 2006 World Athletics Gala in November. Powell tied the 100-meter dash world record (9.77 seconds) at a June meet in England. Richards won U.S. indoor and outdoor titles in the 400 meters.

Meseret Defar of Ethiopia and Liu Xiang of China were each given the Performance of the Year award at the event. Defar broke the 5,000-meter world record, and Liu set the 110-meter world record. Overall, it was a historic year in 110-meter hurdles. For the first time ever, three men ran the race in under 13 seconds.

Defar and Liu's records were only two of many marks that were set during the year (world records, pages 291-293). Women's pole vaulter Yelena Isinbayeva of Russia broke her own indoor record and was also named Laureus World Sportswoman of the Year. Australian Nathan Deakes paced his way to a new world record in the men's 50-kilometer race walk. Ethiopian Tirunesh Dibaba set a new indoor record in the women's 5,000 meters.

Closer to home, it was a big year for Bernard Lagat. A two-time Olympic medalist for Kenya, Lagat became a U.S. citizen in 2004. He captured his first U.S. titles in 2006, winning the 1,500 and 5,000 meters at the USA Outdoor Track and Field Championships.

Sadly, steroids scandals also made headlines in 2006. Two-time U.S. Olympic gold medalist Justin Gatlin tested positive for synthetic testosterone in April. Gatlin said he didn't know how the drug got into his body, but the U.S. Anti-Doping Agency suspended him for eight years.

Trevor Graham coaches Gatlin, as well as superstar sprinters Marion Jones and Tim Montgomery. Graham is in legal trouble over charges that he lied to federal agents in the high-profile steroids investigation.

Speaking of Jones, 2006 was a tough year for America's most famous track star. Claims that she also used steroids turned up in the book *Game of Shadows*. The book made headlines for detailed claims that baseball superstar Barry Bonds used steroids. Other track stars named in the book include Montgomery, sprinter Kelli White, and middle-distance runner Regina Jacobs.

Jones has maintained her innocence, saying that she has never failed a drug test. She is correct, but that almost changed. Jones tested positive for the drug EPO at the 2006 USA Outdoor Track & Field Championships in June. But a backup sample was negative, so she was cleared of the charges. Despite the fact that she won the 100 meters for the

fifth time at the event, her image took another bad blow.

After all the records and scandals, there was one last bit of news. The track world said good-bye to Olympic gold medalist (1,500 meters) and world record holder (1,000 meters) Noah Ngeny of Kenya. Ngeny announced his retirement in November.

Michael Johnson holds world records in the 200 and 400 meter.

2006 USA OUTDOOR TRACK AND FIELD CHAMPIONSHIPS

JUNE 21-25, 2006,
INDIANAPOLIS, INDIANA

Tyson Gay

Men's 100 Meters

ATHLETE	TEAM	TIME
Tyson Gay	Adidas	10.07
Shawn Crawford	Nike	10.26
Jordan Vaden	Nike	10.27

Women's 100 Meters

ATHLETE	TEAM	TIME
Marion Jones	unattached	11.10
Lauryn Williams	Nike	11.17
Torri Edwards	Nike	11.17

Men's 200 Meters

ATHLETE	TEAM	TIME
Wallace Spearmon	Nike	19.90
Jordan Vaden	Nike	19.98
Rodney Martin	Nike	20.14

Women's 200 Meters

ATHLETE	TEAM	TIME
Rachelle Boone-Smith	Nike	22.31
Shalonda Solomon	South Carolina	22.47
LaTasha Jenkins	Nike	22.66

Men's 400 Meters

ATHLETE	TEAM	TIME
Andrew Rock	Adidas	44.45
LaShawn Merritt	Nike	44.50
David Neville	Indiana	44.75

Women's 400 Meters

ATHLETE	TEAM	TIME
Sanya Richards	Nike	49.27
De'Hashia Trotter	Adidas	50.40
Monique Henderson	Reebok	50.71

Men's 800 Meters

ATHLETE	TEAM	TIME
Khadevis Robinson	Nike	1:44.13
Nicholas Symmonds	unattached	1:45.83
Jebreh Harris	Reebok	1:45.91

Women's 800 Meters

ATHLETE	TEAM	TIME
Hazel Clark	Nike	1:59.94
Alice Schmidt	Adidas	2:00.00
Frances Santin	SMTC	2:01.15

Men's 1,500 Meters

ATHLETE	TEAM	TIME
Bernard Lagat	Nike	3:39.29
Gabriel Jennings	unattached	3:39.42
Leonel Manzano	Texas	3:39.49

Women's 1,500 Meters

ATHLETE	TEAM	TIME
Trenier Clement	Nike	4:10.44
Lindsey Gallo	Reebok	4:10.72
Sarah Schwald	Nike	4:11.60

Men's 5,000 Meters

ATHLETE	TEAM	TIME
Bernard Lagat	Nike	13:14.32
Matt Tegenkamp	Nike	13:15.00
Dathan Ritzenhein	Nike	13:16.61

Women's 5,000 Meters

ATHLETE	TEAM	TIME
Lauren Fleshman	Nike	15:12.37
Kara Goucher	Nike	15:14.13
Blake Russell	Reebok	15:19.07

TRACK and FIELD

Men's 10,000 Meters

ATHLETE	TEAM	TIME
Jorge Torres	Reebok	28:14.43
Meb Keflezighi	Nike	28:18.74
Daniel Browne	Nike	28:19.32

Women's 10,000 Meters

ATHLETE	TEAM	TIME
Amy Rudolph	Adidas	32:25.56
Sara Slattery	Adidas	32:29.97
Samia Akbar	Reebok	32:41.84

Men's 110-Meter Hurdles

ATHLETE	TEAM	TIME
Dominique Arnold	Nike	13.10
Terrence Trammell	Mizuno	13.14
Ryan Wilson	unattached	13.22

Women's 100-Meter Hurdles

ATHLETE	TEAM	TIME
Virginia Powell	Nike	12.63
Damu Cherry	Nike	12.64
Michelle Perry	Nike	12.67

Virginia Powell

Men's 400-Meter Hurdles

ATHLETE	TEAM	TIME
Kerron Clement	Nike	47.39
Bershawn Jackson	Nike	47.48
James Carter	Nike	48.44

Women's 400-Meter Hurdles

ATHLETE	TEAM	TIME
Lashinda Demus	Nike	53.07
Sheena Johnson	Nike	53.90
Shauna Smith	Nike	54.76

Men's 3,000-Meter Steeplechase

ATHLETE	TEAM	TIME
Daniel Lincoln	Nike	8:22.78
Steve Slattery	Nike	8:25.54
Daniel Huling	unattached	8:27.41

Women's 3,000-Meter Steeplechase

ATHLETE	TEAM	TIME
Lisa Galaviz	Nike	9:57.58
Kristin Anderson	unattached	9:57.98
Delilah DiCrescenzo	Westchester TC	10:03.31

Men's 20,000-Meter Race Walk

ATHLETE	TEAM	TIME
Kevin Eastler	U.S. Air Force	1:25:09.67
John Nunn	U.S. Navy	1:27:16.83
Tim Seaman	New York AC	1:29:56.84

Women's 20,000-Meter Race Walk

ATHLETE	TEAM	TIME
Joanne Dow	Adidas	1:35:20.76
Teresa Vaill	Walk Usa	1:39:24.07
Sam Cohen	Parkside AC	1:40:29.46

Men's High Jump

ATHLETE	TEAM	HEIGHT
Tora Harris	Shore AC	2.33
Keith Moffatt	Morehouse	2.30
Andra Manson	Texas	2.24

Jennifer Stuczynski

Women's High Jump

ATHLETE	TEAM	HEIGHT
Chaunte Howard	Nike	2.01
Amy Acuff	Asics	1.92
Destinee Hooker	unattached	1.86

Men's Pole Vault

ATHLETE	TEAM	HEIGHT
Russ Buller	Asics	5.80
Toby Stevenson	Nike	5.80
Thomas Skipper	Oregon	5.60

Women's Pole Vault

ATHLETE	TEAM	HEIGHT
Jennifer Stuczynski	Adidas	4.55
Jillian Schwartz	Nike	4.50
Becky Holliday	New Balance	4.45

Men's Long Jump

ATHLETE	TEAM	DISTANCE
Dwight Phillips	Nike	8.08
Miguel Pate	Nike	7.96
Joe Allen	unattached	7.83

Women's Long Jump

ATHLETE	TEAM	DISTANCE
Rose Richmond	Nike	6.93
Tianna Madison	Nike	6.77
Akiba McKinney	Nike	6.63

Men's Triple Jump

ATHLETE	TEAM	DISTANCE
Walter Davis	Nike	17.71
Kenta Bell	Mizuno	17.19
Aarik Wilson	unattached	16.91

Note: Height and distance measured in meters.

Women's Triple Jump

ATHLETE	TEAM	DISTANCE
Tiombe Hurd	Nike	13.86
Yvette Lewis	Hampton	13.42
Simidele Adeagbo	Team XO	13.25

Jeffrey Chakouian

Men's Shot Put

ATHLETE	TEAM	DISTANCE
Jeffrey Chakouian	unattached	20.68
Russ Winger	Idaho	19.34
Jonathan Kalnas	unattached	19.14

Women's Shot Put

ATHLETE	TEAM	DISTANCE
Janae Strickland	unattached	16.59
Abigail Ruston	unattached	16.32
Melinda Lincoln	unattached	15.98

Men's Discus

ATHLETE	TEAM	DISTANCE
Carl Brown	Nike	60.07
Reedus Thurmond	unattached	57.04
William Conwell	unattached	55.23

Women's Discus

ATHLETE	TEAM	DISTANCE
Rachel Jansen	Northern Iowa	52.96
Rachel Longfors	Florida	52.60
Melissa Bickett	unattached	52.59

Men's Hammer Throw

ATHLETE	TEAM	DISTANCE
Cory Martin	unattached	69.97
Brian Richotte	Radford	65.42
Adam Midles	USC	64.57

Women's Hammer Throw

ATHLETE	TEAM	DISTANCE
Melissa Myerscough	unattached	62.77
Keturah Lofton	unattached	62.06
April Burton	unattached	61.39

Men's Decathlon

ATHLETE	TEAM	POINTS
Tom Pappas	Nike	8,319
Ryan Harlan	unattached	7,872
Robert Arnold	Arizona	7,827

Men's Javelin

ATHLETE	TEAM	DISTANCE
Barry Krammes	unattached	73.73
Justin St. Clair	unattached	72.66
Mike Kennedy	unattached	70.40

Women's Javelin

ATHLETE	TEAM	DISTANCE
Samantha Ford	Nwn. St. La.	49.23
Lauren Sexton	Oregon Throw	48.97
Tiffany Zahn	unattached	48.46

Women's Heptathlon

ATHLETE	TEAM	POINTS
GiGi Johnson	unattached	6,183
Hyleas Fountain	Nike	6,148
Fiona Asigbee	unattached	6,030

*Men's 50km Walk

ATHLETE	TEAM	TIME
Kevin Eastler	U.S. Air Force	4:05:44
Philip Dunn	New Balance	4:09:54
John Nunn	U.S. Army	4:14:16

*Women's 50km Walk

ATHLETE	TEAM	TIME
Heidi Hauch	unattached	5:42:55
Karen Karavanic	Western Women Go The Distance	6:21:01
Dora Choi	Western Women Go The Distance	6:33:57

* Held January 28, 2007 in Chula Vista, California

TRACK and FIELD

LEGENDS

■ **Joan Samuelson, marathoner,** b. May 16, 1957, Cape Elizabeth, Maine. Samuelson set the U.S. women's marathon record four times and won the Boston marathon twice, to name just a few of her accomplishments. Most impressive of all, though, may have been her 1984 Olympic marathon gold medal, which she won just 17 days after knee surgery. Samuelson was also the 1984 U.S. women's marathon champion. In 1985, she received the AAU's James E. Sullivan Award, recognizing her as the nation's finest amateur athlete.

■ **Jack Davis, hurdler,** b. September 11, 1930, Amarillo, Texas. A silver medalist in the 110-meter hurdles at both the 1952 and 1956 Olympic games, Davis spent his undergraduate years at the University of Southern California. Davis dominated during his days at USC, winning the NCAA 120-yard hurdle championship in three separate years and coming in first in the 220-yard hurdles in 1953. In an extraordinary run, Davis was undefeated in the 110-meter hurdles and the 120-yard hurdles for two straight years (1953 and 1954).

In 1984, Samuelson became the first American woman to win a gold medal in the Olympic marathon.

AP PHOTO/FILE

■ **Mike Powell, long jumper,** b. October 10, 1963, Philadelphia, Pennsylvania. Powell's record setting jump (8.95 meters/29 feet, 4.5 inches) at the 1991 IAAF World Outdoor Championships in Tokyo set a mark that no long jumper has come close to matching. That world-record performance also marked the first time in ten years that Powell's great rival Carl Lewis did not win the event. Powell was the world long jump champion in 1991 and 1993. He also took home the Olympic silver medal in the long jump twice, in 1988 and 1992, and won the U.S. championship six times.

2007 U.S. INDOOR TRACK AND FIELD CHAMPIONSHIPS

JANUARY 27, 2007
BOSTON, MASSACHUSETTS

Women's 60 Meters

ATHLETE	TEAM	TIME
Hasani Roseby	Nike	7.16
Carmelita Jeter	South Bay Tr	7.17
Marshevet Hooker	Adidas	7.22

Men's 60 Meters

ATHLETE	TEAM	TIME
Dabryan Blanton	Nike	6.56
Marcus Brunson	Nike	6.58
Kyle Farmer	Norfolk Real	6.62

Women's 400 Meters

ATHLETE	TEAM	TIME
De'Hashia Trotter	Adidas	51.95
Monica Hargrove	unattached	52.26
Mary Wineberg	Nike	52.31

Men's 400 Meters

ATHLETE	TEAM	TIME
Greg Nixon	unattached	46.75
Fernada Blakely	Asics	46.97
Darold Williamson	Nike	47.21

Women's 800 Meters

ATHLETE	TEAM	TIME
Nikeya Green	Reebok	2:02.68
Christian Wurth	Nike	2:03.70
Mishael Berger	unattached	2:04.58

Men's 800 Meters

ATHLETE	TEAM	TIME
Nicholas Symmonds	Oregon TC E1	1:48.73
Samuel Burley	Asics	1:49.42
Tim Ramirez	unattached	1:49.59

Women's 1 Mile Run

ATHLETE	TEAM	TIME
Shayne Culpepper	Nike	4:34.42
Sarah Schwald	Nike	4:36.12
Christian Wurth	Nike	4:36.78

Men's 1 Mile Run

ATHLETE	TEAM	TIME
Alan Webb	Nike	4:01.07
Rob Meyers	Reebok	4:01.78
Gabriel Jennings	unattached	4:01.93

Women's 3,000 Meters

ATHLETE	TEAM	TIME
Shalane Flanagan	Nike	8:56.74
Lisa Galaviz	Nike	9:10.75
Emily Field	unattached	9:11.32

Men's 3,000 Meters

ATHLETE	TEAM	TIME
Matt Tegenkamp	Nike	7:46.08
Jonathon Riley	Nike	7:49.73
Sean Graham	Oregon TC E1	7:52.31

Women's 60-Meter Hurdles

ATHLETE	TEAM	TIME
Lolo Jones	unattached	7.88
Danielle Carruthers	Nike	7.92
Nichole Denby	Nike	7.93

Men's 60-Meter Hurdles

ATHLETE	TEAM	TIME
Ron Bramlett	unattached	7.47
David Payne	unattached	7.51
David Oliver	Nike	7.57

Women's 3,000-Meter Race Walk

ATHLETE	TEAM	TIME
Sam Cohen	Parkside Ath	13:51.29
Lauren Forgues	unattached	13:55.90
Loretta Schuellein	Walk USA	14:14.95

Men's 5,000-Meter Race Walk

ATHLETE	TEAM	TIME
Tim Seaman	NYAC	19:24.38
Kevin Eastler	U.S. Air Force	19:28.63
Matthew Boyles	Miami V./Asics	19:47.82

Women's High Jump

ATHLETE	TEAM	HEIGHT
Amy Acuff	Asics	1.92
Gwen Wentland	Nike	1.86
Sheena Gordon	unattached	1.86

Men's High Jump

ATHLETE	TEAM	HEIGHT
Tora Harris	Shore AC/Asics	2.29
Jesse Williams	Nike	2.29
Jamie Nieto	Nike	2.23

Women's Pole Vault

ATHLETE	TEAM	HEIGHT
Jennifer Stuczynski	Adidas	4.60
Lacy Janson	Nike	4.60
Mary Sauer	Asics	4.50

Men's Pole Vault

ATHLETE	TEAM	HEIGHT
Jeff Hartwig	Nike	5.80
Russ Buller	Asics	5.60
Darren Niedermeyer	unattached	5.60

Women's Long Jump

ATHLETE	TEAM	DISTANCE
Akiba McKinney	Nike	6.55
Shameka Marshall	unattached	6.38
Brianna Glenn	unattached	6.35

Men's Long Jump

ATHLETE	TEAM	DISTANCE
Trevell Quinley	unattached	8.06
Brian Johnson	Nike	8.03
Aarik Wilson	Nike	8.00

Women's Triple Jump

ATHLETE	TEAM	DISTANCE
Shani Marks	unattached	13.56
Tiombe Hurd	Nike	13.39
Brandy Depland	unattached	13.17

Men's Triple Jump

ATHLETE	TEAM	DISTANCE
Aarik Wilson	Nike	17.28
Rafeeq Curry	unattached	16.54
Marc Kellman	unattached	16.05

Women's Shot Put

ATHLETE	TEAM	DISTANCE
Jillian Camarena	NYAC	18.46
Elizabeth Wanless	NYAC	17.80
Robyn Jarocki	unattached	16.90

Men's Shot Put

ATHLETE	TEAM	DISTANCE
Christian Cantwell	Nike	21.72
Reese Hoffa	NYAC	21.21
Dan Taylor	Nike	20.32

Women's Weight Throw

ATHLETE	TEAM	DISTANCE
Amber Campbell	Mjolnir Thro	24.54
Erin Gilreath	NYAC	22.40
Kristal Yush	unattached	22.15

Men's Weight Throw

ATHLETE	TEAM	DISTANCE
A.G. Kruger	Nike	24.05
Thomas Freeman	NYAC	23.10
Michael Mai	U.S. Army	22.99

*Won in jump-off.

Note: height and distance measured in meters.

TODAY'S STARS

■ **Asafa Powell, sprinter,** b. November 23, 1982, Kingston, Jamaica. Powell's fifth place finish in the 100-meter dash at the 2004 Olympics came as a disappointment after his series of sub-10-second finishes leading up to the Games had inspired many to consider him the favorite to win gold. Powell was vindicated on June 14, 2005, when he set a new world record (9.77 seconds) at a meet in Athens. To date, Powell has run the 100-meter dash in under ten seconds 25 times. Only Frankie Fredericks, Ato Boldon, and Maurice Greene have recorded more sub-10-second finishes.

■ **Meserat Defar, distance runner,** b. November 19, 1983, Addis Ababa, Ethiopia. Known for a heated rivalry with fellow Ethiopian distance runner Tirunesh Dibaba, Defar asserted herself as a world-class athlete in her own right. Defar won the 5,000 meter gold medal at the 2004 Summer Olympics in Athens and a silver medal in the 5,000 at the 2005 World Championships, coming in second to Dibaba. On June 3, 2006, Defar set a new world record in the women's 5,000 meters, clocking a time of 14:24:53.

Sprinter Asafa Powell was named the IAAF 2006 Male World Athlete of the Year.

AP PHOTO/MARKUS SCHREIBER

■ **Chaunte Howard, high jumper,** b. January 12, 1984, Templeton, California. Templeton is one of the world's premiere high jumpers. In 2006, she took first place at both the Indoor and Outdoor U.S. Track and Field Championships. Her 2.01 meter clearance at the 2006 U.S. Outdoor Championships was a new meet record. She was the runner up at the World, U.S., and NCAA Outdoor Championships in 2005. In 2004, Howard became the first Georgia Tech women's track and field athlete to qualify for the Olympics.

2007 WORLD CROSS COUNTRY CHAMPIONSHIPS

MARCH 24, 2007
MOMBASA, KENYA

Long Race — Men

ATHLETE	COUNTRY	TIME
Zersenay Tadese	Eritrea	35:50
Moses Mosop	Kenya	36:13
Bernard Kiprop Kipyego	Kenya	36:37

Long Race — Women

ATHLETE	TEAM	TIME
Lornah Kiplagat	Netherlands	26:23
Tirunesh Dibaba	Ethiopia	26:47
Meselech Melkamu	Ethiopia	26:48

DID YOU KNOW?

American Dick Fosbury revolutionized the high jump with his head-first, backwards jumping method. Nicknamed the "Fosbury flop," this jumping style helped him win the gold medal at the 1968 Olympics and was soon adopted by all high jumpers.

2006–07 MARATHONS

Chicago Marathon
OCTOBER 22, 2006

MEN	COUNTRY	TIME
Robert Cheruiyot	Kenya	02:07:35
Daniel Njenga	Kenya	02:07:40
Jimmy Muindi	Kenya	02:07:51

WOMEN	COUNTRY	TIME
Berhane Adere	Ethiopia	2:20:42
Galina Bogomolova	Russia	2:20:47
Benita Johnson	Australia	2:22:36

New York City Marathon
NOVEMBER 5, 2006

MEN	COUNTRY	TIME
M. Gomes dos Santos	Brazil	2:09:58
Stephen Kiogora	Kenya	2:10:06
Paul Tergat	Kenya	2:10:10

WOMEN	COUNTRY	TIME
Jelena Prokopcuka	Latvia	2:25:05
Tatiana Hladyr	Ukraine	2:26:05
Catherine Ndereba	Kenya	2:26:58

Boston Marathon
APRIL 16, 2007

MEN	COUNTRY	TIME
Robert Cheruiyot	Kenya	2:14:13
James Kwambai	Kenya	2:14:33
Stephen Kiogora	Kenya	2:14:47

WOMEN	COUNTRY	TIME
Lidiya, Grigoryeva	Russia	2:29:18
Jelena Prokopcuka	Latvia	2:29:58
Madai Perez	Mexico	2:30:16

London Marathon
APRIL 22, 2007

MEN	COUNTRY	TIME
Martin Lel	Kenya	2:07:41
Abderrahim Goumri	Morocco	2:07:44
Felix Limo	Kenya	2:07:44

WOMEN	COUNTRY	TIME
Chunxio Zhou	China	2:20:38
Gete Wani	Ethiopia	2:21:45
Constantina Tomescu-Dita	Romania	2:23:55

WORLD RECORDS — MEN

EVENT	MARK	RECORD HOLDER	DATE	SITE
100 Meters	9.77	Asafa Powell, Jamaica	6-14-05	Athens, Greece
		Justin Gatlin, United States*	5-12-06	Doha, Qatar
		Asafa Powell, Jamaica	6-11-06	Gateshead, England
		Asafa Powell, Jamaica	8-18-06	Zurich, Switzerland
200 Meters	19.32	Michael Johnson, United States	8-1-96	Atlanta, Georgia
400 Meters	43.18	Michael Johnson, United States	8-26-99	Seville, Spain
800 Meters	1:41.11	Wilson Kipketer, Denmark	8-24-97	Cologne, Germany
1,000 Meters	2:11.96	Noah Ngeny, Kenya	9-5-99	Rieti, Italy
1,500 Meters	3:26.00	Hicham El Guerrouj, Morocco	7-14-98	Rome, Italy
Mile	3:43.13	Hicham El Guerrouj, Morocco	7-7-99	Rome, Italy
2,000 Meters	4:44.79	Hicham El Guerrouj, Morocco	9-7-99	Berlin, Germany
3,000 Meters	7:20.67	Daniel Komen, Kenya	9-1-96	Rieti, Italy
Steeplechase	7:53.63	Saif Saaeed Shaheen, Qatar	9-3-04	Brussels, Belgium
5,000 Meters	12:37.35	Kenenisa Bekele, Ethiopia	5-31-04	Hengelo, Netherlands
10,000 Meters	26:17.53	Kenenisa Bekele, Ethiopia	8-26-05	Brussels, Belgium
20,000 Meters	56:55.6	Arturo Barrios, Mexico	3-30-91	La Flache, France
Hour	21,101 meters	Arturo Barrios, Mexico	3-30-91	La Flache, France
25,000 Meters	1:13:55.8	Toshihiko Seko, Japan	3-22-81	Christchurch, New Zealand
30,000 Meters	1:29:18.8	Toshihiko Seko, Japan	3-22-81	Christchurch, New Zealand
Marathon	2:04:55.0	Paul Tergat, Kenya	9-28-03	Berlin, Germany
110-Meter Hurdles	12.88	Xiang Liu, China	7-11-06	Lausanne, Switzerland
400-Meter Hurdles	46.78	Kevin Young, United States	8-6-92	Barcelona, Spain
20-Kilometer Walk	1:17:21.0	Jefferson Perez, Ecuador	8-23-03	Paris, France
30-Kilometer Walk	2:01:44.1	Maurizio Damilano, Italy	10-3-92	Cuneo, Italy
50-Kilometer Walk	3:36:03	Robert Korzeniowski, Poland	8-27-03	Paris, France
4x100-Meter Relay	37.40*	United States (Mike Marsh, Leroy Burrell, Dennis Mitchell, Carl Lewis)	8-8-92	Barcelona, Spain
		United States (Jon Drummond, Andre Cason, Dennis Mitchell, Leroy Burrell)	8-21-93	Stuttgart, Germany

*Pending expulsion

DID YOU KNOW?

The Olympic marathon event commemorates the Greek soldier Pheidippides, who, as the legend goes, ran the roughly 26-mile distance from a battlefield near the town of Marathon to the Greek capital of Athens. Immediately after delivering the message "victory," he reportedly collapsed and died on the spot.

WORLD RECORDS — MEN (cont.)

EVENT	MARK	RECORD HOLDER	DATE	SITE
4x200-Meter Relay	1:18.68	Santa Monica TC (Mike Marsh, Leroy Burrell, Floyd Heard, Carl Lewis)	4-17-94	Walnut, California
4x400-Meter Relay	2:54.20	United States (Jerome Young, Antonio Pettigrew, Tyree Washington, Michael Johnson)	7-22-98	New York, New York
4x800-Meter Relay	7:03.89	Great Britain (Peter Elliott, Garry Cook, Steve Cram, Sebastian Coe)	8-30-82	London, England
4x1,500-Meter Relay	14:38.8	West Germany (Thomas Wessinghage, Harald Hudak, Michael Lederer, Karl Fleschen)	8-17-77	Cologne, Germany
High Jump	2.45 meters	Javier Sotomayor, Cuba	7-27-93	Salamanca, Spain
Pole Vault	6.14 meters	Sergei Bubka, Ukraine	7-31-94	Sestriere, Italy
Long Jump	8.95 meters	Mike Powell, United States	8-30-91	Tokyo, Japan
Triple Jump	18.29 meters	Jonathan Edwards, Great Britain	8-7-95	Goteborg, Sweden
Shot Put	23.12 meters	Randy Barnes, United States	5-20-90	Westwood, California
Discus Throw	74.08 meters	Jurgen Schult, East Germany	6-6-86	Neubrandenburg, Germany
Hammer Throw	86.74 meters	Yuri Syedikh, U.S.S.R.	8-30-86	Stuttgart, Germany
Javelin Throw	98.48 meters	Jan Zelezny, Czech Republic	5-25-96	Jena, Germany
Decathlon	9,026 points	Roman Sebrle, Czech Republic	5-27-01	Gotzis, Austria

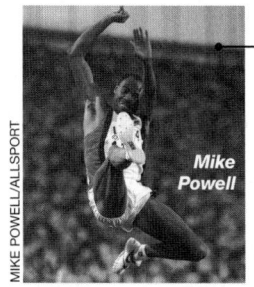

Mike Powell

MIKE POWELL/ALLSPORT

DID YOU KNOW?

In 1974, Herb Washington—the world-record holder in the 50- and 60-yard dashes—signed with the Oakland Athletics. He stole 30 bases in two seasons strictly as a pinch-runner.

WORLD RECORDS — WOMEN

EVENT	MARK	RECORD HOLDER	DATE	SITE
100 Meters	10.49	Florence Griffith Joyner, United States	7-16-88	Indianapolis, Indiana
200 Meters	21.34	Florence Griffith Joyner, United States	9-29-88	Seoul, Korea
400 Meters	47.60	Marita Koch, East Germany	10-6-85	Canberra, Australia
800 Meters	1:53.28	Jarmila Kratochvílová, Czechoslovakia	7-26-83	Munich, Germany
1,000 Meters	2:28.98	Svetlana Masterkova, Russia	8-23-96	Brussels, Belgium
1,500 Meters	3:50.46	Qu Yunxia, China	9-11-93	Beijing, China
Mile	4:12.56	Svetlana Masterkova, Russia	8-14-96	Zurich, Switzerland
2,000 Meters	5:25.36	Sonia O'Sullivan, Ireland	7-8-94	Edinburgh, Scotland
3,000 Meters	8:06.11	Wang Junxia, China	9-13-93	Beijing, China
Steeplechase	9:01.59	Gulnara Samitova, Russia	4-7-04	Iraklio, Greece
5,000 Meters	14:24.53	Meseret Defar, Ethiopia	6-3-06	Randalls Island, New York
10,000 Meters	29:31.78	Wang Junxia, China	9-8-93	Beijing, China
Hour	18,340 meters	Tegla Loroupe, Kenya	8-8-98	Borgholzhausen, Germany
20,000 Meters	1:05:26.6	Tegla Loroupe, Kenya	9-3-00	Borgholzhausen, Germany
25,000 Meters	1:27:05.9	Tegla Loroupe, Kenya	9-21-02	Mengerskirchen, Germany
30,000 Meters	1:45:50.0	Tegla Loroupe, Kenya	6-6-03	Warstein, Germany
Marathon	2:15:25.0	Paula Radclifffe, Great Britain	4-13-03	London, England
100-Meter Hurdles	12.21	Yordanka Donkova, Bulgaria	8-20-88	Stara Zgora, Bulgaria
400-Meter Hurdles	52.34	Yuliya Pechenkina, Russia	8-8-03	Tula, Russia
5-Kilometer Walk	20:02.60	Gillian O'Sullivan, Ireland	7-13-02	Dublin, Ireland
10-Kilometer Walk	41:56.23	Nadezhda Ryashkina, Russia	7-24-90	Seattle, Washington
4x100-Meter Relay	41.37	East Germany (Silke Gladisch, Sabine Reiger, Ingrid Auerswald, Marlies Gohr)	10-6-85	Canberra, Australia

WORLD RECORDS — WOMEN (cont.)

EVENT	MARK	RECORD HOLDER	DATE	SITE
4x200-Meter Relay	1:27.46	United States (LaTasha Jenkins, LaTasha Colander-Richardson, Nanceen Perry, Marion Jones)	4-29-00	Philadelphia, Pennsylvania
4x400-Meter Relay	3:15.17	U.S.S.R. (Tatyana Ledovskaya, Olga Nazarova, Maria Pinigina, Olga Bryzgina)	10-1-88	Seoul, Korea
4x800-Meter Relay	7:50.17	U.S.S.R. (Nadezhda Olizarenko, Lyubov Gurina, Lyudmila Borisova, Irina Podyalovskaya)	8-5-84	Moscow, Russia
High Jump	2.09 meters	Stefka Kostadinova, Bulgaria	8-30-87	Rome, Italy
Pole Vault	5.01 meters	Yelena Isinbayeva, Russia	8-12-05	Helsinki, Finland
Long Jump	7.52 meters	Galina Chistyakova, U.S.S.R.	6-11-88	Leningrad, Russia
Triple Jump	15.50 meters	Inessa Kravets, Ukraine	8-10-95	Goteborg, Sweden
Shot Put	22.63 meters	Natalya Lisovskaya, U.S.S.R.	6-7-87	Moscow, Russia
Discus Throw	76.80 meters	Gabriele Reinsch, East Germany	7-9-88	Neubrandenburg, Germany
Hammer Throw	77.80 meters	Tatyana Lysenko, Russia	8-15-06	Tallinn, Estonia
Javelin Throw	71.70 meters	Osleidys Menéndez, Cuba	8-14-05	Helsinki, Finland
Heptathlon	7,291 points	Jackie Joyner-Kersee, United States	9-23-88/9-24-88	Seoul, Korea

Yelena Isinbayeva, Russia

TRIVIA CHALLENGE

Who was the first American woman to win three track and field gold medals in the same Olympics?

Wilma Rudolph at the 1960 Games.

TRIVIA CHALLENGE

1 In 1960, Ethiopian distance runner Abebe Bikila won the gold medal in the Olympic marathon. What was notable about his victory?
a. He was 40 years old.
b. He ran the race in bare feet.
c. He never raced again.

2 How old was sprinter Florence Griffith-Joyner when she set the 100-meter world record at the 1988 U.S. Olympic trials with a run of 10.49 seconds?
a. 28
b. 23
c. 18

3 How many attempts do competitors in the high jump get to clear the bar before being disqualified?
a. 3
b. 2
c. 1

Florence Griffith Joyner

4 The Czechoslovakian distance runner Emil Zapotek set the world record in the 10,000-meter run how many different times during his career?
a. One
b. Five
c. Nine

5 How many laps are in a 5,000-meter race?
a. 10
b. 12½
c. 15

6 At just under two pounds, which is the lightest?
a. Shot put
b. Discus
c. Javelin

7 In track and field, results achieved on windy days sometimes do not count towards world records.
a. True
b. False

Trivia Challenge: 1. b; 2. a; 3. a; 4. b; 5. b; 6. c; 7. a.

SUMMER OLYMPICS

The XXIX Summer Olympics will be held in Beijing, China, from August 8–24, 2008. An estimated 10,500 athletes from 203 countries are expected to participate in 28 sports. Two new disciplines will be on the schedule: BMX racing and open-water swimming. One men's and one women's BMX race will replace two track cycling events. The women's and men's open-water race will be 10 kilometers (6.2 miles) long. This will be the longest swimming event at the Games.

The 2008 Games will be the last to include baseball and softball. Both sports will be out of the Olympics after Beijing because there are not enough countries participating in them worldwide.

The Chinese government planned to spend $40 billion building venues and improving transportation systems in Beijing, making the 2008 Games the most expensive ever. The host country hopes to get some of that money back in gold medals. China won 32 golds at the 2004 Games, second only to the United States team's 35. Once again, swimmer Michael Phelps, who swam away with eight medals (including six golds) in 2004, will lead the U.S. squad.

The design of Beijing's new Olympic Stadium has earned it the nickname "the Bird's Nest."

GUANG NIU/GETTY IMAGES

BEIJING 2008 SUMMER OLYMPICS SCHEDULE

AUGUST 6
- SOCCER

AUGUST 7
- SOCCER

AUGUST 8
- OPENING CEREMONIES

AUGUST 9
- ROWING
- BADMINTON
- BASKETBALL
- BOXING
- CYCLING
  Road – Finals
- EQUESTRIAN
  Eventing
- FENCING
  Finals
- SOCCER
- GYMNASTICS
  Artistic

- WEIGHTLIFTING
  Finals
- HANDBALL
- JUDO
  Finals
- SWIMMING
  Finals
- WATER POLO
- SHOOTING
  Finals
- ARCHERY
- SAILING
- VOLLEYBALL
- VOLLEYBALL
  Beach

AUGUST 10
- ROWING
- BADMINTON
- BASKETBALL
- BOXING

- CYCLING
  Road – Finals
- EQUESTRIAN
  Eventing
- FENCING
  Finals
- SOCCER
- GYMNASTICS
  Artistic
- WEIGHTLIFTING
  Finals
- HANDBALL
- HOCKEY
- JUDO
  Finals
- SWIMMING
  Finals
- WATER POLO
- TENNIS
- SHOOTING
  Finals

■ **ARCHERY**
Finals

■ **SAILING**

■ **VOLLEYBALL**

■ **VOLLEYBALL**
Beach

AUGUST 11

■ **ROWING**

■ **BADMINTON**

■ **BASKETBALL**

■ **BOXING**

■ **CANOE/KAYAK**
Slalom

■ **EQUESTRIAN**
Eventing

■ **FENCING**
Finals

■ **SOCCER**

■ **GYMNASTICS**
Artistic – Finals

■ **WEIGHTLIFTING**
Finals

■ **HANDBALL**

■ **HOCKEY**

■ **JUDO**
Finals

■ **SWIMMING**
Finals

■ **WATER POLO**

■ **TENNIS**

■ **SHOOTING**
Finals

■ **ARCHERY**
Finals

■ **SAILING**

■ **VOLLEYBALL**

■ **VOLLEYBALL**
Beach

AUGUST 12

■ **ROWING**

■ **BADMINTON**

■ **BASKETBALL**

■ **BOXING**

■ **CANOE/KAYAK**
Slalom - Finals

■ **EQUESTRIAN**
Eventing - Finals

■ **FENCING**
Finals

■ **GYMNASTICS**
Artistic – Finals

■ **WEIGHTLIFTING**
Finals

■ **HANDBALL**

■ **HOCKEY**

■ **JUDO**
Finals

■ **WRESTLING**
Greco-Roman – Finals

■ **SWIMMING**
Finals

■ **WATER POLO**

■ **SOFTBALL**

■ **TENNIS**

■ **SHOOTING**
Finals

■ **ARCHERY**

■ **SAILING**

■ **VOLLEYBALL**

■ **VOLLEYBALL**
Beach

AUGUST 13

■ **ROWING**

■ **BADMINTON**

■ **BASEBALL**

■ **BASKETBALL**

■ **BOXING**

■ **CANOE/KAYAK**
Slalom

■ **CYCLING**
Road – Finals

■ **EQUESTRIAN**
Dressage

■ **FENCING**
Finals

■ **SOCCER**

■ **GYMNASTICS**
Artistic – Finals

■ **WEIGHTLIFTING**
Finals

■ **HANDBALL**

■ **HOCKEY**

■ **JUDO**
Finals

■ **WRESTLING**
Greco-Roman – Finals

Carly Patterson won the women's all-around gymnastics gold medal at the Summer Olympics in Athens in 2004.

■ **SWIMMING**
Finals

■ **WATER POLO**

■ **SOFTBALL**

■ **TENNIS**

■ **SHOOTING**
Finals

■ **ARCHERY**

■ **SAILING**

■ **VOLLEYBALL**

■ **VOLLEYBALL**
Beach

AUGUST 14

■ **ROWING**

■ **BADMINTON**

■ **BASEBALL**

■ **BASKETBALL**

■ **BOXING**

BEIJING 2008 SUMMER OLYMPICS SCHEDULE (cont.)

■ **CANOE/KAYAK**
Finals

■ **CYCLING**
Track

■ **EQUESTRIAN**
Dressage – Finals

■ **FENCING**
Finals

■ **SOCCER**

■ **GYMNASTICS**
Artistic – Finals

■ **HANDBALL**

■ **HOCKEY**

■ **JUDO**
Finals

■ **WRESTLING**
Greco-Roman – Finals

■ **SWIMMING**
Finals

■ **WATER POLO**

■ **SOFTBALL**

■ **TENNIS**

■ **TABLE TENNIS**

■ **SHOOTING**
Finals

■ **ARCHERY**
Finals

■ **SAILING**

■ **VOLLEYBALL**

■ **VOLLEYBALL**
Beach

AUGUST 15

■ **TRACK AND FIELD**
Finals

■ **ROWING**

■ **BADMINTON**
Finals

■ **BASEBALL**

■ **BASKETBALL**

■ **BOXING**

■ **CYCLING**
Track – Finals

■ **FENCING**
Finals

■ **GYMNASTICS**
Trampoline – Finals

■ **WEIGHTLIFTING**
Finals

■ **HOCKEY**

■ **HANDBALL**

■ **JUDO**
Finals

■ **SWIMMING**
Finals

■ **WATER POLO**

■ **SOFTBALL**

■ **TENNIS**

■ **TABLE TENNIS**

■ **SHOOTING**
Finals

■ **ARCHERY**
Finals

■ **SAILING**

■ **VOLLEYBALL**

■ **VOLLEYBALL**
Beach

AUGUST 16

■ **TRACK AND FIELD**
Finals

■ **ROWING**
Finals

■ **BADMINTON**
Finals

■ **BASEBALL**

■ **BASKETBALL**

■ **BOXING**

■ **CYCLING**
Track – Finals

■ **EQUESTRIAN**
Jumping

■ **FENCING**
Finals

■ **SOCCER**

■ **GYMNASTICS**
Trampoline – Finals

■ **WEIGHTLIFTING**
Finals

■ **HANDBALL**

■ **HOCKEY**

■ **WRESTLING**
Freestyle – Finals

■ **SWIMMING**
Finals

■ **WATER POLO**

■ **SOFTBALL**

■ **TENNIS**
Finals

■ **TABLE TENNIS**

■ **SHOOTING**
Finals

■ **SAILING**

■ **VOLLEYBALL**

■ **VOLLEYBALL**
Beach

AUGUST 17

■ **TRACK AND FIELD**
Finals

■ **ROWING**
Finals

■ **BADMINTON**
Finals

■ **BASKETBALL**

■ **BOXING**

■ **CYCLING**
Track – Finals

■ **EQUESTRIAN**
Dressage

■ **FENCING**
Finals

■ **SOCCER**

DID YOU KNOW?

Prior to the 2008 Games, which will be held in Beijing, China, only two Asian cities have hosted the Summer Olympics: Tokyo, Japan, hosted the 1964 Summer Games and Seoul, South Korea, hosted the 1988 Summer Games.

LEGENDS

Lewis won gold in the long jump in four straight Olympics from 1984 to 1996.

HEINZ KLUETMEIER/SPORTS ILLUSTRATED

■ **Carl Lewis, track and field athlete,** b. July 1, 1961, Birmingham, Alabama. Lewis was the best track and field athlete of his era. He won 10 medals, nine of them gold, across a span of four different Summer Olympics. In 1984, he won four gold medals, taking first in the 200 meter sprint, 4x100-meter relay, long jump, and 100-meter sprint. Perhaps the best-known gold medal of his long career came in 1988. Lewis finished a surprising second in the 100 meters behind Canadian sprinter Ben Johnson. Three days later, Lewis was awarded the gold after a post-race drug test showed Johnson had tested positive for steroids. Although Lewis never again won an Olympic medal in an individual race, he continued to win golds in the next two Olympics in the long jump and 4x100-meter relay events.

■ **Ian Thorpe, swimmer,** b. October 3, 1982, Milperra, Australia. Thorpe won the 400-meter freestyle at the 1998 World Championships at age 14, becoming the youngest-ever individual world champion. He continued to dominate the swimming sprint events over the next several years, winning five medals (three gold, two silver) in the 2000 Summer Olympics in Sydney and four more (two gold, one silver, one bronze) in Athens in 2004. He retired in late 2006.

■ **Michael Jordan, basketball player,** b. February 17, 1963, Brooklyn, New York. Before starting his legendary career in the NBA, Jordan won an Olympic gold medal in 1984 playing on the U.S. men's basketball team. At that time, the team was made up entirely of college players. After that restriction was lifted, Jordan returned to the Olympics in 1992 as a member of the gold medal-winning "Dream Team." He is one of only three men's basketball players to win gold as both an amateur and a professional.

BEIJING 2008 SUMMER OLYMPICS SCHEDULE (cont.)

■ **GYMNASTICS**
Artistic – Finals

■ **WEIGHTLIFTING**
Finals

■ **HANDBALL**

■ **HOCKEY**

■ **WRESTLING**
Freestyle – Finals

■ **SYNCHRONIZED SWIMMING**

■ **DIVING**
Finals

■ **WATER POLO**

■ **SOFTBALL**

■ **TENNIS**
Finals

■ **TABLE TENNIS**

■ **SHOOTING**
Finals

■ **SAILING**

■ **VOLLEYBALL**

■ **VOLLEYBALL**
Beach

AUGUST 18

■ **TRACK AND FIELD**
Finals

■ **BASEBALL**

■ **BASKETBALL**

■ **BOXING**

■ **CANOE/KAYAK**
Flat Water

■ **CYCLING**
Track – Finals

■ **EQUESTRIAN**
Jumping

BEIJING 2008 SUMMER OLYMPICS SCHEDULE (cont.)

■ SOCCER

■ GYMNASTICS
Artistic – Finals

■ WEIGHTLIFTING
Finals

■ HANDBALL

■ HOCKEY

■ SYNCHRONIZED SWIMMING

■ DIVING
Finals

■ WATER POLO

■ SOFTBALL

■ TABLE TENNIS

■ TRIATHLON
Finals

■ SAILING
Finals

■ VOLLEYBALL

■ VOLLEYBALL
Beach

AUGUST 19

■ TRACK AND FIELD
Finals

■ BASEBALL

■ BASKETBALL

■ BOXING

■ CANOE/KAYAK
Flat Water

■ CYCLING
Track – Finals

■ EQUESTRIAN
Jumping – Finals

■ SOCCER

■ WEIGHTLIFTING
Finals

■ HANDBALL

■ HOCKEY

■ WRESTLING
Freestyle – Finals

■ SYNCHRONIZED SWIMMING
Finals

■ DIVING
Finals

■ WATER POLO

■ TABLE TENNIS

■ TRIATHLON
Finals

■ SAILING

■ VOLLEYBALL

■ VOLLEYBALL
Beach – Finals

Michael Phelps won eight medals, six of them gold, in Athens in 2004.

AUGUST 20

■ TRACK AND FIELD
Finals

■ BASEBALL

■ BASKETBALL

■ BOXING

■ CANOE/KAYAK
Flat Water

■ CYCLING
BMX – Finals

■ SOCCER

■ GYMNASTICS
Rhythmic

■ HANDBALL

■ HOCKEY

■ WRESTLING
Freestyle – Finals

■ SWIMMING
Finals

■ DIVING
Finals

■ WATER POLO
Finals

■ SOFTBALL

■ TAEKWONDO
Finals

■ TABLE TENNIS
Finals

■ SAILING

■ VOLLEYBALL

■ VOLLEYBALL
Beach – Finals

AUGUST 21

■ TRACK AND FIELD
Finals

■ BASKETBALL

■ CANOE/KAYAK
Flat Water

■ CYCLING
BMX – Finals

■ EQUESTRIAN
Dressage – Finals

■ SOCCER

■ GYMNASTICS
Rhythmic

■ HANDBALL

■ HOCKEY

■ WRESTLING
Freestyle – Finals

■ SWIMMING
Finals

■ SYNCHRONIZED SWIMMING

■ DIVING
Finals

■ WATER POLO

■ MODERN PENTATHLON
Finals

■ SOFTBALL
Finals

■ TAEKWONDO
Finals

■ TABLE TENNIS
Finals

■ SAILING
Finals

■ VOLLEYBALL

AUGUST 22

■ TRACK AND FIELD
Finals

■ BASEBALL

■ BASKETBALL

SIMON BRUTY/SPORTS ILLUSTRATED

- **BOXING**

- **CANOE/KAYAK**
  Flat Water – Finals

- **CYCLING**
  Mountain Bike – Finals

- **EQUESTRIAN**
  Jumping – Finals

- **SOCCER**

- **GYMNASTICS**
  Rhythmic – Finals

- **HANDBALL**

- **HOCKEY**
  Finals

- **SYNCHRONIZED SWIMMING**
  Finals

- **DIVING**
  Finals

- **MODERN PENTATHLON**
  Finals

- **TAEKWONDO**
  Finals

- **TABLE TENNIS**
  Finals

- **VOLLEYBALL**

AUGUST 23

- **TRACK AND FIELD**
  Finals

- **BASEBALL**
  Finals

Allyson Felix won silver in the 200-meter sprint in Athens in 2004.

- **BASKETBALL**
  Finals

- **BOXING**
  Finals

- **CANOE/KAYAK**
  Flat Water – Finals

- **CYCLING**
  Mountain Bike – Finals

- **SOCCER**
  Finals

- **GYMNASTICS**
  Rhythmic – Finals

- **HANDBALL**
  Finals

- **HOCKEY**
  Finals

- **DIVING**
  Finals

- **WATER POLO**
  Finals

- **TAEKWONDO**
  Finals

- **TABLE TENNIS**
  Finals

- **VOLLEYBALL**
  Finals

AUGUST 24

- **TRACK AND FIELD**
  Finals

- **BASKETBALL**
  Finals

- **BOXING**
  Finals

- **SOCCER**
  Finals

- **HANDBALL**
  Finals

- **DIVING**
  Finals

- **VOLLEYBALL**
  Finals

- **CLOSING CEREMONIES**

MATTHEW STOCKMAN/GETTY IMAGES

SUMMER OLYMPICS TRIVIA

1 Which of these has NEVER been an officially sanctioned Olympic sport?
a. Bowling
b. Golf
c. Baseball

2 What was notable about Abebe Bikila winning his first gold medal in the men's marathon in Rome in 1960?
a. He collapsed at the end of the race and had to be hospitalized.
b. He ran the race barefoot.
c. He never again won a marathon.

3 How many times have the Summer Olympics been held in a North American country?
a. 3
b. 6
c. 9

4 Since the modern Olympics began in 1896, only two countries have participated in every Games. Name them.
a. United States and Russia
b. China and New Zealand
c. Greece and Australia

Trivia Challenge: 1. a; 2. b; 3. b; 4. c

TODAY'S STARS

■ **Katie Hoff, swimmer,** b. June 3, 1989, Stanford, California. At 15, Hoff was the youngest member of the 2004 U.S. Olympic team. Although she did not medal, Hoff gained valuable experience. Since Athens she has turned into one of the most versatile swimmers in the world, winning medals in the 200-meter freestyle, 200-meter medley, 400-meter freestyle, and 400-meter medley in international meets. Including relays, Hoff could compete in as many as 13 swimming events in Beijing in 2008.

At the 2006 U.S. National Championships, Hoff set a world record in the 200-meter individual medley.

HEINZ KLUETMEIER

■ **Hicham El Guerrouj, runner,** b. September 14, 1974, Berkane, Morocco. Nicknamed the "King of the Mile," El Guerrouj set numerous middle distance world records during the late 1990s but he failed to capture Olympic gold at both the 1996 and 2000 Summer Games. At Athens in 2004, though, El Guerrouj came through. He won gold in both the 1,500 meters and the 5,000 meters and became the first runner in 80 years to win both of those events at the same Olympics.

■ **Michael Phelps, swimmer,** b. June 20, 1985, Baltimore, Maryland. At age 15, Phelps made his Olympic debut at the 2000 Summer Olympics in Sydney, becoming the youngest American male swimmer to compete at the Olympics in 68 years. Four years later at Athens, Phelps tied an Olympic record by winning eight medals (six gold, two bronze) in a single Summer Games. His six gold medals fell one short of the seven gold medals won by American swimming legend Mark Spitz at the 1972 Summer Olympics. Phelps looks to to add to his career total at the Summer Games in Beijing in 2008.

FAST FACT

Although divided into separate countries after World War II, East and West Germany continued to send a unified team to the Olympics through 1960. From 1964 through 1988, though, each nation sent their own team. Less than two years after becoming one country again in 1992, Germany again had a single Olympic squad.

DID YOU KNOW?

The 1940 Summer Games were canceled because of World War II. They were originally planned for Tokyo, but Japan resigned as host after the outbreak of its war with China in 1937. Helsinki was the next choice, but the International Olympic Committee officially canceled the Summer Games after Soviet troops invaded Finland two years later.

PAST SUMMER OLYMPIC HOSTS

YEAR		HOST	DATES	MEN	WOMEN	NATIONS
XXVIII	2004	ATHENS, GREECE	August 13-29	6,452	4,412	202
XXVII	2000	SYDNEY, AUSTRALIA	September 15-October 1	6,582	4,069	199
XXVI	1996	ATLANTA, GEORGIA, USA	July 19-August 4	6,806	3,512	197
XXV	1992	BARCELONA, SPAIN	July 25-August 9	6,652	2,704	169
XXIV	1988	SEOUL, KOREA	September 17-October 2	6,197	2,194	159
XXIII	1984	LOS ANGELES, CALIFORNIA, USA	July 28-August 12	5,263	1,566	140
XXII	1980	MOSCOW, U.S.S.R.	July 19-August 3	4,064	1,115	80
XXI	1976	MONTREAL, QUEBEC, CANADA	July 17-August 1	4,824	1,260	92
XX	1972	MUNICH, WEST GERMANY	August 26-September 11	6,075	1,059	121
XIX	1968	MEXICO CITY, MEXICO	October 12-27	4,735	781	112
XVIII	1964	TOKYO, JAPAN	October 10-24	4,473	678	93
XVII	1960	ROME, ITALY	August 25-September 11	4,727	611	83
XVI	1956	MELBOURNE, AUSTRALIA	November 22-December 8	2,938	376	72
XV	1952	HELSINKI, FINLAND	July 19-August 3	4,436	519	69
XIV	1948	LONDON, GREAT BRITAIN	July 29-August 14	3,714	390	59
XIII	1944	LONDON, GREAT BRITAIN	Canceled because of World War II			
XII	1940	TOKYO, JAPAN	Canceled because of World War II			
XI	1936	BERLIN, GERMANY	August 1-16	3,632	331	49
X	1932	LOS ANGELES, CALIFORNIA, USA	July 30-August 14	1,206	126	37
IX	1928	AMSTERDAM, THE NETHERLANDS	May 17-August 12	2,606	277	46
VIII	1924	PARIS, FRANCE	May 4-July 27	2,954	135	44
VII	1920	ANTWERP, BELGIUM	April 20-September 12	2,561	65	29
VI	1916	BERLIN, GERMANY	Canceled because of World War I			
V	1912	STOCKHOLM, SWEDEN	May 5-July 27	2,359	48	28
IV	1908	LONDON, GREAT BRITAIN	April 27-October 31	1,971	37	22
—	1906	ATHENS, GREECE	April 22-May 28	77	7	20
III	1904	ST. LOUIS, MISSOURI, USA	July 1-November 23	645	6	12
II	1900	PARIS, FRANCE	May 14-October 28	975	22	24
I	1896	ATHENS, GREECE	April 6-15	241	0	14

SUMMER OLYMPICS

ALL-TIME SUMMER OLYMPIC MEDAL COUNT – NATION

NATION	GOLD	SILVER	BRONZE	TOTAL
UNITED STATES	907	697	615	**2,219**
SOVIET UNION (1952–88)	395	319	296	**1,010**
GREAT BRITAIN	189	242	237	**668**
FRANCE	199	202	230	**631**
ITALY	189	154	168	**511**
GERMANY (1896–1936, 1992–present)	151	154	178	**483**
SWEDEN	140	157	179	**476**
HUNGARY	158	141	161	**460**
EAST GERMANY (1956–88)	159	150	136	**445**
AUSTRALIA	119	126	154	**399**
JAPAN	113	106	114	**333**
WEST GERMANY (1952–88)	77	104	120	**301**
FINLAND	101	83	114	**298**
CHINA	112	96	78	**286**
ROMANIA	82	88	114	**284**
POLAND	59	74	118	**251**
RUSSIA	85	79	84	**248**
CANADA	54	87	101	**242**
THE NETHERLANDS	65	76	94	**235**

ALL-TIME SUMMER OLYMPIC MEDAL COUNT – MEN

ATHLETE, Nation	SPORT	GOLD	SILVER	BRONZE	TOTAL
NIKOLAI ANDRIANOV, U.S.S.R.	Gymnastics	7	5	3	**15**
BORIS SHAKHLIN, U.S.S.R.	Gymnastics	7	4	2	**13**
EDOARDO MANGIAROTTI, Italy	Fencing	6	5	2	**13**
TAKASHI ONO, Japan	Gymnastics	5	4	4	**13**
PAAVO NURMI, Finland	Track	9	3	0	**12**
SAWAO KATO, Japan	Gymnastics	8	3	1	**12**
ALEXEI NEMOV, Russia	Gymnastics	4	2	6	**12**
MARK SPITZ, United States	Swimming	9	1	1	**11**
MATT BIONDI, United States	Swimming	8	2	1	**11**
VIKTOR CHUKARIN, U.S.S.R.	Gymnastics	7	3	1	**11**
CARL OSBURN, United States	Shooting	5	4	2	**11**

Six tied with 10.

ALL-TIME SUMMER OLYMPIC MEDAL COUNT — WOMEN

ATHLETE, Nation	SPORT	GOLD	SILVER	BRONZE	TOTAL
LARISSA LATYNINA, U.S.S.R.	Gymnastics	9	5	4	18
BIRGIT FISCHER, Germany	Canoe/Kayak	8	4	0	12
JENNY THOMPSON, United States	Swimming	8	3	1	12
VERA CASLAVSKA, Czechoslovakia	Gymnastics	7	4	0	11
AGNES KELETI, Hungary	Gymnastics	5	3	2	10
POLINA ASTAKHOVA, U.S.S.R.	Gymnastics	5	2	3	10
NADIA COMANECI, Romania	Gymnastics	5	3	1	9
LYUDMILA TOURISCHEVA, U.S.S.R.	Gymnastics	4	3	2	9
DARA TORRES, United States	Swimming	4	1	4	9
KORNELIA ENDER, East Germany	Swimming	4	4	0	8
DAWN FRASER, Australia	Swimming	4	4	0	8
INGE DE BRUIJN, The Netherlands	Swimming	4	2	2	8
SHIRLEY BABASHOFF, United States	Swimming	2	6	0	8
SOFIA MURATOVA, U.S.S.R.	Gymnastics	2	2	4	8

Eight tied with 7.

ALL-TIME SUMMER OLYMPIC GOLD MEDALISTS

MEN

RAY EWRY, United States	10
PAAVO NURMI, Finland	9
CARL LEWIS, United States	9
MARK SPITZ, United States	9
SAWAO KATO, Japan	8
MATT BIONDI, United States	8
NIKOLAI ANDRIANOV, U.S.S.R.	7
BORIS SHAKHLIN, U.S.S.R.	7
VIKTOR CHUKARIN, U.S.S.R.	7
ALADAR GEREVICH, Hungary	7

WOMEN

LARISSA LATYNINA, U.S.S.R.	9
BIRGIT FISCHER, Germany	8
JENNY THOMPSON, United States	8
KRISTIN OTTO, East Germany	6
AGNES KELETI, Hungary	5
NADIA COMANECI, Romania	5
POLINA ASTAKHOVA, U.S.S.R.	5
KRISZTINA EGERSZEGI, Hungary	5
AMY VAN DYKEN, United States	5
KORNELIA ENDER, East Germany	4
DAWN FRASER, Australia	4
LARISSA LAZUTINA, United Team/Russia	4
LYUDMILA TOURISCHEVA, U.S.S.R.	4
EVELYN ASHFORD, United States	4
JANET EVANS, United States	4
FANNY BLANKERS-KOEN, The Netherlands	4
BETTY CUTHBERT, Australia	4
PAT MCCORMICK, United States	4
BARBEL ECKERT WOCKEL, East Germany	4
INGE DE BRUIJN, The Netherlands	4
YANA KLOCHKOVA, Ukraine	4
DARA TORRES, United States	4

FAST FACT

Yuri Titov, a gymnast from the Soviet Union, competed in three Summer Olympics (1956, '60 and '64). He won a total of nine medals over his career, but only one was a gold medal.

SI KIDS.com
Visit our website for the latest stats and sports info.

WINTER OLYMPICS

The XXI Winter Olympics will take place from February 12–28, 2010, in Vancouver, British Columbia, Canada. Several thousand athletes from across the world will compete in seven sports: skiing (including snowboarding), bobsled, skating, luge, biathlon, ice hockey, and curling. In addition to the events included in the XX Winter Games in Turin, Italy, a new event will be added: ski cross. Also known as skier X, the event got its start at the Winter X Games. The venues for the 2010 Games will include the mountain resort of Whistler, just north of Vancouver. Canada won 24 medals in Turin in 2006. That was just one behind the U.S. for second and five behind Germany for first. The home-slope advantage could help Team Canada challenge for the top spot in 2010.

FAST FACT

The United States ranks second all-time with 216 Winter Olympic medals. Norway, with a total of 280 medals, is first.

Hannah Teter (center) and Gretchen Bleiler (left) of the United States took the gold and silver medals in the women's Halfpipe event.

BOB MARTIN

TURIN 2006 MEDAL COUNT – NATION

NATION	GOLD	SILVER	BRONZE	TOTAL	NATION	GOLD	SILVER	BRONZE	TOTAL
1. GERMANY	11	12	6	29	14. FINLAND	0	6	3	9
2. UNITED STATES	9	9	7	25	15. CZECH REPUBLIC	1	2	1	4
3. CANADA	7	10	7	24	16. ESTONIA	3	0	0	3
4. AUSTRIA	9	7	7	23	17. CROATIA	1	2	0	3
5. RUSSIA	8	6	8	22	18. AUSTRALIA	1	0	1	2
6. NORWAY	2	8	9	19	19. POLAND	0	1	1	2
7. SWEDEN	7	2	5	14	20. UKRAINE	0	0	2	2
8. SWITZERLAND	5	4	5	14	21. JAPAN	1	0	0	1
9. SOUTH KOREA	6	3	2	11	22. BELARUS	0	1	0	1
10. ITALY	5	0	6	11	23. BULGARIA	0	1	0	1
11. CHINA	2	4	5	11	24. GREAT BRITAIN	0	1	0	1
12. FRANCE	3	2	4	9	25. SLOVAKIA	0	1	0	1
13. NETHERLANDS	3	2	4	9	26. LATVIA	0	0	1	1

ALPINE SKIING

MEN

■ Downhill
GOLD – Antoine Deneriaz, France
SILVER – Michael Walchhofer, Austria
BRONZE – Bruno Kernen, Switzerland

■ Slalom
GOLD – Benjamin Raich, Austria
SILVER – Reinfried Herbst, Austria
BRONZE – Rainer Schoenfelder, Austria

■ Giant Slalom
GOLD – Benjamin Raich, Austria
SILVER – Joel Chenel, France
BRONZE – Hermann Maier, Austria

■ Super G
GOLD – Kjetil Andre Aamodt, Norway
SILVER – Hermann Maier, Austria
BRONZE – Ambrosi Hoffman, Switzerland

■ Combined
GOLD – Ted Ligety, USA
SILVER – Ivica Kostelic, Croatia
BRONZE – Rainer Schoenfelder, Austria

WOMEN

■ Downhill
GOLD – Michaela Dorfmeister, Austria
SILVER – Martina Schild, Switzerland
BRONZE – Anja Paerson, Sweden

■ Slalom
GOLD – Anja Paerson, Sweden
SILVER – Nicole Hosp, Austria
BRONZE – Marlies Schild, Austria

■ Giant Slalom
GOLD – Julia Mancuso, USA
SILVER – Tanja Poutiainen, Finland
BRONZE – Anna Ottoson, Sweden

■ Super G
GOLD – Michaela Dorfmeister, Austria
SILVER – Janica Kostelic, Croatia
BRONZE – Alexandra Meissnitzer, Austria

■ Combined
GOLD – Janica Kostelic, Croatia
SILVER – Marlies Schild, Austria
BRONZE – Anja Paerson, Sweden

BIATHLON

MEN

■ 10km Sprint
GOLD – Sven Fischer, Germany
SILVER – Halvard Hanevold, Norway
BRONZE – Frode Andresen, Norway

Julia Mancuso, United States

HEINZ KLUETMEIER

■ 20km Individual
GOLD – Michael Greis, Germany
SILVER – Ole Einar Bjoerndalen, Norway
BRONZE – Halvard Hanevold, Norway

■ 4 x 7.5km Relay
GOLD – Ricco Gross, Michael Roesch, Sven Fischer, Michael Greis; Germany
SILVER – Ivan Tcherezov, Sergei Tchepikov, Pavel Rostovtsev, Nikolay Kruglov; Russia
BRONZE – Julien Robert, Vincent Defrasne, Ferreol Cannard, Raphael Poiree; France

■ 15km Mass Start
GOLD – Michael Greis, Germany
SILVER – Tomasz Sikora, Poland
BRONZE – Ole Einar Bjoerndalen, Norway

■ 12.5km Pursuit
GOLD – Vincent Defrasne, France
SILVER – Ole Einar Bjoerndalen, Norway
BRONZE – Sven Fischer, Germany

WOMEN

■ 7.5km Sprint
GOLD – Florence Baverel-Robert, France
SILVER – Anna Carin Olofsson, Sweden
BRONZE – Lilia Efremova, Ukraine

■ 15km Individual
GOLD – Svetlana Ishmouratova, Russia
SILVER – Martina Glagow, Germany
BRONZE – Albina Akhatova, Russia

■ 4 x 6km Relay
GOLD – Anna Bogaliy, Svetlana Ishmouratova, Olga Zaitseva, Albina Akhatova; Russia
SILVER – Martina Glagow, Andrea Henkel, Katrin Apel, Kati Wilhelm; Germany
BRONZE – Delphyne Peretto, Florence Baverel-Robert, Sylvie Becaert, Sandrine Bailly; France

■ 12.5km Mass Start
GOLD – Anna Carin Olofsson, Sweden
SILVER – Kati Wilhelm, Germany
BRONZE – Uschi Disl, Germany

■ 10km Pursuit
GOLD – Kati Wilhelm, Germany
SILVER – Martina Glagow, Germany
BRONZE – Albina Akhatova, Russia

BOBSLED

MEN

■ Two-Man
GOLD – Andre Lange, Kevin Kuske; Germany
SILVER – Pierre Lueders, Lascelles Brown; Canada
BRONZE – Martin Annen, Beat Hefti; Switzerland

DID YOU KNOW?

Skeleton, the sport in which a competitor rides a sled face-first down a mountain on an icy track, reappeared at the Winter Olympics in 2002 after a 54-year absence.

2006 SPORT-BY-SPORT RESULTS (cont.)

■ Four-Man
GOLD – Andre Lange, Rene Hoppe, Kevin Kuske, Martin Putze; Germany
SILVER – Aleksandr Zoubkov, Filipp Egorov, Alexej Seliverstov, Alexey Voevoda; Russia
BRONZE – Martin Annen, Thomas Lamparter, Beat Hefti, Cedric Grand; Switzerland

WOMEN
■ Two-Women
GOLD – Sandra Kiriasis, Anja Schneiderheinze; Germany
SILVER – Shauna Rohbock, Valerie Fleming; USA
BRONZE – Gerda Weissensteiner, Jennifer Isacco; Italy

CROSS COUNTRY SKIING

MEN
■ Sprint
GOLD – Bjoern Lind, Sweden
SILVER – Roddy Darragon, France
BRONZE – Thobias Fredriksson, Sweden

■ Team Sprint
GOLD – Thobias Fredriksson, Bjoern Lind; Sweden
SILVER – Jens Arne Svartedal, Tor Arne Hetland; Norway
BRONZE – Ivan Alypov, Vassili Rotchev; Russia

■ 30km Pursuit
GOLD – Eugeni Dementiev, Russia
SILVER – Frode Estil, Norway
BRONZE – Pietro Piller Cottrer, Italy

■ 4x10km Relay
GOLD – Fulvio Valbusa, Giorgio Di Centa, Pietro Piller Cottrer, Cristian Zorzi; Italy
SILVER – Andreas Schluetter, Jens Filbrich, Rene Sommerfeldt, Tobias Angerer; Germany
BRONZE – Mats Larsson, Johan Olsson, Anders Soedergren, Mathias Fredriksson; Sweden

■ 15km Classical
GOLD – Andrus Veerpalu, Estonia
SILVER – Lukas Bauer, Czech Rep.
BRONZE – Tobias Angerer, Germany

■ 50km Freestyle
GOLD – Giorgio Di Centa, Italy
SILVER – Eugeni Dementiev, Russia
BRONZE – Mikhail Botwinov, Austria

WOMEN
■ Sprint
GOLD – Chandra Crawford, Canada
SILVER – Claudia Kuenzel, Germany
BRONZE – Alena Sidko, Russia

■ Team Sprint
GOLD – Anna Dahlberg, Lina Andersson; Sweden
SILVER – Sara Renner, Beckie Scott; Canada
BRONZE – Aino Kaisa Saarinen, Virpi Kuitunen; Finland

■ 15km Pursuit
GOLD – Kristina Smigun, Estonia
SILVER – Katerina Neumannova, Czech Republic
BRONZE – Evgenia Medvedeva-Abruzova, Russia

■ 4x5km Relay
GOLD – Natalia Baranova-Masolkina, Larisa Kurkina, Julija Tchepalova, Evgenia Medvedeva-Abruzova; Russia
SILVER – Stefanie Boehler, Viola Bauer, Evi Sachenbacher Stehle, Claudia Kuenzel; Germany
BRONZE – Arianna Follis, Gabriella Paruzzi, Antonella Confortola, Sabina Valbusa; Italy

■ 10km Classical
GOLD – Kristina Smigun, Estonia
SILVER – Marit Bjorgen, Norway
BRONZE – Hilde G. Pedersen, Norway

■ 30km Freestyle
GOLD – Katerina Neumannova, Czech Republic
SILVER – Julija Tchepalova, Russia
BRONZE – Justyna Kowalczyk, Poland

CURLING

MEN
GOLD – Canada
SILVER – Finland
BRONZE – USA

WOMEN
GOLD – Sweden
SILVER – Switzerland
BRONZE – Canada

FIGURE SKATING

MEN
GOLD – Evgeni Plushenko, Russia
SILVER – Stephane Lambiel, Switzerland
BRONZE – Jeffrey Buttle, Canada

WOMEN
GOLD – Shizuka Arakawa, Japan
SILVER – Sasha Cohen, USA
BRONZE – Irina Slutskaya, Russia

■ Pairs
GOLD – Tatyana Totmiyanina, Maxim Marinin; Russia
SILVER – Dan Zhang, Hao Zhang; China
BRONZE – Xue Shen, Hongbo Zhao; China

■ Ice Dancing
GOLD – Tatyana Navka, Roman Kostomarov; Russia
SILVER – Tanith Belbin, Ben Agosto; USA
BRONZE – Yelena Grushina, Ruslan Goncharov; Ukraine

FREESTYLE SKIING

MEN
■ Aerials
GOLD – Xiaopeng Han, China
SILVER – Dmitry Dashinski, Belarus
BRONZE – Vladimir Lebedev, Russia

Tanith Belbin, Ben Agosto, United States

AL TIELEMANS

■ **Moguls**
GOLD – Dale Begg-Smith, Australia
SILVER – Mikko Ronkainen, Finland
BRONZE – Toby Dawson, USA

WOMEN

■ **Aerials**
GOLD – Evelyne Leu, Switzerland
SILVER – Nina Li, China
BRONZE – Alisa Camplin, Australia

■ **Moguls**
GOLD – Jennifer Heil, Canada
SILVER – Kari Traa, Norway
BRONZE – Sandra Laoura, France

HOCKEY

MEN
GOLD – Sweden
SILVER – Finland
BRONZE – Czech Republic

WOMEN
GOLD – Canada
SILVER – Sweden
BRONZE – USA

LUGE

MEN

■ **Singles**
GOLD – Armin Zoeggeler, Italy
SILVER – Albert Demtschenko, Russia
BRONZE – Martins Rubenis, Latvia

■ **Doubles**
GOLD – Andreas Linger, Wolfgang Linger; Austria
SILVER – Andre Florschuetz, Torsten Wustlich; Germany
BRONZE – Oswald Haselrieder, Gerhard Plankensteiner; Italy

WOMEN

■ **Singles**
GOLD – Sylke Otto, Germany
SILVER – Silke Kraushaar, Germany
BRONZE – Tatjana Huefner, Germany

NORDIC COMBINED

■ **Sprint**
GOLD – Felix Gottwald, Austria
SILVER – Magnus Moan, Norway
BRONZE – Georg Hettich, Germany

■ **Individual**
GOLD – Georg Hettich, Germany
SILVER – Felix Gottwald, Austria
BRONZE – Magnus Moan, Norway

■ **Team**
GOLD – Austria
SILVER – Germany
BRONZE – Finland

SPEED SKATING

MEN

■ **500m**
GOLD – Joey Cheek, USA
SILVER – Dmitry Dorofeyev, Russia
BRONZE – Kang Seok Lee, South Korea

■ **1,000m**
GOLD – Shani Davis, USA
SILVER – Joey Cheek, USA
BRONZE – Erben Wennemars, Netherlands

■ **1,500m**
GOLD – Enrico Fabris, Italy
SILVER – Shani Davis, USA
BRONZE – Chad Hedrick, USA

■ **5,000m**
GOLD – Chad Hedrick, USA
SILVER – Sven Kramer, Netherlands
BRONZE – Enrico Fabris, Italy

■ **10,000m**
GOLD – Bob De Jong, Netherlands
SILVER – Chad Hedrick, USA
BRONZE – Carl Verheijen, Netherlands

■ **Team Pursuit**
GOLD – Matteo Anesi, Enrico Fabris, Ippolito Sanfratello; Italy
SILVER – Arne Dankers, Steven Elm, Justin Warsylewicz; Canada
BRONZE – Sven Kramer, Mark Tuitert, Carl Verheijen; Netherlands

WOMEN

■ **500m**
GOLD – Svetlana Zhurova, Russia
SILVER – Manli Wang, China
BRONZE – Hui Ren, China

■ **1,000m**
GOLD – Marianne Timmer, Netherlands
SILVER – Cindy Klassen, Canada
BRONZE – Anni Friesinger, Germany

■ **1,500m**
GOLD – Cindy Klassen, Canada
SILVER – Kristina Groves, Canada
BRONZE – Ireen Wust, Netherlands

■ **3,000m**
GOLD – Ireen Wust, Netherlands
SILVER – Renate Groenewold, Netherlands
BRONZE – Cindy Klassen, Canada

■ **5,000m**
GOLD – Clara Hughes, Canada
SILVER – Claudia Pechstein, Germany
BRONZE – Cindy Klassen, Canada

Shani Davis, United States

DAMIAN STROHMEYER

2006 SPORT-BY-SPORT RESULTS (cont.)

■ Team Pursuit
GOLD – Daniela Anschuetz Thoms, Anni Friesinger, Claudia Pechstein; Germany
SILVER – Kristina Groves, Clara Hughes, Christine Nesbitt; Canada
BRONZE – Yekaterina Abramova, Yekaterina Lobysheva, Svetlana Vysokova; Russia

SHORT TRACK SPEED SKATING

MEN
■ 500m
GOLD – Apolo Anton Ohno, USA
SILVER – Francois-Louis Tremblay, Canada
BRONZE – Hyun-Soo Ahn, South Korea

■ 1,000m
GOLD – Hyun-Soo Ahn, S. Korea
SILVER – Ho-Suk Lee, S. Korea
BRONZE – Apolo Anton Ohno, USA

■ 1,500m
GOLD – Hyun-Soo Ahn, S. Korea
SILVER – Ho-Suk Lee, S. Korea
BRONZE – Jiajun Li, China

■ Relay
GOLD – Hyun-Soo Ahn, Ho-Suk Lee, Se-Jong Oh, Ho-Jin Seo, Suk-Woo Song; S. Korea
SILVER – Eric Bedard, Jonathan Guilmette, Charles Hamelin, Francois-Louis Tremblay, Mathieu Turcotte; Canada
BRONZE – Alex Izykowski, J.P. Kepka, Anthony Lobello, Apolo Anton Ohno, Rusty Smith; USA

WOMEN
■ 500m
GOLD – Meng Wang, China
SILVER – Evgenia Radanova, Bulgaria
BRONZE – Anouk Leblanc-Boucher, Canada

■ 1,000m
GOLD – Sun-Yu Jin, South Korea
SILVER – Meng Wang, China
BRONZE – Yang Yang (A), China

■ 1,500m
GOLD – Sun-Yu Jin, South Korea
SILVER – Eun-Kyung Choi, South Korea
BRONZE – Meng Wang, China

■ Relay
GOLD – Chun-Sa Byun, Eun-Kyung Choi, Dah-Ye Jeon, Sun-Yu Jin, Yun-Mi Kang; South Korea
SILVER – Alanna Kraus, Anouk Leblanc-Boucher, Amanda Overland, Kalyna Roberge, Tania Vicent; Canada
BRONZE – Marta Capurso, Arianna Fontana, Cecilia Maffei, Katia Zini, Mara Zini; Italy

SKELETON

MEN
GOLD – Duff Gibson, Canada
SILVER – Jeff Pain, Canada
BRONZE – Gregor Staehli, Switzerland

WOMEN
GOLD – Maya Pedersen, Switzerland
SILVER – Shelley Rudman, Great Britain
BRONZE – Mellisa Hollingsworth-Richards, Canada

SKI JUMPING

MEN
■ Normal Hill
GOLD – Lars Bystoel, Norway
SILVER – Matti Hautamaeki, Finland
BRONZE – Roar Ljoekelsoey, Norway

■ Large Hill
GOLD – Thomas Morgenstern, Austria
SILVER – Andreas Kofler, Austria
BRONZE – Lars Bystoel, Norway

■ Team
GOLD – Andreas Widhoelzl, Andreas Kofler, Martin Koch, Thomas Morgenstern; Austria
SILVER – Tami Kiuru, Janne Happonen, Janne Ahonen, Matt Hautamaeki; Finland
BRONZE – Lars Bystoel, Bjoern Einar Romoeren, Tommy Ingebrigtsen, Roar Ljoekelsoey; Norway

SNOW BOARDING

MEN
■ Halfpipe
GOLD – Shaun White, USA
SILVER – Danny Kass, USA
BRONZE – Markku Koski, Finland

■ Parallel Giant Slalom
GOLD – Philipp Schoch, Switzerland
SILVER – Simon Schoch, Switzerland
BRONZE – Siegfried Grabner, Austria

■ Snowboard Cross
GOLD – Seth Wescott, USA
SILVER – Radoslav Zidek, Slovakia
BRONZE – Paul-Henri Delerue, France

WOMEN
■ Halfpipe
GOLD – Hannah Teter, USA
SILVER – Gretchen Bleiler, USA
BRONZE – Kjersti Buaas, Norway

■ Parallel Giant Slalom
GOLD – Daniela Meuli, Switzerland
SILVER – Amelie Kober, Germany
BRONZE – Rosey Fletcher, USA

■ Snowboard Cross
GOLD – Tanja Frieden, Switzerland
SILVER – Lindsey Jacobellis, USA
BRONZE – Dominique Maltais, Canada

Shaun White

BOB MARTIN

PAST WINTER OLYMPIC HOSTS

YEAR		HOST	DATES	MEN	WOMEN	NATIONS
XX	2006	TURIN, ITALY	February 10-16	1,611	996	84
XIX	2002	SALT LAKE CITY, USA	February 8-24	1,513	886	77
XVIII	1998	NAGANO, JAPAN	February 7-22	1,389	787	72
XVII	1994	LILLEHAMMER, NORWAY	February 12-27	1,215	522	67
XVI	1992	ALBERTVILLE, FRANCE	February 8-23	1,313	488	64
XV	1988	CALGARY, CANADA	February 13-28	1,122	301	57
XIV	1984	SARAJEVO, YUGOSLAVIA	February 8-19	998	274	49
XIII	1980	LAKE PLACID, USA	February 13-24	840	232	37
XII	1976	INNSBRUCK, AUSTRIA	February 4-15	892	231	37
XI	1972	SAPPORO, JAPAN	February 3-13	801	205	35
X	1968	GRENOBLE, FRANCE	February 6-18	947	211	37
IX	1964	INNSBRUCK, AUSTRIA	January 29-February 9	892	199	36
VIII	1960	SQUAW VALLEY, USA	February 18-28	521	144	30
VII	1956	CORTINA d'AMPEZZO, ITALY	January 26-February 5	687	134	32
VI	1952	OSLO, NORWAY	February 14-25	585	109	30
V	1948	ST. MORITZ, SWITZERLAND	January 30-February 8	592	77	28
--	1944	CORTINA d'AMPEZZO, ITALY	Canceled because of World War II			
--	1940	GARMISCH-PARTENKIRCHEN, GERMANY	Canceled because of World War II			
IV	1936	GARMISCH-PARTENKIRCHEN, GERMANY	February 6-16	566	80	28
III	1932	LAKE PLACID, USA	February 4-15	231	21	17
II	1928	ST. MORITZ, SWITZERLAND	February 11-19	438	26	25
I	1924	CHAMONIX, FRANCE	January 25-February 5	247	11	16

TRIVIA CHALLENGE

Which three cities are finalists to host the 2014 Winter Olympics?

Sochi, Russia; Salzburg, Austria; PyeongChang, South Korea.

TODAY'S STARS

■ **Kimmie Meissner, figure skater,** b. October 4, 1989, Towson, Maryland. Meissner has become one of the world's premiere figure skaters over the past three years. In 2005, the 17-year-old earned a spot on the U.S. Olympic figure skating team by finishing second at the national championships. Meissner came in sixth at the Winter Olympics in Turin, but she went on to win gold in her debut at the world championships later that year. Meissner is one of only two American female figure skaters to have landed a triple axel during competition, and she looks poised to return to the Olympics in 2010.

■ **Joey Cheek, speed skater,** b. June 22, 1979, Greensboro, North Carolina. Cheek won a gold (500 meter) and a silver (1,000 meter) medal in Turin in 2006. But it was after winning both of his medals that Cheek made an even bigger impact. That's when he announced that he would donate both of the medal bonuses that he earned from the U.S. Olympic Committee—a total of $40,000—to charity.

■ **Anja Paerson, alpine skier,** b. April 25, 1981, Umea, Sweden. Paerson, who has ruled the skiing World Cup slopes for the past few years, put on a dazzling show in Turin. She took home three Olympic medals (bringing her career total to five). She won bronze in both the downhill and combined events and captured the gold in the slalom event, after having settled for the bronze in the slalom in 2002.

SIMON BRUTY

Meissner placed sixth in the 2006 Winter Olympics, but went on to win the Worlds later that same year.

FAST FACT

Only two countries that lie south of the equator have ever won medals at the Winter Oympics: Australia and New Zealand.

ALL-TIME WINTER OLYMPIC MEDAL COUNT – NATION

NATION	GOLD	SILVER	BRONZE	TOTAL
NORWAY	98	98	84	280
UNITED STATES	79	79	58	216
SOVIET UNION (1956–88)	78	56	59	193
AUSTRIA	51	64	70	185
GERMANY	68	65	46	179
FINLAND	41	57	52	150
CANADA	38	38	43	119
SWEDEN	43	31	44	118
SWITZERLAND	37	37	43	117
EAST GERMANY (1956–88)	39	36	35	110

ALL-TIME WINTER OLYMPIC MEDAL COUNT – MEN

ATHLETE, Nation	SPORT	GOLD	SILVER	BRONZE	TOTAL
BJORN DAEHLIE, Norway	Nordic Skiing	8	4	0	12
OLE EINAR BJOERNDALEN, Norway	Biathlon	5	3	1	9
SIXTEN JERNBERG, Sweden	Nordic Skiing	4	3	2	9
RICCO GROSS, Germany	Biathlon	4	3	1	8
KJETIL ANDRE AAMODT, Norway	Alpine Skiing	4	2	2	8
A. CLAS THUNBERG, Finland	Speed Skating	5	1	1	7
IVAR BALLANGRUD, Norway	Speed Skating	4	2	1	7
VEIKKO HAKULINEN, Finland	Nordic Skiing	3	3	1	7
EERO MANTYRANTA, Finland	Nordic Skiing	3	2	2	7
BOGDAN MUSIOL, East Germany/Germany	Bobsled	1	5	1	7
THOMAS ALSGAARD, Norway	Nordic Skiing	4	2	0	6
GUNDE SVAN, Sweden	Nordic Skiing	4	1	1	6
VEGARD ULVANG, Norway	Nordic Skiing	3	2	1	6
JOHAN GROTTUMSBRATEN, Norway	Nordic Skiing	3	1	2	6
WOLFGANG HOPPE, East Germany/Germany	Bobsled	2	3	1	6
EUGENIO MONTI, Italy	Bobsled	2	2	2	6
VLADIMIR SMIRNOV, U.S.S.R./ United Team/Kazakhstan	Nordic Skiing	1	4	1	6
MIKA MYLLYLAE, Finland	Nordic Skiing	1	1	4	6
ROALD LARSEN, Norway	Speed Skating	0	2	4	6
HARRI KIRVESNIEMI, Finland	Nordic Skiing	0	0	6	6

ALL-TIME WINTER OLYMPIC MEDAL COUNT — WOMEN

ATHLETE, Nation	SPORT	GOLD	SILVER	BRONZE	TOTAL
RAISA SMETANINA, U.S.S.R./United Team	Nordic Skiing	4	5	1	10
LYUBOV EGOROVA, United Team/Russia	Nordic Skiing	6	3	0	9
LARISSA LAZUTINA, United Team/Russia	Nordic Skiing	5	3	1	9
STEFANIA BELMONDO, Italy	Nordic Skiing	2	3	4	9
CLAUDIA PECHSTEIN, Germany	Speed Skating	5	2	2	9
GALINA KULAKOVA, U.S.S.R.	Nordic Skiing	4	2	2	8
KARIN KANIA, East Germany	Speed Skating	3	4	1	8
GUNDA NEIMANN-STIRNEMANN, Germany	Speed Skating	3	4	1	8
URSULA DISL, Germany	Biathlon	2	4	2	8
MARJA-LIISA KIRVESNIEMI, Finland	Nordic Skiing	3	0	4	7
ELENA VALBE, United Team/Russia	Nordic Skiing	3	0	4	7
ANDREA EHRIG, East Germany	Speed Skating	1	5	1	7
LYDIA SKOBLIKOVA, U.S.S.R.	Speed Skating	6	0	0	6
BONNIE BLAIR, United States	Speed Skating	5	0	1	6
MANUELA DI CENTA, Italy	Nordic Skiing	2	2	2	6

Ursula Disl

AP PHOTO/ITSUO INOUYE

ALL-TIME INDIVIDUAL OLYMPIC GOLD MEDALISTS

MEN		WOMEN	
BJORN DAEHLIE, Norway	8	LYUBOV EGOROVA, United Team/Russia	6
OLE EINAR BJOERNDALEN, Norway	5	LYDIA SKOBLIKOVA, U.S.S.R.	6
ERIC HEIDEN, United States	5	BONNIE BLAIR, United States	5
A. CLAS THUNBERG, Finland	5	LARISSA LAZUTINA, United Team/Russia	5
		CLAUDIA PECHSTEIN, Germany	5

ATHLETES WITH WINTER AND SUMMER MEDALS

EDDIE EAGAN, United States — boxing gold medal (1920) and bobsled gold medal (1932)

JACOB TULLIN THAMS, Norway — ski jumping gold medal (1924) and yachting silver medal (1936)

CHRISTA LUDING-ROTHENBURGER, East Germany — speed skating gold medals (1984 and 1988), silver medal (1988), and bronze medal (1992), and cycling silver medal (1988)

CLARA HUGHES, Canada — two cycling bronze medals (1996) and speed skating gold (2006) and bronze medals (2002)

TRIVIA CHALLENGE

Which winter sport made its Olympic debut at the 1920 Summer Olympics in Antwerp, Belguim?

Ice hockey. (The first Winter Olympics didn't take place until four years later.)

LEGENDS

■ **Eric Heiden, speed skater,** b. June 14, 1958, Madison, Wisconsin. At Lake Placid in 1980, Heiden had one of the greatest Winter Olympics in history, sweeping all the sprint and long-distance speed skating races to win an unprecedented five gold medals. In the process, he shattered four Olympic records and one world record.

■ **Katarina Witt, figure skater,** b. December 3, 1965, Staaken, East Germany. One of the most successful figure skaters in history, Witt dazzled fans at the 1984 and 1988 Winter Olympics, winning gold at both. At the 1988 Winter Olympics in Calgary, the rivalry between Witt and American Debi Thomas came to be known as the "Battle of the Carmens" as both skaters chose to perform their long program to the same music. Witt was only the second woman in Olympic history to win back-to-back figure skating gold medals.

Heiden's five gold medals in one Winter Olympics has never been equaled.

HEINZ KLUETMEIER

■ **Jean-Claude Killy, alpine skier,** b. August 30, 1943, Saint-Cloud, France. Competing in front of his countrymen, Killy won the Triple Crown of skiing at the 1968 Winter Olympics in Grenoble, France. He won gold in the slalom, giant slalom, and downhill events. Killy, who was already the defending World Cup champion, became only the second skier to win skiing's Olympic Triple Crown. Austria's Toni Sailer also did it at the 1956 Winter Olympics in Cortina d'Ampezzo, Italy.

FAST FACT

Two cities have hosted the Winter Olympics twice: Lake Placid, United States, and St. Moritz, Switzerland.

SIKIDS.com
Visit our website for the latest stats and sports info.

SPORTS DIRECTORY

Major League Baseball
245 Park Avenue
New York, NY 10167
(212) 931-7800

Arizona Diamondbacks
Chase Field
401 East Jefferson Street
Phoenix, AZ 85001
(602) 462-6500

Atlanta Braves
Turner Field
755 Hank Aaron Drive
Atlanta, GA 30315
(404) 522-7630

Baltimore Orioles
Oriole Park at Camden Yards
333 W. Camden Street
Baltimore, MD 21201
(410) 685-9800

Boston Red Sox
Fenway Park
4 Yawkey Way
Boston, MA 02215
(617) 267-9440

Chicago Cubs
Wrigley Field
1060 West Addison Street
Chicago, IL 60613
(773) 404-2827

Chicago White Sox
U.S. Cellular Field
333 West 35th Street
Chicago, IL 60616
(312) 674-1000

Cincinnati Reds
Great American Ball Park
100 Main Street
Cincinnati, OH 45202
(513) 765-7000

Cleveland Indians
Jacobs Field
2401 Ontario Street
Cleveland, OH 44115
(216) 420-4636

Colorado Rockies
Coors Field
2001 Blake Street
Denver, CO 80205
(303) 292-0200

Detroit Tigers
Comerica Park
2100 Woodward Avenue
Detroit, MI 48201
(313) 471-2000

Florida Marlins
Dolphins Stadium
2267 Dan Marino Boulevard
Miami Gardens, FL 33056
(305) 623-6100

Houston Astros
Minute Maid Park
501 Crawford Street
Suite 400
Houston, TX 77002
(713) 259-8000

Kansas City Royals
Kauffman Stadium
One Royal Way
Kansas City, MO 64141
(816) 921-8000

Los Angeles Angels of Anaheim
Angel Stadium of Anaheim
2000 Gene Autry Way
Anaheim, CA 92806
(714) 940-2000

Los Angeles Dodgers
Dodger Stadium
1000 Elysian Park Avenue
Los Angeles, CA 90012
(323) 224-1500

Milwaukee Brewers
Miller Park
One Brewers Way
Milwaukee, WI 53214
(414) 902-4400

Minnesota Twins
Metrodome
34 Kirby Puckett Place
Minneapolis, MN 55415
(612) 375-1366

New York Mets
Shea Stadium
123-01 Roosevelt Avenue
Flushing, NY 11368
(718) 507-6387

New York Yankees
Yankee Stadium
161st Street and River Avenue
Bronx, NY 10451
(718) 293-4300

Oakland Athletics
Network Associates Coliseum
7000 Coliseum Way
Oakland, CA 94621
(510) 638-4900

Philadelphia Phillies
Citizens Bank Park
One Citizens Bank Way
Philadelphia, PA 19101
(215) 463-6000

Pittsburgh Pirates
PNC Park
115 Federal Street
Pittsburgh, PA 15212
(412) 323-5000

San Diego Padres
PETCO Park
100 Park Boulevard
San Diego, CA 92101
(619) 795-5000

San Francisco Giants
AT&T Park
24 Willie Mays Plaza
San Francisco, CA 94107
(415) 972-2000

Seattle Mariners
SAFECO Field
P.O. Box 4100
Seattle, WA 98104
(206) 346-4000

St. Louis Cardinals
Busch Stadium
100 S. 4th Street
St. Louis, MO 63102
(314) 345-9600

Tampa Bay Devil Rays
Tropicana Field
One Tropicana Drive
St. Petersburg, FL 33705
(727) 825-3137

Texas Rangers
Rangers Ballpark in Arlington
1000 Ballpark Way
Arlington, TX 76011
(817) 273-5222

Toronto Blue Jays
Rogers Centre
1 Blue Jays Way
Suite 3200
Toronto, Ontario M5V 1J1
  Canada
(416) 341-1000

Washington Nationals
RFK Stadium/
National's Ballpark*
2400 E. Capitol Street, S.E.
Washington, D.C. 20003
(202) 675-6287
(*Expected to open in 2008)

National Football League
280 Park Avenue
New York, NY 10017
(212) 450-2000

Arizona Cardinals
P.O. Box 888
Phoenix, AZ 85001
(602) 379-0101

Atlanta Falcons
4400 Falcon Parkway
Flowery Branch, GA 30542
(770) 965-3115

Baltimore Ravens
1 Winning Drive
Owings Mills, MD 21117
(410) 701-4000

Buffalo Bills
One Bills Drive
Orchard Park, NY 14127
(716) 648-1800

Carolina Panthers
Ericsson Stadium
800 South Mint Street
Charlotte, NC 28202
(704) 358-7000

Chicago Bears
1000 Football Drive
Lake Forest, IL 60045
(847) 295-6600

Cincinnati Bengals
One Paul Brown Stadium
Cincinnati, OH 45202
(513) 621-3550

Cleveland Browns
76 Lou Groza Boulevard
Berea, OH 44017
(440) 891-5000

Dallas Cowboys
One Cowboys Parkway
Irving, TX 75063
(972) 556-9900

Denver Broncos
13655 Broncos Parkway
Englewood, CO 80112
(303) 649-9000

Detroit Lions
222 Republic Drive
Allen Park, MI 48101
(313) 216-4000

Green Bay Packers
Lambeau Field
1265 Lombardi Avenue
Green Bay, WI 54304
(920) 569-7500

Houston Texans
Reliant Stadium
Two Reliant Park
Houston, TX 77054
(832) 667-2000

Indianapolis Colts
7001 W. 56th Street
Indianapolis, IN 46254
(317) 297-2658

Jacksonville Jaguars
One ALLTEL Stadium Place
Jacksonville, FL 32202
(904) 633-6000

Kansas City Chiefs
One Arrowhead Drive
Kansas City, MO 64129
(816) 920-9300

Miami Dolphins
2269 Dan Marino Boulevard
Miami Gardens, FL 33056
(305) 623-6100

Minnesota Vikings
9520 Viking Drive
Eden Prairie, MN 55344
(952) 828-6500

New England Patriots
Gillette Stadium
One Patriot Place
Foxboro, MA 02035
(508) 543-8200

New Orleans Saints
5800 Airline Drive
Metairie, LA 70003
(504) 733-0255

New York Giants
Giants Stadium
East Rutherford, NJ 07073
(201) 935-8111

New York Jets
1000 Fulton Avenue
Hempstead, NY 11550
(516) 560-8100

Oakland Raiders
1220 Harbor Bay Parkway
Alameda, CA 94502
(510) 864-5000

Philadelphia Eagles
NovaCare Complex
One NovaCare Way
Philadelphia, PA 19145
(215) 463-2500

Pittsburgh Steelers
3400 South Water Street
Pittsburgh, PA 15203
(412) 432-7800

San Diego Chargers
Qualcomm Stadium
4020 Murphy Canyon Road
San Diego, CA 92123
(858) 874-4500

San Francisco 49ers
4949 Centennial Boulevard
Santa Clara, CA 95054
(408) 562-4949

Seattle Seahawks
11220 N.E. 53rd Street
Kirkland, WA 98033
(425) 827-9777

St. Louis Rams
One Rams Way
St. Louis, MO 63045
(314) 982-7267

Tampa Bay Buccaneers
One Buccaneer Place
Tampa, FL 33607
(813) 870-2700

Tennessee Titans
460 Great Circle Road
Nashville, TN 37228
(615) 565-4000

Washington Redskins
21300 Redskin Park Drive
Ashburn, VA 20147
(703) 726-7000

OTHER LEAGUES

Canadian Football League
50 Wellington Street, East
3rd Floor
Toronto, Ontario M5E 1C8
  Canada
(416) 322-9650

NFL Europe
280 Park Avenue
New York, NY 10017
(212) 450-2000

PRO BASKETBALL

National Basketball Association
645 Fifth Avenue
New York, NY 10022
(212) 826-7000

Atlanta Hawks
Centennial Tower
101 Marietta Street, N.W.
Suite 1900
Atlanta, GA 30303
(404) 878-3800

Boston Celtics
226 Causeway Street, 4th Floor
Boston, MA 02114
(617) 854-8000

Charlotte Bobcats
333 East Trade Street
Charlotte, NC 28202
(704) 688-8600

Chicago Bulls
1901 W. Madison Street
Chicago, IL 60612
(312) 455-4000

Cleveland Cavaliers
One Center Court
Cleveland, OH 44115
(216) 420-2000

Dallas Mavericks
The Pavilion
2909 Taylor Street
Dallas, TX 75226
(214) 747-6287

Denver Nuggets
1000 Chopper Circle
Denver, CO 80204
(303) 405-1100

Detroit Pistons
Four Championship Drive
Auburn Hills, MI 48326
(248) 377-0100

Golden State Warriors
1011 Broadway
Oakland, CA 94607
(510) 986-2200

Houston Rockets
1510 Polk Street
Houston, TX 77002
(713) 758-7200

Indiana Pacers
125 South Pennsylvania Street
Indianapolis, IN 46204
(317) 917-2500

Los Angeles Clippers
1111 South Figueroa Street
Suite 1100
Los Angeles, CA 90015
(213) 742-7500

Los Angeles Lakers
555 North Nash Street
El Segundo, CA 90245
(310) 426-6000

Memphis Grizzlies
191 Beale Street
Memphis, TN 38103
(901) 888-4667

Miami Heat
601 Biscayne Boulevard
Miami, FL 33132
(786) 777-1000

Milwaukee Bucks
1001 North Fourth Street
Milwaukee, WI 53203
(414) 227-0500

Minnesota Timberwolves
600 First Avenue North
Minneapolis, MN 55403
(612) 673-1600

New Jersey Nets
390 Murray Hill Parkway
East Rutherford, NJ 07073
(800) 765-6387

New Orleans Hornets
1615 Poydras Street
New Orleans, LA 70112
(504) 525-4667

New York Knicks
Two Pennsylvania Plaza
14th Floor
New York, NY 10121
(212) 465-6471

Orlando Magic
8701 Maitland Summit Boulevard
Orlando, FL 32810
(407) 916-2400

Philadelphia 76ers
3601 South Broad Street
Philadelphia, PA 19148
(215) 339-7600

Phoenix Suns
201 East Jefferson Street
Phoenix, AZ 85004
(602) 379-7900

Portland Trail Blazers
One Center Court
Suite 200
Portland, OR 97227
(503) 234-9291

Sacramento Kings
One Sports Parkway
Sacramento, CA 95834
(916) 928-0000

San Antonio Spurs
AT&T Center
San Antonio, TX 78219
(210) 444-5000

Seattle SuperSonics
351 Elliott Avenue West
Suite 500
Seattle, WA 98119
(206) 281-5800

Toronto Raptors
40 Bay Street
Suite 400
Toronto, Ontario M5J 2X2
 Canada
(416) 815-5600

Utah Jazz
301 West South Temple
Salt Lake City, UT 84101
(801) 325-2500

Washington Wizards
601 F Street, N.W.
Washington, DC 20004
(202) 661-5000

WOMEN'S NATIONAL BASKETBALL ASSOCIATION

WNBA
645 Fifth Avenue
New York, NY 10022
(212) 688-9622

Chicago Sky
20 West Kinzie Street
Suite 1000
Chicago, IL 60610
(312) 828-9550

Connecticut Sun
1 Mohegan Sun Boulevard
Uncasville, CT 06382
(877) 786-8499

Detroit Shock
Four Championship Drive
Auburn Hills, MI 48326
(248) 377-0100

Houston Comets
Two Greenway Plaza
Suite 400
Houston, TX 77046
(713) 627-9622

Indiana Fever
125 S. Pennsylvania Street
Indianapolis, IN 46204
(317) 917-2500

Los Angeles Sparks
2151 East Grand Avenue
Suite 100
El Segundo, CA 90245
(310) 341-1000

Minnesota Lynx
600 First Avenue North
Minneapolis, MN 55403
(612) 673-8400

New York Liberty
Two Penn Plaza
New York, NY 10121
(212) 564-9622

Phoenix Mercury
201 East Jefferson Street
Phoenix, AZ 85004
(602) 514-8333

Sacramento Monarchs
One Sports Parkway
Sacramento, CA 95834
(916) 928-0000

San Antonio Silver Stars
One AT&T Center
San Antonio, TX 78219
(210) 444-5050

Seattle Storm
351 Elliott Avenue West
Suite 500
Seattle, WA 98119
(206) 281-5800

Washington Mystics
Verizon Center
401 9th Street, N.W.
Washington, DC 20004
(202) 266-2200

HOCKEY

National Hockey League
1251 Avenue of the Americas
47th Floor
New York, NY 10020
(212) 789-2000

Anaheim Ducks
Arrowhead Pond of Anaheim
2695 Katella Avenue
Anaheim, CA 92806
(877) 945-9464

Atlanta Thrashers
Centennial Tower
101 Marietta Street N.W.
Suite 1900
Atlanta, GA 30303
(404) 878-3300

Boston Bruins
TD Banknorth Garden
100 Legends Way
Boston, MA 02114
(617) 624-1900

Buffalo Sabres
HSBC Arena
One Seymour H. Knox III Plaza
Buffalo, NY 14203
(716) 855-4100

Calgary Flames
Pengrowth Saddledome
P.O. Box 1540
Station M
Calgary, Alberta T2P 3B9
 Canada
(403) 777-2177

Carolina Hurricanes
RBC Center
1400 Edwards Mill Road
Raleigh, NC 27607
(919) 467-7825

Chicago Blackhawks
United Center
1901 W. Madison Street
Chicago, IL 60612
(312) 455-7000

Colorado Avalanche
Pepsi Center
1000 Chopper Circle
Denver, CO 80204
(303) 405-1100

Columbus Blue Jackets
Nationwide Arena
200 West Nationwide
 Boulevard
Columbus, OH 43215
(614) 246-4625

Dallas Stars
American Airlines Center
2601 Avenue of the Stars
Frisco, TX 75034
(214) 387-5500

Detroit Red Wings
Joe Louis Arena
600 Civic Center Drive
Detroit, MI 48226
(313) 983-6606

SPORTS DIRECTORY

Edmonton Oilers
Rexall Place
11230-110th Street
Edmonton, Alberta T5G 3H7
Canada
(780) 414-4000

Florida Panthers
BankAtlantic Center
One Panther Parkway
Sunrise, FL 33323
(954) 835-7000

Los Angeles Kings
1111 South Figueroa Street
Suite 3100
Los Angeles, CA 90015
(213) 742-7100

Minnesota Wild
317 Washington Street
St. Paul, MN 55102
(651) 602-6000

Montreal Canadiens
1275 St. Antoine Street West
Montreal, Quebec H3C 5L2
Canada
(514) 932-2582

Nashville Predators
Gaylord Entertainment Center
501 Broadway
Nashville, TN 37203
(615) 770-2300

New Jersey Devils
Continental Airlines Arena
P.O. Box 504
East Rutherford, NJ 07073
(201) 935-6050

New York Islanders
1535 Old Country Road
Plainview, NY 11803
(516) 501-6700

New York Rangers
Madison Square Garden
Two Pennsylvania Plaza
14th Floor
New York, NY 10121
(212) 465-6000

Ottawa Senators
Scotiabank Place
1000 Palladium Drive
Kanata, Ontario K2V 1A5
Canada
(613) 599-0250

Philadelphia Flyers
Wachovia Center
3601 South Broad Street
Philadelphia, PA 19148
(215) 465-4500

Phoenix Coyotes
5800 W. Glenn Drive
Suite 350
Glendale, AZ 85301
(623) 463-8800

Pittsburgh Penguins
Mellon Arena
One Chatham Center
Suite 400
Pittsburgh, PA 15219
(412) 642-1300

San Jose Sharks
HP Pavilion at San Jose
525 West Santa Clara Street
San Jose, CA 95113
(408) 287-7070

St. Louis Blues
Savvis Center
1401 Clark Avenue
St. Louis, MO 63103
(314) 622-2500

Tampa Bay Lightning
St. Pete Times Forum
401 Channelside Drive
Tampa, FL 33602
(813) 301-6600

Toronto Maple Leafs
Air Canada Centre
40 Bay Street
Suite 400
Toronto, Ontario M5J 2X2
Canada
(416) 815-5500

Vancouver Canucks
General Motors Place
800 Griffiths Way
Vancouver, British Columbia
V6B 6G1
Canada
(604) 899-4600

Washington Capitals
401 Ninth Street, N.W.
Suite 750
Washington, DC 20004
(202) 266-2200

COLLEGE SPORTS

National Collegiate Athletic Association (NCAA)
700 W. Washington Street
P.O. Box 6222
Indianapolis, IN 46206-6222
(317) 917-6222

Atlantic Coast Conference
P.O. Drawer ACC
Greensboro, NC 27417-6724
(336) 854-8787

Big East Conference
222 Richmond Street
Suite 110
Providence, RI 02903
(401) 272-9108

Big Ten Conference
1500 West Higgins Road
Park Ridge, IL 60068-6300
(847) 696-1010

Big 12 Conference
2201 Stemmons Freeway
28th Floor
Dallas, TX 75207
(214) 742-1212

Big West Conference
2 Corporate Park
Irvine, CA 92606
(949) 261-2525

Conference USA
5201 North O'Connor Boulevard
Suite 300
Irving, TX 75039
(214) 774-1300

Ivy League
228 Alexander Street
2nd Floor
Princeton, NJ 08544
(609) 258-6426

Mid-American Conference
24 Public Square
15th Floor
Cleveland, OH 44113
(216) 566-4622

Pacific-10 Conference
800 South Broadway
Suite 400
Walnut Creek, CA 94596
(925) 932-4411

Southeastern Conference
2201 Richard Arrington
  Boulevard North
Birmingham, AL 35203
(205) 458-3000

**Western Athletic
Conference**
9250 East Costilla Avenue
Suite 300
Englewood, CO 80112
(303) 799-9221

OTHER SPORTS

**Association of Tennis
Professionals Tour (ATP)**
201 ATP Boulevard
Ponte Vedra Beach, FL 32082
(904) 285-8000

**Championship Auto
Racing Teams (CART)**
5350 West Lakeview Parkway
South Drive
Indianapolis, IN 46268
(317) 715-4100

Indy Racing League
4565 West 16th Street
Indianapolis, IN 46222
(317) 484-6526

**Ladies Professional Golf
Association (LPGA)**
100 International Golf Drive
Daytona Beach, FL 32124
(386) 274-6200

**Major League Soccer
(MLS)**
110 East 42nd Street
10th Floor
New York, NY 10017
(212) 450-1200

**National Association for
Stock Car Auto Racing
(NASCAR)**
1801 W. International
  Speedway Boulevard
Daytona Beach, FL 32114
(386) 253-0611

PGA Tour
112 PGA Tour Boulevard
Ponte Vedra Beach, FL 32082
(904) 285-3700

United Soccer Leagues
14497 N. Dale Mabry
  Highway
Suite 201
Tampa, FL 33618
(813) 963-3909

**United States Olympic
Training Center**
One Olympic Plaza
Colorado Springs, CO 80909
(719) 632-5551

USA Basketball
5465 Mark Dabling Boulevard
Colorado Springs, CO 80918
(719) 590-4800

USA Cycling
One Olympic Plaza
Colorado Springs, CO 80909
(719) 866-4581

USA Hockey
1775 Bob Johnson Drive
Colorado Springs, CO 80906
(719) 576-8724

USA Luge
57 Church Street
Lake Placid, NY 12946
(518) 523-2071

USA Swimming
One Olympic Plaza
Colorado Springs, CO 80909
(719) 866-4578

USA Track & Field
1 RCA Dome
Suite 140
Indianapolis, IN 46225
(317) 261-0500

USA Water Polo, Inc.
1631 Mesa Avenue
Suite A-1
Colorado Springs, CO 80906
(719) 634-0866

**U.S. Bobsled and
Skeleton Federation**
196 Old Military Road
PO Box 828
Lake Placid, NY 12946
(518) 523-1842

**U.S. Figure Skating
Association**
20 First Street
Colorado Springs, CO 80906
(719) 635-5200

**U.S. Ski and Snowboard
Association**
Box 100
1500 Kearns Boulevard
Park City, UT 84060
(435) 649-9090

U.S. Soccer Federation
1801 South Prairie Avenue
Chicago, IL 60616
(312) 808-1300

U.S. Speedskating
P.O. Box 450639
Westlake, OH 44145
(440) 899-0128

**Women's Tennis
Association (WTA)**
One Progress Plaza
Suite 1500
St. Petersburg, FL 33701
(727) 895-5000